CW00432682

The Orcadian
BOOK OF THE
20th CENTURY

The Orcadian
BOOK OF THE
20th CENTURY

A chronicle of our times

Compiled by Howard Hazell

2000
The Orcadian Limited (Kirkwall Press)

Published by The Orcadian Limited (Kirkwall Press),
Hell's Half Acre, Hatston, Kirkwall, Orkney, KW15 1DW
Tel.: 01856 879000   Fax.: 01856 879001

ISBN 1 902957 03 2

Printed by The Orcadian Limited, Print Centre,
Hell's Half Acre, Kirkwall, Orkney.

With gratitude to all those who have helped
me hack through the public bar of life, and
forgiven so many of my failings on the way

Preface

Many years ago, in the days when a good night out could be had for a pound or two, and people considered it wise to watch television with the lights out, so as not to go blind, a young journalistic contemporary began a story for his newspaper: "History was made today within the walls of an ancient city."

He finished the story, preened himself at his eloquence and we went to the pub. On our return, his work had been pinned to the newsroom wall - the opening paragraph obliterated by red pencil, alongside which the chief sub editor, a man of earthy language and little literary appreciation, had scrawled: "History is made every (expletive) day!"

So to that extent, this is a history book! However, it is by no means the definitive history of 20th century Orkney - for that would have meant reprinting, in entirety, the 5,200 weekly issues of *The Orcadian* from the past 100 years - and then some! Nor does it profess to be a work of great academic weight. The 20th Century has been dubbed the "People's Century" and *The Orcadian Book of the 20th Century* simply aims - in the language of newspapers - to record some of those people and the events, great and small, which have touched their lives in these islands over the last century of the Millennium.

It does not centre only on those who were Orkney-born or of Orkney roots - some were but passing strangers - but, as I state elsewhere in the book, the place of one's death can become powerfully more relevant than the place of one's birth.

It is not possible, within the constraints of one book, to paint an all-embracing picture of the 20th century on one broad canvas. Instead I have striven to capture a series of snapshots in time which, hopefully, will come together in a montage which is both comprehensive and comprehensible. Even so, I must repeat, the content is selective and I apologise for all that has been omitted.

My source for the book, obviously, has been the past 5,000 or so issues of *The Orcadian* - and the paper's sister publications - and I am grateful not only to all those past journalists on the newspaper who did the real work in the first instance, and whose efforts I have plagiarised to some extent, but also to the present managing director, James Miller, for his assistance and encouragement. Also at *The Orcadian*, I must thank Colin Keldie for his conscientious work on the design and production of the book. I would also express my gratitude to Alison Fraser and her staff at the Orkney Library archives department, especially David Mackie, both for their assistance and for the use of many photographs. Acknowledgement is due to Allan Taylor, who provided the details of Orkney's war memorials, and to all those people both within and outwith the county who came forward with the photographs for which they are credited throughout the following pages. I am particularly indebted to Dougie Shearer for the use of his photographs which are in the care of the archives department.

And the book would not yet be complete but for the efforts of my two typists, my wife Myra, and her daughter Arlene Peace, and all the other members of the family who helped.

Reading through *The Orcadian* of past decades soon destroys a few myths. One is that newspapers of today are guilty of previously undreamt-of sensationalist reporting. The truth is that our journalistic predecessors had an equally good eye for the salacious and reported such delights at length. Another cheerful misconception is that there was no wrong-doing in the "good old days." In reality, Orkney is a microcosm of the world and, like every other place on this planet, it's had its villains as well as heroes.

I would also point out that although reference to "the Orkneys" raises hackles amongst today's Orcadians, it was in common usage in the columns of *The Orcadian* in the earlier years of the century. In many cases, the spelling of place-names has changed through the century - for instance, Shapinsay has been spelled in four different ways in *The Orcadian* in the past 100 years. Where possible, I have endeavoured to use the accepted spellings at the end of the century. There will be discrepancies (for instance, it is not my place to alter spellings as inscribed on war memorials) but, in most cases, the modern place-name will be recognisable. There may well be other examples of words or phrases from the past which jar on today's ears. For example, whilst I was compiling this book, a front page story in *The Orcadian* in 1999 dismissed the word "quay" as untypical of Orkney. In fact, the word was used regularly in *The Orcadian* of the 1920s and 1930s.

And, finally, to defend newspapers against the oft-heard accusation that they only use "bad" news, I would stress that news, by its very definition, is the out-of-the-ordinary. Tragedy and misdemeanour is reported because it is still the exception to the norm - it would be far, far worse if it was not reported because it had become accepted as a mundane, everyday occurrence.

Whatever, I trust that I have managed to treat past times of distress with sensitivity. So, through triumph and tragedy, the tears and the laughs, this was your century, this was your life.

Howard Hazell

'Great Storm' hits trawlers

More than 100 trawlermen from the country's major fishing ports were feared to have perished in the worst ever peacetime devastation of Britain's trawler fleet.

Eleven trawlers were lost - with no sign of survivors - in the North Sea and the waters of Orkney and Shetland in the "Great Storm" of February, 1900.

In Orkney, the storm left a trail of

1900

havoc with the wind ripping roofs from houses, and at least 25 small fishing craft, at local piers, wrecked and sunk - remarkably with just one death by drowning reported.

Gunboats HM *Alarm, Sheldrake* and *Jackal* were dispatched to Northern waters to search for the missing trawlers and other vessels which were lost at sea in the storm. Considerable wreckage was washed ashore on several of the islands of Orkney.

The port of Hull suffered the most grievous losses in the tragedy with more than 70 Humberside fishermen presumed drowned in the storm.

The steamer *St Rognvald* lies wrecked on Burgh Head, Stronsay, in 1900.   (Picture courtesy of Orkney Library photographic archive)

Orkney steamer wrecked

Sixty eight passengers were saved as one of the biggest passenger steamers in Orkney waters was wrecked after running aground on Stronsay.

The *St Rognvald*, one of the finest vessels owned by the North of Scotland and Orkney and Shetland Steam Navigation Company, had been built in 1883, with a gross tonnage of 920.

The vessel was on passage from Lerwick when, in poor visibility, it went aground on Burgh Head, Stronsay, on April 24, 1900.

"Passengers rushed upon deck only partially clothed," reported *The Orcadian*. "Few of the passengers took time to dress but rushed on deck almost naked. In all the bustle and confusion, however, there was one pleasant feature worthy of note - the calm heroism of the ladies."

Fifteen people got away in one of the ship's boats within minutes of the stranding, and landed below the farm of Odness, Stronsay. The remainder of the passengers left the *St Rognvald* in another boat within half an hour. All the passengers were given hospitality by the Twatt family at Odness.

Captain John Masson could be seen on the bridge issuing his commands for the lowering of the boats, said *The Orcadian*, and after all the passengers had cleared the stricken ship, he and the crew then left in small boats.

There was a number of cattle, sheep and Shetland ponies on board and all those were reported to have drowned with the exception of one pony which escaped.

Captain Masson - who was to retire later that year after 40 years service - had been off-watch when the ship stranded, and the Chief Officer was on the bridge at the time of impact.

Two days later, the *St Rognvald* began breaking up. A Board of Trade inquiry into the disaster, held four months later, laid the blame with the Chief Officer. The vessel had strayed six or seven miles off course, and he had failed to reduce speed to allow for the poor visibility caused by fog. The inquiry suspended the Chief Officer's master's certificate for three months.

In just a year, a replacement *St Rognvald* was launched at the Aberdeen

shipyard of Hall, Russell and Company, though the new steamer had a narrow escape from a similar disaster in September, 1901, when "with the sea running mountains high" the vessel went on rocks on passage between Lerwick and Kirkwall and only floated to safety after sustaining some damage in dense fog.

Another passenger vessel well known in Orkney waters was to be lost in 1900 - but on the other side of the Atlantic. The old steamer *St Ola*, formerly operated by the North of Scotland Company on the Pentland Firth route between Scapa and Scrabster, foundered off the mouth of the St Lawrence river in Canada, with the loss of 26 crew and passengers.

Schools epidemic

Kirkwall area schools were reopened in January, 1900, after being closed for the last ten weeks of the 19th century due to an epidemic of Measles. A fresh outbreak in 1900 prompted fears that schools would have to shut down again.

Isles minister in scandal

The century began with a scandal worthy of the tabloid press 100 years later as a North Isles kirk minister was revealed to have had an adulterous affair with the wife of the island doctor.

The ensuing divorce case, in December, 1900, saw the former Sanday doctor Edwin Wenyon (47) bring an action against his wife Flora citing her adultery with the Rev Alexander Morrison, parish minister for Cross and Burness in Sanday.

Dr Wenyon had practised in Sanday from 1884-97 and married his wife, daughter of a Glasgow banker, in 1890 after meeting her while she was visiting the island. The Rev Morrison had been parish minister since 1892.

Dr Wenyon told the Court of Session that his wife had confessed that she had been unfaithful with Morrison after the minister had entered, and left, the Wenyons' house by way of the window. The doctor had also found love letters between his wife and the minister.

The Rev Morrison did not appear in court to defend the action, and Mrs Flora Wenyon was said to be working in Calcutta as a nurse after leaving her husband a year earlier. The judge, Lord Low, granted the divorce and ordered the Rev Morrison to pay £100 damages.

A month later, the minister resigned both from his Sanday parish and his status as a minister, but the North Isles Presbytery noted that "it was unaccompanied with any expression of penitence or confession of guilt."

The Presbytery set up a special committee of inquiry and Rev D. Colquhoun Kerr, Moderator, said: "No such calamity has befallen the Presbytery since its institution in the year 1707. A dishonour, worse then bereavement, has come to the Church and has brought shame and sorrow upon us all.

"The investigation of the scandal was a very disagreeable duty for the members of the committee, exposing to them gradually the hideous ulcer which has been feeding so grossly and so long beneath the fair skin of our social life."

It was later reported that the disgraced minister was seeking to join Baden-Powell's police force for active service in South Africa. "The gentleman in question had the reputation of being a fine shot, a good horseman, and full of nerve, and should make a name for himself in his new sphere of labour," commented *The Orcadian* with a degree of irony.

But, in 1901, there was to be a "sensational sequel" to the story when it was revealed that the adulterous wife had indeed emigrated to India - under the name of Flora McLeod - and a child in her care had been found dead in mysterious circumstances.

She had to appear in court in Calcutta to give evidence to a judicial inquiry after the baby boy, whom she was employed to nurse, was found dead in his cot, apparently smothered. She claimed the child had died after a male intruder, armed with a knife, got into the room and attacked her.

In court, she was questioned about her past and the divorce case and admitted that, since her arrival in India, she had formed an "intimate" relationship with a man. She denied that she had been with the man on the night the baby died.

New chief constable

Orkney's Chief Constable Colin Cruickshank, who had been the county's senior police officer since 1898, died in 1900 and was succeeded by Superintendent Richard Atkin, who had joined the force in 1892 after originally being posted to Orkney as a Sergeant Major during his Army career. Superintendent Atkin retired in 1907 and died at the age of 94 in retirement in the Isle of Man in 1935.

Turn of the century

The Orcadian - in common with most of the newspapers of the day - regarded December 31, 1900, as the last day of the 19th century, and January 1, 1901, as the first day of the 20th century

Sir Thomas Clouston, the Orcadian pioneer of the treatment of mental illness, was made a Freeman of Kirkwall in 1908 and knighted in 1911.
(Picture courtesy of Orkney Library photographic archive)

Late opening

Kirkwall's MP Mr Thomas Hedderwick announced his support for a Parliamentary Bill which would see public houses not permitted to open until 10am - instead of 8am, the opening time then allowed. Nine months later, Mr Hedderwick was defeated in the 1900 General Election.

Orcadians in suspense

The start of 1900 saw the arrival in Orkney shops of an article that was to become a fashion icon of the 20th century - for which the world could be for ever grateful to two Orcadians.

For the invention of the suspender belt was credited to Westray men Andrew Thomson and James Drever, who could not only claim to have made one of the most enduring contributions to every day life - but could also go down in history as the men who launched a million pin-up pictures.

To be exact, it was the little clasp fastener, which enabled the stocking to be attached to the suspender, that they can claim as their invention.

Messrs Thomson and Drever had emigrated to the United States and were living in San Francisco at the time they registered their patent - numbered Cal 567, 421, dated September 8, 1896. The preamble to the description of their patent stated: "The invention relates to a clasp or fastening to be used in conjunction with a garment supporter, the clasp serving to secure the stocking or other garment and connect it with a supporting band or strap."

Within five years, it was being mass produced and exported around the world in fashionable suspender belts. It was also to be used on the braces of dungarees, but, somehow, that did not seem to have the same universal appeal to inflame the passions of so many millions of men.

Sporting hall of fame for Orkney solicitor

Angus Buchanan, who from 1883 - 1900 was agent for the National Bank in Kirkwall, represented Scotland in the first ever Scotland - England rugby international and he scored the first try which resulted in the goal that won the match for Scotland.

He was both a banker and solicitor and was a partner in Buchanan and Liddle, Kirkwall solicitors, before returning south to Paisley where he retired in March, 1921, after 59 years service to banking.

He was also a keen cricketer and on one occasion, took all ten wickets, clean bowled, for 46 runs - including a hat-trick - playing for the Royal High School against Edinburgh Academicals in 1871.

He died in 1927, but before then he was to share in the achievements of his explorer son, also Angus, who, in the 1920s, captured the national spotlight when he led a pioneering 15 month expedition across the Sahara Desert.

An outbreak of Bubonic Plague in Glasgow saw the streets and byways of Stromness being cleaned "in a most thorough manner" and the drains being flushed. A special meeting of Kirkwall Town Council was called "to take the necessary steps to have the town put on a proper sanitary footing." This is a street cleaner in the Ayre Road.

(Picture courtesy of Orkney Library photographic archive)

The lighthouse support ship *Pole Star* at the start of the century.   (Picture courtesy of Orkney Library photographic archive)

Lost lightkeepers mystery

One of the maritime world's greatest mysteries at the start of the 20th century involved the Stromness-based lighthouse support ship *Pole Star* and her Orcadian crew.

The *Pole Star* crew were the last men to see alive the three lighthouse keepers on the Flannan Isles - the remote and tiny islands in the Atlantic Ocean, to the west of the island of Lewis - before they seemingly vanished into thin air.

When the *Pole Star* visited the Flannan Isles to deliver stores, all was well but, three days later, the Northern Lighthouse Commissioners' other vessel, the *Hesperus*, making a similar call at the lonely outpost, found the three men in the lighthouse had disappeared from the otherwise uninhabited island.

"And no word has been heard of them since," said Peter Knight, who served on the *Pole Star*, operating from Stromness, for 35 years. "The crew of the *Hesperus* found a half-finished meal but not the slightest sign of the lighthouse keepers."

It was the most mysterious incident he had ever encountered in his lighthouse career, he later told the *Daily Express*.

1901

The end of a reign

Three years to dry out

Kirkwall witnessed the first ever trial in Scotland under the recently introduced Inebriates Act when, at Kirkwall Sheriff Court, on September 20, 1901, a 36 year old Kirkwall hawker was found guilty of being "a habitual drunkard" and ordered to be detained at Perth Inebriates Home for three years.

Since the age of 17, he had faced the courts on 58 occasions and received sentences ranging from ten strokes of the birch to 60 days imprisonment.

Following the enactment of the new legislation, the Perth home had been open for nine months, waiting to receive its first resident. Sheriff Cosens told the accused that, with God's blessing, he would become a good citizen and a respected member of society.

Counted out

The Orcadian announced that a former Kirkwall lobster merchant Jack Roberts had won the 9 stone boxing championship of England with a knockout at the National Sporting Club in London. The following week, a letter from the flattered, but slightly bemused, ex-Kirkwall man pointed out that the newspaper had got the wrong Jack Roberts. Far from being the boxing champion of England, he was working at Billingsgate fish market.

President assassinated

Kirkwall Town Council sent a telegram of condolence to the American Embassy in London following the assassination of the President of the USA, William McKinley, in 1901. McKinley was succeeded as president by Theodore Roosevelt.

Doctor's mercy mission

Dr David Dewar, the medical officer of South Ronaldsay and Burray, had a remarkable escape from death on the wild winter's night of January 31, 1901.

He was on his way across Water Sound to visit a sick child in Burray when the boat was swamped by heavy seas. The boatman, John Wards, of Hill, Burray, was thrown overboard and drowned. He left a widow and six children.

However, the doctor and another occupant of the boat, a boy called David Wylie, were washed ashore and rescued in an exhausted condition, but alive.

Dr Dewar went on to serve as medical officer for South Ronaldsay and Burray for a total of more than 56 years. He died in July, 1928, just two months after his retiral.

Queen Victoria, the only monarch most Orcadians of the day had ever known, having reigned on the British throne since 1837, died in January, 1901.

"The sad intelligence reached Kirkwall shortly after 7pm on Tuesday evening and, as Provost Spence at once ordered the Cathedral bell to be tolled, the mournful news speedily spread all over the place and expressions of regret were universal," reported *The Orcadian*.

A telegram of sympathy was sent by Kirkwall Town Council to the Royal Family, and acknowledged by return. A united memorial service of all dominations was held at St Magnus Cathedral to coincide with the Queen's funeral on February 2.

She was succeeded as monarch by her son, the Prince of Wales, who, at the age of 59, became King Edward VII. In Kirkwall, the reading of the proclamation of the new King was carried out in a severe snowstorm but watched by a large crowd, after a procession through the streets to the Mercat Cross. Shops and businesses were closed for three hours to enable the Orkney Volunteer Artillery and tradesmen to take part.

The Orkney Photo Company of Castle Street, Kirkwall, took a picture of the proceedings - the first time the ceremony had ever been photographed -

and special commemorative copies were sold to the public.

Kirkwall councillor Robert Hewison caused a stir by protesting at having to take an oath of allegiance to "King Edward VII, King of Great Britain and Emperor of India" - making the point that the new monarch was Edward I of Scotland. Councillor Hewison was certainly not anti-Royalist and, at the King's coronation 18 months later, he composed a special poem of tribute which was sent by Kirkwall Town Council to Buckingham Palace.

The coronation of Edward VII was originally scheduled for June 26, 1902, but had to be cancelled at the last minute due to the King's serious illness which required emergency surgery. At one stage, it was feared that he could actually die on his coronation day.

However, he recovered health sufficiently for the ceremony to go ahead on August 9, 1902. Streets in Kirkwall and Stromness were festooned in flags and bunting as Rev Theodore Marshall conducted a special service of celebration at St Magnus Cathedral. A parade of the Orkney Volunteer Artillery, led by the Volunteer band, with the Coastguards, Town Council and Freemasons processed round the town. In the evening there was a torchlight procession and fireworks while celebration bonfires were lit in Stromness and other parishes.

House is blown away

Mr Peter Shearer, from Stronsay, his wife of 12 months, and their new-born baby, had a miracle escape as a cyclone devastated their home and farm in Ballarat, Australia.

"The destruction of the young couple's home was complete - all the fencing, barns, crops and everything else having been swept away," said *The Orcadian*.

Some of their furniture and possessions was later found miles away.

When the cyclone struck, Mrs Shearer was injured by falling timbers. Mr

Shearer carried his unconscious wife to safety then dashed into the house and found the child "covered with fallen debris, though, almost by a miracle, the infant had escaped injury."

Mr Shearer had barely time to rush outside again with the baby before the roof collapsed. "They watched their home being torn to pieces before their eyes," said *The Orcadian*.

A gold watch and a purse containing £10 were in a cabinet that was blown away, but both were recovered by neighbours and returned to the Shearers.

Population below 30,000

The 1901 census showed Orkney's population as 27,723 - a decrease of 2,448 from 30,171 in 1891. Stromness was the only parish in the county to show an increase in population, 2,268 to 2,469. Kirkwall and St Ola had fallen from 4,724 to 4,461. South Ronaldsay and Burray had the biggest fall - from 3,051 to 2,707.

"One explanation of the decrease is that

people are gradually falling into a better style of living and young people - both male and female - prefer going to the South and to the colonies to accepting the current wages in the county. The failure in the fishing in past years has no doubt also had an influence in the decrease of the population," said *The Orcadian*.

Lifeboatmen go on strike

What was believed to be the first strike in the history of the lifeboat service took place in Orkney in January, 1902.

Some members of the crew of the Stromness lifeboat refused to take part in an exercise, and "came out on strike," reported *The Orcadian* of January 11, 1902.

Sufficient volunteers joined the remaining regular crew to allow the lifeboat practice to go ahead.

The exercises - intended to give practice and experience in operating the lifeboat and life saving equipment - were usually held every three months on stormy days to get as realistic conditions for a rescue as possible.

In Stromness, it had been the custom to hold the last quarterly exercise of the year on December 31, but Captain G.G. Bailie, the lifeboat secretary, decided that the weather on December 31, 1901, was too fine to give a worthwhile test to the lifeboat.

1902

Instead, on Friday, January 3, 1902, following a westerly gale of wind, it was decided conditions were more suitable for the exercise and the signal was fired to summon the crew. But a considerable number of the crew refused to go on board and protested against the alteration from December 31.

Mr W.G. Sinclair, second coxswain, and among those who refused to go, said they had remained on shore as a protest. The men would have put to sea in the event of a real emergency.

Captain Bailie said there had never been the least trouble in his 15 years connection with the lifeboat and he contended that the strikers had no grievance whatever.

McGonagall is dead

William McGonagall - the Scot renowned for memorably bad poetry of naive sincerity and tortuous rhythm, such as The Tay Bridge Disaster - died in 1902 at the age of 72.

As a child, his family of hawkers apparently stayed in Orkney for several years, and it was acknowledged that he and his brother received part of their schooling in South Ronaldsay.

Round-the-world

A 22 year old Frenchman, Charles Millot, arrived in Kirkwall in December, 1902, as part of his attempt to walk round the world. He had so far covered 3,140 miles.

He sold postcards of himself to raise money for his living expenses, and he intended to continue on to Shetland and then Norway.

A hotel in lights

A new era of Orkney's hotels began in 1902 as Mackay's Stromness Hotel opened for business. It was the first building in Orkney to be fitted with electric light and "every modern convenience."

The man who conceived the idea of the hotel was Mr John Mackay. Born in Farr, Sutherland, his first hotel was the Station Hotel, Thurso, before, in 1886, he crossed the Pentland Firth to run the Mason's Arms Hotel, Stromness. He even started a "posting service" throughout the Orkney Mainland and bought the farm of Stairwaddy to keep the necessary horses.

In 1899 he asked Stromness contractor Mr S. Baikie to build his new hotel which - after completion in 1902 - came to be recognised as "one of the best conducted hotels in the North of Scotland," said *The Orcadian*.

Inspired by the advent of electricity at the Stromness Hotel, the burgh provost Andrew Wylie proposed that electric street lights should be introduced. A feasibility study which was commissioned suggested such a scheme would cost £2,500, and it was, in fact, another 45 years before Provost Wylie's dream of electric street lights came to fruition in Stromness.

John Mackay went on to become Orkney's major hotelier of the day. He built the Stenness Hotel to cater for fishing visitors and, when the Kirkwall Hotel came on the market, he bought that too. The Queen's Hotel, Lerwick, also came under his management.

A Stromness town councillor and county councillor, John Mackay died in 1928, aged 73, just a few months after the Stromness Hotel had played host to royalty when Prince George visited the town.

Cold justice

A nine year old Kirkwall schoolboy was hauled before Kirkwall burgh police court, in February, 1902, charged with throwing a snowball. He was discharged without punishment.

Capital crimes

Grievous, and in one case fatal, attacks committed by two Orcadians shocked the population of Edinburgh in 1902.

In one case, a young man - said to be a probationer for the Church - was certified insane after being accused of murdering his landlady. In the other, a former Orkney merchant, who had moved to the capital the previous year, bludgeoned his wife and 19 year old daughter nearly to death and then attempted suicide.

New golf course

Orkney Golf Club moved from Pickaquoy to a new nine hole golf course at Grainbank, where a £120 pavilion had been built. The land for the new course had been arranged by Mr William MacLennan, factor of Lord Zetland's estates in Orkney - for which, in 1930, he was to be given life membership of Orkney Golf Club.

Three drown in shipping disaster

A Norwegian barque *Georgesville*, on passage from Glasgow to Christiana, was driven ashore on the east side of South Ronaldsay. Three of the eight crew were lost after they were among four men who were swept overboard. The fourth man was washed ashore and survived.

The captain, mate and two crewmen remained on board until low water when they were "gallantly rescued by several of the inhabitants in the vicinity who crawled out on the rocks through the heavy surf with a rope." The vessel became a total wreck.

School closes

Kirkwall's original Glaitness School was closed on May 30, 1902, and all the pupils transferred to the burgh school, after first being given a half day holiday to mark the occasion.

Battle with the Boers

The 20th century opened with Orcadians caught up in the horrors of war 5,000 miles from home.

Many Orkney families had relatives living or serving in South Africa which had exploded into the bloody conflict of the second Boer War in 1899. Before hostilities ended in 1902, Orkney soldiers would be killed, wounded or posted missing, while others would be honoured for their gallantry on the battlefield.

The war had begun on October 11, 1899, after the Boers - mainly of Dutch descent - had declared independent republics in Transvaal and Orange Free State and demanded the withdrawal of British troops. The major battles were fought in the early months of the war, with the Boers gaining significant victories as the British garrisons at Ladysmith and Mafeking were put under seige.

Back home, the war was portrayed in an atmosphere of patriotic fervour as local men in the Gordon Highlanders, the Black Watch and the Seaforth Highlanders - regarded as Orkney's regiment for most of the 20th Century - served with the Highland Brigade. Several Orcadians were also serving in Canadian and Australian contingents, though it was to the 2nd Seaforths that Kirkwall's Highland Park distillery sent two casks of malt whisky to sustain the local men in battle.

It was not long before the jingoism was deflated by the harsh realities in the front line. A private in the Black Watch wrote home: "The 93rd have got an awful smashing up."

He told of the sight of the wounded passing by - "some on stretchers and others hopping along with the help of men told to help them - nothing but blood and bandages and men with their legs blown off.

"There were three trainloads came in through the night, and the stretchers passed and repassed us the whole night. Since the wounded came here, they are dying about five every day. It is what I never expected to see anywhere."

An Orcadian in Natal wrote home to Kirkwall to report that there were a number of Orcadians in the thick of the action, but adding: "The result of the present war is awful to contemplate. Already the misery and destitution are alarming. We have under-estimated the Boer strength.

"The enemy has surrounded Ladysmith on all sides, throwing shells from the long range guns into the town. Their number is not less than 30,000 while our force is not more than half. The Boers have even refused to allow the women and children to leave."

Orcadians, or those with close Orkney links, were not only involved in the fighting, but also tending to the dreadful toll of the wounded. Among those serving with the Royal Army Medical Corps was Major Henry Halcro Johnston, of Orphir, Dr C.W. Donald, son of James Donald of Kirkwall, and the eminent surgeon William Watson Cheyne, who 20 years later would become Lord Lieutenant of Orkney and Shetland.

John Taylor - a Kirkwall law clerk who emigrated to South Africa in 1895 where he qualified as an attorney in the Supreme Court of Natal - devoted himself to missionary work with the British troops throughout the Boer War.

The British suffered major reverses in battles at the Modder River and Magersfontein and a young Kirkwall soldier, serving in the Seaforths, wrote home to his brother: "A good many of the troops here are a wee bit disheartened over the way we were led into action. It was an awful blunder."

He told how one of his comrades, a Private Oddie from Holm, had been killed. "The poor fellow fell with his face in his hands, and never moved again."

Private H.S. Flett, also of the 2nd Seaforths, wrote to his mother with news that he had been shot through the leg.

"I am not expecting to go back to the front. I think I will get home as soon as I am able to take to the sea. I lost a lot of blood which leaves me weak." An Orcadian comrade Jim Foubister had suffered a neck wound, but he could give no news of fellow Orcadians Cleat, Groat and Eunson, he said.

There was worse to follow. An Orkney policeman, PC Lowden, who had been called up as an Army reservist to serve with the 72nd Highlanders was killed at the Battle of Magersfontein while Flotta man William Flett, who had served in the Black Watch for five years, was among those severely wounded in action.

James Stanger, who had emigrated to South Africa from Sandwick, died 20 days before the relief of Ladysmith.

News of more Orcadians heading for foreign postings came in February, 1900, as the 3rd Battalion Seaforth Highlanders left Fort George en route for Egypt. Their ship was caught in the Bay of Biscay in the great storm of that month and all their horses on board were killed. Back in Orkney, 420 members of the Orkney Volunteer Artillery paraded in a field below Highland Park with companies from Sanday, Shapinsay, Stronsay, Holm, Evie and Birsay as well as Kirkwall and Stromness.

The full impact of the war was made apparent as the British Casualties of the first six months of the war were published. A total of 2,808 had been killed in battle, while a further 2,312 "other deaths" were reported, 4,271 were missing (mostly captured), 4,080 invalided and 10,000 wounded. By March 2, 1900, the casualties of the 2nd Seaforths totalled 20 officers and 400 men.

But news of the relief of Ladysmith and then Mafeking lifted spirits in Orkney. *The Orcadian* of May 26, 1900, reported: "News of the relief of Mafeking reached Kirkwall about 10pm on Friday evening. The news was received with the greatest enthusiasm. Soon large crowds were walking the streets and singing and cheering while the Volunteer band paraded playing patriotic airs till nearly midnight. On Saturday, bunting was everywhere displayed."

Two weeks later, the magistrates declared a public holiday as the news reached Kirkwall of the fall of Pretoria - the Boer capital of the Transvaal republic - to the British Supreme Commander Lord Roberts. Kirkwall Town Council, in a matter of four hours, organised a procession with Orkney Volunteer Artillery and schoolchildren taking part. In the evening there was a firework display and the burning of Boer effigies.

Stromness too put out the flags. "Never before it is said, did the town show such a display. A procession, numbering 2,000, marched through the town, headed by a pipe and drum band," reported *The Orcadian*.

The Supreme Command of the British troops in South Africa was assumed by Lord Kitchener in December, 1900, and the hostilities took on increasingly the shape of guerrilla warfare as Kitchener pursued the Boers with a vengeance.

A letter home in February, 1901, from a Kirkwall soldier told of a 650 mile march to the Transvaal which took nine weeks.

"We also had to burn all the Boer farms on our way, and I may say that it was terrible to witness some of the scenes that took place. Some hundreds of fine farms were burned to the ground and the women and children turned out. They only got ten minutes to clear out and take as much stuff as they could.

"The war has turned into a very serious affair. It looks as bad now as it did at the first. We had a very bad fight about a month ago - we lost our captain severely wounded, and our 1st lieutenant killed, and six of our ranks severely wounded. I am sorry to say that fever has broken out among our division and there are sometimes as many as 20 die every day. I wish I was out of it, but we have not the least idea when we will get home."

The ravages of enteric fever were illustrated when Sergeant Norman Sparke, youngest son of Rev William Sparke of Kirkwall, died of the illness just months after being awarded the Distinguished Service Order for "great gallantry under severe fire" at the relief of Ladysmith. Trooper William Firth, aged 21, of Quoys, Tankerness, died from his wounds in another tragic episode for Orkney.

Trooper Frederick McNiell - son of the Holm United Free church minister - arrived back in Orkney after a year at the front with 15 Company Imperial Yeomanry and was presented with a silver cup by Kirkwall MP Arthur Bignold. The cup was displayed in the window of *The Orcadian* office and drew large crowds. It was not the only honour for Trooper McNiell - Glasgow Corporation awarded him the Freedom of Glasgow.

Trooper Robert Sinclair, of Union Street, Kirkwall, was another to receive a silver cup from Arthur Bignold. Sergeant Thomas Kilpatrick, of the Scottish Horse, whose father lived at Houton all his life, was mentioned in dispatches by Kitchener for "conspicuous bravery."

Corporal Ted Atkin, the son of Orkney Chief Constable Richard Atkin, and serving with the Royal Field Artillery, was another to be mentioned in dispatches after losing the fingers of his left hand under fire from the enemy. He was serving with another Orcadian, Bombadier Bob Taylor, who, said Atkin, deserved the Victoria Cross.

By the start of 1902, British casualties in the field of war amounted to 2,532 officers and 33,349 men killed, wounded or missing. Disease, or other causes, however, had killed or incapacitated another 76,165 officers and men.

Just a week before the war was to end, a Kirkwall trooper, in a letter published in *The Orcadian*, told of a record 75 mile march in 24 hours as the Boers were, by now, on the run. "It was a grand but awful sight to see the Boers fleeing for their lives and gunners dropping shells here and there among them. There were 500 Boers accounted for that day. There is a big move coming off soon which will end the war if peace cannot be settled."

In fact, the peace came on May 31, 1902, as the Boers surrendered to the terms put by the British government under Balfour. The Secretary for War telegraphed a message to Kitchener offering "sincere congratulations on the energy, skill and patience with which you have conducted this prolonged campaign, and would wish you to communicate to the troops under your command the profound sense of the spirit of endurance with which they met every call made upon them, of their bravery in action, of the excellent discipline preserved, and of the humanity shown by them throughout this trying period."

Because Kirkwall Post Office was closed on the Sunday, the news did not reach Orkney untill 7am, Monday, June 2. "Flags were hoisted from public and private buildings, and by breakfast time the town had a gay appearance. The Cathedral bells were also rung," said *The Orcadian*. A half day holiday was declared and a parade of the Orkney Volunteer Artillery was organised for the evening followed by a firework display in which rockets were fired from the tower of St Magnus Cathedral. Portraits of Lord Roberts and Lord Kitchener - the successive commanders of British troops in South Africa - were exhibited in the windows of town shops.

Councillor W.B. Baikie, at a victory reception at Kirkwall Town Hall, said that, from India's sultry sun to Greenland's icy mountains, the mighty deeds of Britain were known. They had concluded a peace with honour, they had fought a desperate fight and they had conquered.

He never hoped for war, and he never wished for war. He had no doubt that the great majority of those in the country had lost relatives in the war. They had now heard peace declared, but he hoped none of them would ever hear peace declared again.

Alas, just 12 years, two months later, Orkney and Orcadians would be involved, with so much of the world, in the Great War which would claim millions of casualties and make the Boer War seem a mere skirmish.

Another world away! Britain was at war in South Africa but this was the peaceful scene at the pierhead at Kettletoft, Sanday.

(Picture courtesy of Kenneth H.S. Foubister)

Salvation for Cathedral

Orkney's St Magnus Cathedral - "the glory of the North" - was saved for future generations by a bequest which caused an unholy row that eventually had to be settled in the courts.

Sheriff George Thoms, who had been Sheriff Principal of Orkney from 1870-1899, died in 1903, at the age of 72, and, after various small bequests, he left the residue of his estate - estimated at around £50,000 - to the Royal burgh of Kirkwall for the restoration and repair of St Magnus Cathedral.

The windfall could not have arrived at a more opportune time. In the previous two years, there had been criticism, not only in Orkney but throughout Scotland, at the parlous state of the Cathedral building, and the standard of some of the emergency repair work which had left the Cathedral covered in scaffolding.

The work had been necessary to make the Cathedral watertight, but some of the measures taken - including the somewhat Heath Robinson construction of iron pipes inside the building to drain away leaking water - were condemned by the Society for the Protection of Ancient Buildings, which claimed: "The spoiling of St Magnus Cathedral is a tragedy that must appeal to a far wider audience than the inhabitants of the islands."

There were complaints that the "fine old dark reddish stone slates have been stripped off the roof of the nave, and their place taken by modern light coloured ones, quite out of tone with the rest of the building."

It was claimed that the original stones had been carted away to be broken up for road mending in an act of "sacrilegious destruction."

One correspondent complained: "All the alterations are in a style which would be very neat and suitable for a mission hall. As applied to an ancient cathedral, it would be ludicrous if it were not deplorable. There is clearly a feeling of great regret among all the more cultured and intelligent of the inhabitants."

The expense of the upkeep of the Cathedral had been underlined in June, 1903, when Kirkwall Town Council agreed that visitors should be charged 6d to be admitted to the building. The money would go to pay for the caretaker.

And so, the announcement of Sheriff Thoms' bequest at the end of 1903, seemed to be a heaven-sent salvation. Unfortunately, there was another obstacle to be cleared before the money would be available.

In July, 1904, it was announced that Sheriff Thoms' will was to be challenged in the Court of Session by the sons of his only brother - who claimed that the late Sheriff was not of a sound mind at the time he made the will.

The nephews' case was that their bachelor uncle was a man "of very eccentric habits." He had elaborate "rules of the house" printed - and fined the servants and even Sambo the cat if the rules were broken. They also claimed that he conceived the idea, although there was no foundation in fact, that he was the chief of the Clan MacThomas of Glenshee.

It was further alleged that he had fallen under the influence of his valet and he had neglected his family and friends. Also the Sheriff - despite leaving an estate at the time of his death exceeding £80,000 - was said to have been "under the delusion that he was a poor man."

Kirkwall Town Council had to defend the case, before a jury, and the Lord Justice-Clerk, in the Court of Session in a five day hearing in Edinburgh in February, 1905.

Several doctors gave evidence that Sheriff Thoms suffered chronic gout but his "mental faculties were absolutely unimpaired." The Lord Justice-Clerk said he had read Sheriff Thoms' correspondence and "found not a single letter showing he was mentally weak."

After deliberating for just half an hour, the jury returned a unanimous verdict that the late Sheriff was of a sound mind and, thus, Kirkwall would get over £40,000 at once, and the remainder of the estate after the death of other beneficiaries who had been granted life occupation of property.

Death of jailed minister

The death in 1903 of Sanday minister Rev Matthew Armour recalled a chapter in Orkney's political history that led to the county's judicial system being held up to national ridicule - and the tragic suicide of a Sheriff.

Rev Armour, of Sanday's West United Free Kirk, a native of Paisley who had served as a minister for 55 years after being ordained in 1848, died at the age of 82. During his life, he had been no stranger to personal tragedy - his wife and daughter had died within four days of each other in 1867 - nor to conflict with authority.

In 1870, he had been called before the Presbytery, and censured, after he allowed a woman - an American Quaker, a Miss Smellie, who was on holiday in Sanday - to preach in his kirk. "This strange phenomenon - a woman preaching in the church - brought a full house and an excited audience," said *The Orcadian*.

And, a few years later, he was to become a household name throughout Scotland after being jailed in the aftermath of an election "riot" in Sanday.

The trouble started at an election meeting in the island during the 1885 Orkney and Shetland General Election campaign contested between Leonard Lyell, for the Liberals, and Thomas Dundas, for the Conservatives. After the meeting, the anti-Dundas feeling had turned into rowdy scenes in which the Conservative candidate was jostled.

If Dundas had won the election, it was believed that no prosecutions would have followed, *The Orcadian* reported later. However, Lyell went on to secure an easy victory for the Liberals.

The result was that on the afternoon of Saturday, January 30, 1886, Rev Armour, then aged 65, faced criminal charges at Kirkwall Sheriff Court. The evidence of the prosecution was that he had heckled the Tory candidate and was said to have given a "spasmodic twitch" to his stick.

Sheriff Mellis imposed four days imprisonment and the minister was sent to the cells to join other Sanday residents who had been jailed for the affray. However, the defence lawyer immediately referred the case to the Court of Session in Edinburgh where the conviction was quashed by Lord McLaren and Lord Young who described it as a "nimious prosecution."

Lord McLaren sent a telegram to Kirkwall ordering the immediate release of Rev Armour, and the minister was awoken by his jailer at 10pm to be freed after just a few hours in custody. "Seldom has our northern capital witnessed such an outburst of joy as on that Saturday night when the minister of the gospel was set free," said *The Orcadian*.

The evidence of the "spasmodic twitch" on which the minister was condemned made the Orkney authorities the laughing stock of the country, said the newspaper, while Rev Armour had become a public hero.

The case was to have a tragic sequel, however, when Sheriff Mellis - the man who had imposed the prison sentence and suffered the derision that followed it - later shot himself to death at his home in Kirkwall.

Kirkwall health warning

Kirkwall's medical officer of health, Dr Benjamin Bell, warned Orcadians from the rural districts and islands that the price they faced for moving to the bright lights of Kirkwall could be death!

"It is an everyday experience that young persons coming from the country districts to our towns, after a short time completely break down, the new surroundings being quite unsuited to their constitutions," Dr Bell told Kirkwall Town Council in his 1903 annual report.

"Members of families who, for generations, have done good and useful work for their country in rural districts, cannot without, in most cases, paying the penalty of deterioration of health and comparatively early death, rush into our

towns, and engage in severe brain work, or, in fact, skilled manual labour.

"Before a parent sends his children into our towns for their professional education or apprenticeship to mercantile life, he should satisfy himself as to what are the conditions under which his son or daughter will live. It must be remembered that persons brought up in the country are much more liable to contract certain ailments, such as Tuberculosis, when they are exposed to the infection, than their town-bred companions."

Dr Bell offered as proof of his contention the fact that in the previous year there had been 17 deaths in Kirkwall of people aged 25-60 years.

Ba' death tragedy

Kirkwall's New Year Ba' game of 1903 was "one of the most terrible ever witnessed" as one player died and another dragged unconscious from the scrum.

The man who died was a Doonie player, Captain Cooper, master of the smack *Caleb*, aged around 45, who left a widow and ten young children. He collapsed and was being carried home when he died.

The "sad and startling" news led to an attempt to get the game stopped "but by this time the Up-the-Gates had got the ball as far up as Tankerness House, and the contest was continued more furiously

than ever," reported *The Orcadian*.

At this point, another player - a Mr Bichan from Quoybanks - was carried out senseless after falling in the middle of the scrum. Fortunately he came round and was able to proceed home in his own trap.

Two months later, a strange twist of fate saw a disaster overtake the vessel of which Captain Cooper had been master. The *Caleb* - owned by Kirkwall merchant Robert Garden - was lost on February 26, 1903, with one of the crew, Thomas Bews, washed overboard to his death.

The only known photograph of the first Orcadian-owned car which was brought to the islands by Mr W.R. Tullock, pictured on the right of this family group.

(Picture courtesy of David Tullock)

Island graves for lost crew

Sanday became the final resting place for the men who perished when their sailing ship was wrecked on the island with the loss of the entire crew.

The brig *Arvio*, from Finland, foundered off the Point of Elsness, but islanders were only alerted when wreckage and bodies were washed ashore at Backaskaill. The funeral of the lost crewmen were held at the Cross Church on the island in October, 1903.

A week earlier, five crewmen of the schooner *Mary Roberts*, carrying 160 tons of coal to Burray, had a more fortunate experience when they made it safely ashore on South Ronaldsay in the ship's lifeboat after their vessel went ashore on the Lowther skerry in the Pentland Firth.

The biggest escape of the year however came when the steamer *St Ninian*, owned by the North of Scotland and Orkney and Shetland Steam Navigation Company, went ashore at Sandside Bay, Deerness, with 30-40 passengers on board. The steamer *Orcadia* helped to tow her to safety a few hours later.

It would be another 12 years before Copinsay lighthouse was built to help avoid similar disasters.

Kirkwall jail break

A 31 year old Stromness labourer earned himself a certain notoriety by escaping from Kirkwall prison - twice.

The offender, who had absconded from the prison on a previous occasion, made his second escape on March 7, 1903, by the not particularly taxing method of placing a ladder against the wall of the exercise yard and climbing over it.

The escapee, who was facing charges of threatening a police constable with a loaded revolver, was recaptured and sentenced to a further nine months imprisonment with hard labour.

Cycle champion

A 27 mile cycle race between Kirkwall and Evie, for a gold medal presented by Kirkwall watchmaker David Sinclair, was won by Kirkwall joiner William Garrioch in 93 minutes 10 seconds, beating Dounby blacksmith Alex Scott by 1 minute 40 seconds. The first two men in the race, in June, 1903, were riding Orcadia cycles while the third and fourth were on St Magnus cycles, manufactured by W.R. Tullock.

On the brink of war

Orkney's first motorised bus service was started in 1905. In the event of a breakdown, the driver sent a telegram for help to Kirkwall. (Picture courtesy of David Tullock)

1904

Britain came to the very brink of war with Russia - with Kirkwall earmarked as a potential front line Naval base - after a North Sea outrage saw the British trawler fleet under fire.

There were angry calls for revenge when the Russian Baltic Fleet made an unprovoked attack on 50 Hull trawlers in an area of sea between Orkney and Denmark. Several vessels were sunk and their trawler crews perished.

Russia was already at war with Japan while, in any new European conflict, it was likely that France would ally with Russia against Britain. *The Orcadian* warned that such a war would cost £200 millions and 50,000 lives.

In the two months before the outrage in the autumn of 1904, there had been increasing conjecture that Kirkwall bay had been chosen as a future Naval base - and warships of both the Channel Fleet and the Home Fleet had arrived in Orkney.

In September, 1904, Kirkwall was invaded by more than 5,000 Naval men when five battleships - *Victorious, Magnificent, Majestic, Jupiter* and *Hannibal* - and three cruisers of the Channel Fleet arrived on a three day visit, with the *Victorious* carrying the flag of Rear Admiral Francis Bridgeman.

A month later, ten ships of the Home Fleet also visited Kirkwall under the command of Vice Admiral Sir K. Wilson in the flagship *Exmouth*, and the burgh saw 500 men of the Royal Marines, with two bands, parade ashore.

The Russian explanation for the attack on the trawlers was that warships had been mistakenly identified amongst the fishing vessels. Fortunately, diplomacy prevailed and it was eventually agreed that the outrage would be dealt with by an international commission of inquiry.

Champagne freedom protest

Sir Henry Craik, Secretary of the Scottish Education Department, officially opened an extension to the Kirkwall burgh school - and was presented with the freedom of the burgh.

The drinks bill at the reception afterwards came to £13 13s 6d and Councillor Robert Reid, a life-long abstainer who had been secretary of the Total Abstinence Society in Kirkwall for 40 years, complained that the guests had drunk too much champagne. He attempted, in vain, to have the bill reduced.

The new school extension included a headmaster's office, school hall, classrooms and science laboratory, with an internal telephone system linking the various rooms.

One classroom seated 100 pupils, and another 80.

Over 600 perish in disaster

Wreckage was washed ashore in Orkney after one of the worst peacetime shipping disasters in the early years of the century when a steamer - carrying 800 Scandinavian emigrants to the New World - struck Rockall and sank within 20 minutes.

A total of 129 survivors from the *Norge* were saved by trawlers and cargo steamers but more than 600 were feared to have perished in the disaster in the summer of 1904. Some of the children had died in the ship's lifeboats and had been buried at sea.

The second mate of the *Norge* was landed at Stromness after being rescued. He had wrapped a 15 month old girl in his coat, helping to save her life by chewing ship's biscuits for her to digest. Other survivors were landed in the Faroes.

Cost of living

Retail prices for groceries and other items in Kirkwall in August, 1904, included the following: a 4lb loaf of bread 6d, one dozen eggs 8d, one stone of potatoes 6d, lobsters 1/3 each and a gallon of beer 1/4.

House sale

Lynnfield House, which, more than 40 years later after World War Two, became Kirkwall's Lynnfield Hotel, was sold in March, 1904, to James Grant of Hobister for £1,300.

The line-up of vehicles owned by the Orkney Motor Express Company. (Picture courtesy of David Tullock)

Record-breaking drive

Pioneering Orkney motorist Edward Robertson Grant, a member of the Highland Park family in Kirkwall, set a new record for driving from John o' Groats to Land's End in the summer of 1904.

He completed his record-breaking drive on the 883 mile run in 42 hours 5 minutes, an average of over 20 mph, beating the previous record by 3 hours 20 minutes. He returned in triumph to Orkney, bring-ing with him his 14 hp Argyll motor car.

The following year, Grant set up Orkney's first motorised bus service, the Orkney Motor Express, managed by W.R. Tullock.

Smallpox hits Orkney

The killer disease smallpox brought fear to Orkney in March, 1904.

The disease broke out among crewmen of the *Hoy Head*, the ferry which served the South Isles from Stromness - and the vessel was ordered to lie in quarantine in the bay at Stromness.

Emergency meetings of Orkney County Council, and the town councils of Kirkwall and Stromness, were held to prepare contingency plans in the event of the disease spreading.

The first case diagnosed by Dr James Grant of Stromness was a Brims seaman Alex Johnston but the disease was thought to have originated with the *Hoy Head* engineer John Corsie who

had recently returned from the South.

The Corsie home was isolated, and the family shop in Bridge Street, Kirkwall, ordered to be closed. All contacts over the age of seven were vaccinated while the bus, on which the sick man travelled from Stromness to Kirkwall, was disinfected.

The emergency meeting of Kirkwall Town Council agreed to find a suitable site to erect a £200 wooden building to be used as a smallpox hospital, with the cost to be shared by Kirkwall, Stromness and the Mainland district committee of the County Council. However Stromness refused to share with Kirkwall and the county council quibbled over the share of the cost.

Stromness, having rejected the Kirkwall plans, then had to make separate provision for a hospital to be built at Midgarth after a third case of smallpox was diagnosed on the *Hoy Head*.

The medical officer of health ordered that the *Hoy Head* would not be allowed to land at Longhope until it had been disinfected and a new crew put on board.

Within two weeks, Kirkwall was officially reported free of the disease and, thankfully, no more cases were recorded in Longhope or Stromness. Which is just as well, for the various councils were still debating suitable sites for a smallpox hospital two years later!

Storm claims 26 lives

1905

A four day storm which raged in January, 1905, left a terrible legacy for the islands of Sanday and Stronsay as at least 26 lives were lost in disasters in Orkney waters.

The first evidence of the weather conditions came as the nine crew of the Hull trawler *Excelsior* were safely landed at Kirkwall after running aground on Egilsay.

But real anguish was to follow. Eight men were lost - and 22 children were left fatherless by the tragedy - when the Portknockie Zulu fishing boat *Evangeline* was wrecked on Stronsay. It was a story of immense personal grief as the death toll included five members of the Mair family and two members of the Wood family, including the skipper, David Wood.

The bodies which were washed ashore in Stronsay were returned to the small fishing port of Portknockie where the funeral procession was estimated at 5,000 people. A disaster fund raised £500 for the families of the victims; a large contribution to the fund coming from the folk of Stronsay.

Sanday was to witness a double tragedy that week. Firstly, the five man crew of the Yarmouth smack *Alice and Ada* perished when the vessel was driven ashore at Kettletoft, on passage from Hull to Iceland.

Then, the *Inclita* of Genoa, which had left Sunderland for Montevideo with a cargo of coal, was wrecked at Hackness, Sanday, with the crew of 13 all feared lost as eight bodies were washed ashore.

The year of 1905 was to continue with a series of serious incidents at sea. In September, 1905, the Aberdeen trawler *Swallow* stranded at Sealskerry, North Ronaldsay, but the eight crew were saved, and two months later, the Aberdeen trawler *Sunbeam* went ashore at Sandwick, where the nine crew managed to scramble ashore to be cared for at the home of Mr John Marwick.

But the cruel sea took its toll again in November, 1905, when 28 men were lost after the Swedish steamer *Johan* and the Russian schooner *Antares* were in collision in the North Sea, to the east of Orkney. Two survivors - the master and carpenter of one of the vessels - were saved by the Hull trawler *Francis Drake* and landed at Stromness.

That same month saw a terrible shipping disaster 1,000 miles away from Orkney which claimed an Orcadian life. Mary Linklater, of Cavan, Twatt, was among the 128 people who died in the English Channel when the steamer *Hilda*, from Southampton, went on the rocks in fog and snow near St Malo,

France. The majority of those killed were French onion sellers returning to Brittany.

But 1905 would also be remembered for another tragedy - and a rescue of heroic proportions - much nearer home as the Grimsby trawler *City of Lincoln* was lost at Papa Westray. The skipper, mate and three of her crew died - but another seven were saved in an epic story of bravery by the islanders.

The *City of Lincoln* was returning from Faroese waters in bad weather and struck rocks having mistaken the light of Noup Head for Suleskerry!

In harrowing scenes, men who had taken to the rigging were washed overboard, but after 12 hours, Papay folk managed to get a makeshift line on board to rescue the remaining crew.

One of the Papay heroes was Andrew Groat, of Kimbland, Papa Westray, a man who had suffered personal tragedy just 18 months earlier when his father, 62 year old Stewart Groat, and two of his brothers David (29) and John (17) were drowned when their small fishing boat was lost in a gale in January, 1904.

Andrew Groat and William Hume, of Kirkholes, Papa Westray, were honoured as heroes by the Royal Humane Society for their bravery in saving the chief engineer of the *City of Lincoln* from the sea. The two men also were awarded the King's Silver Medal for Gallantry.

Later, at the Fatal Accident Inquiry into the disaster, the jury added a rider that the lives of all the trawler crew would have been saved if proper life saving equipment was on the island, and called on the Board of Trade to supply such equipment. The equipment was duly supplied and its value was proved within six months when the newly formed Papay Rocket Brigade - under the command of Andrew Groat - saved ten crewmen from the Aberdeen trawler *Badger* which foundered between Westray and Papay.

Unfortunately one man, the trawler mate Euphraim Mortlock, a father of six from Hull, was washed into the sea and lost, but the rocket brigade managed to reach the scene in a yawl and fire a line aboard the stricken vessel to save his crewmates.

The rescue had a bitter sequel when the eight Papay rescuers were awarded just £6 between them from the Board of Trade for their heroic efforts in the rescue. After representations by Orkney's MP Cathcart Wason, this was later increased to £1 5s per man and £2 10s to Andrew Groat, the man in charge of the rescue operation.

Cruise liners visit

Orkney had an established trade with cruise liners by the early years of the 20th century with hundreds of tourists from Europe and America making summer visits to the county.

In August, 1904, the French steamer *Ile de France* brought 150 French tourists to Kirkwall - they visited the Cathedral, Maeshowe and the Standing Stones at Stenness - while, in July, 1905, the 10,000 ton liner *Hamburg* visited Kirkwall with 234 American and German passengers. The biggest liner to visit was the *Victoria Luise* - a former record holder for the Atlantic crossing - which frequently carried as many as 500 passengers, in the first decade of the century.

Shipping giant spurned

One company could have dominated Orkney's internal and external shipping services as long ago as 1905. In December that year, however, a meeting of shareholders of the Orkney Steam Navigation Company (which, 90 years later, evolved into Orkney Ferries) rejected a £5,000 take-over bid from the North of Scotland and Orkney and Shetland Steam Navigation Company (later to become, in the second half of the 20th century, P&O Scottish Ferries.) The Orkney Steam Navigation Company that year made a profit of £1,179.

Shapinsay shocker

Two fishermen, fishing off Shapinsay in November, 1905, claimed to have seen a mystery sea serpent. "The body is described as massive as that of a horse, covered with a scaly surface and spotted," said *The Orcadian*. The eyes were said to have been as large as a bowl.

General Sir Frederick Burroughs and Lady Burroughs outside their home at Trumland House in Rousay.

(Picture courtesy of Orkney Library photographic archive)

Heroic soldier, tyrant landlord

Hero or villain? The death of Lt General Sir Frederick Burroughs, of Trumland House, Rousay, in 1905, produced contrasting epitaphs from different sides of the community which varied from respect to bitter hatred.

There was no doubt that Burroughs deserved a reputation as the harshest of the 19th century Orkney lairds, but at the same time his distinguished military service was acknowledged as one of courage and heroism.

He was the oldest son of General Frederick Burroughs and, destined for a military career, he was serving in the 93rd Sutherland Highlanders as an officer at the age of 17 and commanding officer by the age of 33. He served throughout the Crimean War and the Indian Mutiny and was recommended for - though never received - the Victoria Cross for his role in the Relief of Lucknow.

By this time, he had already suceeded to the estates of his grand uncle George William Traill of Wyre in 1852, and from 1873-80, he commanded the Brigade of the Orkney Volunteer Artillery.

However, it was his role as laird which provoked the greatest anger in Orkney. He continued the clearances of land in Rousay and caused growing resentment with a policy of increased rents and evictions amongst his tenants.

This culminated in bitter evidence being presented to members of the Napier Royal Commission, whose visit to Orkney led to the Crofters Act of 1886. Burroughs immediately issued eviction notices to those tenants who gave evidence to the commission and it seems likely that he would have cleared the entire estate had not the Crofters Act been introduced to protect the tenancies of crofters.

His reputation was obviously forgiven or overlooked by the establishment because in 1904 he was Knighted by King Edward VII. And presumably, feelings had mellowed somewhat in Rousay for, after his royal investiture, *The Orcadian* reported that he was welcomed home by his tenants singing "He's a Jolly Good Fellow."

He married Eliza Geddes in 1870 but when he died in 1905, at the age of 74, they had no family. His funeral was in London and his pall bearers included the Lord Lieutenant of Orkney and Shetland, and the mourners included at least one Admiral and three Generals. A memorial service was held at the same time in Rousay.

Rev A.I. Pirie said: "Personally I found him extremely kind. He fearlessly contended for what he conscientiously believed to be right and as fearlessly condemned what he believed to be wrong. It

may be honestly said that he lived a model private life, and those who knew him best were most attached to him."

Low wages

A Board of Trade report in March, 1905, said the average weekly earnings of farmworkers in Orkney was 13s 7d (just 68 pence in decimal currency), the lowest in Scotland.

Lighting up time

Orkney and Shetland MP Cathcart Wason voted against a Parliamentary Bill which required motor vehicles to be lit at night, saying it was an intrusion into personal liberties.

Paper fire

Production of *The Orcadian* was disrupted after a fire, in August, 1905, which saw the composing room roof ablaze. The fire was extinguished, however, before major damage to the building.

Royal review

The steamer *St Sunniva* was chartered to take 240 men of the Orkney Volunteer Artillery to Leith for the Royal Review of the Scottish troops at Edinburgh by King Edward VII.

The pioneer of the motor age in Orkney, Mr William Tullock, who founded the company of W.R. Tullock, is seen here outside his first premises in Victoria Street, Kirkwall. At the end of the century, the premises housed the Orkney Health Promotion Service.

(Picture courtesy of David Tullock)

This man was usually to be found at the other side of the camera. It is Tom Kent, one of the greatest pioneers of photography in the county. He was born in Orkney before emigrating to the United States were he learned the developing craft in Chicago. He returned to the islands at the start of the 20th century and opened a photographic shop in Broad Street, Kirkwall. He is pictured here in a Humberette car which was originally purchased from the Royal Navy during World War One by Mr George Drever of the National Bank, and later sold to a Mr Fraser from Scapa Distillery. Tom Kent died in Kirkwall in 1936, aged 73. (Picture courtesy of David Tullock)

Full speed for the motor age

One man was in the driving seat when it came to pioneering the new age of the motor car in Orkney.

William Reid Tullock not only had the first Orkney-owned car and the first ever driving licence in the county, but he was also the man behind the only commercially-manufactured car to be built in Orkney in the 20th century, the St Magnus.

It was little wonder that W.R. Tullock was so enthused by the arrival of the motor vehicle - he could claim to be a personal friend of a man whose fame and achievements would make him an icon of the century - Henry Ford, probably the best known motor manufacturer the world has seen.

But, as we will see later, Ford could have died an unknown engineer had it not been for two men of Orkney roots who helped to get the original Ford Motor Company off the ground.

W.R. Tullock was born in Westray but in 1886, at the age of 20, he emigrated with three of his brothers, George, Jim and David, to the United States where he trained as a marine engineer for five years before joining the famous American malted drinks company of William Horlick where he rose to become chief engineer.

It was during this time that he met Henry Ford but, just as life was prospering in the United States, "W.R." decided to return to Kirkwall in 1901 to set up Orkney's first motor shop.

On the liner back to Britain, he met the great radio pioneer Marconi who, in 1901, for the first time succeeded in transmitting signals across the Atlantic. It was to help prompt W.R. Tullock's later interest in making his own radio sets and gramophones. It is also claimed that he designed and built the first rotary clothes drier, an idea adopted by others and developed around the world.

But it would be his association with cars for which he was best remembered. There had been a car brought to Orkney by visitors in 1901 - it was a one cylinder Daimler which arrived at Stromness on the steamer *St Nicholas* and made a run to Kirkwall at 14mph.

But the vehicle W.R. Tullock brought north in 1903 - a German-made Benz with a 6hp single cylinder engine - was the first Orkney-owned motor car. He paid £45 for it (and two years later it was sold to a Shetland man for £25) and it was also capable of a steady 14mph.

The second Orkney-owned car was soon to follow - a Peugeot purchased by William MacLennan, who, since 1898, had been the Earl of Zetland's factor in Orkney.

It was Mr MacLennan who, in 1904 when vehicle registrations were introduced, ended up with the number plate BS1. It had originally been allocated to W.R. Tullock but he wrote back to the licensing authorities explaining that his lucky number was seven and requesting BS7. This had already been allocated to MacLennan, but the authorities agreed that the two Orkney men could swap.

The result was that BS7 was registered to W.R. Tullock in March, 1904, and BS1 to MacLennan. (Decades later, when personalised number plates became a major business, BS1 was to be owned by the well known circus impresario Billy Smart, while BS7 was owned by the 1976-77 world motorcycle racing champion Barry Sheene.)

W.R. Tullock's first premises were in Victoria Street, Kirkwall, but at the end of 1902 he moved to Junction Road.

In the early days, there was obviously a limited demand for cars so W.R. Tullock manufactured his own bicycles under the brand name of St Magnus. However in 1910, the great entrepreneur went a stage further and unveiled the only Orkney-manufactured car - a two cylinder, four seater - which he also produced under the St Magnus brand and registered on July 12, 1910.

W.R. Tullock also acted as general manager for the first man to run a regular motor bus service in Orkney, Mr Edward J. Robertson Grant, a member of the Grant family of Highland Park distillery.

Mr Grant ran buses between Kirkwall and Stromness from

The Sunday car outing to the country had begun by 1904-1905. This is the Tullock family visiting the Balfours of Breck in Rendall in their Peugeot car.

(Picture courtesy of David Tullock)

W.R. Tullock moved his motor company to Junction Road in the first decade of the 20th century. He is pictured with the only car which was commercially-manufactured in Orkney, the St Magnus, a two cylinder, four seater vehicle seen here on the right in 1910.

(Picture courtesy of David Tullock)

1905 when this form of transport was in its infancy with a fleet of five vehicles including a double decked bus which could carry 44 passengers. *The Orcadian* of July 15, 1905, reported the inauguration of the service: "The company had a pleasant drive to Stromness which was covered in 73 minutes." The new service saw the start of a price war between the motor bus and the traditional horse-drawn coach with fares between Kirkwall and Stromness reduced from 4s to 3s. In the pioneer days of the service, if the bus broke down, the driver would send a telegram back to Kirkwall requesting a relief vehicle.

However, it appeared that the public still preferred traditional horse power and, after three years, Mr Grant withdrew his service and took up farming in South America where he died in Argentina in 1930 having built up a ranch with 3,000 head of Aberdeen-Angus cattle.

The arrival of motor vehicles was swiftly followed by new motoring laws - and one of the first to fall foul of the legislation was a David Collier who, according to *The Orcadian* of July 15, 1905, was fined £1 - or seven days in prison - for "furious driving" in Stromness.

Orkney County Council introduced a register of heavy motor vehicles in 1909 and the first entry was a Leyland lorry with an unladen weight of two tons, 19 hundredweights, and a maximum speed of eight mph.

Stromness merchant Robert Sinclair, of Sinclair's Supply Stores, claimed the honour of being the owner of the first motor van in Orkney while the first six wheel motor van, a Ford, arrived in the county in 1930, delivered to the Kirkwall firm of R. Garden Ltd. The firm's own joiners built the body of the van which would replace the company's horse-drawn van on its rounds.

The popularity of motorcycles soon increased, leading to the first run of the Orkney Motor Cycle Club on May 27, 1914, and the first tractor to come to Orkney was delivered to the county in 1916 for Mr J. Irvine of Stove, Sanday. Four years later, Mr Henry Maxwell of Housebay, Stronsay, took delivery of a four cylinder International tractor.

Motorised traffic quickly grew in the county to the extent that when a traffic census was carried out in 1922, an average of 250 motor vehicles a day passed Tormiston, on the Kirkwall to Stromness road, compared with just 63 horse-drawn

vehicles. In the East Mainland, 135 motor vehicles a day passed Quoyburray, compared to 100 horse-drawn vehicles.

W.R. Tullock's business in Junction Road, Kirkwall, was passed to his sons Mr D.T. Tullock and Mr Robert P.H. Tullock in 1940. By that time, his old pal Henry Ford was a household name, not only in the United States but throughout the world.

But two of Ford's greatest supporters - indeed his partners - in the early days of what became the multi-billion car corporation we know today were virtually unknown outside the company.

Yet - John S. Gray - whose roots trace back to Longhope in Hoy - was the first president of the Ford company, and Gray's nephew Alexander Malcolmson was the man who provided the financial backing which helped to make it all possible at the start.

Malcolmson, whose family apparently came from Seaberry in Longhope, had followed his uncle to the United States and, by 1902, had built up a prosperous coal business in Detroit, where he was a contemporary of Ford.

In August, 1902, the two men agreed a deal to design and produce their first automobile. Malcolmson would take charge of the financial and commercial side while Ford would be responsible for the engineering division - and in June, 1903, the Ford Motor Company was formed with John Gray as president, Ford as vice-president, and Malcolmson treasurer.

In the first 12 months, 364 cars were made, but already there were strains in the working relationship. Malcolmson, it seems, wanted to produce a top-of-the-range vehicle while Ford, of course, championed a "car for the multitude."

Eventually, Malcolmson was squeezed out and in July, 1906, he sold his 255 shares to Henry Ford for 175,000 dollars. It was not a bad return on his investment - the equivalent today would certainly put him in the millionaire bracket - but had he waited another 15 years to sell, it is surmised that he would have made that amount 100 times over, to the extent possibly of becoming the world's richest businessman of the day.

But, back in Kirkwall, W.R. Tullock did not forget his old pal Henry Ford, and, in 1912, Orkney's pioneer of the automobile age travelled south to sign an agreement to become the county's official Ford dealer. W.R. Tullock died in 1948 at the age of 82.

Round-the-world by bicycle

Kirkwall draper William Liddle set off to cycle round the world in 1906 - a journey which was to see him cover 35,000 miles by land and sea.

Liddle (25) and a colleague C.C. Beckett (20) from Birkenhead, started their epic expedition in South Africa where the young Orcadian had remained after the Boer War, when he served for two years in the Cycling Corps.

The intrepid duo had erected a sail behind their bicycle saddles to help speed their efforts, and by February, 1906, it was estimated that they had covered 3,000 miles across Africa.

1906

By November, 1906, they had completed 7,000 miles by cycle when they arrived by steamer in Australia. They had survived their journey across South Africa despite being caught up by the Zulu rising, and they now intended crossing Australia before embarking for New Zealand. Asia and America then lay ahead, they told reporters.

The two cyclists had gathered together a collection of thousands of postcards of places they had visited.

Two years after setting out on his adventure, William Liddle arrived in his native Kirkwall, and he gave a series of lectures about his travels at venues throughout Orkney. He told *The Orcadian* that he planned a holiday before returning to South Africa.

He reckoned by now to have covered a total of 35,000 miles, but how much of this was by bicycle was unclear as he seemed to have "missed" America by sailing by steamer direct from the South Pacific to London.

Orcadians' earthquake horror

Orcadians in the United States of America were caught up in the great San Francisco earthquake of 1906 which left 300,000 homeless and prompted insurance claims of 110 million dollars.

An estimated 100 Orkney exiles lived in the region of California hit by the tremors.

Mr G.W. Johnston wrote home to his father, Peter Johnston in Dounby, to describe the scenes of devastation, in which, remarkably, the death toll was in hundreds rather than thousands.

"For three miles before me stretched a dead empty plain. There was scarcely a vestige of a house here. The wooden houses had absolutely disappeared, the only signs left being, here and there, a brick chimney and the stone steps leading to where the doors had been. It was a queer spectacle.

"You would be surprised to see how cheerful everyone is - in a short time San Francisco will be busy again."

Rescuers are honoured

Longhope shoreboat skipper William Taylor and his crew were awarded the RNLI silver medal for their efforts in saving nine crewmen when the Sunderland steamer *Dinnington* ran aground on Switha, on a passage to Stornoway with a cargo of coal.

Sadly, two of the crew died but the other nine, in the ship's boat, made it safely ashore on Switha, from where they were rescued by the Longhope men. The bodies of the two drowned crewmen were buried at Flotta.

The amount of shipping traffic in Orkney waters in those early days of the century was illustrated in February, 1906, when a snowstorm saw no fewer than 43 trawlers and 14 cargo steamers anchored in Longhope Bay to escape the weather. Fortunately, the nine crew of the Aberdeen trawler *Redcap* were safely landed at Kirkwall after their vessel ran aground on Eday.

But two Orkney parishes were to suffer tragedy at sea in 1906.

In April, two Deerness fishermen, James Bichan (52), father of six of Pickeltillum, and William Bichan (34), father of two of Little Quoys, were drowned when their boat was swamped as they gathered creels off Copinsay. And, in December, 1906, Longhope was touched by tragedy when Samuel Malcolmson, of Aithsdale, and Alexander Hay, of Melsetter, were drowned in another boating accident.

Benefactor honoured

Kirkwall Town Council conferred the freedom of the burgh on Sir Arthur Bignold in October, 1906 - thus honouring the man who was arguably the town's greatest benefactor of the 20th century.

Bignold served as Kirkwall's Member of Parliament - as Conservative MP for the Northern Burghs - from 1900-1910, and was knighted in 1904.

Coinciding with the conferring of the freedom of Kirkwall, it was announced that he would gift the burgh a recreation park and pavilion for the youth of the town. This was to become Kirkwall's Bignold Park, still the venue of Orkney's County Show and the county's major football and hockey matches at the end of the 20th century.

He also presented a chain of office to be worn by the Provost of Kirkwall - it weighed 28 ounces in 18 carat gold!

It is perhaps too easy to be cynical over his motives but, in all fairness, it should be pointed out that much of his philanthropy was directed at those who had no vote.

Each Christmas, he paid the coal bill for all of Kirkwall's poor and distributed free beef - up to 10lbs per family - to the same. He also paid for all the children of needy families to be given free shoes to attend school.

Double-decker bus

Orkney's first motorised double-decker bus arrived in the county in August, 1906.

Carrying up to 44 people, the 40hp Leyland vehicle was operated by the Orkney Express Motor Company, owned by Edward Robertson Grant and managed by W.R. Tullock.

"The machine is equal to the very best motor buses in any part of the kingdom," said *The Orcadian*.

Public executions

Orkney and Shetland MP Cathcart Wason made a plea in the House of Commons for an end to public executions and floggings in the British colonies.

Golf course

South Ronaldsay's new nine hole golf course was opened by the Gray family at Roeberry with a match against players from Kirkwall.

Members of the Stromness life-saving rocket brigade prepare for duty. In December, 1907, they helped to save three men from the Hull trawler *Shakespeare* aground in Hoy Sound. (Picture courtesy of Orkney Library photographic archive)

No escape from the sea

Orcadians, and passing strangers alike, shared the anguish caused by the unrelenting and deadly power of the sea in a series of dreadful disasters in 1907.

The Sanday schooner *Jack Snipe* was lost with her five Orcadian crewmen after sinking to an unknown grave in March, 1907. The vessel had sailed from Kirkwall for the South but, after being reported a month overdue, the families of the crew had to accept the grim reality that their loved ones had perished.

The master, James Sandison, had sailed with his son Benjamin as mate. The other lost crewmen were Thomas Leslie and John Scott, both from Westray, and Robert Cutt from Sanday.

Six months later, four men and a woman drowned, leaving 12 children fatherless, and four orphaned, in Burray.

They were Mr and Mrs David Petrie, a master mariner and first officer of a North Shields steamer; John Bruce, a father of three of Cellardyke, Burray; James Bruce, a father of five of Leith, Burray; and James Copland, the Burray postman and father of four.

They were returning from St Mary's to Burray after a day in Kirkwall. The cause of the accident was a mystery as the only evidence found was their boat, washed ashore the following day.

During the year, more than two dozen

1907

mariners had remarkable escapes after running aground on Orkney shores.

In February, 1907, the Aberdeen fishing boat *Kilrenny* went aground off Deerness in a blizzard. Seven Deerness men who launched a rescue bid could not even locate the scene of the disaster in the blinding snowstorm - but later, as the weather moderated, the nine crewmen of the stricken vessel were saved by another boat with four men from Deerness, before the Stromness lifeboat reached the scene.

The following month, nine crewmen from the North Shields trawler *Irish Prince* reached safety on Copinsay after their vessel ran aground on the island, and, in August, 1907, local people dragged to safety the six man crew of the Chester schooner, *Celtic*, which had been driven ashore in the Bay of Skaill, on passage from London to Oban with a cargo of cement.

But a more dramatic story was to unfold in December, 1907, when the Hull trawler *Shakespeare* went ashore at Breckness in Hoy Sound. Four men

drowned in heavy seas, but three were saved by the local rocket brigade, and another three rescued by Stromness lifeboat, under coxswain Robert Greig.

The funeral of the four lost fishermen was held in Stromness, while the crew of the Stromness lifeboat received £1 each for their rescue, and coxswain Greig was awarded the RNLI silver medal.

But there was to be a sequel of recrimination for the skipper of the fishing vessel as it transpired that the *Shakespeare*, returning South from the fishing grounds, had mistaken the light on Graemsay for the light at Dunnet Head. The Board of Trade inquiry into the loss ordered the suspension of the certificate of the skipper, Arthur Patch, for six months.

Worse was to follow for the luckless skipper when he was arrested, charged with culpable homicide and brought to Kirkwall Sheriff Court to face trial.

Arthur Patch could be grateful for Orkney justice. After retiring for just a few minutes, the jury returned a verdict of not guilty.

Sheriff William Harvey, discharging the skipper, praised "the frank and manly way in which you all along accepted responsibility; and the frank and truthful story you told. I think that does you great credit."

Orcadians in death crash

Six Orcadians, travelling to a new life in the Far West, escaped with their lives in a railway disaster which saw 15 people killed in Canada.

A Canadian Pacific Railway Transcontinental train was derailed and caught fire near Chapleau, Ontario, with nine adults and six children burned to death, in April, 1907.

Two Orcadians - Jim Foubister and William Wards - suffered burns to the face and hands, but four others, including W. Harrold, the son of John Harrold, of Junction Road, Kirkwall, and Bill Mowat, escaped without a scratch.

Another Orcadian, George Inkster, also escaped the disaster. He had gone for a haircut - and missed the train at Montreal.

Mr Harrold wrote home to his father: "In all my life I never saw such a scene. The agonising cries of men, women and children for help which could not be given were awful."

Cold comfort for stowaway

A 14 year old Longhope boy's dream of a life at sea ended in a nightmare, and a narrow escape from death.

For when he decided to set off for a career at sea in exotic climes, he made the mistake of choosing a trawler bound for Iceland.

He crept on board the Aberdeen steam trawler *King Edward* when the vessel called at Longhope, and he hid in the fish-room as a stowaway. Fortunately, the skipper was alerted two days later by knocking and the crew found the huddled boy "half frozen" by the ice which was stored there.

"Prompt steps were taken to bring the youth round, and warmed and fed, and comfortably stowed in a berth, he soon recovered and told his story," reported *The Orcadian*.

School fees abolished

The Kirkwall and St Ola School Board agreed, in February, 1907, that fees for all children attending the Kirkwall burgh school should be abolished. In practice, education had been free for several years, but this decision ended an anomaly whereby children from outwith the burgh could be charged.

Motor vehicles registered in Orkney up to September, 1908, totalled 30 private cars, seven trade vehicles and 36 motorcycles. (Picture courtesy of David Tullock)

No votes for women here!

A Bill to give the vote to women failed to pass through Parliament in March, 1907, after Orkney and Shetland MP Cathcart Wason told the House of Commons he did not think there was any demand on the part of women for the suffrage.

No European country had ever ventured into such a "cauldron of trouble," he warned.

This measure, if passed, would press very severely on the country districts, opined Wason. In his own constituency of some 8,000 electors, they had the greatest difficulty in getting to the polls, and it would be "absolutely impossible for womankind" to get there, except under very favourable circumstances.

Kirkwall canal

A scheme to build a short canal, linking Scapa to Kirkwall Bay, was proposed by a correspondent of *The Scotsman*. Such a project, he suggested, would make Longhope and Scapa Flow a suitable Naval base, thus fulfilling Sir Walter Scott's prophesy of the previous century that Longhope would become "a thriving town."

Pentland baby

What was believed to be the first baby born on the Pentland Firth came into the world, in October, 1907, on the steamer *St Ola* between Scapa and Scrabster when a woman returning home from the herring fishing - the wife of a Glaswegian cooper George Buchanan - gave birth. Mother and child were landed safely at Scrabster.

Reward for vandals

A £50 reward - the equivalent of thousands at 1999 prices - was offered by Kirkwall Town Council, on the advice of the burgh fiscal, for information leading to the conviction of vandals responsible for cutting down 15 trees planted on the Kirk Green.

Not a poor man

Colonel James Balfour, of Balfour Castle, the convener of Orkney County Council since its inception 18 years earlier, died in 1907, aged 79. In addition to property worth over £100,000, he left a personal estate of £43,175.

Veteran minister

Orkney's oldest minister, Rev John Peddie, senior minister of Papa Westray, died in December, 1907, at the age of 96.

Christmas heroes of Faray

1908

Five men of one of Orkney's smallest islands were hailed as heroes - with a personal presentation from King Edward VII - after a dramatic Christmas sea rescue in 1908.

There were only eight families living on the island of Faray but five of the island's menfolk - William Burgar, of Cott, John Hercus of Doggerboat, James Groat of Leaquoy, Robert Reid of Holland and John Drever of Windywall - risked their lives in a small 13 feet boat to save nine men from the Peterhead-registered trawler *Hope*.

The trawler had been driven ashore on the Holm of Faray in a 70mph gale in the evening of December 28, 1908, and in raging seas, the skipper Alexander Youngson and his crew, including Youngson's 17 year old brother, faced a grim death from exposure in the night.

However, the wrecked *Hope* was spotted early the next morning by John Hercus who raised the alarm and the five Faray men made two treacherous journeys in William Burgar's boat across the stretch of Lavey Sound between Faray and the holm to bring, first, five men to safety, and then the other four.

The island was marooned by the storm right over the New Year and it was January 4, 1909, before the rescued men could be ferried to Kirkwall.

The story of the Faray heroes went round the world - gifts were received from as far away as New Zealand - and the Scots philanthropist Andrew Carnegie gave £10 to each of the rescuers.

But the greatest honour was to come in June, 1909, when the men were invited to Balmoral for the presentation of Board of Trade silver medals by King Edward VII.

They journeyed down to Aberdeen by steamer and were met by a royal coach which took them to Balmoral, where as well as the presentation of the medals, they each were given gifts of a pipe and tobacco before a sight-seeing tour of the Castle and grounds.

Some of the Faray men later bought the hull of the wrecked *Hope* from which they salvaged 30 tonnes of scrap metal.

By coincidence, six years later, Captain Alexander Youngson, was to be honoured by King George V, when he was decorated for helping to sink the first enemy submarine of World War One by ramming her with the patrol trawler *Dorothy Gray*, which was under his command, at the entrance to Scapa Flow.

The five heroes of Faray who were given a personal commendation by King Edward VII for their bravery in saving nine men from the wrecked trawler *Hope*. From the left they are Robert Reid, William Burgar, James Groat, John Hercus and John Drever.

(Picture courtesy of Orkney Library photographic archive)

Wife and baby sail to disaster

A tragedy in Orkney waters is still shrouded in mystery after the loss of the Liverpool sailing barque *Isle of Erin* - and her crew of 18 - in a disaster that could have been avoided if North Ronaldsay had telegraphic communications to enable islanders to summon help.

The ship left Sunderland in October, 1908, with a cargo of coal for Montevideo. Captain William McMinn, of Hawick, was accompanied by his wife, Jane, and two year old son Robert. It appears that his wife always wanted to take a trip but the captain would never agree - until this fateful voyage which was to prove the lady's first and final trip.

Among the crew was 25 year old William Angus, of Ramsquoy, Stenness, who had joined the ship as Chief Officer at Sunderland.

On October 19, 1908, the vessel was seen to the south of Start Point, Sanday, running before the wind with full canvas. It seemed to eyewitnesses that the ship was almost on the rocks before danger was realised. At the last moment, the *Isle of Erin* took evasive action but, thrown on her beam ends, it looked as though her cargo shifted because, rounding the point, she appeared to develop a heavy list. It was later suggested that some of the officers and crew were thrown overboard in the violent lurching of the vessel.

That evening the ship was observed by North Ronaldsay folk near the Reef Dyke, flying distress signals. The wind and sea was too strong to launch small boats and the islanders, without telegraphic communication, were powerless to summon help.

Rockets and flares were fired by the crew as the barque was carried north at the mercy of the wind and tide, but no more flares were seen after 11pm on October 19, and, the next day, a ship's lifeboat was found on the North Ronaldsay shore with the identification "*Isle of Erin*, Liverpool."

Although some small wreckage was found, the final fate of the *Isle of Erin* was still a mystery when a Board of Trade inquiry was held in Aberdeen in April, 1909. Witnesses at the inquiry included several from Orkney - Mr Thomas King, Lopness, Sanday; Mr Wilson, Burrian, Sanday; Mr Skea, the Kettletoft harbourmaster; Mr Arthur, North Ronaldsay principal lightkeeper; and three other North Ronaldsay men - Mr James Swanney of Gravity, Mr Hugh Thomson of Bewan and Mr John Swanney of Sangar.

Shortly afterwards, wireless telegraphy was installed in North Ronaldsay.

He wowed the Queen

An Orcadian who rose to one of the top positions in local government in Scotland - and caught the eye of Queen Victoria in the process - was Sir James Marwick who died in 1908. He could claim the distinction of having served as town clerk of both Edinburgh and Glasgow.

Born in 1826, the son of Kirkwall merchant William Marwick, he was educated in Kirkwall before proceeding to Edinburgh University. He was trained for the legal profession before, in 1861, becoming town clerk of Edinburgh.

After 12 years, he moved to Glasgow as town clerk - earning an increase in salary of £1,600. Later his salary rose to £3,500 at a time when Orkney farmworkers earned around £50 a year.

He held sway as town clerk of Glasgow for a period extending over three decades from the 19th century into the 20th century, until his retirement in 1903, and was knighted by Queen Victoria in 1888.

Sir John Samuel, secretary to Glasgow Lord Provosts for 36 years, later recalled: "Marwick was a very handsome man and the Queen had frequently seen him when he accompanied civic deputations to Buckingham Palace. As is known, the old Queen had a keen eye for a good looking man."

Sober Orkney

Orkney - excluding the burghs of Kirkwall and Stromness - was the most sober county in Scotland, with only three cases of drunkenness per 10,000 population in a year, according to a government report.

Kirkwall had the equivalent of 46 cases per 10,000 population, slightly over half the level in Stromness which had the equivalent of 82 cases per 10,000 population. The "most drunken" place in Scotland was said to be Blairgowrie with the equivalent of 1,042 cases per 10,000.

Black Monday

South Ronaldsay was in mourning after the deaths on Monday, March 16, 1908, of four island fishermen when their boat was swamped by a wave off Halcro Head. The victims were James Cromarty of Honeysgoe, Samuel Cromarty of South Cara, James Thomson of Quoybanks and William Guthrie of New London, all South Ronaldsay.

Front page news

A new era began for *The Orcadian* as the edition of December 12, 1908, saw editorial news items displace advertisements on the front page of the newspaper.

Navy in Scapa Flow

"Is it beyond the bounds of possibility that Scapa Bay and Flow may one day become a great Naval station?" asked *The Orcadian* in July, 1908, as Orkney got a glimpse of the future when a flotilla of 24 destroyers arrived in the Flow on an exercise.

The potential value of a Naval base was illustrated as local merchants received orders from the Navy for 1,500 lbs of bread, 3,000 lbs of potatoes and 1,500 lbs of beef for each day the ships were at Scapa.

Meanwhile, Prince Adalbert, the third son of the German Kaiser, was among the crew of the German High Seas Squadron cruiser *Danzig* which called into Kirkwall. He visited St Magnus Cathedral.

Old age pensions

The introduction of a national old age pensions scheme saw people over the age of 70, with an annual income of less than £21, qualify for a pension of five shillings a week for the first time. Applications in Orkney totalled over 1,200 and local committees were set up to decide who qualified.

Monster from the deep

The Aberdeen trawler *Balmedie*, fishing off Orkney, trawled up the skull of what was believed to be an unidentified prehistoric creature, *The Orcadian* reported in July, 1908.

"The skull is of immense size, its dimensions suggesting that the animal was as large as an elephant. It is thought that the relic is part of some prehistoric monster from the Arctic regions which, having been preserved in its ice bed for ages, may have been washed down into warmer latitudes on an ice floe before being deposited in the Atlantic."

Candidate killed

Colin Dunlop, who had stood as the Unionist candidate in the Orkney and Shetland constituency in the General Election two years previously, was killed in a hunting accident while riding with the Dumfriesshire Foxhounds near Lockerbie, in April, 1908.

Great minds think alike

Orkney's contribution to the rarefied world of universities and academia in the first quarter of the 20th century was truly astonishing.

The islands - despite the disadvantages of remoteness and the same problems of poverty and limited elementary education that faced most of the country's ordinary people of the day - could boast a roll call of Orcadian-born professors, totalling double figures, at some of the top universities around the world.

Sadly they had to leave the islands to achieve their success, and so to that extent it can be regarded as a "brain drain" but, at the same time, Orkney's loss was to be the world's gain and the county could be proud of the extent that those men embraced the opportunities that saw Orcadians make their mark not only in Britain but South Africa, Canada and the USA - often carrying out pioneering research work that led the world.

What drove this success is now debatable - it may have been just one of those statistical freaks of history - but nonetheless, a mixture of determination and talent saw a remarkable group of young men educated at Kirkwall Burgh School (later to be Kirkwall Grammar School) proceed to Edinburgh University in the early years of the century.

However, one of Orkney's first professors of the era was not a product of Kirkwall education - but the school room in Flotta. And, in an inspiring story of achievement against the odds, Sutherland Simpson rose from the humble station of dock labourer to become one of America's foremost medical research workers and World War Memorial Professor of Physiology at Cornell University, USA.

Young Simpson, from Saraquoy, Flotta, left the island in 1882, bound for Leith, and with his Orcadian pal John Sinclair he got a job at the docks handling boxes of rhubarb; a task not designed to bring fame nor fortune.

However, Sutherland Simpson eventually got a job as a laboratory boy at Edinburgh University and, in his own time, started attending classes at the university, intending to become a doctor. He graduated in 1897 and taught in Edinburgh before deciding to try his luck in the USA. By 1908, he was appointed to the Chair of Physiology and Biochemistry at Cornell University and, in 1920, World War Memorial Professor of Physiology. He always retained his links with Orkney, however, and his last visit home to Flotta was to be in August, 1923. Sadly, less than three years later, he died on March 2, 1926.

It was at Aberdeen University that another Orcadian made his mark. Professor Trail, born in Birsay, the youngest son of the Rev Samuel Trail, who in 1874 was Moderator of the Church of Scotland, became professor of botany at Aberdeen at the age of 26 and held the post for 42 years, before which time he became one of the first academics to explore the Amazon jungles, visiting remote areas of Brazil from 1873-75. Professor Trail died at the age of 68 in 1919.

Another Orkney student who attended Edinburgh University - in this case going on to become a professor of theology - was Professor John Oman from Stenness who was principal of Westminster College, Cambridge, in the 1920s and 1930s. Born in 1860, the son of Captain Oman, of Biggings, Stenness, the Rev Oman's appointment as Principal of Westminster College in 1922 carried with it a salary of £850 a year and a house! The average annual earnings of his fellow Orcadians back home in Orkney was less than £150.

Professor Ernest Shearer - from Stronsay - was another Orcadian who studied at Edinburgh University from 1897-1904. After working in India and Egypt he was principal of the Edinburgh and East of Scotland College of Agriculture, and professor of agriculture at Edinburgh University. He died, aged 66, in 1945.

He had a string of Orkney contemporaries during his Edinburgh student days, and his fellow undergraduates included several Orcadians who went on to become respected academics around the world.

They included Dr Charles Anderson, the youngest son of John Anderson, of Moa, Stenness, who after graduating both as an MA and a BSc at Edinburgh, went to Australia, where, in 1921, he was appointed Director of the Australian Museum.

Westray-born David Balfour, one of 11 children of the Balfour family of Chalmersquoy, went from Edinburgh University to Jamaica where, in 1908, he became Registrar-General, a post he held until his death in 1922.

John Tait - a brother of Charles Tait of Buttquoy House, Kirkwall - rose to become Emeritus Professor at the McGill University in Montreal, where he occupied the Chair of Physiology. He died aged 66 in October, 1944.

Also at McGill University was Professor George Scarth - also ex-Kirkwall school and Edinburgh University - who had the award of Doctor of Science conferred upon him for his research work in 1933.

Dr Robert Charles Wallace, born in Orkney in 1881, the son of James and Mary Wallace of Deerness, went on to Edinburgh University where he received an MA (1901), BSc (1907) and Doctorate of Science (1912) before - after post-graduate work in Germany - going to Canada where, eventually, he became President of the University of Alberta before, in 1936, becoming Principal of Queens University in Ontario.

When another famous son of Orkney, Sir John Flett, Director of the Geological Survey of Great Britain, visited Canada for a conference in the early 1920s, he was photographed with a group of no less than five Orcadian-born professors in that country.

Shapinsay was the birthplace of Professor James Drever, who, in June, 1931, went on to hold the Chair of Psychology at Edinburgh, and who, in 1937, was invited back to Orkney and his old school in Stromness to formally open a £10,000 extension and rename the school Stromness Academy. Professor Drever's two sons James and Harald were both to emulate their father and become professors later in the 20th century.

Dr John Malcolm, the grandson of Donald Swanson, of Cursiter, Firth, another graduate of Edinburgh University, studied in Germany before returning to Edinburgh where he was lecturer in chemical physiology from 1900 until 1905 when he was appointed to the chair of physiology at Otago University, Dunedin, New Zealand.

A West Mainland son was Professor James Rognvald Learmonth, the son of William Learmonth of Stromness, and a cousin of Mr John R. Learmonth, rector of the Stromness Secondary School from 1927-48. Professor Learmonth was an honorary surgeon to King George V in Scotland and, in 1936, was appointed to the same role for Edward VIII.

A North Isles man who took his medical expertise to South Africa was John Pottinger, from Rothiesholm, Stronsay, who in 1905 was appointed resident surgeon of the Provincial Hospital, Port Elizabeth.

The Gunn brothers, the sons of Mr J.R. Gunn from Kirkwall (their two sisters Robina and Rachel were responsible for running the burgh telephone exchange) both became professors. Professor James Gunn went on to become Professor of Therapeutics at Oxford University and Director of the Nuffield Institute of Medical Research. In the King's honours list of 1947, he was made a CBE.

Professor John W.C. Gunn was Professor of Pharmacology at the University of Cape Town. Also in South Africa was another former pupil of the Kirkwall burgh school, Professor John Bews, Principal of Natal University.

That was the golden age of Orkney academics, but others would follow in the ensuing years. A generation or two later, two sons of Stromness, Professor William Turmeau (Napier University) and Professor Ronald Miller (Glasgow University), achieved distinction in Scotland, while Professor David Scott, from North Ronaldsay, made his career in America.

Kirkwall was twice hit by serious flooding in 1909, in September and again in November. Areas of the town were submerged "until it looked like a loch." The Scapa road was blocked by landslips at the pier where, tragically, one man was killed by lightning. Wooden houses were simply washed away in the deluge. (Picture courtesy of Orkney Library photographic archive)

A survey of housing in 1919 showed that a total of 238 Kirkwall families lived in homes of just one room. Another 314 families, with up to ten children, had the luxury of two roomed homes. In the country areas, it is surprising how some accommodation withstood the force of Orkney's winter storms. (Picture courtesy of Orkney Library photographic archive)

New lifeboat proves a riot

1909

A new lifeboat for Stromness arrived in her home port for the first time - and started a riot!

The streets of Stromness witnessed scenes of mob violence as the police were stoned and, for the second time this century, local lifeboatmen went on strike.

The grievance of the protesters was that the new vessel *John A. Hay* had been brought from London not by the Stromness lifeboat crew but by men from Stronsay.

The original plan had been that the Stromness men would travel down to London to get the new vessel - to replace the *Good Shepherd* - along with the men of Stronsay who were travelling down to collect that island's first ever lifeboat, the *John Ryburn*.

However, when a date in April, 1909, was set, the Stromness crew told the RNLI that was unsuitable as it was the height of the lobster fishing season and a request was made for a delay until June.

The RNLI ruled out any delay and arranged for the Stronsay men to bring both boats North. And the result was uproar. "Stronsay men to fetch the Stromness lifeboat? The thing was absurd!" said the Stromness correspondent of *The Orcadian*.

The new lifeboat arrived in Stromness to an ominous silence, said the newspaper. "Not a cheer was raised." Word was sent round the crew to muster and haul the boat but few of the men turned up, and a scratch crew had to be formed.

And it was the arrival of the steamer *St Ola* which was "the spark which kindled the conflagration."

"A huge crowd had gathered and their demeanour plainly showed the whole grievance was against the Stromness coxswain and members and officials of the local lifeboat committee," said the newspaper.

"The statements of some of the more ardent supporters of the coxswain that they were ready to take the places of the dissatisfied ones led to many heated arguments and not a few threats of the dire results which would follow such a course of action."

When one of the protesters attempted to board the new vessel, Commander F.J. Rowley, from the RNLI, who had been in charge of bringing the lifeboats to Orkney, gave up attempts to reach an amicable settlement and called on police to arrest the "obstreperous" man.

"Excitement was intense as the police searched for their man and, as they emerged with their prisoner, the feeling rose to a pitch such as has seldom, if ever, been witnessed in Orkney.

"The police were simply mobbed as they moved along the street with their charge. Amid the howls of the angry crowd, and even when the more rowdy members of the mob vented their venom on them by the reprehensible conduct of stone-throwing, the officers exhibited a praiseworthy coolness."

Constables Walls and Manson were both struck during the melee, and *The Orcadian* added: "Even when the police had their prisoner safely under lock and key the malicious scenes continued."

Coxswain Robert Greig offered his resignation in an attempt to calm the situation, while the case against the arrested man was dismissed at the Sheriff Court over a legal technicality.

And three weeks later, the strike was forgotten as *The Orcadian* reported that "past differences were sunk" as the new lifeboat put to sea to help local fishing boats in a bad gale.

The *John A. Hay* was to remain as the Stromness lifeboat until 1928. The 43 feet long *John Ryburn*, powered by a 40hp motor, was to remain as the Stronsay lifeboat only until the outbreak of World War One when it was transferred to Peterhead.

A new dawn for Scapa Flow

April, 1909, witnessed an invasion which was to shape Orkney's role in two world wars.

Admiral Sir William May, commander of the Home Fleet, and Vice-Admiral Prince Louis of Battenberg, commander of the Atlantic Fleet, brought an armada of 82 ships into Scapa Flow.

Orkney, and Kirkwall, had frequently been visited by the Navy, of course, but this was undoubtedly the greatest fleet ever witnessed in the Flow up to that time.

HMS *Triton* had been surveying the anchorage over the previous three summers - but this was the first real indication that Orkney could see a permanent Naval presence of huge strength established within the islands.

Ships of the fleet spent much of the summer coming and going in the Flow - the only embarrassment being when the destroyer *Itchen* went ashore below the Head of Work - and Admiral May wrote a letter of thanks to Kirkwall Town Council to say: "Our stay here has been very pleasant."

The Home and Atlantic Fleets again visited Scapa Flow in 1910, and, by June, 1911, it was obvious that the great harbour had friends in high places as the First Lord of the Admiralty Reginald McKenna MP travelled North to tour the Flow.

A few months later, he was succeeded as First Lord of the Admiralty by Winston Churchill, and, in October, 1913, Orkney received an even more high-powered delegation as Churchill arrived in Scapa Flow on the Admiralty yacht *Enchantress*.

He was accompanied by the Prime Minister, Herbert Asquith, and the Secretary of State for War, Colonel Seeley, Asquith and Churchill both visited St Magnus Cathedral but the yacht only stayed a day, en route to the Cromarty Firth, where it was admitted that talks were held on the possible development of Scapa Flow as a permanent Naval base.

At the same time, conjecture grew that an airfield would be built - South Ronaldsay was suggested as a site - to bolster the Scapa Flow defences.

Death and destruction

A man was killed by lightning and widespread damage was reported after a thunderstorm flooded the streets of Kirkwall.

Wooden buildings were washed away, and houses in Mill Street were under water as areas of the town were submerged "until it looked like a loch," said *The Orcadian*.

Highland Park warehouses had four feet of water, while at Papdale Mill, a wall collapsed under the weight of the torrent and two workmen found themselves knee deep in flood water. The Scapa road was blocked by landslips at the pier, where, a driver Peter Hendry, was struck by lightning and killed.

The storm in September, 1909, saw nearly two inches of rain fall in Kirkwall in a couple of hours. But, on November 12-13, worse was to follow as three and a half inches of rain fell in Kirkwall in 48 hours.

Stromness was also hit by floods, after two and a half inches of rain, with walls demolished by the weight of water as closes were turned into rivers of debris.

Billionaire benefactor

One of the world's richest men - and undoubtedly one of the great philanthropists of the 20th century - became a freeman of Kirkwall in September, 1909.

Dr Andrew Carnegie - a household name in two continents, having left his native Scotland to become one of America's wealthiest industrialists - visited the burgh for the opening of the new Free Library in Laing Street.

It was Carnegie who had paid for the building. It had taken exactly six years to become reality, for it had been back in September, 1903, that he had originally offered £1,500 to erect a new Kirkwall library on condition that the Town Council would ensure that £80 a year was provided to maintain its operation.

Kirkwall's MP, Arthur Bignold, had weighed in by offering to pay the cost of a site for the library.

And so Carnegie, then aged 74, arrived at Scapa by steamer, with his wife, and stayed at the Kirkwall Hotel before attending both the opening ceremony of the library, and the conferring of the freedom of the burgh.

The new library was home to a total of 151,000 volumes, reported *The Orcadian*.

Women seek vote

The demand for sexual equality - and the right of women to vote - reached Orkney in 1909.

"If a bombshell had been fired into Kirkwall it could scarcely have caused more sensation than the intimation of the town crier that there was to be a suffragette meeting at the harbour," said *The Orcadian*.

"Several young ladies were seen passing along the principal streets sporting the colours of the suffragettes. The whole force of Kirkwall police were in the vicinity, evidently ready to act if their services were required."

A Miss McNiell and a Miss Hunter made speeches but *The Orcadian* pointed out: "Miss Hunter was subjected to a deal of senseless interruption by some tipsy men."

It led to the formation of the Orcadian Women's Suffrage Society, which met regularly in the years 1909-14. Women over 30, and fulfilling certain property qualifications, eventually were given the vote in the 1918 Representation of the People Act, but it was the 1929 General Election before all women over the age of 21 were able to vote.

Time for short sea crossing

Plans were floated for a so-called short sea crossing over the Pentland Firth from Caithness to Orkney.

In May, 1909, Orkney County Council "resolved to do all in its power to further the proposal for the erection of a pier" at Gills Bay as the Caithness terminal for the shipping service.

By 1911, however, the proposed Gills Bay harbour scheme was estimated to cost £140,000 - the equivalent of more than £10 millions at 1999 prices - and support was obviously faltering.

"Would any sane man dream of such an expenditure for a scheme of this sort?" asked Councillor William MacLennan at a meeting of Orkney County Council in May, 1911. And by December, 1912, Caithness County Council was complaining that no word had been heard on the Gills Bay scheme from Orkney County Council for "months or years."

Sailing ship wreck

The end of the era of sailing ships was drawing closer - a demise that was hastened as the three masted sailing vessel *Edenmore* went ashore on Papa Stronsay.

The ship was four days out of Hamburg with a general cargo for Australia when she was wrecked in bad weather.

Unfortunately, the Stronsay lifeboat was in Kirkwall for repairs to her motor, but the lifeboat crew were able to put to sea in another small boat and they rescued all 25 of the crew of the *Edenmore*.

A Board of Trade inquiry exonerated the master, Captain David Jackson, of all the blame for the disaster, and the wrecked ship was auctioned off to Harray contractor Mr S. Firth for £145.

Motor tax

A tax on motor vehicles was introduced in 1909 - along with a tax of 2d a gallon on petrol. The number of motor vehicles registered in Orkney up to September, 1908, totalled 30 private cars and 36 motorcycles, plus seven trade vehicles.

Anthrax fears

An outbreak of anthrax was discovered at a Rendall farm, with one animal having died. The farm was disinfected and no further cases were reported.

W.R. Tullock became Orkney's official Ford dealer in 1912. You could drive this away for £110, ex works in Manchester. (Picture courtesy of David Tullock)

The German balloonists Distler and Joerdens are pictured with George Leonard (right) at the scene where they landed near Park Cottage, St Ola.
(Picture courtesy of George Leonard)

The first men to fly to Orkney

A new chapter of modern Orkney began as December 4, 1910, went down in history as the first time that men arrived in the county other than by boat.

Two Germans claimed the distinction of being the first men to fly to Orkney. But they arrived, not by aeroplane, but by balloon! And it was all a great mistake in a tragedy which claimed the life of one of their fellow ballooning enthusiasts.

It was certainly a surprise from the skies for Mr George Leonard when, in response to continued ringing of the door bell, he found two strangers in a state of collapse at 10pm.

"Are we in England? We have come in a balloon," was their explanation.

It transpired that they were ballooning enthusiasts Herr Distler, managing director of the Deutscher Touring Club, and Captain Joerdens, a retired German Army officer, who had been blown from Germany

before a strong easterly gale. It was estimated that the balloon had travelled around 1,500 miles.

Three of them had started out from Munich for a 24 hour ascent. At first all went well, but when the wind increased, the balloonists decided to descend to ascertain their position. They got a glimpse of coastline but then the basket struck the sea, with a large wave sweeping away one of the occupants, Herr Metzger, who was never seen again.

The balloon rose again and drifted all day, with attempts failing to alert passing ships below.

Long after dark, they observed lights and the balloon was deflated to attempt a landing. The basket again struck the sea and bounced back into the air as the balloonists hastily threw all ballast overboard.

At last, they knew they were over land and Herr Distler pulled the emergency rope

to let the last of the gas escape. So great was the impetus that wire fences and dykes were torn down as the balloon careered along. Eventually it settled near Park Cottage, St Ola, and the men stumbled to safety. At first the men thought they were in Sweden, but the word "Push" on the door bell revealed that it was Britain.

The balloon had cost £500 - no small sum in those days - and Herr Distler told *The Orcadian*: "Our speed must have been greater than the fastest train in the world."

Captain Joerdens said he would never wish for such an experience again. "For 14 hours, death stared us in the face. The loss of our companion appalled us. We were without hope. It must have been Providence that saved us."

The Germans stayed in Orkney for three days before returning south by the mail steamer on their way home.

A team of helpers load up the balloon basket which carried the first men to arrive in Orkney by air.
(Picture courtesy of George Leonard)

The man who won the West

An unsung pioneer of the development of Canada - indeed, his obituary claimed it was "largely through his efforts that the settlement of the West was made possible" - was Peter Hourie, the son of an Orcadian father and a full-blooded Snake Indian mother.

The "half breed" - as the headline in *The Orcadian* described him following his death in 1910 - had been the "confidant of Governor-Generals, high military officials, Indian chiefs and lowly redskins."

Born in 1827, Peter Hourie had joined the Hudson's Bay Company in his youth and through his upbringing and his work came to know the Indian nations covering thousands of square miles.

"Hourie was by no means a savage or unkempt Indian," said his obituary. "He was a man of great sincerity and a man whose every word could be taken as truth."

The great feature of his work - perhaps something the Canadian Indians would not thank him for today - was helping to place Indians on reservations as the country was opened up to settlers. A fluent linguist in several indigenous languages, he was credited with playing a vital role in negotiations between various Governor-Generals of Canada and local chiefs.

It is possible that Peter Hourie was the first man of native American blood to become a Freemason in Canada. Before his death, he was certainly made an honorary life member of his lodge in Regina, Saskatchewan.

George Leonard (left) surveys the dyke which halted the progress of the two German ballooning enthusiasts.
(Picture courtesy of George Leonard)

The King is dead . . .

1910

Thursday, May 12, 1910, was declared a day of mourning as the death of King Edward VII filled the entire front page of *The Orcadian*.

The 44 year old George V - the second son of the late king, his older brother having died 18 years earlier - ascended to the throne, with Sheriff William Harvey reading the proclamation at Kirkwall's Mercat Cross.

Memorial services were held in Orkney to coincide with the funeral of Edward VII. In Kirkwall, all business was suspended, the streets were silent and flags at half mast, reported *The Orcadian*. The general public "manifested every sign of grief at the great loss the nation has sustained."

The following year, a contingent of 25 men of the Orkney Artillery, under the command of Lt D.B. Peace, went to London for the Coronation of George V.

A Coronation service was held at St Magnus Cathedral but "rain entirely marred the Coronation celebrations in Kirkwall," reported *The Orcadian*.

A 6 feet 8 inch tall Orcadian, William David Gibson, a member of the Metropolitan Police in London, had a special claim to fame with regard to the new King - Gibson, who later emigrated to the United States, was credited with being the tallest man on parade, out of 50,000 troops and police, on the day George V was married.

Skating rink opened

A new roller skating rink, erected in Junction Road, Kirkwall, by D.B. Peace, was officially opened - with the hall packed to overflowing. Admission was 3d, and hire of skates 3d.

The new enterprise lasted three years - in 1913, it was converted into Orkney's first permanent cinema, the Electric Theatre.

Rugby points spree

An Orcadian rugby player set a record when fly half James Drever from Sanday - later to become Dr Drever with a medical practice in South Africa - scored 50 points for Heriot's Former Pupils in their 57-0 defeat of Edinburgh Wanderers in 1910.

Diphtheria at camp

The annual camp in Kirkwall of 353 members of the Orkney Royal Garrison Artillery was hit by an outbreak of Diphtheria. Fortunately, it was proved to be an isolated case.

Town hit by inferno

What was described as the "Great Stromness Fire" completely gutted the premises of the Farmers Supply Stores in the town in February, 1910.

Damage in the early morning blaze at the shop, owned by Mr S. Baikie, was estimated at several thousands of pounds with stock of £5,000 destroyed and the £3,000 building gutted.

"The splendid building is now a mass of ruins," *The Orcadian* reported after flames were said to have leapt 100 feet in the air.

Fishing booms to prosperity

A halcyon period of just four years saw the fishing industry in Orkney prosper to previously unimagined - and subsequently unattained - success.

The years 1909-1912 saw the herring industry in Stronsay boom as annual landings each year reached a new record to the extent that landings more than trebled in those four years.

In 1909, the Stronsay total herring catch was below 50,000 crans but 1910 saw a record unsurpassed in the previous 60 years as the Orkney herring catch - virtually all of it landed in Stronsay - reached 92,109 crans in the season.

The following year, Stronsay's herring fishing for the season reached 113,000 crans, and in 1912, over 130,000 crans. The years 1911-13 saw the value of the Stronsay landings nudging £200,000 a

1911

season - a total value over the three years of £600,000, an equivalent, at 1999 prices, approaching £50 millions.

But although Stronsay ruled the waves as far as the herring fishing was concerned, Kirkwall was also enjoying a period of prosperity as a major port for white fish.

A string of fish curing stations operated around the Peerie Sea, others were opened at Carness, and Captain John Reid, of Shapinsay, had a station at Helliar Holm.

By April, 1910, up to 60 tons a day of fish from trawlers was being landed at the fish-curing stations. In fact, when, in May, 1911, the Grimsby trawler *Uvularia* landed 65 tons of Iceland fish at Kirkwall for local merchants Messrs Cooper and Sons, it was acknowledged to be a record amount for a single trawler landing at the pier at the time. The total landings for that same week in Kirkwall were 230 tons.

By October, 1912, when 550 tons of salt fish from the Faroes arrived in a week for Kirkwall and Shapinsay merchants, Orkney Harbours Commissioners were considering building a Kirkwall fish mart at the pier.

The plans never progressed, and the Kirkwall fish industry could never re-establish the same level of prosperity after World War One.

Fish- curing stations operated at Hatston, Carness and around the Peerie Sea as trawlers landed up to 60 tons of fish a day in Kirkwall.

(Picture courtesy of Orkney Library photographic archive)

Rats leave a sinking ship

Two deck hands promptly signed off the Granton trawler *Malta II* when they saw rats leaving the vessel - a sign of impending disaster in the folklore of the sea - when the vessel called at Kirkwall.

Within hours, the vessel had foundered and sunk off Auskerry, in February, 1911.

The eight crewmen - including two Orkney men, John Herdsman and William Simpson Grant, who had joined the trawler to replace the two who had departed in haste in Kirkwall - took to the ship's boat as the trawler sank and were safely rescued by the Wick drifter *Cordelia*.

There was a closer escape from disaster the following month for the crew of the Sunderland trawler *Alice Dodds*.

The vessel, just six months old having been built at a cost of £6,000, was returning from the Faroes when she struck Seal

Skerry, North Ronaldsay, and became a total wreck.

"When daylight came the islanders found themselves helpless to render any assistance to the distressed seamen," reported *The Orcadian*. "The trawler lay in a smother of foam and unfortunately there was no life saving apparatus on the island."

Thankfully, the trawler crew were able to take to their lifeboat and safely reach the shore through heavy seas.

The waters of Orkney were to be the final resting place not only of British fishermen but also many from continental Europe.

In May, 1910, a French fishing lugger was feared lost with all hands off Westray as bodies were washed ashore, and, in April, 1911, *The Orcadian* reported that a serious shipping disaster - thought to be a German

trawler - had occurred to the west of Orkney as a body was washed ashore on Hoy and quantities of wreckage on Westray and Papa Westray.

A year later, in May, 1912, the Dutch trawler *Dubbelman* was wrecked off South Ronaldsay, although her 16 crew safely made it ashore at Burwick. The wreck was later sold to a Stromness man for just five shillings!

That year was to see both Auskerry and Seal Skerry feature in further trawler disasters. The Aberdeen vessel *Tina Nutten* went ashore on Auskerry and the crew were rescued by the fisheries cruiser *Norna* - which the previous week had arrested the trawler for illegal fishing off Shetland.

And November 4, 1912, saw the Aberdeen trawler *St Nicholas* become a total wreck after running aground at Seal Skerry.

The first Orcadian to fly was airborne by 1911, but it was 20 years later, in 1931, before most Orkney folk had the opportunity to have joy rides organised by Captain Ted Fresson. (Picture courtesy of Orkney Library photographic archive)

Orcadians in the skies

Orkney's first aeroplane pilot - and manufacturer - was Luther Webster, son of the Rev David Webster, minister of Kirkwall's Paterson United Free Church, who built his own aircraft in 1911.

Unfortunately, Orkney never saw the machine - a Bleriot-design powered by a 50hp Jap engine - as young Webster was working in South Africa at the time, having trained as a motor engineer. It meant, however, that he could claim the honour of constructing the first plane to be built in South Africa.

In September, 1911, *The Orcadian* reported that Luther Webster had successfully completed two trial flights and he hoped to compete for a £500 prize offered for a flight from Pretoria to Johannesburg.

A man of Orkney ancestry actually beat Webster, by a few months, in the race to be the first Orcadian to fly.

For an airman called Foulis, the grandson of an Orcadian, was credited with being the first man to fly an aircraft into battle in a war when, with two other Scots called Harkness and Hamilton, he flew aircraft missions in the Mexican revolution in February, 1911.

Acclaimed artist dies

Robert Stewart Clouston, youngest son of Rev Charles Clouston, of Sandwick Manse, where he was born, died on April 25,1911, at the age of 54, having earned a reputation as the top Orcadian artist of his generation.

From 1876, he studied at the Royal Scottish Academy and he exhibited at the Academy's annual exhibitions. His work was also shown at the Royal Academy in London.

He gained a great reputation as an engraver, in the medium of mezzotint, but he was also remembered as an accomplished writer and biographer, publishing books on Arthur Melville the artist and Robert Mannering the designer.

Fewer people again

The 1911 Census showed Orkney's population at 25,896, a decrease of 2,803 on the 1901 figure of 28,699.

Stromness faced the biggest depopulation crisis with the town's population reduced by more than 26 per cent, a fall of 832 residents, over ten years.

Westray's population had fallen by 289 from 1,956 to 1,667 while South Ronaldsay had fallen by over 300 from 2,707 to 2,382. The only two places to show an increase were Stronsay (up by just 33) and Kirkwall (an increase of 73 people).

Four's company

A cow belonging to Mr James Alexander, Hermisgarth, Sanday, presented her lucky owner with a total of four calves in just ten and a half months between April, 1910, and March, 1911.

Home rule bid

Orkney and Shetland MP Cathcart Wason and Kirkwall's MP Robert Munro both announced their support for the Government of Scotland Bill, introduced to the House of Commons by Sir Henry Dalziel, which proposed the setting up of a Scottish Parliament as long ago as 1911. The Bill never progressed and it would be another 88 years before it became a reality.

Orkney heatwave

Kirkwall enjoyed 78.6 hours of sunshine in five successive days, July 9-13, 1911, with temperatures in the seventies Fahrenheit - the highest temperature recorded since 76 degrees 21 years earlier in 1890.

Join the queue

Two brothers called Urquhart who emigrated - one to the USA and one to India - made their fortunes and died leaving £3 million. The 2,000 "relatives" who came forward to claim the estate included two Kirkwall residents.

Power to the people -

It was democracy, but not as we know it. That just about sums up the early years of 20th century politics in Orkney.

The new century dawned with not even "one man, one vote," let alone votes for women.

Kirkwall people were still represented by the MP for the Northern Burghs constituency (which covered the major towns stretching from Kirkwall south to Dingwall) while the rest of the county came within the Orkney and Shetland constituency.

They were curious times in many respects - partly because of the turbulence of the international political and economic situation which prevailed for so long, resulting in the country being ruled by a succession of Coalition or National governments for most of World War One, virtually all the 1930s and throughout World War Two.

But Orkney politics had its own idiosyncrasies:

• One MP was returned to the House of Commons three times in seven years - under a different "ticket" each time.

• The national result of General Elections was known before the voters of the Northern Isles went to the polls in the early years of the century.

• Two Labour governments had been in power before a Labour candidate even contested the Orkney and Shetland seat.

• And, remarkably, on half a dozen occasions in 22 years, the Orkney MP was returned, unopposed, to Westminster without having to face the electorate in a contest.

With the exception of a few months at the start of 1900 and in 1921-22, Orkney and Shetland had just three MPs throughout the period 1900-49. They were John Cathcart Wason (21 years), Sir Robert Hamilton (13 years) and Sir Basil Neven-Spence (15 years).

The election of Wason (for a brief spell of two years before he changed allegiance) and Neven-Spence were notable as the only interruptions of the Liberal domination of the Orkney and Shetland constituency throughout the 20th century.

Kirkwall voters, in the period 1913-18, could claim that their MP, Robert Munro, was at the centre of Government - first as Lord Advocate and later as the Secretary of State for Scotland.

The century began with the sitting MP for Orkney and Shetland being the Liberal, or Radical as *The Orcadian* still labelled him, Sir Leonard Lyell who had represented the Northern Isles for 15 years. But he survived just a few months more, being defeated - albeit by just 40 votes - by John Cathcart Wason, standing as a Unionist, in the first General Election of the 20th century.

(It was opposition to Irish Home Rule that caused the Conservatives to embrace the title of Unionists, rather than any reference to the Union of Scotland and England).

Lyell - a professor at the University College of Wales - had been only 35 when first elected and had obviously done sufficient to be returned to Westminster three times.

But now *The Orcadian* turned on him in vitriolic style. "Sir Leonard Lyell seems to be getting tired of Parliamentary life. He never lifts up his voice in debate; he rarely gives his views to his constituents. Out of 290 divisions, he only took part in 44 of these. When a Member of Parliament fails to address his constituents at least once a year, when he rarely takes part in a debate, he may well be described as useless and should be relegated to private life."

His Unionist opponent Wason was two years older than Lyell, and a man with a strong political pedigree. The barrister son of Peter Wason, who was Liberal MP for Ipswich in three successive parliaments, he had served as an MP in the New Zealand parliament before returning to this country. He compensated for his lack of knowledge of Orkney by playing the patriotic card in powerful speeches about the Boer War which was then being waged.

The result of the October, 1900, General Election contest was Lyell 2,017 Wason 2,057. It hardly meant that Lyell was relegated to private life however. Before his death in 1926, he could play a role in the House of Lords as Lord Lyell.

The level of expenses submitted by the two candidates in the 1900 Orkney and Shetland election campaign was astonishing. Sir Leonard Lyell's expenses totalled £994 while Cathcart Wason reached £1,484 - the equivalent, with inflation over the rest of the century, of £100,000 at 1999 prices!

Voting throughout the country took place over a period of days so it was already known that the Unionists had been returned to power as the new government before Orkney voters went to the polls. In fact, Kirkwall voters knew the identity of their new MP a week before.

Sir Arthur Bignold also won the Northern Burghs seat for the Unionists for the first time in 1900. Bignold, born in Norwich but with a home in Ross-shire for many years, had made a personal fortune in business, before standing for the Northern Burghs seat at the age of 61. He beat the sitting Liberal, or Radical, Mr Thomas C. Hedderwick by 1,154 votes to 1,041 - a result greeted by a display of fireworks in Kirkwall's Broad Street.

Two years later, however, the electorate of the Orkney and Shetland constituency returned to the polls when John Cathcart Wason - in what was headlined as "Mr Wason's Revolt" and was to earn him the soubriquet "Wason the Wobbler" - fell out with the Unionist government and quit the party, his main bone of contention, curiously, being nothing to do with Orkney but the English Education Bill.

At first, Wason declared: "I am more than justified in leaving the Unionist party, crossing the floor and taking up my position as a member of the Liberal party." However, a couple of weeks later, he announced that he would put his change of allegiance to the test. He resigned his seat to contest a by-election.

The 1902 by-election was to be Orkney's first three cornered election contest of the 20th century. Wason stood under the banner of Independent Liberal to face the challenge of an official Liberal candidate McKinnon Wood - a former chairman of London County Council and later to become a Secretary of State for Scotland - and a Unionist Sir Theodore Angier, from Brighton and a member of the London shipping company Angier Brothers.

Wason had obviously developed a powerful personal following in Orkney in just two years because *The Orcadian* - normally a stauch supporter of the Unionist cause - threw its weight behind the rebel candidate as "one who stands up for the weak against the strong."

"During the time he has represented the constituency, he has given himself up wholly to the work, and this is the best guarantee that the electors could have that he will faithfully discharge any business entrusted to him," said *The Orcadian*.

It was easy to understand Wason's magnetic appeal. For a start, he stood 6ft 6inches tall and so, for most of his parliamentary career, he was the tallest MP at Westminster. But also, he had developed the novel habit of knitting socks to relieve the tedium of waiting to make a speech, or waiting for the division bell. He admitted years later that he had learned to knit solely to impress the women of Orkney and Shetland who were unsurpassed experts at the craft.

The by-election, in November, 1902, saw Wason returned with a majority of over 400 in a turn-out of up to 95 per cent of the electorate at some polling stations (this was hardly representative because, at the time, more than half the population was not entitled to vote). The result was: Wason 2,412; Wood 2,001; Angier 740.

the first democracy

The Orcadian Women's Suffrage Society, campaigning for votes for women, met regularly in the years 1909-1914. Members are pictured here canvassing in Stromness. (Picture courtesy of Orkney Library photographic archive)

In the February, 1906, General Election, Wason was adopted as the official Liberal candidate for Orkney and Shetland and, in a straight fight with the Unionist candidate Colin Dunlop he achieved more than 75 per cent of the vote to be returned with an impressive majority of 2,816 as the Liberals nationally swept to power. The result was: Wason 3,837 Dunlop 1,021.

Sir Arthur Bignold retained his Unionist hold over the Northern Burghs seat, however, beating the Liberal candidate William Thomson by 1,362 votes to 1,266.

Sir Arthur had been caught up in allegations of electoral malpractice immediately before the election when it was revealed that he had given Kirkwall £100 to buy a site for a new library. And he was given an ignominious send-off following the announcement of his election victory in Wick where he was caught up in rowdy scenes as, according to *The Orcadian*, "blackguard tactics" were employed by Radical supporters as Sir Arthur was "mobbed" from his hotel to the railway station after the declaration of the poll.

The Orcadian was outraged: "The late R.L. Stevenson was perfectly right when he described the people of Wick as the meanest on earth, and, judging by their conduct on Tuesday night last week, he could have truthfully called them the most cowardly of human beings. Nothing so disgraceful has occurred in the country during the General Election period as the mobbing of Sir Arthur Bignold."

In 1910, the country faced two General Elections in 11 months, and the first, in February, saw Wason increase his majority in the Orkney and Shetland constituency to over 3,000 for the first time as he saw off the Unionist challenge of Thomas Helmsley by 4,117 votes to 994. When the second General Election was called in December that year, the Unionists conceded defeat in the constituency and Wason was returned unopposed to Westminster.

That year was to see the end of Sir Arthur Bignold as Kirkwall's MP. The man who would be remembered for the rest of the 20th century in Orkney as the benefactor who gave Kirkwall the Bignold Park was by now aged 70 and in the February General

Election the voters of the Northern Burghs rejected him. Bignold secured 1,262 votes but Robert Munro, his Radical opponent (with dangerous Socialist leanings, according to *The Orcadian*), was victorious with 1,537 votes. Munro, a barrister, was to become Secretary of State for Scotland during World War One.

Bignold returned to contest the Northern Burghs seat in the December, 1910, General Election but was again defeated by Robert Munro. The result was Munro 1,515 Bignold 1,304. Sir Arthur Bignold - who had been granted the freedom of the burgh of Kirkwall in 1906 - was to die at the age of 76 in 1915.

Kirkwall voters returned to the polls in December, 1913, when there was a by-election in the Northern Burghs constituency after Robert Munro was appointed Lord Advocate. (Under the convention of the day, a man who received a salaried appointment under the Crown had to vacate his seat in the House of Commons, subject to the right of re-election.)

The result - Alexander Mackenzie (Unionist) 1,134 votes, Robert Munro (Radical) 1,577 - saw Munro returned with a record majority in the constituency. He was also the first candidate to win three successive elections in the Northern Burghs.

The Representation of the People Act of 1918 saw the abolition of the Northern Burghs division and so by the next time the voters of Kirkwall went to the polls, their burgh had become part of the Orkney and Shetland constituency and consequently *The Orcadian* no longer had to worry itself about the decorum of the population of Wick.

World War One generally was to mean the suspension of election campaigns, but in 1918, the Representation of the People Act confirmed the right to vote to all men over 21, and for women over 30 (though subject to educational and property qualifications.) It still meant also that hundreds of thousands of men, aged under 21, who had been adjudged old enough to fight for their country had no say in how that country should be governed.

As it was, none of the men and women of Orkney and Shetland was able to exercise the right to vote for another four years because, at the 1918 General Election, John Cathcart Wason was again returned unopposed as MP, this time on the coalition ticket of David Lloyd George Liberals and Andrew Bonar Law Conservatives.

His candidature was a surprise because in October, 1918, it was reported that he had suffered a serious breakdown of health and that he had been ordered by his doctors to end all his parliamentary work. His colleague Sir Leonard Powell even visited Orkney as a potential successor as Liberal candidate for the constituency.

However, on December 5, 1918, Wason announced: "Mercifully restored to comparative good health I, at the earnest request of the Prime Minister, respectfully again offer you my services at the approaching election." No other candidates came forward so, as stated, he was returned unopposed to Westminster for what transpired to be his final term as Orkney's MP.

Nationally, the 1918 General Election saw the landslide return of 528 Coalition candidates. However, an indication of the mood of the time in Ireland was the fact that the next biggest party returned was Sinn Fein with 73 seats - ahead of both the Liberals (26 seats) and Labour (65).

Wason died on April 19, 1921, with his funeral service held at Golders Green, North London. A by-election was called but, in the event, the recently franchised women of Orkney were still denied the opportunity to vote as Sir Malcolm Smith, backed by both the local Liberal and Unionist associations, was returned unopposed as a Coalition Liberal.

Sir Malcolm Smith, born in Shetland and knighted for his service in World War One, was to serve as MP for less than 18 months, and when he died in March, 1935, he was best remembered for his political prominence in the Edinburgh area, including nine years as Provost of Leith.

The General Election of November, 1922, saw the return of a new MP for Orkney and Shetland, a man who was to represent the Northern Isles for the next 13 years. Sir Robert Hamilton, then aged 55, was a former Chief Justice of British East Africa and had also been knighted in 1918. His father was a former Under Secretary for Ireland and, afterwards, Governor of Tasmania, but Hamilton could claim Orkney links - his great grandfather Rev Gavin Hamilton had been a minister in Hoy from 1796-1849.

The election proved to be a contest between the two political wings of the Liberal party. Hamilton stood as the Liberal candidate while Sir Malcolm Smith stood as a Coalition or National Liberal, with the support of Kirkwall Unionist Association.

The result was: Hamilton 4,814 Smith 4,189. The result was greeted with rowdy scenes in Stromness where youths, celebrating Hamilton's victory, carried in "a triumphant procession through the town" a boat containing an effigy of the defeated Sir Malcolm Smith, which at the Market Green was lit into a blazing bonfire.

The *Leith Observer* commented: "We do not know much about the people of Stromness but judging from their actions they seem to be woefully deficient in sporting instinct. To reward their late Member's service by burning his effigy was the acme of base ingratitude, an insult only softened by the reflection that remoteness from civilised manners had interfered with their mental development."

Nationally, the Conservatives were returned to power, thus ending the Coalition government led by David Lloyd George, and the new Prime Minister was Andrew Bonar Law, who - forced to step down by ill health - was swiftly followed by Stanley Baldwin.

But a year later, December, 1923, was to see another General Election and this time Sir Robert Hamilton faced a Conservative challenger - the first Conservative candidate in Orkney since 1910 - in the form of Robert Boothby.

Boothby would later become a major force of the Conservative party over a period of several decades but this early excursion into the election fray saw him defeated by 811 votes. The result was: Boothby 4,318 Hamilton 5,129.

The turn-out was no doubt reduced by the appalling dearth of polling booths in Orkney. For instance, the people of Rackwick had to walk five miles - and then get the *Hoy Head* ferry to Stromness - to register their vote. "These citizens might as well never have the vote," complained *The Orcadian* in an appeal for better facilities.

Nationally, this General Election led to the formation of the country's first ever Labour government - albeit a minority administration - with Ramsay MacDonald as Prime Minister. Philip Snowden, a former Kirkwall customs officer, became the first ever Labour Chancellor of the Exchequer. At this time, there had been no suggestion of a Labour candidate standing in the Orkney and Shetland parliamentary constituency, but at grass roots level, two candidates - Alex Grant and John Muir - stood in the Kirkwall parish council election of November, 1922. They came bottom of the poll.

The first Labour government lasted only months but when it collapsed, and a General Election called for the end of October, 1924, Sir Robert Hamilton was stranded 6,000 miles away on a visit to South Africa. Locally, the Conservatives were too slow to take advantage of such disarray, and so Hamilton was returned unopposed as Liberal MP for another five years, although, nationally, a Conservative government was returned under Stanley Baldwin.

All women over the age of 21 eventually achieved the right to vote in 1928 and so the 1929 General Election was the first opportunity to exercise their newly won equality with men.

It was obviously a right that most (male and female) chose to surrender for the turn-out in the Orkney and Shetland constituency was just 43 per cent.

Sir Robert Hamilton again carried the Liberal standard while representing the Conservative cause for the first time was 40 year old Major Basil Neven-Spence. The former Army officer was the son of a Shetland man, although, through his mother's family, he was also a cousin of Major Harry Hamilton Hebden, Royal Fusiliers, who owned most of the island of Eday as Laird of Carrick.

Neither candidate apparently felt obliged to woo what today would be called the "Green" vote. Neven-Spence had recently entertained readers of *The Orcadian* with a narrative of his expedition in the Sudan shooting lions in which a "thorough good morning's sport" saw his party shoot dead three male lions.

And, not to be outdone, Hamilton suggested to the Orkney Agricultural Discussion Society that fox farming, for furs, might be attempted in Orkney. He later went a step further and offered a reward of 10 shillings for every seal shot dead in the Stenness loch.

The new electoral roll for Orkney - with the vote now extended to women - showed a total electorate in the county of 14,816 - 7,175 men and 7,641 women.

Polling day was May 30 and Orkney's two newspapers divided on partisan lines - *The Orcadian* backing Neven-Spence and the Conservative Unionists, the *Orkney Herald* supporting Hamilton and the Liberals.

The result was: Hamilton 8,256, Neven-Spence 5,404 - majority 2,852.

Nationally, the election saw the defeat of Stanley Baldwin's Conservative government and Ramsay MacDonald returned as Prime Minister at the head of the second minority Labour government of the 20th century.

Philip Snowden, who still had friends and former colleagues in Kirkwall, was named again as Chancellor of the Exchequer in the new cabinet.

Two months after the election, the former Provost Robert Clouston, who was political agent for Sir Robert Hamilton in Stromness, died at the age of 59.

Incidentally, there were still variations in the election practices of the 1920s. For instance, voting for the Orkney Education Authority, which was then elected separately from the county council, was by a system of proportional representation back in 1928.

And ratepayers had the right to vote in local elections, regardless of age. Therefore, schoolgirl Morna Firth, of Victoria Street, Kirkwall, became one of the youngest people in the country to be allowed a vote, when by virtue of being a ratepayer, owning a house in Willow Road, Kirkwall, she voted in the Kirkwall Town Council election of November, 1928.

By 1931, the Labour government had collapsed in economic crisis and a new National government - including Conservatives and Liberals - evolved under Ramsay MacDonald's leadership. It was in this climate that the 1931 General Election was called.

The result was that Sir Robert Hamilton was returned unopposed on a ticket of supporting the National government, after Basil Neven-Spence stood down when Conservative leader Stanley Baldwin announced that the party would not challenge Liberal candidates who pledged their support to the National government.

Neven-Spence returned to the fray however for the 1935 General Election - although *The Orcadian* anticipated a "featureless campaign as neither Unionist nor Liberal organisation has functioned for a number of years."

Neven-Spence attacked Hamilton's luke-warm support of the National government over the previous four years and romped home with a conclusive 2,226 majority at the November 14 poll. The result was: Neven-Spence 8,406, Hamilton 6,180. The turn-out was just 46.6 per cent, but it would be sufficient for Neven-Spence to return as Orkney's MP, unchallenged for the next ten years as World War Two intervened.

Neven-Spence received a telegram of congratulations from Prime Minister Stanley Baldwin, who had been returned at the head of the National government. The defeat of Hamilton reduced the Opposition Liberal representation from Scotland in the House of Commons to just three MPs.

The agreement of political parties that, generally, elections would not be contested during World War Two meant that it was 1945 before Orcadians had the chance to vote again in a General Election.

However, in the intervening period, the voices of opposition parties were heard as both the Liberal party and - for the first time - the Labour party selected prospective candidates for the constituency, who were to come and go.

The first ever Labour prospective parliamentary candidate to be selected for Orkney and Shetland was, in February, 1938, when the Rev Campbell McKinnon (31), a native of Greenock but then serving as the Church of Scotland minister on the Shetland island of Bressay, was adopted.

However, within weeks, he had withdrawn and Councillor John Robertson, a Shetlander resident in Edinburgh, became the new prospective Labour candidate in the county. At the outbreak of war - and elections put on hold - Robertson also withdrew.

In 1938, Lady Glen-Coats, of Troon, Ayrshire, was adopted as the prospective Liberal candidate for Orkney and Shetland. She was to prove a tireless worker - making regular visits to the county - but in June, 1944, she announced that she too was withdrawing.

(The following month saw the death of former Orkney and Shetland Liberal MP Sir Robert Hamilton at the age of 76.)

Polling day for the 1945 General Election was July 5 - although, to allow for the voting of servicemen overseas, the result was not made known for three weeks.

The electioneering had begun by May, 1945, however, when *The Orcadian* asked in an editorial: "Could any reasonable person contemplate without deep misgivings the replacement of a Churchill by an Atlee?"

Three weeks later, *The Orcadian* carried an opinion poll which showed 95 per cent of Kirkwall was "for Churchill" and only two and a half per cent against.

The newspaper sorely misjudged the mood of the nation - and to a large extent, the constituency - as Labour was returned nationally with a landslide 390 seats, 150 more than the Conservatives.

Orkney and Shetland had a three cornered contest in the General Election as sitting Conservative Unionist MP Major

Jo Grimond became one of the great political figures of the 20th century, both in Orkney and nationally as leader of the Liberal Party. But his first venture into Orkney politics saw him defeated in the 1945 General Election.

(Picture courtesy of Orkney Library photographic archive)

Basil Neven-Spence (soon to be knighted and become Sir Basil) was challenged by Major Jo Grimond, a barrister from Fife in civilian life, for the Liberals, and Shetland Merchant Navy man Prophet Smith, the Greenock secretary of the National Union of Seamen, for Labour, the first time the party had contested the Northern Isles constituency.

It had been reported that the Liberals had asked Labour to stand aside to allow the single challenge of the Liberals against Neven-Spence, but Labour had declined.

The result was that the split vote saw Neven-Spence squeeze home although the combined "opposition" was nearly 5,000 more than the Conservative Unionist vote. Neven-Spence's vote fell by 2,000 compared with 1935 but he was elected again as Orkney's MP with a majority of 329.

The result was: Neven-Spence 6,304, Grimond 5,975, Smith 5,208. The turn-out was only 52 per cent but that was the highest in the constituency since the vote had been granted to everyone aged over 21.

The Labour vote recorded by Prophet Smith would remain the highest polled by Labour in the constituency for the remainder of the century.

The campaign of Jo Grimond had, perforce, been hurriedly prepared - he had only a matter of days to devote to electioneering after being released from his military duties - and *The Orcadian* said that "popular opinion" was that Lady Glen-Coats would have gained twice the vote of Grimond had she remained the Orkney and Shetland Liberal Candidate.

However Jo Grimond would return and the second half of the 20th century would see one of the most remarkable careers in British politics evolve in Orkney and Shetland.

Orkney mourns Titanic

1912

Special prayers were said at St Magnus Cathedral as Britain reeled at the sensational news of the loss of the liner *Titanic* on her maiden voyage across the Atlantic.

"When such a leviathan, on her first and last voyage, goes to the bottom in mid-ocean, carrying to an awful and sudden death 1,635 human souls, the imagination stands aghast," said Cathedral minister Rev William Pitcairn Craig.

"The family sorrows and deprivations it has caused, and the far-reaching effects of the calamity that has plunged both America and our own nation into mourning, no human imagination has yet grasped."

As the liner sank, "the band played that beautiful hymn Nearer My God To Thee," said *The Orcadian*. "That is an incident that will live in history."

That same week, the British steamer *Erna*, en route from the Clyde to Newfoundland, virtually in the wake of the *Titanic*, was feared lost with 40 lives, under the command of her Orcadian master Captain Thomas Linklater.

Captain Linklater (60) from Birsay was accompanied on the voyage by his wife Deborah and his ten year old son. They were all presumed drowned.

And Lt C.J. Russell, former adjutant to the Orkney Royal Garrison Artillery , was lost as the P&O liner *Oceana*, en route to India with 240 passengers and crew, collided in the English Channel with a German barque and sank. The liner was reported to be carrying £750,000 in bullion.

On a happier note, Mr Robert Gunn of Kirkwall was presented with a medal from the King of Norway for his bravery at sea in rescuing members of the crew of the Norwegian barque *Euphrates* in February, 1912.

Mr Gunn was a crewman on the steamer *Grampian Range*, on passage to Philadelphia, when he volunteered to man a lifeboat to help rescue eight of the Norwegian crew when their vessel was spotted in distress.

Royal honour for rescuers

The Norwegian barque *Adele* was lost at South Ronaldsay, in January, 1912, in harrowing scenes as men drowned in touch of land.

Two men were lost but, remarkably, nine more survived and four of their South Ronaldsay rescuers were to be personally honoured for their bravery by King George V.

The 400 ton ship, under the command of a Captain Erikson, was on passage to Hull with a cargo of pit props. Heavy seas had already washed away much of the deck cargo when the problems of the *Adele* were compounded by a navigation error which led to the master's calculations being out by 50 miles.

The ship had mistaken Auskerry light for Sumburgh and the Pentland Skerries for Fair Isle.

The result was that, in the early hours of the morning, the ship struck South Ronaldsay in a disaster which saw the vessel "literally broken into matchwood." "The piteous cries of the shipwrecked sailors were heard almost a mile distant," reported *The Orcadian*.

Two crewmen took to the water and made it ashore, but the second mate was never seen again and the steward drowned after getting within yards of the shore before being swept away. "There is a strong feeling in South Ronaldsay that the island should have rocket life-saving equipment," said *The Orcadian*.

It was then that 68 year old William Wards launched his boat, accompanied by William Sinclair and Constable Joseph Cruickshank, and began a perilous rescue mission which, thankfully, saw the other seven survivors of the *Adele* rescued.

"All who witnessed the rescue agree it was a most daring and heroic feat." said *The Orcadian*.

The three rescuers, together with Alexander Wards, the deputy receiver of wrecks in South Ronaldsay, all received bravery awards from the King at Balmoral. Constable Cruickshank also received the King's Police Medal.

Three weeks after the *Adele* disaster, it was the turn of Sanday to witness tragedy when the Aberdeen fishing boat *Crimond* went aground with the loss of four lives. Another four crewmen were rescued by the Stronsay lifeboat while four Sanday men - William Meil, John Muir, William Muir and John King - managed to haul ashore William Walker, the brother of the skipper of the *Crimond*, James Walker, who was saved by the lifeboat.

Another three weeks later and the 1,160 ton Danish steamer *Ceres*, en route from Leith to Iceland, with 14 passengers and general cargo, stranded on the Green Holms between Eday and Shapinsay.

The passengers were taken off the stricken vessel by the Orkney Steam Navigation Company vessel *Fawn*, and eventually the *Ceres* got off the rocks - leaving stranded most of the crew who had taken refuge on the Green Holms.

The following January, the Swedish schooner *Tyra*, on passage from the Baltic to Hartlepool with pit props, went ashore on Papa Westray, with the crew taken off by the Papay rocket brigade, while five crew from the smack *Clestron* were saved after their vessel went aground on Stronsay.

But, as we approached the autumn of the sailing age, Orkney was to see, for the first time, the marine technology of the future as submarines accompanied the British fleet to Orkney.

Unfortunately, one submarine - the 135 feet long *C61* - got a closer glimpse of land than bargained for when, in August, 1912, it went aground on the Pentland Skerries in what was, presumably, Orkney's first ever submarine stranding. The vessel later managed to get off the rocks without serious damage.

Coal crisis

Factories and railways throughout Britain were brought to a standstill as Britain's miners went on strike in 1912. The North of Scotland and Orkney and Shetland Steam Navigation Company had to lay up two vessels and Stromness coal supplies were threatened, but, before serious problems could develop in Orkney, the strike was settled with the introduction of a minimum wage for miners.

Paper pioneer

Mr James Anderson, retired proprietor of *The Orcadian*, died in 1912 - 58 years after he had helped produce the first ever edition of the newspaper in 1854.

The year of 1912 also saw the death, at the age of 83, of Viscount Peel, a former Speaker of the House of Commons, who had been made a freeman of Kirkwall in 1893.

Staff outside one of the shops of Robert Garden, the Aberdonian who became "Orkney's merchant prince" in the early years of the century.
(Picture courtesy of Orkney Library photographic archive)

Orkney's merchant prince

Robert Garden - described by *The Orcadian* as "Orkney's merchant prince" - died in 1912.

His legacy to the county would be what became Kirkwall's Balfour Hospital after his widow bequeathed the money to erect, in his memory, the Garden Memorial Building which opened in New Scapa Road in 1927.

Born in Rayne, Aberdeenshire, he was not only Kirkwall's biggest merchant of the day, but also the owner of a small fleet of cargo vessels and floating shops which served not only the islands but many of the remote and rural areas of the North of Scotland.

The floating shops were a feature of pre-World War One life in Orkney with vessels usually manned by three men - one handling groceries, one feedstuffs and cereals and another drapery. The boats would also collect eggs and lobsters.

The vessels included the *Gleaner*, a 57 feet vessel built in Shapinsay, which could carry 50 tons of cargo, *Endeavour,* *Zoona, Klydon, Thankful, Aberdeen* and the *Lizzie Bain*, lost in a tragic collision that cost the lives of three men.

The shopkeeper skippers included men like John Muir, from Sanday and George Smith, who was succeeded on the *Gleaner* by his son Joe.

As the era of Robert Garden's floating shops came to an end, the *Gleaner*, after World War One, served as an accommodation vessel in Scapa Flow during the salvaging of the German Fleet by Cox and Danks.

Robert Garden: his legacy would be Orkney's new Balfour Hospital.
(Picture courtesy of Orkney Library photographic archive)

The *Endeavour*, one of Robert Garden's floating shops.
(Picture courtesy of Orkney Library photographic archive)

Sanctuary for children

There were so many "pauper" children needing homes in Glasgow that the authorities decided, in 1912, to board them out in Orkney.

"A considerable number of homes of prospective guardians were visited and carefully inspected," said a report to councillors in Glasgow. "The people were all of the small farmer class with well stocked farms and evidently in fairly prosperous circumstances.

"We feel satisfied that there will be no lack of suitable foster parents to be got in these districts."

Meanwhile, back in Orkney, *The Orcadian* reported it had been agreed to extend the Kirkwall Poorhouse to add a "ward for harmless lunatics."

The basin of Kirkwall Harbour saw fishing vessels and trading ships not only from Scotland but many countries of Europe.
(Picture courtesy of Orkney Library photographic archive)

National occasions, especially connected with Royalty, and military ceremonies, prompted great scenes of patriotism on the Kirk Green in front of St Magnus Cathedral. (Picture courtesy of Orkney Library photographic archive)

Perils loom in the sky

The impending perils of war - and for the first time warfare in the skies - loomed large for Orcadians in 1913 as, for the first time, German airships spread their shadow over the islands.

What was believed to be the first German Zeppelin seen over Orkney was reported in March, 1913, when the airship was sighted over Sanday before proceeding rapidly south. Presumably, it was the same airship which was reported to have been seen by people in Deerness the same day.

"Considerable importance was attached to the fact that the craft appeared in daylight, the reported visits to other parts of the country having invariably taken place after darkness had set in," said *The Orcadian*.

A Sanday correspondent wrote to the newspaper: "That there was a great aerial craft seen hovering over this island on

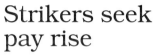

Monday afternoon, March 3, there is not the slightest shadow of doubt.

"What does it all mean? Has our Government been caught napping? It has been Britain's proud boast for centuries that she is mistress of the sea. How is it that our rulers have allowed themselves to be so hopelessly beaten in aerial navigation by Germany?

"That country at the present time has over 20 aircraft carrying crews of 16 men, while Britain at the present moment has only two aeroplanes, carrying two of a crew each, to meet this force if Germany chooses to invade us."

In April, 1913, the threat was under-

lined as reports were received of another airship over Stronsay, hovering over the island, with a bright light seen at intervals for two hours before midnight. "The hum of the engine was distinctly heard, but the airship for a considerable time remained almost stationary," said *The Orcadian*.

What the exact strength of Britain's aerial power was at that time is debatable, but it was in August, 1913, that Orcadians had their first opportunity to see an aeroplane when HMS *Hermes* - the parent ship of the Naval wing of the Royal Flying Corps - arrived in Scapa Flow with hydroplanes on board.

Several successful flights were completed during the ship's ten day stay. Unfortunately, the following week, two planes - a Shorts and a Sopwith - were wrecked when HMS *Hermes* was in the Cromarty Firth.

Strikers seek pay rise

The crews of eight Kirkwall trading vessels went on strike, in May, 1913, in demand of more pay. They were seeking an extra ten shillings a month to give mates a monthly wage of £4/10/-, seamen £3-£4, and cooks £2 a month.

"One skipper got into a wrangle with a stalwart mate, charging him with being the ringleader," reported *The Orcadian*. "The mate at once assumed an aggressive attitude, laying his fist on the skipper's nose."

A month earlier, Kirkwall dockers went on strike, demanding an increase from 7d to 9d an hour for overtime working.

Mermaid ahoy

Longhope fisherman Ralph Taylor and his crew claimed they had seen a mermaid while at the creels off the Old Man of Hoy.

It rose out of the water to a height of three feet and looked like a lady with a shawl round her shoulders. "This is the third occasion it has been seen at close range by them," said *The Orcadian*.

Eagle eyed

Eagles were nesting in Hoy in 1913. James Matches, a telegraph linesman, had watched two of the eagles on the Rackwick road and identified them as golden eagles. However, it was also suggested that they could be white-tailed eagles. They were blamed for carrying away several lambs which had disappeared.

Skatehorn dies

The well-known and much-photographed Orcadian character William Laughton, more familiar as Skatehorn, died in the Orkney Combination Poorhouse in August, 1913, and was buried at St Magnus kirkyard.

According to parish records he was 74 and practically all his life had wandered around the county "living principally on the generosity of folks he met on his way," said *The Orcadian*.

"He was known in all parts of the county and, though quite harmless, his name was often used as a sort of bogey for

quietening children when they were too noisy at night."

In his younger days, he did some hawking and also served five years in the Volunteer Coastguard Reserve.

On one previous occasion, his death had been wrongly reported in the West Mainland and printed in the newspapers. When this was pointed out to Skatehorn, he said: "I saw the report, but I didn't believe it."

Skatehorn is seen here in typical pose.

(Picture courtesy of Orkney Library photographic archive)

Blaze heroes honoured

Mr Andrew Skea, Aikerskaill, Deerness, arrived to find his father's home in flames with the old man, Mr Robert Skea, and Andrew's little niece asleep in the house.

He got through the smoke to his father's bedside and got him to the staircase. He then returned for the child but collapsed unconscious with the girl in his arms.

Robert Skea, although half choked with fumes, managed to pull his son and the child to the staircase, where they were rescued. Both men were later honoured with bravery awards.

Sadly, however, ten years later Andrew Skea died in an accident at the farm when working on mill machinery.

Marathon effort

A Westray man James Stout, of Skelwick, astonished lifeboatmen by rowing his 12 feet skiff all the way from Westray to Tongue in Sutherland - after telling his wife that he was going fishing!

He had been feared lost - and Stromness lifeboat had been launched to find him - before he arrived in Tongue, rowing strongly, said *The Orcadian.*

Train horror

At least one Orcadian - John Moodie (17) from Icegarth, Sanday - died, and another - John Rendall, Clay Loan, Kirkwall - was injured when eight people were killed and 50 hurt in a train disaster near Ottawa. The train was carrying Scots immigrants who had recently arrived in Canada to take up farming.

Chart topper

Mr J.G.S. Flett, of Harray, was acclaimed as a song writer and lyricist in the USA, as thousands clamoured to buy his music hall song "Out with Angeline in an Airship" which was released by American music publishers in 1913.

Murder threat

A man headlined by *The Orcadian* as a "dangerous Kirkwall lunatic" was ordered to be detained indefinitely, at Edinburgh Sheriff Court, after threatening to murder two doctors at the Royal Asylum in the capital.

Good Friday

Unemployment benefit, under the National Insurance Act, was introduced for the first time in Orkney with benefits payable on a Friday, commencing January 24, 1913.

Royal visitor in Scapa Flow

King George V, on the left, is seen talking with Admiral Sir David Beatty, Commander-in-Chief of the Grand Fleet, during the King's visit to Scapa Flow in 1917.

(Picture courtesy of Orkney Library photographic archive)

Death of Orcadian who became King

Captain Daniel Sutherland Rich took to his grave an unequalled honour - he was the only Orcadian of modern times to be crowned a King.

Captain Rich, a native of Rackwick where he was born in 1829, began a career at sea as a teenager and, after securing his sea captain's ticket, he went to Australia, where he spent some time in the goldfields and, according to his obituary in *The Orcadian* in 1914, met and befriended Lord Robert Cecil, later to become the Marquis of Salisbury and Prime Minister of Great Britain, 1885-6, 1886-92 and 1895-1902.

After a spell in Tasmania, Captain Rich went to Fiji where he was appointed marine pilot and where he remained for 20 years, during which time he was crowned King of one of the islands.

He held, it was said, "almost autocratic sway over thousands of fierce natives, many of whom secretly practised cannibalism."

And it was supposed that he was chiefly instrumental in persuading King Thakambau to consent to the annexation of the Fiji islands by Britain.

Captain Rich retired back to Tasmania where he died in Hobart, aged 85, in 1914.

1914

A fateful blow

Dr Samuel Linklater could have been remembered for his contribution to medicine. Instead he gained the unwanted distinction of being the first Orcadian to be knocked down and killed by an electric tram!

Born in 1853, he was educated at Stromness school before graduating in medicine and surgery at Edinburgh University in 1882. A year later, he intended to emigrate to Australia but he broke his journey in the United States to visit his sister in Hillsboro, Oregon - and instead stayed there to set up a medical practice as a physician and surgeon.

And, it was in Oregon in 1914, that he suffered the fate of being killed by a tramcar.

Kirkwall headmaster - £260 a year!

Dr J. McEwen resigned through ill health as headmaster of the Kirkwall Burgh School (later to become Kirkwall Grammar School) in July, 1914, after 35 years service.

In that time the average attendance had grown from 350 to 700. It was agreed to advertise for a successor at £260 a year!

The job went to Dr Hugh Marwick, a native of Rousay, who had been chief master of English at Burnley Grammar School, Lancashire, after gaining his degrees at Edinburgh University.

Dr Marwick soon established his reputation as a Norse scholar with several historical publications, before becoming Orkney's county education director in 1929. He was made an OBE in 1938, and in 1946, the year of his retiral, he was appointed a Chevalier (First Class) of the Royal Order of St Olav by King Haakon in honour of his war services to Norway.

Bid to revive oyster fishery

An attempt was made to revive the previously flourishing oyster fishery in the Bay of Firth - with the hope that Finstown would be the centre from which several boats would operate.

Many years earlier, *The Orcadian* reported, it had been "one of the finest, largest and most prolific oyster fisheries in Britain" but the beds had been destroyed.

It was now hoped, under a Fishery Board for Scotland scheme, formally opened in October, 1914, that stocks had been replenished. Unfortunately, by 1922, the directors of the Orkney (Bay of Firth) Oyster Fishery Ltd admitted that the restocking appeared to have failed with the low temperatures of the water blamed for killing the oysters.

1915

Orcadian designs on military success

Hundreds of thousands of greatcoats issued to the fighting services during and subsequent to World War One owed their creation to a Kirkwall tailor Peter Shearer.

Mr Shearer - who ran his firm Peter Shearer & Sons, then in Albert Street, Kirkwall, from 1883 to his retirement in 1925 - originally designed his version of the coat for Admiral Sir Stanley Colville, who from 1914-16 was Admiral Commanding Orkney and Shetland.

The pattern and design was brought to the attention of the War Office and duly approved for issue to the services, first of all going to France with a contingent of the Lincolnshires.

After World War One, many thousands of the coats were dyed and sold to the general public as surplus war stock.

Mr Shearer, born in Stronsay, served his tailoring apprenticeship in Edinburgh and Leith and, after returning to Kirkwall, he opened his first shop in Broad Street and later moved to bigger premises in Albert Street.

In his early years in business, he used to visit London at least once a year - an ambassador of the Orkney tweed trade - and well known people in his clientele included Sir Thomas Ritchie, a former Home Secretary; Sir Richard Webster, a former Solicitor-General (afterwards Lord Alverstone); and Lord George Hamilton, a former Secretary for India.

World War One ended his trips to London but the presence of the Grand Fleet at Scapa Flow brought new business and his customers in Albert Street included Admiral Sir John Jellicoe, and Prince Albert, who was later to become Duke of York and King George VI, who served for a time in Orkney waters.

Peter Shearer died on June 8, 1933, at his home at Cedar Lea, Holm Road, Kirkwall. His sons continued the business.

* * *

Sir Arthur Bignold, former MP for Kirkwall, left an estate worth £123,788 when his will was published.

* * *

Orkney cattle were selling at up to £26 at Aberdeen mart in the Spring of 1915. The increase in the retail price index over the remainder of the century would make that an equivalent price in 1999 of around £2,000. Compared, with the increase in average earnings over the same period, the equivalent 1999 price would be even higher - nearer £5,000.

When this view looking east from St Magnus Cathedral was taken at the start of the 20th century, the background behind the East Kirk was open countryside. By the end of the century, the same view would be dominated by the houses of Papdale.

(Picture courtesy of Orkney Library photographic archive)

The harvest is safely gathered in. Surprisingly, the first motorised tractor arrived in Orkney as early as 1916, although horses would reign supreme for another 30 years.

(Picture courtesy of Orkney Library photographic archive)

Death of a famous Orkney son

"One of Orkney's most brilliant and talented sons" was the tribute paid to the Orcadian pioneer of the treatment of mental illnesses, Sir Thomas Clouston, who died in April, 1915.

He was born, the son of Robert Clouston of Nisthouse, in 1840 and, after education at Edinburgh University, at the age of 23, he was appointed medical superintendent of the Cumberland and Westmoreland Asylum, Carlisle, in 1863.

In 1873 he became Physician Superintendent of the Scottish Metropolitan Asylum for the Insane, and ten years later, his book of clinical lectures on mental diseases established his reputation throughout the English speaking world.

He was made a freeman of Kirkwall in 1908 and knighted in 1911.

Less than a year before his death, Sir Thomas had been involved in a public debate with Orkney and Shetland MP John Cathcart Wason who had dismissed vivisection as "cowardly" and "brutal."

Sir Thomas Clouston wrote to *The Orcadian*: "I am proud to say that the men who practise experiments on animals to increase our knowledge are, as might be expected, as kind-hearted, brave, chivalrous and philanthropic as the very best of our citizens."

This Tom Kent photograph shows a military funeral in Kirkwall in August, 1912. (Picture courtesy of Orkney Library photographic archive)

The Kirkwall Burgh School, decades later to become the headquarters of Orkney Islands Council, in School Place.

(Picture courtesy of Orkney Library photographic archive)

1916

Chinese nights on a deserted island

Orkney mariner Robert Heddle Lennie - later to become Captain Lennie, master of the Liverpool steamer *Benholm* - was the hero of an amazing wartime escape when he helped save a ship's crew of 52, including 43 Chinese, after their vessel hit rocks off the Saltee islands off the Irish coast of Wexford.

After, a fortunate escape from the sinking ship, the men were marooned on the uninhabited island for four days from December 30, 1916 - January 2, 1917.

The ship ss *Lennox*, with Robert Lennie sailing as chief officer, had put to sea from Barry docks, South Wales, with a cargo of 6,000 tons of coal for Egypt. However, in thick fog, the vessel struck the rocks and huge seas washed away the bridge and two of the lifeboats.

Lennie, along with seven of the Chinese, managed to get into the Number three lifeboat with a line - the intention to get a connection from ship to shore. All eight were washed out of the lifeboat, which was smashed to pieces, but miraculously, they all made ashore, along with rations of seven 6lb tins of corned beef, 20lbs biscuits and two casks of water. They had also saved the ship's dog.

However, they still had to climb 200ft high cliffs to reach the top of the island. In daylight, Lennie helped supervise the evacuation of the remainder of the crew from the stricken ship to the island. The last to come ashore were the captain, third officer and an apprentice.

After lighting bonfires on the island shore, their plight was seen from the Irish mainland and they were rescued by the lifeboat from Kilmore where they were landed on January 2, 1917.

Zeppelin surrenders to *The Orcadian*

A Zeppelin airship, brought down by gunfire in the Thames estuary, produced a personal story of triumph for *The Orcadian*.

For the 15 German crewmen of the floundering airship surrendered to Lieutenant William Mackintosh RNR, the younger son of the proprietor of *The Orcadian*, who was in command of the steam trawler *Olivine* on patrol off the English coast.

Later in 1916, it was announced that Lt Mackintosh had been awarded the Distinguished Service Cross for "zeal, gallantry and success" whilst in command of a patrol boat in another episode of war.

1917

Sheriff courts trouble over year

A storm of protest - with questions asked in the House of Commons - followed the revelation that the Sheriff Principal of Orkney, Caithness and Shetland had dealt with just two cases in a year!

And for deciding those two cases, the Sheriff Principal had been paid a salary of £775.

That was the equivalent at the time of twelve years' wages for an Orkney farm-worker - or the price of a large farm in the isles.

Anger over eviction

Public outrage was directed at a Kirkwall kirk minister after it was revealed that he was evicting two widows, just days after their husbands perished at sea.

The men were lost with the steamer *Ruby*, owned by Messrs William Cooper and Son of Kirkwall, early in 1917. Almost immediately, their homes in Olaf Place, Kirkwall, were advertised for rent in *The Orcadian* by the landlord, a minister in the town.

A correspondent to *The Orcadian* protested: "This was the first intimation given by the reverend landlord to the widows of the two tenants referred to, and as such was a cold blooded, contemptible and cruel action towards the bereaved at a time when their loss and grief were scarcely more than realised.

"It may be stated that the landlord in question had previously called on the two widows in his ministerial capacity and professionally condoled with them in their lamented loss, but refrained from making any allusion to his intention of evicting them from their homes."

A public relief fund raised £200 for the widows and orphans of the crewmen.

* * *

A Portsmouth serviceman appeared in court in Kirkwall when it was discovered that he had bigamously married a Kirkwall woman when he already had a wife back home in "Pompey."

* * *

Fire at Scapa distillery destroyed the kiln roof completely after grain ignited in the middle of the night in June, 1917.

* * *

Orkney's first tractor was delivered to county in 1916 for Mr J. Irvine of Stove, Sanday. Despite the war, it was a year for farming innovation - the first Friesian bull was brought to the county by Mr T. Leslie of Glaitness, Kirkwall.

1918

Orkney's masters of the roads

A national report aimed to improve the lot of Orkney's tinkers in the community.

The Departmental Committee which produced the report said that Orkney had 76 tinkers - with 19 serving in the Army through World War One. Nationally, Scotland had a total of 2,728 tinkers, of whom 304 lived in tents, 15 in caves and 20 in shelters made of branches. The remainder lived in vans, sheds or houses.

"Everywhere, it is stated, strong drink is the bane of the tinker's life," said the report. "Most of the witnesses testified to the evil effects of drink. They seem unable to avoid getting on the spree now and again, one witness observes.

"The tinker endures a great deal in order that he may realise his ideal of living. He travels long distances, usually heavily laden. Such work as he performs is carried through under conditions of great discomfort, the saving clause being that he remains his own master.

"The misery of his life may be gauged from the fact that he finds his highest enjoyment in the insensibility produced by alcohol."

But the tinker was "a member of a community with definite ideas of right and wrong. It may be said tinkers as a class are singularly free from disease and that, apart from the vice of intemperance, they constitute a race many of whose characteristics might with advantage be grafted on the community in general."

It was reckoned that 400 houses were needed for the Scottish tinker population, with tuition given to the women to read and write. A register of all tinker families in each county should be prepared, said the report.

Two members of the committee - including the Duchess of Atholl - dissented to the proposal that total prohibition should be applied to tinkers on the ground that it would attach a social stigma and be an interference with individual liberty.

Cathedral minister

Rev William Barclay was appointed the new second minister of Kirkwall's St Magnus Cathedral, to succeed Rev W. Pitcairn Craig, who moved South in 1918. A year later, the Rev John Rutherford retired after 36 years as first charge Cathedral minister and the two charges were combined under Rev Barclay. The Rev Rutherford died in 1922.

Epidemic leaves trail of deaths

Schools throughout Orkney were closed in the Autumn of 1918 as an epidemic of influenza swept the islands, causing several deaths. All three resident doctors in Kirkwall were affected by the outbreak, reported *The Orcadian*, and subsequent complications were proving "fatal over the whole country."

Nationally in 1918, deaths from the flu totalled 112,329 - the worst death toll in Britain since the cholera epidemic of 1849 - and most of the deaths were aged under 35, many of them girls working in munitions factories. The deaths continued into 1919 - making a total national death toll of 151,446 from the epidemic.

Farm wages

The Northern Counties District Agricultural Wages Committee decided on a minimum agricultural wage of 26 shillings a week. The employers had suggested 25s and the workers' representatives had asked for 45s.

Crowded housing

Kirkwall Town Council decided that the building of a minimum of 200 houses was required in the burgh in 1919 as a survey revealed massive overcrowding of local housing.

A total of 238 Kirkwall families were living in one roomed homes, while 314 families had just two rooms.

A national survey in 1918 said that Orkney was home to 76 tinkers, mostly living in sheds, but sometimes tents and even caves at the shore.

(Picture courtesy of Orkney Library photographic archive)

These Stromness Volunteers are pictured at a camp in Edinburgh.   (Picture courtesy of Orkney Library photographic archive)

A world of war

Orkney paid a dreadful price for the Great War - the war that was to end all wars, but failed. One in seven of the Orcadians who went off to fight for King and Country never returned as nearly 600 men in the prime of their life made the supreme sacrifice and were killed in battle, far from home and, invariably, in scenes of utter carnage.

The Seaforth Highlanders - traditionally Orkney's regiment - suffered as dreadful a toll as any other military unit. During World War One, a total of 50,000 men of all ranks served in the Seaforths. Of those, more than 8,000 were killed in action and thousands more left seriously handicapped by injury.

Twenty five years later, Orcadians were well aware of the threat of hostilities months, even years, before the actual outbreak of World War Two. But, in 1914, when *The Orcadian* and the *Orkney Herald* provided the only news for the majority of the population, especially in the isles and rural areas, the declaration of war came with little warning. (National radio broadcasts did not start until ten years later). Indeed, if there was to be fighting, most people would have expected it to be civil war in Ireland. Instead, within weeks and months, the names of faraway places - often not even shown on Orkney schoolroom maps - would become part of everyday conversation as Orcadians died in Mons, Ypres and Gallipoli and other theatres of war.

The bombshell came in *The Orcadian* dated August 1, 1914, tucked inside the newspaper on page five, that Austria had declared war against Serbia. (*The Orcadian* spelt it as "Servia"). There had been general mobilisation of the Serbian army and partial mobilisation of the Austro-Hungarian forces. It was anticipated that Germany would follow suit, in support of Austria.

That week, unbeknown to most Orcadians, Captain John Gilbert Oringsell Coke was recalled from retirement by the Navy to be King's Harbourmaster at Scapa Flow. Captain Coke had retired from the Navy in 1912 but now, just seven days before the official outbreak of war, he was recalled to prepare the Scapa Flow defences. (Captain Coke was to survive the war and he died, aged 62, in the South of France in 1937).

Although the defences were flimsy, the credit for what preparations had been made was due in part to Admiral Sir William May. In 1905 he became Commander of the Atlantic Fleet and from 1909-11 he was Commander-in-Chief, Home Fleet, during which time it was largely through his endeavours that Scapa Pier was brought up to Admiralty standards, paving the way for the use of Scapa Flow throughout World War One. Indeed, when he died in October, 1930, the national press, with masterly overstatement, described him as "the man who discovered Scapa Flow." Relevant as his contribution may have been, we can safely assume that Orcadians suspected its existence all along!

In fact, there were several Naval top brass who claimed the credit for "discovering" Scapa Flow including the First Sea Lord Admiral Sir John "Jacky" Fisher, later to be Lord Fisher, who died in 1920. He claimed that he had signalled the use of Scapa Flow as the base for the British fleet as early as 1905 when he had sent a hydrographic vessel to Orkney to survey the suitability of the anchorage. (This was later disputed by Admiral A. Mostyn Field who said that it had been arranged for HMS *Triton* to visit Scapa Flow anyway.) Another who later also claimed some credit for the early defences of the Flow was Admiral Sydney Fremantle.

However, whatever the collective exertions by Admirals May, Fisher and Fremantle on behalf of Scapa Flow, it was still by no means certain that the Orkney harbour would be used by the British Fleet. In January, 1914, even *The Orcadian* was describing the Cromarty Firth as "the finest war harbour in the kingdom, designed to become the strategical base of the British Fleet." Indeed, just seven months before the declaration of war, the Admiralty refused to sanction expenditure of £1,475 to widen the pier at Scapa. Orkney Harbours Commissioners were told that Admiral Lowry believed that any traffic congestion at the pier could be relieved by "ordinary police supervision." The Commissioners were told: "He is surprised that the harbours commissioners should anticipate difficulty in obtaining the services of a constable on the comparatively rare occasions of the congestion complained of."

Within a few months, there would be congestion aplenty - as the first German prisoners of war were handed over at Scapa pier.

It was *The Orcadian* dated August 8, 1914, which carried the front page headline: "Britain at War." The newspaper explained: "A British ultimatum was addressed to Germany protesting against the German violation of Belgium's neutrality and demanding a reply before Midnight. The British request was summarily rejected, and the British government have declared to the German government that a state of war exists between the two countries as from 11pm on August 4." In the House of Commons, the Prime Minister Mr Herbert Asquith read a message from the King saying he was calling out the army Reserve and embodying the Territorials.

The first Orcadians to be directly aware of the impending hostilities were the Territorials of Orkney Royal Garrison Artillery. *The Orcadian* reported: "So long ago as Wednesday of last week (July 29), special service sections of the Orkney Artillery were called out and sent to their appointed sections. On Sunday (August 2) the remainder of the force was mobilised and further detachments at once sent forward to certain points which are understood to be of strategical value. The remainder of the men were allowed to proceed home but had instructions to hold themselves in readiness for an immediate call. The orders to mobilise came on Monday evening (August 3) and all night long the men from the out-stations were arriving at headquarters where the Kirkwall companies had already reported for duty.

"The calling out of the Orkney Artillery at such an early stage in the crisis created great excitement in Orkney, especially in view of the fact that at one time it was decided to disband the corps, and it was only with great exertion on the part of those concerned that this was averted."

Soon after, units of Royal Marine pensioners - many of them aged over 50 - were sent to Scapa Flow to help augment the defences already provided by the Orkney Royal Garrison Artillery.

Several Orcadian Naval reservists who immediately proceeded to Portsmouth were dispatched home to Orkney, however, "their services not being at present required."

Lord Kitchener accepted the post of War Minister while Admiral Sir John Jellicoe was appointed to the supreme command of the British Home Fleets, with Rear Admiral Charles E. Madden his Chief of Staff. Admiral Sir Stanley Colville was Admiral Commanding Orkney and Shetland, a position he held until 1916 when he was appointed Commander-in-Chief at Portsmouth. In a message to Jellicoe, the King expressed "his confidence that the officers and men of the fleets will revive and renew the old glories of the Royal Navy and prove once again the sure shield of Britain and her Empire in the hour of trial."

It was to prove to be far more than a mere hour of trial, but it is a tragic truth that, alongside the dreadful toll of death during wartime, the county economy in Orkney, in both World War One and World War Two, was to be boosted to levels which it could seldom attain in peacetime. The provisioning of the Military and Naval authorities meant growing business for local merchants and other Orkney concerns. For instance, the

and Orkney woe

Stromness shipbuilding yard at Ness, which in 1856, had built the *Royal Mail*, the first steamer to carry the mails across the Pentland Firth to Orkney, once again became a flourishing industry. In 1913, Mr Fred Stanger had installed new power-driven equipment which enabled him to secure Admiralty contracts, and during the war the Admiralty took over the yard entirely for war work.

(Unfortunately, the return to peacetime would see the end of the heyday of the yard. After the war, Mr Stanger began building a 250 ton motor-powered vessel but he died in 1924 and the vessel remained unfinished - though it was later purchased by Norwegian ship brokers who planned to use it for sealing in the Arctic. Work ceased in the yard and, in August, 1928, the fall of the auctioneer's hammer marked the end of Stanger's era.)

Within 24 hours of the declaration of war, Orkney saw the reality of the conflict at first hand. Two enemy ships were reported sunk off the Northern Isles and German prisoners were landed in the county as early as Wednesday, August 5, 1914.

The Orcadian explained: "The police passed along the road with two foreign looking gentlemen in charge, and shortly after, the Superintendent of Police and the Fiscal were seen hastening towards the Police Station. A motor car went off with an officer, and two men fully armed, then followed a strong detachment on foot, and last of all an officer on a motor cycle.

"At Scapa Pier, the escort were drawn up at one of the landing steps with bayonets fixed. After a short wait, a large and powerful steam pinnace came alongside and a petty officer, who was accompanied by several Marines carrying rifles stepped ashore, and handed over 13 German fishermen to Lt Dennison, the officer in charge of the escort. These men formed, it is said, the crew of a German trawler caught in the North Sea by a British warship."

Sadly, Lt James Dennison, a Shapinsay member of the Orkney RGA, would be one of the many Orkney servicemen who did not survive the war.

Kirkwall Town Council held a special meeting on August 6 "to consider what provision ought to be made for the care of the sick and wounded who might at any time be landed on our shores." It was agreed that the burgh school be utilised as the Naval Emergency Hospital and an appeal went out for funds and equipment to provide at least 50 beds. "Any doctors, medical students or nurses willing to give their services are requested to send their names to Doctor Sinclair, Kirkwall," appealed *The Orcadian*, while county convener Alfred Baikie appealed to civilians to conserve foodstuffs, coal, oil and other commodities likely to become scarce.

Within weeks, Orkney was, in effect, under the rule of Martial Law as the Defence of the Realm Act introduced a catalogue of Draconian powers. *The Orcadian* reported: "We have had no actual experience of war of any serious kind in this country since the time of Cromwell and we hardly yet realise how entirely we are in the hands of the war authorities.

"They can without any civil proceedings or ceremony enter any house by force, order the lights to be put out, require all persons within any area to remain indoors between stated hours. They have the power to take possession of any land, building and any moveable property they like. They can demolish your house, arrest you without any warrant, order whole communities to leave specified districts, and close public houses.

"It sounds a little strange to us in this fair land of liberty and freedom, but happily we all know that wisdom and discretion will govern the operation of these martial regulations. War is a ruthless business and all private considerations have to give way before the necessities of the State."

And despite the war, all of the major agricultural shows in Orkney - the West Mainland, South Ronaldsay and the County - all went ahead, not only in 1914 but 1915 too.

In fact, from the correspondence columns of *The Orcadian* it would almost appear that as much energy was expended on the war against drink as the actual war against Germany in the following weeks and months.

The first restriction under the new martial powers saw the closure of Kirkwall public houses brought forward to 9pm and then, in October, 1914, to 8pm, with members of the United Free Church Presbytery of Orkney urging complete prohibition for the continuance of the war. The Defence of the Realm Act was employed equally in Shetland where the entire staff of Lerwick Post Office found themselves under arrest by the military authorities!

In Orkney, the first prosecution under the Defence of the Realm regulations was taken before Sheriff Mercer at Kirkwall where a Stromness licence holder was charged with supplying whisky, rum and black beer to a member of the Territorial forces whilst on duty. He was fined £40 (the equivalent of thousands at 1999 prices).

Under the headline "The drink problem," *The Orcadian* complained that there were "scenes of debauchery and drunkenness" in Kirkwall, and argued that restrictions should apply "not to the Navy and Military alone, but to the civilian population as well."

The annual report of the Orkney police showed that the number of crimes and offences in 1915 had risen to 571, an increase of 365 cases over 1914, and 517 people had been apprehended - of whom 382 were said to be under the influence of drink when they committed their misdemeanours. Of those apprehended, 208 were handed over to the Naval authorities. Interestingly, we obviously had not yet reached the era of the troublesome teenager. Of the hundreds of miscreants who were convicted, the number aged between 16-21 was just seven!

On December 9, 1916, the Defence of the Realm Act introduced a complete ban on spirits and a "no treating" rule in Orkney pubs, with licensing hours restricted to 12noon-2.30pm and 6pm-8pm. In the week before the ban came into force, "hundreds of gallons of whisky" were bought up and stockpiled, reported *The Orcadian*.

Long before this, *The Orcadian* had announced: "All the North Scotland mainland and the islands are now prohibited areas from which aliens, both neutral and belligerent, are barred."

There were certainly belligerent aliens just off the Orkney coast. As early as August 15, 1914, *The Orcadian* reported: "Kirkwall was greatly excited on Saturday evening by the rumour that a German submarine had entered one of the harbours in the islands. The rumour is probably without foundation."

With hindsight, the rumour could equally well have been true. Certainly in October, 1914, the captain of the steamship *Leander* reported four German submarines off Orkney, and one of them could well have been responsible for one of the first major sea casualties of the war in Northern waters when the 7,350 ton cruiser HMS *Hawke* was sunk by a U-boat, with up to 400 men lost. The trawler *Ben Rinnes* landed most of the 55 survivors in Aberdeen, but four men - who had survived by clinging to a raft for 23 hours - were brought to Orkney and taken to a hospital ship. "The enemy's submarines hovered round the raft, their crews watching and laughing at the terrible plight of their victims. They offered no aid but showed evident delight as sailor after sailor gave up the struggle and dropped into the sea," said *The Orcadian*.

Elsewhere the newspaper commented: "Germany has thrown off the mask and is disregarding the laws of war in a way that places her outside the pale of civilised nations. Her methods of war are those of the barbarous Middle Ages."

And there was no doubting how close the U-boats could get to Orkney shores on November 23, 1914, when the German submarine *U18*, commanded by Heinrich Von Hennig, earned the distinction of being the first officially-confirmed enemy submarine to breach the defences of Scapa Flow.

An official communique reported that a British patrol vessel had spotted and rammed the intruder at 12.20. "She was not sighted again till 1.20 when she was seen on the surface, the crew on deck and waving a white flag. Shortly after this she foundered, just as the destroyer *Garry* came alongside and rescued three officers and 23 of her crew, only one being drowned."

The news of the capture quickly spread and, in all quarters, was the sole topic of conversation, said *The Orcadian*. The survivors were taken south as prisoners to Edinburgh Castle.

However, it was the great war on land that was to claim so many lives of Orcadians and their fellow countrymen. The British Expeditionary Force had landed in France and Belgium by the third week of August, 1914, and a month later saw the first reports of Orkney casualties in the war with Private Ernest Arthur, a former Kirkwall Post Office worker, wounded during the retreat with the Royal Scots from Mons and two of his comrades "fearfully mutilated and instantly killed." Corporal Donald Thomson of Flotta was another wounded and in hospital, as was Sergeant Hugh Tulloch of Hooking, North Ronaldsay, serving with the Scots Guards in France.

On December 1, 1914, Private John McKenzie, of the Gordon Highlanders, was the first soldier belonging to South Ronaldsay to die on the battlefield. He left a widow and two children at home in Grimness. Sapper Daniel Sutherland, son of the late tenant of the Kirkwall Hotel, was also among the first Orcadians to be killed in action, serving in France with the 2nd Highland Field Company RE.

At this stage, the military authorities were still relying on voluntary recruits to fight the war and Orkney did as much, or as little, as the rest of the country to answer the call of King and Country. *The Orcadian* published a weekly "Legion of Honour" of those men who had enlisted in each island and parish. The percentage of the population who had signed up varied, from parish to parish, from one per cent to seven per cent, but that included all the local Territorial members of the Orkney Royal Garrison Artillery, so the number of Orkney men in regular units overseas during the first four months of World War One would have been in the dozens rather than the hundreds or, indeed, the thousands which it became.

A number of young men from Westray came forward to join the Orkney RGA after a recruiting meeting in the island, but a correspondent to *The Orcadian* in October, 1914, complained: "Our country is in the throes of the greatest war in the world's history, and yet the great majority of the people in Orkney are going about their business in the usual placid style, never thinking that any day there may come along a Zeppelin and wipe them out, and all their hoarded possessions."

If further weight were needed to his warning, six weeks later the Germans shelled the ports of Hartlepool, Whitby and Scarborough and the first bomb to fall on British soil from an enemy plane landed on Dover on Christmas Eve, 1914. And after several aerial bombardments by Zeppelin of towns in Norfolk, from Cromer to King's Lynn, the Admiralty issued a list of precautions to people in Orkney and other coastal areas, especially warning them against gathering in crowds.

But fears that the Germans had invaded Copinsay proved unfounded. A trawler was dispatched to the island after a black flag was seen flying. However it was discovered that workmen engaged on building the lighthouse had run out of food and provisions.

Orcadians were not only caught up in the war in Europe, however. William Dennison of Shapinsay was among the crew of the 4,800 ton *Benmohr*, sunk, en route to Australia, by the rogue German cruiser *Emden*. Other Orcadians in exile returned home to fight for British regiments while others were enlisted in Canadian, Australian and New Zealand units.

It soon became obvious, however, that more men were needed. "Lord Kitchener wants another 100,000 men and he wants them at once," said *The Orcadian* in November, 1914 - the same week that income tax was doubled! Recruiting campaigns were aimed at all men aged 19-38, or, in the case of ex-soldiers, up to the age of 45.

As the German spy Karl Lody was shot at the Tower of London, there were sporadic outbreaks of "spy fever" among the population - but reports of a German captured in Caithness, in a car laden with cans of petrol and maps of Orkney, were denied. Nonetheless the general mood of anti-German feeling had grown to the extent that a well known visitor to Scapa Flow, Admiral Prince Louis of Battenberg - the father of the future Lord Mountbatten - was forced to resign as First Sea Lord. Born in Austria, he had joined the Royal Navy in 1868 on becoming a naturalised British subject. However, he had no property in the UK but still owned a castle and estate in Germany.

As the reality of war hit home, a correspondent to *The Orcadian* recommended that Kirkwall Town Council should insure St Magnus Cathedral against "war risks" with Lloyds underwriters.

But it was correspondence from the trenches of France which made the most poignant reading. For a few months in 1915, *The Orcadian* reprinted letters home to his family in Sandwick from Private James Brass, 2nd Battalion Seaforth Highlanders. The correspondence was a compelling mix of bravado and brutal honesty about the horrors of the war.

To his mother, he wrote: "We are still holding our own here, and I think if our Navy manages to get at the Germans on the sea, the war will soon be at an end.

"Some time ago provisions were rather short and for two days we only received two biscuits each. Lying in the trenches in this weather is not very comfortable - among the mud and the dirt.

"About 50 out of our company have been killed or wounded. I am thankful that I have come through it so far without a scratch. One day five of us were told to discover the enemy's position. I was one of that five. Two of us got shot, one through the heart - a groan and all was over. A chum of mine got two of his fingers blown off. God knows how he managed to get away." To his sister, he wrote: "We are going to give the Germans a treat. I long to get at them with the bayonet. When the shells are bursting near our trenches we cuddle up like sardines in a tin."

In March, 1915, he was serving alongside another Orcadian, Jack Reid from Stronsay. Private Brass wrote home: "For four days in succession we had to stand in trenches with water up to our knees. Once four of us got into a trench in the morning after being on outpost duty all night. We expected an easy time but the trench soon began to fill with water and we had to stay in it till Midnight."

Another letter to his mother read: "I think, and so does everybody, that the war will last till April or May, so there will be some rare work to do yet. We have been staying in a piggery for the last three days and it is just like a madhouse or a menagerie."

Alas, Private Brass's war probably did only last a few months for, presumably, he was the same Private James Brass whose death, aged 22, with the Seaforths in France, is recorded on the Sandwick war memorial.

His frighteningly frank word pictures of life at the front can have done little to encourage recruitment back home in Orkney where the Central Recruiting Committee in January, 1915, issued a letter verging on emotional blackmail to every man aged 19-38 in the county appealing for volunteers: "Answer honestly to your conscience the question: 'Have I a real reason for staying at home or am I merely sheltering behind the bayonets of men with greater spirit than myself?' A million men are absolutely needed and needed instantly. It is a sacrifice for every one of these men to come forward, just as much as it is a sacrifice for you, and for a generation to come men will be judged by their answer to that question. We believe that no Orkney man would like to answer it in such a way as to forfeit his own self-respect or the good opinion of his friends."

Four months later, Orkney and Shetland MP John Cathcart Wason complained in the House of Commons that the voluntary recruiting system was unfair - it was only the willing horses who went, and the loafers and shirkers stayed at home, he said. He stopped short of calling for conscription but demanded what he called "universal service." The fact was, said the MP, that the country did not realise that a terrible waging war was going on not far from our shores.

By the end of 1915, Lord Derby's recruiting scheme was launched - the final step before compulsory conscription - with teams of canvassers visiting every Orkney household seeking men aged 18-40, with the pledge that call-up would be prioritised so that married men would be the last to go into uniform.

The Orcadian commented: "Among so-called slackers there is a very considerable body of men who, not for the want of patriotism, but simply for the want of means, are holding back." Forced enlistment of these men could see their homes broken up and "the removal of their families to the nearest slum," warned the newspaper.

Under the Derby scheme, local tribunals were set up to arbitrate on which men should be enlisted. Within two weeks, over 200 more Orcadians had signed up. Nationally, an astonishing total of 2,246,630 men came forward. Yet even then, it was not sufficient, and *The Orcadian* commented: "Still the broad fact remains that two million men did not see their way to answer the call." And on January 24, 1916, the law was passed introducing conscription throughout Britain.

New maritime regulations in Orkney saw Scapa Flow closed for civilian navigation in February, 1915, and the Pentland Firth steamer *St Ola* ceased sailing to and from Scapa, operating instead via Hoy Sound directly between Scrabster and Stromness.

But there were Orcadians at sea all around the world. Captain David Cromarty Thomson, originally from Quindrie, South Ronaldsay, was honoured for bravery for his part in rescuing ten men from the Norwegian barque *Elim* off Cape Finisterre. Tragically another Orkney mariner, Pat Shearer - son of Kirkwall coal merchant Peter Shearer - died trying to save a Chinese sailor who fell overboard from the SS *Hangchow* off the Chinese coast on November 11, 1914.

In the Dardanelles and at Gallipoli, there was fighting on land and sea, and the first deaths were reported of Orcadian exiles, fighting with Australian and New Zealand forces. More than 25,000 British deaths were suffered at Gallipoli before the area was evacuated.

When HMS *Triumph* was lost in the Dardanelles, there was a "feeling of great uneasiness in Orkney, it being known that at least three Orcadians were on board," reported *The Orcadian*. In the event, all three seamen - John Kirkpatrick from Longhope, J. W. Linklater, born in Sanday, and Thomas Wylie from Burray - survived to be repatriated to Britain.

An appalling disaster nearer home saw 158 lives lost - including at least one Orcadian in a troop train disaster at Gretna Green. However, more fortunate was Private Peter Skea (20) of the Royal Scots, from Pool in Sanday, who was in hospital in Carlisle with burns and a broken leg after crawling out of the blazing wreckage.

The minister of St Magnus Cathedral, Rev W. Pitcairn Craig, was called up as a chaplain to the forces - and would serve in France - as *The Orcadian* gave the first reports of poison gas being used by the Germans against British troops around Ypres. A greater blow to morale was in May, 1915, with the loss of the *Lusitania* liner, torpedoed off the Irish coast and sinking within eight minutes. Just 658 were reported to have survived from 2,160, including 980 British and 188 American passengers, on board.

There had been a steady stream of tragic dispatches from the theatres of war around the world but, nonetheless, Orcadians, like the rest of the country, must have been horrified when the casualties of the first 12 months of World War One were revealed. The British casualty list of the first year showed: killed - 4,965 officers, 70,992 men; wounded - 9,973 officers, 241,086 men; missing - 1,501 officers, 53,466 men. It added up to a total of nearly 400,000 killed, wounded or missing - and the war was to continue for another three years yet, despite an optimistic headline "Is the end approaching?" in *The Orcadian* in March, 1915. Eventually, those casualty figures would increase ten-fold.

It was not easy to escape the hardships. Income tax - which had been doubled ten months earlier - was further increased by 40 per cent in September, 1915, while the people of Kirkwall - despite a new £20,000 Wideford Hill reservoir scheme - were suddenly told, on November 6, 1915, that owing to a shortage, water would now only be available to the town's inhabitants between 8am and 1pm. Also, a bacterial analysis showed the water was only 4th class and thus "only suitable for domestic use after bleaching."

It was, no doubt, as a diversion from the war that *The Orcadian* published the story of Emma Moules, of White Hart Lane, Wood Green, North London, aged 73, who, as the mother of 23 children had married, for the second time, a man with 17 children. She had also raised 28 foster children - making a record of having raised 68 children. At that time, she had 107 grandchildren and 11 great grandchildren. Mrs Moules' second husband was said to be away fighting for King and Country, having enlisted at 20 years below his real age.

The British Naval authorities in Kirkwall and Scapa Flow intercepted many vessels sailing under the flags of neutral countries in Orkney waters to ensure that their cargo was not bound for Germany. By March, 1915, so many American vessels had been detained at Kirkwall, because of suspicions over their ultimate destination, that diplomatic relations with the United States were becoming slightly strained, especially when the British government refused a request that an American consul be allowed to be stationed in Kirkwall.

In July, 1915, when the Norwegian steamer *Bergensfjord* was escorted into Kirkwall by British forces, on board was found to be the Kaiser's special envoy, Herr Dernburg, returning from a German propaganda visit to the United States. He was granted safe passage to proceed, reported *The Orcadian*.

However, the extent of the blockade was such that a total of 743 ships of neutral countries were intercepted and sent into Kirkwall for inspection in the year of 1915 alone.

Each night, the so-called Jellicoe train - named after Admiral Sir John Jellicoe - would run from London to Thurso - given special priority to enable it to complete the run in a time far quicker than anything achieved in peacetime - carrying hundreds of officers and men to the Fleet in Scapa Flow.

Many of those men came together, in June, 1915, for what can undoubtedly be regarded as the biggest Church service ever conducted in Orkney - when a congregation of an estimated 14,000 servicemen gathered at the back of Whanclett in Flotta for an open air service at which the Archbishop of York, Dr Cosmo Lang, officiated. Dr Lang also conducted a service for several thousand in Walls. Soon after, the Very Rev Dr Wallace Williamson, Moderator of the General Assembly of the Church of Scotland, visited servicemen in Orkney and preached at St Magnus Cathedral in Kirkwall.

A month later, King George V visited the Grand Fleet in Scapa Flow on July 7-9, 1915. He was welcomed by his son Prince Albert (later to become King George VI) and Admiral Cecil Colville and stayed at the Longhope Hotel, which had been requisitioned. Throughout World War One, there was a direct telegraph link from the Longhope Hotel to the inner sanctums of Government in London's Whitehall.

The King later recalled to Provost James Marwick of Stromness that he enjoyed a round of golf with Admiral Sir John Jellicoe. He also apparently enjoyed a dinner on HMS *Iron Duke* in the company of no less than eleven Admirals.

He landed in Flotta - at a spot which became known as the King's Hard for the rest of the century - where 4,500 servicemen were on parade, and later estimated that he had seen 35,000 men in two days. The King returned to Scapa Flow in June, 1916, and again on Midsummer's Day, 1917.

The Prince of Wales, later to be Edward VIII, visited Scapa Flow from August 18-24, 1915, while his brother Prince Albert was being dispatched south for hospital treatment for suspected appendicitis.

Two other visitors to Orkney during 1915-16 were the Count Alexis Tolstoy - a descendant of the famous Russian dynasty which included the author of the epic *War and Peace*, Count Leo Tolstoy, who visited British ships in Scapa Flow - and the American motor magnate Henry Ford who arrived at Kirkwall, but was not permitted to land, aboard the so-called "Peace Ship" *Oscar II* which was part of Ford's ill-conceived mission to end the war in Europe.

If truth be known, Ford was more concerned about the loss of his European market for cars rather than any great philanthropic drive for peace. Anyway, when he arrived in Kirkwall Bay in December, 1915, Ford sent a message ashore to his former contemporary, the Kirkwall motor dealer W.R. Tullock, whom he had met and befriended 20 years earlier when Mr Tullock was in the United States. Unfortunately, William Tullock was away in Edinburgh and so Ford left Orkney without seeing him. He had no more luck with his peace mission which the British press derided as the "Ship of Fools." Just over a year later, the USA had joined the war.

Nearly 2,000 men died in just three great tragedies of World War One in Orkney waters - the loss of HMS *Hampshire* in 1916, HMS *Vanguard* in 1917, and the destroyers HMS *Opal* and HMS *Narborough* in the same incident in 1918. But probably hundreds more died, during 1914-18, with the loss of dozens of other ships - both military and civilian - which foundered, either as a result of acts of war or the same peacetime perils in Orkney of bad weather and rocky shorelines.

The dual danger of mines and submarines faced not only military vessels but also the merchant ships and trawlers which continued their work. The potential terror of torpedo-firing U-boats was soon made apparent in Orkney as German submarines launched a series of attacks against "soft targets" of British and Allied shipping.

Usually, the civilian crews were given a warning and a chance to abandon ship; but sometimes not. U-boats were obviously in action off Orkney through much of June, 1915, when the 53 crewmen of the cargo liner *Iona*, en route from Middlesbrough to Montreal, were landed at Kirkwall after their ship was sunk by enemy submarine between North Ronaldsay and Fair Isle. The ship's chief officer was James Petrie was Burray.

On June 3, 1915, three trawlers fishing off Orkney were sunk by U-boat within hours of each other. Another met the same fate three weeks later. Then, between July 22-25, eight trawlers were sunk by U-boat, four of them on one day, July 25. So in less than eight weeks, 12 fishing boats were destroyed by enemy action in Orkney waters. However, the single biggest attack on fishing vessels saw *The Orcadian* of July 3, 1915, report that 16 drifters had been sunk in a raid by U-boats off Shetland, although all the crews were saved.

There appeared then to be a gap of some 18 months before U-boats again turned their attentions to fishing boats, but between February and June, 1917, another five trawlers at least were sunk by torpedo. That gives a minimum of 17 trawlers lost to German submarines around the islands in just two years - around a quarter of the total loss of ships in local waters in World War One.

One of the methods chosen to counter the lurking threat of enemy submarines was the introduction of so-called Q ships - disguised merchant vessels equipped with weapons - which were sent forth from Scapa Flow to hunt for U-boats.

Several Orcadian civilian mariners were recruited for this work and at least three were honoured by King George V for destroying submarines.

One of those honoured was Captain William Moodie, of Finstown. In July, 1915, he had a first hand encounter with a submarine when he was in command of the 130 ton trading schooner *Sunbeam*, owned by Finstown merchant W.B. Firth. A U-boat emerged at the eastern end of the Pentland Firth and ordered Captain Moodie and his three Orcadian crewmates - William Laird of Burray, James Seatter of Westray and Robert Walls of Firth - to abandon their vessel before the submarine destroyed it.

Captain Moodie and the crew made it safely ashore and, not long afterwards, he was given command of his own Q ship, the *Ready*, which, in June, 1917, gained a measure of revenge by sinking a U-boat off Cornwall - for which Captain Moodie

received the medal of the Distinguished Service Cross. Again he had an all-Orcadian crew, including John Sinclair from Kirkwall, and Messrs Walls and Seatter, his fellow survivors from the sinking of the *Sunbeam* two years earlier.

Captain James Dunnet Thomson, a native of North Ronaldsay, also won the Distinguished Service Cross for his part in sinking a German submarine in the North Sea. He was in command of the Granton trawler *Commissioner*, which like several fishing vessels was converted to a Q ship to fight the U-boat menace. Captain Thomson successfully identified and destroyed an enemy submarine. (In peacetime, he rose to be commodore skipper of the trawling fleet belonging to Messrs T. L. Devlin and Sons, Granton, but he died at a comparatively young age of 61 in 1930.)

Another North Isles master to be honoured was Captain John Irvine, of Papa Westray, who was awarded the Distinguished Service Order by King George V in 1917 for sinking a German U-boat in Mid-Atlantic.

Approaching her 50th birthday in World War One was the Northern Isles steamer *St Clair*, owned by the North of Scotland and Orkney and Shetland Steam Navigation Company. She also saw wartime action with a German submarine off Fair Isle when several members of her crew were killed. The *St Clair* - 205 feet long and built at Govan in 1868 - later became the *St Colm* and she was one of the oldest ships on the British register when, in 1937, she was sent to a breakers yard - in Germany!

But, regardless of the risks of war, mariners still had to contend with the natural perils of Orkney waters which did not distinguish between peace or conflict - and half a dozen ships were wrecked either on the shores of the North Isles, or close by. One of the first was the 1,200 ton Norwegian ship *Skotfos* which ran aground and caught fire when lost on Seal Skerry off North Ronaldsay in January, 1915, en route for Manchester. Ten North Ronaldsay men were praised as heroes when they launched three boats to battle through wild sea conditions to rescue the *Skotfos* crew off the rocks where they had been exposed to the elements for 18 hours.

The ten heroes were named as Hugh Muir, Sholtisquoy; Thomas Tulloch, Garso; Robert Tulloch, Sandback; William Thomson, Dennishead; John Tulloch, Scourygar; William Tulloch, Lochend; Thomas Tulloch, Rue; Hugh Thomson, Bewan; John Swanney, Sangar; and W. Swanney, Vincoin.

In just the first week of 1915, a total of 46 shipwrecked mariners were landed at Kirkwall after three separate disasters in which at least 13 men died. Seventeen crewmen from the 1,500 ton iron barque *Pilgrim*, from Boston, USA, were brought to safety in Orkney after being rescued in mid-Atlantic by a Norwegian steamer. Also the 23 crew of the Norwegian steamer *Bjorgvin* were landed at Kirkwall by another Norwegian vessel *Brynhild* after abandoning ship and taking to their lifeboats. A further six crewmen from the Norwegian barque *Maryetta*, en route from Denmark to Brazil with cement, were saved and delivered to Orkney but 13 of their fellow crewmen were drowned when their lifeboat capsized after being forced to abandon ship in stormy conditions. Kirkwall was also to welcome the crew of the Danish steamer *Canadia* after the vessel was wrecked on Fair Isle. A Russian-Finn crewman was said to have climbed up a 300 feet high cliff with a line to help the rest of the ship's company to safety.

In February, 1915, it was to be a British Naval vessel, the destroyer HMS *Goldfinch*, which was to meet a sad end - being wrecked on Sanday. Ten months later, Sanday became the final resting place of an Admiralty trawler HMS *Response*.

Westray was to witness the stranding of three big merchant vessels during World War One - the 3,000 ton American tanker *Llama* foundered in October, 1915; the 1,800 ton Swedish cargo vessel *Birka* with all hands - including the body of a woman washed ashore in Papa Westray - was lost in January, 1916; and another Swedish vessel, the *Scandinavia* in February, 1917.

Stronsay claimed another merchant vessel - the 1,600 ton Norwegian ship *Marco Polo* - in December, 1915.

The ss *Active*, managed by the Hudson's Bay Company, was lost off Orkney with all her crew - the tragedy only discovered when lifeboats and bodies were washed up at Deerness, Shapinsay, Stronsay and Papa Stronsay, and Rousay.

But the single biggest loss of ships and men would be in a major theatre of war - the Battle of Jutland, the last great engagement, in which fleet confronted fleet, in British Naval history.

On May 30, 1916, more than 70 ships, under the command of Sir John Jellicoe, sailed from Scapa Flow - 16 battleships, 12 cruisers of various types and 44 destroyers - to meet up at sea with another 70 British ships from the Cromarty Firth and the Forth.

The next day they came face to face with their German counterparts in the seas between Orkney and Denmark.

The result of the open bombardment by the two Navies was inconclusive, but 6,000 of the 60,000 men of the British fleet died as 14 ships were lost including the battlecruisers *Indefatigable, Invincible* and *Queen Mary,* the cruisers *Defence* and *Black Prince,* with the *Warrior* disabled, and five destroyers, *Tipperary, Turbulent, Fortune, Sparrowhawk* and *Ardent.*

The Germans lost slightly fewer men and ships, but, in retrospect, it was to prove a British success in as much as the German fleet never again ventured out of harbour to face such open combat for the rest of the war.

Among those engaged in the action at the Battle of Jutland was 32 year old Gunner William Johnston, from Stromness, who was on HMS *Marlborough,* a ship which "acquitted herself magnificently" in the North Sea battle, according to the Press Association report.

Gunner Johnston wrote to his mother, at home in Khyber Pass, Stromness, on June 10, 1916: "Well, dear mother, we have at last attained our object, but conditions were rather rotten, but it was fine while it lasted and the blighters took to their heels for safety; not before I had my guns at play.

"It was a sight that I'll never forget, not that I had much time to think at the time, for I was too busy pounding them. We had an accident (being struck by a torpedo) which gave us two casualties but that was all. It was quite enough and we must thank God that we are here to tell the tale, for while it lasted, it was simply Hell. We are 'ready, aye ready' and I only hope for another pop at them."

Gunner Johnston survived the war but, tragically, was killed by a motor accident in Plymouth in 1930.

Some of the victims of the Battle of Jutland were to be laid to rest at Orkney's Naval War cemetery at Lyness.

They included the only non-combatant to be buried in the cemetery at that time - a Chinese cook Zu Sing Kang from the Royal Fleet Auxiliary vessel *Tuscalusa.* He died of wounds suffered under fire during the battle while he was nursing an injured signaller - a man called Macgregor who recovered and subsequently went on to become an Australian senator.

Along with those from the Battle of Jutland were also buried the bodies of some of those lost, less than a week later, in another great tragedy of Orkney's war - the sinking of HMS *Hampshire* and the death of Lord Kitchener.

The Orcadian of June 10, 1916, reported: "Today we record one of the great disasters of the war - the loss of HMS *Hampshire,* having on board Lord Kitchener and staff - which occurred off the west coast of Orkney on Monday night. The news came upon the country with startling suddenness and there is no gainsaying that the blow was a staggering one, but already the people exhibit their wonted calm, and instead of being cowed by what is apparently the work of German assassins, their determination is more resolute than ever that the sword should not be sheathed till Prussian militarism is laid in the dust."

The first opportunity that most Orcadians had to see an aircraft was when HMS *Hermes* visited the islands in 1913. The parent ship of the Naval wing of the Royal Flying Corps arrived in Scapa Flow with a flight of hydroplanes on board and during a ten day stay entertained Orkney folk to a series of successful flights. Aviation was not yet an exact science, however, and a week after leaving Orkney, two aircraft from HMS *Hermes* were lost when they crashed into the Cromarty Firth.

(Picture courtesy of Orkney Library photographic archive)

Tragedy and enigma -

It was a riddle wrapped in a mystery inside an enigma, to borrow the words of Winston Churchill (on another subject on another occasion.)

And more than 80 years later, the events of June 5, 1916 - the sinking of HMS *Hampshire* with the loss of 643 lives including the British War Secretary Lord Kitchener of Khartoum - still constitute what many would regard as the greatest mystery of 20th century Orkney.

It certainly left a lasting mark on the islands, and the lives of Orcadians, as witnessed by the stone tower still overlooking the Atlantic Ocean from Marwick Head, standing as a memorial to the disaster, and Kitchener. It was constructed after the people of Orkney raised the money through public subscription, to which the British government contributed nothing.

Whatever, strip away the rumours and gossip, malicious mischief-making and conspiracy theories (the disaster can probably claim a place in history for spawning the first great international conspiracy theories of the modern era) and what remains is still one of the worst single tragedies of World War One.

It was by no means the worst Naval tragedy of wartime, nor Orkney. Just a week earlier, ten times as many British lives were lost at the Battle of Jutland; a year later, 1,000 lives would be lost when HMS *Vanguard* blew up in Scapa Flow; the same graveyard of the *Royal Oak*, with the loss of 833 lives, in World War Two.

But what elevated the Hampshire disaster to such a level of horror in the public consciousness was that the death toll included Kitchener, a colossal warlord of the Empire with an almost mystical status in the eyes of the British people. The nation was shocked - perhaps to an extent that we only saw at the end of the century with the death of Princess Diana - that the War Secretary could have perished in the care of the Royal Navy, on a supposedly secret mission, only a few miles from the Naval stronghold of Scapa Flow.

Wartime censorship, and the reluctance of the authorities to disclose information, led to wild speculation about the cause of the explosion which tore a great hole in the hull of the 450 feet long, 10,900 ton cruiser as she fought her way in the teeth of a fierce storm, en route to Russia, off Orkney's west coast of Birsay. But, all the facts in later years seem to conclusively confirm that the *Hampshire* struck a mine.

Sadly, what can never be confirmed is just how many more men could have been saved if Orcadians had been encouraged - or even allowed - to mount organised rescue efforts. In fact, it was later claimed they were turned away from the area at gunpoint by the military authorities - and the Stromness lifeboat crew was ordered to remain in port on pain of being locked up for mutiny!

There can be no wonder that in Orkney there were to be bitter recriminations, and scarcely veiled resentment, over the actions of the authorities. What followed was to produce a picture often clouded by allegations of official ignorance, incompetence and misjudgement. Many people argued that it amounted to criminal negligence that the tragedy had just 12 survivors.

Kitchener's mission had been intended as a morale-boosting rendezvous with the Czar of Russia, with the aim of reviving the flagging relationship between the two countries and offering practical support for the war effort. What that practical support could have been is, today, irrelevant - but at the time it led to rumours, later to become an unshakeable conviction for some, that the *Hampshire* was carrying millions of pounds worth of gold bullion.

It had originally been intended that the War Secretary would depart for the Russian port of Archangel from the Clyde, but he wanted to see the state of the British fleet, in the aftermath of the Battle of Jutland, and instead plans were made for him to embark from Scapa Flow. So it was that in the early morning of June 5, 1916, Kitchener arrived by train in Thurso.

Two of the last - if not the last - civilians to see Lord Kitchener alive were Christina and Jessie Harper, the sisters who, in 1936, came to Orkney to take over the Standing Stones Hotel in Stenness. In 1916, however, they had the Admiralty contract to feed all the servicemen passing through the town, at the Drill Hall in Thurso, and it was there that they saw the VIP visitor. "He passed through the Drill Hall, a very handsome man, and spoke to the men on his way to the destroyer that was to take him to the *Hampshire*, " said Jessie Harper in a later interview with *The Orcadian*.

In fact, another comment in that same interview, gave a clue to the almost obsessional idea that pervaded the public perception at the time that Britain was over-run by spies. "Many a time we saw people being taken down from Scapa Flow, all chained together," said Jessie Harper. "We knew they were spies and that they would be shot as soon as they got to Inverness." In fact, it is unlikely that many - if, indeed, any - of them were spies, and it is probable that most were simply the day-to-day miscreants of military routine.

Kitchener crossed from Thurso to Scapa Flow in the commander-in-chief's dispatch vessel *Oak* and lunched with Admiral Sir John Jellicoe before boarding the *Hampshire* with his party of military and civilian staff, including, as will be explained later, a Metropolitan Police officer whose presence on the fateful voyage was still unacknowledged 80 years later.

The *Hampshire*, under the command of Captain Herbert Savill, set sail in the late afternoon, accompanied by a destroyer escort of HMS *Unity* and HMS *Victor*. Straightaway, the first misjudgement of the mission became apparent as it was obvious that the weather forecasts had been misinterpreted. The weather had been deteriorating all day, the barometer falling and a big sea running as Orkney was pounded by north easterly gale force winds. For that reason, it was decided that the *Hampshire* would take a route hugging Orkney's west coast, offering some protection from the wind.

Professor Alexander McAdie, who held the chair of meteorology at Harvard University, later wrote: "The decision proves that those present did not comprehend what type of air structure was prevailing at the time. For within an hour, the storm centre had passed and the wind backed sharply to the north west. The conditions were exactly the reverse of those anticipated. Even fiercer than the north east gale was the north west blast that swept the swelling waters against the jagged coast."

The result was that the two destroyers could not maintain the 18 knot speed of the *Hampshire*, they fell behind and were soon ordered to return to Scapa Flow, leaving the *Hampshire* to proceed alone. "It was the most terrific gale in my experience. It whipped the sea to a fury," said one of the survivors, Petty Officer Wilfred Wesson, in a statement later.

And there it was, at 7.45pm, about a mile and a half off shore between Marwick Head and the Brough of Birsay, the *Hampshire* was rocked by explosions. The evidence of two other survivors tells its own story.

One recalled: "A terrific blast went through the ship, shaking her from stem to stern. Something out of the ordinary had happened, and the fumes which began to spread gave evidence that we had probably struck a mine."

Stoker Alfred Reed said: "It was as though an express train crashed into us, first on one side then on the other."

The *Hampshire* had sailed with 655 men on board. Some, presumably, now died below decks as fire broke out and ammunition stores exploded. As the ship began to founder, the lifeboats were smashed against the hull in the fury of the storm.

the death of a warlord

The ship apparently went down bow first, with her stern rising into the air. The explosions had cut the power and there was no opportunity for a distress signal.

The evidence later established that as many as 200 men did get away from the ship in three liferafts, ten feet long, eight feet wide, and encircled with cork. Such a number was obviously well over the capacity of the rafts, already unstable in such horrendous sea conditions, but two of the rafts drifted into geos between Marwick and Skaill and the third came ashore in Skaill Bay, where more men died - either battered against the rocks or from exposure and exhaustion as they struggled ashore to find no rescue parties to offer first aid or other assistance.

Those fortunate few who made it ashore found refuge at various houses in Sandwick - including the home of the Harvey family at Stockan, the Whitelaws at Linnahowe, the Phillips at Garson and the houses of Garricott and Pallast (the Brass family).

The body of Kitchener was never found. At the time of the first explosion, he was resting and reading in his cabin, but was then apparently escorted immediately to the bridge by a Naval officer, uttering the now immortalised line: "Make way for Lord Kitchener."

Once on the bridge, Kitchener was joined by members of his staff and urged to take to the lifeboats by Captain Savill. It appears he refused. Eye witness accounts indicate that there were four uniformed Army officers near to Kitchener and he was talking to Colonel Oswald Fitzgerald. Leading Seaman Charles Rogerson, another of the survivors, insisted later: "He went down with the ship."

According to Rogerson: "Captain was calling to Lord Kitchener to get to a boat but Lord Kitchener apparently did not hear him or else took no notice. He had walked calmly from his cabin when the explosion occurred and waited equally calmly while preparations were made to abandon ship."

What is now accepted as an accurate account of the cause of the disaster emerged, in piecemeal fashion, over decades rather than months or even years. And the man generally credited with destroying the *Hampshire*, by laying mines off Orkney's west coast, was Lt Kurt Beitzen, commander of the submarine mine-layer *U75*.

There is still some conjecture how, when and why the mission was carried out, but it seems that Beitzen was one of 18 German U-boats ordered to patrol the major strategic Naval seaways around Britain in late May - just before the Battle of Jutland - and that *U75* was dispatched to lay the mines in case that was the route that the British fleet chose to take from Scapa Flow. Beitzen arrived at the agreed position on May 29, and in three hours, laid a formidable total of 34 mines. If that was the case, it was just ill-fortune that led to the *Hampshire* being the victim.

However, in Germany, a more complicated story was to emerge later that suggested, by some luck and good intelligence, the Germans had stumbled across the fact that the British intended to use that very route for an important mission.

In 1934, the German magazine *Berliner Illustrierte Zeitung*, while confirming that no spy had informed the Germans of the *Hampshire's* journey or her important passenger, gave a novel twist to the story, suggesting that it was a wireless code decipherer in Neumunster who first realised that something urgent and important was to take place off Orkney and warned the German naval authorities in time for them to lay the sequence of mines in the area.

According to the magazine, one night in May, a message was intercepted at Neumunster which attracted attention because it did not relate to the then manoeuvres of the British fleet. It was a report from a British torpedo boat destroyer to the Admiralty in London stating that, according to instructions, a certain route west of Orkney had been searched and found free of mines. Suspecting that this suggested that some unusual transport, by a fairly unusual route, was imminent, the decipherer passed the information to the German naval authorities.

The rest of the story tallied with the account of the actions of *U75*, and it was reported that Lt Beitzen had returned home, reaching the submarine base of Heligoland on June 3 - although it would be four days before the Germans realised what they had achieved and that the *Hampshire* had been sunk and Kitchener lost.

The Orcadian originally tended to dismiss this account, pointing out that it was contradicted by the fact that, after the loss of the *Hampshire*, British vessels swept the area and brought to the surface mines which were barnacle-encrusted, indicating that they had been there some time. However, this would equally rule out the accepted theory that Beitzen had laid the mines as a prelude to the Battle of Jutland.

(A year after the *Hampshire* disaster, the *U75* torpedoed and sank the ss *Palatine* of Glasgow, commanded by Captain Balfour Miller of Westbank, Kirkwall. The master and crew of the *Palatine* were taken prisoner by the submarine and Captain Miller - who was to spend the next 17 months in captivity in Germany - was certainly told by the German crew that they had been responsible for the mine that claimed the *Hampshire*.)

Back in Orkney, as realisation dawned as to what had happened to the *Hampshire*, the verbal flak began to fly as the inquests revealed that British intelligence reports of submarine activity in the area had been ignored or downgraded in importance. Two interceptions of German signals dated May 31 and June 1 were to do with the *U75* and its position west of Orkney, but the staff of Admiral Sir John Jellicoe apparently gave no warning of this to the *Hampshire*.

Jellicoe was later to be described by Churchill as "the only man on either side who could lose the war in an afternoon." It certainly became clear that he had been guilty of complacency, at least, as regards the dangers of submarines, and mines, to the *Hampshire*.

Admiral Jellicoe, later to be Lord Jellicoe, wrote afterwards: "It was practically impossible that this route could have been mined owing to the dark period in northern latitudes being confined to a couple of hours, during which no ship could expect to approach the shore and complete her minelaying without being sighted," and he dismissed the threat of submarine minelayers by adding: "Mine laying by enemy submarines had been confined to waters well to the southward of the Firth of Forth."

But the Admiralty later admitted: "The waters in the vicinity of the ordinary eastern exit made by the Fleet were frequently visited by enemy submarines. One had appeared there less than a week before and had fired a torpedo at one of the fleet minesweeping vessels and been hunted without success by destroyers. At the time, there was good reason for considering both the eastern and western channels under suspicion."

Certainly, the German raider *Mowe*, a 4,600 ton surface vessel which operated under bogus neutral colours, commanded by a Count Dohna Schlodien, was known to have laid 250 mines in the western approaches to the Pentland Firth five months earlier in 1916.

And reports claimed the Admiralty drifter *Laurel Crown* was lost to a mine in Orkney waters on June 2, 1916 - just three days before the *Hampshire* sailed. (The date of the loss of the *Laurel Crown* was later disputed - some claimed after the war that the drifter was not lost until June 22.)

A court of inquiry into the sinking of the *Hampshire* was held aboard HMS *Blake* on June 7, 1916, but the findings were kept secret until 1926 when much of the evidence formed a major part of a government report that was finally published following growing public concern about the events on the night.

By then it was accepted - in Orkney at least - that the gravest blunder had been the appalling shambles after the sinking which had seen a failure by the authorities to organise any properly equipped search and rescue parties with local knowledge. In fact, the Admiralty ordered Jellicoe to make Orkney's west coast out-of-bounds to local people, in case any of the secret documents being carried by Kitchener should float clear of the wreckage and be washed ashore.

One of the most damning stories to emerge was that help was refused from Stromness lifeboat. The secretary, Mr George Thomson, after hearing of the loss of a vessel off Marwick Head, spoke to Stromness Naval HQ only to be told: "We cannot discuss the movements of warships." He was further rebuffed, it was reported, when Captain F. M. Walker, the senior officer on duty at Stromness, told him: "You have no right to interfere in Naval matters. It is none of your bloody business. And what's more, if you attempt to launch the lifeboat, it's mutiny. Mutiny, do you hear? Any more nonsense or argument and I'll have the whole lot of you locked up."

By 1926, Captain Walker was dead and unable to defend himself against these allegations and, therefore, it can only be conjectured to what extent he was made a scapegoat. The official Government report of 1926 pointed out that, because of Captain Walker's death, it was impossible to obtain first hand reasons why the Stromness lifeboat was not called upon - but Naval men at the scene were unanimous that the lifeboat would have been unable to reach the *Hampshire* disaster in the conditions prevailing at the time.

Jellicoe said later that he did not think anything more could have been done which was not done, but misunderstandings, in fact, began almost as soon as the *Hampshire* was sunk.

Gunner Joe Angus - later to become a Stromness grocer - was on duty at the lookout post at the Earl's Palace at Birsay when the ship loomed through the grey backcloth of the Atlantic. "I hadn't been looking very long when all of a sudden a cloud of smoke and flame burst up from behind the bridge," he recalled. Gunner Angus reported what he had seen to a Corporal Drever, a Sanday man, who headed to Birsay Post Office to transmit the message by telegraph to the Commander of the Western Patrol in Stromness: "Battle cruiser seems in distress between Marwick Head and the Brough of Birsay."

Apparently there was some confusion when that message was received (the *Hampshire* was a light cruiser rather than a battle cruiser) and the only action taken by Captain F. M. Walker was to order two vessels to stand by in Stromness harbour until more information was received. Around an hour later came a further message: "Four-funnel cruiser sunk 20 minutes ago. No assistance arrived yet. Send ships to pick up bodies." It was almost 90 minutes after the fateful explosion before six vessels were put to sea; too late to save a soul.

One obvious cause of confusion in the controversy which followed after the war was that British Summer Time was in operation at the time of the loss of the *Hampshire* and civilians gave the time accordingly. However many of the Admiralty reports later gave timings in Greenwich Mean Time - hence the timing of the original telegram from Birsay was given by civilians as 8.45pm (BST) but it was received by the Navy at Stromness at 8.31pm (GMT).

Kirkwall man Robert "Winkle" Cumming was one of the few Orcadians who was able to get to the shore to join attempts to rescue survivors of the *Hampshire* disaster. In fact, he had to endure the gruesome task of recovering bodies.

In 1916, he lived in Victoria Street, Kirkwall, and worked in the business of Peter Shearer, coal merchant. On the night of the disaster, he apparently hired a car and headed to the West Mainland.

He later made a hand-written statement, relating the grim facts, which only came to light years later when it was found by his daughter, Muriel. This is what Robert Cumming wrote:

"I arrived home about 9 p.m. feeling very tired, having been out in Kirkwall Bay coaling a neutral diverted steamer for two whole days and one night.

"I gladly slouched down in the first available chair, near the fire, when I was off-handedly informed that information had been received in Kirkwall that a British cruiser was in distress off Marwick Head in Birsay.

"Half dreaming and half sleeping, I took the information somewhat coolly at first, only to be stirred by a horrible dreamy spectacle of crowds of men scrambling about in the water.

"My first thought, then, was to see what I could do to help and I decided that I should hire the largest motor car in town and proceed to the position of the wreck.

"This I did and was joined by the hirer, he having volunteered to accompany me through my expedition. Petrol had to be procured and this was done from another local hirer, without any demure.

"Oilskins and seaboots having been donned, we left Kirkwall, I should say about 10 pm and arrived at the Post Office, Birsay, only to be informed that the cruiser had sunk off Marwick Head and that owing to the wind blowing in a north westerly direction, any rafts or boats would probably drive ashore about the Bay of Skaill.

"We didn't delay here many minutes, but proceeded to Skaill at full speed. Here, we were met by three or four mariners and a young Naval surgeon who was beginning to turn over some bodies with a view to determining whether or not there was any of the men alive.

"The sights here are better not described and it was 15 minutes before I could harden my mind to face the gruesome spectacle.

"One raft - the largest - had about 50 or 60 bodies in it and a little way along the rocks, we found a smaller raft, entirely hung up between two rocks, having washed up there by the force of the waves and tide ebbed from it.

"This raft was suspended about 15 feet from the lower ledge of rocks and was about ten feet from the top of the small ravine, making it impossible to work from the top side.

"We were now feeling the pinch very much for the want of suitable gear, namely stout ropes and blocks and tackles etc, and all we could do at this juncture, was to cut the rope bottom out of the raft and let the bodies fall below.

"This was done by lowering one of our party down by a rope procured from one of the neighbouring farms.

"At this stage, I saw that, with a few men at hand, the undertaking would have lasted at least three days so suggested to the six or seven men there that I should make this representation to the surgeon.

"It was then I was informed that this officer had to retire from the scene of operations owing to the fact that he had taken a nervous turn and was assisted to the nearest farmhouse.

"I immediately went up to the house and interviewed him but with very little material assistance.

"Grasping the situation, I received pen and paper from the good people of the house and wrote something after the following words: 'Request that signal be sent to SNO Kirkwall and air stations for 150 men and four motor lorries urgently to Bay of Skaill also rope ladders, ropes and blocks and tackles.'

"The young officer signed this happily and addressed same to O/C Hoy 1 Battery, Stromness. I set off right away and arrived at Stromness at about 6 o'clock in the morning.

"After a little trouble I was allowed to interview the Commanding Officer and a few minutes from then, he set the ball a-rolling.

"Between 8 am and 9 am we had plenty of assistance, men and lorries at Skaill.

"The work at this point was taken over by two officers of high standing who carried out the work in a most efficient manner.

"By this time however, we had salved about 43 bodies and had carefully carried them up the rocks from the large raft to a place of safety (from the tide) in a field nearby.

"Touching on the pathetic side of the story, I shall never forget the sight before my eyes of the remains of a young signal boy lying with a smile on his lips, having a signal message clasped tightly in his hand - so tight that we found it impossible to take it from the hand.

"I left a surgeon with this body and he stated that the signal would necessarily have to be treated as confidential and that he would have to extricate same."

The First Lord of the Admiralty told the House of Commons in July, 1926, that, on receiving the first telegram at Stromness, Captain Walker had contacted by telephone the Vice Admiral and received orders to send out every available vessel and to make arrangements for motor cars for a shore rescue party. Captain Walker quickly put that business in hand and then put to sea in the ocean going tug *Flying Kestrel*. Four destroyers had sailed on the rescue mission by 9.20pm (GMT) and another five destroyers joined the search for survivors in the early hours of the morning.

The First Lord of the Admiralty dismissed suggestions of spies and sabotage. "It is ridiculous to suggest that the Admiralty would not know if two spies had been shot on the *Hampshire* a short time before," he said.

No survivor saw Lord Kitchener in a lifeboat and stories that he got away from the ship and reached the shore were clearly imaginary, said the Government report issued in August, 1926.

The report - dismissed by *The Orcadian* as a "Naval white-wash" - rejected claims in Orkney that local assistance had been spurned. "Many of those living near the coast had actually seen or heard of the accident and were therefore already aware, without being warned, that there might be an opportunity of rendering assistance and possibly of saving life south of Marwick Head," said the report.

It added: "The suggestion that the rescue parties would repel any assistance in saving those lives is as contemptible as it is untrue.

"On the following morning, when large numbers of bodies were being collected, with adequate facilities, ordinary police measures had to be taken to prevent the tendency of members of the public to crowd upon and impede the operations. This appears to be the only foundation for the allegation that local inhabitants were prevented from engaging in rescue work."

However that contradicted the evidence of local Orcadians. There were many who were not aware of the tragedy - in one case, until a survivor arrived at the house seeking help - and some of those who did offer help were ordered away.

One man quoted in *The Orcadian* said: "I went down to see what could be done but I was told by a soldier that all civilians were to remain in their houses and not venture near the shore or we should be fired on." Another man quoted by *The Orcadian* years later said: "The men saw one of the rafts reach the shore, but it was overturned by a wave and the men on board thrown out. They wanted to help, but the soldiers turned their guns on them. They were very disturbed about it for the rest of their lives. It was something they never forgot."

Wounded Orcadian feelings were hardly salved when Admiral Brock, writing to Jellicoe to suggest that the part played in the rescue by some Orcadians should be recognised, added the appallingly patronising postscript that it should not be a financial reward because the people were "not of a class to which money could be sent; I am of the opinion that a letter of thanks would be much more highly prized, although the persons concerned are mostly poor."

The official secrecy of the times, of course, had the opposite effect to that intended - it simply provided the fuel for rumours and wild claims of saboteurs, spies, IRA plots and political conspiracies to destroy Kitchener. Many of the stories were scurrilous fabrications: one of the most ridiculous featured a man called Arthur Vectis Freeman, who formed an organisation called the Kitchener League.

Freeman, who wrote under the name Frank Power in a publication called *The Referee*, claimed that Kitchener had, in fact been murdered by a German spy and his body buried in Norway. He announced that he would bring back Kitchener's body to Britain - and, later, a coffin arrived in London. It was opened in the presence of the Westminster coroner and the Home Office announced that the coffin had never contained any human remains.

It was later discovered that Freeman, when in Orkney for the unveiling of the Kitchener Memorial, had bought the coffin from the woodyard of Samuel Baikie, of Bea, Stromness, who had himself purchased the coffin the previous year at a sale of surplus stock at Lyness. Freeman had arranged for the coffin to be shipped south in a bizarre hoax.

Later, years after the event, there were two excellent books published which centred on the disaster - *The Mystery of Lord Kitchener's Death* by Donald McCormick and *The Kitchener Enigma* by Trevor Royle - which were both quoted at length by *The Orcadian*. But some of the publications in the 1920s and 1930s were much more fanciful in their accounts.

Another story, which featured in several publications between the two world wars was that the sinking of the *Hampshire* had been masterminded by a German spy Ernst Carl, working with two Irish Sinn Fein confederates who, as crew members of the *Hampshire*, had carried aboard two time-fuse bombs before the vessel sailed. The plausibility of the story, however, was stretched beyond belief by Carl's claim that, from a hotel window, he had been able to watch the ship leave Scapa Flow and then blow up off Birsay.

Another so-called "suspect" for the destruction of the *Hampshire* was a German sympathiser, a Boer called Captain Fritz Duquesne. His motive, it was claimed, was revenge against Kitchener for outrages committed against his family by Kitchener's troops in the 1899-1902 Boer War. It was true that the British government was seeking a German agent of that name in connection with sabotage of the British liner *Tennyson*, with the loss of three lives, in July, 1916.

In May, 1932, the authorities in New York arrested a man they claimed to be Duquesne, and linked him to the *Hampshire* disaster because he was said to be carrying a diary detailing the sinking of the warship. However, at the time, a book entitled *The Man Who Killed Kitchener*, which purported to be Duquesne's story, written by Clement Wood had just been published. Friends in South Africa dismissed it all, claiming that Duquesne had been shot dead in Mexico, and the story was eventually accepted as fiction.

The fact is that pre-planned sabotage of the *Hampshire* as a means of killing of Kitchener was virtually impossible as the ship was only chosen for the voyage at the very last moment - to the extent that several officers were totally unaware of the mission even on the day! Cyril Kinmond, who owned the Scapa Flow island of Cava, confirmed that those officers were enjoying lunch at Cava Lodge on June 5 when an orderly arrived to say their presence was required on board immediately. "They went off promising to visit us the next afternoon, and half an hour later we were surprised to see the *Hampshire* steam out to sea," said Kinmond.

But one story which kept resurfacing was the belief the *Hampshire* was carrying gold bullion - and that various secret salvage attempts had been made to retrieve it.

In 1933, the German magazine *Berliner Illustrierte Zeitung* - and several American newspapers - reported that the site of the *Hampshire* had been located in 1932 and an unsuccessful salvage attempt made. In April, 1933, a new attempt was begun when a salvage ship returned with three expert divers - a German deep sea expert Hans Weissfeld, an American Charles Courtney and an Australian called Costello. The divers had to work a full week clearing away sand and mud, and they made a total of 26 dives in 17 days, after using explosives to blow their way into the *Hampshire*. Eventually, in the captain's cabin, a strongbox was opened and an estimated 50,000 dollars of gold retrieved. However, when they returned to tackle the ten main strongboxes, an explosion ripped through an ammunition store in the ship. The divers escaped with their lives but they were forced to abandon the operation and return to Germany, suffering serious injuries.

The Admiralty responded in a statement: "If these salvage operations on HMS *Hampshire* are proved, the British Admiralty will certainly take action against the parties concerned. The information is new to us, and we must now wait until this salvage ship sails again from Germany to continue her work. Then we shall take the necessary steps to stop their operations, unless some agreement is arrived at."

On June 15, 1934, the American diver Charles Courtney - he was also the president of the Master Locksmiths' Association of America - arrived in Britain on the liner *Leviathan*. He told reporters he was going to the Admiralty to hand over rings and items of apparel which he said belonged to Kitchener and which he claimed to have recovered from the *Hampshire*.

"I really took them as souvenirs of my descent to a wreck 65 fathoms deep," he said. Courtney added that, if he was assured of gold on board, it would be salvaged. He was to meet people in Germany and something might be attempted the following autumn, but he would not discuss his plans.

The Orcadian had originally been sceptical about salvage claims but, on March 30, 1939, the newspaper was quoting an authoritative source as substantiating the German salvage effort on the *Hampshire*. American intelligence sources had gathered evidence to confirm that Charles Courtney had indeed been in the employment of Germany on an expedition to the Orkney islands. It was stated that a German salvage ship had conducted operations off the Orkney West Mainland, and divers had been lowered to the wreck of the *Hampshire*, sunk in 30-40 fathoms. It had now been established that the German salvage ship, in the course of several voyages back to Germany, landed injured divers, including Courtney, suffering from the Bends after being trapped inside the wreck, and two of his fellow divers subsequently died. Experts who had dismissed the story now accepted it was quite possible. "One expert goes so far as to say that today such a feat would rank as nothing more remarkable than a commonplace Naval diving inspection," said *The Orcadian*.

Salvage interest was to continue right into the second half of the 20th century - in 1977, a Swedish vessel *Deep Diver* operated over the site, and, amidst controversy in the 1980s, the vessel *Stena Workhorse*, equipped with a 100 ton crane, began hauling artefacts to the surface - including the 50 ton propeller and shaft which was later to be handed over to Orkney Islands Council and displayed at the wartime museum at Lyness.

The Marwick Head memorial today is a fitting reminder both of the tragedy, and an apparent official reluctance by the government to mark the disaster which killed Kitchener. But, even now, more than 80 years after the event, Orkney's great

mystery of the 20th century still throws up new twists.

For at least one man was totally unacknowledged amidst the toll of death that night. The official communique at the time only named six of Kitchener's staff on the fateful voyage - Lt Col Oswald Fitzgerald, Brigadier General W. Ellersham, Second Lt R.D. Macpherson, Mr B. Obeirne, Sir H.F. Donaldson and Mr L. Robertson. In fact there were 13 members of Kitchener's staff who sailed with him for Russia, and amongst them was a Detective Sergeant Matthew McLaughlin of the Metropolitan Police Special Branch - he was Kitchener's personal protection officer.

He would have remained forgotten but for some painstaking research in 1996 by a modern day London policeman, Mr R. McAdam.

McLaughlin, he discovered, was born on February 6, 1879, in Tipperary, Ireland, and came to Britain as a teenager, working as a building labourer before he was accepted into the Metropolitan Police on September, 1900, as PC 161D, Marylebone Police Station. He appears to have served there until 1909, when, as a Detective Sergeant he transferred to the Special Branch. In the years leading up to the World War One, he was apparently involved in top level protection assignments for King Edward VII and George V as well as the Secretary of State for India, Sir Curzon Wylie, later to be shot dead by an Indian extremist.

Prior to his last fateful assignment, McLaughlin was serving with General Kitchener at General Headquarters, St Omers in France.

It is impossible at this late stage to ascertain if McLaughlin died at Kitchener's side in the disaster but Mr McAdam says: "One suspects that given his reputation as a loyal and devoted protection officer that he would either have been close to him, or at least on his way to him when the ship sank." Like Kitchener, the body of Detective Sergeant McLaughlin was never found.

But there was no memorial to McLaughlin. The Commonwealth War Graves Commission, while having records of all servicemen aboard, did not have records of the policeman because he was not a member of the Armed Forces on active service.

In fact the only epitaph to this unsung hero of the police was the coldly bureaucratic language of Police Orders of June 7, 1916, which recorded his death with the comment: "Pay to 5th instant." Sergeant McLaughlin left a wife and child who were awarded £53 1s and £10 12s a year pension, respectively.

Civilian casualties at sea continued up till and throughout World War One. Pictured here are members of the crew of the Swedish schooner *Tyra* who were rescued by the rocket life-saving brigade after being wrecked on Papa Westray in January, 1913.

(Picture courtesy of Orkney Library photographic archive)

The toll of King and Country

A memorial service for Kitchener and the men of HMS *Hampshire* was held in Kirkwall's St Magnus Cathedral on Sunday, June 11, 1916, and almost immediately an appeal fund was launched in the county for a Kitchener memorial.

However, although the *Hampshire* tragedy had struck at the heart of the community, Orcadian families were now to suffer increasingly the anguish of personal loss as the toll of the war in France and Belgium grew at an alarming rate with the onset of the Battle of the Somme. By mid-1916, *The Orcadian* was reporting four or five deaths a week on war service. It was to get worse with Orkney's regiment - the Seaforth Highlanders - suffering major casualties to the extent that, early in 1917, as many as 12 Orcadians a week were reported killed, and a similar number wounded or falling to the ravages of disease.

Tribunals were set up to decide on applications for exemption from call-up for military duty - and scores of cases were reported in *The Orcadian* - but, by the end of 1916, the need for more fighting men led to the order that there would be no exemptions under the age of 26.

Many, many Orkney men had answered the call of King and Country by this time. Mr Robert Hourston of Quoyberstane, St Ola, received a letter from the King commending him on the fact that all his six sons were serving in the Army. Mr G. Miller, Fernibrae, Eday, also had six sons in the forces, while Mrs Velzian of Garth, Quholme, Stromness, anxiously awaited news of her five sons who were all serving. William Reid of Stronsay had four sons in the forces - one of whom, Archibald, would die in the service of the Gordon Highlanders.

It was the son of Mr Robert Hourston, Lance Corporal A.J. Hourston, who was credited by *The Orcadian* as being Orkney's first soldier to be awarded the DCM, the Distinguished Conduct Medal, in World War One. Educated at Kirkwall Burgh School, he was serving with the 29th Battalion of the Second Canadian Contingent. His act of bravery - rescuing a wounded comrade under fire - also saw him awarded the French Military Medal. Sadly, Mr Robert Hourston had more tragic news nine months later when it was reported that another of his sons, Alexander, had been killed in action with the Royal Scots.

Lance Corporal George Inkster of Rousay also received the DCM, fighting in the ranks of the Canadian Light Infantry. His heroism could not ensure that he survived the war - he was killed six months later in 1916 on active service.

During World War One, nearly 100 Orcadians would be decorated, or mentioned in dispatches, for bravery and service beyond the call of duty - and, remarkably, in just a few weeks of the summer of 1916, seven Orkney men were honoured. Captain William Archibald Miller, who had set up his Kirkwall doctor's practice just before World War One, was awarded the DSO, Distinguished Service Order, with the Royal Fusiliers, while Acting Lt James Towrie Muir (29) of Sanday was the recipient of the DSC, Distinguished Service Cross, for his work in command of a division of drifters, helping to protect merchant shipping in the English Channel in the Dover Patrol.

Lt William Mackintosh, younger son of the proprietor of *The Orcadian*, also received the DSC for "zeal, gallantry and success" while in command of a patrol boat. He had been an officer with the Blue Funnel Company, operating steamers to Australia, before World War One.

Lt J. M. Davie, of Crantit, Kirkwall, and the Royal Scots, was awarded the Military Cross for "conspicuous gallantry," as was Lt Robert Ramage, the son of Rev Granville Ramage, the UF church minister on Shapinsay. Captain John Cecil Macrae, son of Orkney Procurator Fiscal Mr John Macrae, received the DSO for his services with the Indian Army.

Captain David Pottinger, of Hobbister Farm, Orphir, was awarded the Military Cross for showing "an utter disregard of danger" in his work in charge of stretcher bearers.

So often, however, the medals were earned at a terrible cost.

Crowds gather to pay their respects as a military coffin, draped in the union flag, is carried into the graveyard of St Magnus Cathedral during a funeral in August, 1912.
(Picture courtesy of Orkney Library photographic archive)

HMS *Vanguard* pictured in Scapa Flow in World War One. When the great warship blew up at anchor off Flotta in July, 1917, wartime censorship restrictions limited *The Orcadian* report to just five lines, with no mention that the tragedy, with the loss of around 1,000 lives, had occurred in Orkney waters. There were only two survivors of the blast but another 95 men escaped the explosion as they were off duty and away from the ship. Remarkably, one of those fortunate few was reported, 22 years later, to have survived the *Royal Oak* disaster in Scapa Flow. (Picture courtesy of Orkney Library photographic archive)

Lance Corporal John Flett RE, of the Bu, Flotta, was awarded the Military Medal for bravery on the field in France - but the price he had to pay for his heroism was to have a foot amputated.

Another Flotta hero, Lt R.W. Taylor (23) died in action in France just days after being awarded the Military Cross for bravery.

Tens of thousands of men were taken as prisoners of war - but Orcadian Leading Seaman James Marwick, from Kirkwall, had one of the most unusual experiences at the end of 1915 when he and his shipmates found themselves marooned in the Libyan desert "with a tribe of savage Arabs as their guardians."

Leading Seaman Marwick was a member of the crew of HMS *Tara* which was torpedoed and sunk by the German submarine *U35* while on patrol in the eastern Mediterranean. Rescued from the water, they were taken prisoner and 97 survivors were landed in Africa. They were forced to march 175 miles in desert temperatures as they were kept prisoner for "five months of torture," during which many of the men succumbed to dysentery.

However, just as hope for their survival was waning, Leading Seaman Marwick told *The Orcadian*, they were freed by a column of armoured cars under the command of the Duke of Westminster.

On July 1, 1916, *The Orcadian* reported that it had been announced in the House of Commons that 34 conscientious objectors had been sentenced to death! The sentence in every case was commuted to penal servitude; however, it was the strongest indication yet of the lengths that the Government would go to ensure that men enlisted for the war.

The King issued a statement in May, 1916: "I desire to take this opportunity of expressing to my people my recognition and appreciation of the splendid patriotism and self-sacrifice which they have displayed in raising by voluntary enlistment, since the commencement of war, 5,041,000 men - an effort far surpassing that of any other nation in similar circumstances recorded in history. I am confident this magnificent spirit will inspire my people to endure the additional sacrifice now imposed on them and it will, with God's help, lead us to victory which shall achieve the liberation of Europe."

The youngest Orcadian serving King and Country at this time was 14 year old Bugler Robert S. Johnston, son of Mr James Johnston of Kirkwall, who was in the uniform of the Highland Light Infantry.

In civilian life, sacrifices were also being made for the war effort. Orcadians collected £400 for the purchase of an ambulance - to be named "The Orkney Ambulance" - for use at the Front. On March 11, 1916, after several years of carrying page one news, *The Orcadian* reverted to advertisements on the front page as restrictions of paper and labour reduced the size of the newspaper.

Women, as well as men, were now being recruited for war work. In many cases, with their menfolk away in uniform, Orcadian women were helping to keep the farms and crofts of Orkney in business. By September, 1916, they were being asked to answer a new call with *The Orcadian* reporting a "great demand for strong women" to work in munitions factories in the South. Their railway fares would be paid and they would receive wages of 22s 6d to 27s a week, with 12s deducted for board, lodgings and laundry.

The year of 1916 ended with changes at the highest level in the Government of Britain. Herbert Asquith resigned as Prime Minister, with a new government formed by David Lloyd George. Admiral Sir John Jellicoe was appointed First Sea Lord and Sir David Beatty became commander of the Grand Fleet.

The Orcadian bemoaned the fact that, ten years earlier, the chance had been missed to build a Channel Tunnel. The newspaper complained that "but for the adverse decision of the Committee of Imperial Defence in 1907, we might have had direct rail communication with France today. The tunnel would have more than paid for itself in the past two years." In fact, it would be another 75 years before Britain and France would be linked by railway through a Channel Tunnel.

And rather than developments underground, it was developments in the skies - and the coming of the age of aerial warfare - that would make more headlines. The Royal Flying Corps (RFC) had been formed and now we had deaths in the air, as well as on land and sea. One of the first victims was Second Lt James Stevenson, aged just 20, from Evie who was killed on a flying mission with the RFC over Scotland.

Kirkwall Bay is dominated by American minesweepers in August, 1919. (Picture courtesy of Orkney Library photographic archive)

The Aberdeen trawler *Strathelliot* sits high and dry after running aground on Hoy. Twelve men were saved from the vessel in a dramatic rescue operation in October, 1952. (Picture courtesy of Orkney Library photographic archive)

Airship pioneers soar

Orkney had its first glimpse of aircraft when, prior to World War One, HMS *Hermes* came North with a flight of experimental seaplanes. But the impetus of war was to see huge advances in the development of aerial power through 1914-18.

More seaplanes arrived at Scapa in August, 1914, and large hangars were built for their accommodation at Scapa beach. Also a large air station, for seaplanes, was established at Houton Bay, while a Royal Naval airstrip was prepared at Swanbister, Orphir.

But one of the biggest military establishments was at Caldale, near Kirkwall, where an auxiliary station for airships was built, with huge hangars dominating the valley.

Airships, of course, never developed as a long-term weapon of war, but it's a fact that in World War One, from a network of British coastal stations of which Caldale was one, airships on patrol covered more than two million miles in 88,000 flying hours.

The need for airships was vital to help protect British merchant shipping which, as we have already seen, was often at the mercy of U-boat attack. The idea was conceived that airships could be used as submarine spotters, accompanying merchant convoys over long distances. In contrast to the limited reliability and scope of operation of the early wartime aircraft, the airships could not only carry a reasonable payload of bombs at a speed of between 40-50mph but, in the event of engine failure, could remain aloft.

Until the end of 1916, attacks on Allied shipping were so frequent and devastating - cutting off Britain's supply lines of food and other provisions from the Empire - that it was later surmised that the country had been within weeks of being starved to defeat in the war.

John McDonald, who 70 years later researched and wrote a series of excellent articles for *The Orcadian* on Orkney's wartime heritage, said: "The remarkable fact is that, except on one occasion, no ship was ever sunk while under escort by an airship. It is fair to say that, while airships themselves did not win the war, without these rudimentary flying machines the war might well have been lost."

Caldale was commissioned in July, 1916, and two giant hangars - one 200 feet by 70 feet and another 150 feet by 45 feet - were built to house the airships. There was also a camp of huts to accommodate the ground staff required for the launch and landing of the airships.

At the behest of the then First Sea Lord, Lord Fisher, a committee of senior Royal Naval Air Service officers had drawn up desired specifications for a new type of airship to be called a Submarine Scout - capable of carrying a two man crew with wireless telegraphy, 160lbs of bombs and enough fuel for eight hours flying.

The Royal Naval Air Service quickly achieved a satisfactory result by cannibalising the fuselage of a BE2C reconnaissance biplane which, powered by a 70hp Renault engine, was slung underneath a small training airship. Within just three weeks, it had proved its performance and entered service as SS1, while another 58 SS class airships were built later.

In August, 1916, two of these airships SS41 and SS43 were sent north from Kent to Orkney - and on August 20, SS41 was ready for service at Caldale. A week later, the airship made five flights over Orkney; then on August 30, a trip as far as Fair Isle and another short demonstration trip carrying Admiral Sir John Jellicoe himself.

Landing of the airships was still not an exact science. For instance, in windy weather conditions, the air crew relied on dropping a rope which the ground staff had to grab to haul the craft to safety.

The following year a more powerful SSP class airship was built, and in May and June, 1917, SSP2 and SSP4 arrived safely at Caldale. However, in the next six months, both were to encounter the extremes of Orkney weather - gales and snowstorms - and both were to be lost in accidents, claiming the lives of four crewmen.

On November 3, 1917, the SSP2 airship proved her worth when she escorted the Fleet's Battlecruiser Squadron for 80 miles into Scapa Flow - but, three weeks later, engine failure led to the SSP2 being lost off Westray, although two of the crew were rescued.

A month later, all three crew members on the SSP4 were lost in a crash in a snowstorm.

"These two tragedies in such close succession hastened the end for Caldale as an air station since the SSPs were not replaced," said John McDonald. "It was decided instead to entrust the aerial patrol and reconnaissance of Orkney waters to the big reliable flying boats which would operate from the newly constructed base at Houton."

Caldale now became No 20 Kite Balloon Station, and for the rest of the war, maintained and supplied manned observation balloons to Admiralty trawlers and larger vessels of the Grand Fleet. The balloons were inflated at Caldale and then carried by motor lorry to Scapa or Kirkwall - a trip not always free of problems on a day of blustery wind conditions.

However, those problems paled into insignificance compared with trials going on in Scapa Flow which were to be a fore-runner of the development of the aircraft carrier. For, in August, 1917, Orkney witnessed a moment in history when, for the first time, an aircraft successfully landed on a ship underway at sea.

There had been previous experiments with flying aircraft from ships - in fact, as far back as 1910, an American airman Eugene B. Ely had flown from a biplane off the USS *Birmingham* while the ship was steaming in Chesapeake Bay. And in 1912, the Royal Navy had successfully repeated a similar feat when Lieutenant C. R. Samson flew a plane off a ramp built on HMS *Africa*, anchored off the Kent coast.

But, in the early days of World War One, the use of aircraft from ships was a cumbersome business. Seaplanes had to be hoisted in and out of the water - and once an aircraft had taken off there was no guarantee that the machine would ever be able to return to the ship. In Scapa Flow, the planes had to either ditch in the sea, or land at Smoogro for ferrying back to the ship.

The Battle of Jutland, however, emphasised the useful role that aircraft could play in the war - if only to provide reliable information about the movements of the enemy fleet. A conference of senior Naval officers, held at Longhope, led to the formation of a Grand Fleet aircraft committee - and the conclusion that more aircraft could be taken to sea if a large and fast ship could be requisitioned for conversion to a carrier of fighter aircraft.

The ship chosen was the cruiser HMS *Furious*, then being built on the Tyne. It was decided to amend the design of the vessel to incorporate a large hangar for the aircraft, and, on the roof of the hangar, would be built a 220 feet long, 50 feet wide, runway.

The ship was commissioned in June, 1917, and with her establishment of 800 officers and men, joined the Fleet in Scapa Flow. Also, on board were 80 men of the Royal Naval Air Service, with three Short seaplanes and five Sopwith Pup scout aircraft. They were under the command of Squadron Commander Ernest Dunning, the man who was to make the historic flight and land on a ship underway at sea.

Trial flights - without an actual landing - were carried out before, on August 2, 1917, Dunning had the perfect conditions to carry out the landing.

above the Orkney skies

Commander Ernest Dunning makes the historic first landing of an aircraft on a ship underway at sea. The picture below, however, captures the moment when, a few days later, the plane went over the side of the ship, and Dunning was tragically killed.

(Pictures courtesy of Orkney Library photographic archive)

After circuiting the *Furious*, he made his approach into a 21 knot wind as the ship was steaming at 26 knots - the effect being that the aircraft was virtually stationary over the ship - and then, inelegantly but effectively, the watching group of officers grabbed the fuselage of the aircraft and physically pulled it on to the deck.

"The practicability of landing wheeled aircraft on the deck of a moving carrier had been proved and with it the very beginning of carrier operations," John McDonald wrote in *The Orcadian* later.

Tragically, further trials five days later were to illustrate the fatal dangers of trying to land on a deck still cluttered with all the other paraphernalia of a military vessel.

On August 7, 1917, Dunning completed another successful landing but, on his next attempt, the aircraft clipped the edge of the deck and went over the side of the ship. By the time help reached the pioneering pilot, he had drowned.

However, his contribution to the development of the aircraft carrier would be remembered and, a year later, HMS *Argus* entered service - the world's first carrier with an uninterrupted flight deck. And in 1992 - the 75th anniversary of Dunning's achievement - a memorial was erected at Smoogro, on the shores of Scapa Flow, to commemorate the event that made aviation history.

Slaughter at sea

The entry of the United States into the war in 1917 would soon see 100,000 Americans in France. Orkney would also welcome an American presence as ships of the US Navy arrived in local waters. "The celebration of Independence Day last Thursday will be long remembered in Kirkwall," reported *The Orcadian* of July 11, 1918. "Citizens of the United States of America came to town in force and from early morning till late afternoon the streets were thronged with visitors."

But Orkney was still destined to witness more tragedies before the end of the hostilities. The total Royal Naval Casualties of World War One were: killed - 2,466 officers, 30,895 men; wounded - 803 officers, 4,378 men; missing or taken prisoner - 237 officers, 985 men. The Merchant Navy suffered an equally grievous toll. Throughout 1917, an average of 20 UK merchant ships a week were lost to mines, torpedoes or other machinery of war.

It was to be a Royal Navy disaster - the loss of HMS *Vanguard* by an explosion that ripped through the ship - that would claim Orkney's biggest death toll in World War One, however. Curiously, it was a disaster that somehow never struck the public consciousness in the same way as the earlier loss of HMS *Hampshire* or the loss in World War Two of the *Royal Oak*.

Part of the explanation was obviously the fact that the loss of HMS *Vanguard* - with around 1,000 men killed in the waters of Scapa Flow - was scarcely reported. Wartime censorship regulations meant that the report of the fatal explosion that blasted through the warship filled just five lines in *The Orcadian* of July 21, 1917 - with no mention at all that the disaster had even occurred in Orkney waters. Under a tiny sub-heading "British battleship blown up - only two survivors," the report stated: "It is officially announced that the British battleship *Vanguard* blew up from internal explosion on July 9 and sank immediately. There were two survivors." In fact, another 95 members of the crew could claim to be survivors - they escaped the blast as they were ashore at the time.

The disaster at 11pm on July 9, 1917, had occurred just two weeks after a visit to Scapa Flow by the King. It was nearly 18 months later before censorship restrictions allowed *The Orcadian* to make any further mention of the incident in Orkney. On December 26, 1918, the newspaper's Flotta correspondent gave an eye witness account:

"From outside the house at the distance of a couple of miles or thereby we saw the battleship "go into the air," the awful catastrophe which sent into eternity in the twinkling of an eye "twice 400 men!"

"First there was the V-shaped column of flame between sea and sky, then the frightful detonation, then the spreading over the great harbour of innumerable blazing fragments of everything combustible, then the smoke and glare arising from our own hill of Golta, off which the doomed ship had been lying, and the heather on which had been set on fire.

"The marvel was indeed that a number of the nearer houses, around which much blazing material also fell, escaped the general conflagration. Nor was it a matter for less surprise that none of the houses on the island collapsed from the fearful shock, the force of which may be judged by the fact that, though we had left the door closed, we found on re-entering the house that it had extinguished the lamp!

"We may add that when learning of the relic of the *Vanguard* (in the form of a diary) only now picked up some three miles from the scene of the explosion, and another relic (a framed photo) being in the possession of the Bishop of London, we thought of how many *Vanguard* mementoes - bits of charred wood, fragments of clothing, scraps of powder stained paper etc - must be in the keeping of the people on the Scapa Flow border. We ourselves have a photo of a civilian seated, and a little boy in a sailor suit standing beside him, which we found in our West Hill some days after the catastrophe, and, which, had we been at liberty to send it for newspaper publication, might have been identified by some sorrowing relative."

The destruction of the *Vanguard*, not by a deliberate act of war but as a result of a tragic accident, almost resulted in the perished crewmen becoming the forgotten victims of Orkney's war. Years later, there was a local outcry whenever it was sug-

The loss of the cargo vessel *Express* in February, 1918, brought tragedy to Orkney. Her 11 crewmen, all from the county or with Orkney roots, perished after their ship was in collision with HMS *Grenville*. (Picture courtesy of Orkney Library photographic archive)

The Aberdeen trawler *Keith Hall* after running aground on Birsay in November, 1921. (Picture courtesy of Orkney Library photographic archive)

gested that salvage work could be carried out on the *Hampshire* or the *Royal Oak* - an outcry which forced the Admiralty to declare the *Royal Oak* as an official war grave in 1957.

However, the Admiralty permitted salvage work to go ahead on HMS *Vanguard* for several years with little more than a murmur of concern expressed.

However, if the restrictions of censorship limited the reporting of the *Vanguard* disaster, the loss of the destroyers HMS *Narborough* and HMS *Opal*, wrecked off the east side of South Ronaldsay while returning to Scapa Flow on January 15, 1918, received even less mention in *The Orcadian*, despite the fact that there was only one survivor as 200 men lost their lives. A two line report in the newspaper of January 26, 1918, simply recorded: "Two British destroyers were wrecked during a gale on the Scottish coast. All hands were lost except one."

In fact the destroyers were caught in blizzard conditions in 60mph winds and, completely blinded by the weather, one vessel had apparently followed the other to oblivion. On the Orkney Mainland, deep snow drifts accumulated as the temperature dropped to 16 degrees of frost. "This has probably been the severest snowstorm we have had in Orkney for more than half a century," said *The Orcadian*.

Seventy five years later, a memorial commemorating the loss of the two destroyers, and their 200 men, was unveiled in South Ronaldsay.

Understandably, it was another disaster at sea which was to touch Orkney more personally in the early weeks of 1918. The ss *Express*, owned by Messrs William Cooper and Son of Kirkwall, was sunk in the early hours of February 9 after a collision ten miles south east of Copinsay. All hands were lost - 11 crewmen, all from Orkney or with Orkney roots, and two servicemen.

The 138 feet long *Express* was en route to Kirkwall with a cargo from Leith when she was in collision with HMS *Grenville*, leading a flotilla of destroyers towards Scapa. "The announcement of the vessel's loss, when so near port, came as a great shock to the community, and at first the news could hardly be credited," said *The Orcadian*.

The *Express* - formerly the *Hebridean* - had only been purchased the previous year by Messrs Cooper to replace the *Ruby*, the victim of another sea tragedy in 1917. The steamer was

reported to have been purchased for £5,000 - something approaching five times the vessel's pre-war value. Her value obviously could not prevent the boat sinking almost immediately, and, a week later, only one body had been found.

The crew of eight married men and three single men were identified as the master Robert Heddle (40) of Leith, mate John Cooper (42) of Holm, chief engineer Charles Peace (32) of Kirkwall, second engineer George Rendall (48) of Kirkwall, firemen George Leslie (29) and Robert Craigie (34) both of Kirkwall, deckhands William Foulis (36) of Papa Westray, James Fox (18) and George Foulis (38) both of Kirkwall, steward John Rendall (52) of Leith, and trimmer William Budge (18) of South Ronaldsay.

John Cooper, brother of the owner of Messrs Cooper, had been making a single trip as relief for the regular mate, while the steward, John Rendall, had intended that this should be his final trip on the *Express* before coming ashore to work a small farm he had just purchased in the North Isles.

Right up to the official end of hostilities, Orkney would be living with the threat of casualties at sea. The minesweeper *Ascot* was torpedoed in the North Sea - with the loss of 52 lives - on November 10, 1918, less than 24 hours before the Armistice.

And an enemy submarine tried to penetrate Scapa Flow, also just before the Armistice. The U-boat appeared to have been manned almost entirely by officers, with 11 torpedoes. "It is certain that a dramatic blow would have been struck had the hazardous enterprise succeeded," stated *The Orcadian*. As it was, the submarine was detected near the entrance to the Flow and destroyed by the explosion of mines. A number of bodies were subsequently recovered, and a portion of conning tower retrieved and taken to St Margaret's Hope.

(Eighteen months later, Lt Commander Hugh Woodward and HMS *Ophelia* were granted £35 bounty for the sinking of the German submarine *U83* while off the Pentland Skerries in September, 1918.)

But, the end of 1918 was to see another island community suffer the most grievous tragedy when on New Year's Eve, more than 200 men from Lewis lost their lives as HM Yacht *Iolaire*, taking Naval ratings home on New Year leave, was lost just outside Stornoway harbour in the Western Isles.

A land fit for heroes?

The good people of Papa Westray - ever ready for a party - celebrated the end of World War One a month too soon.

The Orcadian of October 17, 1918, explained: "Last week a statement was circulating in Orkney that Germany had surrendered unconditionally. Coming as it did from a source which since August, 1914, has proved consistently unreliable, Kirkwall was unmoved, and most parishes were distinctly sceptical - though it is asserted that one district in the West Mainland got out the length of flying flags. Papa Westray, however, swallowed the pill. We are told that farm workers were summoned from the fields, treated to a dram, and given a half holiday. The whole island was soon agog and gave way to merrymaking."

There had been a gradual easing of tension in Orkney throughout 1918, with the Admiralty agreeing that the *St Ola* could resume sailing to Scapa as early as January, 1918 - although, in the South, air raids over London were still claiming as many as 200 casualties in a day.

Day-to-day life was still by no means normal. *The Orcadian* reported: "The food shortage is now becoming noticeable in Kirkwall. On Saturday night several butchers' shops were completely sold out." But confidence had risen to the extent that 21 East Road, Kirkwall, formerly the house of the Rev W. Pitcairn Craig, the St Magnus Cathedral minister who was moving South, was sold for £845 - nearly £200 over the upset price. And five building sites for new houses in Berstane Road, Kirkwall, offered for sale by Kirkwall Town Council, were snapped up at £10 each.

Orkney aimed to raise £100,000 in war savings to purchase a submarine for the war effort. An indication of a certain prosperity was apparent as Orcadians, in fact, beat the target easily, raising a total of £233,954 (a figure nearer £20 millions at 1999 prices.) And the Orkney Steam Navigation Company reported an annual profit for 1917 of £1,589.

Government confidence in the eventual outcome of the war was presumably high when, at the start of 1918, Admiral Sir John Jellicoe was honoured by the King and adopted the title of Viscount Jellicoe of Scapa!

Nonetheless, the precautions of war were being continued. On May 18, 1918, *The Orcadian* reported that "the greatest minefield that has ever been laid" existed in the North Sea, embracing 121,782 square nautical miles - including Orkney and Shetland. It was estimated that 70,200 mines had been laid across an area 25 miles wide off Orkney.

Six months later, at the conclusion of hostilities, it was announced that 400 craft would start clearing the mines in the North Sea off Orkney. Volunteers were sought to crew the minesweeping vessels - officers would receive an extra £4 a week and men £2 a week more.

Although, Orkney had escaped the war without a major attack from the air, it now became apparent that enemy airships had passed over the county. The German Zeppelin commander Von Butlar had crossed the North Sea to Yorkshire and then flown north to Scapa Flow before continuing to Norway and then back to Germany in a marathon mission lasting nearly six days in which he claimed to have photographed the British fleet in the Flow.

The Orcadian commented: "At least twice we had reports of enemy airships being sighted in the vicinity of the Orkneys though, at the time, confirmation was not obtainable. The first was following one of several occasions when an 'all lights out' order had come through from Longhope. The second was more recent when patrols in Deerness reported seeing an airship. It was understood that the authorities came to the conclusion that the airship belonged to the enemy." (The progress in the development of airships was illustrated in July, 1919, when the British airship R34 completed an epoch-making voyage of some 6,500 miles to New York and back to East Anglia).

On October 31, 1918, the conclusion of the war was obviously close as *The Orcadian* carried the headline: "Germany's request for peace." It can be conjectured now how long the British public would have allowed the hostilities to continue if the Germans had not sued for peace at that stage. Certainly, it had looked at times as though many workers of the country were careering towards a general strike. In London, in September, 1918, not only were thousands of railwaymen on strike, but also 10,000 policemen, in dispute over pay and other grievances.

In the event, Kirkwall heard the news of the Armistice an hour and a half before London. *The Orcadian* announced the official announcement of the abdication of the Kaiser and reported: "The King, Queen and Princess Mary had a magnificent reception as they drove through the crowded streets to attend the thanksgiving service at St Paul's.

"The news of the signing of the Armistice with Germany was received in Kirkwall on Monday evening. The announcement was received with intense enthusiasm. The shipping in the harbour, and the streets of Kirkwall were quickly bedecked with bunting, whilst the steamers in port voiced the feeling of all by the continuous sounding of sirens. All through the day the manifestations of joy continued; as ship after ship entered the bay the glad tidings were announced to the mariners by renewed blowing of whistles.

"All places of business in the town were closed in the afternoon, and a joint service of thanksgiving, in which the ministers of the town took part, was conducted in St Magnus Cathedral at night."

Now the public learned the dreadful price of the war in human deaths and suffering. The British casualties of World War One were officially announced as: killed - 37,896 officers and 620,829 men; wounded - 92,644 officers and 1,930,478 men; missing or held prisoner - 12,094 officers and 347,051 men. It added up to a horrifying total of 3,040,992 men.

The Kirkwall City Pipe Band owes its origins to the first memorial service held by World War One comrades in St Magnus Cathedral for those who fell in the conflict. After the service, it was agreed that the pipe band which formed for the occasion should be continued as a permanent town institution, with Charles MacGregor as president and J.A. Forsyth as Drum Major.

In many cases, the hoped-for repatriation of prisoners ended in disappointment. One in four of prisoners held in Turkey was reported to have died. And, in November, 1918, as the first details of demobilisation were published, families in Orkney were still receiving notifications of deaths in battle more than three months earlier.

And certainly the men who had returned home with the promise of land from the government were betrayed to a large extent. It was reported in the House of Commons that the number of ex-service applicants for land in Orkney was 163. But, by December, 1920, not one single Orkney application had been granted, Orkney and Shetland MP Cathcart Wason was told. A scarcity of large farms in Orkney, and the reluctance of farmers to sell, was blamed.

One Orkney ex-serviceman was reported to be walking 750 miles from Aberdeen to Brixham in Devon. He had reached Teddington, outside London, said the *Surrey Comet*, and hoped to stay with relatives in Devon while waiting for a war pension to be approved.

Private R. Cursiter of the Seaforth Highlanders returned home to Sanday after nearly eight months as a prisoner of war, having been captured in March, 1918, when the Seaforths found themselves outnumbered three to one when a German offensive began.

The prisoners were forced to march two days without food before being driven into sheds at a camp where they had to sleep on the ground. The next day they were loaded on to cattle trucks for a four day train journey, without food, into Germany. At the German camp in Munster, all possessions were taken from the men and they were kept on starvation rations, reported Private Cursiter. "Many died in camp owing to want of nourishment and the terrible hardships they had undergone before arrival."

Sadly, one young Orcadian had no story of wartime service to tell. He appeared in the court of Bow Street magistrates in London, accused with falsely wearing the uniform of an RAF major, with the ribbons of the Victoria Cross, Distinguished Service Order and the Military Cross.

He told the magistrate that he had tried to enlist four times but had been rejected on health grounds. He had purchased the uniform and medals from an army surplus store to save himself the taunts of friends.

Another Orkney man claimed that he had helped Britain win the war but had gone unrewarded. Schoolteacher Thomas Bathgate, of Tankerness, went before the War Compensation Court at Edinburgh, to claim £44,000 for inventions which he said he sent to the War Office during the conflict.

Among his inventions, he claimed £15,000 for an amphibious tank, £10,000 for a portable military bridge and £18,750 for an anti-Zeppelin bullet. "I maintain that Zeppelins were brought down by bullets which were used exactly as I stated," he told the court. Unfortunately for him, the court dismissed the claim as being outwith its jurisdiction.

There was increasing frustration and anger back in Orkney at the painfully slow return to civilian normality - and the promised land fit for heroes. Although censorship of letters from HM Ships was cancelled in November, 1918, "high handed actions" by the military authorities caused a row as the Navy prohibited passengers - including many servicemen - en route from Shetland landing at Kirkwall. "It was a grave injustice that those serving their country for a shilling a day should be forced, practically under guard, to live for lengthy periods afloat under the same conditions," thundered *The Orcadian.*

Too much had been allowed to go on under the shelter of the Defence of the Realm Act, the newspaper complained.

"It is an undoubted fact that the Navy has stood between the country and defeat. Yet, equally true is it, that Orkney is convinced from sad experience that in no service are there to be found so many officers in positions of authority where, with a minimum of efficiency, they succeed in giving a maximum of annoyance to the civilian population.

"There is a whole host of subjects which require to be seriously taken in hand - such as matters connected with measures to save life after HMS *Hampshire* was mined, and many questions affecting the public purse."

The last remark was a reference to the public alarm at the growing expenditure on the air stations at Caldale, Houton, Stenness and Swanbister - with £45,000 spent, including the requisitioning of the Standing Stones Hotel, before discovering that the Stenness Loch was unsuitable for sea planes - and high rates of pay being earned by an army of imported workmen at the Lyness base.

An estimated £297,000 had been spent on works and buildings at Lyness up to March 31, 1920 - the equivalent at 1999 prices of around £25 millions.

In February, 1919, *The Orcadian* complained: "Last week disgraceful scenes were witnessed in Kirkwall almost nightly. Servicemen appear to have obtained drink somewhere in town and became so obstreperous that even the police were unable to deal with them adequately."

It would be another six months - following the signing of the Treaty of Versailles in June, 1919 - before the system of permits to enter or leave Orkney was abolished.

The signing of the peace treaty saw a salute fired by the British warships in Scapa Flow while in Kirkwall "the sirens of the vessels in port were sounding for hours and ships festooned with flags," said *The Orcadian.*

"Motor cars and cycles decked with the Allied colours were in evidence in all parts of the burgh whilst the younger element, and the servicemen at the base, gave vent to their feelings of delight in patriotic airs and music hall ditties.

"The celebrations would have been incomplete without the burning of effigies of the Kaiser and this was duly done in Harbour Street and in Broad Street."

King George V, in a message to Sir W. Watson Cheyne, Lord Lieutenant of Orkney and Shetland, said: "I desire to express my admiration of the courage and endurance displayed by the sailors, soldiers and airmen of your county during the past five years of war. I am grateful to all the brave men and women of Orkney for their devoted and patriotic service." The King expressed sympathy for the bereaved and the wounded and added: "I rejoice with you today at the restoration of peace which I trust will bring to us all unity, contentment and prosperity."

The Orcadian used the occasion of the Treaty of Versailles to fire a final broadside at the permit system which, it said, had failed to keep "undesirable strangers" out of the county. "Why should Orkney remain a restricted area? Is it that the Naval authorities are unwilling to have attention drawn to the lavish and unnecessary expenditure of public funds that has been made in these islands? They may rest assured that they will never keep the fact to themselves."

Although *The Orcadian* aimed the flak at the Naval authorities - pointing out that, nationally, the cost of the Navy had increased from £34millions in 1904 to £140millions in 1919 - it was, in fact, the newly formed Royal Air Force which was now responsible for several of the air stations in what was tagged the "Orkney RAF scandals" as, in late 1919, Sir W. Joynson Hicks MP laid down a series of questions in the House of Commons regarding "deficiencies discovered when closing some of the air stations in the Orkney and Shetland islands."

In reply the Under Secretary for Air admitted that there had been a deficiency of £1,000 at a Shetland base, but avoided spelling out the total cost of all eight air stations in Orkney and Shetland which had been the base for 292 officers and 1,836 men. All of the air stations, he said, had by now either closed down or were in the process of being reduced to "care and maintenance" status.

Two years later, in 1921, it was reported that the Houton air base was being considered as an internment camp for 2,000 prisoners arrested during the troubles in Ireland but, whether the rumour was correct or not, it certainly never came to pass.

To help in the "big sweep" of the North Sea Barrage, as the huge North Sea minefield was known, a large United States minesweeping fleet - the American Minesweeping Detachment - was stationed at Kirkwall for six months under the command of Rear Admiral Joseph Strauss, who a year later was to be appointed Commander-in-Chief of the US Atlantic Fleet.

The arrival of the American minesweepers saw the Bignold Park host its first ever international baseball match as a team from USS *Black Hawk* beat the representatives of USS *Lake View* by a score of 20-2 in front of a large crowd of Orcadians in May, 1919. American Independence Day a few weeks later saw 2,000 US servicemen come ashore to celebrate in Kirkwall.

The Orcadian, after months of sniping at the British Naval authorities, appeared, by comparison, to be completely besotted with the slick public relations machine of the Americans. Some weeks up to ten per cent of the newspaper's editorial content was devoted to the social events of the visitors from the USA.

The fact that the streets of Kirkwall were now patrolled nightly by servicemen, with guns, from a foreign power brought no adverse comment from the newspaper - even when a Wild West style shoot-out disturbed the calm of the night in the centre of town.

The Orcadian in September, 1919, reported: "On Monday night, about 10 o' clock, a crowd which had gathered at the top of Mounthoolie Lane watching a struggle between members of the American Naval patrol and some sailors, was soon dispersed by the firing of a revolver. Apparently, among those concerned in the squabble was a petty officer who suddenly whipped out a revolver and fired up the lane. The crowd, as soon as they saw the flashes of the shots, took cover, and the women folks ran up the street. The members of the patrol immediately doubled down Albert Street for assistance and during their absence the sailors and petty officer made their escape. The petty officer was arrested later."

At sea, the mine-clearing exercise did not proceed without mishap. In July, 1919, the trawler *Richard Buckley*, attached to the American Minesweeping Detachment, was lost with her eight man crew.

Others were unfortunate victims of fate - including the *Olive* from Stronsay which hit a mine while fishing with all six of her crew blown up, also in July, 1919. The men who died were W. Williamson, Peter Chalmers and William Leslie (all Stronsay), David Flett (Finstown), William Muir (South Ronaldsay) and Andrew Wilson (Fair Isle).

But Orkney was soon to say goodbye not only to the Americans but also much of the British fleet. The Royal Naval headquarters at Kirkwall closed down on September 15, 1919, and in February, 1920, Vice Admiral Robert Prendergast, Admiral Commanding Orkney and Shetland, bid farewell to the county as his flagship HMS *Victorious* returned to Devonport. Scapa Flow finally reverted to a peacetime role on December 1, 1920, when the headquarters of the Commanding Officer of the North of Scotland Naval Area was switched from Lyness to Invergordon.

It was not exactly peaceful, however, for a party of airmen who visited Kirkwall on leave one Saturday night in March, 1920. They were subjected to a "hostile demonstration and left town in their motor lorry followed by a crowd of yelling youths" as the fracas assumed an ugly appearance, reported *The Orcadian*. A possible cause of the grievance, suggested the newspaper, was "that the ladies seem still to prefer the man in uniform to the mere civilian."

And, unfortunately, even the erection of a Kirkwall war memorial could not be agreed without an acrimonious dispute. At one stage, county clerk Duncan Robertson threatened to withdraw his consent for his son's name to be included on the memorial in protest at a proposal to use names of the fallen, and their regiments, only in abbreviated form. Eventually, a compromise was reached, but it was to be five years after the Armistice before the Kirkwall memorial was officially unveiled.

Before that, however, a new chapter in Orkney's history had begun as, into the midst of the islands, sailed thousands of defeated Germans and scores of German warships.

Under the terms of the Armistice, the British Admiralty had ordered the surrendered German vessels to sail with reduced crews and no ammunition. The fleet surrendered to Admiral Sir David Beatty, Commander-in-Chief of the Grand Fleet, on November 22, 1918, off the Firth of Forth - and was diverted north to be interned in Scapa Flow. The ships and their crews were "absolutely awful - without spirit left," said *The Orcadian*.

"Now the product of Germany's dream of sea power lies in ignominy, beneath the shadows of the hills of Hoy," said the newspaper. "There they lie, filthy and rusty, indicative of the sure fate which would have befallen them, had they but dared to put to the test their loud-toned boasts of invincibility."

The pride of the Kaiser, the great German Fleet, steams into Scapa Flow to be held captive for the next seven months. In June, 1919, the ships' German crews would deliberately scuttle the vessels in one of the most dramatic episodes of 20th century Naval history.

(Picture courtesy of Orkney Library photographic archive)

Roll of honour

Mr Allan Taylor and Mr Richard Shearer, of Kirkwall, have compiled
the following list of names inscribed on the war memorials of Orkney
to commemorate those who died in World War One:

BIRSAY

A.F. Aitkin, Boardhouse
C.S. Ballantyne, Quoylonga
J.V. Bias, Eastabest
G.S. Duthie, Oxtro
A. Flett, Glebe
G.S. Flett, Millgoe
W. Flett, Glebe
W.A.D. Flett, Millgoe
G.F. Harvey, Howquoy
E.G. Johnston, Waird
W.P.H. Kirkness, Glower
A. Moar, Briton
J. Newlands, Bigbreck
J.T. Phillips, Waird
J.B. Sabiston, Grew
G.R. Scarth, Twatt
A. Scott, Mossiter
C.M. Selbie, FC Manse
J. Spence, Doverhouse
J.R. Spence, Makerhouse
J.W. Spence, Midhouse
T. Spence, Houseby
J.W. Yorston, Dale

BURRAY

John K. Allan, Seaforth Highlanders
Peter Allan, Seaforths
Thomas Allan, *HMHS Karapara*
James K. Bruce, Lab Corps
James Copland RNR
Peter S. Duncan, Seaforths
Alexander Laird RNR
David B. Laird, Lab Corps
John Osborne, Seaforths
Alexander M. Park RFA
George Petrie RNR
John R. Woodrage, Seaforths

DEERNESS

Cpl D. Cormack, Delday
L/Cpl J.H. Craigie, Grindigar
Pte W. Craigie, Breck
Pte J.W. Cromarty, Littlequoys
PO J.C. Dick, Keigar
Cpl R. Foubister, Watermoss
Gunr T. Irvine, Sandside
Pte D. Linklater, Braebuster
Pte J. Mowat, Cellardyke
Sgt D. Ritch, Free School House
L/Cpl J. Scott, Wood Cottage
Pte J. Wick, Cutpool

EDAY

David Drever
James W. Groat
Stewart Groat
Robert Harcus
William Miller
Charles Peace
George P. Peace
James Reid
Richard Rousay
David Scott
George Seatter
James Stout
James S. Tulloch
John A. Wallace

EGILSAY

Pte James Bews, Maeness

EVIE

Pte Andrew Anderson
Str Malcolm H. Leonard
Pte Charles W. Louttit
Gunr Ralph A.T. Louttit
Pte George Manson
Sgt Marcus Robertson
Pte Robert Seatter
Sgt Lt James Stevenson
Cpl James B. Wilson

FIRTH

David Flett, Kingsdale
George R. Harvey, Burnside
John I. Heddle, Horraldshay
Alexander T. Horrie, Turriedale
James C. Hourston, Grimbister
William S. Kent, Savil
William G.C. Linklater, Millquoy
Arthur E. Mackay, Schoolhouse
Thomas Newlands, Greenfield
Robert Rendall, Southbrake
James G. Scarth, Binscarth
Thomas S. Sclater, Settiscarth
George Stevenson, Smograth
Alfred Taylor, Woodbine
James Taylor, Cruan
James Taylor, Woodbine
William S. Turfus, Holland

FLOTTA

Signaller James Flett
LS Adam I. Norquoy
Pte William Norquoy
Capt William I. Norquoy
Sgt James Sutherland DSM
Pte John Sutherland
Gunr James T. Sutherland
Pte William Sutherland
Lt R.W. Taylor MC
Sgt Donald S. Thomson

HARRAY

A. Aitken, Estaquoy
J. Anderson, Appiehouse
C.A. Borwick, Lynneth
W.V. Bruce, Lamaquoy
J.W. Corrigall, Geroin
D.M. Cullie, P. School
W. Flett, Newmill
W. Flett, Nisthouse
D.J. Garriock, South Lyde
T. Gray, Furzbreck
M. Harray, Upper Bigging
A. Ironside, Midhouse
J. Isbister, Moan
G.R. Johnston, Flaws
W.J. Johnston, Garth
A. Newlands, Harray
I. Newlands, Harray
J. Newlands, Harray
A. Scott, Mossiter
J. Spence, Garth
J.F. Spence, Post Office

HOLM

Kenneth Alexander, St Marys
John S. Budge, St Marys
John S. Cutt, St Marys
George W. Dishan, St Marys
Archibald Garrioch, Westerbister
John W. Garrioch, Northhouse
David Hourston, Millfield
John A. Laughton, Annfield
William Laughton, Easterbister
Thomas Louttit, Woodstock
Patrick K. McNeill, West UF Manse
William A. McNeill, West UF Manse
John Meil, Hurteso
Henry I. Runciman, East UF Manse
William W. Runciman, East UF Manse
James W. Sinclair MM, Kirkbreck
William Sinclair, Blowmuir
John Sutherland, St Marys
John C.C. Walls, Gutterpool

HOY

Pte John Mowat
Pte William Mowat
L/Cpl John Omand
Pte Harry Ritch
Seaman John Robb
James Sabiston RNR
Pte John Thomson

Roll of honour - continued

KIRKWALL

Pte Kenneth Alexander, Seaforths
Pte Edwin I. Barnett, Seaforths
Pte John W. Barron, Canadian forces
Pte James W. Borwick, Australian forces
Pte John H. Brass, Seaforths
Cpl William Brass, New Zealand forces
Pte Alexander Buchan, Seaforths
Capt Arthur Buchanan, Royal Engineers
Pte James Burgess, New Zealand forces
Pte John W. Clouston, Seaforths
Lt Alfred H. Cooper, RNR
Pte James Cooper, Royal Scots
Pte James Cooper, New Zealand forces
L/Cpl John W. Cooper, Royal Scots
John Cooper, ss *Express*
Rifleman William Corner, PO Rifles
Cpl James Corse, US forces
Capt Gordon Cowper, Gordons
Surgeon William P. Cowper, RN
Pte James Craigie, London Scottish
Robert Craigie, ss *Express*
Pte William Craigie, Middlesex Regt
Gunr Thomas Cutt, RGA
Cpl David B. Donaldson, KOSB
Pte George Drever, Scots Guards
Pte John Drever, Seaforths
Pte Thomas Drever, Seaforths
Cpl James Dunnett, Royal Engineers
Pte William I. Dyce, Royal Scots
Gunr George Eccles, RMA
David Findlayson, ss *Express*
Lt David Flett, Highland Light Infantry
Second Lt Frederick Flett, Seaforths
George T.F. Flett, ss *Era*
Gunr George Foubister, RGA
George Foulis, ss *Express*
William Foulis, ss *Express*
James Fox, ss *Express*
CPO Adam Frisken, RN
Pte William Frisken, KOSB
Cpl David Gordon, RGA
L/Cpl Albert Gullion, Seaforths
Pte William D. Gunn, Seaforths
William J. Halcrow, ss *Cape Cross*
James Harcus, Seaforths
Seaman Robert Harcus, RNR
Pte Thomas Harcus, Scottish Rifles
L/Cpl David Harrold, Canadian forces
Pte James W. Harrold, Seaforths
Pte Robert Hay, Seaforths
Pte William Hay, Seaforths
Robert Heddle, ss *Express*
Pte James W. Holland, Seaforths
Sgt Alexander Hourston, Royal Scots
Pte Archibald Hourston, New Zealand forces
Lt David W. Hourston, Camerons
Pte Anderson Ireland, Northumberland Fusiliers
Pte George H. Johnston, Australian forces
Staff Sgt John Johnston, RASG
Pte William P. Johnston, Royal Scots
Second Lt Thomas R. Kirkness, RAF
Pte George M. Laird, Canadian forces
Seaman Alfred I. Learmonth, RNR
Pte James A. Learmonth, Seaforths
Pte Alexander Leask, Seaforths
George Leslie, ss *Express*

Pte Robert E. Leslie, Seaforths
Pte William Leslie, Royal Scots
Pte Alfred Liddle, Canadian forces
Pte David S. Linklater, Seaforths
Pte John Linklater, New Zealand forces
Pte Robert Linklater, Seaforths
Pte Edwin Mackay, Seaforths
Pte James Mackay, Seaforths
L/Cpl David Manson, Canadian forces
Pte Joseph Manson, Seaforths
Sdlr Hugh Marwick, RASC
James Marwick, ss *Ruby*
Pte John J. Marwick, Royal Scots
William Mason, ss *Ruby*
Pte John K. Maxwell, Gordons
Rev George Miller, Chaplain to the Forces
Pte William Milne, Highland Light Infantry
Dmr Donald Morgan, Canadian forces
Pte Robert Mowat, Seaforths
Pte John Muir, Australian forces
Fireman Stanley J. Muir, RNR
Spr Robert Newlands, Royal Engineers
Pte Andrew Nicolson, Seaforths
Pte Alfred Osborne, Seaforths
Charles Peace, ss Express
Pte James Reid, Gordons
George Rendall, ss *Express*
George I. Rendall, ss *Express*
Second Lt Archibald G. Robertson, Black Watch
Gunr James Robertson, RGA
Pte William C. Robertson, Seaforths
Pte John Rosie, KOSB
Pte Gordon Sandison, Seaforths
Gunr John Scarth, RGA
Cpl Thomas Scolley, Seaforths
Pte Charles F. Scott, Seaforths
A/Paymr Donald M. Scott, RNR
Pte Robert T. Scott, Scottish Rifles
Pte George S. Shearer, RS Fusiliers
Pte James Shearer, Seaforths
Pte Leslie Shearer, Canadian forces
Pte James Simison, Seaforths
Pte George W. Sinclair, Seaforths
Spr John Sinclair, Royal Engineers
Gnp Robert Sinclair, RNR
Pte Thomas Sinclair, Royal Scots
L/Cpl William J. Sinclair, Seaforths
Sgt Alexander Smith, Canadian forces
Driver David J. Smith, RASC
L/Cpl Robert M. Smith, RS Fusiliers
Sgt John G. Spence, Highland Light Infantry
Major Anderson Sutherland, RFA
Lt Goodwin Sutherland, Gordons
Pte James H. Sutherland, Camerons
Seaman James Tulloch, RN
Pte James W. Tulloch, Black Watch
L/Cpl John Tulloch, Canadian forces
Pte Dick Velzian, RS Fusiliers
Sgt George F. Velzian, Royal Scots
Pte John Velzian, RASC
Pte James Voy, Canadian forces
Lt William B. Watson MC, RFA
Pte James Watt, Gordons
Pte J. Duncan Webster, Seaforths
Pte John Wick, Australian forces
Pte James Willits, Seaforths
Pte Stewart Wilson, RS Fusiliers

Cpl James Wishart, Camerons
Pte John E. Work, Seaforths
Pte William Work, Seaforths
Pte William J. Work, Seaforths
Pte Alexander Yule, Seaforths

NORTH RONALDSAY

John Angus, Holland Farm
Samuel Cutt, Milldam
Thomas Swanney, Holm
Charles Thomson, Cursetter
Thomas Thomson, Quoybanks
John Thomson, Quoybanks
John Tomson, Howatoft
William Tulloch, Upper Linay

ORPHIR

Thomas Anderson, Gyre
John H. Brass, Outer Dale
Samuel R. Donaldson, Donaldsons
James S. Farquhar, Nearhouse
Charles Johnston, Scows
John Muir, Kirbuster
George Robson, Grays Inn
Victor Sclater, Kebro
Charles Scott, Swanbister
Alexander Shurie, Greenigoe
James Sinclair, New Place
John Stevenson, Glenrae
William Wishart, Braebrecks

PAPA WESTRAY

George Foulis, Quarryhouse
William Foulis, Roadside
David Irvine, Hinsobrae
Thomas Irvine, Hinsobrae
Thomas G.D. Miller, Daybreak
John Rendall, Roadside
Robert Sinclair, Backaskaill
William Tulloch, Newhouses

RENDALL

William Brass, New Zealand forces
Henry Hay, New Zealand forces
Alfred Osbourne, Seaforths
David Spence, Canadian forces
John W. Yorston, Seaforths

ROUSAY

Pte George Craigie, Triblo
Pte John Craigie, Ploverhall
Pte David Flaws, Hammerfield
Pte Alfred Gibson, Langskaill
Pte Alfred C. Gibson, Avelsay
Pte Hugh Gibson, Oldman
L/Cpl John D. Grieve, Falldown
L/Cpl George Inkster DCM, Knapper
Pte John A.M. Inkster, Essaquoy
Pte John Logie, Grindlesbreck
Engineer Isaac Marwick, Essaquoy
Pte John H. Marwick, Quoys
Pte David Munro, Old School
Pte Harry Reid, Brough
Pte Edward Seatter, Banks
Capt A.Graham Spark, Manse

Roll of honour - continued

St. Andrews
Robert S. Baikie, New Zealand forces
John T. Eunson, RAF Can
John J. Fairweather, Seaforths
Henry H. Garrioch, Seaforths
James W. Holland, Seaforths
Clifford A. Johnston, Royal Scots
Thomas Laughton, Seaforths
James W. Paterson, RN
Alfred Pottinger, RN
James Scott, Machine Gun Corps

Sandwick
Pte William C. Allen, Mount Pleasant
Pte James A. Brass, Instabellie
Pte John G. Corrigall, North Unigarth
Pte Peter Corrigall, North Unigarth
Spr Simon J.M. Corrigall, North Unigarth
Gunr John A. Crichton, Hourston
Pte George Esslemont, Millhouse
Pte John W. Firth, Bockan
Pte John G. Forbes, Vetquoy
Pte David S. Garson, Gerstie
Pte James W. Harvey, Yeldaday
Pte Peter L. Johnston, Westfield
Cpl Charles Kirkness, Hammerclett
Pte John G.B. Kirkness, Queenamoan
David Linklater RNR, Skaill
Pte George J. Linklater, Cruaday
Pte William G.C. Linklater, Pow
Pte Edward B. Moar, Brae
Pte William Poke, Rango
Lt James A. Sabiston, Overhouse
Pte John G.L. Scott, Housegarth
Pte David Sinclair, Bookan
Pte George Taylor, Bain
Pte William Taylor, Voy

Sanday
John Angus, Tofts
James Brown, Stove
Magnus Brown, Stove
James A. Burnett, Boloquoy
James Campbell, Skaill
James Clyne, Howe
Charles Cutt, Kettletoft
John C. Dearness, Nouster
James Dick, Roadside
Richard Dick, Roadside
David Drever, Grecemay
Walter Fairburn, Viggie
James Fea, Boloquoy
William Flett, North Myre
Peter Fotheringhame, Nearhouse
Peter Fotheringhame, Templehall
Robert L. Garrioch, Balaclava
James Guthrie, Elsness
Robert M. Hay, Kettletoft
William Hay, Kettletoft
David M. Learmonth, Mid Breckan
James A. Learmonth, Hermisgarth
William M. Learmonth, Ortie
George Lennie, Howland
James Lyall, Stove
Alfred Mackinson, Clickimin
David Manson, Corsdale
James Moodie, Icegarth
John Moodie, West Hill
Archibald Muir, Roadside
James Muir, Ortie
John Muir, Neigarth
William Muir, Rue
George F. Paul, Backaskaill
William Robson, Howe
James Scott, Feastown
William Sinclair, Ayre
William Sinclair, North Myre
John Swan, Holland
John Swanney, Colligarth
John H. Tait, Parlgo
William Towrie, Clickimin
John Tulloch, Ortie
Andrew Wallace, Lettan
James Wallace, Mid Langamay
William Wallace, Newark

Shapinsay
Gunr James Craigie, RGA
Lt John Dennison, RGA
Pte James Drever, RAMC
Pte Thomas Drever, Seaforths
Capt David L.I. Hepburn, Camerons
Lt Dennis P. Hepburn, Canadian forces
Pte John R. Hepburn, Seaforths
Pte Robert R. Hepburn, Canadian forces
Cpl John Irvine, RGA
First Officer John MacDonald, Mercantile
    Marine
Pte Robert S. Mowat, Canadian forces
Gunr Robert Sinclair, RGA
Pte William Swanney, Royal Scots

South Ronaldsay
Pte John H.N. Annal, Gordons
Dkh John Brown, RNR
Gunr William Bruce, RGA
Pte John D. Cormack, Scots Guards
Pte William R. Cromarty, US forces
L/Cpl William Cumming, Seaforths
Pte William Dass, Seaforths
Pte Magnus Dearness, Seaforths
Pte William Duncan, NF
Cpl James Dunnett, Royal Engineers
Pte William Esson, Seaforths
Pte Robert Gunn, Seaforths
Pte Robert Henderson, Seaforths
Pte William MacDonald, Seaforths
L/Cpl John MacKenzie, Gordons
Pte John R. Marwick, New Zealand forces
Pte Donald Norquoy, New Zealand forces
CSM Magnus Norquoy, Highland Light
    Infantry
Cpl William Petrie, Scots Guards
Eng John Simpson, HMT service
L/Cpl Archibald Sinclair, Machine Gun
    Corps
Pte Richard Spence, Machine Gun Corps
Gunr James Sutherland, RGA
Pte Robert Sutherland, Canadian forces
Pte Gilbert O. Thomson, Canadian forces
Sgt Joseph Thomson, Scots Guards
Dkh John G.H. Thomson, RN-MMR

Stenness
James A. Burnett, Grievehouse
Robert Coghill, Stoursdale
William M. Findlay, Burnside
William M. Irvine, Seattersquoy
Harold T. Leask, Coldomo
John Linklater, Nisthouse
Thomas F. Muir, Cumminess
Alexander L.W. Pottinger, Nether Bigswell
James Pottinger, Nether Bigswell
James Sinclair, Redbraes
James Sinclair, Breck
William Sinclair, Breck
John F. Spence, Lochend
James W.S. Tait, Brig o' Waithe
John Thomson, Burnside
Caleb Walter, Quoyer

Roll of honour - continued

STROMNESS

Pte Herbert E.S. Angus, Canadian RAMC
Major Charles P. Atkin MC, RFA
PO John Christie, RNR
Engineer John S. Clouston, HM Transport
Pte William G. Clouston, RASC
Pte William Corrigall, Machine Gun Corps
Pte Robert Fiddler, Australian forces
Pte William Finnie, Canadian forces
Pte James Firth, Canadian forces
CSM David Flett, L'pool Scottish
Pte John R. Garson, RH
Pte David C.S. Harvey, Seaforths
Pte John Harvey, Seaforths
Pte James W. Harvey, RSF
Pte Charles F. Hutchison, RASC
Pte Dan E. Johnston, South African forces
L/Cpl John Johnston, Canadian forces
Seaman Charles Kilpatrick, RNP
L/Cpl Henry Linklater, Australian forces
Pte James W. Linklater, Highland Light
   Infantry
Sgt John McIntyre, RFA
ABS Isaac Manson, Mercantile Marine
Pte David Matheson, Australian forces
Pte Joseph Matheson, Scots Rifles
L/Cpl James Miller, Royal Engineers
Pte James Mowat, New Zealand forces
Seaman John Mowat, Mercantile Marine
Sgt J.A. Mowat, PPCLI
Sgt William Mowat, RGA
Pte John W. Omand, Seaforths
Pte William S. Porteous, South African
   forces
Pte Robert M. Rendall, Seaforths
Pte Charles Robb, Canadian forces
Steward George Robb, Mercantile Marine
Pte George Robertson, Canadian forces
Pte John Scott, Camerons
Seaman Frank S. Shearer, RN Patrol
Pte John Simpson, RSF
Seaman John E.L. Sinclair, HM Transport
L/Cpl James W. Sinclair, Seaforths
Pte William G. Sinclair, RMLI
Pte Alex Smith, Seaforths
Second Lt D.Stewart Spence, RFA
Sgt David Steven, Argyll and Sutherland
   Highlanders
Seaman William R.S. Stout, RNR
Captain James Sutherland, Mercantile
   Marine
Seaman Charles Taylor, RNR
Lt R.W. Taylor MC, RFA
Cpl Robert Wilson, Canadian forces
Pte Samuel Wylie, Seaforths

STRONSAY

William D. Brownlie, Royal Scots
Richard Caithness, West Yorkshire Regt
William Croy, New Zealand forces
David Dearness, Seaforths
James Dennison, Seaforths
James Drever, RAMC
Thomas Drever, Seaforths
Robert B. Fotheringhame, RGA
James Groat, RGA
Peter C. Irvine, Seaforths
George Logie, RGA
John Millan, RNR
John Miller, Seaforths
Peter Miller, Canadian forces
Andrew Mowat, Seaforths
John Mowat, Gordons
Archibald Reid, Gordons
Alexander Robertson, RGA
James Shearer, ASC
James W. Shearer, Seaforths
Peter Shearer, Scots Guards
Robert Shearer, Seaforths
Robert Shearer, Canadian forces
William Shearer, Canadian forces
James W.B. Stevenson, London Scottish
John Stevenson, RGA
John Stevenson, RNR
George I. Stout, Seaforths
Anderson Sutherland MC, RFA
Goodwin Sutherland, Gordons
James Tulloch, RGA
John M. Tulloch, Seaforths
Thomas Twatt, Seaforths

WALLS

Gnr Andrew W. Chalmers, RNR
Pte James R. Chalmers, Canadian forces
L/Str John Coutts, RN
Pte Malcolm Groat, Argyll and Sutherland
   Highlanders
Pte John Heddle, Highland Light Infantry
Lt Frederick N. Robertson, Gordons
Gnr William Shearer, RGA
Pte Isaac W. Stout, Seaforths
Pte William Stout, Seaforths
Gnr George S. Sutherland, New Zealand
   forces
Pte George M. Swanson, Seaforths
Pte Harry A. Taylor, Canadian forces

WESTRAY

William T. Bain, Newhouse
James Burgher, Ness
John Cooper, Newbigging
Thomas Cooper, Newbigging
James Drever, Cot o' Howan
John Drever, Broughton
Thomas Drever, Sangar
John Foulis, Links
Thomas Foulis, Links
George Gray, Brandies
James B. Groat, Feuld
Andrew Harcus, Tirlot
Andrew Harcus, Broughton
James L. Harcus, Heatherbank
John Harcus, Old Glen
Thomas Harcus, Pow
William Heddle, Hammers
John E. Hewison, Pierowall
Thomas Kent, Greenwall
William Leslie, Pierowall
William Manson, East Thorn
David Reid, Rebuilding
William T. Reid, Rose Cottage
Alex Rendall, Breck of Aikerness
David Rendall, Saverton
George S. Rendall, Nether Brough
John Rendall, Quoynabreckan
John T. Rendall, Bell Towers
John T.S. Rendall, Floss
Robert R. Rendall, Floss
Stewart Rendall, Nether Brough
Thomas Rendall, Angerquoy
William Rendall, Millhouse
William G. Rendall, Ouseness
George Seatter, Daisybank
Thomas R. Seatter, Burness
Robert Sinclair, East Hill
Henry Stevenson, Berriedale

WYRE

Pte John Craigie, Bu'

The great sea monster of Hoy

A colony of sea monsters living in deep submerged caves off Hoy was suggested after a mystery creature was seen by crewmen of Longhope lifeboat.

Mr John Mackintosh Bell, of Roundstonefoot, Moffat, was fishing off Brims on August 5, 1919, when the monster appeared between Brims Ness and Tor Ness.

His story was supported by four local men who were in the boat with him - John Swanson, coxswain of the Longhope

1919

lifeboat, William Mowat, second coxswain, Charles Mowat, second engineer, and Donald Mackay.

"About 25-30 yards from the boat, a long neck, as thick as an elephant's fore leg, was sticking up," said Mr Bell. "On

top of this was the head, which was much smaller in proportion. The neck, I should say, stuck about five to six feet, possibly more, out of the water.

"My friends thought it would weigh two or three tons, some thinking four to six. If the neck stretched say to eight feet, the neck and body would be 18-20 feet long."

He suggested that such monsters frequented the rocky caves, always covered by deep water, off Hoy.

Strike battles for teachers and bakers

Wartime hostilities were replaced by industrial strife in Orkney in 1919. The county's schoolteachers voted for strike action over a pay dispute and many of Orkney's master bakers went on strike in protest at the price of bread!

Teachers were campaigning for a minimum salary of £100 per annum, and all the teachers at the Kirkwall Burgh School signed a letter to the school board,

pointing out that Kirkwall had not suffered financially as a result of the war "but had rather enjoyed greater prosperity."

The Orkney branch of the teachers' organisation, the Educational Institute of Scotland, voted by 56-35 for strike action.

However, the dispute was resolved as the Education (Scotland) Act saw the introduction of national pay scales, and the formation of a new Orkney Education

Authority which would have a budget of £22,015 for teachers' salaries throughout the county. Mr Frank Young was appointed as the first Orkney director of education.

In August, 1919, Orkney master bakers took strike action over the price they could charge for bread. Thousands of loaves were imported from South before the dispute was settled.

Airmen conquer Atlantic - by boat!

The race to make the first non-stop flight over the Atlantic saw two pioneer airmen arrive in Orkney having crossed the ocean!

Alas, they had to abandon their aircraft in mid-Atlantic and they were fortunate to complete the journey by boat.

The *Daily Mail* had offered a £10,000 prize for the first non-stop air crossing of the Atlantic, and that was the challenge facing Harry Hawker, a 25 year old Australian-born airman who, in 1916, had set a world altitude record by flying to 24,000 feet.

Hawker took off in his red Sopwith aircraft from St John's, Newfoundland, on May 18, 1919, aiming to fly 1,880 miles to the west of Ireland.

He was accompanied by Commander Kenneth Mackenzie Grieve acting as navigator. Commander Grieve had previously worked on the Cunard liner *Campania* which in World War One saw service in Scapa Flow, having been converted to an aircraft carrier.

On May 22, 1919, *The Orcadian* reported that no news had been heard of Hawker or his companion. "It is believed at St John's that disaster overtook him soon after the start."

However, on May 25, Hawker and Grieve arrived in Scapa Flow. The airmen - driven off course by a northerly gale - had come down in the sea, with engine trouble, about 14 hours out of Newfoundland.

Fortunately they had been picked up by the Danish steamer *Mary*.

They were transferred from the *Mary* to the British destroyer *Woolston* which safely delivered the aviators to the Flow where they were entertained as guests of Admiral Sir Sydney Fremantle on HMS *Revenge*.

An American vessel *Lake Charlottesville* later salved the red aircraft, and landed it

in Cornwall, so, to that extent, both the plane and airmen had crossed the Atlantic!

However a month later, the names of Alcock and Brown went into the record books as the men who completed the first non-stop air crossing of the Atlantic.

Harry Hawker was to be killed in an air crash at Hendon aerodrome two years later on July 12, 1921.

Peacetime disaster averted

What could have been the worst ever peacetime disaster in Orkney waters was narrowly averted when a ship, carrying more than 1,000 troops, plus women and children, hit trouble off North Ronaldsay.

The White Star liner *Vedic*, on a voyage from Northern Russia to Leith, stranded on the Reef Dyke in wild weather in September, 1919.

British Naval vessels and ships of the American Minesweeping Detachment,

based at Kirkwall, were alerted to the rescue of the 9,332 ton vessel.

However, the emergency passed as the liner was able to refloat under her own steam.

There was worse news of two other vessels. The schooner *Janet* of Kirkwall, en route from Leith to Kirkwall, and the schooner *Isabella* of Wick, en route to Stromness, were both posted missing at Lloyds in 1919.

Weather pioneer

The man who supplied the Navy in Orkney with daily weather reports throughout World War One died in 1919, aged 65.

Mr Magnus Spence, the schoolmaster at Deerness, where he operated his weather station, would be remembered as a

botanist, writer and scholar as well as for the early meteorological records of the county. One of his Deerness pupils was Dr Robert Charles Wallace who, ten years later, became President of the University of Alberta in Canada.

The great eclipse

On the longest day, the sun finally set on the German High Seas Fleet - the greatest spectacle that Orkney would witness in the 20th century as more than 50 warships went to the bottom of Scapa Flow.

Another 20 drifted grotesquely ashore in their death throes while hundreds of men had to swim for their lives - in some cases, in a hail of bullets - as the drama unfolded of the suicide of what had been the pride of the Kaiser, sinking eerily to an alien maritime graveyard on June 21, 1919.

They went in just four hours in the greatest scuttle in history - ordered by the Vice-Admiral Ludwig von Reuter in a breathtaking act of defiance or, as it was seen then, treachery, which would cause debate among military commentators for years to follow. A fleet of ships worth millions - *The Times* estimated the value at £60 millions - was reduced to scrap metal.

The momentous events were watched by hundreds of Orcadians from the shores of the Flow, and, even more remarkably, by upward of 200 Stromness schoolchildren who were caught right in the midst of the scuttle, on a Saturday pleasure boat cruise through the warships.

The German ships had been interned since the Armistice of November, 1918. They were first taken to the Firth of Forth and then, during the last week of November, started their journey north to what would be their final resting place in Scapa Flow. Seventy four vessels would spend the next six months languishing at anchor - the large battlecruisers and battleships around Cava and towards Houton, while the destroyers and cruisers lay off Fara and Rysa, towards Lyness - while negotiations on the Treaty of Versailles to agree the terms of peace seemed to drag on interminably.

Vice Admiral Sir Sydney Fremantle had sailed from Scapa Flow on the morning of Saturday, June 21, with his British First Battle Squadron to carry out routine exercises. His departure left the Germans to their own devices - and, soon before Noon, the signal from von Reuter went round the Kaiser's ships for the scuttle to begin. The Germans threw open hatches, seacocks and watertight doors of the vessels and the water of Scapa Flow rushed in. The interned would become the interred.

As it transpired, it was no spur-of-the-moment decision by von Reuter - it later emerged that he had planned his great eclipse for a month - though there would be controversy afterwards over whether von Reuter - who was designated Admiral-in-Charge, German Ships at Scapa - had been ordered, from Germany, to destroy the vessels; and whether the British authorities, aware of such orders, turned a diplomatic blind eye.

Von Reuter claimed in the aftermath that he had acted on his own initiative. He knew that the terms being demanded of Germany would mean the decimation of the German Navy, whatever. Also, he knew that the peace talks on the Treaty of Versailles had stalled and it looked that, at worst, hostilities would resume or, at least, all the interned, unarmed German ships in Scapa Flow would be unilaterally seized by the Allies. Von Reuter saw a "third way" to ensure that none of the Kaiser's fleet would fall to the possession of an enemy, and so evolved the audacious plan for the great scuttle.

But none of that was known in Orkney that summer's afternoon as the news of the events in Scapa Flow swept round the population. Hundreds of people headed to the vantage points at the Houton air station from where *The Orcadian* gave eye witness accounts.

The "Abandon Ship" signal first sounded from the former flagship *Friedrich der Grosse.* Pandemonium followed and there is now no doubt that some fleeing, unarmed German sailors were shot dead. At the time, however, following five years of

The foreground illustrates just part of the major development that grew up at Houton during World War One when the bay was a base for sea planes.

(Picture courtesy of Orkney Library photographic archive)

of the German fleet

brutal war, it was not a climate of public opinion in which the word "atrocity" would have been used - though it was a horror that perhaps remained with some of the watching schoolchildren for the rest of their lives.

"The battleships, as a rule, gradually submerged until their decks were awash, turned turtle, and quietly slipped out of sight," reported *The Orcadian*. "A slight boiling on the sea, repeated at intervals for more than an hour afterwards, and the bluish tinge on the water caused by the release of oil, were all that marked the spot where for months before had lain the one-time pride of a nation.

"The light cruisers settled by the stern. As the after part of the ship disappeared, the bows and a hundred feet or more of the hull projected sheer from the sea, looking like some huge whale leaping through space.

"The Naval authorities hurried all available craft - drifters, trawlers, destroyers, tugs and a mass of smaller craft - to the scene, and whilst the earlier information which reached the shore gave hope that a considerable portion of the fleet would be saved, events have proved that the Germans had once more, with characteristic thoroughness, done their work so well, and made their plans so carefully, that the efforts of the British seamen were almost wholly futile."

Under the terms of the Armistice, there were no British guards on board the ships which had been entrusted to their German skeleton crews.

A total of 20,000 Germans had originally arrived in the Flow on the interned German ships, but around 15,000 were quickly returned home, and by June 21, 1919, fewer than 1,800 German officers and men were left in charge of the Fleet - nearly 3,000 having been shipped out to be repatriated to Germany the week before - otherwise casualties could have been much higher. As it was, even the battlecruisers and battleships had only 60-75 men aboard, and the destroyers and cruisers only a couple of dozens each.

At 10.30am that morning, at the invitation of the Admiralty, parties of Stromness schoolchildren had gathered at the town pier to board the *Flying Kestrel* - usually used to carry fresh water to the British fleet - for a tour of Scapa Flow.

The Orcadian reported: "The Stromness schoolchildren, on their return from their thrilling outing on Saturday, reported having witnessed a British officer shoot dead a German who persistently maintained a mutinous bearing."

There were other vivid eye witness accounts reported, both at the time and later. The proprietor and editor of *The Orcadian*, James Mackintosh, wrote in his newspaper of June 26, 1919: "A number of German sailors came alongside Houton pier early in the afternoon but were refused permission to land and directed to report to the flagship. I was told, though I was unable to obtain confirmation, that among these was the German Admiral who made an appeal for assistance to save his men.

"Strong patrols of Royal Marines were landed from the battle fleet shortly after five o'clock, and these took up positions along the beach presumably to deal with any of the German seamen who may have swum ashore. As I left Houton, my attention was directed to a mooring buoy some short distance off the Houton shore to which I could clearly see a man clinging. I was told that he had been observed swimming from the direction of a sinking warship."

A week later, *The Orcadian* reported the eye witness account of marine artist B. F. Gribble, who had been sketching some of the German ships from the patrol trawler *Sochosin* when the former flagship *Friedrich der Grosse* began to sink and the cruiser *Frankfurt*, her decks awash, began to list and drift ashore.

He said, that the German crewmen, taking to their lifeboats, were ordered back to their floundering ship - and shots were fired at them when they failed to obey the order. Germans were seen to wave white flags, he said, and a German officer cried out: "You have killed four of my men and we have no arms. I want to look after the men. It's not our fault. We are carrying out orders."

Gribble added: "Although the Germans declared that they had no arms I have good reason to believe that automatic pistols were found in the possession of some of the officers. While our rifle fire was proceeding there was a good deal of crossfire which lasted for, I should think, three quarters of an hour, and it is impossible to say whether the Germans actually did use firearms, but probably some shots did come from the Germans. Their intention evidently was to keep out to sea as long as they could in order to give their vessels time to sink."

Although reports were unconfirmed, *The Orcadian* added: "It seems certain that machine guns were freely used; and a destroyer is said to have run down a group of boats or a raft containing a large number of men who were endeavouring to make their escape."

Another unconfirmed report included: "A member of a drifter's crew alleges that a German officer who presumably either refused to sanction the action taken by his crew, or was roundly hated by them, was strung up at the mast and went down thus with his ship."

The Orcadian reports of the schoolchildren's trip through the Flow included the claim that "Germans were seen in small boats stabbing each other, and the German officers were frequently observed to be using their revolvers against their men." There was an account of a German surgeon laying dead with stab wounds in his back, and a suggestion that Admiral von Reuter had asked for protection against his own men.

Two of those on the *Flying Kestrel* trip that day were later to tell BBC documentaries of seeing and hearing men being shot. "Men were in boats and I definitely saw one man shot. He dropped right out of the stern of the boat. The other men were standing with their hands up," said Mrs Rosetta Groundwater in one interview.

Another, later to be a prominent Orkney councillor, J.R.T. Robertson, recalled: "We saw what appeared to be hundreds of men on the surface swimming and as we got further away we heard small arms fire - machine guns and heavier guns too."

The Orcadian later recorded the recollections of retired Kirkwall schoolteacher Mrs Peggy Gibson - who had been aged ten when she joined the day out in the *Flying Kestrel*, expecting to see the British fleet, as well as the Germans. "However we were told they had gone to sea on exercise earlier that morning. But we were not disappointed - we were going to see the Germans," she said.

"We went out of Stromness and across the Flow. The first time we knew anything about the scuttling was as we were sailing through an avenue of destroyers all in rows, two and two. And then a trawler came towards us and a man on board using a megaphone shouted: "Turn back! The German fleet are sinking!" But the captain thought it would have been stupid to turn back when so many ships were sinking. And I saw the light on the Admiral ship - that was the signal for the flags to go up, so they all sank with flags flying."

She recalled that they had headed towards HMS *Victorious*, being used as a hospital ship. "During that time we watched the marvellous display as the German ships sank all around us. I counted them, 12 capital ships going down. Some went up by the bows, some by the stern, and some stood right up in the water. It really was a marvellous display.

"In a way it was a very sad sight to see all these men getting

The great scuttle of the German fleet. Here, crewmen from a German destroyer are pictured taking to the boats on June 21, 1919.
(Picture courtesy of Orkney Library photographic archive)

Destined for a watery grave. The German battle cruiser *Derfflinger* is seen just four minutes before sinking to the bottom of Scapa Flow.
(Picture courtesy of Orkney Library photographic archive)

into their boats; you really wondered what would happen to them. They had lost all their possessions. The whole thing was done in such a peaceful way. It was just the air escaping from the ships as they went down that caused the turbulence on the sea.

"And the German officers were in their boats - they were all in full uniform. I don't know how I knew that, but it impressed me that, although they were going down as a defeated fleet, they were going down in full uniform. We saw rafts with Germans on them in the water. There would be one with eight on it and one with two. And we saw them swimming ashore and scrambling up on to the islands. I don't know how anyone who saw it could forget it.

"Every pier in Stromness was crowded with people waiting to see this boat return with all the children on it. There was great rejoicing when we finally arrived back at the warehouse pier in the early evening, the 300 children plus teachers and crew."

More than one academic would later suggest that the British had tacitly connived in the great destruction - including the Orcadian professor George W. Scarth, of McGill University, Montreal, who suggested that the convenient absence of the British Battle Squadron during the fateful few hours was because the British did not want to distribute the German ships to other nations.

The battle squadron, led by Vice-Admiral Sir Sydney Fremantle, in the flagship *Revenge*, certainly returned from exercises at full speed as the message was received of the events back in Scapa Flow. They arrived back in the anchorage to find the scene of devastation and debris. Since their departure that very morning, 52 German ships had sunk.

At the bottom of Scapa Flow were 15 battleships and battle-cruisers - *Prinz Regent Luitpold, Kaiser, Kaiserin, König, König Albert, Friedrich der Grosse, Grosser Kurfurst, Kron Prinz Wilhelm, Markgraf, Bayern, Seydlitz, Moltke, Von der Tann, Derfflinger* and *Hindenburg*; five light cruisers - *Brummer, Bremse, Cöln, Dresden* and *Karlsruhe*; and 32 destroyers.

(The battleships *König, Kron Prinz Wilhelm* and *Markgraf* and the cruisers *Brummer, Cöln, Dresden* and *Karlsruhe* would remain in that final resting place for the remainder of the 20th century).

Just one of the giant battleships had failed to go down - the 28,000 ton *Baden* which was beached. Three cruisers were also saved - the *Nurnberg, Frankfurt* and, irony of ironies, the *Emden*, which had been the flagship of the mastermind of the whole operation, Vice Admiral Ludwig von Reuter. A total of 18 destroyers also remained above the water.

The Orcadian had to protest to the Admiral Commanding the Orkneys and Shetlands that the Naval authorities stopped reporters from transmitting their dispatches from Kirkwall post office, thus preventing the news reaching the Saturday after-noon editions of the London papers. The telegrams were finally allowed to be sent after a five hour delay.

Von Reuter was taken aboard the *Revenge* and formally surrendered. Through an interpreter, Vice-Admiral Fremantle told the defiant German officer: "Before I send you ashore as a prisoner of war I would like to express to you my indignation at the deed which you have perpetrated and which was that of a traitor violating the arrangements entered into by the Allies. The German fleet was, in a sense, more interned than actually imprisoned. The vessels were resting here as a sort of good-will from the German government until Peace had been signed. It is not the first occasion on which Germans have violated all the decent laws and rules of the seas. We have had on many occasions to regret the fact of having to fight a nation which takes no notice of civilised laws on the high seas." The *Daily Sketch* was more forthright, quoting Admiral Sir Percy Scott: "It serves us right for trusting the Huns."

A casualty list of nine Germans had died (or been killed) and another eight injured. An Admiralty statement confirmed the stark details of the day: "The German rear admiral and most of the Germans from the ships are in custody on board HM ships. Some boats from the ships refused to stop when ordered

The final plunge of the German battleship *Bayern* as the great ship is scuttled in Scapa Flow.
(Picture courtesy of Orkney Library photographic archive)

and were fired on, and a small number of Germans were killed and wounded." Just one British serviceman faced any charges over the deaths - a 20 year old sailor on the *Resolution* who was accused of murdering a German prisoner, Kuns Eversberg from the cruiser *Frankfurt*. However, in February, 1920, a verdict of not proven was returned in just 30 minutes by a jury at the High Court in Edinburgh. "There was considerable applause in court and the accused was heartily congratulated by his Naval friends," reported *The Orcadian*.

The 1,800 Germans who survived the day were immediately dispatched to Invergordon as prisoners of war, leaving their ships in their lonely, watery graveyard - a legacy for Orkney that they could have scarcely imagined nor intended.

In the last week of June, the British Admiralty announced: "Where they are sunk, they will rest and rust. There can be no question of salving them."

Of course, what governments say and what they mean are, invariably, totally different and, within weeks, some rescue efforts had begun with 15 German destroyers adjudged suffi-ciently seaworthy to be towed to Rosyth. Unfortunately it devel-oped into a comedy of errors of calamitous proportions. At the start of 1920, eight of the destroyers were towed South, even-tually reaching their destination, but, in a total shambles, another seven were caught in a storm in the Pentland Firth. One, in an attempt to tow it back into the shelter of the Flow, apparently sank off Flotta; another ran aground on Sanday - and the other five were lost forever in the waters of the Pentland Firth.

After that, the Admiralty decided that further salvage efforts should not be at public expense - and certainly not at the risk of public ridicule. The task was soon handed over to the expert-ise of men whose names would become bywords in skill and courage in 20th century Orkney.

The German High Seas Fleet would be salvaged in one of the greatest feats of engineering the world had ever known. Ludwig von Reuter died at the age of 75 at the start of 1944 but his legacy would see an industry grow up which would inject the equivalent of £100 millions into the Orkney economy at a time of world depression. Gratitude can be earned in curious ways.

Church burned down in parish feud

1920

A feud between squabbling factions in an Orkney parish led to "horror, indignation and disgust" as a local Church was burned down in a suspected fire bomb attack.

The Holm East United Free Church was gutted by fire in the early hours of Sunday, February 29, 1920. Only the bare walls of the building, erected in 1814, were left standing.

It was the final outrage after a series of malicious acts perpetrated at the kirk and an arson attack was immediately suspected after the discovery of paraffin oil flasks inside the debris.

It was thought the culprit, or culprits, had entered by one of the windows alongside the pulpit. "The police are hopeful that they will be in a position to make one or more arrests in a day or two," said *The Orcadian*.

The news had created "a great sensation" in Kirkwall and large numbers of people visited the scene.

But police hopes of a quick solution to the case were dashed as a story unfolded of feuding acrimony stretching back years.

In the 19th century, there had been separate United Free Church parishes for Holm East and Holm West. However, the real troubles began in 1913 when the parishes were united. At first, services alternated between the two kirks but then it was decided by the Presbytery that the West Church alone would be used. After a dispute, this decision was reversed and it was declared that the East Church would be the sole place of worship.

"Feeling in the district has run high and windows of the East Church have been smashed on more than one occasion," said *The Orcadian*. The suspicion was that the East Church had been deliberately burned down by supporters of the campaign to restore services at the West Kirk.

Rev A.B. Taylor, Moderator of the Orkney United Free Church Presbytery, said: "We have been familiar for some time with the fact that a section of the Holm congregation, considerable in number, has been openly defying the instructions of the Presbytery.

"This, no matter by whom it was done, is rebellion. I have never heard of such a thing being done before in all the history of our church.

"It is an old, old feud and I fear the spirit of the feud has been handed down from one generation to another.

"If this destruction of the East Church in Holm has been the act of a person or persons connected with the West Church party, it is to be hoped that party, or at least the majority of them, will dissociate themselves from what has been done."

Rev A.P. Bathgate - a luckless newcomer to Orkney who had arrived in the county to be told by the Presbytery that he had been elected interim moderator for the warring parish - said the burning down of the kirk had caused "horror, indignation and disgust throughout Orkney."

Orkney Presbytery referred the dispute to the Kirk's General Assembly and a special committee of inquiry was set up under the chairmanship of Dr Robert Forgan of Aberdeen. In the meantime, services were held at the Drill Hall of Holm's wartime battery.

In November, 1920, Dr Forgan reported: "The grave allegation of incendiarism has not been proved and we have reason to believe that the authorities of the Crown have decided not to institute a prosecution."

This statement merely fanned the flames of the feud with a Holm elder, Mr Hepburn, contending that the authorities had ample proof.

Dr Forgan's committee of inquiry eventually recommended that services should be held at the West Church in Holm and called on parishioners to "put away all incriminations and recriminations" and to exercise the judgment of charity.

Such hopes were futile. Within a month - in July, 1921 - a petition from Holm called for a dissolution of the union between the East and West Kirks. "Though the culprit was never discovered, no reasonable person has any shadow of doubt that the destruction of the church was an act of incendiarism," stated the petition, signed by 119 members of the congregation who were now holding their services in the local school.

In August, 1924, four and a half years after being destroyed by fire, the Holm East UF Church was re-opened after being rebuilt at a cost of £1,700 with free labour provided by parishioners. With seating for 300, it was "now one of the most handsome churches in the county," reported *The Orcadian*.

A year of tragedy in Orkney waters

Three separate tragedies in and around the waters of Scapa Flow saw the loss of ten lives - five Orcadians and five Naval sailors - in boating disasters during the year of 1920.

The first, in March, 1920, saw the deaths of William Wooldrage, of Weddell, Burray, Andrew Sutherland of Warebanks, Burray, and 16 year old Annie Robson of Redbanks, Hunda, as their boat capsized as they crossed Kirk Sound from Burray to Holm.

Blockships, which had been placed in the channels during World War One, were blamed for changing the currents in the area.

However two men survived - William Budge (25) of Mosshouse, Burray, and Edward Ritch of Diamonds, Deerness - and Budge was acclaimed as a hero. He only had the use of one arm after a war injury but he managed to drag himself and Ritch on to the sunken blockship *Palerna*, from where they were rescued.

There was no such salvation three months later when five sailors, belonging to HMS *Lucia*, perished off Orakirk, Orphir, when they were caught in a squall making for Stromness in a small boat.

And, in November, 1920, Robert Johnston and his son, of Greenhill, Hoy, were both drowned when their boat was swamped in a storm which washed away part of the road at Scapa and damaged Scapa Pier.

Highway robbery

The first case of "highway robbery" reported by *The Orcadian* was in August, 1920, when Mr Robert Clouston, The Castle, Outertown, Stromness, was set upon, beaten and robbed of £8. A Stromness man was arrested and sentenced to 12 months hard labour.

An era of prohibition

The people of Orkney went to the polls and ushered in an era of prohibition which, in Stromness, would remain in force for the next 27 years.

The Temperance (Scotland) Act of 1913 allowed burghs and parishes to vote on whether they wanted to ban drinks licences.

Most of the major cities in the South - Glasgow, Aberdeen, Inverness and Perth included - had rejected prohibition, but, in the North, Wick and Lerwick went "dry" by a big margin of votes.

Their example was supported in Stromness where the population voted: No change 183, No licence 286. It meant that no certificate for the sale of liquor would be granted for inns or hotels except in "special cases."

The Stromness result caused "a great sensation" when news was received in Kirkwall, said *The Orcadian*.

Orkney United Free Church Presbytery congratulated the people of Stromness and expressed the hope that voters elsewhere would follow their example. Rev R.W. Haggie said Stromness had given a shining example which should be reflected in other areas.

The Church urged "our faithful people to exercise their new found liberty and seek to secure the fullest benefit from the Act by voting 'no licence'."

The Rev A.B. Taylor, minister of the Paterson Kirk in Kirkwall, addressed a "no licence" campaign meeting at Kirkwall Town Hall and claimed that, in 1919, the country had spent £386 millions on drink. "We are face to face with a crisis affecting the highest well-being of our town. We are seeking to get rid of what is unquestionably a great evil. The drinking customs of our country are a national calamity, a gigantic evil."

The lobby for the continuation of drinks licences for public bars warned that prohibition would lead to "night clubs" and secret drinking. The Temperance Act, they argued, favoured the wealthy who could still stock their cellars from wholesale merchants. It was not a campaign to reform drink laws, it was a campaign to reform the working classes.

Seventy per cent of those qualified turned out to vote in the temperance poll in Kirkwall, and the result was: No change 629, No licence 672.

However, the majority of 43 was not big enough to see Kirkwall go dry. (The Act said that 55 per cent of the vote was needed for the resolution to succeed). Instead, it would mean a limiting of licences in Kirkwall with the number of drinks certificates in the town reduced by a quarter. The result was that the Imperial Hotel in Albert Street and the Queen's Hotel at Kirkwall waterfront both had their licences withdrawn. The Queen's had held a licence for 120 years.

The parishes of Evie and Rendall and Holm both voted to go dry while the parishes of Walls and Flotta and Westray both voted to carry on drinking.

In 1923, Stromness voted to remain dry (in fact, it would be 1947 before prohibition would be overturned there) while Kirkwall voted to continue the limitation of licences.

A national review of the impact of the various temperance bans was published in 1923.

In Orkney the Superintendent of Police reported a "complete absence from crime of any kind. Benefits derived in Orkney cannot be over-estimated."

In Stromness, Rev William Muirhead reported: "Streets quieter and more respectable. Soakers now living soberly and their homes comfortable. Social functions are nicer. Shopkeepers have not so many bad debts. The new system is bearing good fruit, which is not only my testimony but also that of our local police. It has removed a great deal of temptation from our young men."

In 1926, Kirkwall, in fact, voted to further limit the number of licences in the town. The certificate of the Castle Hotel and the off-licence of John Slater in Bridge Street, Kirkwall, were both withdrawn. It meant that the town, by 1927, had only two hotels with public bars - the Kirkwall and the St Ola - and two off licences.

Epidemic precautions

An epidemic of scarlet fever in 1920 saw the former wartime Scapa seaplane station acquired as a hospital for infectious diseases. It had 30 patients - and one nurse.

A hut at Carness was also rented from the Admiralty as a precautionary small-pox hospital as an epidemic of the disease threatened in Glasgow.

Two years later, Orkney County Council paid £400 for the former Scapa seaplane station building to be converted into the county's tuberculosis hospital.

First woman JP

Miss Alice Walker of Dundas Crescent, Kirkwall, was in the first list of women JPs to be appointed in Scotland in July, 1920, following the change in the law to allow female justices. She was a member of Kirkwall parish council and Kirkwall school management committee.

Bread prices rise

With the abolition of wartime price controls on bread, the price of a 4lb loaf in Kirkwall rose to 1s 6d - at a time when Orkney farm workers were earning as little as 25s a week.

The final whistle

A football match between RAF Houton and Kirkwall Britannia had to be abandoned with the airmen leading 3-0. The ball had been kicked in the sea - and floated away!

Kirkwall doctor celebrates century

Special presentations were held to mark the 100th birthday of Dr James Logie, born in May, 1820, the son of Rev William Logie, minister of Lady, Sanday, and later St Magnus Cathedral.

He had studied at Edinburgh University, becoming a licentiate of the Royal College of Surgeons in 1841 at the age of 21. He worked as a doctor in Newcastle and Carlisle before returning to Kirkwall in 1845 and setting up a practice covering the whole county. At that time there were only two doctors outwith Kirkwall - one in Stromness and one in Sanday.

Dr Logie became an elder of St Magnus Cathedral in 1855 - a position he held for 65 years. Eventually, in old age, he handed over his medical practice to his partner Dr Benjamin Bell who died in 1915, when the practice was sold to Dr William Park.

Dr Logie received a telegram of congratulations on his 100th birthday from King George V but, sadly, could enjoy his century for only two months before dying in July, 1920.

Scout's honour for Antarctic trip

One of the world's great explorers of the 20th century, Sir Ernest Shackleton, set off on a major expedition to the Antarctic in 1921 - accompanied by a 16 year old Kirkwall boy scout.

Shackleton had offered to take a boy scout on the trip to serve as cabin boy. Hundreds volunteered and a short list of ten was drawn up to be interviewed by Shackleton in London.

Shackleton, unable to decide on just one boy, selected two - an Aberdeen patrol leader J.W.F. Marr and Patrol Leader Norman Erland Mooney, a member of the 2nd Orkney Troop of Boy Scouts, whose home was in Cromwell Road, Kirkwall.

News of Mooney's selection preceded his return home. After his arrival at Scapa, he was carried shoulder high by fellow scouts to Broad Street to be welcomed by a large crowd. He received telegrams of congratulations from the Prince of Wales and Sir Robert Baden-Powell, the Chief Scout.

Shackleton was no stranger to Orkney. Following his 1914-16 expedition to the Antarctic, he visited Kirkwall en route to Archangel for service with the British forces operating on the River Dwina in World War One. Commander F.A. Worsley - who accompanied Shackleton on the 1914-16 voyage and who was to be navigator on the 1921-22 expedition - gave a lecture on the mission to the people of Kirkwall in April, 1921.

In September, 1921, Mooney left to join

1921

Shackleton's ship *Quest* which would sail, in the first instance, to Cape Town via Madeira. The *Quest* left London Bridge on September 17, 1921, cheered by a crowd of thousands.

Unfortunately, Mooney's chapter in history was to be wrecked by the sea conditions of the Bay of Biscay.

Shackleton reported: "I regret that Scout Mooney has been continuously sea sick, but he is always willing. I am taking him as far as Madeira, hoping that he will enjoy better health. But doctors consider he is not strong enough for the whole voyage."

A week later, Shackleton reported from Funchal that he was sending home Mooney and the camera operator J.C.B. Mason. "Both are unable to stand the continuous pitching and rolling," he said. They arrived back in Southampton on the liner *Avon* on October 22, 1921.

In a farewell letter to the two, Shackleton said that the doctors had warned "it would be endangering your life to allow you to continue further, however much you desire to do so, especially as later on, we may expect even worse weather. I have watched your

endeavours to carry out your duties despite your continual sickness and have nothing but praise for what you have done."

Mooney - who had anticipated being away for up to two years - was back in Orkney within two months. It was not only his last Antarctic expedition, it also proved to be the final voyage of Sir Ernest Shackleton. The pioneering explorer died and was buried in South Georgia - his coffin at the funeral on March 5, 1922, being carried by six Shetlanders from the whaling station there.

Norman Mooney did not live to old age either. He died in 1946, at the comparatively young age of 42, working in Nigeria where he was employed as a government surveyor on a road building project.

One man who completed the 1921-22 Antarctic expedition did return to Orkney - Commander F.A. Worsley, who had been chief navigator of the *Quest* in the south polar regions.

Unfortunately his return to Orkney was less than auspicious. In 1924, he was master of the four masted schooner *Kathleen Annie* which was wrecked off Eday. The vessel was en route from Bremen to Newfoundland with 17,000 cases of spirits. Fortunately, Worsley and his eleven crewmen were all able to clamber to safety on the Muckle Green Holm, and his cargo was later salvaged and transferred to another ship to be returned to Bremen.

Bank fraud brings financial ruin

Hundreds of Orkney investors faced financial ruin as they lost their deposits in the collapse of a bank.

Farrow's Bank Ltd had opened a branch in Junction Road, Kirkwall, only months before its collapse, offering interest rates of up to five per cent. The bank, established in 1904, had 75 branches throughout Britain, and its deposits in Scotland alone were said to total £8 millions.

But Orkney customers arriving at the local branch on Christmas eve, 1920, were met by a notice - presumably intended for members of staff - saying: "Suspend payment. Do not open bank."

It was estimated that Orkney depositors were affected to the extent of "fully £60,000." A petition of compulsory liquidation was being sought, and officials from the Official Receiver's office were taking charge of the documents at the various branches, said *The Orcadian*.

In the House of Commons, it was admitted that "widespread hardship" would be caused but the Government refused a request, from the new Orkney and Shetland MP Sir Malcolm Smith, to

recompense investors who had lost out. The Government blamed the collapse of the bank on "losses in trading and errors in management extending over a series of years."

In fact, it soon became apparent that investors had been hoodwinked by false accounting by the bank.

In June, 1921, the bank's founder, Thomas Farrow - a "noted philanthropic

and religious worker" - and bank director Walter Crotch were sentenced to four years penal servitude for conspiracy and fraud. The bank's auditor was also jailed for a year after a trial at London's Old Bailey. Farrow was to be released from Parkhurst Prison after serving three years, and, eventually, by 1925, investors managed to recoup a total of 5/3 in the pound from their lost deposits.

Great expectations fall flat

Blacksmith Peter Taylor, of Buttquoy Place, Kirkwall, was waiting to discover whether he would inherit part of what was said to be a £5 million fortune, in 1921, stowed in four mysterious chests in a museum in Haarlem, Holland.

They had been left there since the death of a man called Pieter Tayler van der Hulst. He had apparently gone to Holland from Stirling in 1709 as plain Peter Taylor but, after changing his name, had amassed a fortune in Britain, America, France and Holland.

He was related to Andrew Taylor, who was the great, great grandfather of the Kirkwall blacksmith Peter Taylor.

According to reports, the wealthy ancestor had left the four chests in the museum strongroom with a request that they be opened 100 years after his death and the contents distributed to his nearest kin.

Unfortunately, the story had no romantic, nor financially rewarding, conclusion. In 1925, the Supreme Court in The Hague rejected any claim by descendants to any fortune, real or imagined.

Eclipse silences the birds

The partial eclipse of the sun on Friday, April 8, 1921, was "seen in Kirkwall to excellent advantage."

The Orcadian reported: "Between 9.30 and 10am, the middle of the eclipse occurred, when the state of semi darkness, which had gradually been reached, gave the landscape a peculiar aspect. The sky had taken on a dull greying tinge and the shadows became rugged, while the atmosphere became decidedly chilly.

"The change from bright sunshine to twilight had a remarkable effect upon poultry, some of which went to roost."

An Orkney film

The Lunatic at Large, a book by Orkney writer Joseph Storer Clouston, later to become county convener, was made into a film - the first Orkney book to be filmed. "It was really funny. And good British fun too," said the reviewer of the *Daily Mail*.

Birth of the Legion

Kirkwall ex-servicemen agreed to amalgamate their organisation, the Comrades of the Great War, with the Scottish Federation of Discharged Ex-Servicemen and Officers Association under the name of the British Legion. Kirkwall's first British Legion club premises were opened in West Castle Street.

Icebergs warning

A warning notice was posted at Kirkwall harbour office in September, 1921, when two icebergs were reported as far south as the same latitude as Orkney, but 200 miles to the west.

Freedom of Kirkwall

James Johnston, of Coubister, Orphir, the Orkney County Council convener, was presented with the freedom of the burgh of Kirkwall in 1922.

He had been a member of the county council since its formation in 1889, and became vice-convener in 1904 before becoming convener. At the ceremony, he recalled that he had been in Kirkwall's Paterson Kirk when the freedom of the burgh had been bestowed on the former British Prime Minister Mr W.E. Gladstone and the Poet Laureate Lord Tennyson in 1883.

Bridge plunge

Mr Herbert Bichan, a son of the Bichan family of Redbanks, Tankerness, died when he fell 110 feet during construction work on the Dennison Harvard Bridge in Cleveland, USA. He had been married just a week.

Orkney Golf Club members extended their course to 18 holes in 1922 but these barefoot boys had to practise their golfing skills in the street.
(Picture courtesy of Orkney Library photographic archive)

Sad departure

There's no fortunate way to be shot dead - but the death of luckless Orcadian John Isbister seemed particularly unfortunate.

He lost his life during the troubles of 1922 in Johannesburg, South Africa. Whilst cycling, he was ordered by police and soldiers at a checkpoint to stop. Paying no attention, and continuing to cycle past, he was shot dead.

"Sad to relate, later inquiry showed that he suffered from deafness," said *The Orcadian*.

Return home

The Earl of Ronaldshay - who, as heir to the Earl of Zetland, still owned estate properties in Orkney - left India in 1922 to return to Britain after five years as Governor of Bengal. "Cheering crowds lined the route, the demonstration being a remarkably popular tribute to the recent Governorship," said *The Orcadian*.

* * *

Orkney Golf Club rented part of Muddiesdale Farm, Kirkwall, in 1922 to extend the Kirkwall golf course to 18 holes.

Stromness soon followed suit with a new home and the official opening of the 18 hole course at Ness, Stromness, was performed by a Harley Street physician Dr McNeish, a regular visitor to the county, on Thursday, July 30, 1925.

Falling population

The 1921 census showed the population of Orkney at 24,109 - 1,788 or 6.9 per cent less than in 1911 - of which 11,454 were males and 12,655 females.

Even the two burghs had shown a fall in population - Kirkwall from 3,810 to 3,697, and Stromness from 1,770 to 1,665.

Museum director

Dr Charles Anderson, youngest son of John Anderson, of Moa, Stenness, was appointed Director of the Australian Museum in February, 1921.

* * *

Rev James Irvine, a native of Sandwick, celebrated 50 years as a minister in South Ronaldsay where St Peter's Kirk had the second biggest congregation of the Established Church in Orkney, after St Magnus Cathedral.

* * *

A Government-appointed commission recommended that Kirkwall Prison be closed - although the cells would remain licensed to hold prisoners for up to 14 days. In fact, it stayed open until 1954.

* * *

Veteran music hall star and comedian Charles Coborn walked from London to John o' Groats - and then crossed to Orkney where he gave a performance at the Kirkwall picture house.

Nine perish in New Year trawler tragedy

"Never did Stromness lifeboat men acquit themselves better than they did on New Year's Day, battling against the fiercest of elements for nine long hours in a bleak winter's day. Covering over 50 miles of the worst sea in Britain, they covered themselves with honour," said *The Orcadian.*

The lifeboat, under coxswain William Johnston, was launched to assist the Grimsby trawler *Freesia,* which sank opposite Midhouse in Evie, with nine of her 11 crew perishing.

The *Freesia* was returning home from the Faroes with 500 boxes of fish when she struck rocks and was holed. The ship's boat was lowered but smashed. The skipper organised the building of a makeshift raft which nine crewmen climbed aboard while two other crewmen, the mate William Saxby and third hand Albert Dartnell, the eventual survivors, leapt into the water, sharing a lifebelt.

"When we came to the surface, we saw the raft but there was no one on it and the ship was gone. We struck out for the raft and got on it," said the mate. They

1922

saw three other crewmen in the water but, before they could help, the sea engulfed them.

On shore, the two men were spotted clinging to the raft and the people of Evie were called from kirk to launch two yawls to attempt a rescue. Two boats from Rousay also crossed Eynhallow Sound to help.

However, the lifeboat eventually rescued the two men from their makeshift raft after they had been in the water for three and a half hours. They were transferred to the Rousay mail boat and landed at Evie.

Curiously, the mate did not know the name of his late trawler skipper - he had always been known to the crew simply as "Faroe Tom."

The disaster led to calls for a Kitchener Memorial Lighthouse to be erected at Birsay to prevent similar disasters.

The *Freesia* was the second trawler in a month to hit the rocks in Birsay. A month earlier, one man died, and another nine crewmen were rescued by the Stromness lifeboat, when the Aberdeen fishing boat *Keith Hall* went aground.

The skipper William King afterwards complained that the crew's possessions had been looted from the wreck of the *Keith Hall,* and Orkney's reputation for hospitality was tarnished in February, 1922, when ten men of the West Mainland appeared in court accused of stealing from the stranded vessel. They received fines of up to £3/10/- or 18 days imprisonment. The defence argued that it was a local custom to go aboard wrecks to take away souvenirs.

There was better news in September, 1922, when the crews of two Aberdeen trawlers, *Cornet* and *Phyllis Belman,* were all saved after running aground in the North Isles. The Stromness lifeboat, in the rescue of the crew of the *Cornet,* covered a total of 120 miles - a record distance covered by a lifeboat in Britain at the time.

Big names in Orkney

The top 32 most common surnames in Orkney in 1922 were, in the following order: Sinclair (208 households of that name were recorded in the census), Flett (115), Rendall (111), Johnston (110), Spence (107), Thomson (101), Sutherland (99), Muir (89), Drever (84), Tulloch (78), Miller (75), Smith (69), Shearer (68), Mowat (64), Harcus (61), Linklater (61), Taylor (60), Craigie (55), Clouston (53), Foubister(53), Wilson (52), Mackay / McKay (45), Moar (44), Harvey (43), Ritch (42), Corrigall (41), Swanney (39), Isbister(39), Baikie (34), Tait (31), Wylie (28), and Laird (28).

Cold comfort

The building of a 70 mile railway line over the Florida Keys in the USA was blamed by weather expert John Harrison, of the Clapham Observatory, for diverting the flow of the Gulf Stream across the Atlantic Ocean.

Now, instead of going north of Ireland to Orkney, the Gulf Stream appeared to go south of Ireland into the English and Bristol channels. This explained phenomenally low winter temperatures which had been experienced in the Northern Isles in recent years, he claimed.

Pauper's death for aristocrat

A man believed to be the Honorable Alexander Edward Fitzmaurice, the younger brother of the Earl of Orkney, died in poverty, aged 48, in lodgings in Brighton.

He had gone to the south coast resort in 1904 and was a prominent and wealthy figure in the town - a member not only of Brighton Union Club but also several leading London clubs.

But practically all his capital was invested in Russian stocks and this was lost when the Bolsheviks seized power in Moscow, said *The Orcadian.*

Fitzmaurice had relinquished his flat in prestigious Oriental Place and took rooms, under the name of Maurice, in Albert Road, Brighton, where he died a pauper.

Mrs Amelia Purser, his landlady, said: "He always seemed to be living with the ghosts of a past affluence. He would sometimes say: 'I was somebody once.'" He once told her: "When I lost my money, I lost my friends."

She could only recall him ever having two visitors - a man and a wife who bore a Russian name.

The modern title of Earl of Orkney had no connection with the ancient Orkney earls of Norse times, but was revived in 1696 when Lord George Hamilton, the fifth son of William, Duke of Hamilton, was created Earl of Orkney by William III. The first Lord Orkney had two claims to fame - he later became the first man to hold the rank of Field Marshal in the British services, and he also married Elizabeth Villiers, the mistress of William III.

The modern earls of Orkney had no links with the county at all, nor indeed, since 1864, when the 5th Earl of Orkney sold Glenapp in Ayrshire, had they any residence in Scotland.

The title passed through the female lineage, to the Fitzmaurice family and the Earl of Orkney in 1922 could claim little more status than the fact that he was chairman of the parish council at Stewkley, Buckinghamshire.

Orkney welcomes all mod cons

1923

Orkney took a giant leap forward to embrace the new technology of the 20th century in the early 1920s. A period of just two years saw the arrival in Kirkwall of mains electricity, public telephones, radio broadcasting and a publicly-owned mains gas system.

The rate of progress was rapid. In May, 1922, Orkney was the only county in Scotland not to have a telephone service, and the county council called on the Post Office authorities to install one! It was to be officially opened just 15 months later.

Also, in May, 1922, Kirkwall Town Council revealed plans for a burgh electricity scheme with a generating station to be built on the corner of St Magnus Lane and Junction Road. That scheme was up and running just 20 months later.

Kirkwall had enjoyed a gas supply for nearly a century but, in 1923, that too came under public ownership as Kirkwall Town Council agreed to pay £5,500 to take over the privately-owned Kirkwall Gas Company which was founded in 1838.

The first telephone installed at *The Orcadian* offices in September, 1922, provided a private link between Kirkwall and the newspaper's correspondent in Stromness.

A week later, however, the district manager for telephone services in Aberdeen, announced that telephone exchanges were to be built at Kirkwall and Stromness, and public call offices in various parts of the islands. Submarine telephone cables would connect Orkney to the North of Scotland.

By October, 1922, over 50 subscribers had been secured for the new phone system in Kirkwall and Stromness, which would ensure a 24 hour service, Sundays included.

Kirkwall telephone exchange was opened on Thursday, September 20, 1923. Provost John White made the first call to his counterpart in Thurso. The telephone switchboard was wired for 80 subscribers but had a total capacity for 120. At this stage, Thurso and Wick was as far away as could be telephoned because Kirkwall was not yet linked with the telephone trunk line to Tain.

The Kirkwall telephone exchange was operated by sisters Rachel and Robina Gunn and, in those early days, subscribers used to collect to give them an annual Christmas present.

The Stromness exchange opened on Monday, October 8, 1923, with a call to Kirkwall, and it was announced that agreement had been reached for public call boxes at the post offices at Holm, Burray, St Margaret's Hope, Shapinsay, Stenness and Sandwick.

By 1925, the Northern Lighthouse Board at Stromness was linked up by wireless telephone to the lighthouses as far away as the Flannan Isles and the Butt of Lewis.

Also in 1923, Kirkwall Town Council agreed it was time to bring the burgh's gas supply into the 20th century. The plant to produce coal gas had been built, and the gas mains laid, in 1838 at a total cost of £1,487 10s. In those early days, the gas was used almost solely for lighting purposes.

Now in 1923, the gas company works manager Mr Thomas Gourlay and his directors recognised that the future success of the company lay in popularising their product for commercial and household purposes, as well as lighting, said *The Orcadian*.

By November 27, 1923 - the date Kirkwall Town Council took over the gas company - the annual production of gas had increased to over eight million cubic feet. Modernisation plans were also underway in Stromness where the town council planned to erect a new gasometer which had been purchased for £75 from the Admiralty at Houton.

But a new rival to gas power was about to arrive in Orkney - mains electricity.

There had been private generator-driven electrical schemes in the county for more than 20 years. Electric light was first introduced in Orkney in 1901 by John Mackay at his Stromness Hotel, which was then under construction, followed by Highland Park Distillery and then Kirkwall merchant Robert Garden in 1911. W.R. Tullock and the Electric Theatre picture house soon followed.

And, of course, World War One had seen the Admiralty invest large sums of money to introduce electrical power at the military bases at Houton and Lyness. It was much of this generating equipment purchased from the Admiralty which was to power Kirkwall's new public electricity scheme.

Kirkwall Town Council agreed to borrow £10,000 to finance the scheme, and, in May, 1923, the Kirkwall Electricity Order was approved in the House of Commons. It was agreed that the street lights would switch from gas to electricity, and Mr J.R. Wilson, of 19 East Road, Kirkwall, was the first resident of the burgh to specially wire his house for the introduction of mains electricity.

(They were obviously expansionist times - Kirkwall Town Council also agreed to borrow £60,000 to finance the building of 44 new homes at the Carter's Park housing scheme in 1923.)

The new electricity scheme opened on February 15,1924, with William Roy as manager and Robert Walls his assistant. In the first instance, power was only available in an area of Junction Road, Broad Street, Albert Street, Bridge Street, Kirkwall Pier and Harbour Street - and the first electric lights to be illuminated were those at Kirkwall Pier. More than 200 consumers had signed up to take electricity from the scheme and, within six months, the mains cables had been extended as far as Berstane Road. Kirkwall's scheme was the most northerly public electricity supply in the country and the cost per unit - varying between 4d and 9d a unit - was 30 per cent cheaper than the other public supplies in the north of Scotland, said engineer Mr James Liddle, the man who oversaw the installation of the scheme.

A few weeks later, Orkney had its first chance to see a new world of consumer goods as an exhibition of electrical products at the Kirkwall power station introduced local housewives to an array of vacuum cleaners, radio sets and other household "essentials."

The growth of Kirkwall electricity department was illustrated by the increase in the number of units generated over the first five years - from 3,108 units in 1923-24 to 131,353 units in 1927-28. When Mr William Roy resigned as manager of the Kirkwall scheme in 1928 to take up a similar job in Wick, the town clerk was instructed to advertise for a successor at £208 a year.

Although, mains electricity was confined to Kirkwall and St Ola for the next 20 years, this did not prevent innovative Orcadians from enjoying the benefits of electricity. Mr Sinclair Mowat and Mr Norman Mowat, of Slack, Hoy, built their own hydro electric generating plant at the Braebuster burn, where a water turbine engine was connected by 600 yards of underground cable to the house and farm buildings.

The years 1923-24 also saw the arrival of the first mass market wireless receivers in the county, enabling Orcadians to tune into radio broadcasts from around the world. Often, a wireless set would be purchased by a community, allowing people to attend what were called "listening in" concerts. Kirkwall's British Legion Club installed its first radio set in February, 1924, allowing nearly 50 members to be entertained by "a varied programme from practically all the British broadcasting stations, and the School of Arts, Paris."

The staff of Kirkwall's St Ola Hotel prepare for a function at the hotel in the 1920s.   (Picture courtesy of Orkney Library photographic archive)

Disaster strikes the merchant fleet

More than 20 lives were lost - despite the heroic efforts of the men of the Stromness and Longhope lifeboats - in a year of tragedy for merchant shipping vessels in Orkney waters. The year of 1923 would end with the Longhope lifeboat crew honoured by both the Royal Navy and the King of Sweden - but it began with fears, fortunately unfounded, that the Stromness lifeboat had been lost.

The Stromness lifeboat was "missing" for 12 hours after answering a distress call to the Kirkwall steamer *Cormorant*. Battling against a gale for hours, the engine's petrol supply gave out, and the lifeboat drifted off Orkney's west coast throughout the night until taken in tow by the Findochty drifter *Lizzie Birrell* and taken back to Stromness.

The Orcadian was lavish in its praise for the lifeboatmen. "Never had they had more trying experiences under such terrible conditions. In doing their utmost to save life, these men risked their all. Orcadians all over the world will learn of their deeds with a glow of pride."

The *Tamara XII* of Hamburg, en route to her home port from Leith, was lost off Orkney, with all hands, and the only clues were the wreckage washed up after an easterly gale hit the islands. One of the ship's boats, with the body of a young

seaman, was washed up in Sanday.

Also lost was the ss *Valur*, belonging to a Hull company, which foundered off Orkney en route from Shetland to Liverpool.

Eight crewmen were saved by the Aberdeen trawler *Star of the Realm* and landed at Longhope, but the master, Captain Arthur Wigglesworth, and mate, Frank Miller, both drowned.

To complete a grim few weeks, the Grimsby fishing boat *Aralia* called into Stromness after three of her crew had been washed overboard to their deaths off Iceland.

But it was to be another cargo steamer tragedy which would see the men of the Longhope lifeboat praised as heroes around the world.

In September, 1923, the Swedish steamer *Citos* - on a voyage from the Baltic with a cargo of wood - lost her propeller in the Pentland Firth and, drifting dangerously towards rocks, 15 of the crew took to the ship's boat. Six of those men drowned but nine were rescued by HMS *Vivacious* which landed the survivors at Kirkwall.

Another eight men, who had stayed on board the *Citos*, were saved by the Longhope lifeboat, *Annie Miles*, under the command of second coxswain William Mowat, and landed at St Mary's

village. It was a rescue of such epic proportions that the lifeboat crew were given a special presentation of £50 by Rear Admiral George H. Baird as a mark of the admiration of the officers and men of the British Fleet who witnessed the operation.

A greater honour followed the following year when, at a ceremony in Kirkwall, silver cups were presented, on behalf of the King of Sweden, to the Longhope crew who took part in the rescue - William Mowat, T. Gunn, Alex Johnston, Fred Johnston, George Johnston senior and junior, D. Mackay, Wilson Nicolson, S. Mowat, A. Barnett, J. Robertson and J. Stout.

The *Citos* incident was to have a sequel in the High Court for some other Orkney mariners. The crew of the Stromness-based lighthouse support ship *Pole Star* managed to save the drifting Swedish ship from the rocks and later towed it to the safety of Inganess Bay. They then claimed £6,000 in salvage reward from the Swedish owners. The crew eventually accepted an offer of £3,500 - but only after they had taken their claim to the Court of Session in Edinburgh where the judge, Lord Blackburn, said £800 was "not an inadequate reward." The crew also had to pay their own legal expenses for the court case.

Acclaim for Scotland football star

Scottish international Andy Wilson was acclaimed as the only Orcadian to achieve significant national success as a footballer in the early years of the 20th century.

And in 1923 he signed for Chelsea for a fee of £6,000.

He was born Andrew Beattie Wilson on October 28, 1895, a son of Sergeant Major Andrew Wilson and his wife Susan, of the Drill Cottage, Stronsay. Sergeant Major Wilson had been posted to the island six years earlier as instructor to the Stronsay company of the Orkney Volunteer Artillery.

He did not stay on the island long afterwards as the family are believed to have moved to Lanarkshire - which is where some of Wilson's former clubs actually claim he was born.

In fact, he started his career with Cambuslang Rangers but had just joined Middlesbrough when World War One broke out. He fought in the war - in which his left arm was shattered - but he battled back to fitness to play for Hearts and Dunfermline before returning to Middlesbrough in 1921 where he scored 31 goals in 32 games in a season to win a place as a regular Scottish international.

After his move to Chelsea in 1923, he spent eight years at Stamford Bridge before moving to West London neighbours Queen's Park Rangers and then spending two years with Nimes in France.

In October, 1934, he became manager of Walsall FC, in the English Midlands, and in his first season guided the club to fourth in Division Three South - the highest position Walsall had ever achieved at that time. He remained at Walsall until April, 1937, during which time he signed Bert Williams, the goalkeeper who eventually went on to play for Wolverhampton Wanderers and England.

Before the outbreak of World War Two, he returned to Chelsea in a coaching capacity - but, after the war, he achieved fame in another sport as an international bowls player. Andy Wilson died in 1973 at the age of 77.

Another Orkney player to sign for a professional club was Tommy Cooper, Kirkwall Rovers centre forward, who joined Raith Rovers in 1938 after leaving Orkney to take up studies at Heriot Watt College, Edinburgh. Cooper was only 16 when he made his inter-county debut against Shetland in 1933 and he had played for Orkney in every representative game until he left the county.

He had also received an offer from Scottish first division team Third Lanark, said *The Orcadian*. However, the outbreak of World War Two was to end aspirations of a professional football career.

Orcadian in medical breakthrough

The same year that David Hepburn, the headmaster of Stromness school, retired after 33 years service, his son, Dr John Hepburn received acclaim around the world for the part he played in one of the major advances in medical science in the 20th century.

Dr Hepburn completed his medical studies at Toronto University, where he played a supporting role in early research work on the treatment of diabetes with the discovery of Insulin.

Clinical trials by Professor John James Macleod, Sir Frederick Banting and Charles Best proved that an efficient remedy for diabetes had been found - and the three men shared the 1923 Nobel Prize for their achievement. Professor Macleod paid tribute, however, to the contribution made by Dr Hepburn in the research work.

Never too old

Barbara Peace, neé Wilson, born at Skaill, Sanday, on December 10, 1823, celebrated her 100th birthday at her home in Chester. She had decided to leave Sanday and move to England at the age of 90!

Hong Kong posting

Dr W.L. Paterson, who had served as a general practitioner in Rousay and Kirkwall, after being awarded the Military Cross for gallantry with the Royal Army Medical Corps in World War One, left Orkney in 1923 to take up the post of Medical Officer in Hong Kong.

Seven year old sent away

The harshness of the school truancy regulations of the day were illustrated in 1923 when a seven year old Westray boy, who in the previous year had 230 school attendances out of 399, was ordered by Sheriff Martin Laing to be sent away to an Industrial School Reformatory until he was 14.

Royal engagement

Orkney County Council sent a telegram of congratulations in February, 1923, to mark the engagement of the Duke of York (later to become King George VI) to Lady Elizabeth Bowes-Lyon (who, in August, 1999, celebrated her 99th birthday as the Queen Mother.)

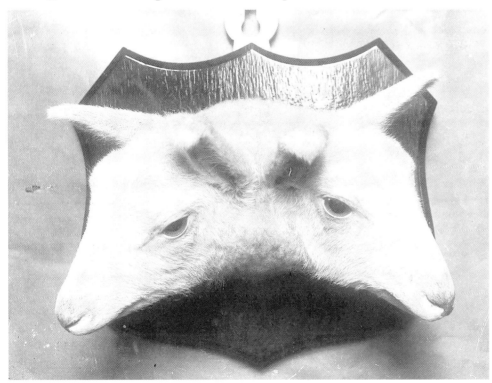

Two headed lamb

A two headed lamb was born at Winksetter, Harray, along with a normal lamb, delivered by veterinary surgeon Captain L.F. Eady. The lamb appeared to breath alternately from one head to the other. The lamb was destroyed and Captain Eady had the two heads stuffed and mounted. (Picture courtesy of Orkney Library photographic archive)

The land of a thousand lairds

One of the major reasons for Orkney's relative economic stability - and the development of the county's agricultural industry - throughout the 20th century has been the fact that, thankfully, the islands have largely escaped the restraints of the all-powerful, and often absentee, landlords who ruled in many other island and rural areas of Scotland.

Orkney farmers were fortunate that, quite early in the century, the major lairds were prepared to sell off property to their tenants - and the tenants were prosperous enough to be able to purchase!

The result was that Orkney had a far greater proportion of owner-occupied farms than any of her northern neighbours. It was an exaggerated comment, but valid to some extent, that everyone was a laird in Orkney.

The biggest sale of the century was undoubtedly that of the land and properties belonging to the Earl of Zetland's estates in Orkney. The task of organising the sell-off fell to Mr William MacLennan OBE, a Ross-shire man who

1924

came to Orkney in 1898 as factor to the Earldom estates. By the time of his retiral in 1929, his crowning success had been to carry through the sale of the whole of the Earldom lands to their occupiers - about 700 in number, said *The Orcadian*.

The nearest Orkney had come to anything approaching the Highland Clearances in the 19th century had been suffered in Rousay under the harsh lairdship of General Sir F.W.T. Burroughs. But he had died in 1905, and in 1921, the trustees of his estate offered the farms for sale to the tenants. The same year, the Hobbister and Elsness estates in Sanday and Stronsay were sold off, in most cases to those occupying the land.

And, in 1924, another of the biggest lairds in Orkney, Colonel W.E.L. Balfour, of Balfour and Trenabie, sold off most of

his properties on the Orkney Mainland and in the North Isles - giving the first option of purchase to the tenants. In March, 1928, he went a step further and wrote to his tenants in Shapinsay saying that he intended to dispose of most of the island, and offering the tenants the opportunity to buy their properties.

It was only after he had sold off most of his Shapinsay farms that Col Balfour retired to Balfour Castle to live in August, 1930, after a career which was largely spent in London and overseas. He was educated at the Royal Military Academy, Woolwich, before joining the Army in which he saw active service in Ceylon and Africa, after which he pursued his business interests in London. He died at Balfour Castle in April, 1934, aged 79.

By then, however, he had played his part in creating an Orkney agricultural industry based largely on owner-occupied farms and, in 1924, it was estimated that the first 25 years of the century had seen at least 1,000 tenants buy their lands from the Zetland and Balfour estates and others.

Kirkwall's own Chancellor of the Exchequer

Britain's first Labour government, a minority administration led by Ramsay MacDonald, came to power in 1924 - with a former Kirkwall customs officer as Chancellor of the Exchequer!

Born in Yorkshire in 1864, Philip Snowden came to Kirkwall in 1886 as a young civil servant and worked as a Customs and Excise man until 1889. He lodged in Shore Street, Kirkwall, and was remembered for attending the local meetings of the Young Men's Literary and Debating Association.

A cycling accident, however, was to

leave him crippled and it was while bedridden that the young Liberal, as he then was, began to study the doctrines of Socialism. It was to change his life and lead to him becoming Britain's first Labour chancellor in January, 1924.

He was again Chancellor of the Exchequer in Ramsay MacDonald's second Labour government of 1929 but, after being created Viscount Snowden in 1931, he resigned from the National government in 1932. His autobiography was published in 1934, and he died in 1937.

He returned to Kirkwall for a visit in

1926 and spent a weekend with old friends in the county, including Kirkwall Provost John M. Slater, a man with whom he maintained contact for most of his life.

Woman legal pioneer

Mary Mowat, of Albert Street, Kirkwall, became the first Orcadian woman to qualify as a law agent in January, 1924. After starting her career with the Kirkwall solicitors of Drever and Heddle, she moved to the Edinburgh firm of Dundas and Wilson.

The potato famine that never was

The steamer *Castle Rock* arrived in Kirkwall in June, 1924, with a cargo of 150 tons of potatoes from Poland after, somehow, the rumour went abroad that Orkney had been hit by a potato famine.

The story had it that islanders were unable to feed themselves as the potato shortage had seen prices rocket to £24 a ton. In fact, potatoes were as plentiful

as they ever were and prices were just £10 a ton.

"The whole transaction seems to have been one big misunderstanding," said *The Orcadian*. The "super cargo" looked set to rot until a Shetland merchant bought 10 tons and the rest of the consignment was taken to Stronsay to sell to those in the herring industry.

Orcadians escape disaster

The British steamer *Port Elliott*, en route from New York, was wrecked in January, 1924, off New Zealand, but all aboard were rescued - including no less than five Orcadian crew members: David Baikie, Thomas White and Peter Knight, all Stromness; Robert Wilson, Graemsay; and George Johnston, Longhope.

Pioneers of the skies

In 1924, two men flew from Orkney to America. In 1930, an Orcadian with only hours of flying experience bought a second hand plane and - taking a packet of sandwiches to fortify him on the journey - set off for Australia. Not only that, but he got there too!

It prompts a cynic to wonder, 70 years later, why there are days when it is impossible to fly on a scheduled flight from Orkney to Wick.

But in the pioneering days of aviation, Orkney was at the forefront of many developments in flying - to the extent that, by 1930, proposals were revealed at the highest levels of the fledgling industry for a scheduled airline service from Orkney to Canada.

From the start, Orcadians embraced the new air age. The first time that most would have seen a flying machine was before World War One when HMS *Hermes* came North with a flight of seaplanes. More seaplanes arrived at Scapa in August, 1914, and the impetus of war was to see huge advances in the development of aircraft through 1914-18, including the experiment which proved to be the fore-runner of the aircraft carrier when, for the first time, an aircraft landed on a ship underway at sea, in trials in Scapa Flow.

But even before then, Orkney had made a mark in aviation history for an airman called Foulis, the grandson of an Orcadian, was credited with being the first to fly an aircraft into battle in a war when, with two other Scots called Harkness and Hamilton, he flew aircraft missions in the Mexican revolution in February, 1911.

It was such tales of derring-do that, no doubt, encouraged the adventurous spirit of young Orcadians and, in 1916, Orkney's first glider was built by three Kirkwall teenagers working from plans published in a boys' magazine. The finished machine - made of cotton material round a wooden frame with the addition of discarded aircraft material given to the boys by men of the Royal Navy Air Service at Scapa - was a bi-plane jump glider with an 18 feet wingspan. The gliding ground was on the steep slope below Highland Park Distillery. The pilot, strapped into the contraption, had to run down the slope and eventually found himself lifted into the air. The longest flight extended to 20 seconds, covering 200 yards. Each night the machine was dismantled and taken home before being re-assembled the next night.

After several successful flights, there was disaster, although the pilot fortunately escaped injury. In completing a flight of record distance, the wings clipped the ground and the craft was wrecked - though the wreckage was later utilised to make a "man-lifting" kite. Wartime service followed for the boys, in which at least one of the three was killed.

At the conclusion of World War One, activity in the air over Orkney was to be limited. But that was all to change in the summer of 1924 when the islands became the centre of world attention. We were to witness the first men to fly from Orkney to America.

Of course, by then John Alcock and Arthur Brown - they were both knighted for the exploit - had become the first to fly the Atlantic in 1919 when they flew a Vickers Vimy aircraft from St John's, Newfoundland, to County Galway in 16 hours 27 minutes.

But this was different: Houton had been chosen as the take-off point for the first leg of an air crossing of the Atlantic as part of an American attempt to fly round the world!

Elaborate and costly organisation by the American government had seen five US military pilots set off in bi-seaplanes from Los Angeles on March 17. They had flown in stages to Alaska, across to China, and then flown through Asia and Europe before reaching England and flying North to Orkney to start the attempt over the Atlantic by the so-called Northern route.

By this time, two of the five pilots had dropped out, but the three who reached Orkney were Lieutenants Lowel M. Smith, Leigh Wade and Erik Nelson.

They arrived at Houton on July 30, 1924, to be welcomed by the county convener James Johnston, and a raptuous reception from a big crowd, which was said to have been as large as that which had gathered five years earlier when news of the great scuttle of the German fleet had spread round the county. There was added interest for the Orcadian spectators, for the three planes had been serviced by Air Mechanic James Simpson, son of the Simpson family of Little Bu, Flotta, who worked for the American aviation company which supplied the aircraft for the round-the-world attempt.

Also awaiting the arrival of the airmen in Houton Bay was the cruiser *Richmond* and other US war vessels, whilst patrolling the route between Orkney and Greenland were US ships, stationed at ten mile intervals to ensure the safety of the aviators. The *Richmond* was full of US newspapermen, photographers and newsreel cameramen to record the progress of the marathon which, it was estimated, cost the American government £40,000, without including the cost of the Atlantic maritime patrol.

On August 1, the three airmen took off from Houton and straightaway ran into heavy fog which forced Lieutenants Smith and Wade to return. Lt Erik Nelson, however, continued and reached Iceland at 6pm that evening. Smith and Wade set off again on August 3. This time Wade crashed off the Faroes and his aircraft was wrecked, but Smith safely reached Iceland, and a month later the two pilots Lt Erik Nelson and Lt Lowel M. Smith wrote themselves into the record books as they successfully reached the USA and duly completed their round-the-world circumnavigation by air.

Hard on the heels of the Americans came another world flier - the Italian airman Antonio Locatelli and his flying companion Tullio Crosio, and two support crew, who arrived at Houton, from Hull, in their Dornier seaplane on August 9, 1924.

In contrast to the Americans, they were greeted by a reception committee of one newspaperman and a score of curious onlookers.

The air attaché at the Italian embassy in London, a Major Scaroni, had arranged with Mr F.C. Thornley - managing director of the Thornley Binders seaweed factory - that the Italian team should make Stromness their headquarters, so Signor Locatelli set off to Stromness where he moored to a buoy in the harbour.

Locatelli tried to take off on August 13 but bad weather forced him to return after 90 minutes, so it was August 15 before he was able to make the flight to the Faroes and then Iceland. On the next leg of the journey, however, Locatelli met disaster - and he had good reason to be grateful to his American rivals. Locatelli was forced by engine trouble to land on water 125 miles east of Cape Farewell. He drifted for 100 miles and was ultimately rescued by the cruiser *Richmond*, the flagship of the American round-the-world bid. Sadly that was the end of the Italian effort which, compared to the huge logistical support, and accompanying ballyhoo, of the Americans, had somehow produced a much more dashing and cavalier style. Antonio Locatelli was killed in Abyssinia in 1936.

The next five or six years saw occasional visits to Orkney by flying boats - usually on survey work or military test flights - but Tuesday, August 27, 1929, was "a red letter day in the history of Evie," said *The Orcadian*, with the arrival of what was heralded as the first privately-owned aeroplane to land in Orkney, carrying Cecil and Leslie Horne who had rented the shooting rights and Woodwick House for the season. They flew from London in a DeHavilland Gypsy Moth in under six hours flying time, plus a 45 minute stop for fuel at Leuchars. The plane

Two of the Italian team who attempted to fly from Orkney to America in 1924, believed to be Antonio Locatelli and Tullio Crosio, are pictured taking a stroll in Stromness.

(Picture from the files of The Orcadian)

landed in Mr John Craigie's grass field at Walkerhouse, Evie, and - soon dubbed as "Evie's Air Force" - the airmen later flew to South Ronaldsay and landed in a field at the farm of Berriedale.

But Orcadians were already involved in the development of aviation around the world and, at the end of 1929, an astonishing feat of bravery saw James Cusator, from St Margaret's Hope, acclaimed as one of the first heroes of the pioneering air age in Northern Canada.

Employed as a mechanic by the Canadian United Air Transport company, he risked death to climb from a plane, at a height of 300 feet and, in a 70 mph slip stream, and sub-zero temperatures, crept along the fuselage to hold a broken ski in position to allow the pilot, Geoffrey Home-Hay, to land in the snow of Prince Albert, Saskatchewan. Cusator went on to become a well-known pilot in Canada!

A real red letter day, however, must have been Friday, July 11, 1930, as hundreds of Orcadians saw one of the great symbols of the 20th century when the famous German airship Graf Zeppelin passed over Scapa Flow as the ex-German battleship *Hindenburg* was being raised from the sea. Passengers waiting at Scapa to join the steamer *St Ola*, and also people in Stromness, had a perfect view - the number on the side D-LZ127 could be clearly seen - as she passed almost noiselessly overhead, heading south, although apparently causing cattle on Graemsay to stampede. A year later, on June 30, 1931, the Graf Zeppelin, with 12 passengers plus crew, made another visit to Orkney, again flying over Scapa Flow and dipping in salute to the beached 25,000 ton battleship *Prinz Regent Luitpold* that had just been salvaged.

It was a day of fine weather as the airship passed overhead at 600-800 feet. *The Orcadian* recorded: "Quite slowly, like a giant cigar, glistening white in the rays of the setting sun, this world renowned Zeppelin moved slowly along, passing immediately over Stromness golf course. All the players on the course abandoned their game and waved to the stranger overhead. The name 'Graf Zeppelin' painted red on her fore-end was easily read with the naked eye."

The year of 1930 saw some major moments in Orkney's aviation history and the next excitement was to be a new attempt to fly the Atlantic from Orkney - this time by a one-legged German.

The challenger was 28 year old Wolfram Hirth, technical adviser to the Wurttenberg Aviation Company. An early pioneer of gliding in Germany, he had an artificial leg following a crash in 1923, but, accompanied by journalist Oscar Weller, he intended to fly from Kirkwall across the Atlantic via Iceland to Labrador in his Klemm monoplane, weighing just 650 lbs and capable of 70 mph for 20 hours at a stretch.

The aviators arrived at Kirkwall on Sunday evening, July 27, 1930, from Hanworth, via Turnhouse, Edinburgh. At the Bignold Park, a large white sheet had been laid out and a smoke box prepared to indicate wind direction. But bad weather set in, the airmen could not identify the park and they instead landed on a field adjoining New Scapa Road, belonging to Mr Charles Anderson of Corse. The Germans were welcomed by Provost John M. Slater and the German vice-consul Mr Fred Buchanan. It was explained where the Bignold Park was, and Wolfram Hirth took off again to fly there. The plane was covered in tarpaulin at the Bignold and five boy scouts - Angus, Fred and Tommy Buchanan, Al Cumming and Angus Fraser - were deputed to mount an all-night guard on the aircraft.

Hirth soon announced that the Bignold Park was far too small for a fully laden plane to take off, so the aircraft was later flown to the Naval aviation ground at Swanbister, Orphir, and, it was from there, after being delayed by bad weather for three days, that Hirth and Weller took off on the morning of Friday, August 1. Mr Colin Park, who had served with the air force in World War One, turned the propeller, the engine roared into life and, watched by a small crowd of 50 Orcadian observers, the blue and silver monoplane accelerated down the hill and, heavily laden with fuel, cleared the dyke at the end of the field by six feet before climbing over Scapa Flow and setting a course over the Atlantic. Seven and a half hours later, the aircraft was sighted over Hornafjord, Iceland, and a message from the airmen to vice-consul Fred Buchanan later confirmed their safe arrival at Kaldarnes after a flight of nearly 12 hours.

However, a week later, hopes that Orkney had played its part in a new aviation milestone were dashed. Reuters reported that Hirth and Weller had abandoned their flight from Iceland and were instead sailing to Greenland with their plane.

But, by then, top men in the fledgling aviation industry, were convinced that the Northern route over the Atlantic was the safest and most viable for regular commercial flights and, in 1930, proposals were revealed that could have made Orkney a major aviation hub of Europe with plans for a scheduled airline service from Orkney to Canada, via the Faroes and Iceland. This was certainly no "pie in the sky" scheme suggested by bar room gossip. Major General James MacBrien, president of the Aviation League of Canada, confirmed that three routes were being considered for a trans-Atlantic service - but the route via the Azores and the route from Newfoundland to Ireland involved long flights over the ocean, and therefore the Orkney - Faroes - Iceland - Greenland - Baffin Land - Winnipeg option seemed the safest route with no flight of more than 470 miles over sea.

Trial flights were being considered for the following summer and such a service would reduce the journey time between Winnipeg and London to just two and a half days. "If the scheme materialises, it is probable that the Orkney islands will be a chief link in the chain," said Major General MacBrien.

By now, several flights had been made via the Northern route, but the arrival in Kirkwall in 1931 of an American, William Cramer, was a cause for sadness rather than celebration - he was seeking news of his brother Parker, an airman who had disappeared while flying from America to Denmark. Wreckage of his plane had reportedly been found off Sanday.

Another early pioneer, Charles Lindbergh, the man who made the first solo flight over the Atlantic in his aircraft *Spirit of St Louis* in 1927, carried out a reconnaissance flight over the Northern route in 1933 but chose to land in Shetland rather than Orkney.

In the event, of course, the scheme for a North Atlantic air service never developed. The industry was moving at such a pace, with longer range aircraft being introduced, that the growing number of airlines could safely bypass Orkney. The opportunity was lost.

But, nonetheless, Orkney could celebrate in 1930 when one of the most audacious feats of the era saw an Orcadian fly solo to Australia. It was a tale straight from the pages of a Boy's Own adventure story and captured the imagination of the world's press who nicknamed the pilot the "Sundowner of the Skies."

He was 27 year old Oscar Garden, son of Robert Garden and grandson of the late Bailie Robert Garden of the well-known Kirkwall firm R. Garden Ltd, the same family who had been the major benefactors in providing a hospital for Kirkwall, and after whom the headquarters of Orkney Health Board, Garden House, was named 60 years later.

Amy Johnson had made her famous flight to Australia earlier in 1930 but Garden was soon to follow.

Astonishingly, he had only learned to fly in the previous six months, and had a total of only 40 hours flying experience, when he purchased his small, second hand, blue and silver Gypsy Moth aircraft which he named *Kia Ora* - Maori for "Good Luck" - and announced his intention to fly Down Under.

With the confidence of youth, and his total provisions a few sandwiches to fortify him on the way, he set off from Croydon Aerodrome on October 16, 1930, announcing that his first destination was Munich.

He had gone to Australia with his parents as a child and he said: "I don't know why there should be any fuss about this trip. Heaps of other people are flying to Australia nowadays, and really it is my way of returning home from my holidays over here. I have to go back and I thought I might as well fly back."

He took off despite a last minute plea from his mother to drop the whole idea. An hour later, it seemed that mother knew best when bad weather forced him down, 50 miles away, in Kent! Undaunted, however, Garden took off again and later reached France. His flight across Europe did not appear to be reported to London, but on October 28, Reuters reported that he had reached Calcutta. There he met up with the famous woman air pioneer, the Hon Mrs Victor Bruce, who was flying her own aircraft, and they flew on to Rangoon. Garden had a scare at Jhansi in India when his plane overturned and the propeller smashed but he was able to carry out repairs and continue, flying from Rangoon to Siam (Thailand) and Timor island.

And, on November 4, Reuters reported that Oscar Garden had arrived in Western Australia, having completed his journey in 19 days, or just 13 days flying time. He later carried on to Christchurch, New Zealand, where members of his family now lived, and he was welcomed by a civic reception. Lack of meals, continuous exertion and nervous strain had caused him to lose one and a half stones in weight on the epic journey.

But, by now, Garden was seriously smitten with the flying bug and in May, 1932, the "Sundowner of the Skies" set out on another solo flight, this time from Capetown to Britain, via Cairo and Paris. Unfortunately this effort came to an end when he was forced to land in the jungles of Tanganyika, however. He was a regular visitor to his grandmother's home in Orkney and, in 1934, he returned to Kirkwall when he was offered a pilot's job with Highland Airways, although the following year he moved on when he was appointed manager of United Airways in the Isle of Man.

And at the start of 1934, it was an Orcadian-Australasian contemporary of Garden who was to make the headlines when a young pilot Thomas Corrigal made the first amateur solo flight to Mount Cook, New Zealand's highest mountain at 12,349 feet, in a Gypsy Moth aircraft. Mr Corrigal's father Frank had emigrated to New Zealand from Finstown.

In 1933, the focus returned to Orkney, however, when another pioneer aviator John Grierson made an attempt to cross the Atlantic in his seaplane. This was to be the first British attempt to fly from Orkney to America. Grierson arrived in Orkney on August 5, 1933, and moored his plane in the shelter of Scapa Pier before flying to the Faroes the next day. However, in Iceland, the plane was badly damaged and Grierson had to give up. He did complete an Atlantic crossing in 1934 - but taking off from Northern Ireland, instead of Orkney.

However, Orkney did see the ocean conquered in 1934 - when the first trans-Atlantic air tourists from America arrived in Kirkwall on September 6.

They were pilot Dr Richard Light (25) and his companion, wireless operator Mr Robert Wilson (22) who landed in Kirkwall Bay in their red and green single engined Bellanca Skyrocket mono-seaplane, which had made the trip averaging seven miles to a gallon of fuel. The two had set off on their flying holiday to Europe from Newhaven, 70 miles from New York, flying to Labrador, Iceland and then Kirkwall, via the Faroe islands.

The two lunched at the Kirkwall Hotel, had their passports checked by Supt John Tulloch of Orkney police, and then continued their flight, taking off for Rochester in Kent.

However, before departure, Dr Light earned a place in the history books as the first man to challenge Orkney's high cost of air fares. Referring to newly started services to the county he said: "I would have thought that flying would be much cheaper - the fares are much higher for the mileage than is the rule in the United States. I suppose that through time your British air fares will be reduced. The more popular your local services become, the cheaper flying will be." If only!

A few weeks later, *The Orcadian* - caught up in the growing excitement of the aviation age - launched what was probably the newspaper's most ambitious column of the 20th century: "Learn to fly with Captain H.C. Biard" in which the "famous instructor and test pilot" gave weekly tips and advice on how to pilot a plane.

By now, several air charter companies had grown up. In fact, as far back as May, 1931, a Desoulter Sports Coupé plane landed in the New Scapa Road field of Corse, bringing Mr H.P. Hamilton, of the National Utility Poultry Society, and his wife. They had done the 600 mile trip from Reading in five and a half hours, piloted by Mr J.B. Wilson, chief pilot of National Flying Services stationed at Reading. Mr Hamilton had come to Orkney to speak to farmers on the need to eradicate poultry diseases.

A month earlier however, at the same field of Corse, Orkney had witnessed a landing which was to mould the history of the islands for the rest of the century. Miss Helen Pauer arrived in her dual-controlled Gypsy Moth bi-plane which she owned. The purpose of the visit was to organise a return flight in August when Orcadians would be offered joy rides of three minutes for 5s 6d a time. Miss Pauer was acknowledged as the first woman to land from an aircraft in Orkney - but it was not that which made the flight so memorable. It was her companion, and the pilot who landed the plane, who was to become a major Orkney figure of the 20th century.

That day was the first visit to the county of Ted Fresson - and it was to mark the birth, not many months later, of Orkney's civilian air age and regular scheduled services which were to make the islands the pioneers of British aviation.

The Flow surrenders

It was called the greatest salvage operation in history - and only the churlish would dispute it. Over a period of less than 15 years, a massive effort succeeded in cajoling and bullying the dark waters of Scapa Flow to surrender up most of the great ships of the scuttled German High Seas Fleet which had been sent so ignominiously to the seabed in 1919.

There were many skilled and able men - many of them Orcadians - who risked life and limb in the perilous work to defy the laws of nature and retrieve what had been thought to have been lost forever. But the names and achievements of two of those men would forever be inextricably linked with that remarkable pioneering era. They were an Englishman Ernest Cox, from the Isle of Sheppey, and a Glaswegian, Thomas McKenzie. From 1924 to 1939, they shared over two decades a string of salvage triumphs that remain unmatched.

McKenzie, who lived with his family in Lyness for close on a quarter of a century, was to go on to earn respect and acclamation not only in Orkney but throughout Europe, and not only in peace but wartime too, honoured by the King for his work in liberated French ports after D-day.

The salvage operations in the Flow were to become a vital part of the Orkney economy. It was dangerous work but saw the men rewarded accordingly with the first £10 a week manual wage - nearly four times the average in the county at the time - as the equivalent, at 1999 prices, of something like £50 millions went into the pay packets of Orcadians involved in the project over a generation.

Ernest Cox first travelled to Orkney to survey the German wrecks in 1923. He was the proprietor of a firm of iron and steel merchants Cox and Danks (his erstwhile partner Danks no longer had any connection with the company) which had branches in London, Sheffield, Birmingham and Manchester. Mr Cox, then approaching his 40th birthday, had never salvaged a ship in his life, though he did know about ship-break-

ing, having previously broken up a pair of redundant British battleships.

Anyway, he was obviously encouraged sufficiently by what he saw to make a deal with the Admiralty. Ernest Cox - to be immortalised as "The Man Who Bought A Navy" in a book of that title - paid £24,000 in the first instance, in 1924, to buy 28 of the ships, most of them destroyers but including the 28,000 ton *Hindenburg*, the pride of the German fleet which had gone down without ever firing a gun in anger. (It obviously seemed a good deal because that same year, Hughes Bolckow and Company paid the Admiralty £77,000 for the British battlecruiser HMS *Lion* which was broken up on the Tyne).

With Thomas McKenzie and Ernest McKeown, a former Royal Navy man, appointed as his joint chief salvage officers, Cox invested a further £40,000 in two tugs, an ex-German floating dock and other equipment that he would need to raise the fleet.

There had already been some salvage work carried out in Scapa Flow prior to 1924. The Royal Navy had started operations, followed by two or three locally-based companies, including an Orkney concern started by Mr John Mowat and a Shetland company headed by Mr J .W. Robertson, who had been involved in salvaging the first German ship to be raised by a civilian company in the Flow, a destroyer which was towed to Stromness to be broken up in December, 1922. Robertson bought and salvaged a total of four destroyers.

But the arrival of Cox and his right hand men McKenzie and McKeown was to see an unimagined scale of operations and expertise.

The first German destroyer was raised on August 1, 1924, and work continued at a rate of a vessel a month until, by April 30, 1926, less than two years of work had witnessed the company raising 25 of the wrecked vessels. None of these had been in particularly deep water and they were able to be hoisted from the Flow by mechanical muscle, sealed up and the water

One of the greatest feats of marine engineering ever achieved during the 20th century saw salvage teams raise to the surface the sunken German fleet at a rate of a ship a month in the 1920s. (Picture courtesy of Orkney Library photographic archive)

her ghost ships of war

It was dangerous work for the divers who worked on the salvaging of the German fleet. However, it could be rewarding. Men employed by Metal Industries were the first manual workers in Orkney to earn £10 a week. (Picture courtesy of Orkney Library photographic archive)

pumped out, before being dispatched to the breakers. Initial breaking was carried out at Lyness before the bulk of the work went to Rosyth. One ship, in December, 1925, did not make the trip South, breaking away from her tow and running ashore on the coast near Fraserburgh.

But, undeterred, Cox soldiered on, investing in a second floating dock - and turning his attention to the biggest challenge he had faced so far, the *Hindenburg*. The Cox and Danks men worked through the General Strike - using coal retrieved from the *Seydlitz* to fuel their efforts - and proceeded to plug with cement every hole in the giant vessel to allow the water to be pumped out. Cox had purchased the *Hindenburg* because she had sunk on an even keel and the refloating had appeared, at first sight, to be relatively straightforward. However, when the salvage men first raised the vessel, she immediately threatened to capsize and they had to take the demoralising decision to re-sink her. The great hulk would remain there for four years before being re-raised. When she was finally brought to the surface in July, 1930, it was the culmination of Cox's greatest dream but it had involved the salvors in a loss of about £30,000 as scrap metal prices collapsed.

Undaunted, however, Cox turned his attentions, back in 1926, to new challenges and the relatively recent idea of forcing compressed air into sunken ships, a technique which had been successfully used in the Mediterranean to bring wrecked vessels to the surface. Although this was to be grim, dangerous work, involving men in having to enter the sunken hulls, it was successfully employed over the next four years to salvage the 22,000 ton *Moltke*, the 25,000 ton *Seydlitz* and *Kaiser*, and the cruiser *Bremse*.

The departure of the *Moltke* on May 28, 1928, would see a new first for Cox and his men - the battleship was towed upside down, with living quarters built on the bottom of the hull, on the 200 mile journey to Rosyth, ironically pulled by three German tugs. The *Seydlitz* soon followed by the same method. The *Hindenburg*, when she went to Rosyth in 1930, made the trip in conventional style in just three days, however, again towed by German tugs.

Sandy Robertson, from Hoy, joined Cox and Danks in December, 1925, as a 17 year old labourer before serving his time as a diver's linesman. "It was a job that had great responsibility," he recalled later to *The Orcadian*. "You were in charge of their life, putting their suits on for them, connecting them up and lowering them down. They picked someone they thought was trustworthy."

At the time, he said, the men hardly considered that they were taking part in the largest salvage operation in history. "It was just a job to us, and something to get on with," he explained. "It wasn't just about being a linesman. You had to be a carpenter's mate and joiner's mate - you learned a bit about everything because you had to do a bit of everything."

There were around 200 people working on ship and shore on the salvage project with Cox and Danks at that time - most of them locally recruited - with a team of 40 dedicated salvage workers. "In Cox and Danks' time, there weren't many compressors and that led to a few narrow escapes. There was never a dull moment for the divers. There was a lot of gas - methane - around down there so it was dangerous cutting. You were never far from danger, but when you were young you didn't give a damn," said Sandy Robertson.

The jobs were as secure as any in those tough economic times but he remembered that around 20 men were usually laid off temporarily at the end of most months. "Most would be brought back on the payroll the next month, though if he didn't like the look of you, you'd be out," he recalled.

There were other salvage attempts going on at the time. In Holm Sound, in response to demands from local mariners that the eastern approaches to Scapa Flow should be cleared of blockships, the Orkney County Council had persuaded the Admiralty to contract the Thames and Lorne Salvage Company to try to remove the old steamer *Thames*, which had been sunk in the early months of World War One as an anti-submarine precaution.

And it was even suggested in *The Orcadian* of December 11, 1930, that an invention of a French scientist - an adaptation of an acetylene blowpipe which could be used underwater to a depth of 100 feet - would allow HMS *Hampshire* to be raised off Orkney's west coast.

But, back in the Flow, Cox had turned his attention to another two mammoths of the German fleet - the 20,000 ton *Von der Tann* and the 25,000 ton *Prinz Regent Luitpold*. History would show these to be the last two vessels to be raised by the firm of Cox and Danks.

During the period of salvage work undertaken by Cox and Danks, just three lives were lost. One victim was a 45 year old diver from Portsmouth, Herbert Hall, who had worked for Cox since the start of the Scapa Flow operations five years earlier, when he was killed in an accident while working on the salvage of the *Kaiser* in May, 1929.

But in November, 1930, came the great escape when four men, including McKenzie, were caught in rising water up to their necks after an explosion trapped them inside the *Von der Tann* for three hours. Rescue came in the nick of time.

Six months later, however, tragedy was to strike again when, working on the *Prinz Regent Luitpold*, an explosion killed a carpenter, William Tait from Thurso, and seriously injured three workmates including two Orcadians Robert Johnston and Robert Mowat.

By the end of 1931, Cox and Danks had raised 32 vessels, including six of 20,000 tons or more. Between 1924-31, the firm spent a total of £450,000 on the Scapa Flow salvage - a big proportion of which was pumped into the Orkney economy in wages.

But, at the start of 1932, with more than a dozen large vessels still languishing in the Flow, Cox and Danks announced that due to the "general depression," the firm would cease the salvage operation. Mr Cox's daughter told the *Daily Herald*: "Vast sums of money were spent and now that task is over it has been found that very little profit has been yielded. But my father has gained tremendous knowledge. Today he has the finest knowledge of salvage in the world." He died, with that epitaph, at the age of 76 in 1959.

There was said to be no market for scrap metal so the last two salvaged ships - the *Von der Tann* and the *Prinz Regent Luitpold* - were beached and left to rust until, in 1933, they were sold to Metal Industries Ltd. A new chapter was about to begin and, under the command of re-appointed chief salvage officer Thomas McKenzie, Metal Industries decided to take over, and resume, operations in Scapa Flow. The *Prinz Regent Luitpold* was towed upside down to Rosyth by three tugs from Bremerhaven flying the Nazi swastika. The *Von der Tann* soon followed.

At that time, the *Prinz Regent Luitpold* was still the largest ship salved by compressed air from any depth.

However that was soon to change as a new salvage triumph by McKenzie saw the 28,000 ton battleship *Bayern* raised from a depth of 120 feet in Scapa Flow. Never before in the annals of marine salvage had such a vessel been raised upside down from the sea bottom in 20 fathoms of water. The achievement in raising the *Bayern* - 630 feet long and with a 100 feet beam - far eclipsed the raising of the *Hindenburg* which had been in comparatively shallow water.

Eighty workmen had carried out the salvage of the *Bayern*, working from the salvage steamer *Bertha*. Seven huge airlocks up to 100 feet in length were fitted to the bottom of the *Bayern* to enable workmen to enter the hull, working under air pressure up to 50 lbs to the square inch. The *Bayern* was taken to Lyness in September, 1934, and prepared to be towed to the Forth to be broken up.

In 1935, the *König Albert* was retrieved and, in 1936, the *Kaiserin*, before Scapa Flow surrendered another of her victims in May, 1937, when the 25,000 ton *Fredrich der Grosse* was raised, after nine months work, from a depth of 23 fathoms - acclaimed by *The Orcadian* as the greatest triumph yet of the Metal Industries salvage team - at a spot between Cava and Houton. The *Friedrich der Grosse*, estimated to have been built at a cost of millions, was valued at £150,000 for scrap metal. She was the tenth capital ship to be raised since the salvage operations began a dozen years earlier. A year later she was followed by another 25,000 ton wreck when the *Grosser Kurfurst* was raised to the surface off Houton Head.

An indication of the importance of the Scapa Flow operations to the Orkney economy came in June, 1938, when it was announced that the 130 men working for Metal Industries on the salvage of the *Derfflinger* were to receive pay increases that gave the top wage earners (those working in the most dangerous conditions in compressed air) a weekly wage in double figures - the first manual workers to attain such status in Orkney. Depending on the nature of their work, increases would range between 30 shillings and £3/15/- a week, giving an average weekly wage for most of around £6. The men, who also qualified for bonuses on the successful raising of each wreck, would also receive the unheard-of luxury of holidays with pay. Meanwhile, for comparison, it was announced that for crewmen on the Northern Lighthouse ship *Pole Star*, their minimum wage of £2/16/- would be increased by six shillings. A year later council employees in the Kirkwall burgh yard went on strike in protest at their weekly wages between £2/8/- and £2/12/-.

However, World War Two was to intervene and the Metal Industries salvage operations were to end in 1939 with the 26,700 ton *Derfflinger* raised from 150 feet. Although McKenzie thought it possible to raise the remaining ships, the Royal Navy now needed Scapa Flow unhindered by civilian salvage work - and Metal Industries men would be required to devote their full resources to Naval operations, with McKenzie appointed Chief Salvage Officer for the Northern Area of the Royal Navy.

The *Derfflinger* was trapped in Orkney by the arrival of war and she was to remain off Rysa until 1946 when she went South to be broken up at Faslane. An indication, however, of how the national mood judged the achievements of Metal Industries came in November, 1939, when Sir Donald Pollock, the chairman of the company, easily won the election to become the new rector of Edinburgh University, beating the Orcadian writer Edwin Muir by 1,010 votes to 367.

But, with World War Two over, *The Orcadian* of September 19, 1946, gave the announcement of the impending demise of Metal Industries' link with Orkney - the company had decided to transfer all operations from Lyness to Faslane. The move would directly affect around 100 Orkney families and reduce the county's spending power by around £2,000 a week, it was estimated. The aggregate wages paid into the Orkney economy by the various salvage companies over 25 years amounted to more than £1.25 millions, estimated *The Orcadian*, while the value of the salvaged sunken ships - and attacked ships which were saved in wartime - ran into several million pounds.

The gates closed at Metal Industries' Lyness base on Wednesday, March 19, 1947, and the company bid a farewell to Orkney. However, a year later, under the command of Thomas McKenzie's son-in-law Harry Taylor, men of Metal Industries returned to salvage some of the dozen World War Two blockships off the Churchill Barriers to help contribute 60,000 tons of scrap metal during a national shortage of iron and steel which reached crisis proportions in the immediate post-war years.

The salvage men left behind seven German ships still at the bottom of Scapa Flow - the cruisers *Brummer, Karlsruhe, Cöln* and *Dresden* and the bigger *König, Kron Prinz Wilhelm* and *Markgraf*.

But a generation later, these ships would also be seen - by thousands of diving enthusiasts who travelled from around the world for the chance of an underwater glimpse of sunken history. In the 1980s, a new industry grew up with a small fleet of dive boats catering for those seeking the unique opportunity to dive on warships.

Admiral Ludwig Von Reuter's legacy to Orkney was still making a pound or two for the local economy.

A false dawn for Stromness

The success of the company would "render the name of Stromness a household word throughout the British Isles."

That was the promise of Mr F. C. Thornley as he announced the formation of his Thornley Binders company which would, he said, herald an era of new prosperity for Stromness.

The idea was not only to extract potash, iodine and other chemicals from Orkney seaweed, but also - through a new process patented by Thornley - to produce a residue which could be mixed with coal dust to form coal briquettes.

He planned a new factory which would contribute to the employment of hundreds as production of his new product could reach as much as 2,000 tons a week.

Within two years, a total approaching £100,000 had been spent on the project - and within another two years, it had all ended in failure!

The company of Thornley Binders first appeared on the Stromness scene in 1923. The chairman of the firm was Colonel J.F. Scott but the driving force was managing director F.C. Thornley. He was a consulting engineer who was recognised as an authority on coal distribution. As an engineer for the Baltimore, Ohio and Eastern Railways, he originated and constructed the largest and fastest coal loading terminal in the world. The first organised fuel distribution yard was designed and built by him for the US government in Washington.

His newly patented seaweed processes were a new venture, but he and Colonel Scott were obviously eloquent salesmen because in July, 1923, Stromness Harbours Commissioners agreed to build a new £10,000 200-feet long pier which would form a basin to store seaweed alongside a new £50,000 factory to be operated by Thornley Binders.

A few weeks later, plans were approved for the 160 feet long factory and adjoining power house.

By 1924, the company had thrown itself into local community life - donating a Christmas tree to Stromness and forming a football team to compete in Orkney competitions. As construction work went ahead, both of the pier and the factory, unemployment in Stromness was virtually non-existent, said *The Orcadian*.

In fact, by August, 1924, Orkney's unemployment total was down to only 50 men as, along with the Thornley Binders project, men were being recruited for the salvage of the German fleet in Scapa Flow and the installation of Kirkwall's new electricity scheme and

1925

Orkney's new telephone service. Throughout this period, Orkney's unemployment was just a quarter of the level of that in Shetland, to the North, and Wick, to the South.

However, some warning bells obviously began to sound even before the completion of the factory. The building of the new pier caused some controversy - leading to the resignation of the chairman of Stromness Harbours Commissioners, John Mackay.

Nonetheless, in April, 1925, Thornley Binders anticipated being up to 500 tons a week production within two months. And the new North Pier at Stromness, which would serve the factory, was officially opened at the end of June, 1925. "The whole town was en fete, surrounding buildings were decorated with bunting and all vessels in harbour had dressed ship," reported *The Orcadian*.

Thornley Binders operated its own ships to transport its production to the South and, at the end of 1925, there was near disaster when the SS *Whinstone*, owned by the company, was lost off the Humber, but the crew of six, all Orcadians - John Groat and John Marwick, from Stromness, Peter Smith and Edward Scollay, both Kirkwall,

Hubert Sinclair, St Margaret's Hope, and Tom Kirkpatrick, Longhope - were rescued by breeches buoy by the Humber lifeboat; a rescue that resulted in bravery awards for the lifeboatmen.

But economic disaster could not be staved off. After just two years of operations, it was announced in March, 1927, that Thornley Binders was in voluntary liquidation and a meeting of creditors appointed a firm of London accountants as liquidators. Three months later, the entire business was offered for sale by the accountants but there were no takers for the company as a going concern and the factory closed down.

It was a double blow for Stromness that year for it also appeared that efforts to revive the town's once thriving herring industry had failed. In 1901, catches worth over £50,000 had been landed in Stromness, but the industry had died in the town by 1910. However, the attempt at relaunching the industry in 1927 saw only 2,000 crans landed at Stromness - a tiny fraction of the 60,000-80,000 crans that were landed annually at Stronsay in the mid 1920s.

Over the next 20 years, there were occasional attempts to revive the seaweed industry in Stromness, and, in 1933, it was reported that the Thornley Binders factory was set to be taken over by another company, Segro Ltd, with the promise of 50 jobs, processing chemicals from seaweed. Again, it did not prove a long term success.

St Magnus discovered after 800 years

An examination of two skeletons found in St Magnus Cathedral, Kirkwall, during restoration work, identified the remains as those of St Magnus and St Rognvald.

The examination was carried out in 1925 by Professor R.W. Reid of Aberdeen University, attended by Rev Dr George Walker of Aberdeen's East Parish Church.

Dr Walker said that in March, 1919, the unsuspected presence of part of a skeleton was discovered in a pillar in the South side of the Choir. The skull, which was in a fairly good state of preservation, had evidence that a heavy, sharp instrument had penetrated to the brain - in accord with the story of the murder of St Magnus.

"Those acquainted with the circumstances of the murder of St Magnus could have little hesitation in believing that the skull bore the veritable mark of his death wound and that these were the relics of the saint" said Dr Walker.

The identification of another skeleton on the opposite side of the Choir as that of St Rognvald appeared to be almost certain, he added.

The bones in question, he supposed, were hidden in the pillars to guard against theft. "In the case of St Magnus, the secret was known to so few, and so well kept, that all knowledge of their existence had for centuries been lost till they were accidentally discovered in 1919."

The 1925 researches of Professor Reid and the anatomical evidence of the bones - including the respective ages and statures of the two persons - entirely proved the identification, said Dr Walker.

General Strike, general strife

1926

A national state of emergency was declared as millions of workers joined the 1926 General Strike - "this drastic and most momentous strike decision in history which aims at paralysing the nation's life," reported *The Orcadian*.

In fact, the General Strike, although a major milestone in the history of British industrial relations, was significant more in its symbolism than its impact. It was settled in a relatively short time and its effect in areas like Orkney was modest.

The General Strike, called by the Trades Union Congress, began on Monday, May 3, 1926, joining Britain's miners who had been in dispute for months. It would affect railways, sea transport and docks, the printing trade including newspapers, the iron and steel industry and building workers, amongst others.

Troops were drafted into potential flash-point areas in Britain's industrial heart-lands. But the most serious effect in Orkney, according to *The Orcadian* of May 6, 1926, was that the price of eggs in Kirkwall had fallen to 11d a dozen in anticipation that thousands of dozens would have to be stockpiled if shipping was disrupted.

The Orcadian published as normal throughout the strike period after print-ers joined the stoppage for just one day. The mail service was curtailed to three times a week but the Pentland Firth steamer *St Ola* continued sailing. Dockers at Kirkwall did join the strike - but vessels were discharged by volunteer workers -

and in Stromness, all was peaceful with "no stoppage of work of any kind in the town."

By the week of May 13, 1926, *The Orcadian* headlines reported: "Strike fizzles out." Locally, Kirkwall dockers, in a row over non union labour, stayed on strike for over two weeks, and, nation-ally, the miners' industrial action con-tinued throughout the summer.

It was the first time in a major national crisis that Orcadians had the benefit of up-to-date news bulletins via radio broad-casts. But, by the time, the General Strike had ended, it was estimated that the cost of the disruption would be less than the coal strike of 1921 which was said to have cost the country £200mil-lions.

In fact, Britain's million miners staged strikes in both 1920 and 1921. The 1920 dispute over pay saw the sailings of the *St Ola* reduced to three a week, and mail deliveries were curtailed, but, otherwise, Orkney was unscathed by the stoppage which was settled after a fortnight.

The impact was far greater nationally in the next miners' strike, six months later in April, 1921, in a row over wage cuts being imposed. At one stage, it threat-ened to develop into a general strike

verging on civil war as Prime Minister David Lloyd George declared a state of emergency and called out 70,000 Army reservists.

Lloyd George sent a telegram to the Provost of Kirkwall asking for urgent steps to be taken to recruit local defence force units with the enlistment of "loyal citi-zens." The pay would be the same as the Regular Army.

In fact no defence force units were ever formed in the county and, by June, 1921, Army reservists were stood down after the railwaymen and transport workers had broken ranks with the miners, and the so-called Triple Alliance, and pulled back from strike action.

Kirkwall Gas Company estimated it had sufficient coal stocks for three months and other coal stocks in Orkney were reckoned to be ample for a summer period. "Beyond a trivial inconvenience, through a restricted mail service, and through the distribution of coal on permit only in half hundredweight lots, the county has been totally unaffected," stated *The Orcadian*.

The 1921 miners strike was eventually settled after three months and on July 14 it was announced that permits were no longer needed to purchase coal in Orkney.

Kirkwall dockers did join a national dockworkers strike in 1924 but it was reported to have little effect on shipping at the pier as the employers immediately hired 40 unemployed men to replace them.

The seaplanes of the American pilots who, in 1924, not only completed the first flight from Orkney to America, in a series of short "hops," but also the first circumnavigation of the world by plane. (Picture courtesy of Orkney Library photographic archive)

Orkney's memorial to Kitchener

"Surely never before had a ceremony so stirred the heart of a county," said *The Orcadian*. "The people of Orkney, who had raised this tower, were there in their thousands. From East and West, from North Isles and South Isles they came, each to pay a tribute to a great company of the dead."

The Kitchener Memorial - a great stone tower erected on Orkney's Marwick Head to commemorate the loss of more than 600 men, including Britain's Secretary for War, Lord Kitchener, in the sinking of HMS *Hampshire* in 1916 - was officially unveiled on July 2, 1926.

The day was declared a public holiday in Orkney and many made their way to see the tower which they had paid for with a memorial fund which, in public subscriptions plus interest, raised £924. In a day of deep emotion, several people were overcome by the heat during the unveiling ceremony.

The new memorial was 48 feet high with walls 4 feet 6 inches thick at the base, designed by Kirkwall architect Mr J.M. Baikie and built by Orphir contractor Mr William Liddle. The official unveiling was performed by General Lord Horne, a soldier who had served with Kitchener, and a long-time friend, and the man who was commander of Britain's First Army in World War One.

Lord Horne was welcomed by the Lord Lieutenant of Orkney and Shetland, Sir William Watson Cheyne, and county convener James Johnston, who had latterly chaired the Kitchener Memorial Committee.

A guard of honour was formed by Orkney ex-servicemen. Among the ex-officers on parade was Kirkwall's Roman Catholic priest, Father Bruno Murphy, who before taking up the ministry, was an officer under Lord Kitchener in Egypt. Officers and ratings from HMS *Royal Sovereign* and HMS *Wessex* also attended.

But, for the most part, it was a day that the Establishment stayed away. No senior Government figure attended. Admiral of the Fleet Earl Jellicoe - a man who had faced some criticism over the loss of HMS *Hampshire* - sent his apologies for not attending the ceremony.

Lord Horne told the throng of thousands: "And so this tower stands, and will stand, a landmark to those at sea, erected by a people who understand all that life at sea means - in memory of, and typical of, a great soldier - a mark of appreciation of the people of Orkney of a man who set his duty before him and did it."

He then unveiled the granite memorial tablet inscribed: "This tower was raised by the people of Orkney in memory of Field Marshal Earl Kitchener of Khartoum, on that corner of his country which he had served so faithfully, nearest to the place where he died on duty. He and his staff perished along with the officers and nearly all the men of HMS *Hampshire* on June 5, 1916."

As it was undraped, HMS *Royal Sovereign*, lying off Marwick Head, fired a Field Marshal's salute of 19 guns.

Lord Horne told the guests at the Stromness Hotel afterwards: "I do not want to let this occasion pass without a reference to the extraordinary rumours circulated to the effect that the loss of HMS *Hampshire* and Lord Kitchener's life resulted from preventable causes. Allegations have been made of lack of foresight and neglect to provide protection, and very serious reflections cast on, and gross injustice done to a great Admiral and the Royal Navy. The First Lord of the Admiralty has stated repeatedly in Parliament, and I take the opportunity of restating it, that there is not a word of truth in such allegations. They are as ridiculous as they are unfounded, they are as cruel as they are false."

And for those who wanted to remember Kitchener for ever, the age of the souvenir had arrived. China replicas of the Kitchener Memorial, five inches high and bearing an inscription and the Orkney coat of arms, were sold at three shillings each.

Ordeal at sea

Five crew from the Faroese schooner *Rosenhjem* landed on the west side of Westray after 24 hours in their open lifeboat after having to abandon ship when their vessel sank 40 miles off Noup Head in November, 1926.

The giant stone tower which stands as a memorial to Lord Kitchener on Orkney's Marwick Head.

(Picture courtesy of Orkney Library photographic archive)

Motor tragedy at pier

One of the worst tragedies of Orkney's newly-born motor age saw two Orcadians - Andrew Bews (23) of St Mary's, Holm, and Andrew Shearer (58) of Wilderness, Holm - drown when their car fell into the basin at Kirkwall Pier. A third man in the car, John G. Corse, Bridge Street, Kirkwall, escaped and swam to safety.

Treble chance bonus

A cow belonging to Thomas Groat, Skenstoft, Shapinsay, had three calves on December 4, 1925, and then gave birth to another set of triplets on November 28, 1926 - a total of six calves within 12 months!

Crimean war veteran

The man thought to be Orkney's last surviving soldier of the Crimean war, in the mid 19th century, died in September, 1926, at the age of 87.

Former Sergeant Major William Keetley, born in Ireland but resident in Orkney for nearly 60 years, was Rendall sub postmaster from 1894-1925, when he retired at the age of 86.

Mr Keetley had served in the Crimean War at Sebastopol with the Royal Artillery at the age of 16. He also saw service in China before, in 1868, being sent to Orkney as Sergeant Instructor of Number 7 Company Orkney Artillery Volunteers at Finstown.

They came from all over Orkney to witness the unveiling of the Kitchener Memorial in 1926, a day which saw many people collapse from the effects of hot weather and emotion.

(Picture courtesy of Orkney Library photographic archive)

The Kitchener Memorial stands proud on Marwick Head overlooking the Atlantic Ocean and the final resting place of HMS *Hampshire* which was lost with more than 600 men in 1916 after striking a mine while on passage to Russia.

(Picture courtesy of Orkney Library photographic archive)

Good health! New hospital opens

A new chapter in the story of Orkney's health services began when the new Balfour Hospital - the Garden Memorial Building, gifted by the family of Kirkwall merchant Robert Garden - was officially opened on April 6, 1927.

Until 1927, the hospital had been in Main Street - and the fever hospital would remain there for another ten years - but the opening of the new Garden Memorial Building in New Scapa Road would see Orkney's main hospital services remain on that site for the remainder of the 20th century.

The new hospital was designed by Kirkwall architect Mr T.S. Peace and built by Kirkwall contractor John Firth. The opening ceremony was performed by Alfred Baikie of Tankerness, Vice-Lord Lieutenant of Orkney and Shetland, and chairman of the Garden Memorial Building Committee.

The hospital - until becoming part of the National Health Service 20 years later - would be administered by a board of trustees, who had capital funds of £15,000 but otherwise relied on voluntary donations to maintain and operate the hospital.

Barbara Cartland marries Orkney tenant

One of Britain's best known and most prolific authors of the 20th century, Barbara Cartland, married Alexander McCorquodale, tenant of Swanbister House, Orphir, in 1927.

The romantic novelist, born in Birmingham in 1901, went on to have over 400 titles published in her literary career.

Her marriage to Alexander McCorquodale did not last - they divorced in 1933 - and, in 1936, she married his cousin Hugh McCorquodale. Her daughter, Raine, became the stepmother of Diana, Princess of Wales.

Captain Alexander McCorquodale maintained his links with Orkney, and, in 1949, he caught 129 trout in five days on the Harray Loch, fishing with Sandwick boatman J.R. Esslemont.

He died in 1964, a year after his cousin Hugh.

Double drowning horror

A double drowning tragedy rocked Stromness in January, 1927, as Bailie Thomas Mowat, a draper in the town, and his brother John Mowat, chemist and optician, lost their lives as they were swept off rocks at Yesnaby on a Sunday afternoon excursion.

The scene was witnessed by Thomas's wife, Mrs Cissie Mowat, who said her husband was engulfed by an enormous wave. John Mowat (34) ran to help but, as he grasped his brother to haul him from the sea, another wave washed the two men away to their deaths.

Tom Mowat (40) had served in World War One and returned with the rank of Captain, and became a member of Stromness Town Council.

John Mowat had won the Military Medal for his World War One service in France. Now, the Carnegie Hero Fund Trust posthumously honoured him for his tragic rescue attempt of his brother, adding his name to its Roll of Heroes.

Sea turns to milk

A "most remarkable phenomenon" in the Hoy Sound saw the sea turn white - and "milky" in appearance - in July, 1927.

Fisherman John Sinclair said the water seemed to be coloured by a chalky substance. So thick was the colouring that it was impossible to see fish which were being hauled, which would normally be plainly visible at several fathoms deep.

When taken on board, fish appeared to be "bleached" but regained their natural colour when dead. The occurrence was blamed on a tidal wave in the Pentland Firth, a few days earlier, which was said to have disturbed chalk deposits on the seabed.

Shooting tragedy

The people of Holm were stunned by the shooting to death of a local farm-worker and the young wife of a neighbouring farmworker in an apparent suicide pact.

Police chief dies

Orkney's Superintendent of Police, Robert Wood, died after 27 years service in the county force, in February, 1927.

A native of Wyre and a champion ploughman before joining the police, he entered the force in 1900 and served as a constable for seven years before becoming Superintendent on the retiral of Superintendent Richard Atkin in 1907.

On July 1, 1905 - the fifth anniversary of his joining the force - he saved a drowning man at Kirkwall Pier, for which he received a bravery award from the Royal Humane Society.

During World War One, Superintendent Wood was in charge of the Police arrangements at Longhope while King George V was visiting Scapa Flow.

His obituary in *The Orcadian* reported: "Superintendent Wood, in his contact with delinquents, showed diplomacy and skill."

Sergeant John Tulloch was appointed the new Superintendent of Orkney Police.

Bravery award

Policeman hero Constable David Allan received a bravery award, and a cheque for three guineas, after carrying to safety pensioners from a blazing house occupied by six women, three of them aged in their 80s. The house in St Margaret's Hope was completely gutted but all the women were rescued.

Earthquake drama

An earthquake was felt in Orkney, lasting 20 seconds and sounding like thunder after three separate tremors in the early hours of January 24, 1927. Houses were shaken but no damage reported.

Otter invasion

Flotta man Malcolm Ross was woken by screams from his mother that she had found a 43 inch long otter in her bedroom. Mr Ross, of Bow, Flotta, and his neighbour Joseph Simpson killed the creature which had climbed into a clothes press.

Battle for St Magnus Cathedral

Orkney's St Magnus Cathedral - "the glory of the county from time immemorial" - was at the centre of a legal row that threatened to see the cathedral's traditional ownership taken away from the people of Kirkwall.

The ownership for centuries had been vested in the town council of Kirkwall by Royal charters and an Act of Parliament but the introduction of the Church of Scotland (Property and Endowments) Act 1925 saw the general trustees of the Church of Scotland claim that ownership of the building, as a Kirkwall parish church, should pass to them.

Kirkwall Town Council agreed to contest any change in the ownership and the dispute went to a court hearing in Edinburgh before Sheriff J.C. Pitman, in October, 1928.

In the early years of the century, there had been concern whether the Cathedral

1928

would be able to retain even a roof as major repair work was required. Fortunately, a bequest from Sheriff George Thoms, and the setting up of a permanent maintenance fund, had seen the Cathedral saved. (In the 22 years, 1912-34, a total of £53,000 was spent on the restoration of St Magnus Cathedral - an amount approaching £5 millions at 1999 levels.)

For several years, the town council made a charge for visitors to the Cathedral to help pay for the caretaker, but the charge was dropped in 1927 when the Thoms trustees agreed to make provision for the caretaker's salary.

Sheriff Pitman, commenting that the town council "resents being deprived of what I might call that proudest possession," continued the case for one month to allow the two sides to reach an amicable agreement. " If no arrangement is come to, and the matter is referred to me, I will give judgement in due course," he said.

However, by the end of the year, agreement had been reached. The town council would continue to hold and retain the fabric and site of the Cathedral, vested in it by Royal Charter, but formally acknowledge that the property is held in trust for the community and nation, and be made available as and for a Church of Scotland parish church. In return, the general trustees of the Church of Scotland agreed to withdraw their petition and not renew it.

Secrets of Skara Brae unearthed

Life 5,000 years before became a story of the 20th century as the secrets were laid bare of Orkney's unique village of Skara Brae.

The village had been revealed, of course, by a great storm in the mid 19th century, and some excavation work had been carried out in the intervening period, both by local historians and Professor Boyd Dawkins prior to World War One. However a further big storm in 1926 had laid bare further ruins and threatened the whole village with destruction.

HM Office of Works, under the care of which the site had been placed, was

thereby forced to take steps to preserve the monument, and Professor Gordon Childe, of Edinburgh University but an Australian by birth, was invited by the Chief Inspector of Ancient Monuments to oversee operations, in 1928, on behalf of the Society of Antiquaries for Scotland.

The actual excavation work was carried out, in the first instance, by Kirkwall contractor John Firth, and Professor Childe was in no doubt at the value of the discoveries. "Nowhere, except in Egypt or at Pompeii, is a prehistoric settlement to be found, the streets, huts and even

domestic furniture of which are in such perfect preservation.

"Eventually the office of works will have under its charge a national monument of absolutely unique interest - nothing less than a complete prehistoric village. This season's work has not only rescued a wonderful passage in immediate danger of irreparable collapse and disclosed to the public a building which for completeness has no equal of like age in the British Isles; it has also brought to light a number of relics that will splendidly adorn our national collections."

Flags fly for a Prince

Prince George, a son of King George V, was welcomed to Stromness, with the streets bedecked in flags, to officially name the new Stromness lifeboat and, later, to cross Scapa Flow to name the Longhope lifeboat, in June, 1928.

Provost Corrigall of Stromness welcomed the Royal visitor with the words: "I am sure that in all the British Empire there are no more loyal subjects than we, the natives of the Orkney islands.

"From our earliest youth we have been brought up to reverence our King, and the more we know of the world in general the more convinced we have become that nowhere is to be found a King, Queen or Royal family to compare with ours. It is

then a proud day for us that Prince George has deigned to visit a small town like Stromness."

It was a special day for Sanday pupil Helen Scott, from the Burness School, who was presented with a challenge shield by the Prince - her prize for winning a lifeboat essay competition.

Six years later, when Prince George became Duke of Kent and married Princess Marina of Greece, both Stromness and Kirkwall town councils declared a public holiday. Stromness town council gave the Prince a wedding gift of an Orkney chair, made by D. M. Kirkness, while Orkney schoolchildren donated £19/15/11 to a national wedding gift fund.

Round-the-world

International solo sailor Captain Thomas Drake (64) arrived in Kirkwall in his 35 feet schooner *Pilgrim* which he built himself in Seattle, USA. The English-born mariner had gone to the USA in 1889 where his single-handed exploits had earned him the nickname "The Lone Sea Rover."

He had made an earlier voyage of 32,000 miles in his first yacht *St Francis I*, and then began his world voyage in *Pilgrim* on May 28, 1925. He took two years to reach Britain and he then headed for Orkney where visitors were able to look over his boat for 3d admission charge, and where he was given a guided tour of Kirkwall by Provost John Slater.

In November, 1928, it was reported that the *Pilgrim* had been totally wrecked off the Netherlands.

UNVEILING OF KIRKWALL & ST OLA WAR MEMORIAL, 17-10-23 -T.K.

Plans for a Kirkwall memorial for those who died in World War One were dogged by acrimony with, at one stage, the county clerk Duncan Robertson refusing to allow the name of his son to be included in protest at the way names and regiments were to be abbreviated. Happily, harmony was eventually restored, although it was 1923 before the memorial was officially unveiled alongside St Magnus Cathedral.

(Picture courtesy of Orkney Library photographic archive)

Death of 'the man who won the war'

The death of Field Marshal Earl Haig, on January 29, 1928, was marked by tributes in Orkney churches and a special memorial service in St Magnus Cathedral, Kirkwall.

There would be later criticism of Haig over his responsibility for thousands of deaths in the Battle of the Somme and other World War One theatres of conflict, but the German President Hindenburg had described the British soldier as "the man who won the war," and his name was to live on through the Poppy Fund he founded.

Cathedral minister Rev William Barclay said: "Perhaps not from the fifth day of June, 1916, when Earl Kitchener, his staff and the officers and men of the ill-fated *Hampshire* sank to rest in the angry waters that surround your western coast, has the heart of the nation been so deeply moved."

An Orcadian George S. Begg - son of Mr and Mrs George Begg of Stromness - was the operator who sent the first high speed telegram transmission across the Atlantic to New York when the new Western Telegraph office was opened in Belfast in 1928.

The service was opened with Begg transmitting a message from the Lord Mayor of Belfast to the Mayor of New York, and receiving a reply from 3,000 miles away within eight minutes.

* * *

A four legged chicken was hatched at Fillets, Graemsay. "Mr Linklater did not relish the idea of having a monstrosity about his house, so he killed it. Our friend, Mr S. Wilson, has skinned it and we hope to have it set up for Stromness museum," reported *The Orcadian*.

* * *

Dr Kenneth Albert Wilson (41) who was medical officer for Eday from 1922-24, was jailed for 18 months for performing an illegal abortion on a young woman. The doctor had hit hard times after moving to London where a serious illness reduced him to living on charity, staying at a sailors' lodging house, the court in London was told.

* * *

A new road was opened from Hoy to Rackwick. The first motor car to use the road was driven there by Mrs and Miss Begg, the wife and daughter of the Procurator Fiscal in Kirkwall. However, the car broke down and Mr Albert Wick, of Burnmouth, was hired with his horse to tow the disabled vehicle 15 miles from Hoy to Longhope so the car could be shipped back to Stromness via the *Hoy Head*.

* * *

W.R. Tullock & Son, Kirkwall, was selling the new Ford Tudor saloon car - capable of 50-55 mph, 30-35 miles per gallon - for £185 ex works, bumpers £6 extra.

* * *

The whaler *Scapa*, owned by a Leith company, was lost in January, 1928, with 13 of her Norwegian crew off the South Orkney Islands in the South Atlantic.

By 1927, only two companies were engaged in whaling from Scotland - one operating from Olna Firth, Shetland, and another from Harris in the Hebrides. Seven vessels were involved in the 1927 season and they caught 314 whales, compared with 459 in 1926. They were manned almost exclusively by Norwegians, reported *The Orcadian*.

* * *

The first slot machine for stamps was installed at Kirkwall post office - while the telephone was linked up for the first time to Hoy post office.

From boom to bust –

Of all the Orkney stories of "what might have been" in the 20th century, the conflicting fortunes of the Stronsay fishing serve to tell a powerful tale of the decline and fall of an empire.

The industry - based on herring - developed and died in just 50 years. But, while it lasted, the name of Stronsay was known the length of the coast from Shetland to East Anglia. The island's population would grow to 5,000, with an international invasion from not only western Europe but beyond, and visits by ships of thousands of tons - to be welcomed by the biggest bar north of Inverness, a cinema, Italian ice-cream shops and itinerant market traders from as far away as Turkey. They were heady cosmopolitan days which, produced an economy worth the equivalent today of £100 million over a few years at the peak of the bonanza.

Stronsay had its own police station, for a time its own lifeboat, its own customs office and a team of marine pilots to guide in ships from America and Russia. In 1930, the revenue from Stronsay harbour dues was greater than all the other piers in Orkney put together. When Orkney councillors asked for government assistance for Stronsay, they argued that it was in the "national interest," so great were the financial benefits. Stronsay, alone, could provide 25,000 tons of fish a year for the nation, though, in fact, most went abroad.

How much the people of Stronsay gained from all this is debatable - but it can be reckoned to be just a fraction of the total turnover.

For, although it was an industry *in* Stronsay, it was not an industry *of* Stronsay. Most of those involved were outsiders who descended on the island for just three months of June, July and August each year.

The end when it came was sudden. The advent of World War Two was generally blamed for the demise of the Stronsay herring industry but, in fact, it had been in its death throes for the previous three or four years. The herring industry nationally met a crisis in the late 1930s with the fishing authorities denouncing the lack of government support.

In fact, a truer reason for the decline was that the laws of nature would not conform with the routine of man. There were undoubted changes in the herring migration patterns and the "silver darlings" did not always arrive to suit the traditional schedules of the fishermen and the fish curers which had become established over the years. For years, the routine had grown up - the fishing boats, and their accompanying army of shore workers, would start the season in the North and then follow the shoals as they progressed down the east coast of first Scotland and then England, with the season ending in Yarmouth or Lowestoft. A change in migration patterns of just a month could mean the difference between boom or bust for the herring ports.

This was illustrated vividly in Stronsay's case in 1937 - the year the industry hit rock bottom. A premature halt to the season was called after catches worth just £11,950 had been landed at Whitehall village. The curers and the fisher girls moved on - and it was too late to return six weeks later when the seas around the north of Orkney were reported to be awash with heavy shoals of herring.

It had been all so different 30 years earlier. Records show that Stronsay sold herring to the Dutch as far back as the 16th century, but it was the start of the 20th century which was to see the birth of the modern day era of the Stronsay herring industry - and a couple of generations of prosperity.

At the end of the 19th century, there had been bigger herring stations in Orkney - at Holm and Burray, Stromness and Kirkwall and, in the North Isles, it was Sanday which could claim one of the most modern herring factories - but fate was to see Stronsay grow into the headquarters of the industry.

It started with the establishment of what became known as the Station, at the lower end of Whitehall village, where men from Fair Isle, other islands of Orkney and the North East of Scotland settled, and worked from the Station pier which was built towards the end of the 19th century. A former Stronsay resident, Mrs Margaret Miller, was later to tell *The Orcadian* that as many as 50 children would go to the local school from the Station.

Major harbour developments followed and in the first decade of the 20th century, Whitehall witnessed the completion of, first, the Steamers pier and then the building of the West pier. It was said that it was possible to walk right across Whitehall harbour, stepping from fishing boat to fishing boat. An annual invasion of as many as 300 drifters - mainly from the areas of Banff and Buckie - would descend on the island as their base for 12 weeks of fishing, to provide the raw materials for the hundreds of fisher girls working at 17 curing stations in Stronsay and another five in Papa Stronsay. They were joined by salesmen and merchants, dozens of coopers who manufactured the barrels, and a whole battalion of coal workers - loading and unloading the huge coal hulks which sat off the shore to service the steam drifters.

The Orkney Steam Navigation Company operated special charter trips to transport to Stronsay the hundreds of itinerant fish workers, men and women who arrived in Orkney from all over Scotland, Ireland and England. The women would sleep on sacks of straw in dormitories of six in wooden accommodation huts. There were some Stronsay women who joined the annual summer work at the fish curers, and there were Stronsay coopers who operated throughout the year, but, mainly, it was an invasion of outsiders. The 1921 census showed the permanent population of the islands of Stronsay and Papa Stronsay to be 1,061 - but the population from June to August would balloon to five times that number.

And the islanders undoubtedly benefited from the spin-off of the industry. It provided a captive market for Stronsay's farmers who could sell all they could produce, and led to the growth of shopping facilities which many a small town would envy today - ten general merchants' shops, three bakeries, five butchers and as many travelling grocery vans, as well as the fish and chip cafes, barber shops and confectioners. Astonishingly, there were five ice cream parlours, three of them owned by Italians. Perhaps the best known was Adam Gillinotti. One of his first employees was Livio Zanre who later went on to run the Central Cafe in Kirkwall for many years.

From 1909, it was felt necessary to have a lifeboat, the *John Ryburn*, stationed in Stronsay to safeguard the fleet. Its crew featured some well known Stronsay names - Miller, Shearer, Leslie, Stout, Fiddler, Eunson and Williamson - but the station closed at the outbreak of World War One and, although representations were made, and a volunteer crew came forward, for the lifeboat to be reinstated in 1930, it never returned, having been transferred to Peterhead. In fact it was 1952 before a lifeboat was again stationed in Stronsay.

Much of the Stronsay herring went to Germany and Russia, but there could be as many as ten big freight vessels, up to 3,000 tons from Spain, the Scandinavian countries, even America, arriving at any one time to load the fish - guided into the harbour by a team of marine pilots competing for business with such rivalry that more than one dispute ended up in Kirkwall Sheriff Court.

The original Stronsay Hotel was built, with the luxury of gaslight, and what was claimed to be the biggest bar in the North of Scotland, while along the road the Stronsay cinema provided nightly entertainment. Margaret Miller recalled for *The Orcadian*: "The Kirkwall Pipe Band and Brass Band came

the Stronsay fishing

At the start of the century, the island of Sanday played as big a part as Stronsay in the herring industry. This huge herring factory dominated the scene at Kettletoft, Sanday, for several decades. (Picture courtesy of Kenneth H.S. Foubister)

to the island in the summer on a Saturday amid great excitement, and the shops - which hardly ever closed anyway - would stay open until 1am." Work ceased on Sundays and she added: "The singing in the church was something worth hearing as hundreds of fisher folk joined in with the locals. After the service, the Salvation Army would hold another at the head of the pier."

The Stronsay industry had survived the difficulties of World War One — partly thanks to intervention by the government which, in 1919-20, guaranteed a market and a price for herring. This was not without its problems. By December, 1920, it was reported, the government was left with 800,000 unsold barrels of herring as Continental markets collapsed.

In 1922, the fisher girls in Stronsay complained that they had earned only 30 shilllings for a month's work. Had it been better fishing, they could have earned £10-£12 a month. Nonetheless, the total catches landed at Stronsay that year realised £23,100 and steam drifters were said to have grossed between £600 - £1,200 each, and in the following post-war years the industry gradually recovered. In fact, the value of catches landed in Stronsay during the three month season of 1924 was £113,000 - the equivalent figure being nearer £10millions at 1999 prices!

Unfortunately, it could not last, and the first voices of concern were raised as early as 1927 when it was reported that the curers, who had made big preparations for heavy landings, had finished the season with sizeable losses. The fishing in 1927, from June 7 to August 24, and the start of the 1928 season, was said to be "poor."

The Stronsay folk had more serious concerns just before the start of the 1929 season, however, when the island was hit by an epidemic of poliomyelitis. The outbreak was reported to the county council in May, 1929, by the medical officer of health Dr Walter Bannerman.

"Two cases have died of the disease, the rest are progressing favourably. The epidemic is well under control," he said. The following week, however, saw the further death of a 14 year old Stronsay girl. One school was ordered to be shut and it was possible that all schools would have to be closed for a fortnight. Eventually, there was a total of 17 cases of polio - 11 of them among children aged under 15 - and four fatalities, including three young men, aged 16, 21 and 26.

In the end, the 1929 Stronsay herring season finished with improved figures. As the curers closed down and most of the women workers left in August, it was revealed that the season's total had amounted to 60,418 crans, valued at £88,414, against 52,660 crans, worth £86,970, at the corresponding date in 1928. That was an equivalent value, at 1999 prices, approaching £10 million.

When the Secretary of State for Scotland, Mr William Adamson, visited Orkney in June, 1930, the county council sought to win government grants for vital harbour works at Stronsay to sustain the fishing industry. It was in the national interest, Councillor Alex Calder told the minister, and the financial burden could not be shouldered by Orkney. "The fishing is entirely carried on by interests outside the county. Boats and personnel are brought to the county for the season," he said. And whatever the success of the herring fishing, it could not sustain Stronsay's population which, by the 1931 census, had fallen by 100 to 943.

The plea for government help obviously fell on deaf ears because in October, 1936, the main pier of Whitehall harbour was said to be in imminent danger of collapse with Stronsay representative Mr Ralph Fotheringhame lambasting the Orkney harbours commissioners for concentrating all their spending on Kirkwall improvements.

While Stronsay's herring industry took the spotlight, Orkney still had its own indigenous inshore fishing industry. However by the early 1930s that was in a parlous state, leading to public protest meetings in Westray and Papa Westray where the blame was directed at the deep sea trawlers of Aberdeen and Humberside which were accused of plundering the seas around Orkney.

Coinciding with the decline of the fishing was a crisis in the kelp industry. In 1906, the county's output exceeded more than 2,000 tons, and earned more than £12,000, mainly for the North Isles. By the 1930s, there were still 300 families in North Ronaldsay, Westray and Papay, Sanday, Stronsay and Evie who relied on the annual seaweed harvest to supplement their income. However, cheap imported supplies used in the manufacture of iodine and other products were now coming into Britain from Japan and Chile, and prices tumbled to the extent that, in 1935, it was feared that no Orkney kelp would be purchased.

Mr William Traill of Holland, Papa Westray, warned: "Unless something is done to revive the fishing industry, a great many people will be in very straitened circumstances." If the area was closed to trawlers, he said, a large and valuable food supply would be secured for the county, and even for export, instead of the incongruous situation prevailing whereby Orkney depended on imports of fish from Shetland or Aberdeen.

Spurred on by the alarm of Westray and Papay, at the start of 1935, the county council sent a petition to the Scottish Secretary, pleading for a complete ban on deep sea trawlers in inshore waters, and asking for a fishery cruiser to be stationed at Pierowall to police such a ban. The council regarded with dismay how "the erstwhile flourishing fishing industry in Orkney has been reduced by the complete lack of regard and protection afforded it."

The statistics quoted by the council were certainly a dramatic illustration of the decline in fish caught by line and landed in Orkney. In 1890, a total of 78,452 hundredweight was landed to a value of £19,797 - and the number of fishermen engaged in the industry was 2,142. By 1933, the catch had fallen to 2,735 hundredweight, valued at £2,746, and only 596 fishermen were said to be engaged in the industry.

"The ruin of the fishing industry has caused many of the younger generation to turn from rural to urban industry with the result that the population of Orkney has shown a steady decrease during the present century," complained the council. Excluding, the burghs of Kirkwall and Stromness, the population of the county had fallen from 22,538 in 1901 to 16,966 in 1931.

Crisis too was looming for the Stronsay, indeed, the national herring industry with reports in July, 1937, that the season's fishing had been a "complete failure" so far. Although prices had risen because of a scarcity of fish, the landings were so small that curers and shore workers were left idle. One worker was quoted as saying: "The herring industry has been going down and down, but this is about the last straw." A new Norwegian-built plant which had been installed in Stronsay to manufacture fish meal from the herring offal was to stand unused.

The season was brought to a premature close in the first week of August with the total catch for the season only 6,950 crans - about ten per cent of the levels ten years earlier - valued at just £11,950. Infuriatingly, six weeks later, after the fisher folk had gone, huge shoals of herring appeared off the north of Orkney. Elsewhere, more vocal protests were being raised and a mass demonstration at Britain's "herring capital" of Yarmouth heard calls for the government to act to save the industry. There were complaints that Hitler was building up the German fishing fleet while Britain's was being left to flounder.

A minimal revival in 1938 saw landings and values of herring at Stronsay double to 15,600 crans worth £23,300, just a

This photograph from around 1920 shows an apprentice cooper Andrew Young who was employed by Moar's Cooperage in Stronsay. (Picture from the files of *The Orcadian*)

quarter of the levels of a "poor year" in the 1920s, and 1939 was another disaster with just 3,994 crans, valued £6,731, landed. The war intervened but it is probable that few of the fisher folk would have returned the following year even if peace had reigned.

Throughout the great era of Stronsay, with a population at times of more than 5,000, the island had relied on sending emergency messages by telegraph. Ironically, as it all ended, Stronsay was linked to the national telephone service.

And one of the first emergencies to be reported by the new telephone system was to be in August, 1939, when one of the main symbols of the island's prosperity of the herring age, the Stronsay Hotel, was destroyed by fire. The two storey building, owned by county councillor D.J. Macrae, was completely gutted, with damage estimated at £2,000, although fire-fighting efforts prevented the blaze spreading to other properties in Whitehall village. Two months later, the Orkney Licensing court granted a licence allowing the hotel to be "moved" along the street to Armadale House.

But other memories would remain. In the 1990s, a £100,000 interpretation centre opened in the former fish mart, incorporating a museum telling the story of the time when hundreds of boats thronged the harbour of one of the major herring ports of Britain.

And, fittingly, it was to be Stronsay men, the Reid brothers, who would play a leading role in pioneering Orkney's new fishing era, with the establishment of the county's £20 million white fish trawler fleet, in the second half of the 20th century.

The union of two great Churches

It was "one of the most memorable days in the history of Scotland," said Rev C. A. Gray, minister at Kirkwall's Paterson Kirk as the union of Scotland's two great Churches - the Church of Scotland and the United Free Church - took place on Wednesday, October 2, 1929.

A series of thanksgiving services for "Union Sunday" were held in Orkney Kirks to mark the successful conclusion of years of discussions. Until the Union, the Church of Scotland congregation of

784 members in Kirkwall worshipped at St Magnus Cathedral, while 812 members of the United Free Church congregation worshipped at the Paterson (or East) Kirk.

The Church of Scotland had 27 charges in Orkney at this time, with a membership of 4,450, while the United Free Church had 26 charges and 5,649 members. However, no fewer than eight Church of Scotland congregations were without a minister and seven United Free Church charges were vacant. Sanday, at this time, had a total of four ministers.

A report by the General Assemblies of the two Churches had proposed that, in several parishes, the ministries of the two Kirks should be combined. The proposals would mean a reduction, within a few years, of 24 ministers.

Kirkwall turns to drink

The electorate of Kirkwall went to the polls to allow new licences to be granted for the sale of alcoholic liquor.

Kirkwall had voted to impose restrictions on licensed premises in 1920, continued at further polls in 1923 and 1926.

The 1929 vote - under the auspices of the controversial Temperance Act of 1913 - saw a lively month-long campaign by both sides to woo the electors.

Stromness, Wick and Lerwick had voted to remain "dry" and an advertisement in *The Orcadian* by the Kirkwall branch of the Scottish Temperance Alliance urged: "Kirkwall electors should, at the coming poll, rid their town of this dangerous and unchristian traffic, and follow the example of Stromness, Lerwick and Wick."

A rival advert from the Anti-Prohibition Campaign Council proclaimed: "What

right have the Pussyfoots to assume that the children of today require the shackles of Prohibition to make them upright and honourable citizens?"

The first meeting of the new unified Orkney Presbytery of the Church of Scotland also appealed to Kirkwall to vote "no licence" while the Orkney Local Veto Defence Association pointed out that Kirkwall had no convictions for drunkeness in 1929.

The entire front page of *The Orcadian* on the eve of the poll was taken up by advertisements from the anti-drink lobby. It did them no good, however, as 1,323 people out of Kirkwall's electorate of 1,670 turned out to vote for the repeal of the prohibition legislation by a majority of just 46 votes.

The vote was: Repeal resolution 678 No licence 632

Aukney

It is generally accepted that the last ever Great Auk was shot in Papa Westray in 1812 (and that specimen could be seen at the British Museum.)

However, there was a flurry of excitement in birding circles in 1929 when the publication *Bird Notes and News* reported that a Great Auk had been seen in Norway's Lofoten Islands. There were even reports that two had been seen in Orkney - at Hoy Head and on the island of Suleskerry.

* * *

The old-established Stromness distillery - dating back to 1784 and formerly known as the Old Man o' Hoy Distillery - was sold by Messrs Sinclair and McConnell, the owners since the end of the 19th century, but distilling of Highland malt whisky would continue under the supervision of Mr F.C. Kelly.

* * *

Mr Hugh Marwick, headmaster of Kirkwall burgh school, was appointed as the executive officer of Orkney Education Authority in succession to Mr Frank Young, who was appointed Principal of Dundee Technical College and School of Art. Mr Marwick was succeeded as headmaster by Mr Alexander Leask, already second master and principal teacher of science at the school.

* * *

Orkney punters were celebrating, it was reported, after a five year old horse called Old Orkney - owned by Irish millionaire Mr J.J. Murphy, who made his fortune from tea planting in India - won the Goodwood Cup, one of Britain's major races.

* * *

Kirkwall Town Council accepted an offer of £1 each, from Kirkwall engineers W. & J. Leslie, for the four cannons which stood in front of St Magnus Cathedral.

Stromness - the hub of Europe?

Oh, what might have been! Instead of Rotterdam becoming the greatest port of Europe, it could have been Stromness.

In 1929, the Canadian government investigated the possibility of a regular shipping service between Churchill, on the Hudson Bay, to Stromness, carrying Canada's surplus wheat crop to Orkney. Stromness would act then as the distribution centre to all of Europe.

The new service was being considered because the railway from Canada's western provinces now extended as far as Churchill. It certainly was not simply

"paper talk" because, by March, 1929, *The Orcadian* reported that Mr Alexander McOwen, a Canadian government representative, had already visited Orkney for preliminary discussions.

There was talk of a fleet of fast grain carrying ships operating to a British port and "it is asserted that, strategically and historically, Stromness answers all the requirements."

The idea apparently disappeared down the plughole of the great depression that hit both sides of the Atlantic.

Tragedy as five die in Westray

Sunday, June 16, 1929, will be remembered as a day of dire tragedy for Westray and Papa Westray after a sea disaster in which five Orcadians - three women and two men - lost their lives.

The five perished in Sandquoy Bay after their 14 feet skiff sank after being swamped in strengthening winds half a mile from shore when the party was

returning from a visit to Papay.

The victims were brothers Thomas and John Rendall, and two teenage daughters Maggie Ann, daughter of Thomas, and Maggie, daughter of John, and Mary Foulis, a sister-in-law of the brothers.

A public appeal fund for the victims' families later raised over £200.

Steamer disaster but 65 saved

One of the most familiar sights in Northern ports, the mail, cargo and passenger steamer *St Sunniva*, was totally wrecked after going aground on the island of Mousa, Shetland, in dense fog. All 42 passengers and 23 crew were safely evacuated.

Stromness lifeboat was called out - leaving at 5.40am and arriving at Lerwick at 7.20pm - but was not required, and eventually got back to Stromness at 1.45pm the following day after a total trip of 240 miles. (Fortunately, soon after this, the first Shetland lifeboat station opened at Lerwick.)

All the passengers of the *St Sunniva* were roused and taken off the stricken

1930

steamer by the three port lifeboats. "Captain Williamson and the whole ship's company behaved magnificently, as also did the passengers, including the women," said *The Orcadian*.

"The stewards and stewardesses knew their emergency duties and carried them out calmly while the captain himself assisted to launch the lifeboats," said passenger Captain L. R. Anderson, who was travelling with his wife and son,

when the stranding occurred on April 10, 1930.

Several thousands of pounds were feared lost as 130 bags of mail were given up to the sea. Ironically, the four bags of mail which were later found contained income tax demands! It was the second, and final, drama for the *St Sunniva* in two years.

In May, 1928, 45 passengers were safely taken off the ship by the Peterhead lifeboat when the 864 ton *St Sunniva*, owned by the North of Scotland and Orkney and Shetland Steam Navigation Company, went ashore in dense fog near Peterhead. On that occasion, the vessel was later refloated and continued to Aberdeen.

Centenarian or hoaxer?

Was he Orkney's oldest man - or the county's biggest hoaxer?

In 1930, Orcadian William Groundwater was said, at the age of 101, to be Britain's oldest working tailor, according to national newspapers who visited him at his business in Pendlebury, Manchester.

He claimed to have been born in Orphir in 1829, and that his mother had also lived to over 100. He had left Orkney in his youth, obtaining work as a draper's assistant in Glasgow where, according to Mr Groundwater, he played for the original Glasgow Rangers football club.

He later moved to Manchester where he started his own business and told those

who cared to listen that, at the age of 100, he could still walk 20 miles a day, having spent only half a crown on doctors during the previous 50 years.

He was said to be acknowledged as one of the "greatest living experts" of violins and Orkney fiddles, of which he had made several.

In 1932 - having outlived his wife and three children - he returned to Orkney to live in Rendall, where he died in October, 1936, apparently at the age of 107, having enjoyed a daily drink of beer and been a chain smoker right up to the end.

His name did not appear in local baptism records so there was nothing to

substantiate his true age - but relatives suggested he had added ten years at least to his true age.

Rabbits - breeding like rats

A freak of nature, claimed the Stromness correspondent of *The Orcadian*, James Marwick, had seen rats and rabbits inter-breeding on Stromness's Outer Holm - producing a hybrid rabbit with a long tail and the feet of a rat.

One specimen had been found "by one of the Wishart boys" who lived at Ness, and the creature was said to be about the size of an ordinary half grown rabbit with the head and body of a rabbit. "This rare hybrid was seen by several highly-reliable townspeople who declare that they never before have seen such a creature," said *The Orcadian*. Unfortunately, the animal had now been destroyed and disposed of, added the report.

However, the story prompted an immediate slump in the rabbit trade of local butchers. One Kirkwall dealer reported later that he had not sold a single rabbit since the offending article had appeared in print.

It was later suggested that the mystery creature could have been an escaped Canadian musk rat, kept for fur farming.

* * *

The world draughts champion Robert Stewart visited Kirkwall in May, 1930, and simultaneously played 41 local opponents on different boards. Of that number, only six of the Orkney players succeeded in managing a draw against the champion in the exhibition staged at Kirkwall Temperance Hall.

Few jobs for the boys at the council

Local government reorganisation saw a newly constituted Orkney County Council come into being - and the demise of Orkney's parish councils.

The administrative work of the new council would come under one official, Duncan J. Robertson, and Mr William Isbister became his assistant. Mr Robertson's salary as county clerk, treasurer and collector, for the year from May 16,1930, was set at £650. Councillors on the new county council would receive expenses of 15/- a day.

In 1930, *The Orcadian* reported that just 39 men and five women were employed in national and local government positions in Orkney (this obviously did not include school teachers).

The first convener of the new county

council was Mr J. Storer Clouston, and vice-convener Mr Alexander Calder.

The parish councils had been set up in 1895. Major William Robertson, Elwickbank, Shapinsay, held the appointment of chairman of Shapinsay parish council from its inception to its abolition, a total of 35 years. William Tait was also chairman of St Andrews and Deerness parish council for the entire 35 years.

At the end of 1930, the county council decided to adopt a new coat of arms for Orkney. A "wealthy, patriotic and anonymous gentleman" had agreed to finance the registering of the new county standard with the Lyon King of Arms. The new coat of arms would consist of an impaled shield, having on one side a sailing galley and on the other the lion rampant holding an axe.

Police guard for the SWRI

"You are a set of cowardly young hooligans," Sheriff George Brown told eight Birsay youths who appeared at Kirkwall Sheriff Court charged with annoying and molesting the members and friends of the Birsay branch of the Scottish Women's Rural Institute.

The Fiscal explained the SWRI had started in Orkney in the 1920s. The branch meetings were "a source of great interest to many of the countywomen who hitherto did not have very much to brighten their lives."

Around the county, meetings were conducted in the most orderly and peaceful manner - except at Dounby and Birsay where it was necessary to have a policeman to keep order.

The Sheriff, imposing fines of £2, or 20 days imprisonment, said he did not understand why their mothers and sisters did not get the men in the neighbourhood "to give them a good thrashing."

* * *

Dozens of livestock were killed as houses were struck by lightning and hailstones fell as big as marbles in what was said to be the worst thunderstorm to strike the islands in living memory in September, 1930.

* * *

A new Morris Minor cost £140 ex works, and a Morris Six, with coachbuilt saloon, cost £299 from J. & W. Tait, Kirkwall.

* * *

There were enough Orcadians in Brooklyn, USA, for an Orkney Rovers football team. A game on November 15, 1930, saw Orkney Rovers beat Brooklyn Thistle 3-1. The man-of-the-match, played at Marine Manor, Brooklyn, was said to be right back Harry Begg of Stromness.

* * *

William Learmonth, of Saither, lost his watch while competing in the 1929 West Mainland Ploughing Match. It was found 12 months later by James Craigie, Lyking, when ploughing the same ground.

* * *

Bishop of the Peculiar People

William Heddle, a native of Stromness, born at Redland, son of John Heddle, became Bishop of a sect known as the Peculiar People, an organisation he joined after leaving Orkney at the age of 18.

The sect, based in Southend, Essex, was founded by James Banyard, a Wesleyan preacher, in 1837.

In the case of illness, sect members refused medical aid and believed in the power of prayer to cure all ills.

Such beliefs obviously did no harm to Bishop Heddle who, in 1930, at the age of 85, celebrated his golden wedding with his wife, Emma. He continued as Bishop until 1942 when he retired on account of his age, and in August, 1946, he celebrated his 100th birthday in Southend with his wife, to whom he had, by then, been married 66 years.

A four masted, 132 feet long Danish schooner, the *Olga*, carrying a cargo of timber for Kirkwall merchants W.B. Peace and Son, had a miraculous escape after leaving Sweden on the voyage which usually took three weeks to Orkney.

For weeks she had been reported missing and was feared lost when, after 64 days at sea, most of which time she had been drifting helplessly in gale force conditions after the master was washed overboard and drowned, she was towed into Aalesund in Norway in January, 1930.

* * *

Three Stromness fishermen J. Folster, J. Sinclair and William Black landed a halibut weighing 168lbs with a handline in Hoy Sound.

* * *

Mr Alfred Baikie was appointed Lord Lieutenant of Orkney and Shetland in succession to Sir William Watson Cheyne, who resigned through ill health. Sir William, a distinguished surgeon who reached the rank of Surgeon Rear Admiral in World War One, had served as Lord Lieutenant since 1919. Alfred Baikie - who succeeded to the Tankerness estates on the death of his brother William Dover Baikie - had served as county convener from 1909-17.

The one-legged German aviator Wolfram Hirth who attempted to fly from Orkney to America in 1930. He took off from Orphir and safely completed the first leg of the trip to Iceland, where he was forced to abandon the venture.

(Picture from the files of *The Orcadian*)

Farming in crisis -

The fall-out from the black clouds of economic depression that hit the world at the end of the 1920s and beginning of the 1930s did not spare Orkney farmers. The crisis in agriculture was so grave that thousands took to the streets in the greatest public protest rally to be seen in Orkney in the 20th century.

In the last five years of the 1920s, Orkney agriculture had expanded significantly. Farm statistics showed that between 1925-29, the number of cattle increased by 17 per cent from 30,441 to 35,306, while the number of sheep increased by 60 per cent from 34,892 to 54,507. Cattle exports had grown to an estimated 10,000 animals in 1929 - while egg exports stood at an annual 2.5 million dozens.

And the county already had a national reputation for quality, with ten Orkney bullocks being purchased at £24 10s each for the King's Royal Farms at Windsor in the Spring of 1930.

As a rough guide, that amount can be multiplied to provide an equivalent 1999 price approaching £2,000 per animal - a figure that today's farmers would accept with gratitude.

Similarly, Orkney's egg exports in 1933 were valued at £148,000 - the equivalent approaching £10 millions at the end of the century.

The farmers of today would probably wonder what their predecessors were complaining about. Two year old cattle were selling at the markets for around £22 in 1928; the champion Aberdeen Angus bull at the annual bull show of Orkney Agricultural Society at Kirkwall Mart that same year went for £72 to Mr W.F. Brown, Breckowall, Westray; and pig prices at Aberdeen mart in 1929 reached new heights of 63s, a 1999 equivalent of around £200.

Col T. Smith Peace must have been relatively satisfied with the state of the economy when he announced that on his 80th birthday on July 16, 1928, he would retire after 53 years from his business as auctioneer and cattle salesman, and transfer the Kirkwall cattle mart to his nephew David Balfour Peace.

"It may reasonably be claimed that Orkney leads the Kingdom" in the quality of beef, said *The Orcadian* of January 31, 1929. "It is time we realised it and gave the matter the widest publicity."

Certainly, Orkney agriculture was already moving into the modern mechanised era with the harvest at Swanbister, Orphir, being gathered by an Albion binder pulled by a 28 hp Fordson tractor in the autumn of that year. (Not everyone was in favour: a debate on the merits of horses and mechanical traction at a meeting of Orkney Agricultural Discussion Society and the West Mainland Farmers Union at Dounby in January, 1931, saw 17 vote for traditional horsepower and only nine for tractors. In 1935, members of the mutual improvement societies of Firth and Sandwick went a step further and voted by 15-11 in favour of a motion that agriculture would benefit from the abolition of motor transport.)

The warning signs of impending crisis for Orkney farmers came, though, in January, 1928, when Mr W. Ritch of Kierfold, Sandwick, told Orkney Agricultural Discussion Society: "Agriculture as an industry is at present passing through a time of depression."

This was underlined by the fact that male dairy workers in Orkney received the lowest weekly wages in Scotland of 23 shillings (including the estimated value of board and lodgings), according to the Scottish Board for Agriculture. For women, it was just 21s, while casual workers earned between 9d-10d per hour. (At the time, a pair of boots could cost 30 shillings and a bottle of whisky 12s 6d.)

There was obviously still a market for farms, however. The upset price for the 45 acre farm of Uppertown, Hoxa, South Ronaldsay, at public auction was £470. It sold for £515.

But by 1930, the industry nationally was reeling as a result of cheap subsidised imports - to the extent that on February 28, 1930, a mass protest rally saw 5,000 farmers, their families and supporters pack Broad Street and the Kirk Green in Kirkwall to voice their anger.

The Isles steamers and motor buses from all the Mainland districts ran special excursion trips to hear the county vice-convener Joseph Storer Clouston tell the demonstration: "This subsidised dumping business is not free trade at all. It is like a man going into the boxing ring armed with a six shooter. We are quite ready to fight the fellow but we cannot as long as he has a gun and we have not. It will not be a question of fighting at all, but merely a bullet followed by a funeral, and it will be our funeral."

Mr William Corrigal, Northbigging, Harray, president of the West Mainland Agricultural Society, said the depression in farming had intensified to alarming proportions in the previous months, with the price of home-produced grain falling to five shillings a hundredweight, and potatoes unsaleable. "Are we to be satisfied with eating the crumbs that fall from the foreigner's table?" he demanded.

Jobs of farm workers were threatened, he warned. "We have examples already in Orkney of large farms being laid down to sheep pasture, and not employing a third of the manpower that was formerly on the farm."

Cheap imports of grain and potatoes would be followed by beef, mutton and eggs. A loss of just a penny a dozen on local eggs would cost Orkney £10,000 a year - nearer £1 million at 1999 prices. "That, you must admit, would spell disaster," he told the assembly.

No wonder, many Orcadians were still being lured to Canada - "the land of opportunity" - with promises of "farms for families, work for farm labourers, homes for domestics and jobs for boys." When a representative of the Canadian Pacific company visited Kirkwall in 1928, he was offering Canadian government-assisted passages of £2, free for under 17s. (Incidentally, at this time, a second class cabin on the steamer from Kirkwall to Aberdeen cost £1 12s 6d)

The fur trade department of the Hudson's Bay Company was still advertising for "sturdy youth 18-21 of good courage, having the spirit of adventure and prepared to rough it. They must have good average upper school education, good manners, ambition to improve their position, be physically fit and of irreproachable character. Preference given to youths with a knowledge of swimming."

News from Australia was less encouraging. A letter from an Orcadian exile to *The Orcadian* in January, 1928, said: "I am writing to warn any Orcadian contemplating emigrating against coming here, as there is a general dearth of employment with thousands out of work and destitute."

In fact, it was a world slump that had hit farming - illustrated when *The Orcadian* reported in May, 1931, that sheep in Queensland, Australia, had been selling at six shillings a dozen (6d each) because of the collapse in wool prices.

Things were not helped back in Orkney in June that year when outbreaks of Foot and Mouth Disease in England and Scotland led to a nationwide standstill order on all movements of cattle, sheep and pigs except by licence, and then only for slaughter. There was no sale at Kirkwall Auction Mart, as a result, and the shipping companies could not accept animals for transport from the Isles. Representations were made to the Ministry of Agriculture for Orkney to be exempted - on the grounds that there had been no recent imports of cattle to Orkney - but no concessions were made.

The importance of farming to the Orkney economy was illustrated by the 1931 census which showed that more than half of the working population - 4,611 - were involved in

the great demonstration

agricultural occupations. However, this was a 16 per cent decrease over ten years.

The Orkney Agricultural statistics for 1933 showed 30,000 acres under oats, another 2,500 under bere/barley, and over 12,000 of turnips/swedes. The county had a cattle population of 37,079, plus 64,882 sheep and there were still 5,434 horses. The poultry population was a massive 482,153 - 20 chickens for every man, woman and child in the county.

Again the voices of farmers were being raised in protest, however. In 1932, Rev T.T. Alexander, a former Orkney minister, was appointed the organising secretary in Scotland of the Agricultural Party, set up to organise the industry for political purposes, and in 1934, Captain Angus Buchanan, brother of Kirkwall solicitor Fred Buchanan, became leader of the Farmers League, a new organisation which was "taking direct action to save the Scottish agricultural industry from ruin."

Captain Buchanan, a well known explorer as well as a qualified architect, had surveyed large areas of Northern Canada for the Saskatchewan government, and, after three years service in the Royal Fusiliers in East Africa, had twice crossed the Sahara desert, making a film of a 16 month expedition from Nigeria to Algiers.

He said: "Last year (1933) was a year of disaster for agriculture. Prices were ruinous. Our crops were sold under cost of production. This year the outlook is even more dark, for 1934 has begun very badly. To my mind it is clear we are being betrayed."

However, West Mainland Agricultural Society members were confident enough to purchase five acres from Mr J. Flett of Curcabreck for a new showyard and to enclose the ground with a five feet wall. The new showyard was used for the first time at the 1934 show in August.

And an example of Orcadian innovation that same year came when farmer William Baikie, Lower Arsdale, Costa, Evie, built his first tractor - converting a 11.9 hp Phoenix touring car for the job - and completing all his season's ploughing with the vehicle.

Farmers did not have to build their own. In *The Orcadian* advertisements for tractors were beginning to appear - John Scarth, Ayre Road, Kirkwall, selling Fergusons, and J. & W. Tait offering Internationals, Massey Harris and Allis Chalmers. There were 26 licensed tractors in Orkney in 1938. However, as most farmers continued to use horses, remarkably there were work oxen in use as late as 1940 when Roland Barnett, of the Cottage, Flotta, was still ploughing with three oxen. There were drawbacks to working with animals. In 1930 *The Orcadian* reported that, after having his right ear almost severed by a bite from a horse, David Laughton, of Lynnfield, Holm, walked four and a half miles to have medical attention and, after having his ear stitched back on, he walked all the way back to work again.

Janetta Logie of Westray was judged champion dairymaid at the Scottish National Fatstock Show of 1936. It would not have made her wealthy - by 1938 cattlewomen's wages rose to 27s a week, but those who milked just 10 cows would get 11s 6d week. Male general farmworkers were now on 32s but their working week varied from 44 hours mid-November to mid-February, 50 hours mid-February to mid-November, and 60 hours during six consecutive weeks of the corn harvest. (Also deductions could be made from the foregoing pay rates if the workers were supplied with milk, potatoes or peat).

Milking of cows by machine was started by Mr Charles Anderson of Corse Farm, St Ola, in 1938. That year there were 160 Orkney herds certified free from Tuberculosis but the main concern in the West Mainland was the discovery of a case of Anthrax in a two year old bullock at a Harray farm. The diseased animal was cremated by police, and the Ministry of Agriculture notified. Fortunately, it appeared to be an isolated case.

That same year, a new £1,000 limited liability company, Stromness Auction Mart, was formed with 200 £5 shares to operate livestock and general auction sales, after taking over the mart premises on a 20 year lease. James Wood of Garson Farm, Sandwick, became the new chairman. It was Mr Wood, who, in 1939, would lead the way in Orkney with experiments on silage production in trials organised by Mr Gordon Watt, the Orkney county organiser for the North of Scotland College of Agriculture.

New innovations were proceeding apace in the run-up to the outbreak of war. January, 1939, saw the advent of the battery laying poultry system at Heathfield, St Ola, where Mr William Scott had installed 324 battery cages and was planning to triple the size of the operation. There was no doubt that the system had come to stay, said *The Orcadian*. That year's County Show also saw electric fences for farm fields exhibited for the first time.

However, it was not only the arrival of new technology that was to now revitalise Orkney's farming economy - it was also the arrival of tens of thousands of men - soldiers and civilians - who descended on these shores in the wartime emergency. Within weeks, farmers had a huge new captive market. Virtually all of Orkney's production of cattle, sheep and pigs could go to feed not only the islands but also the demands of the military, with huge ships to be supplied daily in Scapa Flow as well as all the shore establishments.

Subsidies were introduced to encourage greater cultivation of fields - doubled from £2 to £4 an acre in 1944 - and dozens of new tractors, despite the problems of war, were imported into the county. Not only that, but farm employees benefited with agricultural wages literally doubling within six years so that, by 1944, a general farmworker was paid £3 5s a week and shepherds £3 12s.

There were occasional snags - for a while it looked as though the scarcity and expense of feedstuffs for hens would threaten the wartime viability of the Orkney industry; and in 1942 it was reported that Orkney was suffering a shortage of cabbages (for which farmers were being paid £16 a ton). But, generally, after the depressions of the 1930s, the farmers of the county could enjoy a new confidence.

It was in such expansionist mood that, in October, 1941, egg producers, co-operatives and merchants in the county linked up in a new company, Orkney Egg Producers Ltd. (There were an estimated 4,000 egg producers in Orkney at the time). A new egg packing station was opened in Cromwell Road, Kirkwall, and more than 100,000 eggs were handled in the first week of operations. By 1946, the 1,042 producers in membership of Orkney Egg Producers - now based at the Ayre Mills packing station - had produced 30 million eggs during the year, and the turnover of the company for the first time was over half a million pounds - £500,071 - the equivalent of £12 millions at 1999 prices. By 1947, the Ayre Mills packing station was acknowledged as the largest in Scotland, with 8.75 million eggs handled in just eight weeks up to May 28, 1947. (A setback that same week saw Orkney's farmers warned to cancel all imports of chicks into the county as fowl pest swept through poultry flocks in the South).

It was not only the poultry sector that was buoyant, however. Livestock prices generally were at a healthy level. Top price at the 1943 Orkney Agricultural Society Aberdeen Angus bull sale was 98 guineas, or £102 18s, and at the Perth bull sales, Orkney cattle dealer John T. Flett paid 220 guineas, or £231, for a Shorthorn.

The end of the hostilities saw the loss to Orkney of the

temporary wartime population, but there were encouraging signs in 1946 that - with the desperate need to feed the nation - Orkney farmers were winning back export markets.

In 1946, a total of 6,455 cattle and 15,600 sheep were shipped from Kirkwall and Stromness. A further 2,600 cattle and 5,200 sheep served home consumption. It was estimated that cattle, sheep and pigs earned over £393,000 in the year - around £10 millions at 1999 prices.

And farmers must have felt that the "years of plenty" had arrived as prices boomed. At Aberdeen mart, in September, 1947, pedigree Border Leicester ram lambs sold to £250, average £101, while gimmers sold to £60, average £36, and ewe lambs averaged £35.

Those prices are the most vivid illustration of the crisis that the industry was to face at the end of the 20th century - for 50 years later, farmers in Orkney were often only attaining the same price that prevailed in 1947. (In the same 50 year period, the average wage in Britain increased nearly forty-fold).

Also, two year old Orkney bullocks were selling strongly to £52 while, despite the advent of the tractor, Orkney-bred Clydesdale horses were still selling at up to £145.

The era of the horse was coming to an end, however. The 1946 Evie ploughing match was the first in Orkney to hold a competition for ploughing by tractor power - the winner was John Baikie of Dale, Costa - and other shows quickly followed suit.

During the war years, 94 per cent of all the tractors produced in Britain had been Fordsons - the Fordson Major cost £237/10/- ex works in 1945 - but September, 1946, saw the dawning of a new era for Orkney farming as that stalwart of the county, the "little grey Fergie," was introduced on the market, price £343. The Ferguson had been produced in the United States for Harry Ferguson Inc for the previous seven years, but would now be mass produced by Standard Motors in Coventry where 10,000 men and women would produce 500 tractors a day.

The agricultural returns for 1947 showed that the number of people in farming had halved in the previous 50 years - with a total of 1,894 men and women now employed full time on Orkney agricultural holdings. They were looking after an estimated total of 33,850 beef cattle, 11,982 dairy cattle and 55,468 sheep. Although the number of horses in the county had fallen by 40 per cent in ten years, down to 3,447, the poultry population had rocketed to an astonishing 692,000 (30 hens for every person in the county).

The 1947 County Show reflected, however, the industry's buoyant economic health that year with new record gate receipts of £630 from an estimated attendance of 6,500. That August produced a drought with Orkney getting just seven hundredths of an inch of rain. Water services were threatened and a hose pipe ban was in place. So at least they had something to complain about again!

The motorised age brought benefits for all, not least Orkney's farmers who, as this photograph illustrates, now had some novel transport methods to get their animals to and from the mart. (Picture courtesy of Orkney Library photographic archive)

A treasure trove for Orkney

A cornucopia of treasures opened up for Orcadians as what was described as "the most richly laden ship to founder in Orkney waters" was wrecked on the island of Swona.

The 6,000 ton Danish freighter *Pennsylvania* was en route from New York to Oslo when she fell prey to fog in July, 1931, and ran aground. The 32 crew safely got away - but they left behind a cargo not only of wheat and flour but also a treasure trove of the latest consumer goods from America.

A gang of 40 men from Wick employment exchange was recruited to remove the cargo of the stranded vessel before it broke up and disappeared - but Orcadians beat them to it, and boat loads of men from the South Isles were reported to be plundering the *Pennsylvania* to lay claim to typewriters, gramophones, cash registers, even a piano.

A Customs officer was sent from Aberdeen to Swona to protect the cargo but, by then, there were few homes in the South Isles which were not adorned with pickings from the ship, said *The Orcadian*.

Another ship to go aground that month was the Norwegian steamer *Borg* - bound from Leningrad to Belfast - which was deliberately beached by her master at Birsay in an attempt to save the vessel, after being holed at sea.

The crew of 15, plus the wife and daughter of the captain, all got ashore safely - and the following weekend 2,000 people turned out to see the wrecked ship on the shore. Plans were made to sell her cargo of timber locally.

Dense fog was the culprit for a series of strandings during July and August of 1931 - but one incident led to four islanders of North Ronaldsay being acclaimed as heroes for saving the lives of four Germans from the trawler *Ludwig Sanders*.

The Germans, all non swimmers, were thrown into the sea as they tried to refloat the trawler grounded at Bride's Ness, North Ronaldsay. They were rescued by John Tulloch, North Ness, his 15 year old son George, John Thomson (62) of South Ness, and his son Martin.

The following week there was an epic experience for passengers - many of them tourists - coming north on the steamer *St Rognvald*. The ship eventually berthed at Stromness 60 hours late, on what should have been a 12 hour voyage, after being caught in dense fog off Wick for three days.

Earthquake shock

The effects of the "biggest earthquake in intensity and area ever recorded in the British Isles" were felt in Kirkwall and Stromness on Sunday, June 7, 1931. It was estimated that the centre of the tremor was south of Hull, with shocks felt as far away as Norway and France. There had been a previous tremor felt in Orkney on January 24, 1927.

The sea freezes over

What was described as the heaviest snowfall in living memory in Kirkwall saw the Basin at the harbour icebound on March 2-3.

Storm force winds and blizzards brought Orkney to a standstill with all communication cut off by the dislocation of telegraph and telephone services. A coffin had to be taken to a Stromness funeral on a horse drawn sledge.

Teachers' pay cut in crisis

A national financial crisis saw the Government order a cut in the pay of school teachers in October, 1931, as part of a package of austerity measures.

The salaries of Orkney teachers were cut by seven and a half per cent in 1932 to help make economies in the county education budget, but the following year the education committee decided there would have to be a further reduction - making a total cut of eight and a third per cent. It would be June, 1935, before the Government agreed to restore teachers' pay levels.

Spending on education in Orkney had nearly trebled in less than 20 years. Education statistics showed the total cost of education in 1913-14 was £18,703; in 1918-19 £24,602; and in 1930-31 £52,394, although the number of pupils had decreased from 3,797 in 1913-14 to 3,243 in 1930-31.

The cost per pupil in those years was (1913-14) £4.84, (1918-19) £6.46, and (1930-31) £16.04, while the cost of education per head of population in Orkney for the same three years was 14s, 19s and 47s.

Plans were announced in 1931 for a new North Walls school costing £1,500.

Orkney misses dramatic milestone

The Orcadian exclusively announced that there was a possibility of the submarine *Nautilus II*, with the intrepid explorer Sir Hubert Wilkins, making a dash for the North Pole from Orkney waters.

The *Nautilus* was leaving New London, Connecticut, USA, for Europe and the plan was for the submarine to pass under the ice of the North Pole, whilst simultaneously the German airship Graf Zeppelin would cruise over the Pole and rendezvous with the submarine, within 10 miles of the Pole, along with the Russian icebreaker *Malyguin*, in early July.

"Surely there has been no more dramatic assembly in history," proclaimed *The Orcadian*. But, in the event, the project - which never did start from Orkney - ended in failure.

New homes for Kirkwall

The single biggest housing project ever launched in Orkney began when Kirkwall Town Council agreed to a new housing scheme of 50 homes to be built on the Council's ground at what was known as the Cabbage Park and the Reservoir Park at Papdale. The three new streets were later named Thoms Street - after Sheriff George Thoms, benefactor of St Magnus Cathedral; George Street - after King George V; and Slater Street - after the then Provost of Kirkwall John Slater. Rents in the new houses would range from 7s to 10s 6d a week, including rates.

Orkney population falls

The 1931 census showed the fifth successive fall in Orkney's population since 1881, with the number of residents dropping to 22,077 - 10,617 males and 11,460 females - a decrease of 2,034 on the 1921 figures, and a decrease of 10,322 on the peak population of 1861.

Of the total population, 20,158 - or 91.3 per cent of the total population - were born in Orkney; 1,511 were born elsewhere in Scotland; 251 in England; 33 in Ireland and six in Wales.

The figures suggested that emigration from Orkney was running at around 200 a year. The total number of households in the 240,847 acres of the county was 5,773.

More than half the working population - 4,611 people - were involved in agricultural occupations - but this showed a decrease of 874, or 16 per cent on 1921.

There were 711 female domestic servants, but the decline in fishing was shown with the number giving their occupation as fishermen down by 139 to 234.

There were 718 employed in commercial occupations; 558 in transport and communications and 342 in professional occupations.

The total population of the Orkney Mainland was 13,352 - which included 4,397 in Kirkwall and St Ola and 1,592 in Stromness. Island populations included South Ronaldsay 1,702; Westray 1,269; Hoy 955; Sanday 1,160; Stronsay 943; Eday 470; North Ronaldsay 298; Shapinsay 584; Flotta 282; Rousay, Egilsay and Wyre 597; Graemsay 114; and Papa Westray 237. Fara, in Scapa Flow, still had a population of 28 and Cava 14.

Illegitimate births

The number of illegitimate births in Orkney in 1931 was, in percentage terms, the highest in Scotland and showed that "one in every eight babies entered the world bearing a stigma that can only be removed, socially, by the subsequent marriage of the parents," stated *The Orcadian*. The statistics showed the county's death rate, at 16.2 per 1,000 population, was also the highest in Scotland over a three month period.

Bird attack

A three day old lamb, belonging to Mr D. Pratt of Ocklester, Holm, was carried off by a bird and found over a mile away at Nigley, none the worse for its experience. *The Orcadian* report did not identify the bird - but a few months later it was revealed that a golden eagle had returned to Hoy after an absence of several years.

End of the well

The well - variously known as Login's Well or Franklin's Well - at the South end of Stromness was filled in, after being used for centuries to supply some of the most famous ships in history - Captain Cook's two vessels *Resolution* and *Discovery* in August, 1780, and Sir John Franklin's ships *Erebus* and *Terror* in 1845.

The well - which also provided water for the Hudson's Bay Company vessels - had been covered over since Stromness's town water system became operative 30 years earlier.

Flu disruptions

A proclamation of marriage had to be announced from the steps of St Magnus Cathedral, after being signed by two elders, because the minister was unable to take a Sunday morning service as an epidemic of influenza closed schools and businesses.

Lost in the post

A search was started the length of Britain after 20 year old Eday-born Rose Hercus was reported missing, having "disappeared" travelling from Broadstairs in Kent to her parents' home in Orkney. *The Orcadian* made a dramatic appeal for its readers in London and Edinburgh to help in the search.

And that was all rather embarrassing for Rose Hercus when she read the story!

She explained to the newspaper the following week that she had started a new job at an Edinburgh hotel and her letter, informing her parents of this, must have gone astray in the post.

First post

The first Air Mail post from Australia reached Orkney.

Name change

Orkney Education Committee agreed the change of name of Kirkwall Secondary School to Kirkwall Grammar School.

International honour

Stromness hockey player Norma Rossie - eldest daughter of Stromness draper William Rossie - was selected for the Scotland ladies hockey team for a six week tour of the USA, visiting Boston, Chicago, St Louis and Baltimore. She was working as a PE teacher at Kilmarnock Academy.

Dance abandoned

The New Year dance at Eday had to be abandoned in a fracas. Two men were later fined for riotous conduct.

Wireless licences

The total number of wireless licences in Orkney had risen to 491 - about one household in twelve.

Misadventure

An intruder who broke into a Kirkwall house accidently gassed himself to death after inadvertently switching on a gas tap. "Overtaken by the deadly fumes, he had been unable to make his escape before paying the penalty for his nocturnal escapade," reported *The Orcadian*.

Museum grows

After a worldwide appeal for funds to purchase the neighbouring old Stromness Town Hall, Orkney Natural History Society's extension to Stromness Museum was formally opened by the Lord Lieutenant for Orkney Alfred Baikie.

Car sales

The 7.8 hp four cylinder Austin Seven car was selling at £130 at D. Wishart's Stromness garage.

Baby kidnap horror touches Orkney

1932

The after shocks of one of the first, and most tragic, human interest stories of the new age of international mass media were to strike home deeply in Orkney.

American aviation pioneer Charles Lindbergh, born in 1902 in Detroit, made history when he completed the first solo, non-stop trans-Atlantic flight, taking off from New York and landing in Paris on May 31, 1927, in his *Spirit of St Louis* aircraft.

But five years later, he had to pay a terrible price for his fame when his two year old son was kidnapped and murdered in America. And that dreadful event caught up an innocent young girl, Betty Gow, whose relatives came from Orkney.

She was the nurse who was in charge of the Lindbergh baby at the time of the outrage. It was Betty Gow who, on March 1, 1932, discovered the disappearance of the child from a second floor nursery - with a ladder lying outside.

A huge search over two and a half months, and involving thousands of police and state troopers, even saw Al Capone, the "Csar" of American gangsters asking to be released from jail to help in the search. Lindbergh actually paid a ransom of 50,000 dollars, but it was not established whether this was to the genuine kidnappers, or a cruel hoax.

Eventually the skeleton of the baby boy was found in May, 1932, just five miles from the Lindbergh home.

Still in shock after the ordeal she suffered following the child's disappearance, Betty Gow returned to this country and stayed with relatives near Glasgow, although she did make a visit home to Orkney, where her grandmother still lived, in 1933.

Long investigations by the New Jersey Police resulted in 1934 in the arrest of a German born carpenter Bruno Hauptmann. He was sentenced to death and, despite appeals, executed in 1935.

Following the tragedy, Lindbergh and his wife Anne - driven out of the USA by American tabloid newspaper harassment, and fears for the safety of their other son, John, aged three - moved to Britain for some years.

Epic battle to save an island son

The harsh existence of island life was nowhere better illustrated than on Copinsay which, in the 1931 census, was one of the few places in Orkney to show an increase in population.

This was due entirely to the family of farmer James Groat who had 12 children on the island (and another two in Stromness.) The family moved to Copinsay from Deerness in 1927, and, by 1932, the eldest of the children was 22 and the youngest three. The only other residents on the island were the lighthouse keepers and their families.

But the Groat family's first emergency came in January, 1932, when 15 year old David Groat was hit by a paralysing illness, which was feared infectious. It was later to be diagnosed as Poliomyelitis.

The Mainland was alerted to the problem by wireless link between the lighthouse and the Stromness shore station of the Northern Lighthouse Commissioners. Mr James Groat meantime battled in his boat *Copinsay* against heavy seas and engine problems to get from Copinsay to Deerness to seek the help of Dr William Park of Kirkwall, who ordered the immediate removal of the boy to hospital - which was carried out by Mr James Ritch and his son William who ran the weekly mail boat to Copinsay from Deerness, the *Pearly Dawn II*.

Orkney's Medical Officer of Health Dr Walter Bannerman later crossed to the island to examine the other children and, as a precautionary measure, the school was closed for a month.

David - treated in the hospital in Main Street, Kirkwall - recovered, though the illness left him lame.

A generation later, however, the old hospital was sold and became the West End Hotel. Its owner over four decades was Mrs Eva Currie, neé Groat, the sister of that same young boy who had grown up in Copinsay.

Queen of the Orkney tinkers

Orkney's "Queen of the tinkers," Mrs Isaac MacPhee - better known as Nellie Newlands - died at the age of 82.

She never slept a single night in a house but tradition had it that her good looks in her youth made her the "loveliest girl in Orkney." Her enjoyment of smoking a pipe, later in life, probably amended that view somewhat.

She died at her encampment in a quarry at the Brae of Clouster, near Stromness, on April 17,1932. She had been born in 1850 in Stromness, the daughter of Willie Newlands and "Leezie" White, and was not into her teens when she first hit the road as one of Orkney's itinerant hawkers.

She would ride bare-back on a bay mare, her good looks turning many a head, and in pre-World War One days, many Orkney visitors made a point of meeting her, and she was much photographed, said *The Orcadian*.

Her first husband was Duncan MacPhee and her second husband, who also pre-deceased her, was Isaac Newlands - descendant of a well-known Caithness clan.

She claimed she never slept in a house all her life, but she enjoyed whisky and smoked a pipe, whilst raising a family of two daughters and two sons, George and Isaac. (Isaac also pre-deceased her).

By the 1920s, the "tribe" - as they were affectionately known - had progressed to hawking their wares by motor transport, and there were few areas of Orkney where they were not well-known visitors.

* * *

What was claimed to be the first baby show to be held in Orkney was staged, at a packed Dounby Masonic Hall, by Dounby SWRI with 50 children in four age categories, judged by Medical Officer of Health Dr Walter Bannerman and Nurse Margaret MacKenzie of Finstown. The under threes section was won by twins Grace and Betty Combe of Stromness.

Distilleries in crisis

Orkney whisky production faced extinction in 1932 as the Highland Park distillery of James Grant and Company stood idle for more than a year.

The company wrote to the Chancellor of the Exchequer Neville Chamberlain pleading for a reduction in whisky duty as a bottle of whisky still cost half a week's wages in Orkney.

"Our distillery (the most northern of the Empire, and established for over 130 years) has been silent since April last, and, if something is not done soon to relieve the pressure, it, with many others, is doomed," said the company.

Two years later, the Scapa distillery was temporarily wound up when a meeting of shareholders of Scapa Distillery Ltd placed the company in voluntary liquidation.

The distillery, founded in 1885, had produced up to 40,000 gallons of whisky a year. Westray man James Thomson, who was brewer at the Scapa distillery for 40 years, was estimated to have walked 50,000 miles to and from work, from his home in Kirkwall during his employment there.

The great Stronsay coalmine hoax

A 57 year old man was fined £2 - or 20 days jail - at Edinburgh police court after he admitted fraudulently obtaining 5s each from 17 men. They had handed over the money in return for a promise that the confidence trickster would secure jobs for them at what he claimed was "a newly discovered coalmine on the island of Stronsay."

Gang warfare

Rival gangs were engaged in "guerrilla warfare" with juvenile rioting in the streets of Kirkwall after dark, reported *The Orcadian*. One boy had lost an eye after "pitched battles between opposing gangs." The new housing scheme at Papdale was a favourite battleground.

Trout poaching

Indiscriminate night poaching, particularly in the burns feeding the West Mainland lochs, had robbed the waters of so many thousands of fish that Orkney trout fishing faced disaster, said Orkney Trout Fishing Association.

Police costs

The total cost of the police service in Orkney for the year was £1,618 11s 6d.

Bargain cars

An auction sale at Kirkwall saw three cars sold at £6 15s, £13 5s and £17 5s respectively.

Harvest time

Mrs James Gray, of Horraquoy, Harray, brought in her 71st successive harvest at the age of 85. Her husband had died two years earlier.

The sheep population of Orkney was estimated to have grown by 60 per cent from 34,892 to 54,507 in just five years between 1925-1929, an era of huge growth in the county's agricultural industry.
(Picture courtesy of Orkney Library photographic archive)

Sir William dies, age 79

Sir William Cheyne, eminent Scottish surgeon, and former Lord Lieutenant of Orkney and Shetland, died aged 79 in 1932. A Shetlander, he was Lord Lieutenant from 1919-1930. In World War One, he held the rank of Surgeon Rear Admiral and he received a baronetcy in 1918. He had worked with the world's then greatest known surgeon, Lord Lister, at King's College Hospital, London, in the 1870s.

He carried out his last operation in his 77th year, long after his retirement, when he was travelling to New Zealand on holiday on the liner *Tamaroa*. Two days out of Southampton, he successfully operated to save the life of a young woman suffering from appendicitis - a particularly magnanimous act because, *The Orcadian* pointed out, the woman was only travelling as a third class passenger

An estimated £5,000 damage was caused when the shop of Peace & Low, outfitters, drapers and milliners, on the corner of Broad Street and Castle Street, Kirkwall, was destroyed by fire in 1932. By the end of the century, this was, of course, the site of the Clydesdale Bank, Kirkwall.

(Picture courtesy of George Currie)

The civil air age dawns

The pace of the development of Orkney's civilian air services was extraordinary. Within a period of just three years, Orkney progessed from having no service at all to a situation whereby the county was served by two competing airlines offering services to Inverness, Wick, Thurso and Aberdeen - and connections as far away as London and mainland Europe.

They were halcyon pioneering days. Stromness had its own airport, Kirkwall had two, while a regular inter-island service was established, with not only the country's first domestic air mail service but also Britain's first air ambulance service. Orkney really was at the forefront of civil aviation developments.

And much of the credit was due to one man, Ted Fresson. He had made his first visit to the county in 1931 and immediately realised the potential for an air service. It took him less than two years to get one off the ground.

Captain Fresson had started flying in 1916 when he joined the Royal Flying Corps and qualified as a pilot in Ontario after just four and a half hours instruction. After World War One, he helped to organise the first aircraft factory in China - and test piloted that country's first ever aircraft - and was for some time flying instructor to the Chinese military authorities. However it was while operating with the Cheshire-based North British Aviation Company that he earned the title of the "Joy Ride King" - performing in a single engined Avro aircraft at local shows - and it was that business that first brought him to Orkney.

In August, 1931, he visited the county offering short pleasure trips over the islands and established the first of many aviation milestones when he flew 18 year old Miss Agnes Shearer - a reporter of *The Orcadian* - to Wick. Miss Shearer, later to become Mrs Scott Moncrieff and an author of some repute before being tragically drowned in the Moray Firth in 1943, thus became the first Orkney resident to fly over the Pentland Firth.

By April,1932, however, Ted Fresson was running regular charter flights and he flew to Kirkwall with Major John Shearer, of Kirkwall, as a passenger from Edinburgh - a journey time of 150 minutes - and announced that he would start operating an air service between Kirkwall and Wick that summer. It was soon reported that the North British Aviation Company had 200 provisional bookings but then plans had to be postponed when the aircraft which was being built for the service crashed during trials.

So it was February,1933, when it was announced that an airfield of around 30 acres at Wideford Farm, on the Kirkwall - St Andrews road, had been approved and licensed to allow Captain Fresson to start a service between Orkney and Inverness. Kirkwall building contractor James Craigie was employed to level out the new airfield, and a new company called Highland Airways would operate the flights.

Highland Airways Ltd, registered on March 24, 1933, was the first company to be formed and registered in Great Britain for internal air traffic with a scheduled programme. Captain Fresson would be chief pilot and general manager of the company, which was launched with an initial capital of £3,500. The subscribers were motor engineer R. Donald and solicitor R. Wotherspoon, both of Inverness. The first landing at Wideford was a trial flight made by Captain Fresson on March 26, 1933. He announced that the service would operate with a twin engined Monospar aircraft - named "City of Inverness" - which would carry three passengers, at a cruising speed of 115 mph. Kirkwall - Inverness would cost £3 single, Kirkwall - Thurso £1 single.

And so it was that Monday, May 8, saw the first scheduled flight, piloted by Ted Fresson, land at Wideford Farm from Inverness, via Wick, to be welcomed by county convener Storer Clouston and Provost John Slater of Kirkwall. The aircraft "presented the appearance of a silver bullet crossing the sky," said *The Orcadian*. The first passengers to use the service were Sir Edmund Findlay, president of the Scottish Newspaper Society and a proprietor of *The Scotsman* newspaper, which would now be flown to Orkney daily by the new service; Mr D.S. Gabriel, of Inverness, northern manager for the Anglo-American Oil Company Ltd; and Mr D.L. Smith, Inverness, of White Horse Distillers Ltd of Glasgow.

The Monospar was followed into the airfield by a De Havilland Moth biplane, piloted by Flt Officer W.B. Caldwell, owned by the Scottish Motor Traction Company, carrying two "overflow" passengers - Harriet, Lady Findlay and Mr Peter Findlay - mother and brother of Sir Edmund Findlay.

Mr William Norn, the Kirkwall groundsman for Highland Airways, ignited a smoke beacon to help guide the planes' landing, and during his break in Kirkwall, before returning South, Ted Fresson played a round of golf with county surgeon Mr Ian McClure.

The first Orcadian to use the new service was Miss Marjorie Clouston, daughter of the county convener, who flew from Kirkwall to Inverness on Tuesday, May 9. Already the vagaries of Orkney's weather were making an impact. On the flight North, Captain Fresson had been unable to locate Wideford in the fog and had to land instead at Hatston, which he used for charter flights over the previous two years. *The Orcadian*, for the first few weeks of the service, published the name of every passenger. The service had other uses - day old chicks could now be flown North to Orkney farms.

From 1933 - 35, the services operated without radio communication,but the popularity of the air link soon saw expansion plans. In June, 1933, Highland Airways announced the purchase of an eight seater De Havilland Dragon to augment the Kirkwall - Inverness service, and the following month an extra pilot was recruited - Flt Lt George Holmes, a man with 19 years flying experience and another veteran of the Royal Flying Corps and RAF, with five years flying experience in Canada where he was Inspector for Civil Aviation.

In the first year of service, Highland Airways operated with 95 per cent regularity, and from July, 1933 - January,1934, Flt Lt Holmes carried 950 passengers, flying 26,000 miles. Holmes who lived in Kirkwall with his wife and daughter, left the company later in 1934 but tragically the pilot was killed at the age of 43 in March, 1937, when his Imperial Airways airliner crashed in Germany.

By 1934, Highland Airways had increased the fleet of aircraft to three twin engined seven-seaters, with a new Aberdeen - Kirkwall service, with a journey time of 100 minutes, and a new inter-isles service between Kirkwall and the North Isles and Hoy. The aircraft company, Shorts Brothers, brought a twin engined Scion monoplane to Kirkwall on a trial flight to assess the machine's suitability for the Thurso service. The plane - which needed only 120 yards for take off and landing and could carry five passengers - was piloted by a New Zealander H.L. Piper, who, like Orcadian Oscar Garden, had also flown from England to Australia in 1930.

And 1934 was to mark two major aviation milestones in Orkney - the Postmaster General approved the first domestic air mail service, allowing a letter posted in Orkney to be delivered 18 hours later in London, and the launch of Orkney's - and Britain's - first air ambulance service.

The new airmail service was inaugurated on May 29, 1934, with more than 400 people travelling in special buses to Wideford airport to await the arrival from Inverness of the

What was believed to be the first landing of a monoplane on North Ronaldsay. (Picture courtesy of Jean Tulloch)

Highland Airways suffered an accident in September, 1935, when this plane, piloted by John Rae, and carrying five passengers, crashed approaching the Trumland airfield in Rousay, careering through trees and ending up against a wall.

(Picture courtesy of George Currie)

The first Orcadian to fly over the Pentland Firth was Miss Agnes Shearer, then an 18 year old reporter with *The Orcadian*, who was flown to Wick by Captain Ted Fresson in 1931.
(Picture courtesy of Orkney Library photographic archive)

Highland Airways plane carrying the Royal Mail badge. A newsreel cameraman from Gaumont - British films was there to record the scene, as was the well known national BBC broadcaster S.P.B. Mais. To collect the first historic delivery of airmail, the crimson motor mail van from Kirkwall office was driven by Jack Barnett, a great grandson of James Barnett, the first mail carrier ever employed by the Postmaster-General in the Orkney islands. The Royal Mail plane, piloted by Ted Fresson, landed at 12.22pm to rousing cheers and General Sir Fredrick Williamson, director of the Royal Mail postal services, who had flown North to inaugurate the service, handed over the first airmail letter from the Postmaster-General Kingsley Wood to Kirkwall's Provost John Slater.

To mark the occasion, *The Orcadian* issued free souvenir envelopes which were dispatched all over the world by the new service. Kirkwall head postmaster Mr J.J. Tait said that the first inward mail had totalled more than 6,000 letters, and the outward bound 12,000 letters carrying the special "first day cover" date stamp of May 29, 1934. The outward mail was put aboard the plane within 20 minutes of the box closing at the head post office at 1.35 pm.

The Orcadian also ensured a permanent record of the "Red Letter Day" by sending a communication to the British Museum via the new service, and the newsreel film of the occasion was shown at the Albert Kinema at the end of June.

The following month, the Moderator of the General Assembly of the Church of Scotland, the Rt Rev Dr P.D. Thomson was tagged the "Sky Pilot" as he flew into Wideford airport for a visit to Orkney - the first time that a Moderator of the Church of Scotland had ever used air transport in his official duties. The following week the Moderator of the United Free Church of Scotland, Rev Bruce Blackwood, also flew into the county.

On August 6, 1934, the Highland Airways air service was extended to provide a trial service between Kirkwall, North Ronaldsay, Stronsay, Sanday and Westray, twice a week with the return fare of 22s between Kirkwall and Westray.

These trial flights laid the foundations, in October, 1934, for Orkney's first official air ambulance service, with a county council scheme, in conjunction with the Department of Health

for Scotland, to transport hospital patients by Highland Airways aircraft. Doctors would be able to use the service in cases where "transport by aeroplane is essential or, at least, eminently desirable".

The ambulance charter flights would, in the first instance, be paid for by the county council, with grants later claimed from the Department of Health for Scotland and also reimbursement of some of the cost sought from those patients who could afford to pay. "Having regard to its primary responsibility as a public service company, Highland Airways cannot guarantee that a plane will always be available for this particular service," said Captain Fresson. "Every endeavour will, however, be made by the company to meet all emergency calls." Because free landing facilities had been provided in North Ronaldsay, Sanday, Rousay, Westray and Walls, Highland Airways would make a 50 per cent reduction in their ambulance charter charges to those islands.

In fact, it was 12 months earlier, in 1933, that Orkney made history with the first ever air ambulance "mercy flight", when Dr William Sinclair of Kirkwall, who served as a GP in the town for 25 years, became the first doctor in Britain to use an aircraft to deal with a case and the first to fly a patient for treatment by air. It was a serious case in Sanday which prompted Dr Sinclair to take off in a Dragon aircraft of Highland Airways. The patient was put into the plane in Sanday and brought back to Kirkwall where the Wideford airport was unlit at night. This caused serious problems and the plane had to circle Kirkwall in darkness for an hour while motorists were recruited to light the airfield with their car headlights, and smoke beacons lit to show wind direction. The plane eventually made a perfect landing.

Dr Sinclair went on to make several flights to the islands, often in hazardous weather, dealing with other cases in Sanday, North Ronaldsay and Westray. He retired from his Kirkwall practice in December, 1946 - sooner than the Dragon aircraft which had made the first air ambulance flight, registration G - ACIT, which Captain Ted Fresson was still flying at the end of the 1940s.

The first patient to be carried outwith Orkney by plane was 30 year old David Knight, an auxiliary postman of Nouster,

North Ronaldsay, who was flown from Kirkwall to Inverness, in July, 1933, to have "an obstruction" removed. It transpired he had swallowed his denture in his sleep!

In June, 1935, Orkney witnessed what was then the longest air ambulance flight ever undertaken in Britain when Highland Airways pilot John Rae flew an Orkney patient from Kirkwall to Renfrew for transfer to a Glasgow hospital.

After just 16 months of Orkney air services, ambitious plans for expansion were already underway. September, 1934, saw the proposal of an east coast air service from London to Orkney with Captain Duncan Sinclair, of the British Aviation Corporation, having discussions with Captain Fresson over co-operation on the project which would see the establishment of a chain of municipal aerodromes at Hull, Newcastle, Edinburgh and Elgin.

But, by now we had also seen the dangers of the new civil air age. The first major civilian aircraft crash in Orkney was on August 29,1934, as the Highland Airways' Kirkwall - Inverness mail plane came to grief in taking off at Kirkwall in heavy rain. Fortunately, the seven passengers and pilot, E. Coleman, escaped with their lives as eye witnesses saw the aircraft tail hit the Wideford aerodrome's south wall and crash into the adjoining turnip field. The crash was blamed on the water-logged state of the runway which had reduced the plane's take-off speed.

The pilot was praised for his actions in helping the passengers who included Mr Gilbert Archer, managing director of R. Garden Ltd of Kirkwall, his wife and son. The cargo of mail was rescued intact, and the following week Captain Fresson had to appeal in a letter to *The Orcadian* for people to return parts of the plane which had been taken away by souvenir hunters.

Four months later, Highland Airways - and the unfortunate pilot Coleman - had their second crash when the mail plane from Inverness was forced down in the Moray Firth - giving a ducking to the two passengers, Mr and Mrs William Firth, Dunsyre, Harray, who were returning from their honeymoon after marrying on Christmas Eve. The plane had just taken off from Inverness when it ditched into the sea some 50 yards from the shore in about five feet of water. The pilot and passengers broke their way out of the fuselage and were rescued by boat, sustaining only minor injuries. The company denied that there had been an engine failure.

Highland Airways - who wooed the affections of Kirkwall children by flying in Father Christmas each year - now prepared to face competition on their Orkney routes, however. Passenger fares during the summer of 1934 had been: Inverness - Kirkwall £5 return; Aberdeen - Kirkwall £5 10s return and Wick - Kirkwall £1 15s return. It was now announced that, for the winter of 1934-35, there would be a reduction with the Kirkwall-Inverness fare cut by ten shillings to £4 10s.

The reason was soon apparent as a new contender, Aberdeen Airways, emerged to challenge for business on Orkney air routes. The managing director of Aberdeen Airways was Mr Eric Gandar Dower, a veteran of flying back to World War One, and also the proprietor of the new Aberdeen Airport at Dyce. (At the time, Highland Airways operated their Aberdeen flight to Kintore). Gandar Dower's chief pilot was Eric A. Starling, who 50 years later, was to have a British Airways plane named after him. Aberdeen Airways - with a fleet of six purple and yellow aircraft - was also in discussions with Dutch airline KLM on a possible Amsterdam - Aberdeen - Iceland service. The original intention of the new company was to open an airfield at Grimsetter, three miles out of Kirkwall, and the site of what was to eventually become Kirkwall's civilian airport in 1947, but when the service began, it was not to Kirkwall, but Stromness!

The new Stromness Airport was at Howe, Cairston, which was farmed by Mr Thomas Scott, a Westray man, and it was there that the first Aberdeen Airways scheduled passenger flight, piloted by Eric Starling, landed on Monday, May 27, 1935, to be welcomed by Provost James Marwick. A week later,

the company planned to inaugurate its Aberdeen - Edinburgh - Newcastle - Hull - London route, making it possible to travel from Orkney to London in six or seven hours.

Gandar Dower boasted the biggest fleet of aircraft outside London but he denied that he would be entering a price war with Highland Airways, saying that his fares would be based on the same mileage rate as his rivals. However, he was considering employing four engined aircraft on an Orkney - Shetland service, he added.

Encouraged by the rapid development of air services, Orkney County Council approved in principle its support for acquiring a county aerodrome, and sites at Quanterness, Hatston, and Grimsetter as well as the airstrip at Wideford Farm were all considered - despite a warning from Gandar Dower that "a public aerodrome would be a heavy burden on your ratepayers." In fact, in 1937, the Air Ministry suggested that the most satisfactory site for a municipal airport for Orkney would be at Skeabrae, Sandwick, although Hatston could remain as a "feeder" airport to serve Kirkwall. The second choice would be a site at Mill Dam, Tankerness, but that could require the demolition of Voltigar and Quoyburray farms. Skeabrae could be easily developed to provide runways 700 yards long, 150 yards wide, said the Air Ministry - a premise that was proved correct three years later when the wartime air station at Skeabrae became operational.

Highland Airways suffered a third major accident in September, 1935, when a plane, piloted by John Rae, and carrying five passengers, crashed approaching the Trumland airfield in Rousay, careering through trees and ending up against a wall. The pilot's head went through the cockpit windscreen and the passengers were all thrown from their seats, although everyone escaped with minor cuts and bruises. The small planes did have their advantages - a few weeks earlier, a Highland Airways De Havilland Dragon, with just enough fuel for ten minutes of flight, managed to land in a field of cattle near Kirkwall, after being caught in a blanket of fog.

The first crash on Aberdeen Airways' Orkney service came a year later when a De Havilland Rapide, piloted by James Hay with four passengers aboard, came down in a cornfield in fog near New Portsligo, soon after taking off from Dyce for Orkney. Everyone escaped injury.

The most dramatic accident, however, came in July, 1937, when Orkney passengers had to be dragged from the blazing wreckage of a plane. By that time, Aberdeen Airways had become Allied Airways (Gandar Dower) Ltd and the company's aircraft landed at St Margaret's Hope "by request." The accident happened as the Silver Ghost crashed on take-off at Thurso, bound for Aberdeen. The plane, piloted by Flt Lt G. Hinckley, apparently hit an airfield wall and came down in a neighbouring field where it burst into flames. In a courageous rescue, the pilot and seven passengers were pulled to safety before the plane was completely destroyed in the fire.

The passengers were Mr J.W. Towers, of the Union Bank, Stromness, and his wife; Miss E.R. Stocks of Stromness Academy; Mrs Peter Murray, wife of the proprietor of the Murray Arms, South Ronaldsay; Mrs Andrew Banks, Smiddybanks, South Ronaldsay, and her sister Minnie Sinclair from Canada; and Mrs Annie Hughson from Shetland.

Heroes at the scene included a local motor driver William MacKay and neighbouring farmer's son John Green, who climbed on the plane and opened the emergency exit to help pull people out while others were pulled from the cabin door. Mrs Murray, whose clothes were burning, was the last to be pulled out by Mr MacKay.

Mrs Minnie Sinclair, from Hamilton, Ontario, said: "It was terrifying - I won't forget this holiday. I was home visiting my people in St Margaret's Hope after an absence of 12 years. With my sister, Mrs Banks, I was going south to see the King and Queen in Edinburgh."

She said Mrs Murray was thrown on the floor in the crash. "We saw flames and it was a case of every man for himself. Flames started to shoot up through the floor beside where Mrs

Murray was lying. I tried to force open the door - it wouldn't move." She eventually escaped through the emergency exit in the roof. "Clambering on to a seat, I managed to pull myself through and I found myself near one of the wings. I ran along the wing and jumped to the ground. By this time the plane was well ablaze. Several others got out before I did but Mrs Murray was still lying inside the plane. Her life was undoubtedly saved by Mr MacKay. A terrific heat came off the burning aircraft, but Mr MacKay remained at the door and, though he is not a big man, pulled Mrs Murray from certain death."

Mrs Murray, Mrs Banks and Mrs Towers were detained in hospital in Thurso with minor injuries and, two weeks later, the luckless Mrs Murray, when returning home, was involved in another near miss when the De Havilland Dragon crash-landed, damaging the undercarriage, as it landed at Berriedale, South Ronaldsay.

In February, 1938, there was another footnote in local aviation history when an Allied Airways aircraft, flying from Quanterness, near Kirkwall, to the Stromness airport at Howe, with pilot "Bill" Baillie and ground engineer F.E. Baxter aboard, was forced to land at Girnigoe, Shapinsay, by a snowstorm. A telephone fault, however, meant that they could not inform Kirkwall that all was well - and a three hour search was started on the Mainland before a message finally got through. In the meantime, the first ever police message from Orkney had been broadcast on the BBC radio, appealing to the public for information.

Highland Airways was also to undergo a name change and in April, 1938, became Scottish Airways. The company had already consolidated its position more than two years earlier when it combined with four other airlines - United Airlines, Northern and Scottish Airways, Spartan Air Lines and Hillman Airways - in a conglomerate operating under the title of British Airways. The routes of the new concern would serve 25 towns and cities in Britain and Europe over an area stretching 2,200 miles, and it meant that, as early as 1935, Orcadians could fly from Kirkwall to Europe on a single ticket. They had to wait until May, 1936, when Orkney and Shetland were linked for the first time by wireless, for Highland Airways to inaugurate the first air service from Kirkwall to Shetland.

The problems of operating to Shetland were soon illustrated in January, 1937, when, in storm force winds, air services had to be cancelled when the new wireless station engine hut at Sumburgh aerodrome was blown away. There were gales recorded on 27 days out of 31 that January and the air service proved its worth for North Ronaldsay (not for the last time) when pilot Adam Smith managed to fly his De Havilland Rapide into the marooned island with four hundredweight of food from R. Garden Ltd. Cargo, which had been loaded on to the steamer *Earl Sigurd* on January 9, had still not reached the island by January 28, so islanders were in a desperate plight with all foodstuffs, apart from those locally produced, totally exhausted by the time the pilot made his flying mercy mission.

Another advantage of the air age was that Orkney could receive newspapers the same day as publication. In 1937, national newspapers - carrying reports of the Joe Louis-Tommy Farr world heavyweight boxing championship fight, which Louis won on points in front of a 60,000 crowd - were flown to Orkney by a special charter aircraft, a three engined Spartan Cruiser. Three months later, another special charter flight was used to bring national papers with the news that former Labour Prime Minister Ramsay MacDonald had died.

Ted Fresson was determined that no island should be left without the opportunity of joining the air age - and in August, 1937, he made the first landing of an aircraft on Stroma to survey a possible landing strip for air ambulances. Until May, 1938, Highland Airways not only operated the flights but the company's staff also carried out all the air traffic control duties. That ended when the first Air Ministry radio control station in Scotland came into operation at Mayfield, near Kirkwall's Wideford aerodrome, with the appointment of Air Ministry air traffic control officer John Graham.

By 1939, Scottish Airways' fleet was three seven-seater De Havilland Rapides, four seven-seater Spartan Cruisers and three seven-seater De Havilland Dragons - a total passenger capacity of 70 seats. Scottish Airways services were still using the Wideford Farm airfield while Allied Airways (Gandar Dower) used both Wideford and, in some cases, Quanterness. Now, however, the Air Transport Licensing Authority announced that only Wideford would be licensed, although Allied could continue using the Stromness airfield for the Thurso - Stromness service. The licensing authority refused Allied a Stromness - Shetland service, and also ruled that Allied and Scottish Airways should share some Orkney services.

Nonetheless, Scottish Airways was able to celebrate the sixth anniversary of Orkney's civil air services with new schedules which meant it was possible to fly from Kirkwall at 6.25am and arrive at Croydon Airport, London, at 12.30pm.

The potential of the air age for the tourist industry was illustrated in June, 1939, when the first 25 holidaymakers from the North of England arrived under a new "See Orkney by Air" package holiday scheme, organised by James Wilson of the Royal Hotel, Kirkwall, Crosville Motor Services, and Allied Airways (Gandar Dower) Ltd. It was expected that 400 English tourists would visit Orkney during the summer under the package deal.

But, of course, World War Two was to intervene. The outbreak of war not only halted the inter-island services, but saw the end of Stromness's civil airport. Clardon airfield in Thurso was actually destroyed for security reasons in 1940. However, Scottish Airways - with some interruptions when the company's aircraft were mobilised for service in France - continued an external air service for Orkney throughout the next six years.

The outbreak of war, however, provides the opportunity to analyse what Ted Fresson's company had achieved in six years - and it was an achievement of which he could be justly proud. For instance, from July, 1937, to December, 1938, Scottish Airways operated the Kirkwall - Inverness service with 100 per cent regularity - not one flight was missed in 18 months. During the two years prior to the war, Scottish Airways carried 30,168 passengers, 200 tons of mail and 100 tons of freight.

Even during the war years, the company's record of reliability was impressive with the worst regularity achieved in a year being 97 per cent, and the best 100 per cent. One blemish came in March, 1940, when six passengers and the pilot had to scramble to safety from their blazing plane which was destroyed after hitting a wall while taking off from Kirkwall's civilian airfield.

From September, 1939, to September, 1945, Scottish Airways carried 170,831 passengers, 1,246,348 lbs of freight, 4,287,300 lbs of mail, and the total distance flown was 5,109,547 miles.

The end of the war, and the election of a Labour government, was to see the end of Orkney's privately operated air services, however, and the dawn of a new era of nationalisation.

A legacy of the war was that Orkney had been left with four major airfields, and Scottish Airways operated both from Hatston and Grimsetter before, in 1947, it was settled that Grimsetter would be Orkney's civilian airport for the remainder of the 20th century. It has often been murmured since that either of the two West Mainland airfields, Skeabrae or Twatt, both less liable to fog, would have been a preferable choice.

Orkney now saw some different planes introduced on local routes. In August, 1946, Ted Fresson brought a 24 seater Dakota aircraft to Orkney on a trial. The modified wartime plane, which promised Kirkwall - Glasgow flights of 75 minutes, included, for the first time on Orkney routes, an air hostess. Not long after, 12 seater Jupiter aircraft - in reality ex-German Junker 52s - were introduced on Scottish routes.

By now, both Scottish Airways and Allied Airways (Gandar Dower) Ltd had been swallowed up by the nationalised corporation of British European Airways. There were grumbles that Orkney - despite being the pioneer of Britain's scheduled air services in 1933 - would get a raw deal under the new set-up, and there were anxious calls for the reinstatement of the inter-island services, suspended at the outbreak of war, and the continuation of the air ambulance service. A consolation for Orkney was that the new North of Scotland manager for British European Airways was none other than Ted Fresson. And Fresson was quick to show his loyalty to the islands in January, 1947, when he made three flights to land on North Ronaldsay's flooded pre-war airstrip after the island had been marooned by weather for 17 days. The Post Office had chartered the De Havilland Rapide aircraft to clear a backlog of more than 1,000 lbs of mail.

How would Orkney fare under nationalisation? The first omens were not good. In October, 1947, British European Airways imposed 30 per cent fares increases with the Kirkwall - Glasgow fare going up from £4 15s to £6 3s.

But worse was to follow. There was an outcry in March, 1948, as Ted Fresson was sacked, as an economy measure, from his job as North of Scotland manager of BEA. (The company also made redundant 71 pilots, all ex-RAF personnel, and 15-20 radio operators). The dismissal of Fresson led to angry protest meetings in Kirkwall and Inverness and questions asked in Parliament.

"There will be general resentment and anger at this flagrant breach of faith with the pioneers who had the vision and courage in 1933 to embark on providing air services for Scotland," said *The Orcadian*. It was reported that Fresson got a tax-free pay-off of £2,000 but he "should not have been discarded like an old boot," Orkney's MP Sir Basil Neven-Spence told the House of Commons.

The regard for the new nationalised airline further diminished when BEA refused twice in 24 hours to answer SOS air ambulance requests from Westray - resulting in a six year old girl with appendicitis and a 76 year old farmer having to be ferried to Kirkwall by boat. Later in 1948, BEA did set up a dedicated air ambulance service but with planes based in Aberdeen and Renfrew.

And it was hardly encouraging when the airline axed the Orkney-Edinburgh service and, for a time, suspended the daily Aberdeen-London return flights as unprofitable. There was, of course, no competition to BEA on passenger services, but a company called Air Cargo Distributors - of which Sir Basil Neven-Spence was chairman - attempted to launch an Orkney freight service, and also carried out some trial air ambulance flights.

Despite the gripes, however, Kirkwall Airport handled 1,360 aircraft movements in the four months of February- May, 1948. That was more than Inverness, Aberdeen or Edinburgh!

BEA even brought a double decker bus to Orkney, to transport passengers to and from the airport - but Kirkwall Town Council refused permission for the vehicle to use Victoria Street. And there was a narrow escape in July,1948, when a BEA Dakota on the Orkney - Aberdeen - London route made a forced landing in a Northamptonshire wheat field but the 18 passengers and crew scrambled out before it burst into flames.

BEA - again temporarily switching back to Hatston from Grimsetter for the 1948 winter schedule - also attempted to boost passenger figures by reducing prices. (Neven-Spence complained that, on one occasion, he was the only passenger on a flight south). The standard Orkney-London return fare was cut from £24 to £21 2s. The Retail Price Index increased 25-fold between 1948-99 so that gives an equivalent price of around £525 at the end of the century.

But Captain Ted Fresson - the pioneer of Orkney's air services and the man who had put the islands at the forefront of civil aviation progress - was so disillusioned by the events of the previous few months that he quit flying and left Britain. As a farewell gesture, he offered his own Gypsy Moth aircraft to the recently-founded Orkney Flying Club, and announced he was off to Kenya as managing director of a brewery!

He left with a final parting shot at BEA: " No commercial undertaking ever succeeded on such dictatorial methods and until those in charge change their outlook, the losses will continue to increase."

The scene at Inverness on May 29, 1934, as the Inverness-Kirkwall air mail service is inaugurated. The occasion was captured in this painting by Edmund Miller which was presented to Inverness Airport to commemorate the pioneering spirit of Captain Ted Fresson, the founder and managing director of Highland Airways. (Picture courtesy of Highlands and Islands Airports)

Steamers on crest of wave

It was not only the dawning of the air age that was to bring Orkney's transport links into the 20th century. The period from 1928 - 38 also witnessed great improvements to the county's shipping fleet.

Half a dozen new vessels were to be launched - in some cases replacing ageing steamers dating back to the middle of the 19th century - as the various companies serving the islands enjoyed an era of success. For instance, in the annual report for 1927, the Orkney Steam Navigation Company - later to evolve into the Orkney Islands Shipping Company and, later still, Orkney Ferries - announced a record net profit of £2,076 14s 11d. (This was in an age when there were no shipping subsidies and when the average weekly wage in the county was around 30 shillings.)

At that time, the company operated two vessels serving the North Isles - the *Countess of Bantry* and the *Orcadia*.

However, in March, 1928, the *Earl Thorfinn* was launched at the Aberdeen yard of Hall, Russell and Company to replace the *Countess of Bantry* as a passenger, cargo and cattle-carrying steamer. The new ship - 150 feet long and 27 feet broad - had first and second class accommodation for 250 passengers. Unfortunately, a delegation from the Orkney Steam Navigation Company failed to attend the launching, delayed by bad weather in the Pentland Firth.

Captain John Craigie, the company's senior officer, assumed command of the *Earl Thorfinn*. Captain Craigie, born in Rousay in 1865, had sailed as mate on the *Lizzie Burroughs* and then the *Fawn* on the Rousay, Egilsay and Wyre route until, after qualifying as master in 1894, he took command of the *Orcadia*.

Captain John Bremner now became master of the *Orcadia*, but it would only be three years before he too had a new ship to command. The *Earl Sigurd*, also built by Hall, Russell and Company, was launched in December, 1930 - a 117 feet long vessel to carry 200 passengers, with a crew of ten, with first and second class accommodation and separate cabins for women, as well as compartments for cargo and livestock. "The *Earl Sigurd* is fitted throughout with electric light and is in every way arranged on the most modern and up-to-date lines for a vessel of that type and dimensions," said *The Orcadian*. Captain Bremner and crew travelled down to Aberdeen to take charge of the new ship which averaged 10 knots on her first trip North.

It signalled the end for the *Orcadia* (really the *Orcadia II* as she was the successor to a previous *Orcadia*, a converted sailing vessel of older date) which had served the isles for 63 years after being built in 1868 at the South Shields yard of Messrs Readhead, Softley and Company and engined by Hall, Russell and Company in Aberdeen.

The *Orcadia*, after being lengthened by 19 feet in the 19th century, was 140 feet in length with a beam of 20 feet. A single screw vessel, she was registered to carry 66 first class passengers and 90 second class, with a crew of eight. Her seven masters during her six decades of service to the Orkney Steam Navigation Company were: Captain James Pottinger, James Bremner, George Robertson, David Charleson, John Robertson, John Craigie and John Bremner.

In March, 1931, having been made redundant by the arrival of the *Earl Thorfinn* and *Earl Sigurd*, the *Orcadia* was sold to Messrs W & J Leslie, Ayre Road, Kirkwall, and then two months later to Mr D. Chalmers, Whitehall, Stronsay. The old ship languished in Whitehall harbour for three years until being sold to a firm of shipbreakers. In September, 1934, she left Orkney on her final voyage, towed by tug, to be taken to the breaker's yard of Messrs Thomson and McGregor in Bo'ness.

And, whatever the advantages of the new steamers, they were still at the mercy of the great scourge of fog. Dense fog in September, 1930, caused the *Earl Thorfinn* to take seven hours to get the few miles from Eday to Stronsay, while the ss *St Rognvald* took 25 hours to get from Aberdeen to Kirkwall. At this time, Orkney passengers could travel from Kirkwall, Stromness or St Margaret's Hope to either Leith or Aberdeen in the South, or Shetland in the North. A first class cabin, Kirkwall - Leith, cost 66s 6d, twice the average weekly wage of the period. Meanwhile, at the end of 1930, Stromness bid farewell to the old Northern Lighthouse Ship *Pole Star* which had served the lighthouses of the North for 38 years, with a crew of 30, of whom 28 were Orcadians. She had lived through an era during which mercy missions to take a doctor from Stromness to Auskerry or Fair Isle, or further still, had been common occurrences.

Her replacement, the new *Pole Star*, was the last vessel to be built by Wm. Beardmore and Company at Dalmuir on the Clyde. She was handed over to Captain Robert Swanney and his crew on Hogmanay, 1930, and arrived at her home port of Stromness for the first time on January 21, 1931. Captain Swanney retired in 1934 after 40 years at sea, including the last 21 years in the service of the Northern Lighthouse Commissioners. Kirkwall-born, he went to sea at the age of 15 in 1894, and sailed in Australian waters for some years, but in 1903 he succeeded Captain Robert Robertson as master of the RMS *St Ola*, a command he kept until he joined the NLS *Pole Star*, becoming master in 1918.

The former *Pole Star*, pensioned off in 1931, was being prepared for a new challenge in other climes, however. She was bought from the Northern Lighthouse Commissioners by a company called the Argonaut Corporation and was renamed the *Orphir* while her new owners refitted her for marine reconnaissance and salvage work. In July, 1934, *The Orcadian* reported that she had been fitted with submarine film equipment and it was thought that one of her first missions would be to photograph the wreck of the liner *Lusitania* in 276 feet of water off Ireland, sunk in 1915 by a German U-boat with the loss of 1,195 lives.

It was conjectured that the *Orphir* would ultimately make an attempt to recover some of the treasures lying in the Bay of Navarino, situated off Peloponnesus in Greece, where 130 Turkish and Egyptian vessels had been sunk in 1827 by the combined British, French and Russian fleets. Modern technology now made it possible to salvage the bullion and other treasures from these ships and it was estimated that there was bounty to the value of £10 millions (at 1934 values) to be recovered.

August, 1939, saw the introduction of the Northern Lighthouse Commissioners' new motor vessel *Hesperus* - a replacement for the ship of the same name - on the west coast patrol. The 214 feet vessel carried a crew of 27.

While the Orkney Steam Navigation Company operated passenger services within the isles, the external services to Shetland, Aberdeen and Leith were operated by the confusingly similarly named North of Scotland, Orkney and Shetland Steam Navigation Company - later to evolve into P&O Scottish Ferries.

In April, 1931, the North of Scotland company launched a new 250 feet long, 35 feet beam *St Sunniva* designed to carry 400 passengers. She had been built at the Aberdeen yard of Hall, Russell and Company to replace the ship of the same name lost off Shetland in 1930. The new *St Sunniva* would be lost in war service off Canada in 1943.

In December, 1936, at a cost of £86,000, a new *St Clair* was launched by Hall, Russell and Company for the North of Scotland company. The new 250 feet long vessel, capable of over 15 knots speed, could accommodate 420 passengers and would be "the finest vessel of her class on the coast," boasted company director Thomas Adam. When, four months later, she paid her first visit to Kirkwall, she was welcomed by a crowd of between 1,500-2,000, taking advantage of the recently completed £30,000 pier extension, and the blaring sirens of the North Isles steamers *Earl Thorfinn* and *Earl Sigurd*, lying at the pier. The master of the *St Clair* was Captain William Leask, holder of the Distinguished Service Cross for his good work in World War One.

In 1939, the North of Scotland company faced competition when a new shipping company, Orkney Direct Line, began services linking Kirkwall and the North Isles with Leith, using the steamer *Rota* owned by a Dundee-based Orcadian Mr Robert Tulloch.

Although the Orkney Steam Navigation Company could claim to be the major shipping operator within the islands, it was by no means the only one - with several smaller concerns serving several of the islands. In fact, in February, 1938, Captain John Bremner left the Orkney Steam Navigation Company to go into business on his own account . With three partners, John Hourie, John Gray and Andrew Wilson, he took over the South Isles steamer *Hoy Head* which had been owned since 1922 by Alexander Swanson and Robert Towers. The people of North Ronaldsay made a presentation of banknotes to Captain Bremner as he made his final call at the islands, and Captain John Groat - a native of Longhope - became master of the *Earl Sigurd*.

The Burray, St Margaret's Hope and Scapa service was operated by the steamboat company of John and James Laird who, until 1938, operated the *Sutors* which could accommodate 50 passengers. However that year they acquired the 80 feet long ss *Ailsa* which was certificated for 130 passengers. The Lairds had also earlier purchased the Kirkwall steamer *Cormorant* which had previously been operated, until 1933, by R Garden Ltd on routes down the West Highland coast. And in 1935, *The Orcadian* reported that the people of Westray were investigating buying their own steamer to serve their island.

One of the longest running operations, however, was the Dennison company which served the island of Shapinsay with the steamer *Iona*. The original master of the *Iona* - registered on May 25,1893 - was William Dennison of Balfour Village, who before his death at the age of 73 in 1937 had handed over to his son, also William. The *Iona* was to celebrate her 50th "birthday" in 1943 but continued sailing for another 20 years after that, having diesel engines installed in 1949.

In 1930, it was reckoned that there were 78 men employed in shipping in Orkney - but there would be as many again employed in other waters. *The Orcadian* published a weekly list of ships on which Orkney mariners were sailing round the world's oceans, with their latest ports of call recorded so that relatives could keep in touch. The number at sea can be illustrated by the fact that this list often ran to as many as 75-80 ships, of which up to a dozen had Orkney masters.

By this time, the "grand old lady" of the Orkney steamers was the North of Scotland company's mail steamer *St Ola*, which celebrated her 50th anniversary in Orkney waters in March, 1942 - nine months before the retiral of her longest serving master, Captain George Swanson, who made 18,000 crossings of the Pentland Firth during 31 years in command.

One of Captain Swanson's most alarming moments in the peacetime service of the *St Ola* had been in July,1936, when, with 22 passengers aboard, she ran aground at Hunda, after sailing from Scapa for Scrabster in thick fog. The ship's two lifeboats had been lowered, and passengers transferred to them, before being picked up by launches from Burray and St Margaret's Hope in, fortunately, flat calm conditions. The Scapa Flow salvage vessel *Imperieuse* helped refloat the *St Ola* and escorted her to Lyness where divers could inspect the damage.

While the *St Ola* was out of action that year, Captain William Spence, from Yell, had an epic eight hour crossing of the Pentland Firth in the relief steamer *Earl of Zetland* as winds reached 88mph in gusts. It was 51 years to the day since he made his first voyage as a young seaman from Glasgow to the Mediterranean, he told *The Orcadian*.

There was disappointment in Orkney in 1937 when the North of Scotland company declined an invitation from the Admiralty for the *St Ola* to join the Coronation Review of ships by the King at Spithead. It would have been a fitting pinnacle to the career of what was one of Orkney's finest servants of the 20th century, and the rejection of the idea by shipping company bosses was regarded as niggardly, to say the least.

Despite the importance to the islands of the *Earl Sigurd, Earl Thorfinn, St Sunniva, St Clair* and *St Ola*, these ships were often dwarfed in size by other visitors to Orkney. Nowadays, it is often thought that the arrival of cruise liners has been a development of the latter years of the 20th century, but not so. In fact, liners were visiting the islands in the years prior to World War One, and between the wars, Kirkwall frequently played host to visiting liners of up to 17,000 tons.

Many of the liners were German, or German-American, owned, but there were British and Scandinavian vessels as well, either calling into Kirkwall Bay or passing through Scapa Flow. For instance, in 1928, these included the Royal Mail Steam Packet Company liners *Arcadian* and *Avon* and the Cunard liner *Carinthia* as well as the 9,000 ton German ship *Orinoco* which had just completed her maiden voyage to the West Indies. Other visitors were slightly more exclusive - like the 732 ton oil burning yacht *Sans Peur*, which visited Kirkwall in August, 1928, with a crew of 33, and carrying on board the owners, the Duke and Duchess of Sutherland, and their guests, Lord and Lady Ednam and Lord Wodehouse.

(Also, tankers were a common sight in Scapa Flow, long before Orkney's oil age. In December, 1930, for example, the Fleet oil tanker *War Krishna* arrived from the Persian Gulf oil port of Abadan with a cargo of 8,000 tons of oil for the Admiralty tanks at Lyness. The chief engineer on board was a Stromnessian, Mr John R Flett).

It was on the more luxurious Hamburg-Amerika liner *Resolute*, which visited Kirkwall on July 19,1933, that the passengers included Queen Marie of Romania, her daughter Princess Ileana and the Archduke Anton. The following year, Kirkwall City Pipe Band marched from the Town Hall to the Pierhead to welcome 550 passengers off the 16,600 ton *Milwaukee*, including Sir John Maynard, a former Vice-Chancellor of the Punjab University, and Lady Maynard. A 1936 visitor, the Swedish cruise liner *Drottingholm*, was said to be one of the fastest ships on the New York - Baltic route when she called at Kirkwall with 749 passengers. The following year, the 17,000 ton P&O liner *Moldavia* visited - although Orkney interest centred more on the launch of a new liner, called *Orcades*, owned by the Orient line, which made her maiden voyage on a cruise to the Mediterranean.

But, of course, the arrival of World War Two was to end, for the time being, Orkney's interest in the developing cruise liner trade.

More alarmingly for Orkney, the war seemed to mark a watershed in the fortunes of the Orkney Steam Navigation Company. Over a period of 20 years, the firm's profits had varied - from £2,076 in 1927, to £579 in 1932 to £1,005 in 1943 - but always remained above the waterline.

But, suddenly, in July, 1947, it was revealed that the company had hit a financial crisis. The company, which had two steamers serving the North Isles, was losing £500 a month - the equivalent of an annual loss approaching £200,000 at 1999 prices - even though freight charges had increased by 75 per cent compared with pre-World War Two levels. Calls were made - led by Sir Basil Neven-Spence MP - for government subsidies to protect the service.

The year of 1947 also signalled the beginning of the end for the faithful steamer *St Ola*. The North of Scotland company announced that a replacement ship was to be built at Aberdeen. However, with a shortage of materials and skilled manpower, it would be another three years - and into the second half of the 20th century - before Orkney would see the new vessel.

Trawler tragedies and

The sea makes heroes of men, and widows of women. Orkney waters have seen more than their fair share of tragedies throughout the 20th century to justify that statement. It would have been many more had it not been for the courage and seamanship of generations of Orcadian lifeboatmen who risked their lives in appalling conditions to pull off scores of heroic rescues to cheat the Grim Reaper.

Nonetheless, the toll of the sea produces grim statistics, and too many men from the trawler ports of Hull, Grimsby, Fleetwood and Aberdeen died a terrible death far from home as they strove to earn a living in that dangerous industry. That's the real price of fish, as they used to say in the Hessle Road in Hull.

In the first quarter of the 20th century, the men of the fishing communities had good cause to be grateful to the Stromness lifeboat *John A Hay,* a vessel with both sail and motor power, which saved 102 lives in 35 call-outs between 1909-28 - the majority of them from trawlers.

Just a random selection from the roll of honour of the *John A Hay* vividly illustrates her valiant service: October 5, 1909, ten saved from the trawler *Ocean Prince*; December 17, 1914, ten saved from the trawler *Lorenzo*; January 27, 1920, ten saved from the Aberdeen trawler *Ulster*; October 10, 1920, nine saved from the trawler *Ben Namur in* Skaill Bay; November 27, 1921, nine saved from the Aberdeen steam liner *Keith Hall* off Birsay; and October 4, 1924, ten saved off the trawler *Hessonite* also off Birsay.

And that did not include the shocking loss of nearly 20 trawlers sunk by German submarines in Orkney waters during World War One.

But the toll of lost fishing vessels in peacetime, and loss of life amongst fishermen, was to grow until it was acknowledged as a national problem - to the extent that, in May, 1933, the Board of Trade ruled that formal inquiries should be held in the event of all trawler disasters because of grave anxiety being caused by the serious fishing tragedies that were increasingly occurring. In 1932, no fewer than 76 British trawlers or drifters suffered serious casualty with the loss of 33 lives. In just the first five months of 1933, 35 trawlers of over 100 tons had suffered disasters, with the loss of 61 lives.

Orkney had been the scene of too many of those incidents. Between 1928-38, nearly 70 lives were lost in peacetime shipping tragedies in Orkney waters - more than half of them trawler men. Thankfully, nearly 400 were rescued - half of them by Orkney lifeboats.

Stromness lifeboat undertook no rescue missions for five years between the end of 1914 and the beginning of 1920. But, with the end of World War One, it was soon business as usual again, and the lifeboat, under coxswain William Johnston, saved the ten crew - and the ship's dog - when the Aberdeen fishing boat *Ulster* went aground off Graemsay in January, 1920.

In October, the same year, two lives were lost, swept overboard, but nine crewmen saved, as the Aberdeen trawler *Ben Namur* ran aground in thick fog to the north of Skaill Bay. (The Board of Trade later suspended the trawler skipper's certificate for nine months).

There was drama in the Pentland Firth too, in July, 1920, when the ss *Grayson*, with 3,000 tons of coal from Virginia, USA, for Sweden, ran aground on Stroma with a crew of 30, who were forced to abandon ship.

Stromness lifeboat saved the ten crewmen of the Hull trawler *Hessonite* which went aground on Orkney's west coast in dense fog in October, 1924. Such disasters could see the crews stranded penniless in Orkney with the trawler owners of Humberside often seemingly reluctant to even pay the fares

home of rescued men. In this case, the Shipwrecked Mariners Society paid the men's passage home, it was reported.

Alas, there was no homecoming for some. In January, 1925, as a body and wreckage was washed ashore in Westray, it was reported that the North Shields trawler *Princess Mary* had been posted missing for three weeks.

Stromness lifeboat took off 31 members of the crew, and landed them at Kirkwall, in June, 1926, when the Norwegian cargo steamer *Hastings County*, on a voyage from Hamburg to Montreal, stranded in thick fog below Auskerry lighthouse. The master and eight crew remained on board to enable the cargo to be salvaged.

That autumn, the new Stromness lifeboat house and slipway was brought into use for the first time, beginning a new chapter in the town's long lifeboat history.

The end of January, 1927, saw Orkney battered by what was described as "the worst storm for 30 years" and the islanders of Eday distinguished themselves with a dramatic rescue. The North Shields trawler *Ben Meidie* was driven ashore on Eday by the hurricane force winds but the islanders saved the ten crew with an improvised breeches buoy.

It was not surprising that vessels were attracted to the rich fishing grounds of the county - in February, 1928, fish landings from Orkney waters landed at Aberdeen totalled 195 tons in a week - but, in fact, most of the vessels which met disaster off the Orkney West Mainland, the North Isles or Hoy had not been fishing locally - they were going to, or returning from, the fishing grounds off the Faroes or Iceland, or even beyond.

Such was the case in October, 1927, when the Hull trawler *Amethyst* - a sister ship of the *Hessonite* lost off Birsay three years earlier - ran aground on the Kame of Hoy in bad weather, returning from the Faroese fishing grounds with a full hold of fish.

The crew fired rockets and set fire to their bed sacks to attract the attention of rescuers and, fortunately, the trawler's SOS sirens were heard at the house of Weaverhall, Stromness, and the lifeboat alerted. The rescue of the ten crew was carried out in just two hours.

The crew of the *Amethyst* included third hand Alfred Jackson, who had attended Stromness Secondary School during World War One when his father was skipper of a mine sweeper working out of Stromness.

Worse was to follow on Sunday, March 18, 1928, when eight fishermen of Hull perished when the trawler *Lord Devonport* (H273), homeward-bound from Iceland with 950 kit of fish, struck Hoy Head in darkness. The supply of emergency rockets was washed overboard and no signals of distress could be made. But, amazingly, six men were to be rescued in what was a dramatic baptism for the new Stromness lifeboat, which had arrived home just two weeks earlier to replace the *John A Hay.*

The 137 ton *Lord Devonport* was no ageing rust bucket but one of the pride of the fleet, being one of the newest and best trawlers fishing out of Hull. Owned by the Pickering and Haldane steam trawler company of St Andrews Dock, Hull, she had only been built in 1926 and "fitted with every modern convenience for deep-sea trawling."

The disaster was not discovered until the next morning when two Stromness lobster fishermen Isaac Robb and James Johnston, coincidentally the assistant motor mechanic of the Stromness lifeboat, came across the scene of devastation at North Loop. Robb and Johnston were to become heroes of the rescue as they alerted the passing Peterhead steam drifter *Guiding Star* which blasted "Ship Ashore" in morse on her steam whistle. Fortunately this was heard and deciphered by Mr John G. Sinclair, of Langhouse, Stromness, who had been a wartime signaller, and he was able to alert the honorary sec-

isles lifeboat heroes

retary of Stromness lifeboat Mr George L. Thomson. The lifeboat was launched by coxswain William Johnston, joined by James Johnston, who was able to act as pilot.

The new £12,000 51-feet lifeboat, capable of a range of 135 miles carrying 80 people and a speed of 8.75 knots driven by two six-cylinder 60 hp engines, had been launched just two months earlier at Cowes, in the Isle of Wight, to replace the long-serving *John A. Hay*. She was described as a "triumph of marine engineering" and had a full time engineer, William Cursiter, but at that stage the lifeboat had not even been officially named. (Prince George, later to be Duke of Kent, would visit Stromness in June, 1928, to name the vessel *JJKSW*, in memory of the legators who financed her.)

The lifeboat was able to fire a line aboard the stricken trawler and, one by one, the six survivors were hauled through the sea to safety, and to tell their grim story. Bosun Harry Claxton was an eloquent witness. "It was a most awful experience and we were in a terrible plight. There were nine of us altogether on the verandah. Our decks were awash at times and, sometimes, when a big roller came along we were all under water for a while. This soon began to tell on us. One by one the men died and as their hold loosened they dropped off. It was a terrible sight indeed."

The death toll left ten children fatherless. The eight victims included the skipper John Hanson, Icelandic-born but a naturalised Briton, the youngest crew member, boy learner Herbert "Dickie" McLean, and the steward, father-of-four Ernest Tate, a brother of one of the six survivors, third hand Stanley Tate. One man gave his life in an heroic attempt to bring help, for firemen Walter Noviss volunteered to attempt to swim ashore. Bosun Claxton explained: "He slipped over the side and swam gamely for a bit. The distance to the beach did not seem so very far, but the cold gripped him after his long exposure, and his head went forward and we all saw that he was done for."

Fireman Noviss's body was later recovered from the sea and the funeral of the 36 year old father of two was held at Stromness cemetery, with his six surviving crewmates among the many mourners. Another black night for the Hessle Road!

The final word went to the mate of the *Lord Devonport*, William Bates, who said: "I never spent such a terrible night and hope never to do so again. We've lost everything." In his case, including the title deeds to his home in Hull, which had been in his pocket at the time of the wreck.

A few days later, the Aberdeen trawler *Avon Glen* arrived in Stromness with ten crewmen from another Aberdeen fishing vessel, the *Strath Moray*, which was lost after striking a rock off North Rona.

A year later, Stromness lifeboat coxswain William Johnston was to be honoured with a RNLI bronze medal, with a monetary award for his crew, after another dramatic operation. The crew of 12 on the Grimsby trawler *Carmania II* were rescued after going ashore at Kirk rocks, Stromness, in what *The Orcadian* described as "a most gallant piece of work - in fact an epic of the sea. At times the lifeboat was entirely enveloped in the huge breaking seas." An indication of the savagery of the conditions came when the salvage vessel *Henry Lancaster*, en route to Stromness to try to recover the stranded trawler, was driven 50 miles off course in gale force winds and blinding snow showers.

Beyond salvage was the 138 ton Grimsby trawler *Jeria*, built in 1916, which was a total loss after running ashore, again homeward-bound from Iceland, between St John's Head and the Old Man of Hoy. The 12 crew had to take to their lifeboat from which they were rescued by another trawler, in September, 1929. That year was to end with a Christmas storm of 70 mph southerly winds which saw fish lifted over a 200 ft high cliff in Copinsay. A few miles away, at the height of the gale, the nine crewmen of the Aberdeen trawler *Strathugie* were rescued by breeches buoy after their vessel stranded ashore beneath the farm of Redbanks, Tankerness.

The year of 1930 had no sooner begun than the men of Longhope lifeboat were called to another trawler tragedy in a rescue which was to earn Longhope coxswain Jack Swanson the RNLI silver medal. (When Jack Swanson retired in 1934 after 56 years lifeboat service from the age of 14, he had participated in the saving of 146 lives. He died at the age of 75 in October, 1939).

The lifeboat had been alerted by local shepherd William Stout, of Melsetter, whose wife had been awoken by the distress calls of the stricken vessel. The lifeboat found that the Aberdeen trawler *Braconmoor* had gone ashore at Torness Point after being caught in wild weather and sea conditions in the Pentland Firth. Sadly the trawler skipper, Archie Brown, died but eight other crewmen were safely rescued by the Longhope lifeboat by breeches buoy. (The Longhope lifeboat *KTJS* had also been named by Prince George in June, 1928. The 45 ft vessel, capable of six knots for 30 hours, had been built in the Isle of Wight at a cost of £8,333.)

Three months later, however, it was to be the Stromness lifeboat that was to make history in the annals of the British lifeboat service with an epic voyage that was to earn the crew £10 each for their efforts (the equivalent of more than a month's wages for most at that time). The drama saw the Stromness boat undertake a record 130 mile trip, each way, in an attempt to aid the Aberdeen steam trawler *Ben Doran* which was lost with all hands on the notorious Vee Skerries in Shetland. Alas, by the time the lifeboat reached the scene, the *Ben Doran* had almost completely disappeared and no trace could be seen of any of the seven crew. The Stromness boat had left her home port at 4.45pm on Sunday, March 30, 1930, and arrived at Scalloway for re-fuelling at 7.30am on the Monday - a passage just 15 minutes short of 15 hours. The lifeboat arrived back in Stromness at 10.30pm Tuesday, a 17 hour passage in the teeth of a gale, after her round trip of 260 miles. The lifeboatmen had clocked up a stamina-sapping 55 hours of continuous service.

The crew of the lifeboat on that epic voyage were William Linklater (acting coxswain), William Cursiter (engineer), R. Greig, J. Folster, J. Johnston, James Towers, Thomas Wishart and William Sinclair. The lost skipper of the *Ben Doran* was James Caie, well known in Stromness because, being a firm adherent of the Sabbath, he always put into port on Sundays when he refused to fish.

Two weeks later, Stromness lifeboat returned to Shetland in a another marathon round trip of 240 miles, in a time of just under 28 hours at sea, when the steamer *St Sunniva* was lost, fortunately with all crew and passengers saved. Soon after this, Shetland got that county's first lifeboat, based at Lerwick, and Stromness boat was spared further excursions so far north.

Both the trips by Stromness lifeboat to Shetland were under the command of acting coxswain William Linklater, and he was now promoted to coxswain on the retirement through ill health of Graemsay-born William Johnston, a crew member for 23 years and cox for 16 years.

It was coxswain Johnston who had set the previous record trip of 114 miles for a lifeboat which the Stromness boat had done round the Orkney mainland and North Isles in September, 1922, when nine men were saved from Aberdeen steam trawler *Cornet* ashore at the point of Ayre in Sanday. The same year he was awarded the RNLI bronze medal for service to the Grimsby trawler *Freesia* when the vessel foundered off Evie on New Year's Day, 1922. Tragically, on that occasion nine fishermen drowned, but two were saved off a small raft of planks by the lifeboat. During his long service William Johnston shared in saving a total of 99 lives, and sadly he died in February, 1931.

Fog, of course, was a deadly danger in this era of limited marine instrumentation, and June, 1930, witnessed the loss of skipper W. Jenner, drowned at Swona, when the Grimsby trawler *Lord Percy* struck the island in a dense "pea souper", homeward bound from a fishing trip to Faroese waters. The remaining crew of nine were all rescued safely.

And 1930 was to see more drama as the North Shields registered trawler *Ben Earn*, owned by Richard Irvin and Son, Aberdeen, was wrecked on the North Taing, Sanday, in an 85 mph November gale. It was not where skipper James Mair, from Banff, expected to be, for it soon became apparent that the luckless Mr Mair, returning from the Faroes with the vessel's first catch in six trips, was 40 miles off the course he thought he was on.

The folk of Sanday were alerted to the disaster in the early hours and Sanday Rocket Lifesaving Brigade members under the command of Andrew Slater and with their rocket apparatus taken to the shore by horse and cart, were able to rescue the crew of ten. It was then that skipper Mair explained how snow, rain and hail had obliterated his vision and a light that he took to be Hoy (Graemsay) had turned out to be North Ronaldsay. However, Sanday folk "wallowed" in free fish for days as the catch had to be abandoned to assist in attempts to refloat the trawler.

At the height of the westerly gale, across the Pentland Firth, the 29 crew of the ss *Linkmoor* were safely landed by breeches bouy operated by the Scarfskerry lifesaving crew in Caithness.

Unfortunately, the navigational error of skipper Mair was not uncommon. On Sunday, March 1, 1931, the Aberdeen trawler *Hannah E. Reynolds* ran ashore in a blinding blizzard at Bow Head, Westray, after mistaking the Noup Head light for North Ronaldsay light, returning from a 16 day fishing trip to the Faroes. For five hours, the vessel languished on off-shore rocks before being carried ashore when the ten crew were taken off by breeches bouy, and Stromness lifeboat, after a six hour voyage, arrived to find the crew safe. "I don't think I was ever in the lifeboat when she found deeper holes to plunge into, causing her to almost stand on end at times, and to dive about in the most vicious fashion," said the lifeboat engineer William Cursiter.

The mate of the *Hannah E. Reynolds*, J.H. Smith, had obviously experienced similar emotions. "With a blizzard raging round us, we thought we were done for," he said. "The waves were breaking completely over us." Remarkably, however, the trawler was salvaged the following week.

At the same time, two Orkney seamen had an escape, which surely deserves to be described as miraculous, after their water logged and disabled boat was tossed about for 15 hours in a mountainous sea 30 miles from the nearest land.

John Linklater, of Longhope, and William Work, Flotta, had travelled to Leith to take over the 68 ft, 80 ton motor vessel *Tomega*, recently purched by William Sutherland of Flotta. Skipper Linklater explained that they hit bad weather near Fraserburgh and then the boat sprang a leak. The hand pump managed to keep the boat clear, but then the pump broke. "We had to set about baling the water out with buckets. This proved to be inadequate and the water rose to such a level that within an hour the engine room was flooded and the engine stopped. We were now left drifting before the wind in a helpless condition. For nine hours we battled in the raging sea and though we kept baling all the time, the water was gaining. For the last two or three hours, we were standing up to our waists in water."

One trawler passed without seeing the stricken boat. "For several more hours we kept a look-out. Then after we had drifted helplessly for some 15 hours, the Hull trawler *Amethyst* was sighted. The skipper immediately saw we were in dire distress." The rescued men were taken to Hull and returned to Orkney the following week. It was a favour repaid - three years earlier the *Amethyst* (or a boat of the same name) had

come to grief on the Kame of Hoy and her crew of ten were saved by the Stromness lifeboat.

In the next four years, more than 150 trawlermen were to be saved in Orkney waters - including the biggest trawler rescue that the county was to witness in the 20th century.

The crew of 15 on the Hull trawler *Cape Crozier* safely made it to shore in their lifeboat after the vessel, later refloated, ran aground at the Riv, Sanday, in April, 1931. A month later, a dramatic race againt time, with nine lives at stake, saw the Aberdeen trawler *Conductor* safely reach Kirkwall, with smoke belching from her hatches, after fire broke out 30 miles off Copinsay. Soon after, the Grimsby trawler *Gambri* had to make a similar dash for Stromness after fire broke out 125 miles off Hoy.

Longhope coxswain Jack Swanson was honoured again by the RNLI for his gallantry in a rescue in January, 1932, when the Hull trawler *Dorbie* came to grief on Torness Point, Hoy, returning from the Faroes in gale force conditions. Three of the crew swam to the shore - an amazing feat in those sea conditions - while eight other men clung to their doomed and partially submerged vessel for five hours before being plucked to safety by Longhope lifeboat which had crossed the Pentland Firth, and back, in 70 mph winds, searching for the vessel after flares had been spotted from Hoy. It was a dramatic return to Orkney for the mate of the Dorbie, Herbert Harris, who had been stationed in Kirkwall and Scapa Flow for three months in World War One. The same week, another nine crewmen on the disabled trawler *Tom Jenkerson* were brought safely to Kirkwall after their disabled vessel was towed 100 miles in gale force winds by the Aberdeen fishing boat *Ben Breac*.

A few months later, the Duke and Duchess of Montrose visited Longhope where local lifeboatmen were honoured for their heroism in saving the crew of the *Dorbie*. Those given awards were coxswain Jack Swanson, second cox William Dass, bowman Tom Gunn, engineer Robert Johnston, second engineer Charles Mowat, brothers George and Robert Johnston, John Norquoy and Sinclair Mowat. (The two Robert Johnstons were cousins.)

Surprisingly, until then, North Ronaldsay lighthouse did not even have a fog siren, but, in 1932, one was installed, along with a wireless beacon signal. In the Westray Firth, the crew safely rowed to Westray after abandoning ship when the Grimsby trawler *Athenian* went aground on Skea Skerries, heading home from the Faroes in a gale. The vessel was later refloated by the Aberdeen salvage tug *Henry Lancaster*.

In 1933, the lifeboat *KTJS* was transfered to Shetland and Longhope was given a new vessel, the *Thomas McCunn*. Built at Cowes, she was 45 ft long, devided into eight watertight compartments, driven by two 40 hp engines, capable of more than eight knots and with a range, at full speed, of 116 miles. With capacity for 100 people, she had a line throwing gun, electric searchlight, and was fully lit by electricity. She was soon in action, completing her first rescue when she saved 13 men from the stranded Grimsby trawler *Silanion* which went aground at Torness point, on the south coast of Hoy, proceeding to Iceland with 230 tons of coal and 70 tons of ice aboard. The *Silanion*, a vessel of 144 tons, was not yet three years old. On Sunday, February 27, 1933, local sightseers were able to walk around the vessel, stranded by a big ebb tide. Customs and exise men patrolled the vessel to ensure the security of the trawler's bond of tobacco and alcohol.

Ten men had to abandon the sinking Aberdeen trawler *Avondow* and row for four hours to safety on Eday, after running aground returning from the Shetland fishing grounds in a gale. The skipper later had his skipper's certificate suspended for 12 months by a Board of Trade inquiry.

Although most of those in the trawlers were from Aberdeen or Humberside, there were Orcadians in the fishing industry as well - and James Swanney, from Westray, had a narrow escape when he was pulled to safety as eight of his crewmates died following a collision in a snowstorm between the Granton trawler *Succession* and the Liverpool steamer *Atheltarn*, 100 miles off Aberdeen, which sank the trawler in two minutes.

Back in Orkney, the Longhope lifeboat saved the 18 crew - including a 17 year old girl - off the Icelandic trawler *Geyser* which went aground at Torness, Hoy, in November, 1933, while the Stromness lifeboat went to the assistance of the Hull trawler *Cape Sable*, aground in thick fog on the Fore-berry, Hoy Head, helping tow the trawler to safety at high tide. And, in April, 1934, the 11 crewmen from the 274 ton Hull trawler *Strato* were rescued and landed by Stromness lifeboat at Kirkwall, after the vessel ran aground at Tresness, Sanday. The trawler, with 140 tons of coal aboard, was later salvaged and towed to Kirkwall. Two months later, the Grimsby trawler *Lord Birkenhead* sank in the Pentland Firth but the 16 crew were safely transferred to another of the company's vessels, the *Lord Harewood*.

To illustrate that the sea did not only vent its wrath on trawlers, the 22 crew of the 1,600 ton Finnish steamer *Gertrud* had to take to their lifeboats after the vessel ran aground on Stroma and later sank. All the crewmen reached safety.

There were obviously hundreds of men who had cause to be grateful to the lifeboats of Longhope and Stromness. And the death of Bill Mowat, a name renowned all around the coast of Britain, was mourned by many in October, 1934, when he died aged 72 in his native Longhope where he served the lifeboat for 53 years until his retirement as second coxswain in 1932, after helping to save 107 lives. The Chief Inspector of Lifeboats, Mr E.D. Drury, sent this tribute: "He was one of the finest specimens of lifeboatman you could possibly come across - a man who had no fears and was willing to go anywhere and do anything."

He had received a silver cup from the King of Sweden for his part, in 1923, in rescuing eight men from the steamer *Citos*. However, in 1929, he was rescued by his own lifeboat after running into difficulties with engine problems in his fishing boat off Hoy.

Sometimes rescue did not arrive so swiftly. In March, 1935, the crew of ten of the Aberdeen trawler *Strath Atholl* were adrift in an open boat for 16 hours, after abandoning their sinking vessel, before being picked up by the Danish steamer *Royksund* off Auskerry.

Thick fog was the culprit again in August, 1935, when the

The "Queen of the Pentland Firth." The steamer *St Ola* operated on the lifeline shipping route between Orkney and Scrabster for 59 years, including both world wars, before the North of Scotland Shipping Company built her namesake successor, a motor vessel, in the early 1950s.

(Picture courtesy of Orkney Library photographic archive)

Stronsay lifeboat saved six men from the Grimsby-registered fishing vessel *Tanana* when she ran aground in the Westray Firth in 1958.
(Picture courtesy of Orkney Library photographic archive)

3,300 ton Swedish motorship *Gunnaren* stranded on Swona. Longhope lifeboat took off 26 crewmen, and 41 bags of mail from America, while the captain and eight officers remained on board. However, they too were taken off later, when it was deemed impossible to refloat the ship, and part of the ship's cargo of apples was retrieved and sold in Kirkwall.

The year of 1936 saw five trawler disasters in Orkney waters - with ten deaths and 69 crewmen rescued.

The fatal tragedy was the first, in February, 1936, when the 125 ft Grimsby trawler *Merrivale* stranded in thick fog and sank off the Pentland Skerries. The Longhope lifeboat managed to reach the scene but there was no sign of life. It was sadly accepted that the ten crewmen had perished and that their bodies would never be found.

The following week, however, Longhope lifeboat made the biggest trawler rescue of the 20th century in Orkney - an operation that was to see the local lifeboatmen honoured by the French government.

Forty one crewmen were saved off the French factory trawler *Neptunia* after the 619 ton, 175 ft vessel had run ashore at Brims, en route for Iceland. The lifeboat - manoeuvred alongside by coxswain William Dass - got the last man off just five minutes before the trawler sank to the stern in a south easterly gale, and the 41 rescued fishermen, including five 14 and 15 year old boys, were taken to the Longhope Hotel. Some excitement was created in Brims the following day when a three month old pig - which was to have been slaughtered for fresh meat on the voyage - escaped from the wreck and swam ashore. After two days of liberty it was caught and penned up to await "further orders."

Coxswain Dass later was to receive the RNLI bronze medal for his part in the rescue, but greater acclaim was to follow. In October, 1936, the Longhope lifeboatmen travelled to Kirkwall to be honoured by the French government at a special ceremony to mark their role in the single biggest rescue from a fishing vessel in Orkney's history.

Coxswain Dass was presented a silver medal, while the French presented bronze medals to the rest of the crewmen - second cox Sinclair Mowat, engineer-mechanic Robert Johnston, second engineer Eric Mowat, bowman George Johnston and boatmen Robert Johnston, John Norquoy and John Robertson.

Prior to the *Neptunia* rescue, the Stromness lifeboat had carried out one of the biggest rescues, in terms of lives saved, in Orkney waters when, on June 13, 1925, a total of 31 men were rescued, and landed safely in Kirkwall, after a Norwegian vessel, the ss *Hastings County* of Bergen, was wrecked on Auskerry.

Another dangerous mission saw the Stromness lifeboat rescue 11 men from the Hull trawler *Siberite* wrecked in fog at Rora Head, Hoy, returning from the Faroes with 700 boxes of fish in March, 1936. "We had to go astern several times to avoid being smashed against the trawler," said coxswain William Linklater. "Whenever we got near enough, a man or two would jump on board, then out we would go and back again for more men."

In May, the crew of nine - including the Orcadian chief engineer Arthur Isbister, who lived in Cleethorpes - were saved as the Grimsby trawler *Morvina* became a total loss after stranding on the northern point of Egilsay.

A small consolation of the disaster was that it led to a reunion for Mr Isbister with his two Stromness sisters, with whom he had lost touch 20 years earlier.

The eight crewmen of the Aberdeen trawler *Danella* were able to scramble ashore in Deerness after their vessel, sheltering in Deer Sound, was driven ashore in 70 mph winds at Scarvataing after her cable chain broke in October, 1936. The vessel was later refloated.

But there was to be no salvation three months later when the worst sea disaster in Orkney waters since World War One saw 30 people - including women and children - perish in the Pentland Firth as the 5,500 ton Finnish motorship *Johanna Thorden* was wrecked, returning from her maiden voyage to New York, on Tuesday, January 12, 1937.

Maiden voyage to disaster

The loss of 30 people - including women and children - in Orkney's worst peacetime shipping disaster of the 20th century - was to leave anguish and recrimination - and mystery!

Although the entire ship's personnel of the Finnish motorship *Johanna Thorden* - returning from her maiden voyage to New York - got clear of the wreck in two of the vessel's lifeboats, the first boat, with 25 men, women and children, met with disaster and perished in the raging storm.

In the other boat, five of the 13 occupants, including the 55 year old Captain Lahja Simola, were also lost when the boat came to grief on the east side of South Ronaldsay. Just eight survivors made it ashore.

General cargo valued at two million dollars was lost. The surmise of local lifeboatmen was that she had run aground on Swona - the same site as the wreck of the Swedish vessel *Gunnaren* in 1935 - although the survivors maintained that it was the Pentland Skerries that claimed the ship. The missing lifeboat, and several bodies, were later washed ashore at Deerness.

First warning of the disaster came at 11am on Tuesday, January 12, 1937, when Mr John Peace, Whistlebrae, South Ronaldsay, saw men scrambling up the shore. He went to St Margaret's Hope to alert Constable Robert Tulloch, Dr Stephen Mouat and the deputy receiver of wreck Mr James Macdonald, who all went to the scene to give first aid to the survivors.

The wireless operator, George Moliis, explained the ship had left New York on New Year's Day for Gothenburg and other Swedish ports. In the Pentland Firth, they encountered a southerly gale with winds up to hurricane force. The collision with the rocks wrecked the radio so no SOS could be sent, though they fired 30-40 rockets. The ship was plunged into darkness as the engine room flooded. The first lifeboat included the wife and son of the chief engineer, also the wife and son of an engineer from the company which installed the ship's engines. The two boys were aged just four and six.

George Moliis explained that the first lifeboat got away from the ship at 6.15 am - 30 minutes after stranding. " In addition to the women and children, the first boat carried the first, second and third officers, chief engineer, chief steward, motormen, seamen and saloon boys.

" I saw those women and children leave the ship and go not to safety but to death."

The second lifeboat, under the command of Captain Simola, left the ship at 7.15 am. " Only eight of us were alive three hours later when our boat reached the shore," said the wireless operator.

The Swedish vessel *Gunnaren* broke in two when she ran aground on Swona in 1935.
(Picture courtesy of Orkney Library photographic archive)

"The boat upended three times in succession, throwing us all into the sea. We were washed ashore, along with the boat. Our Captain and unfortunate comrades who died were battered so severely that I do not think they were drowned. They were killed probably in the first smash."

Bodies, washed ashore, were taken to St Peters Church in South Ronaldsay. Others came ashore in Flotta, Copinsay, Deerness and Sanday.

Another of the survivors, a seaman H.J. Blomkvist, told how, once ashore, they had gone to a house where "a lady took us to her fire and boiled food for us. We each got a tiny little nip of whisky and it did us a lot of good. We needed it badly."

For the first time in any major peacetime disaster in Orkney, air power was used in the subsequent investigation with a plane flying over the area surveying the scene - however, there was criticism that the Highland Airways had not been called in earlier to help in the search for the lifeboat.

Captain George Swanson, master of the *St Ola*, was to say later: "It will never be known now whether the ship originally ran on the Pentland Skerries, on Stroma or Swona or anywhere else. If it could have been definitely determined that the stern, as well as the bow, was at Swona, then one could take it that the original stranding was at Swona. If only the bow was at Swona, then it means that the ship stranded somewhere else."

There was some criticism because the Longhope lifeboat - which had turned out soon after noon following the first report of

the disaster - had originally been recalled because of a misunderstanding that all the crew of the ship were accounted for. It was later established that only the occupants of one lifeboat were accounted for, and there was another lifeboat with 25 people still missing. So a further two hours had elapsed before the Longhope lifeboat returned to the Pentland Firth.

Had the lifeboat been permitted to proceed on its first call, which was to the east side of South Ronaldsay, it is possible that the missing boat would have been located. On the other hand, so tremendous were the seas that two small boats might have been within a mile of each other and never seen the other.

Three weeks later, George Moliis wrote to *The Orcadian* : "The survivors wish to express their deep gratitude to the people of the Orkneys, especially those of St Margaret's Hope and Kirkwall, for the kindness shown to them all after the disaster of their ship. May we also tender to those who helped us so much on our landing at Newark Bay, our sincere thanks and heartfelt gratitude."

At this time, 12 bodies were still unaccounted for. There was to be a sad sequel to the disaster in the first week of February, 1937, when four of the victims who had been buried in Flotta, Deerness and Sanday were exhumed on warrants signed by the Sheriff, applied for on behalf of the vessel owner, Mr Gustaf B. Thorden of Helsingfors, so their bodies could be returned to Finland for burial, along with those which had already been returned home. It was a poignant final journey.

The real price of fish

By March, 1937, the sea was taking its toll of the trawler fleet again when 11 men were saved off the Aberdeen fishing boat *Loch Buie* by Stromness lifeboat as the vessel foundered off Westray. The lifeboat, which had been alerted at midnight by Kirkwall Coastguard that distress flares had been seen at Mull Head, arrived at 5 am. The following month, the trawler, which had been returning home from Faroese waters with 240 boxes of fish, was refloated and towed to Kirkwall. Some trawler skippers were still prepared to take extra risks and, in May, 1937, an Aberdeen skipper, caught fishing within the three mile limit off Rackwick, was fined £200 (this was when many people earned £2 a week) or six months in jail, at Kirkwall Sheriff Court.

The sea was no respecter of nationality either. In June, 1937, 23 Norwegians from the 225 ton Haugesund herring trawler, *Shetland*, after taking to their lifeboat when their vessel sank off Start Point, Sanday, were landed safely at Kirkwall by the Aberdeen trawler *Loch Assater.*

However, tragedy was never far away and in February, 1938, it descended once again like a thief in the night, leaving 23 children fatherless as all 15 crewmen of the Grimsby trawler *Leicestershire* perished off Hoy when the state-of-the-art 157 ton stern trawler, built only 18 months earlier, was lost returning from a fishing trip to Iceland.

The cause of the disaster was a mystery as there had been no warning of a vessel in distress and the first the Longhope people knew of the tragedy was when bodies started to be washed ashore, followed by wreckage. Many of the victims could be indentified by tattoos but two unidentified bodies were interred at Longhope kirkyard, and a memorial to the 15 dead was dedicated in the South Walls cemetery. Most of the crew came from Grimsby, or neighbouring Cleethorpes, and it had been skipper Evans' first trip in the *Leicestershire*.

The wreck of the trawler was later found off the Berry of Hoy - the same spot where, seven months later, the Grimsby trawler *Worsley* was wrecked, but, thankfully, all her crew were saved.

And Stromness paused to mourn the passing of one of that town's pioneers of the lifeboat service. Robert Heddle Greig, who died at the age of 83 in March, 1938, was born in Kirkwall but he joined the crew of the first lifeboat to be stationed at Stromness, the *Saltaire*, rising to become coxswain of the next lifeboat, the *Good Shepherd*, in 1898. He was the first coxswain

of the first motor boat at Stromness, the *John A. Hay*. He retired in 1915 after 17 years as coxswain, during which time he was awarded the RNLI silver medal for the rescue of three men off the Hull trawler *Shakespeare* wrecked off Breckness, with four fishermen drowned, in 1907, and was awarded a vellum parchment signed by the Prince of Wales, later to become King Edward VIII, then Duke of Windsor.

That year, 1938, saw another member of the Greig family take command of the Stromness lifeboat when Robert Greig, a member of the crew since 1902, and second coxswain since 1930, became the new coxswain following the retiral, at the age of 66, of William Linklater, the man who had led the lifeboatmen on that recording-breaking 55 hours service when making the epic 1930 trip to Shetland. In his lifeboat career, he had shared in saving 137 lives; 48 during his eight years as coxswain.

The months leading up to World War Two proved to be the calm before the storm, with Orkney's lifeboats spared a single major incident. However, when the hostilities came, an epic rescue in November, 1939, was only indirectly the result of war, when the 8,600 Norwegian steamer *Mim*, on her maiden voyage loaded with grain from Australia to Norway, ran ashore on Reef Dyke, North Ronaldsay. The Norwegian shipowners later blamed the stranding on the poor navigation of a British Naval officer who had been put aboard the ship to escort it into Scapa Flow for inspection. After a 100 mile battle in darkness, through heavy seas, Stromness lifeboat landed the 31 crew at Kirkwall. Five days later, the Norwegian steamer *Hesni* ran aground at the same spot, and the 16 crew taken ashore on North Ronaldsay. Normal service had resumed.

(Wartime was to see the death in 1945 at the age of 71 of Graemsay-born George Thomson, who was secretary of Stromness lifeboat for four decades. His funeral was attended by all the staff and senior pupils of Stromness Academy, a mark of the achievements of his career, in which he was created a life governor of the RNLI and decorated with the MBE for his services to the lifeboat. In 1946, the RNLI honoured Mr William Sutherland who retired as secretary of the Longhope lifeboat after 24 years - during which 272 lives were saved. He was succeeded by his daughter Miss M. Sutherland. That same year, William Dass, coxswain of the Longhope boat for 12 years and with a total of 51 years service, retired to be succeeded as coxswain by Fred Johnston.)

Longhope lifeboat made the biggest trawler rescue of the 20th century in Orkney waters in 1936 when 41 crewmen were saved off the French factory trawler *Neptunia* which is pictured here after running aground at Brims, with the Pentland Firth steamer *St Ola* standing by in the background.

(Picture courtesy of Orkney Library photographic archive)

The 1931 census showed Copinsay as one of the few places in Orkney to show an increase in population. This was due entirely to the family of farmer James Groat who had 12 children on the island (and another two in Stromness). This family reunion of members of the Groat family, who as children all grew up on Copinsay, took place more than fifty years later. Back row, from the left: Joseph Groat, Sinclair Groat, Ernest Groat, Bobby Groat, Ralph Groat, Jimmy Groat and Bill Groat. Front: Kathleen Kemp, Ethel Harcus, Bessie Coghill, David Groat, Isabel Groundwater, Eva Currie and Alice Hepburn.   (Picture courtesy of George Currie)

The Orkney Steam Navigation Company vessel *Earl Sigurd*, launched in 1930, would serve the North Isles for four decades.
(Picture courtesy of Myra Hazell)

Tragedy of 'Lady of Hoy'

1933

One of Orkney's saddest and most poignant stories was unearthed in Hoy when the discovery of a coffin, containing a girl's body, revived a controversy of 150 year earlier.

The discovery was made, unwittingly, by a team of Hoy peat diggers - John Davidson of Garson, Alex Robb, of Quoys, and his sisters Annie and Bessie Robb. As they cut the turfs, in May, 1933, they came across the coffin, at a depth of 2 feet 7 inches, at the boundary of the Walls and Hoy parishes.

The men notified local postmaster Isaac Moar, with whom they later opened the coffin to reveal the sad contents - the body of the tragic young woman, with her long dark hair around her shoulders, and still in a remarkable state of preservation, although her skin, stained by the peat, now had a tinge of brown.

A piece of rope, which had been the noose which ended her life, apparently lay beside the body but turned to dust when exposed to the air.

And so emerged the story of Betty Corrigall - a hapless victim of a fickle lover and an unforgiving Church which refused burial rights for those who committed suicide.

Her burial site, it transpired, dated back to the 1770s and the reason for her lonely resting place was tied up in the customs and religious practices of the late 18th century.

Betty Corrigall lived at Greengairs Cottage, Rysa. (In 1933, the ruins of the house were still visible between Rysa Lodge and Rysa Mill House). Aged 27, she discovered she had fallen pregnant to a sailor who had jilted her and departed for the whaling.

According to the folklore of the day, Betty - either ashamed of her predicament or fearful of the consequences - decided to commit suicide. Her first attempt to end her life by walking into the sea, and drowning, was unsuccessful and she was rescued. But days later, the tragic woman hanged herself in a barn.

Now she was to be denied a Christian burial. In those days, the accepted Church law was that those who took their own life could not be buried in the consecrated ground of the graveyard. (In fact, the Church refused to allow suicides to be buried in parish churchyards until late in the 19th century).

At the same time, neither the Laird of Hoy nor of Melsetter would allow the body of Betty Corrigall to be interred on their estates. And so, the solution was reached that she would be buried in the unsanctified ground right on the parish boundary between Hoy and North Walls.

It was said that, at one time, a cairn of stones had marked the grave, but this had either been removed by her family to conceal the memory, or had simply fallen away over the years.

Whatever the folklore, the fact was that Betty Corrigall's coffin cut right through the parish boundary line - and the peat bank where her body was discovered that day in 1933.

The Kirkwall police were immediately informed and, after a visit to Hoy, the Procurator Fiscal ordered the reburial of the body at the same spot it was found. Many people from Hoy and Walls visited the grave on Sunday, May 21, 1933, either out of morbid curiosity or in a spirit of pilgrimage.

However, it was to again prove to be a disturbed resting place, as six years later Hoy witnessed the arrival of thousands of service personnel and civilian war workers. At the beginning of 1941, a working party of soldiers, digging on the peat bank to erect telegraph poles, also stumbled across the coffin of the girl they called "The Lady of Hoy."

Although the grave was quickly covered again, it seems that, sadly, the story of the preserved body aroused morbid interest among new arrivals of servicemen and some made the excursion to dig up the grave and view the body - the continual exposure to the air quickly causing the remains to deteriorate.

Fortunately, officers eventually heard of this and put an end to the unsavoury practice by moving the grave 50 yards and placing a heavy concrete slab on top of the coffin, which otherwise remained unmarked other than by a stick.

However, after the war, Harry Berry, a Londoner who served in Hoy with the forces and then settled on the island, was approached by an American minister who asked if he would erect a headstone for the grave. In the first instance, a small wooden cross was made and a fence erected around the site. Later, a glass fibre headstone - light enough not to sink into the peat bog - was put in place at a short service of dedication. Betty Corrigall could finally rest in peace.

There may be other unfortunates, however, whose final resting place was in the peat banks of Hoy. According to folklore, another unmarked grave is that of a Kirk minister who hanged himself in North Walls and was also buried in unconsecrated ground at the parish boundary.

Royal honour for artist of courage

The bravery and talent of an Orkney artist, born without arms, was recognised by a special tribute from the Queen.

Miss Harriet "Hettie" Scott of Twargarn, Harray, overcame her handicap by teaching herself to paint and do needlework using her feet.

Her paintings won many prizes and her work adorned many homes in Orkney and, in 1933, an example of her handicraft - a fancy needlebook and two pincases, bearing paintings in water colours - were sent for presentation to Queen Mary and Princess Elizabeth.

A message was returned to Miss Scott from Buckingham Palace: "Her Majesty was much impressed by the courage shown by Harriet Scott in overcoming her great affliction by such patience and perseverance as she must have done to create such great work." Accompanying the message were photographs of the Queen and of the Princesses Elizabeth and Margaret Rose, daughters of the then Duchess of York.

A decade later, in her autobiography *Brightening Her Corner*, Hettie Scott said: "Ever since I can remember, I have been able to use my feet as others use their hands. I have been able to sew and paint and also to write and knit a little."

Examples of her work, including many of her paintings and embroideries, were exhibited at the Harray Hall, 50 years later, in 1999 to raise funds to help the deprived in Eastern Europe.

First public telephone

Kirkwall had its first public telephone kiosk and it was now possible to speak, via phone, to 29 countries from Orkney, and by radio telephone link to another 20 countries, including Australia, South Africa, United States and Canada.

Giant fireball lights the skies

The skies of Orkney were illuminated by a giant fireball, believed to be an exploding meteor, which travelled through the heavens, trailing a tail of flame on March 5, 1933.

Travelling from the North East to the South West over the county, it went at a speed later estimated by experts at over 50,000 mph.

It was reckoned to be the largest and most brilliant meteor ever seen in Orkney, creating a vivid purple and white light which was witnessed by hundreds in the Northern Isles.

Royal visitors sail in

Orkney has often played host to members of the British Royal family - but, in 1933, Kirkwall welcomed four members of the Romanian and Austrian ruling families.

Queen Marie of Romania, her daughter Princess Ileana and her husband the Austrian Archduke Anton, with their 12 month old baby Prince Stefan, were among the passengers who came ashore when the Hamburg-Amerika liner *Resolute* visited on July 19.

Queen Marie was following in family footsteps by visiting Orkney - in January 23, 1882, her father, the then Duke of Edinburgh, was granted the freedom of Kirkwall.

In glorious weather, the royal party was escorted around Kirkwall by the Rev William Barclay, minister of St Magnus Cathedral, shadowed by two British detectives and two members of the Austrian secret service. With cheering crowds gathering around them, they not only visited the Cathedral and the Palaces but visited several shops, buying knitwear from Peace and Low's drapery store.

Seven years later, in 1940, Queen Marie's son, King Carol II, was overthrown in Romania.

Football accolade

Jim Findlay of Orphir played in the Orkney team which beat Shetland 1-0 in the 1933 intercounty football match - thus becoming the fifth Findlay brother to be "capped" against Shetland.

A crowd of more than 3,000 at the Bignold Park contributed to gate receipts of £72 10s 1d.

The referee - who flew to Orkney especially to officiate - was Aberdonian Peter Craigmyle, who had previously refereed three Scottish Cup finals and several major internationals in front of 100,000 people.

Mr Craigmyle - who was a regular visitor to Orkney and a major supporter of football in the county over three decades - had refereed his first Rangers - Celtic game at the age of just 24.

Ba' tragedy escape

What could have been the worst accident in the history of Kirkwall's Ba' game was narrowly averted, by good fortune, when a car ran into the crowd watching the New Year Ba' in Broad Street.

Four people - an elderly man and three women - were injured but a baby, in the arms of one of the women who was knocked down, was miraculously thrown clear to avoid injury. The car driver was later fined £3 at Kirkwall Sheriff Court.

Down in the mouth

Auxiliary postman David Knight, of Nouster, North Ronaldsay, became the first hospital patient to be carried outwith Orkney by plane - after swallowing his denture while asleep. He was flown on a scheduled Highland Airways flight from Kirkwall to Inverness for specialist treatment to have the "obstruction" removed.

Author of courage

Orkney welcomed the American author Helen Keller, a woman who had become world renowned for her inspiring victory over adversity, after losing her sight and hearing as a baby.

Despite her handicaps, she learned to speak, read and write and graduated from college to write her autobiography before travelling the world campaigning for the education of handicapped people. She spent several weeks in 1933 in the Northern Isles, twice crossing the Pentland Firth on the *St Ola*, and later corresponded with the ship's master, Captain George Swanson.

* * *

Kirkwall Town Council agreed to buy the burgh's first motorised refuse vehicle for £250, putting an end to horse drawn carts.

* * *

The Orcadian was the first Scottish county newspaper to publish a photograph (of the Orkney badminton team) taken with the aid of flash bulb - instead of exploding magnesium powder, which had traditionally been used to illuminate photographs. The picture was taken by James W. Sinclair, of the Castle Street Studio, Kirkwall.

* * *

Three Orcadian musicians - piper David Laughton, of Victoria Street, Kirkwall, violinist James Johnston of Deerness and accordeonist Francis Wood, of Quarrybanks, St Ola - went to the studios of the Parlophone company in Glasgow to make their first Orkney gramophone record.

* * *

The authorities decided that Twatt's Mortification - a charitable endowment fund bequeathed for education in Orkney - should be renamed the Orkney Educational Trust.

* * *

The most dreadful disaster at Gresford Colliery in North Wales led to Orkney's Lord Lieutenant Alfred Baikie and Kirkwall's Provost John Slater launch an Orkney appeal fund to aid the dependants of 264 miners who lost their lives.

* * *

Ferdinand Vetesse, born in Belgium but of Italian nationality, was a Paris-trained fashion designer who, in 1934, at the age of only 23, set up in business as Kirkwall's only dress designer, next door to the Victoria Street cafe run by his brother. Ill health forced him to close the business early in 1939.

Lord Chamberlain bans Dounby SWRI play

1934

There was a sensation in Orkney community drama circles when the Lord Chamberlain - arbiter of public decency - banned a play to be performed by the Dounby SWRI team at the 1934 drama festival in Kirkwall.

The original script *A Marriage Took Place,* by local drama enthusiast David Towers, could not be licensed for performing, ruled the Lord Chamberlain.

The one act play, a tragedy, had a theme of an incestuous marriage as a means of revenge. Based at a fictional Cursiter House in Orkney, it tells how - in a web of intrigue - a wedding is allowed to take place in which the bride and groom are, unwittingly, brother and sister. The play ends with the bride's mother - who 20 years earlier had been wronged by the groom's father - taking her own life.

Mr Towers said: "I have no hesitation in saying that the Lord Chamberlain's decision has robbed us of the premier honour at Kirkwall. I cannot say if the play will ever be performed locally."

He went on to write several plays which were performed at drama festivals over the following years, and he also acted in several productions as he become a well-known stalwart of the local drama scene.

Caithness invasion hits Cathedral

Hundreds of visitors, travelling to Scapa on the steamer *St Clair,* descended on Kirkwall for the annual trip of Caithness folk and prompted complaints of vandalism and desecration in St Magnus Cathedral.

Cathedral minister Rev William Barclay told Kirkwall Town Council that electric lamps were wrenched from the walls and either smashed or taken as souvenirs.

"Is your council aware that the Bell Tower was once again used as a place of public convenience and that the behaviour on the stairway leading to the tower was outside the bounds of decency?"

The Cathedral was "the wonder and glory of all the North" and should not have to suffer the invasion of a mob of men who were "quite evidently C3 both mentally and morally."

The council agreed to measures to stop future problems by charging 6d admission to the Cathedral and limiting the size of parties who could ascend to the tower.

Flotta fire tragedy

Flotta was hit by tragedy when brother and sister John (77) and Jessie (82) Simpson died when their house, Cauldhame, was gutted by fire. The police recovered a metal box containing £500 from the ruins. The same week, the Mill of Cairston in Stromness, which dated back to the 16th century at least, was destroyed by fire, including a new McCormick reaper which had just been delivered.

It was the same year that Eday's recreation hall - originally bought at the Admiralty displenishment sale at Houton Air Station in 1922 - was destroyed by fire.

* * *

The death occurred in 1934, at the age of 93, of Stenness's oldest parishioner of the day, William Macleod, of the Brig o' Waithe, who held the distinction of having landed Orkney's record trout - a 29lb specimen. An expert angler and boatman, he was well known to visitors to the Stenness loch.

* * *

Members of the crew of the German oil tanker *Kattegat,* berthed at Lyness, celebrated Hitler's birthday by marching, headed by their officers, to Lyness Naval Cemetery to pay tribute to the memory of the several hundreds of their compatriots lost in World War One or during the great scuttle of the German fleet in Scapa Flow.

* * *

The annual meeting of Kirkwall Chamber of Commerce discussed a proposal for an annual Kirkwall Shopping Week.

* * *

Orkney County Council rejected, by 15 votes to eight, a proposal from Stromness that the steamer *St Ola* - instead of calling at Scapa and South Ronaldsay - should proceed direct from Stromness to Scrabster, via the west of Hoy.

Weather leaves trail of destruction

Two men died in weather-related tragedies as Orkney suffered the extremes of climate during 1934.

Parts of the roads at Scapa and Carness were washed away, and houses in Stromness flooded in a storm on January 18. Three weeks later, strong winds continued at 73mph or more for five days - reaching a hurricane force 88mph - the strongest winds of the century so far. (The highest strength winds ever recorded in Orkney at that time was 94mph on November 17, 1893. However that was surpassed on January 23, 1938, when wind speeds reached 100mph in Kirkwall - the first time the "century" had been reached.)

In April, 1934, gale force winds and heavy rain combined to force water through the defective copper spire of St Magnus Cathedral, making it impossible to occupy the pulpit for the Sunday service.

Fog was the culprit in July, 1934, when a party of 140 Evie and Rendall Bible Class members, on their annual trip, were marooned overnight in Stronsay after the *Earl Sigurd* was prevented from reaching the island.

A thunderstorm flooded Kirkwall streets to a depth of 12 inches, in September, 1934, and killed a 22 year old North Walls man, James Baikie, by lightning.

Another tragedy followed the following month when one of Orkney's most promising footballers John Sinclair, son of Finstown merchant William Sinclair, was killed when he was thrown from his bicycle in a gale. Just three months earlier, while still a pupil at Kirkwall Grammar School, he had made his debut for Orkney, at left half, in the county game in Shetland, at the age of 17.

* * *

Two Finstown men were jailed for setting fire to a haystack as Sheriff George Brown pointed out that it was only as recently as his father's time that the death penalty was removed for this offence.

* * *

The St Magnus Cathedral wedding of Marjorie Clouston - daughter of county convener J. Storer Clouston, of Smoogro, Orphir - to Leicestershire architect Henry Goddard received a report in *The Orcadian* of more than 5,000 words - including a full list of all the presents, and their donors.

Golden age of the silver screen

Orkney was to be in the front row when it came to celebrating the great era of cinema; an age that came to a glorious climax when Kirkwall played host to a world premiere of a film that was both written and filmed in the islands.

The film was *The Spy In Black* and the star-studded occasion of its first showing was at the Albert Kinema, Kirkwall, on Saturday, April 8, 1939.

The thriller had been written by Joseph Storer Clouston, Orkney's county convener, historian and novelist. In fact, this was the second Storer Clouston novel to be transferred to the screen - his book *Lunatic At Large* was made into a film in 1928.

But *The Spy In Black* was to be a commercial and critical success - it was still shown on British television more than 50 years later - made by Columbia - British, and directed by Michael Powell, who, with his Hungarian collaborator Emeric Pressburger, was to go on to become one of the top British film directors of the 1940s and 1950s with productions like *49th Parallel, I Know Where I'm Going* and *A Canterbury Tale*.

Filming of *The Spy In Black* - apparently in Canada it was shown under the title *U-boat 29* - began at the film studios in Denham in October, 1938, starring the Berlin-born actor Conrad Veidt, by now a naturalised Briton. It had originally been reported that Vivien Leigh had been wanted for the female lead part, but when filming began, the role was given to Valerie Hobson. (She was later to become Mrs John Profumo, but that's another story).

Location filming soon switched to Orkney, with local amateur dramatic society members, as well as Orphir schoolchildren and Stromness dock workers and the crews of the vessels *St Ola* and *Pole Star*, featuring among the extras at location shots in Stromness and Longhope - including the Longhope Hotel and the bedroom where King George V once slept. In the book, the manse of St Nicholas in Orphir featured as the hide-out of the "Spy", and the film camera work of Bernard Browne, with atmospheric scenes of Scapa Flow, was to be highly praised when the film was released.

It was a gripping espionage drama of a German U-boat commander involved in a mission to sink British ships at Scapa Flow in World War One, explained the pre-publicity in what was to seem eerily prophetic six months later when the *Royal Oak* was lost to a submarine attack.

As well as Conrad Veidt (he died four years later while playing golf in America) and Valerie Hobson, the film included some star names of the period - Marius Goring, Sebastian Shaw, June Duprez, Helen Haye, Hay Petrie and Margaret Moffatt.

Both Storer Clouston and Michael Powell attended the premiere of the film at the Albert Kinema, from which all the proceeds would go to aid the Balfour Hospital. They were welcomed by the Albert manager Mr Thomas S.P. Shearer, whose sister Norma Shearer was at that time achieving some acclaim as a film actress in America.

Although several films for cinema and television were shot in Orkney, mainly in the second half of the century, *The Spy In Black* probably remained the most memorable. It was certainly the crowning glory of the 18 years that the Albert Kinema was in existence.

The acknowledged pioneer of cinema in Orkney was the Albert's owner, Mr David Balfour Peace, a cabinet maker by trade and a native of Shapinsay. Although there had been magic lantern shows and primitive moving pictures brought to Orkney by travelling showmen as early as the 19th century, it was Mr Peace who, in 1913 opened Kirkwall's first permanent cinema, the Electric Theatre, in what for the previous four years had been a roller skating rink which he had built in his Junction Road wood store.

This was to be the age of Charlie Chaplin and, for 14 years, the Electric Theatre screened the silent movies of the day, accompanied by the music of a wind-up gramophone.

It was not the only picture house, however. Stronsay, with its summer population of thousands for the herring fishing, could also boast a cinema, and the Orkney isles and parishes could also enjoy visits from Sinclair's Up-To-Date Cinema, which, at the start of 1928, was showing news reels of the salvage of the German battleship *Von Moltke* in Scapa Flow, the launching of the new Longhope lifeboat and the unveiling of the memorials at Longhope and Kirkwall.

In March, 1928, D.B. Peace decided that Kirkwall was ready for another picture house, and he began converting his former cabinet-maker's shop in Albert Street to accommodate his new cinema. On September 21, 1928, the Electric Theatre closed its doors and business transferred to the new Albert Kinema which opened on September 26 with the spectacular Russian romance *Michael Strogoff* from the novel by Jules Verne.

For another three years, however, the Kirkwall cinema audiences had to settle for musical accompaniment to silent films - or they could go along to grand variety entertainment shows at the Kirkwall Temperance Hall where, in January, 1931, the "Latvian Hercules" Martin Breedis was offering a £50 challenge to Orcadians to match his feats of strength which included driving a six inch nail through three inches of wood with his bare hands.

But a new chapter of Orkney's cinema history was to begin in June, 1931, when a full house packed the Albert Kinema to see and hear the first "talkie" to be screened.

Orkney's MP Sir Robert Hamilton called for an end to the imposition of entertainment tax on cinema-goers in the cheapest seats - but his move in the House of Commons failed in 1934 - so Orkney film fans were still being taxed when the Hollywood epic *Mutiny on the Bounty*, starring Clark Gable and Charles Laughton, came to the Albert Kinema in 1936. The part of the Orcadian midshipman Stewart, who was caught up in the actual events of the mutiny, was played by Douglas Walton.

By now, Stromness too had regular access to film shows. The Stromness Cinema operated twice weekly in the Town Hall in the 1930s - and continued after the war - while Metal Industries Ltd, the company working on the salvage of the German fleet in Scapa Flow, operated its own cinema in the Lyness recreation hall.

In April, 1939, the former Electric Theatre in Junction Road, Kirkwall, was relicensed as a cinema - and it looked that film fans would have a choice of venues. In the event, war intervened and the building instead became a wartime drill hall.

But the war, of course, was to produce a mushrooming of picture houses to entertain the influx of servicemen sent to the islands. Kirkwall's Temperance Hall became the Kirkwall Naval Cinema, while the huge cinemas in Flotta and Lyness were as big as any in the country. A new civilian cinema, the Strond, was built to seat 350 in St Mary's, Holm, by Mr and Mrs John Marwick of St Mary's Inn. It opened on June 10, 1943, but burned down 18 months later.

January, 1943, witnessed the death at the age of 91 of Orkney cinema pioneer D.B. Peace. His daughter, Mrs J. F. Shearer, took over the management of the business, along with her sons Tommy and Dougie. But four years later disaster struck.

The Albert Kinema, Kirkwall, was gutted by fire on Thursday morning, May 8, 1947. The alarm was raised by Mr John Cooper, storeman next door at Boots the Chemist. The whole building - which had provided seating for 400 - was ablaze within 20 minutes with huge clouds of smoke billowing over the town. The oil tanker *Pass of Leny*, carrying petrol, kerosene and gas, was approaching Kirkwall pier at the time and had to be diverted to safety. The men of the fire service were joined by British and Polish soldiers to help save adjoining premises, and, finally, after six hours, the fire was contained.

The Albert Kinema manager Dougie Shearer announced that film showings would transfer to the Temperance Hall. And that's where they stayed for the next eight years.

In the meantime, the Orkney education authorities launched the Rural Cinema Service with the first showing in Shapinsay on January 5, 1948. In the first 20 weeks of operation, 96 shows were given around the county with a total attendance of 11,101.

Eventually, after a long search for a suitable site, a new 650 seat cinema in Kirkwall was built for D.B. Peace junior, and the Shearer family, in what was thought to be the most costly venture by a private Kirkwall firm at that time. Inevitably, it was called the Phoenix and it opened on Tuesday, June 14, 1955. The first film to be screened was *Doctor In The House* starring Dirk Bogarde.

However, the television age was to reduce the attraction of cinemas and, after varying economic fortunes, the Phoenix was eventually purchased by Orkney Islands Council in 1985. In 1989, it was to be the venue for the premiere of another Orkney film *Venus Peter.*

The Phoenix - for a long time the most northerly cinema in Britain - continued until November, 1998. In its 43 years of existence, more that 5,000 films had been screened - the biggest box office successes apparently being *Grease*, which attracted an audience of 4,220 in September, 1978, just beating the previous record of *Jaws* in April, 1977. The last film to be shown, on November 28, 1998, was the wartime drama *The Land Girls.*

Two months later, the curtain rose on another chapter of 20th century film-going in Orkney when a modern cinema - the New Phoenix - was opened as part of the new £7 million Pickaquoy Leisure Complex in Kirkwall.

Right is the theatre and music hall star Evelyn Laye, who visited Orkney during World War Two to entertain the troops, while, below, is a scene from one of the local halls following the introduction of the rural cinema service in 1948.

(Pictures courtesy of Orkney Library photographic archive)

Thousands celebrate Royal silver jubilee

Flags were flying to celebrate the silver jubilee of King George V and Queen Mary after 25 years reign. Loyal messages to the Royal couple were sent by the Lord Lieutenant, the county council, Stromness and Kirkwall town councils, the British Legion and Stromness Secondary School.

A day of celebrations, on May 6, 1935, began in Kirkwall with the 702 Kirkwall Grammar School pupils, led by Kirkwall Town Band, marching to Broad Street where they were presented with souvenir medals. At noon, the scholars marched to the Willows where they planted the first of 700 trees before joining a carnival procession with the

1935

Kirkwall City Pipe Band. It was estimated that 3,000 people packed Broad Street.

In the evening, the Kirkwall Amateur Operatic Society gave a charity performance of *The Desert Song* and there was a hospital dance before at 11pm the lighting of a beacon on Wideford Hill - one of a chain of bonfires stretching the length of Britain.

In Stromness, pupils received silver

jubilee mugs and scholars marched to St Peter's Church where they heard live radio coverage of the thanksgiving service relayed from St Paul's Cathedral. The Stromness celebration bonfire was at Brinkie's Brae. As beacons were lit in the parishes and isles, revellers in South Ronaldsay said that a total of 30 bonfires could be seen.

The week of celebrations ended with a thanksgiving service in St Magnus Cathedral.

But Kirkwall Town Council abandoned plans to provide children's playgrounds after it was stated that the response of Kirkwallians to a public appeal for funds was nil.

County Show washout

Orkney Agricultural Society's diamond jubilee County Show, for which a record entry of stock had been put forward, was ruined by torrential rain as only 2,000 people attended.

* * *

School attendance returns for Scotland showed that Orkney pupils had the best attendance record in the country in 1934 - with an average daily attendance of 93.8 per cent. The total school roll in Orkney was 3,136.

* * *

Mr Livio Zanre, the Italian proprietor of Kirkwall's Central Cafe, presented a trophy to the Orkney County Football Association for an inter-town competition between Kirkwall and Stromness.

* * *

The year 1935 saw the introduction of a 30mph speed limit in built-up areas - and a driving test for motorists. The price of a Ford Popular car was reduced to £100.

* * *

Aberdeen FC manager Paddy Travers visited Orkney to assess the possibility of Scottish FA senior affiliation for Orkney football which could see an Orkney team playing in the Qualifying Cup and - if successful - in the Scottish Cup, with the possibility of teams like Celtic and Rangers travelling to Orkney.

* * *

Kirkwall marksman David Dunnet was the best in Britain in 1935. The member of Kirkwall and District Smallbore Rifle Club achieved the gold medal in the nationwide Royal Silver Jubilee Commemorative Competition - against competition from 12,495 entries from throughout Britain. In the contest, Mr Dunnet scored 80 consecutive bulls.

Scores of children turned out in fancy dress and on decorated bicycles to join the procession marking the celebrations in Kirkwall of the silver jubilee of King George V and Queen Mary. (Picture courtesy of Orkney Library photographic archive)

Three die in blaze disaster

Friday, December 13, 1935, was a day of tragedy for Longhope when three people died in a fire which gutted the two storey house of Greenhill, believed to have been started by the accidental overturning of an oil lamp. The victims were Captain Walter Dunnet (56) retired shipmaster;

James Taylor (86) retired farmer; and Mrs Isabella Taylor (80).

Mrs Jessie Dunnet - Captain Dunnet's wife, and daughter of Mr and Mrs Taylor - escaped to raise the alarm but rescuers found themselves powerless to enter the blazing property.

The great constitutional crisis

1936

The old King - George V - died on Monday, January 20, 1936, and his mortal remains were laid to rest at Windsor eight days later. Half an hour after the funeral, the biggest congregation ever accommodated in Kirkwall's St Magnus Cathedral gathered at a memorial service. Such was the strength of feeling for the monarchy in those days.

Little did those who gathered that day realise but they were about to live through Britain's greatest constitutional crisis of the 20th century - and be betrayed by a disgraceful conspiracy of silence by the national Press barons of the era.

Entertainments and social functions were closed as a mark of respect throughout Orkney as the news of the death of George V reached the county.

(Just two weeks earlier, Stromness policeman Constable Thomas Mainland had been awarded the King's Police Medal for Gallantry after stopping a runaway horse in Stromness).

A crowd of 1,500 or more, including all the staff and pupils of Kirkwall Grammar School, gathered at the Market Cross, Kirkwall, to hear the proclamation of the accession of the new King, Edward VIII, by Sheriff George Brown. Proceedings at Kirkwall's annual bull show were suspended so that farmers and buyers at the mart could attend the proclamation.

At least 1,700 people took part in the memorial service for George V at the Cathedral, conducted by ministers of four churches, including 115 members of the Boys Brigade, of which George V had been patron for over 40 years.

A fund was later started to raise money for a King George V Memorial Playing Field - although it was another ten years before Kirkwall Town Council got round to preparing a site at Pickaquoy that had been purchased for £1,205.

But, of course, there was never to be a Coronation for Edward VIII - nor would the British public be allowed any debate over the relationship of the new King and the twice married American Mrs Wallis Simpson, as Britain's national newspapers concealed the full truth of the crisis precipitated with the cabinet headed by Stanley Baldwin.

King Edward VIII did take part in the Armistice Day ceremony at the Cenotaph in London on November 11, 1936 - and chosen to be a member of the King's bodyguard was young David Ford of Bignold Park Road, Kirkwall, who had been a member of the Royal Air Force for just three weeks.

But it was December 10, 1936, that the matter exploded into sensation. *The Orcadian* revealed that "grave news" was expected regarding "the King and his marriage," quoting statements of Prime Minister Baldwin in the House of Commons.

By the afternoon of Thursday, December 10, the news of the Abdication of Edward VIII was confirmed by a telegram from London which was immediately displayed to the public from a window of *The Orcadian* office. The Duke of York, brother of the abdicated monarch, was proclaimed as King George VI - the proclamation in Kirkwall being made on December 15 by Sheriff George Brown before a crowd of around 1,000.

The Stromness correspondent of *The Orcadian* James Marwick pointed out: "Many townsfolk who had relatives in America, and had received newspapers and periodicals from them, were conversant with the facts which led up to the abdication long before they were known by the general public here."

The Coronation of George VI went ahead the following May, 1937, with criticism of Provost John Slater for not representing Kirkwall at the ceremony. The Ven Archdeacon Edward Kissack, of St Olaf's Episcopal Kirk, said: "It was a great disappointment to many that Kirkwall's chief magistrate had not found it his duty to be present at the Coronation ceremony in London." Orkney Guides were represented at the Coronation by Acting Lieutenant Joyce Leask from Stromness.

A public holiday was declared for the occasion and KGS pupils planted another 600 trees at the Willows before marching to the Cathedral to be presented with souvenir bronze medals from the town council. The Coronation service was broadcast by radio from Westminster Abbey. Between 2,000 - 3,000 people witnessed the afternoon carnival procession in Kirkwall, and a grand Coronation ball was held in the Town Hall in the evening while the Wideford Hill bonfire was lit at 11pm.

Stromness pupils too received Coronation medals, and an afternoon parade of fancy dress tableaux, followed by sports in the evening. At 11pm, 200 signal rockets, courtesy of the NLS *Pole Star*, were fired as part of a grand firework display. Other celebrations were organised in most isles and parishes.

In the Coronation honours list, Maurice Bloch, proprietor of Scapa distillery, was knighted to become Sir Maurice.

Coronation silver medals, awarded by the King, went to, amongst others: county clerk Duncan J. Robertson, his assistant William Isbister, Orkney medical officer Dr Walter Bannerman, and education director Hugh Marwick, Kirkwall town clerk William Heddle and Kirkwall Provost John Slater, Stromness town clerk John Robertson and Stromness Provost James Marwick, Captain George Swanson, master of the *St Ola*, Robert Wilson of Kirkwall Post Office, and Superintendent John Tulloch and Constable David Allan of Orkney police.

Cathedral changes

Rev William Barclay, minister for 17 years of St Magnus Cathedral, left Orkney in 1936 to take the ministership of Shawlands Old Church, Glasgow. During his time in Kirkwall, 500 new members of the congregation had been admitted, 250 couples married and 300 children baptised.

He was succeeded by Rev George Arthur Fryer (29) assistant minister of Greenside Church, Edinburgh. Lincolnshire-born but educated in Scotland, he was a graduate of Glasgow University, and the son of an Ayrshire minister.

Orkney heatwave

The month of June, 1936, saw Orkney enjoy 262 hours of sunshine, with 88.6 hours of sun from June 18-23 - an average of nearly 15 hours a day. Sunday, June 21, saw an estimated 1,000 people on Scapa beach as temperatures reached the 70s in Fahrenheit. The dry weather prompted the Medical Officer of Health to advise that all well water be boiled before use.

* * *

Miss R.M. Johnston and Miss Margaret Coghill, Breck Cottage, Marwick, Birsay, received a postcard which was posted in Gourock on July 2, 1904 - 32 years previously.

* * *

Kirkwall and Finstown merchants Messrs James Flett and Sons gave up their last two double-horse-drawn retail vans in favour of Albion motor vehicles.

* * *

Two hundred years of Freemasonry in Kirkwall was celebrated at Kirkwall's Kilwinning lodge with a series of commemorative bicentenary events.

Orkney's greatest sporting accolade

One of the most momentous sporting gatherings of the 20th century was undoubtedly the infamous 1936 Olympic Games in Berlin. It was to be Hitler's promotion of the German master race, staged under Nazi flags - but, to the chagrin of the Fuhrer, ended up being acclaimed for the achievements of the black American athlete Jessie Owens who won four gold medals, set two world records and equalled another.

Not only did an Orcadian compete for Britain at the Berlin Olympics - but he met, and was photographed with, the great Jessie Owens.

The Orkney sportsman was Tom Ward, remarkable as much for his modest personality as his powerful physique, who was selected as one of the British wrestling team at the games.

He was the son of county councillor W. Cowper Ward of Scar House, Sanday, and had only taken up wrestling in 1932 after going to London and joining the Metropolitan Police as a constable.

Standing 6 feet 2 inches and weighting 13 stones 9lbs, he soon won a string of police and district titles before becoming the light heavyweight wrestling champion of Britain, which secured his selection for Berlin.

Unfortunately, a points defeat at the hands of a Turkish wrestler meant that he never progressed as far as the medal rostrum - unlike his new pal Jessie Owens who won the gold medal in the 100 metres, 200 metres, long jump and 400 metres relay.

Two year later, Tom Ward - still the British champion - was seen on the international stage again when he was selected to represent Scotland at the 1938 Empire Games in Australia - necessitating a 28,000 mile round trip by sea which required four months leave of absence from the Metropolitan Police.

He was beaten by an Australian called Scarf and a South African called Greenspan to take third place in his competition.

Tom Ward returned to Orkney in 1945 and took part in an exhibition bout at Kirkwall Temperance Hall.

One of the great sporting icons of the 20th century, the American athlete Jessie Owens, who claimed four gold medals at the 1936 Berlin Olympic Games, is pictured with the Orcadian wrestler Tom Ward, from Sanday, who represented Great Britain at the Games. (Picture courtesy of Pat Harris)

Tom Ward, who was national light heavyweight wrestling champion of Britain, and who competed in both the 1936 Olympic Games and the 1938 Empire Games, is pictured here, second from the left in the front row, with a line-up of other wrestling champions from the Metropolitan Police.
(Picture courtesy of Jean Ward)

The most magnificent spectacle in the North

1937

A mid-summer pageant - a people's play to celebrate the 800th anniversary of Earl Rognvald laying the foundation stone of St Magnus Cathedral in Kirkwall in 1137 - saw the eyes and ears of the world on Orkney in 1937.

Thursday, July 29, heralded what was described as "the most magnificent dramatic spectacle ever seen in the North" as 700 performers performed the Pageant of St Magnus telling "the history of the Cathedral, the story of St Magnus, the glory of Orkney" in eight scenes celebrating the 800th anniversary of the founding of the Cathedral.

A special grandstand and bandstand had been erected for the occasion - which was declared a public holiday - and admission to Brandyquoy Park, behind the Earl's Palace, was set at standing room 1s, seats from 3s to 7s 6d, and an official programme 1s.

Plans had been announced in January when Orkney writer Eric Linklater issued an appeal for 400 local people to come forward to join the cast - with a request to Kirkwall Chamber of Commerce to release workers to take part. The organising committee included Eric Linklater, Orkney director of education Hugh Marwick, the county convener, author and historian J. Storer Clouston, the Lord Lyon of Arms Sir Francis Grant, and the Orkney-born director of the National Gallery of Art in Edinburgh, Stanley Cursiter.

Dr Olaf Kolsrud, Professor of Church History at the University of Oslo, said that the King of Norway would appoint representatives to attend the celebrations, and Karl Holter, a premier Norwegian actor, was to take part with 20 other performers from Norway.

The great day dawned with a Cathedral service followed by afternoon and evening performances of the Pageant. The Cathedral service brought together an impressive array of clergy. The Cathedral minister Rev Arthur Fryer was joined by his predecessors Rev William Barclay (1919-36) and Rev W. Pitcairn Craig (1905-18) as well as the Moderator of the General Assembly of the Church of Scotland, Rt Rev Dugald Macfarlane, and the Bishop of Nidaros, Norway, Rt Rev J. Storen, as well as other local ministers.

However, just two weeks before the event, an ill-tempered meeting of Orkney Presbytery put a cloud over the preparations with complaints from Rev T.T. Alexander (Sandwick), Rev George Cox (Harray St Michaels) and Rev D. Wilson Baird (St Andrews North) that the Presbytery had not been adequately consulted and complaining at the small role that the Moderator of the Church of Scotland, Rt Rev Dugald Macfarlane, would play in the service.

Cathedral minister Rev Arthur Fryer defended his position: "The arrangements that have been published are made by me, as minister of the church, without requiring the sanction of Presbytery." Rev Alexander complained: "I distinctly object to the whole temper in which Mr Fryer is speaking." The Presbytery retired into private session to discuss the matter for an hour.

A crowd of 2,000 gathered at the Kirk Green to see the congregation of 1,500 arrive for the Cathedral service - including such guests as Jon Baldvinsson, president of the Iceland United Althing (Parliament) and representatives of the King of Norway.

But the main focus of attention was to be on the Pageant. The pageant master was Sir Ronald Sinclair of Barrock, with Rodney Shearer, Kirkwall, as his assistant. Director of music was Mrs Ian McClure, wife of the county surgeon, while joint authors of the pageant were Eric Linklater and J. Storer Clouston. Music was by Kirkwall Amateur Orchestral Society (conductor James Williamson); Kirkwall Town Band (conductor Robert Spence) and Kirkwall City Pipe Band (led by Drum Major David Nicolson.)

Producers were D. B. Peace junior and William Hourston, Kirkwall; Donald McInnes and Ian Paterson, Stromness; Mrs Marjorie Linklater; Karl Holter, the Norwegian actor who also played the role of Earl Rognvald; and Sir Ronald Sinclair; the pageant master who also produced the grand finale of the drama.

The occasion saw the first ever live broadcast from Kirkwall as BBC radio programmes relating to the octocentenary celebrations were broadcast while *The Orcadian* published a four page pictorial supplement detailing the Cathedral's eight centuries of history.

All the 1,500 seats for the afternoon performance of the Pageant had been sold and several hundred folk had to be turned away from Brandyquoy Park, although everyone was able to see the evening performance, where a number of the higher priced seats remained unsold. They heard Eric Linklater, in his prologue, proclaim: "Eight hundred years have gone, but the faith of Earl Magnus and the splendour of Earl Rognvald are living things, and their Cathedral church is the heart of Orkney and the head of all our pride."

Karl Holter, the Oslo State Theatre actor who played the role of Earl Rognvald, making a presentation of 250 volumes of Norse literature to the city of Kirkwall, told an evening reception: "Let us hope and believe that although the political ties may never be bound between the old Norse countries, the cultural bonds, the bonds of the hearts and the blood which mean so much more, will be tied so much faster that they will never be broken."

(Unfortunately, these turned out to be weasel words from Holter. Orcadians were shocked four years later when *The Orcadian* revealed that Holter was supporting the Quisling Norwegians and went to live in Berlin in 1941-42.)

Orkney's Cathedral celebrations ended on Saturday, July 31, 1937, with a pilgrimage to the ruined Church of St Magnus on Egilsay, near where St Magnus was murdered, where 400 people took part in a commemorative service.

A cinema film of all the proceedings over the three days was recorded at the expense of D.B. Peace, owner of Kirkwall's Albert Kinema. The octocentenary celebrations made a loss of £96 9s 8d - but this was covered by local guarantors.

Peedie Charlie's

The shop occupied by watchmaker Mr R.G. Harrold in Albert Street, Kirkwall, was sold to Mr Loretto "Charlie" Celli, who for the previous four years had worked at the Albert Street confectioners of Mr Livio Zanre. Mr Celli planned to open a "first class refreshment saloon" complete with ice cream freezer and soda fountain.

* * *

Robert Groat, Skelwick, Westray, who became a postman at the age of 13, retired after 56 years service.

She married an alien

One of the great victims of 20th century Orkney was the luckless Mrs Kate Albrecht, née Mackintosh, who faced years of discrimination and prejudice in a 20 year battle with the county licensing authorities.

Mrs Albrecht's misfortune stemmed from the fact that she married a German, whom she helped to manage Kirkwall's Royal Hotel for seven years from 1910.

Her solicitor, Mr J.E.P. Robertson, from Stromness, later explained: "Mrs Albrecht's husband was of German nationality, and during the war there was a natural feeling of resentment against an alien holding a certificate. Through this antagonistic feeling, Mr Albrecht left Kirkwall. Mrs Albrecht last heard of her husband in 1916 when he wrote that he was going to Alaska. In 1917 she lost her certificate through this anti-German feeling. But Mrs Albrecht was not an alien - she was a native of Skye. There should be no hostile feeling now!"

But hostility there was galore from the licensing authorities. The "dry" decade of the 1920s in Kirkwall meant that it was 1930 before Mrs Albrecht could reapply for a drinks certificate for the Royal Hotel. In the next few years she fought a futile battle - her applications were either rejected by the Orkney Licensing Court or the Licensing Appeal Court.

Her solicitor's claim that there was no general climate of hostility towards her in Kirkwall was underlined, in 1931, when her application was supported by a petition signed by 638 local people and a statement of no objection from the police. It cut no ice with the court which retired to secret session to refuse her application, with the Lord Lieutenant Alfred Baikie, who was chairman, refusing to reveal how the board voted.

In 1937, Mrs Albrecht gave up and sold the Royal Hotel to Thurso hotelier James Wilson. Mr Wilson was granted a licence at his first request.

* * *

Kirkwall telephone operator Robina Gunn gave the alarm by telephone to the fire brigade when the switchboard burst into flames, and then joined her sister Rachel Gunn in fighting the blaze.

An Academy of excellence

The name of Stromness Secondary School would change to Stromness Academy, it was announced, as a £10,000 extension to the school was formally opened by Dr James Drever, Professor of Psychology at Edinburgh University, a native of Shapinsay and an old boy of the school.

Cold comfort

February, 1937, ended with snow-drifts 15 feet deep in the West Mainland. At this time, the county council owned two horse drawn snow ploughs.

Oops!

An attempt to wind up Orkney Canine Society, because of a lack of support, ended in failure when nobody turned up for the closure meeting.

On tour

Robert Nicolson, Junction Road, Kirkwall, began Nicolson's circular tours - a five and a half hour, 54 mile bus excursion of the sights of the Orkney Mainland - including the Kitchener memorial, the Birsay palaces and Maeshowe - fare 4s 6d.

In the wrong court

William Costie, 12 Main Street, Kirkwall, admitted using his tennis court for public dancing without a licence. He was admonished by Kirkwall burgh police court.

Monsters ahoy!

A sea monster was reported off the Pentland Skerries. Lighthouse keeper John Brown said: "A great object rose up out of the water, anything up to 20 to 30 feet. It was round shaped and there appeared to be a head on it."

Meanwhile, diver Colin Heddle, working in Kirkwall basin, had to abandon his work when a shark, measuring up to 30 feet, swam into the harbour.

Monstrosities ahoy!

The first major environmental row of the 20th century saw outrage being expressed as Kirkwall Town Council gave permission for work to begin on the erection, in Shore Street, Kirkwall, of a new oil depot for Scottish Oils and Shell-Mex Ltd.

There would be four tanks - two of 250 ton capacity and two of 100 ton capacity - but the project was to unite some of Orkney's best known personalities in deploring the eyesore it created.

The leading Orcadian artist Stanley Cursiter, who was born in Kirkwall, and who, in 1937, was director of the National Galleries in Edinburgh, condemned the work as a "scandalous desecration" of Shore Street. The forefront of the town had been destroyed, he said.

His views were immediately supported by the county convener and author, J. Storer Clouston, and the Orkney writer Eric Linklater who both accused Kirkwall Town Council of allowing "vandalism."

Murder death sentence

A 17 year old girl Sheila Sutherland - who had left Burray with her family 15 years earlier - was found dead half a mile from her home in the New Forest, Hampshire. A 21 year old farmworker, employed by her father, Mr Daniel Sutherland, was accused of her murder and, although at his trial he was said to have a mental age of only nine or ten, he was sentenced to death by hanging.

Death of Orkney Presbytery's oldest member

Rev James D. Anderson, the oldest member of Orkney Presbytery, died after 42 years as minister of Hoy. The manse in which he lived and died had been visited by Sir Walter Scott, who gained some inspiration from the scene for his later novel *The Pirate*.

Rev William Bremner became the new minister for Flotta - after the charge had been vacant for nine years!

The end of Orkney's private police force

1938

The New Year of 1938 saw a chapter end - and a new one begin - in the history of Orkney's forces of law and order.

It marked the end of Orkney's "private" police force - paid for, through the rates, by the county council - and the inauguration of a new official county force, operating within the terms of the Scottish Police Acts, and funded by government finances, under the control of the Scottish Office.

The change was probably long overdue - the chief constable of the old independent force was aged 72!

The prospect of a shake-up had first been voiced in 1935 when the HM Inspector of Constabulary for Scotland, Brigadier General R.M. Dudgeon, recommended several changes, including linking up with either the Caithness or Sutherland forces.

At that time, Orkney had a Chief Constable - Superintendent John M. Tulloch - and six constables - three at Kirkwall, two at Stromness and one at St Margaret's Hope. During the summer, one Kirkwall constable and one Stromness constable went to Stronsay.

The Inspector recommended that an extra constable be recruited to be based in Stronsay, to cover the North Isles. He also recommended that the Orkney force be provided with a car of 10hp or under, and the Kirkwall prison building taken over by the police and the cells utilised for sentences up to 30 days.

But his most far reaching recommendation would see the end of Orkney's independent force with either the Chief Constable of Sutherland or Caithness also becoming Chief Constable of Orkney. The title of deputy Chief Constable would be held by the senior officer in Orkney who - after the retirement of Superintendent Tulloch - would hold the rank of Inspector.

Within six months, Orkney County Council had agreed by 14 votes to 12 to proposals which would see the end of the Orkney force's independence - and a merger, instead, with the Sutherland force. The idea was not without its critics, with councillor Peter Flett warning his colleagues that they would be worse off in 50 years. "The last vestige of freedom and independence will go if this is adopted," he said.

As it was, Orkney retained its independence after negotiations broke down between Orkney and Sutherland.

But nonetheless, in May, 1937, the county council voted by 16-12 to create an official Orkney force - within the national Police Act - which, it was said, would provide a better service and save the ratepayers £400 a year. At this time, it seemed likely that Orkney would share a Chief Constable with Shetland if that county also decided to adopt the Police Act. But, in the end, it was agreed that the new Orkney force would remain a separate entity.

In December that year, Orkney's first Chief Constable, under the Scottish Police Acts, was named as Mr W. Colin Campbell (43) who had 25 years police service in Stirlingshire, after starting as a constable at Bannockburn in 1912. He was the unanimous choice of the Orkney police committee, out of 20 applicants.

Depute Chief Constable, with the rank of Sergeant, would be 33 year old Constable Gathorne Hardy Cheyne from the Argyllshire Constabulary, who was selected from 25 applicants.(Cheyne would later become Chief Constable when Colin Campbell moved to take up the post of Chief Constable of Wigtonshire. In 1948, Colin Campbell died of a heart attack at the comparatively young age of 53.)

The Orkney County Council police committee would continue only in an advisory capacity when the new force came into operation at the start of 1938.

And it meant the retirement of Superintendent John M. Tulloch, at the age of 72, after almost 44 years service. He had joined the Orkney constabulary on April 1, 1894, and following two months probationary duty as a constable in Kirkwall, was posted to Stromness as junior officer there. On April 27,1898, he became senior constable in Stromness, was promoted to sergeant nine months later and remained in charge at Stromness until October, 1903, when he was transferred to St Margaret's Hope. In 1908 he was transferred to Kirkwall, becoming Superintendent there on April 1, 1927.

Before his appointment as Superintendent, Mr Tulloch - a native of Sanday who worked in the shoe trade before joining the police - served under four previous Superintendents - Messrs Grant, Cruikshank, Atkin and Wood. He also served for ten years in the 1st Kirkwall Company of the Orkney Brigade of the Royal Garrison Artillery (Volunteers).

Sheriff Harvey presides at Kirkwall Sheriff Court while, seated at the table from the left, are W.P. Drever, Procurator Fiscal James Begg, Sheriff Clerk John White and the Orkney County Clerk Duncan Robertson. (Picture courtesy of Orkney Library photographic archive)

One of Orkney's most famous daughters, the Hollywood actress Greer Garson, in 1943, the same year she won the Oscar for best actress in the film *Mrs Miniver*.

(Picture courtesy of MGM)

'Peculiar' Orkney practices

Court of Session judges had to grapple with the legal complexities of what they called "peculiar" Orkney practices in a case where a farm girl claimed paternity against a neighbouring farmer who she said was the father of her illegitimate baby daughter.

The Lord Justice Clerk said there was evidence in Orkney that there was a practice of young men visiting young women after midnight. His Lordship did not know whether that was merely a modern laxity of morals or whether, as he rather thought, it was a survival of a very old custom in that part of the country. The woman had claimed that the defender had visited her around 50 times over six years in such circumstances.

The woman had expressed no shame or hesitation in having received men through her window by use of a farm ladder, said Lord MacKay, and all concerned in the case "seemed unanimously to treat these - to our more sophisticated mind - somewhat peculiar calls as illustrations of a perfectly innocent social custom."

The judges decided that the woman had failed to prove the man was father of the child.

Laid to rest in a foreign field

A 23 year old Chinese seaman was laid to rest 6,000 miles from home - as Chinese funeral rites were observed at the graveside at St Olaf Cemetery, Kirkwall.

The man, Low Ah Kue, who died on the Royal Fleet Auxiliary vessel *War Afridi* was interred by his father and four fellow countrymen. He was one of 40 Chinese - natives of Shanghai - on board the ship.

Orkney's Chief Constable Colin Campbell attended the funeral along with British Naval officers. It was reported that Low Ah Kue had died from a stomach ailment after the *War Afridi* had docked at Lyness from Trinidad.

Blaze destroys Kirkwall merchants

There were calls for Kirkwall to be equipped with a proper fire engine after the premises of the town's biggest merchants, R. Garden Ltd, were totally destroyed, causing £12,000 damage.

The night-time blaze gutted the drapery, grocery, china, hardware and general office sections of the 200 year old building in Bridge Street, Kirkwall.

Firemaster David Oddie had to take special precautions to prevent the spread of the fire to the new oil depot in neighbouring Shore Street. Six months later saw the official opening of the first Scottish Co-operative Society shop in Orkney at 25 Bridge Street, Kirkwall.

Golfers back on course

It was hoped that golfing relations between Orkney and Caithness could be resumed following a three year rift between the two counties following the loss of the valuable Wilson Cup - a trophy donated in 1906 by Lord Ashmore for competition between golfers in Caithness, Orkney and Shetland.

In 1935, it became clear that Wick, the holders of the trophy, could not explain the whereabouts of the cup which had been valued at £30 thirty years earlier. The Orkney clubs decided they would not play for a trophy that did not appear to exist, and consequently did not compete for three years.

However, it was now reported that the trophy had been found in the attic of a Wick Golf Club official's home.

Names the same

The three most popular boys names in Scotland were John, James and William, and for girls, Margaret, Mary and Elizabeth - exactly the same as 80 years earlier in 1860, said the Registrar General for Scotland. Likewise, the three most common surnames were still the same as 1860 - Smith, MacDonald and Brown.

Magnus memorial

A memorial cairn was unveiled in Egilsay to mark the traditional scene of the murder of Earl Magnus, in whose memory Kirkwall's St Magnus Cathedral was built. The cairn was erected by the congregation and minister of the Cathedral, and by Rev H.J. Fynes-Clinton, rector of St Magnus the Martyr Church, London.

* * *

Firth's new £3,000 school, with accommodation for 160 pupils in four classrooms, was opened by Sir James Peck, secretary of the Scottish Education Department.

* * *

Papa Westray's isolation was ended when the island was linked with the British Post Office telegraph service to Sanday.

* * *

Orkney Presbytery asked congregations not to hold raffles or other "gambling" games at fund-raising events. At Kirkwall Sheriff Court, a touring entertainer was fined £1 for giving a kettle as a prize in an illegal raffle.

* * *

A busload of police and civilians was sent from Kirkwall to assist local men in Orphir fighting a hill fire which was blamed on a discarded cigarette thrown away by two lovers who had parked a car at the scene.

The great mutiny in Hoy

1939

Two days work in Orkney was two days too much for 42 men from the area of Ashby-de-la-Zouche in Leicestershire.

Not even a wage rate of 1/3 an hour could prevent them downing tools and demanding to be sent back home.

They were recruited by a firm of sub-contractors to carry out work in connection with tunnelling at Lyness for the military authorities. A total of 58 men were recruited in Leicestershire - through Labour Exchanges and local newspaper advertisements - after 27 Orcadians had already been taken on. (At this time, Orkney shared with Rutland the enviable record of having the lowest unemployment in Britain.)

The 58 men arrived at Lyness on January 16, 1939. They were put to work road-making on January 17 and remained at work that day and the following day. But on the evening of January 18, 42 of the men intimated to the contractors that they did not intend to remain on the job any longer. The Unemployment Assistance Board arranged for the men to travel home to England.

The incident led to questions being asked in the House of Commons and the Minister of Labour, Mr Ernest Brown, said that the men had been told in advance by a representative of the employers that the work was arduous and in an isolated area. He emphasised that he only wanted volunteers to undertake the work and urged any of the men who had any doubts not to accept the job.

Each man engaged through the Labour Exchange service had been given written particulars of the employment conditions.

Mr Brown said: " The firm did, in fact, pay 1/3 per hour, and the arrangements for board and accommodation were in accordance with the particulars furnished, and compared favourably with road-making schemes in other parts of Scotland. Action has now been taken to ascertain the firm's total requirements with a view to securing the necessary labour, if possible, from the coal-mining areas in Scotland."

The arduous and dangerous nature of some of the military preparations in Orkney was further illustrated, however, when a lorry carrying workmen, engaged on the Scapa Flow defence work, plunged over a 25 feet cliff onto the shore at Stromness, killing a Stromness man and injuring nine other workmen.

Great ideas of our time?

Kirkwall Town Council agreed to seek legal advice on whether they could sell the Bignold Park - possibly for house-building - because of its unsuitability as a playing field.

Royal patronage

The Longhope Hotel, built in 1905 by Thomas Middlemore, was bought by James Wilson, proprietor of Kirkwall's Royal Hotel.

King George V slept in one of the rooms when visiting Scapa Flow in World War One. Another was subsequently used on an occasion by the then Prince of Wales (later Edward VIII, then Duke of Windsor.) Brass plates on the bedroom doors commemorated the Royal patronage.

The Ayre Hotel, Kirkwall, which had reverted to a private residence soon after World War One, was reopened as a hotel by Mr Robert Matches, who had recently returned to Kirkwall after 30 years in the USA.

Royal telegram

Thomas Maxwell, of Orquil Farm, St Ola, received a greetings telegram from the King on his 100th birthday on May 7, 1939. A native of Stronsay, he had nine grandchildren and eight great grandchildren. He died in 1940 at the age of 101.

Housing delay

The outbreak of war caused the deferment of Kirkwall Town Council plans to build 39 houses off the Clay Loan, Kirkwall. Government permission to proceed with the houses was eventually given in 1944.

* * *

Membership of the nine hole golf course in Rousay, at Westness Farm, reached 60.

* * *

Mr Robert Sinclair, the head of Sinclair's Supply Stores, Stromness, who died in 1939 at the age of 56, claimed the honour of being the owner of the first motor van in Orkney.

Horror as 99 die in submarine disaster

A desperate 500 mile race against time by an Orkney rescue squad was too late to save the lives of 99 men trapped by a submarine disaster.

The men from the Metal Industries base at Lyness - now acknowledged as the world's leading experts on underwater salvage - were summoned by Government SOS appeals to join the rescue operation on the British submarine *Thetis* which was trapped on the seabed, off Liverpool, with 103 men on board.

The team under the command of Thomas McKenzie, the senior salvage manager at Lyness, included Lyness divers James Thomson and Daniel Johnston, from Melsetter, who were flown south on their mercy mission by Scottish Airways.

They worked for 48 hours on the salvage operation but, tragically, despite their heroic efforts, 99 men of the 103 had died before rescue could be made.

Orkney's first international sportsman

The first Orcadian to represent Scotland as an international Rugby Union player, Colonel Henry Halcro Johnston CBE DSc MD CM DL, died in 1939 at the age of 83.

Colonel Halcro Johnston, of Coubister, Orphir, a Deputy Lieutenant of Orkney, could not only claim ancestry of the Royal Norse family of Halcro but could also trace his roots back to the times of Robert the Bruce, from whom the family was given a Scottish coat of arms and the motto: "We'll put it to a Venture."

Henry Halcro Johnston represented Scotland as a back in international rugby matches in 1877, before joining the Army Medical Department in 1881 and seeing service in the Sudan, the North-West Frontier and South Africa, as well as postings to Singapore and Gibraltar.

In World War One, in retirement, he was administrator of all military, war and territorial general hospitals in the Glasgow area, and later Assistant Director of Medical Services at York.

Wrath of war returns

World War Two arrived with the Autumn in 1939 - and the Fates swiftly conspired to bring the conflict directly to the heart of Orkney.

From the moment of the declaration of war with Germany by Prime Minister Neville Chamberlain on Sunday, September 3, the islands were pre-destined to be in the main line of fire.

The lack of military hostilities elsewhere in Europe during the early months was later to be labelled by historians as the Phoney War. But for Orkney it was real enough as the county was forever written into military record books.

For a small community of just 22,000 civilians, it was remarkable how powerfully the conflict was to touch Orkney between the Autumn of 1939 and the Spring of 1940. Within the early days and weeks, the impact of war was both immediate and deadly:

An Orcadian died in the very first act of the war at sea as the liner *Athenia* was sunk - and two Orcadians were killed when the aircraft carrier HMS *Courageous* was torpedoed two weeks later.

Disaster in the night followed as more than 800 men perished in Scapa Flow as HMS *Royal Oak* was destroyed.

The first German bomb to land on British soil hit Hoy as air attacks disabled HMS *Iron Duke* - and Orkney gunners brought down the first enemy plane to be felled by anti-aircraft fire from the ground

Orkney was declared a Closed Area, with entry prohibited without a permit and photography banned. A night time curfew was to follow.

Mass communal burials were held for more than 80 men killed in German attacks on merchant shipping in Orkney waters.

Orkney witnessed work beginning on the biggest civil engineering challenge of World War Two - the construction of the Churchill Barriers to seal Scapa Flow; a feat that was to claim the lives of a dozen construction workers.

Another tragic milestone of the hostilities saw an Orcadian become the first civilian of World War Two to be killed by German bombs on British soil.

Just six months of war had passed, yet Orkney had witnessed, at close hand, more than 1,000 deaths, and endured more than 50 air raids.

This obviously was not the outcome anticipated by *The Orcadian* 18 months earlier when, in a misplaced judgement that "peace for our time" had been secured by the Munich Agreement, the newspaper had chosen to serialise the life story of Adolf Hitler!

They were indeed curious times. Less than three months before the outbreak of war, 30 Kirkwall Grammar School pupils had gathered at the Pier to sing the German national anthem in tribute to departing German sailors.

In fact, the clouds of war had been gathering throughout the 1930s. *The Orcadian* had reported as far back as September 18, 1930: "Fighting between Communists and National Socialists occurred in Berlin at the close of the General Election campaign. One man was killed and several were wounded while 200 arrests were made."

In April, 1936, Neville Chamberlain, then Chancellor of the Exchequer, allocated an extra £50 million for defence - and increased income tax by 3d to pay for it. As early as October, 1936, Government leaflets were distributed to every household advising on precautions to be taken in the event of gas attacks by air, and six months later, Orkney County Council and the town councils of Kirkwall and Stromness were ordered to set up special committees to deal with air raid precautions.

The staff and employees of the civil engineering company of Sir William Arrol who built the Lyness oil tanks in 1937.

(Picture from the files of *The Orcadian*)

Councillor Charles Archibald told Kirkwall Town Council at their April meeting in 1937: "There will be no safe places anywhere in these islands if war breaks out."

Some preparations for war were underway. The first of what was to grow into an army of civilian construction workers arrived in Orkney to join local Orcadians in the erection of a number of oil fuel tanks at Lyness. Contractors Sir William Arrol and Company employed 130 men at Lyness throughout 1937. Huge tunnels were to be driven into the hillside; a dangerous task which claimed its first death of a workman in April, 1937. Two months later, the project claimed a second life - that of 26 year old Longhope Lifeboat crewman James Taylor.

By July, 1937, Government agitation was becoming apparent at Orkney's lack of preparedness for war. The county's doctors and nurses were put through a course under the auspices of the Air Raids Precautions Department of the Home Office, with the Kirkwall mortuary being used as a "gas chamber" which the medical staff entered wearing the latest issue of gas mask.

The Orcadian stressed that Home Office officials were anxious for Orkney to be properly prepared because of the strategic importance of Scapa Flow, and fears that the anchorage could be taken over by an enemy fleet of aircraft carriers.

The newspaper stated: "Even with London immune from serious attack in the early stages of a war, it is believed that with Scapa Flow in the possession of an enemy, London would then be at the mercy of the enemy's aircraft."

There was a major flaw in this argument - namely, that London was as close to many German cities as it was to Orkney - but nonetheless Scapa Flow's importance could not be underestimated.

And *The Orcadian* went on to warn: "It is stated that there is some anxiety at Whitehall because no steps have yet been taken by the Orkney local authorities. It is emphasised that should war break out, we may not have a formal declaration of war. The first intimation of war may quite possibly be the appearance of enemy aircraft overhead. These airplanes are already capable of dropping high explosive bombs, incendiary bombs or gas bombs, with much greater accuracy than was possible a short time ago."

However, confirmation of a certain unwillingness to consider anything at all to do with war came when Kirkwall branch of the British Legion - after a series of poor attendances - decided to take no further part in Armistice Day parades. (Increased interest in the Legion in 1938 saw this decision rescinded).

It would certainly be understandable if Orcadians were slow to accept the threat of impending hostilities, for they were receiving very mixed messages from the authorities.

For just a week after the Home Office call for action, two German liners, the *General Von Steuben* and the *Milwaukee* were allowed into Kirkwall with 1,000 tourists who were welcomed to a service in St Magnus Cathedral - in which the sermon was preached entirely in German - conducted by a visiting German Lutheran minister Dr Rudolf Muusz and Cathedral minister Rev Arthur Fryer, with musical accompaniment by Fritz Holzel, organist of Berlin Cathedral.

And, by October, 1937, three months after trying to goad the local population into wartime contingency measures, *The Orcadian* changed tack again and, following a visit to Germany by a "well known Orcadian" professional man quoted him as saying that the German people had as much freedom as the people of Britain. Hitler, it was apparent, was tremendously popular with his people, and the Orkney man questioned whether there was more anti-Jewish feeling in Germany than in parts of Britain.

Even into 1938 - with the announcement that the Territorial Army was to be reconstituted in Orkney and the Scapa Flow defences strengthened - there appeared to be no general feeling of imminent danger among the Orkney population. At the March meeting of Orkney County Council, it was reported that the council's efforts to organise the defence of the civilian population in the event of enemy attack had seen just nine volunteers, from the entire county, come forward to act as air raid wardens or auxiliary nurses. In Kirkwall, the volunteers consisted of a 15 year old boy, a 24 year old woman and three men over 30. There were no volunteers at all from Stromness.

Yet this was the week that German troops invaded Austria.

It was the arrival of Orkney's newly appointed Chief Constable, Colin Campbell - and presumably the news from Austria - that finally galvanised a public response. The Chief Constable took up the duties of Air Raids Precautions Officer, and set about drawing up a civil defence plan for the county, and Cathedral minister Rev Arthur Fryer agreed to attend a War Office school to become an authorised lecturer on air raid precautions.

Chief Constable Campbell took his campaign to a new power-base of Orkney - the women who made up the membership of the Scottish Women's Rural Institutes in the county. One of his first tasks was to address a meeting of SWRI members in Kirkwall. Scapa Flow, he told them, would almost certainly be a magnet to draw enemy aircraft. Enemy planes, failing to discharge their bombs on the warships, were quite likely to target Kirkwall or Stromness instead. He tended to discount the threat of poison gas bombs, however, with Orkney's windy conditions likely to prove a natural ally in quickly dispersing any danger from gas.

The Chief Constable revealed the details of his new civil defence scheme, with volunteers - men and women - asked to report to their local police station for duties in Observer Corps, Special Constabulary, Air Raid Warden force, rescue squads, first aid parties, ambulance wagon crews, fire brigades and decontamination squads. It was anticipated that SWRI members would come forward for many of these duties, and volunteers would receive training in incendiary bombs and anti-gas precautions.

Plans were announced for the control and distribution of food stuffs in the event of war, and it was announced that recruitment would begin for the 80 Orkney men, aged 18-38, required for the Orkney section of the 226 Battery (Anti-Aircraft) Royal Artillery, also for a searchlight corps of the Royal Engineers.

When General Sir Walter Kirke, Director General of the Territorial Army, visited Kirkwall in May, 1938, recruitment was proceeding apace - with the honour falling to ship's carpenter John Drever Nicholson, Slater Street, Kirkwall, of being the first recruit to be enrolled at the Kirkwall headquarters of the anti-aircraft battery.

"A gun" was now available and would soon be in position on a site near Kirkwall. Other guns would eventually be mounted at various sites around Scapa Flow.

The 80 members of the Orkney section of the 226 Battery (Anti-Aircraft) Royal Artillery (TA) marched through Kirkwall in their uniforms for the first time, in August, 1938, cheered by a large crowd, led by the Kirkwall Town Band and with the salute taken by the Lord Lieutenant of Orkney and Shetland Alfred Baikie. Three days later the men left for their first training camp in Wigtonshire.

Stromness was still slow to respond. The September meeting of the town council was told that no volunteers had come forward to be air raid patrol wardens, despite appeals over six months.

Again, it was understandable that scepticism remained over the likelihood of war as the German liner *Berlin* brought to Orkney 560 tourists who, bizarrely, on finding most of the shops closed during their Sunday visit, in July, 1938, took advantage instead of a Royal Navy invitation to go aboard HMS *Sovereign* which was open for inspection. Unfortunately for the Germans, the *Berlin* ran aground on a sandbank 300 yards north of the Kirkwall coastguard station - though the liner was able to quickly refloat under her own power.

As Britain's rearmament gathered strength, Orcadians were getting a preview of the aerial power that was being developed. Seven RAF Hawker Hector aircraft landed at the Wideford Farm Airstrip on a long distance training flight. However the appearance of two other RAF planes over the Hoy hills was a harbinger of tragedy. They were looking for a missing Vickers

Wellesley bomber which had disappeared on a training flight after being seen over Longhope. The Air Ministry announced that the three crewmen, who had taken off from Upper Heyford, Oxfordshire, to test the endurance of the new plane, were presumed dead.

With German demands on Czechoslovakia, the full enormity of the threat to European peace was plainly apparent to most, however, by September, 1938. Suddenly the fleet was mobilised and Naval reservists were called up - forty men had to leave Kirkwall in one day to answer the call-up - and the officers of the Orkney Territorial Army Association were authorised to recruit more than 300 men for two new TA units, a Heavy Battery, Royal Artillery, and a Fortress Company, Royal Engineers. A TA drill hall would also be built at Weyland, it was announced.

As "prayers for peace" were being held daily at St Magnus Cathedral, Kirkwall British Legion members promised they would construct air raid shelters if the town council would provide the land. Gas masks would soon be available for everyone in Orkney, said the Chief Constable.

Blackout precautions were tested throughout the county in a 90 minute exercise. The result was not a total success - "Women were molested in the streets by gangs of rude young men," reported *The Orcadian*.

The newspaper's political allegiance at this time, of course, was unreservedly for the Conservative and Unionist party - a loyalty that approached blind faith in its intensity. In fact, any criticism of Prime Minister Neville Chamberlain was presented almost as treasonable in the editorial leader columns of the paper. And so it was that *The Orcadian* threw its weight behind Chamberlain's policy of dialogue with Hitler - a policy that elsewhere was being denounced as appeasement and betrayal.

As Chamberlain returned from his first talks with Hitler, *The Orcadian* of September 22, 1938, under the headline "War Would Not Be Justified," praised the Prime Minister's "magnificent gesture" and said it would be "an unthinkable folly to allow the matters which have been in dispute to lead to the calamity of a world war."

"It is, of course, a travesty of the action of the Government to describe it as one of peace at any price," stated *The Orcadian*. Britain had no obligation to take any action in the Czech dispute with Germany, said the paper, adding: "It would be

A gunner prepares one of the giant searchlights which eventually formed part of the air defences of Scapa Flow.

(Picture courtesy of Orkney Library photographic archive)

inexcusable to allow a general war to take place in order to resist the claims of the minorities in Czechoslovakia."

The following week - as Chamberlain returned from signing the Munich Agreement, averting war at that stage - *The Orcadian* embraced Chamberlain's claim of "peace with honour" to such an astonishing extent that it began publishing the serialised "Life of Adolf Hitler" by Phillip Bouhler. Its uncritical, almost laudatory tone was questionable, to say the least, taken in context with what was to happen in Scapa Flow 12 months later.

The Fleet's in town

The machinery of war - both at sea and in the air - was a familiar sight for Orcadians through the 1920s and into the 1930s.

They were given a close-up view of some of Britain's most deadly military firepower during the annual visits to Scapa Flow by the Atlantic Fleet; renamed the Home Fleet in 1932.

The arrival of the ships brought not only a bonanza of trade for Kirkwall businesses as thousands of sailors poured ashore - more than once threatening to drink the town dry - but also gave Orcadians the opportunity to watch some dazzling flying displays by dozens of planes from the giant aircraft carriers.

Prince George - later to become the Duke of Kent - was a VIP guest with the Fleet when the ships, under the command of Admiral Sir Hubert Brand, arrived in the Flow in June, 1928. The Prince had actually travelled north by train but stayed overnight on HMS *Nelson* before going the next day to Stromness and Longhope, where he was to officially name the local lifeboats. (He had visited Orkney previously when serving on HMS *Temeraire* - and had signed the visitors' book at the Kirkwall Hotel on July 20, 1920.)

Three years later, in 1931, the Atlantic Fleet, under the command of Admiral Sir Michael Hodges, arrived in the Flow to fire a royal salute for King George V's birthday on May 27.

The year 1932 was marked by a fine flying display of 25 aircraft from the carriers HMS *Furious* and HMS *Courageous*,

reported *The Orcadian*. Over 30 vessels of the Home Fleet were anchored at the Scapa end of the Flow as the Naval anchorage recaptured its atmosphere of World War One during a two week visit. The battleships *Malaya* and *Valiant* were accompanied by HMS *Nelson*, flagship of Admiral Sir John Kelly, Commander-in-Chief of the Home Fleet, HMS *Rodney* and the battle cruiser HMS *Hood*, as well as the cruisers *Dorsetshire*, *Norfolk*, *York*, *Exeter* and *Centaur*.

The following year the fleet had grown - with 25 destroyers as well as tankers and support vessels joining the battleships and cruisers - with nearly 100 aircraft reported to be on board the carriers. Under the command again of Admiral Sir John Kelly, they arrived in Scapa Flow in temperatures of 73 degrees on Sunday, June 4, 1933.

The "tropical" weather brought sharks into the Flow, with as many as 16 being seen. One died after being in collision with the NAAFI vessel *Muriel*. After being struck, the bleeding 27 feet long creature thrashed the side of the vessel several times before seeming to attack a smaller motor launch *Emily* which had to take evasive action to escape the danger, reported *The Orcadian*.

One spectator, Kirkwall apprentice draper Jack Smith, got a closer view of the fleet than he bargained for, after falling from the cliffs of Gaitnip. He was rescued by the Navy and treated in the sickbay of HMS *Nelson*.

Invasion of civilian army

Whatever Chamberlain's public pronouncements, the Government was, by the start of 1939, preparing Orkney for war with a zeal. To join the civilian workforce at Lyness came another 1,000 workers to start building the new Hatston aerodrome. Before long, the Kirkwall to Stromness road was to become part of the runway. The general public could continue to use the highway, although it was no longer a public thoroughfare, until a new road up Hatston Brae was completed.

The new aerodrome runway and associated works was to cost £292,645. "RAF tenders dash along Orkney roads, bent on mystery work, performed by mystery workmen. It's all part of the National Government scheme to make Orkney safe for Orcadians in event of war," *The Orcadian* assured readers. However, there were complaints from Orkney churchmen that work was proceeding at Hatston on Sundays.

While 26 men - one third of the town's Air Raid Wardens - began a ten week training course under Rev Arthur Fryer at the ARP depot in Main Street, Kirkwall, the Department of Health for Scotland said that in the event of a national emergency, Orkney would not be used as a reception area, nor would any evacuation take place.

The war preparations, however, did much to fuel Orkney's rumour factory. One story was that there had been a secret police swoop on suspected spies and all cameras, binoculars and telescopes confiscated. "Needless to say," said *The Orcadian*, "There is not a vestige of truth in the rumour at all. No persons have been interrogated officially, not even by our established and non-secret constabulary, the Military or the War Department."

However, mystery lights seen in Scapa Flow were officially investigated by the authorities. "The theory that submarines of a potential enemy stole into the Flow and laid mines may now be dismissed from mind. Officialdom is satisfied as to the safety of the Orkneys," said *The Orcadian*.

The arrival of more civilian workers prompted the launch of a public bus service between Lyness and Longhope - despite fears that it would encourage Lyness workers to drink at the Longhope Hotel. But women workers at Lyness had other concerns in June, 1939, when they had to heroically fight a blaze of heather which was threatening to engulf an ammunition magazine at Lyness. There were other problems for the civilian population as the influx of workers saw potato supplies dwindle to the extent that *The Orcadian* ran a headline asking: "Is Orkney on the brink of a potato famine?" At the same time, local firms were being hit by staff shortages as their workers were dispatched to TA training camps and other duties.

By May, 1939, Mr Ian MacDonald, secretary of the Orkney County National Service Committee, reported that 585 men and 199 women volunteers had enrolled for local air raid precautions and similar voluntary work in the previous month. Nightly appeals for volunteers were made at Kirkwall's Albert Kinema.

For some, there was no choice. At the end of April, 1939, the Government announced compulsory conscription for all men, aged 20-21, for six months intensive Army training. An estimated 300-400 Orcadians were immediately affected.

The announcement of conscription led to an extraordinary incident at St Nicholas Church, Orphir, when Orkney's county convener Joseph Storer Clouston walked out of the morning service in protest at the sermon of missionary Quintin Finlay, who was denouncing the military preparations.

Storer Clouston, whose family had worshipped at the church for generations, stood up and told Mr Finlay: "This is a most disgraceful and unpatriotic sermon - I leave the church!"

The preacher then continued his sermon which ended: "The excuse given for conscription is that it is in defence of small nations. To my mind, beggars cannot be choosers - the weak nations must take their chance and we should mind our own business."

Mr Finlay, an ex-serviceman, who had previously served in Holm and Shapinsay, was said to be somewhat upset by the incident, but Storer Clouston remained unrepentant. "It was a very painful, and unpleasant thing for me to do," he said. "I was actuated by my sense of public duty and my indignation at this abuse of the pulpit for the dissemination of dangerous and unpatriotic doctrines."

Across Scapa Flow from Orphir, there was patriotic work aplenty going on. Lyness - which at the start of the century was simply a farm - was by now virtually a town of workmen, housed in camps.

World War One had seen Lyness converted into a Naval fuel oil depot and shore base; and it had then become the headquarters for the salvage of the German Fleet. By 1938-39, the Admiralty had embarked on several secret schemes - including the imposing series of tunnels - to reinforce the defences.

The civil engineering firm of Baldry, Yerburgh and Hutchinson Ltd had 300-400 workmen - 65 per cent of them Orcadian - working in shifts; the single men sleeping in dormitories, the married staff in bungalows "that would solve Kirkwall's municipal housing problem overnight." Linking the various parts of the residential camp were well built roads, lit by electricity.

The firm had its own dance orchestra and application was being made for a beer licence for a new 120ft social club that was being erected.

Surprisingly, in June, 1939, just three months before the start of the war, the permanent Orkney staff of the Royal Navy was constituted solely by Commander O.M. Frewen, Naval Officer in Charge and King's Harbourmaster at Scapa, and his civilian secretary Miss Ivy Eunson from Stromness. It was Commander Frewen - a cousin of Winston Churchill - who welcomed to Scapa Flow that month five ships of the French Navy - the battleships *Dunkerque* and *Strasbourg* and the cruisers *Montcalm, Gloire* and *Georges Leygues*.

Three miles away in Kirkwall was a more unlikely visitor - the German Navy fishery protection vessel *Weser*, commanded by Captain Karl Jung.

The crew played out a 2-2 draw in a football match with Kirkwall Rovers at Bignold Park, and then attended a dance with members of the Orkney Territorial Army (Royal Artillery) at the Junction Road Drill Hall. "British khaki and German navy blue mingled in the best of spirits, and the men of both countries - and the girls of Kirkwall - made up a very happy assembly," reported *The Orcadian*. When the Germans returned to their ship at midnight, 30 Kirkwall Grammar School students sang the German national anthem at the Pierhead.

Such jollity did not prevail everywhere. Two sailors from HMS *Greenwich* were fined £6 each at Kirkwall Sheriff Court after admitting driving away a new £600 bus from Kirkwall Pier.

And then the waiting was over. The impending arrival of war was signalled in Orkney in different ways - Kirk Sound, Skerry Sound, East Weddel Sound, Water Sound and Burra Sound were all declared "no longer navigable" after block ships and other obstructions were placed in the channels; the Caithness - Orkney inter-county football match, scheduled for August 30 in Wick, was postponed on account of the international situation; and Bombardier John Leslie and nurse Ruby

Marwick were the first couple to be married at the Lyness camp of Metal Industries Ltd, after the planned Church wedding had to be cancelled when Bombardier Leslie was called up for duty.

One of the last Britons to get out of Germany before war broke out was Lady Glen-Coats, the prospective Liberal candidate for Orkney and Shetland, who was touring Europe. She and her private secretary John Junor - later to become editor of the *Sunday Express* - managed to get on a train from Berlin to Amsterdam just hours before the Prime Minister's announcement.

A transcript of the Prime Minister's speech, when it came on Sunday, September 3, was read to the congregation of St Magnus Cathedral by the minister, Rev Arthur Fryer.

All schools in Orkney were closed until further notice - they remained shut for two weeks - as was the Albert Kinema, which was open again in a week. Water restrictions were imposed in Stromness, there were appeals for blankets and blood donors, and Kirkwall's Balfour Hospital was evacuated of all patients to await the expected arrival of war casualties. Civilian air services were also cancelled for a week, while air raid shelters were in the course of construction in Kirkwall, in The Strynd, the Earl's and Bishop's palaces, and at the old Castle in Main Street.

The Orcadian appealed to the public not to listen to, or repeat rumours, while Orkney Presbytery agreed a motion recording approval of the Government's action in declaring war on Germany - but only after some members had forced a vote.

"While recognising that war is an evil which ought to be outlawed from the civilised world, the Presbytery believe that no other course was open to Britain than resort to arms against a ruthless regime which threatens the freedom and independence of the nations of Europe." This wording was eventually agreed by 11 votes to three after the Rev Harald Mooney (Deerness), who stated he did not agree with parts of the motion expressing approval of war, put forward an amendment.

Outside, in the real world, a German steamer *Hannah Boge* was seized at Kirkwall and the vessel requisitioned by the British authorities.

And Miss Hetty Chalmers, clerkess in the Junction Road, Kirkwall, veterinary surgery of Messrs George Johnson and John Simison, organised the assembly and depot distribution of Orkney's 21,000 civilian gas masks, helped by a team of 60 volunteers.

Orkney was at war - and it would not be long to wait for the first casualties. In fact, Britain's - and Orkney's - first death of World War Two came just hours into the conflict when 90 civilians were killed after the liner *Athenia*, outward bound for Canada, was attacked and sunk by torpedoes from a German submarine off Ireland.

The death toll included Elizabeth Brookes, nee Scott, of Dundas Street, Stromness. In a massive rescue operation, however, most of the 1,400 passengers and crew were saved.

Two weeks later, Orkney was hit by the first casualties of the war among servicemen when Leading Stoker George Robertson (40) of Kirkwall and Artificer John Delday (43) of Birsay were both killed when 500 men were lost as the aircraft carrier HMS *Courageous* - a well known visitor to Scapa Flow - was torpedoed by enemy submarine. Mr Delday had, in fact, retired from the Navy after 22 years service in 1937, but had been recalled to duty in the wartime emergency.

The massive mobilisation of troops was to see Orkney's wartime population increase nearly threefold to 60,000 with a huge influx of servicemen and civilian workers - plus another 100,000 afloat in Orkney waters. The aerodrome at Hatston was just about complete by the onset of war and work was progressing on other airfields at Grimsetter (later to be Kirkwall's civil airport), Twatt and Skeabrae, which would open in 1940. The Lyness camp of Baldry, Yerburgh and Hutchinson had now grown to more than 800 men.

The influx created huge logistical problems - the men had to be fed, their welfare and entertainment looked after - and law and order maintained. The near doubling of Orkney's population in the run up to, and at the start of, the war saw the Chief Constable's annual report reveal that the number of crimes and offences in the county had trebled. However, lest it be thought that total lawlessness prevailed, it should be stressed that, in 1939, offences in Orkney averaged just one a day. Of the 335 people apprehended, the most (76) were held for motoring offences, followed by breach of the peace (65) and being drunk and incapable (60). The strength of the Orkney police force, with wartime reservists, had been increased to 21. In addition, 43 special constables had been enrolled.

To help feed the nation, farming subsidies were increased and Orkney farmers were called on to cultivate an extra 8,000 acres of land. Experiments with silage were launched at Garson Farm, Sandwick, in trials organised by farmer James Wood and Mr Gordon Watt, the Orkney county organiser for the North of Scotland College of Agriculture, in order to conserve animal feedstuffs. By October, 1939, food rationing details were announced. Petrol was also on ration at 1s 9d a gallon.

The organisation Toc H - originally founded by the Rev P.H. "Tubby" Clayton in Belgium in World War One - was to play a big part in caring for the welfare of the servicemen in Orkney. The Rev Clayton had been a frequent visitor to the islands before the war and now he was back, often for months at a time, helping to organise rest and recreation centres which would eventually be set up throughout the county. Woodwick House in Evie was to become a Toc H rest home which, during the course of the war, would provide comfort for more than 2,000 service patients.

And, of course, the war had to be paid for! As Warsaw fell to the Germans on September 26, 1939, the first wartime Budget saw income tax raised from 5s 6d to 7s 6d (it would later be further increased to 8s 6d) - and a bottle of whisky increased from 12s 6d to 13s 9d.

For some, whisky was not available at any price. The Chief Constable Colin Campbell said the proprietor of the Longhope Hotel, James Wilson, had voluntarily stopped serving men in uniform after "several very bad nights over there."

As the new austerity set in, however, Kirkwall was able to put out the flags to welcome King George VI in the first week of October, 1939.

The Naval authorities had given the Royal Burgh 24 hours notice of the royal visit and the King was given "a rousing reception by crowds" who gathered in front of the Kirkwall Hotel - which served as HMS *Pyramus* throughout World War Two, having been HMS *Cyclops II* during World War One - where the monarch was greeted by Provost John M. Slater before he inspected the ranks of servicemen on parade. Sadly, Kirkwall car hirer John Mackay, who drove the King that day, was to be killed in a road accident a year later.

The King met 85 year old Kirkwall veteran Alexander Ronald, of the Clay Loan, Kirkwall, who held seven military medals dating back to the age of 19 when he joined the 83rd Argyll and Sutherland Highlanders. He had served in India, Afghanistan, Egypt and South Africa at the end of the 19th century; with the Royal Naval Volunteer Reserve in World War One; and later as a special constable in South Ronaldsay.

King George, who went on to meet airmen of the Fleet Air Arm at Hatston, also visited ships of the Home Fleet in Scapa Flow. "I have been much impressed with the keen and cheerful spirit that unites you in a determination to bring the war to a successful conclusion," he told the Commander-in-Chief Home Fleet. Because of wartime censorship restrictions, this was all reported in *The Orcadian* as taking place in "a town in the North."

Just one week after the King's visit to Scapa Flow, the Germans were to achieve the unthinkable and breach the defences and strike a mortal blow against HMS *Royal Oak*.

From the unsinkable –

It was "a remarkable exploit of professional skill and daring." The reluctant admiration of Winston Churchill, as he announced to the world that the battleship HMS *Royal Oak* had been sunk by U-boat was obvious. But, behind the words, Churchill, then First Lord of the Admiralty, was devastated at what occurred in Orkney in the early hours of October 14, 1939.

Not only a battleship, and more than 800 lives, had been lost but Scapa Flow - Orkney's great secure anchorage that had been believed to be impenetrable - had proved frighteningly fallible; her defences had been breached and a mortal blow struck against the pride of the Royal Navy. The blow to morale was huge; the suffering of hundreds of bereaved families adding a human dimension of tragedy that was immeasurable.

Recrimination would swiftly follow.

Scapa Flow, with the help of barrage nets and block ships, had proved secure in World War One. It was true that, at the behest of Orkney County Council in the early 1930s, the Admiralty had agreed to salvage some of the block ships and re-open channels to shipping, but, in 1938-39, replacement vessels had been dumped there. A few days before the outbreak of war, a public notice to mariners had announced that Kirk Sound, Skerry Sound, East Weddel Sound, Watter Sound and Burra Sound were no longer navigable. Built at a cost of £2.5 million, the 27,000 ton *Royal Oak* had been presumed unsinkable by submarine attack within Scapa Flow - but the unsinkable became the unthinkable as German U-boat commander Lt Gunther Prien evaded the flimsy defences in the submarine *U47* and attacked at the heart of the British Navy.

The architect of the operation was Germany's chief Naval Commander Admiral Karl Doenitz. German surveillance of Scapa Flow had revealed the weakness in the defences of Holm Sound, then protected only by three blockships. With careful navigation, Doenitz decided, it would be possible to either pass between them or on either side of them.

Doenitz personally planned the mission, it was reported later, and personally chose Prien to carry it out.

Unfortunately, ten years later in 1949, Sunday newspapers and American magazines created a fanciful story of the German submarine being guided into Scapa Flow by a German spy, a Swiss watchmaker living in Kirkwall called Albert Oertel. Nobody in Orkney had ever seen, nor heard, of such a man - though several pointed out that the name closely resembled "Albert Hotel" - and the Lord Lieutenant of Orkney Mr Patrick Sutherland Graeme denounced the whole account as fiction and "a monstrous lie."

In fact, Prien's own log tells the story of those fateful few hours in 1939 which were to change Orkney forever.

Prien's log showed that *U47*, with a crew of 40, lay off Orkney on October 12-13. On the evening of October 13, the submarine set course, on the surface, for Holm Sound. Prien had a scare when he sighted a merchant ship and had to submerge but, at 23.31, he surfaced again and entered Holm Sound. Soon after midnight, *U47* was in Scapa Flow.

In his log, Prien reported: "It is disgustingly light. The whole bay is lit up. To the south of Cava, there is nothing. I go farther in. To port, I recognise the Hoxa Sound coastguard to which, in the next few minutes, the boat must present itself as a target. In that event all would be lost.

"We proceed north by the coast. Two battle ships are lying there at anchor, and, further inshore, destroyers. Cruisers not visible, therefore attack on the big fellows. Distance apart 3,000 metres. Estimated depth 7.5 metres. One torpedo fixed on the northern ship, two on southern. After a good three and a half minutes, a torpedo detonates on the northern ship; of the other two nothing is to be seen."

The *U47* turned and fired three torpedoes from the bow. "After three tense minutes comes the detonation on the nearer ship. There is a loud explosion, roar and rumbling. Then come columns of water, followed by columns of fire and splinters fly through the air. The harbour springs to life. Destroyers are lit up, signalling starts on every side and on land, 200 metres from me, cars roar along the roads. A battleship has been sunk, a second damaged and the other three torpedoes have gone to blazes. All the tubes are empty.

"I decide to withdraw because (1) with my periscope I cannot conduct night attacks while submerged; (2) On a bright night I cannot manoeuvre unobserved on a calm sea; (3) I must assume that I was observed by the driver of a car which stopped opposite us, turned round and drove off towards Scapa at top speed; (4) Nor can I go further north, for there, well hidden from my sight, lie the destroyers which were previously dimly distinguishable."

At 01.28, after just an hour in Scapa Flow, Prien made his escape. "At high speed both engines, we withdraw. Everything is simple until we reach Skildaenoy Point, then we have more trouble. It is now low tide, the current is against us. Engines at slow and dead slow, I attempt to get away. I must leave by the south, through the narrow, because of the depth of the water. Things are again difficult. I pass the southern blockship with nothing to spare. The helmsman does magnificently.

"At 02.15, we are once again outside. A pity that only one was destroyed. The torpedo misses I explain as due to faults of course, speed and drift. The crew behaved splendidly throughout the operation."

On October 17, Prien and the *U47* entered Wilhelmshaven at 11am, and four hours later, he was flown to Berlin for a personal audience with Hitler.

(Although Prien was to take the credit for the sinking of the *Royal Oak*, the torpedo gunner on board *U47* was a man called Herbert Herrman who in 1989, the 50th anniversary of the disaster, returned to Orkney to take part in a commemorative wreath-laying service at the Lyness Naval Cemetery, where he met the man who was then the oldest survivor of the *Royal Oak*, George Langlands from Wallsend, Tyneside.)

Back in Orkney in 1939, the military authorities and civilians alike were having to confront the horror of human suffering that Prien had left in his wake in Scapa Flow. The first official list showed the number of survivors given as just 424 out of a crew of 1,234, though the death toll was later given as 833.

About 300 of the *Royal Oak* survivors were picked up by the drifter *Daisy II*, and another vessel in the vicinity, the *Pegasus*, but between 60-70 men swam ashore, a race against time ahead of the spreading sea of burning oil which had been thrown up by the explosions of the torpedoes. Those survivors, having reached the shore, still had to clamber up the cliffs below Gaitnip Farm, St Ola.

Astonishingly, it was reported, one of the *Royal Oak* survivors had also survived the blowing up of HMS *Vanguard*, when more than 1,000 men died in Scapa Flow in 1917. Twenty two years had passed but tragedy remained.

Three Orkney men were on the *Royal Oak* - Bertie Johnston from St Mary's village, Holm; William Baker from Stromness; and James Moar from Birsay. The three pals had served in the Navy for just a year and the *Royal Oak* was their first ship after shore training. Baker, aged just 18, and Moar (19) both died in the disaster.

As Prien was preparing for his audience with Hitler on Tuesday, October 17, Winston Churchill gave the news to the House of Commons. The analysis by British intelligence forces of what had happened was remarkably accurate.

"The battleship *Royal Oak* was sunk at anchor by a U-boat

to the unthinkable

in Scapa Flow approximately at 1.30am on the 14th inst," began Churchill's statement. "It is still a matter of conjecture how the U-boat penetrated the defences of the harbour. When we consider that during the whole course of the last war this anchorage was found to be immune from such attacks on account of the obstacles imposed by the currents and net barrages, this entry by a U-boat must be considered as a remarkable exploit of professional skill and daring."

A Board of Inquiry was now investigating the exact circumstances, but Churchill added: "It appears probable that the U-boat fired a salvo of torpedoes at the *Royal Oak*, of which only one hit the bow. This muffled explosion was at the time attributed to internal causes, and what is called the Inflammable Store, where the kerosene and other such materials are kept, was flooded. Twenty minutes later, the U-boat fired three or four torpedoes, and these, striking in quick succession, caused the ship to capsize and sink.

"She was lying at the extreme end of the harbour and therefore many officers and men were drowned before rescue could be organised from other vessels. The lists of survivors have already been made public, and I deeply regret to inform the House that upwards of 800 officers and men have lost their lives. The Admiralty immediately announced the loss of this fine ship.

"Serious as this loss is, it does not affect the margin of security in heavy vessels which remains ample. Meanwhile, an intensive search of the anchorage has not yet yielded any results. It is clear, however, that after a certain time the harbour can be pronounced clear as any U-boat would have to rise to the surface for air or perish. All necessary measures are being taken to increase the precautions which in the last war proved

effectual. For the rest, I must await the report of the Board which is now examining the event in full technical detail."

The extent of the new defensive measures would not have been imagined in Orkney at that time, but the following Spring Churchill returned to Scapa Flow and set in motion the greatest civil engineering challenge of World War Two - the construction of a series of barriers that would permanently seal the eastern approaches to the Flow. The enormous engineering feat would claim the lives of a dozen civilian workers; how many lives of Royal Navy personnel it may have saved is incalculable - but, by then, of course, more than 800 men of the *Royal Oak* had already paid the ultimate sacrifice.

In Bérlin, and the ports of the German Navy, Gunther Prien was lauded as one of the first war heroes of Hitler's Third Reich. He could not enjoy the accolades for long - Prien was soon to be killed in action against the Royal Navy - but, nonetheless, the legacy of what Churchill had described as "a remarkable exploit of professional skill and daring" would remain in Orkney until the end of the 20th century.

A memorial plaque to the men of the *Royal Oak* was erected in Kirkwall's St Magnus Cathedral. It was unveiled on October 14, 1948 - the ninth anniversary of the tragedy - by Rear Admiral W.G. Benn, who was captain of the warship on the night she sank in just ten minutes, at a service attended by several other survivors of the terrible events of war back in 1939.

In 1949, it was reported that a private individual, astonishingly, had offered the Admiralty £50 for the salvage rights to the *Royal Oak*. This was rejected, and though the Admiralty did consider a survey of the sunken ship to assess the possibility of salvage, the site was to be declared an official war grave - still marked today by a buoy in Scapa Flow.

The massive firepower of HMS *Royal Oak*, sunk by U-boat in Scapa Flow in 1939, with the loss of 833 men, before she had the opportunity to fire her guns in anger in World War Two. (Picture courtesy of Orkney Library photographic archive)

The first enemy bombs

There was to be no respite for Orkney. Two days after the horror of the *Royal Oak* tragedy, the focus switched from submarine attacks to war in the skies as Scapa Flow became the target of the first sustained air raids of the conflict. Air raid warnings sounded eight times on Tuesday and Wednesday, October 17-18, 1939.

What was claimed to be the first enemy bomb to fall on British soil landed on the potato field of John Manson at Ore Farm, Hoy. It created such a large crater that potatoes actually rained on the next door house of Peter Wilson, Orraquoy.

Fourteen German planes made two raids over Scapa Flow and two aircraft were said to have been shot down. One certainly came down in flames near Pegal Burn on Hoy, the victim of the accurate fire of Orkney's 226 Battery. There had been an air attack on the Forth Bridge the day before, in which the RAF had shot down the first enemy aircraft on British soil, but the plane shot down on Hoy on Ocotber 17 was acknowledged as the first German plane to be brought down in Britain by anti-aircraft artillery. One of the German crew baled out and was taken to a Scapa Flow hospital ship.

Chief Constable Colin Campbell had to appeal to souvenir hunters in the Lyness area to return parts of the wrecked German plane. He also had to issue a stern warning that aerial warfare was not a spectator sport. Lives were at risk, he said, if people continued to go outdoors to watch air raids - especially as shells and shrapnel were falling all over the South Isles.

And the attack by the German Junkers had left some serious damage behind as bombs were dropped on HMS *Iron Duke*. Although no direct hits were suffered in the first air attack of October 17, two bombs did fall within yards of the veteran warship, built in 1912 and the flag ship of Admiral John Jellicoe in the Battle of Jutland. And she was damaged and suffered serious flooding after taking two hits in follow-up attacks, to the extent that most of the vessel's company were ordered to abandon ship.

The old ship was not finished yet, however. Despite this serious setback after just six weeks of war, the *Iron Duke* was to continue to function for the next six years - on the beach!

After the attack, a volunteer skeleton crew took the ship to Ore Bay where men of Metal Industries Ltd - who, in peacetime, had been involved in the salvaging of the German Fleet - were able to carry out patch-up repairs which allowed the warship to be towed to Longhope and beached. And despite suffering further damage in an air raid of March 16, 1940, the incapacitated *Iron Duke* operated for the rest of the campaign as the base ship for the Scapa Auxiliary Patrol - responsible for the victualling, clothing and payment of more than 50 attached vessels, involving a total of some 1,600 officers and men. Her bakery had a daily issue of more than 1,000 lbs of bread throughout the war, but in March,1946, her ovens were cold and it was announced that the ship would be towed south to be broken up by Metal Industries.

The loss of the *Royal Oak*, and the following air raids, meant that Orkney was no longer seen as the safe haven that had been presumed. Temporarily, the Fleet withdrew from Scapa Flow. Later, on the orders of Winston Churchill, a "dummy" fleet would be moved into the anchorage as merchant ships were camouflaged with wood and canvas to look like warships. The *Pakeha* was made to represent HMS *Revenge*, the *Waimara* became HMS *Resolution*, and the *Mamari* became aircraft carrier *Hermes*. The former HMS *Centurion* was reconstructed as a replica of HMS *Anson* and actually sailed to India in her new guise, the only embarrassment being when one of her wooden guns fell off and floated away!

Back on the home front, conscription was soon extended -

by the end of 1940, everyone up to 35 had to register - and, as soon as October, 1939, Orcadian women were going into uniform when the first recruits of the Kirkwall division of the Women's Royal Naval Service began their training. More than 70 women, aged 18-50, were required, with rates of pay from 30s - to 43s 6d.

(In July, 1942, former Kirkwall Grammar School pupil Betty Scollay, daughter of Mr and Mrs William Scollay of Thoms Street, Kirkwall, became the youngest recruit to the Women's Auxiliary Air Force, when she volunteered for service, and was accepted, before her 17th birthday.)

In the first three months of the war, air raid alarms were sounded 42 times in Orkney. There was anger in November, 1939, when children, sent home from school after an air raid alert, were caught in the middle of artillery flak from both north and south of Kirkwall as a German plane flew overhead.

"The air quivered and houses trembled; the noise overhead was like a dozen high-note thunderstorms," said *The Orcadian*. "Many children were scared by the terrific outburst of firing, the fiercest yet heard in the town of Kirkwall." Kirkwall Grammar School pupils were later instructed to take cover under their school room desks in such circumstances.

Schools in the Walls and Flotta area were closed after a shell crashed through the roof of Fara school in Scapa Flow. At the same time, parts of Stromness Academy and schools in South Ronaldsay were requisitioned by the military authorities. The school roll in Fara had fallen to just two - girls of 11 and 12 - when the school was closed and lessons at home, by correspondence, were introduced under the control of Orkney's newly appointed director of correspondence studies, Mr John D. Mackay. Participating in the Orkney correspondence scheme were the county's 28 one-teacher schools plus those which had been closed in the air raid danger zone around Scapa Flow. In the future, it was hoped to extend the scheme to include not only academic lessons but also such subjects as poultry keeping. In the event, the scheme continued for only the first 18 months of war.

Red tape, of course, thrived in the war. An Orkney joke of the time featured the foremen of two work parties discussing the respective progress of their labours. "Another six loads and we'll be finished," said one. "Great," said the other. "Another six chits signed and we'll be able to start."

The civil police and the courts certainly kept the wheels of bureaucracy turning. A St Ola shop assistant - cited for not having a rear red light on his bicycle - was fined 21s - (near half a week's wages) and told by Provost John Slater that he could have killed someone, despite the Chief Constable stating in mitigation that wartime restrictions meant it was almost impossible to obtain such lamps. An infantry sergeant, ordered by a senior officer to drive a car without lights, was then promptly stopped by the civilian police, and admonished at Sheriff Court - presumably a more preferable penalty than the alternative at court martial for disobeying the orders of an officer.

Of course, some wartime regulations were essential, especially during the period when Orkney was suffering air raids, and in November, 1939, a Kirkwall hotelier was fined £5, with the option of 30 days jail, in the first prosecution in the county for failing to observe blackout precautions.

By this time, Orkney mail was subject to censorship. Indeed, about 100 people were employed on the task in Inverness. Each envelope from Orkney was opened. If there was no sensitive information revealed, it was resealed with a gummed label, bearing the words "Opened by Censor" and released for forwarding. Innocent references to movements of troops or ships were cut out with scissors, while what appeared to be more suspicious revelation of details was passed to a supervising examiner. However, the censors found themselves caught

fall on Orkney soil

up in a Commons row when the Secretary for War was asked on what grounds an ex-Brigadier General on the Inverness censorship staff had also secured the appointment of his wife, son and daughter. "A number of these appointments are looked upon in the district as being a case of gross nepotism and favouritism," the War Minister was told. In January, 1940, *The Orcadian* informed readers that they were not even allowed to mention the weather in their letters.

The most Draconian restriction of war for the islands came on November 23, 1939, when the War Office announced that Orkney was to be a "Closed Area". No person - other than residents, servicemen or police - would be allowed to remain in, or enter the area without a permit, and travel would only be allowed to and from prescribed ports - Aberdeen, Leith, Wick and Thurso, and the airports of Aberdeen, Inverness and Wick. The use of cameras out of doors was now prohibited in Orkney and, in fact, this ban was later extended to include indoor photography as well.

The Admiral Commanding Orkney and Shetland issued a strong warning to Orkney's gossip mongers, who were threatened with expulsion from the county.

"It has come to my knowledge that information which would be of undoubted value to the enemy is being talked of quite openly by the general public in the Orkneys," he said. "Some of this information is undoubtedly the result of personal observation and the fact that this information is known by some of the general public cannot be avoided. Some may come from the fact that the Naval personnel and the general public live in such close contact that indiscreet statements made by the former come to the knowledge of the latter. Steps are being taken to ensure that any such indiscretion by Naval personnel will be severely dealt with.

"In order to prevent information which might be of value to the enemy reaching him it is particularly important that it should not reach people who can convey it outside the Orkneys. This particularly applies to persons whose normal vocation takes them out of the Islands. In future if proof is obtained of the fact that information, which should be secret, is being publicly discussed by any persons, consideration will be given to removing such persons from the area where such information can be obtained."

"There is only one safe rule and that is not to discuss Service matters, however small, which might convey information, unless it is your duty to do so, and never do this in public, and I appeal to the general public to enforce this rule."

The appeal to the public to be alert for suspicious behaviour had its lighter moments, however. Two suspected spies - reported hiking towards Stromness - turned out to be officials of the forces entertainments body ENSA, returning from a visit to the Stone Age village of Skara Brae.

ENSA was just one of the organisations helping to bring some entertainment to the troops. A Kirkwall Naval Base Sports Club was founded and, initially, members played their football matches in the colours of Nottingham Forest FC after the gift of a full set of jerseys, boots and footballs from the English club was passed on to Kirkwall by the secretary of the English Football Association, Stanley Rous.

Because of the hostilities, Orkney's traditional festive Ba' games were cancelled. The Naval Base Sports Club instead planned to organise an Uppies versus Doonies tug of war.

However, events elsewhere were to ensure that there would be few luxuries on the festive dinner tables of Orkney during that first wartime Christmas. The entire stock of 312 crates of chocolate goods and fancy biscuits, consigned to be sent to Orkney for the Christmas trade, was destroyed by fire at the Edinburgh premises of Cadbury and Fry's.

And if Orcadians needed any reminding that it was a world theatre of war, they received it that first Christmas with the news of the first Orcadians to be taken prisoners - not in Europe but in South America.

Alfred Walls, from Hermisgarth in Sanday, and John Laurenson of Sandwick were taken captive on the German pocket battleship *Admiral Graf Spee* after their merchant ships were sunk in the South Atlantic. John Laurenson was landed at Montevideo in Uruguay - before the German officers of the *Graf Spee* scuttled their ship in the River Plate rather than confront the Royal Navy - and he was able to return to Britain and sign on another ship within weeks.

(Incidentally, Vice-Admiral Sir Henry Harwood, who was credited with the elimination of the *Admiral Graf Spee* from the war in December, 1939, when he commanded the Royal Navy's South America division, was later to have much closer links with Orkney when, in March, 1944, he was appointed to succeed Admiral Sir Lionel Wells as Flag Officer Commanding Orkney and Shetland.)

Alfred Walls had a less fortunate experience after his capture. He was transferred as a prisoner to the German auxiliary ship *Altmark*, and spent 11 weeks in Nazi hands, including "celebrating" his 28th birthday on the prison ship which was to take him, and 400 other prisoners, to Germany. However, help was at hand and Mr Walls was to become Orkney's first prisoner of war to be freed when the *Altmark* was cornered by HMS *Cossack* in a Norwegian fjord and all the British prisoners released. Mr Walls was later landed at Leith and allowed to return to Sanday on leave.

Merchant seamen in Orkney waters were having to endure dangers just as grave as the South Atlantic. Fishing was a perilous enough task in peacetime. In wartime, the trawlermen of Hull, Grimsby and Aberdeen faced even worse.

At the end of October, 1939, the 15 crewmen of the Hull trawler *St Nidan* set some sort of unwanted and luckless record when they were blown out of the water by a German U-boat twice in 12 hours. They were fishing north of Orkney when the first attack sank their vessel and they were forced to take to their lifeboat. They had no sooner been picked up by the Grimsby trawler *Lynx II* than that vessel was also attacked by submarine, forcing the total of 25 crewmen from the two fishing boats into the lifeboats again. Fortunately, this time they were picked up by the Hull trawler *Lady Hogarth* and landed safely ashore.

But worse was to follow on Orkney's doorstep. Although, in January, 1940, the 40 crew of the Danish tanker *Danmark* were safely taken off the vessel after an explosion ripped through the ship, the month was to end in a grim week of attacks on British and neutral merchant shipping as between 80-90 lives were lost - 20 of them British, many of them Shetlanders - in Orkney waters. Mass communal burials had to be organised as scores of bodies came ashore on the East Mainland, South Ronaldsay, Copinsay, Shapinsay and the outer North Isles.

The greatest anguish came in South Ronaldsay - where the Cromarty Hall was converted into a temporary mortuary - after the 2,000 ton steamer *Giralda*, a regular Orkney trader, was attacked and set on fire by two enemy aircraft off Grim Ness on January 30, 1940. The 23 crew, seven from Shetland, were able to take to a lifeboat but 500 yards from shore - where Coastguards, police, doctor and nurse were waiting to help - the boat capsized and they were all drowned.

The same week, the Danish steamers *Fredensborg* and *England* and the Norwegian vessels *Faro* and *Hosanger* were all sank off Orkney with the loss of 60 lives.

The second mate of the *England* was the sole survivor of his ship after he was picked up after 32 hours on a raft. Deerness life saving team managed to save the skipper and six men by breeches buoy from the *Faro*. The injured survivors were cared for at the Balfour Hospital in Kirkwall.

Eight of the victims were buried on February 1, another 21 on February 4, and eight on February 8, following graveside services conducted by Cathedral minister Rev Arthur Fryer at St Olaf Cemetery. A commemorative stone to the men of the *Giralda* was erected in the cemetery in 1942.

The tragedy continued into February, 1940. Ten survivors from the 3,300 ton Swedish steamer *Oriana* were safely landed ashore when their vessel sank in three minutes after being torpedoed by U-boat - but the Captain, his wife and 12 crew were missing. Fortunately, another 46 crew off the Norwegian steamer *Vestoff* and the Swedish ship *Lagaholm* were rescued after their vessels were also sunk by German vessels.

After 17 hours exposure, 37 men, three women and two children were landed at Kirkwall after being rescued from the Norwegian ship *Cometa* which was torpedoed off Orkney while on voyage to Buenos Aires. One of the men, the three women and the two children, one just a babe in arms, were part of a team of Swedish missionaries going to Brazil.

Another 12 crew perished - though 14 were saved after eight hours in a lifecraft - when the Oslo steamer *Navarra*, which had been on her way home with a cargo of coal from Wales, was torpedoed. The tragedy was to unfold a poignant human story 40 years later. The then-unidentified body of Nils Jorgen Nilssen, the chief officer of the *Navarra*, had been washed ashore on Westray where he was buried in an unmarked grave for many years. However in 1981, appeals by the Orkney Norway Friendship Association in Norwegian newspapers led to Mr Nilssen being identified by his wedding ring. Sadly his wife Olga had died but his daughters Karin and Bjorg, from near Oslo, were able to make the journey to Westray to see the erection of a headstone with his name. And, in 1999, Bjorg, who was only five months old when her father died, made another pilgrimage to the grave of the father she never knew when a special service of dedication saw the unveiling of a war grave commission headstone over his resting place.

Also, in 1941, the Swedish tanker *Sveaborg* and the Norwegian steamer *Tosca* were both sunk by German submarine, with the loss of three men, while 64 survivors were landed in Orkney by a British patrol ship. Still the death toll mounted as the crew of 12 on the salvage boat *Disperser*, which had been working in Orkney waters, were lost when the vessel foundered.

The dreadful merchant shipping casualty list in early 1940 caused an outcry in Orkney - to the extent that the Lord Lieutenant Alfred Baikie felt obliged to make a public statement defending the authorities.

Mr Baikie wrote to *The Orcadian*: "The Naval authorities in Orkney have become aware of rumours being spread about that sufficient effort to save life from sinking ships is not being exerted, more especially if the subject be a merchantman.

"I wish to state authoritatively that all possible speed and all available means are used on every occasion, irrespective of the service - Naval or mercantile. When an effort fails, it is owing to insurmountable obstacles such as time, distance, gales and tides.

"I think the public will help the nation if it will abstain from carping criticism, and rely on the zeal, courage and resourcefulness of the men who are guarding our lives and property so ably."

An indication of military deaths followed as bodies from the minesweeper HMS *Sphinx*, which had been sunk after being bombed by German aircraft, came ashore near Longhope. And military casualties were not confined to the Allied cause. Two unidentified German airmen, whose bodies were recovered from the sea, were buried at Burray and Copinsay.

As the build-up of troops continued, the authorities introduced compulsory billeting for servicemen because of a shortage of people coming forward to volunteer accommodation in the county - though reports that all Orkney's children were to be evacuated to the Highlands of Scotland were

Winston Churchill would make a number of visits to Scapa Flow, both as First Lord of the Admiralty and then Prime Minister. It was in the wake of the loss of the *Royal Oak* in 1939 that he visited Orkney in 1940 to put in train the building of what would become the Churchill barriers linking the Orkney Mainland to Burray and South Ronaldsay. (Picture courtesy of Orkney Library photographic archive)

denounced as cruel rumours, without truth. Payments of 21 shillings a week, in addition to their wages, were authorised for "South" workers in Orkney in order for them to pay their lodgings.

The arrival of thousands of men from throughout the country, and the crowded conditions in which they lived, brought a new crisis as the county, both servicemen and civilians, was hit by an epidemic of Meningitis. It was a serious infectious disease formerly very uncommon in Orkney, said Medical Officer of Health Dr Walter Bannerman, and he asked people with 'flu-like symptoms to seek medical aid. Classes at Kirkwall Grammar School were sent home, and the outbreak claimed its first civilian death, that of 16 year old Charles Flett, a very promising young footballer who had already represented a Kirkwall Select X1 versus the Fleet Air Arm. The following year, Diphtheria was the threat and, after several cases, a mass innoculation programme was started for local children.

A few weeks after the Meningitis scare, however, the focus of Orkney was to return to casualties of war as bombers of the German air force again attacked the Fleet anchorage at Scapa Flow and Orkney suffered the loss of the first civilian to be killed by enemy bombs on British soil.

1940

Duncan J. Robertson OBE retired at the age of 80 in September, 1940, after 50 years as Orkney County Clerk - a record of local government service unequalled in Britain.

Mr Robertson, of Crantit House, St Ola, the only son of Sheriff James Robertson, became County Clerk in 1890. He also served as clerk of Orkney Harbours Commissioners and the Balfour Hospital as well as being factor for several large Orkney estates.

He served as Kirkwall's vice consul for Denmark, Sweden and Norway and was honoured by the monarchs of all three countries.

Mr Robertson - who was succeeded as County Clerk by Aberdeen law agent Douglas Wood (33) - died at the age of 81 in 1941, just eight months after his retiral.

* * *

Three boys, who stole cakes and jam from a back shop, were birched in Kirkwall, with a doctor in attendance.

* * *

Twelve hens were taken in crates into the Kirkwall Sheriff Court as evidence in a case of an isles couple accused of receiving the said hens as stolen property. The hens grew so noisy during the trial that the Sheriff ordered their removal - but only after four of them had laid eggs!

* * *

One way traffic regulations were introduced to Bridge Street, Albert Street and Victoria Street, Kirkwall.

* * *

Mr William Bertram, East Road, Kirkwall - who was Scotland's oldest working saddler until his retirement in 1938 - died at the age of 86.

* * *

Provost John M. Slater of Kirkwall died at 71 after over 14 years as provost. He was succeeded by Peter C. Flett OBE.

* * *

Warnings were given that the Corncrake was a "disappearing" bird in Orkney in 1940.

* * *

Dr William Park of Kirkwall, who held the unique distinction of having been both a teacher at Kirkwall Grammar School in his early career and then, after medical training, a doctor in Orkney, died at the age of 73.

* * *

Seven registrars - in Kirkwall, Stromness, Sanday, Stronsay, Westray, South Ronaldsay and Walls - were now authorised to perform civil weddings in Orkney under the new Marriage (Scotland) Act.

1941

Orkney police were able to use the latest criminal-detection technology to catch offenders as the county's population was swollen by an influx of soldiers and civilians engaged on war work.

In 27 cases in 1941, fingerprints of criminals were sent to New Scotland Yard and Glasgow City Police for identification. Glasgow provided identification in seven cases and New Scotland Yard in two cases.

* * *

Longhope was touched by New Year tragedy when Mrs Freda Manson (née Norquoy) was buried in her wedding dress following her death just four days after her marriage to Mr William Manson. The newly wed bride had fallen ill the day after her wedding.

* * *

Kirkwall shellfish company D. Meil and Sons had a lobster measuring 30 inches across and weighing 9lbs 4 ounces. Despite the war, the firm was still handling 3,500 lobsters a week.

* * *

A workman from a Glasgow contracting firm was jailed for 15 months at Kirkwall Sheriff Court for the night-time theft of £297, the weekly payroll for workers in Flotta, engaged on war work.

* * *

An Orcadian exile in South Africa, William Johnston, a farmer originally from Birsay, died at the age of 81 - leaving a legacy of £18,605 to be shared by relatives in Orkney.

* * *

Mr Robert Flett and his wife Elizabeth, of Furso, Harray, celebrated 65 years of married life.

* * *

Orkney's oldest resident in 1941 was "Granny" Mainland, of Victoria Street, Kirkwall, who celebrated her 101st birthday. Born at Banks, Frotoft, Rousay, she died in 1942, four weeks after her 102nd birthday.

* * *

A man from Glasgow was jailed for 12 months for bigamy when Kirkwall Sheriff Court heard he married a woman in Orkney when he already had a wife - with 15 children - back in Glasgow.

* * *

Tributes were paid in Orkney following the death of George Balfour MP - the founder of the civil engineering company of Balfour, Beatty and Company, the firm then engaged on the construction of the Churchill Barriers, linking the Orkney Mainland to Burray and South Ronaldsay.

1942

A mystery carcase of a 24 feet long "monster" was washed ashore at Deepdale in Holm - and nicknamed Scapasaurus because it was said to resemble the extinct plesiosaurus.

Provost James Marwick of Stromness who wrote the weekly nature notes for *The Orcadian*, and who had seen the carcase, said that he was now prepared to believe in the Loch Ness monster. He thought it resembled an extinct family of reptile Ichthopterygia.

Provost Marwick dispatched sketches, and samples of the carcase to museums and universities in the South. However as monster mania swept Orkney, museum experts dismissed the find as a decomposing basking shark - although a lecturer in biology at Durham University agreed with Marwick that it was a sea reptile.

A week later, a second "monster", 28 feet long, was found at Hunda and put on show at St Margaret's Hope, where it was also identified as a shark.

Neither of the finds could rival Orkney's biggest unexplained phenomenon - the 1809 "Stronsay Monster", a 55 feet long, six-legged creature with a 15 feet neck, which was found on the island's shores.

* * *

Orkney was shocked by the frenzied killing, by 126 stab wounds, of a woman well known in the county - Mrs Eva Sandeman, the wife of Surgeon Commander Charles Sandeman, who served as locum doctor on Rousay.

Following the horrific death in an incident in Cornwall, a 16 year old girl was charged with her murder. She was later found guilty of manslaughter and sentenced to five years in prison.

* * *

A Kirkwall woman who harboured an Army deserter for five days was admonished at Kirkwall Sheriff Court.

* * *

Winds reached gale force on 111 days in 1942, with gales recorded on 20 days in December, 1942.

* * *

The Secretary of State for Scotland, Mr Tom Johnston, visited Orkney and opened the new county council offices at 6 Broad Street, Kirkwall.

* * *

A total of 254 people were apprehended or cited for offences of drunkeness in Orkney in 1942 - compared with 460 in 1941.

* * *

Rev David Muir was inducted as minister of the North Church, Stromness, as successor to Rev James Christie who retired in 1939 after 42 years service.

As construction work went ahead on the Churchill barriers, Orkney witnessed a railway system for the first time.

(Picture courtesy of Orkney Library photographic archive)

The Orkney countryside was transformed as, within a matter of weeks, the giant Rockworks complex grew up to provide the blocks for the building of the barriers.

(Picture courtesy of Orkney Library photographic archive)

Death from the skies

The planes came at dusk, *The Orcadian* reported with powerful simplicity. The German raiders attacked the Fleet anchorage in Scapa Flow but they were to leave behind them the first civilian to be killed by enemy bombs on British soil. And the tiny Orkney hamlet of Brig o' Waithe, Stenness, was to be reduced to a scene of devastation and carnage, from which, miraculously, two babies escaped with their lives.

It was Saturday, March 16, 1940, that 14 German aircraft descended on their deadly mission. Mrs Ellen Farquhar, approaching her 70th birthday, had a little confectionery shop, which operated in conjunction with a boot and shoe repair business run by her son William, at the Brig o' Waithe. She explained later: "I just saw a blue and white flame which dazzled me at the same moment as a terrible explosion shook everything. The shop window crashed in and I was half choked with dust. I saw William sagging against the wall at the door. He was half doubled up and I knew he had been hit. Blood was pouring from a wound in his thigh."

Next door, however, was greater tragedy. James Isbister had been killed - although his wife Lily and three month old baby son Neil escaped unhurt despite broken glass showering the baby's clothes in his pram. The fatally injured man was carried into his house, recounted Mrs Farquhar. "They got James Isbister laid out on the bed and William asked me if anybody would have any whisky. He was not able to get any . . . poor James Isbister was beyond help anyhow."

Alfred Linklater, who lived beyond the Isbisters' house, had also been injured - but he pushed his wife and baby son Alfred to safety under a table for protection during the bombing. Outside his car was completely wrecked between flattened hen houses amidst 22 gaping craters.

Miss Isabella McLeod's house was a direct hit but, amazingly, she was able to crawl from the wreckage. Also injured were Mr James Jamieson of Bankburn, Stenness, and Mrs Jane Jessie Muir of Cumminess, Stenness, widow of Captain Frederick Muir, who had been lost, at the age of 39, while on minesweeping duties in 1917. Medical aid arrived and an ambulance took the injured to the Balfour Hospital.

Blacksmith John Isbister, the brother of the bomb victim, had hurried to his home at Upper Onston to ensure the safety of his family when the air raid began. "Suddenly there was a series of explosions and I looked out in time to see bursts of flame on the ground at the Bridge of Waithe houses. The children were screaming, frightened by the terrific explosions, and I was relieved to hear the noise of the planes growing fainter.

"I left the house and ran down to the Bridge of Waithe, a few hundred yards. In the moonlight I saw pits every here and there - bomb craters. I was shocked to see what a havoc had been caused. The first house I made for was that of my brother Jim. There was a bomb crater just across from his house. I feared the worst, and learned with horror that Jim had been killed. They told me he had been hit by a bomb splinter."

It was not only the Brig o' Waithe that was hit. Many other civilians had escapes as bombs fell on Kirkwall, Holm and the South Isles. Fourteen bomb craters were counted near Craigiefield House, to the east of Kirkwall, and 120 incendiary bombs fell in Holm, as well as scores of high explosive bombs in Stenness during the 85 minute attack. In fact, the 52 acre farm of Housequoy, Stenness, was said to have suffered a bomb for every acre.

Seven Naval personnel in Scapa Flow were injured in the attack which was announced by the Admiralty at 1pm on Sunday, March 17. "A considerable number of bombs were dropped, one hitting a warship which sustained only minor damage. Bombs were also dropped on the land; no military objectives being hit; but one civilian was killed and seven wounded, including two women, and five cottages damaged. One enemy aircraft was shot down," said the stark announcement.

The attack - and the war's first civilian bombing casualty - saw murmurs of criticism from national newspapers. *The Daily Telegraph* suggested that there must be something wrong with the Scapa defences, otherwise more enemy aircraft would have been shot down.

However Prime Minister Neville Chamberlain, in a statement in the House of Commons on Tuesday, March 19, played down the impact of the raid. Seemingly without expressing any sympathy for the victims, he stated: "I am rather surprised at the importance attached to what was a very unimportant affair. Does anybody think a war of this kind can go on without innumerable raids of this kind? If it was a raid on the Fleet in Scapa Flow, it must be classed as a failure. Not more than 20 bombs were dropped in the Flow. No capital ship in Scapa Flow suffered any damage whatsoever.

"The only difference between this raid and raids which preceded it is that on this occasion, for the first time, an attack was made upon the land. One hundred and twenty one high explosive bombs with 500 incendiary bombs were dropped on land covering 100 square miles and, as a result, there were several civilian casualties, including one death.

"The excuse given was that they were bombing military objectives. The responsibility for the consequences must rest with the authors."

It had been an alarming moment in Orkney's wartime history. Yet, as events unfolded, James Isbister was to be one of only three civilians to die in air raids within the county in World War Two. The second air raid death came in March, 1941, when a civilian workman died, and five were injured when a Junkers 88 aircraft bombed an RAF installation being built at Start Point, Sanday. The third air raid death of the war was in June, 1941, when enemy aircraft bombed and strafed the Grimsetter airfield, killing one man in the neighbouring civilian worker's camp.

Tragic though that was, the death toll was thankfully light in comparison to other parts of Britain, especially the industrialised cities. Up to October 1, 1943, a total of 48,282 people were killed by air raids in Britain, and another 61,192 injured.

In fact, more Orcadians, or people with Orkney links, were probably killed in just one night, on March 13-14, 1941, when German air attacks on Clydeside killed 1,100 and seriously wounded nearly 1,000.

The Brig o' Waithe tragedy, however, did bring home the perils of war. The dangers of the civilian highway still seemed to be unappreciated in the county. It's a grim statistic that ten times more people were killed by road accidents, as by bombs, in Orkney in the years 1939-45. In fact, March, 1947, was the first month for ten years in which Orkney police were not called to deal with a road accident. The high death toll on the roads is made more astonishing by the fact that, at the outbreak of war, the number of cars registered in Orkney totalled just 683, and motorcycles 727.

(Another 30 deaths were recorded in accidents at work among civilian workmen engaged on construction projects in Orkney in the run up to, and during the war years).

Nonetheless, Orkney had suffered many more enemy attacks than most rural areas, and the final casualty list from World War Two air raids was three deaths, 11 seriously injured and five slightly injured. In all, 228 bombs and two parachute mines fell on land in the county in 16 major attacks, and other isolated raids.

Hoy suffered the most attacks, having been bombed five times, South Ronaldsay three times, Sanday and Flotta twice, Shapinsay and Burray once. Bombs fell on the Mainland parishes of Deerness, Holm, Kirkwall and St Ola, Stenness and Tankerness. In addition, Stromness suffered on one occasion an attack by a raiding aircraft which machine gunned the town along its entire length.

Deaths in battle

Surprisingly, the following meeting of Orkney Presbytery did not appear to devote any great time to expressing sympathy for the victims of the Brig o' Waithe bombing. Instead the churchmen "deplored the amount of drunkenness in Kirkwall", calling for restrictions in the sale of drink, and agreed to write to all employers asking them to immediately cease Sunday working. The minister of St Magnus Cathedral, Rev Arthur Fryer, then aged 32, would not be able to take a role in the debate - he was, that week, called up for duty as an Army chaplain.

Conscription obviously created difficulties in Civvy Street. The Orkney education committee reported a serious shortage of teachers as men were called away - by mid-1941, everyone up to 41 was liable - and there was a problem for the manager of Kirkwall Ministry of Labour when his entire staff of three clerks registered for service.

There was a possible "escape" of military service - conscientious objection - but this was no easy opt-out. In the first seven months of conscription, Orkney's total seeking to be registered as conscientious objectors totalled eight men. However, they had to prove their case before a Conscientious Objectors Tribunal in Inverness. In April, 1940, four from Orkney appeared in one week and, in every case, the tribunal members were unconvinced that the applicants had genuine conscientious objections, and removed their names from the roll of conscientious objectors. This would usually mean that they would still be liable to service of a non-combatant nature. They had perhaps an even heavier penalty to pay when they returned to Orkney - they were all named by *The Orcadian* so the public knew who they were!

By this time, Germany had invaded Denmark and Norway, coinciding with increased enemy air attacks on Orkney. Six bombs fell on Flotta, and both Kirkwall and Stromness were strafed by German aircraft. Some degree of revenge, if not compensation, for the bombing of the Brig o' Waithe was secured as no less than four German planes were shot down in dog fights over the county, although two more civilian casualties, not serious, were suffered in Hoy when German aircraft made another attack on Scapa Flow on April 2, 1940.

Kirkwall became a staging post both for German prisoners of war and for Norwegian refugees. Between March-May, 1940, nearly 200 captured German airmen and seamen, taken prisoner in Norway, passed through the town, under armed guard, en route for internment in the South. At the same time, scores of Norwegian refugees escaped from Aalesund in small fishing boats, to make the perilous crossing to freedom in Orkney and Shetland, after the German forces arrived at the Norwegian port.

And now - as what had been called the Phoney War in Europe came to an end; with retreat from France and the evacuation from Dunkirk; and the imminent start of what was to become the Battle of Britain - Orkney, with the rest of Britain, had to accept news of casualties from other theatres of war. At the end of April, Sergeant Robert Mainland died on active service - the first Orcadian RAF pilot, and the first Rousay man, to be killed on active service. No island, however small, was to be spared a dreaded War Office communication. Able Seaman Gillies Hercus, of Faray, was one of 79 men who perished when HMS *Alfridi* was bombed and sunk off Norway.

Back at home, the formation was announced in May, 1940, of the Local Defence Volunteers, who initially would be trained to fight the potential menace of landings by parachute troops.

The radio announcement of the force (later to be immortalised by the television comedy series "Dad's Army") saw a rush of volunteers to Kirkwall police station. More than 50 men came forward in the first 24 hours and, within two weeks, more than 300 Orkney volunteers had registered. In fact, the Orkney force was the first in Britain to go into active service - although recruits had to wait another six months to receive their full uniforms. The name of the new force was soon changed to the Home Guard and Orkney was to have two battalions, the 2nd Orkney Battalion of the Home Guard earning the nickname of Orkney's Foreign Legion, so called because most of the members were civilian workers from the South.

New wartime regulations saw the introduction of an 11pm curfew from July 15, 1940. It was scrapped after three months, but only after dozens of people had appeared in Orkney courts for breaking the restriction. Other disruptions to ordinary life would see the continuance of British Summer Time throughout the winter and, in 1941, Double Summer Time (the clocks two hours ahead of Greenwich Mean Time) was introduced. The sale of silk stockings was banned from December 1, 1940, and, two months later, the strength of beer was reduced by ten per cent. There would be no 1940 County Show (nor indeed would it be held throughout the war years) but Westray went ahead with the island's annual flower and industrial show.

The impending fall of France - and General Charles de Gaulle's move to London as leader of the Free French forces - saw the mobilisation of Orkney's Scottish Airways planes to help the evacuation across the Channel. One aircraft managed to take off from Bordeaux just as German tanks appeared at the airfield. Another was forced to land on one engine in Jersey - only to find that all the British military establishment had already left the island. However the pilot, Captain Donald Prentice, was able to cannibalise parts of a Jersey Airways plane before taking off just before German troops landed on the Channel Island.

Capt. John Hankin, a New Zealand pilot who flew with Scottish Airways for three years, left Orkney in August, 1940, to take up RAF service. In 1943, he was awarded the Air Force Cross.

The fall of France saw a rush of notifications of Orcadians who had been taken prisoner. The youngest prisoner of war so far was Driver William Firth, of Kirkwall, aged 18, of the Royal Army Service Corps, who was captured prior to Dunkirk. Double ill fortune was suffered by a Burray family - Private Charlie Park of the Seaforth Highlanders was reported a prisoner while his brother Seaman Gunner James Park was posted missing after his ship was sunk by enemy action.

Despite the anguish, or perhaps because of it, Orkney rallied to raise large amounts of money for wartime funds and savings schemes. The first effort was the Orkney Spitfire Fund, later renamed Orkney Fighter Fund, which in six weeks of the summer of 1940 raised £6,000. It eventually reached over £8,000 and Lord Beaverbrook, Minister of Aircraft Production, sent a commemorative plaque with the inscription: "In the hour of peril, the people of Orkney earned the gratitude of the British nations, sustaining the valour of the Royal Air Force, and fortifying the cause of freedom, by the gift of one Spitfire aircraft."

August, 1941, saw the organisation of Orkney War Weapons Week with a target of £100,000 to be invested in savings schemes. Opened by Vice-Admiral Sir Hugh Binney, the week of events included an exhibition of weapons, a march past of troops, a fancy dress carnival parade and a flypast of aircraft over Kirkwall. In fact, the target was exceeded fourfold as the amount pledged climbed to over £393,000 - an impressive total which would pay for just 47 minutes of the war against Hitler.

A year later, Orkney's Warship Week was opened by Vice-Admiral Lionel Wells, Flag Officer Commanding Orkney and Shetland. The total invested in 1942 was £243,500 - double the target of £120,000 - encouraged by a series of sporting and

and prisoners of war . . .

carnival events throughout the county. "South Ronaldsay was Gay," announced *The Orcadian*. The county officially adopted the Corvette HMS *Ness*.

Orkney's fourth major wartime fundraising venture, in June, 1943, was the Wings for Victory week, aiming to raise £140,000, which was officially opened by Air Vice Marshall Raymond Collishaw, a Canadian air ace who shot down 68 German planes between 1916-1918. A crowd of 6,000 gathered in Kirkwall for the ceremony which was followed by a march past, led by the military band of the Argyll and Sutherland Highlanders, 300 men of the RAF and the RAF Regiment, 60 Royal Marines, 60 WRNS, 100 men of an Anti-Aircraft Detachment, 90 WAAFs, 60 Air Training Corps boys, 40 Girls Training Corps members, a band of the Royal Marines, 80 ratings from the Royal Naval Air Station at Hatston, 100 ATS girls, a Highland infantry company, 100 Home Guard members and a Home Guard pipe band, and 80 Army Cadet Force boys as well as hundreds of representatives of local Civil Defence and uniformed youth organisations - a total of around 1,500 people. Every island and parish had been set a financial target and, eventually, a total of more than £300,000 was pledged, enough to finance 15 Catalina flying boats for Coastal Command of the RAF, and a Spitfire.

A year later, the Salute the Soldier savings campaign coincided with the Allied D-day landings. With the opening of the Western front, large numbers of servicemen had left Orkney, but, after being inaugurated by Major General J. N. Slater, General Officer Commanding the Orkney and Shetland Defences, the week achieved investments totalling over £265,000.

Orkney's wartime savings weeks saw a total of £1,217,000 pledged. In November, 1945, a Thanksgiving Week was organised with a target of £100,000. It eventually reached £209,000 - making Orkney's total, from 1940-45, a massive £1,426,000 (an amount that can be multiplied 25 to 30 times to give an indication of a 1999 equivalent). It really was an astonishing achievement by Orcadians during very austere times.

But, back in 1941, there was still more than four years of war for Orcadians to endure, now under the leadership of Winston Churchill who had replaced Neville Chamberlain as Prime Minister in 1940. (Chamberlain was to die on November 9, 1940.) More demands had to be made on the people - by September, 1941, all men up to the age of 60 had to register for Civil Defence duties, while Orkney schoolchildren and SWRI members were recruited to collect sphagnum moss and various other wild plants, including dandelion root, and stinging nettles, for use in the preparation of medical dressings and drugs. Iron railing were requisitioned for the war effort and milk was to increase from 3d to 4d a pint, but a limited supply of oranges was available for children with the correct ration books. However, when war booty fell from the skies, the civil authorities were quick to ensure that no individuals benefited. Four island farmers who cut up and shared material from a barrage balloon they found on the shore, to use as covers for farm stacks, were fined up to £5 each.

There were other dangers to be found on the shore. Land mines had been placed around the Orkney coastline as part of local defences. They were never needed to repel invaders - although leaflets were published advising the public what to do in the event of invasion - but on Christmas Day, 1943, they claimed the life of a 20 year old Able Seaman Frank Rose, of Stanley, County Durham, who was out catching rabbits with snares. Earlier, in 1941, two 12 year old Kirkwall schoolboys were killed in a holiday accident, and two workmen died, and three were seriously injured, in an explosion as they investigated a mystery object which was washed ashore as they waited to board an Orkney ferry. The tragedy led to urgent appeals to the public not to touch objects on the beach.

Orkney, which as well as *The Orcadian* had the *Orkney Herald* newspaper, was now to have a third publication, the *Orkney Blast*, a weekly paper for the Forces which was launched on January 17, 1941, and continued publication until November 24, 1944.

Blockships were required to obstruct the channels in the eastern approaches into Scapa Flow while the construction of the barriers went ahead.

(Picture courtesy of Orkney Library photographic archive)

A Blast of fresh air

Orkney's wartime newspaper, the Orkney Blast, brought the pizzazz of Fleet Street to the islands - and can claim to be the publication that introduced the "pin-up" picture to the county.

The *Blast* - it ran to 202 issues - was aimed at the 60,000 wartime troops based in Orkney, and the original idea came from the well-known Orcadian novelist, Eric Linklater, then Major Linklater, commander of the Orkney Fortress company of the Royal Engineers (TA), and his colleague Lt Col G.N. Tuck.

The production facilities of *The Orcadian* were used with *The Orcadian* continuing to publish on Thursdays while the *Orkney Blast*, the editorial offices of which were in Stromness, came out on Fridays.

In the first issue of January 17, 1941, Eric Linklater wrote: "The need for a service newspaper in Orkney is so evident that we will not say very much about it. We are civilised people, and to civilised people, books and newspapers are necessary things. We cannot live without them. The Nazis, who hate and fear civilisation - because they do not know how to behave in a civilised world - began their campaign in Germany by burning books and suppressing newspapers. Because, as they know very well, books and newspapers are the weapons of civilisation. They can be loudspeakers for freedom, and arguments for justice. So the Nazis set out to destroy them, for Nazidom cannot exist in the same world with freedom, justice and civilisation."

In fact, Linklater was soon transferred to the War Office Directorate of Public Relations, but, by then, responsibility for the production had fallen to a young Private Gerry Meyer, who had worked in Fleet Street in his native London, and Gunner Geoffrey Halton, a journalist from the *Yorkshire Post* in Leeds.

A luckless third colleague was Bombardier Gaston du Pasquier, a veteran of World War One with more than 20 years journalistic experience. To get the articles for the first issue through to Kirkwall, he had to walk eight miles through snowdrifts from Orphir. The result was that he caught pneumonia and so ended his career on the *Orkney Blast*.

The Orcadian of the 1920s and 1930s was acknowledged as rivalling the quality of any weekly newspaper in Scotland, but the *Blast*, after the first 17 issues in broadsheet format, was to bring the tabloid look to the county, and, in May, 1941, it became the first to include pin-ups, with front page photographs of Hollywood actresses and starlets. Comedian Arthur Askey sent 1941 Christmas greetings to readers of the *Blast*, assuring them that there were worse places to celebrate the festivities.

The paper, with a weekly circulation of 6,000 but a readership three or four times greater, could claim the distinction of being the only British newspaper to reduce its cover price, from 3d to 2d, during the war.

In May, 1944, the *Blast* told of things to come, of a record breaking flight across the Atlantic when a Mosquito aircraft was reported to have covered 2,200 miles in just five hours, 40 minutes. And a month later, the *Blast* declared: "The Allies have won the battle of the beaches in Normandy and the bridgehead is solidly established."

The opening of the new front in Europe saw thousands of troops, and readers of the *Orkney Blast*, leave Orkney, and gradually the justification for a forces paper diminished until, on November 24, 1944, the final issue was published.

The man who did so much to create the unique publication would make a bigger contribution yet to Orkney journalism, however. Gerry Meyer - demobbed as Sergeant Meyer - returned to London and Fleet Street for a while but, in 1947, he returned to the islands as editor of *The Orcadian*, a role he was to play for 36 years.

Private Stanley Eldridge and an ATS girl catch up on the latest news from the *Orkney Blast*.

(Picture courtesy of Orkney Library photographic archive)

Gracie Fields featured regularly in the columns of the *Orkney Blast*. She is pictured here being welcomed to Hatston by Captain H.S.J. Fancourt in 1941.

(Picture courtesy of Orkney Library photographic archive)

Royal visitors in Scapa Flow

Both *The Orcadian* and the *Orkney Blast* covered several royal visits to the county and, in August, 1941, Orkney morale was lifted when King George VI paid his second visit to the county in less than two years. The King arrived by air "escorted by the most powerful air armada seen by Orcadians in any daylight flight since the start of hostilities," reported *The Orcadian* after scores of Spitfires and Hurricanes were seen over the county. The King, on a three day visit, toured military bases, the Lyness dockyard and saw the work of civilian contractors before, watched by a crowd of several thousand spectators - he reviewed national forces, including an inspection of the 2nd Orkney Battalion of the Home Guard. The King was to come North again with the Fleet in June, 1942.

Another Royal visit in 1941 saw the Duke of Kent in Orkney to visit various establishments of the Toc H organisation. Sadly, the Duke was one of 15 killed the following year when a Sunderland flying boat crashed en route to Iceland on war duties.

Winston Churchill sailed from, and returned to, Scapa Flow when he crossed the Atlantic for talks with the American President Franklin Roosevelt.

King George VI paid his third visit of the war to Kirkwall, and his fourth to Orkney, in March, 1943. The King, who was welcomed by Admiral Sir John Tovey, Commander-in-Chief Home Fleet, arrived in the destroyer HMS *Milne* which took him amongst the Fleet and the three 35,000 ton battleships *King George V, Duke of York* and *Howe*. He came to Kirkwall on March 20, landing at Scapa before being driven to the Royal burgh in a convoy led by PC Alfred Cromarty on his motorcycle. Big crowds had assembled in Junction Road to greet him before he continued to the West Mainland to visit the Fleet Air Arm station at Twatt. On the Saturday evening, he attended Leslie Henson's ENSA show at Flotta, and his photograph was shown in *The Orcadian* of April 1, pictured in the audience, relaxed, laughing - and smoking a cigarette!

The King was to go to sea again with the Home Fleet during four days of August that year, again coming ashore for a Naval concert and a church service. The following year, the King returned, from May 10-13, to visit the Naval base in the run-up to D-day. Another VIP visitor at the same time was General Bernard Montgomery - but what was particularly significant about that visit of 1944 was that there were three reigning monarchs in Scapa Flow at the same time: King George VI, Hakon III of Norway and King George II of Greece.

Although the main focus of Scapa Flow was always on the Royal Navy, there were other men afloat who made a significant, if often over-looked contribution to the war effort - namely the crews of the North of Scotland and Orkney and Shetland Steam Navigation Company, a company which had operated on Orkney and Shetland lifeline routes since 1790, and which was later to become part of P&O Scottish Ferries. The North company's role in World War Two saw 21 servants of the shipping line perish at sea; another four died as a result of enemy action on land or in the air; and 12 men and one woman were to be decorated for their war service.

The worst tragedy was on November 14, 1940,when the *St Catherine* was sunk by enemy air attack off Aberdeen with the loss of one passenger and 14 crew, including the master Captain James Norquoy. Three passengers and 14 crew were rescued. The *St Sunniva* was requisitioned for war service and was lost off Nova Scotia, with all hands, in February, 1943. The ss *St Clair* served as the base ship, HMS *Baldur*, at Reykjavik.

The *St Ninian* was attached to the Home Fleet in Scapa Flow and crossed the Pentland Firth 3,000 times between Lyness and Scrabster, steaming over 100,000 miles and carrying 900,000 serviceman and civilian personnel during World War Two. The *Earl of Zetland*, operating from Stromness mainly on Army personnel transport, carried another 600,000 military personnel.

And of course, the faithful steamer *St Ola* - which in March, 1942, completed 50 years service in Orkney waters - continued her regular scheduled Pentland Firth sailings throughout the war, including, on May, 1941, pulling off a "top brass" rescue when saving five occupants of a British military plane, including Vice Admiral Hamilton and his Flag Lieutenant, from the Firth. The master of the *St Ola* for 31 years, Captain George Swanson - a native of Wick who had grown up in Longhope - made over 18,000 crossings of the Pentland Firth before his retirement at the end of 1942. (Captain Swanson died aged 75 in October, 1945, but he lived long enough to be reunited with his son George who had been a prisoner of war of the Japanese.) Eighteen months before his retirement, George Swanson was honoured with the award of the MBE in the King's birthday honours list. It was just one of a significant number of military and civilian honours which were bestowed on Orkney men throughout World War Two.

This photograph featured in *The Orcadian* a week after King George VI was pictured, cigarette in hand, enjoying a concert at Flotta.
(Picture courtesy of Orkney Library photographic archive)

King George VI inspects a parade of personnel at Hatston during one of the King's several visits to Orkney over the course of World War Two. (Picture courtesy of Orkney Library photographic archive)

A line-up of aircraft at the Royal Naval Air Station at Hatston in the early days of the war. The Hatston aerodrome was completed and ready for action within weeks of the declaration of war. (Picture courtesy of Orkney Library photographic archive)

Heroes, heroines and honours

Orkney's contribution to the war effort was illustrated by the roll of honour of those who were decorated - in battle and in civilian life - for their efforts.

What follows cannot claim to be a definitive list of Orkney war heroes - if such is possible - but it is a representative sample and does show the international diversity of the foreign theatres of war in which Orcadians fought on land, at sea and in the air. And the extent of the bravery of so many is undoubted.

Others would claim no heroism; they were simply civilians doing their job, they would say. But nonetheless they more than played their part in the public service that was required to support the huge machinery of war in Orkney.

Not all were Orcadian-born - for several Orkney was an adopted home - but, as these pages reveal, in times of war, the place of one's death can become powerfully more relevant than the place of one's birth.

In fact, most of the early honours of World War Two were for civilian achievements. And, when Orkney awoke on New Year's Day, 1941, the King's honours list included no less than seven Orkney names - the most ever decorated in any single list of the 20th century. Orkney's Lord Lieutenant Alfred Baikie, by now aged 80 but still president of the Orkney Territorial Army Association, became a Companion of the Order of the Bath (CB), while Orkney's Chief Constable, Wilson Colin Campbell, the architect of the county's civil defence preparations, became a CBE. Also made a CBE was a man who was to be honoured twice during the war: Thomas McKenzie, who for nearly 20 years had worked on salvaging the German fleet from Scapa Flow, first for Cox and Danks and then, for ten years, as manager of Metal Industries at Lyness. One of McKenzies's colleagues, diver Jimmy Thomson of Lyness, also became an MBE, while South Ronaldsay shipmaster Captain Malcolm Gray was made an OBE. The British Empire Medal was also awarded to two members of the local telephone service - Robert Duncan Crighton, Chief Inspector of Telephone Communications for Orkney, and Miss Robina Gunn, supervising telephonist at Kirkwall telephone exchange. (She was a sister of Professor James Gunn of Oxford University.)

It was not long however before those in the front line would be honoured for their courage, and a month later Lt Erlend Clouston, the younger son of Orkney's county convener Joseph Storer Clouston, was awarded the Distinguished Service Cross for "courage and resource" in sinking an enemy submarine.

That same year, the Royal Navy and the Fleet Air Arm avenged the loss of HMS *Hood* by sinking the "unsinkable" German battleship *Bismark*. Three Fleet Air Arm men from HMS *Sparrowhawk* at Hatston were honoured for their "gallantry, daring and skill" in the operation: Commander Geoffrey Rotherham (DSO), Lt Noel Goddard (DSC), and Leading Airman John Armstrong (DSM).

Orkney RAF station commanding officer, Acting Group Captain Geoffrey Ambler, of Hobbister, Orphir, who already held the Air Force Cross, became an OBE. In June, 1942, he was to be appointed commandant of the Royal Observer Corps.

A former Stromness Academy pupil William Ollason, son of Suleskerry lighthouse keeper William Ollason, received both the DFC (in 1941) and the DSO (in 1943) during his wartime RAF service. In 1948, Squadron Leader Ollason was promoted by the RAF to Senior Air Staff Officer for Scotland.

Honours came not only from the British government. Merchant Navy Captain John Cromarty, from Stove in Sanday, whose first job at sea had been with the Orkney Steam Navigation Company, was awarded the Polish Cross of Valour. He had rescued 500 Polish soldiers and refugees from the French port of Nantes and safely carried them to Britain through mined waters, although attacked by artillery and enemy bombs. His ship was the last to leave Nantes before the Germans arrived and, on berthing at Plymouth, he received a letter of congratulations on his heroism from the British Foreign Secretary Anthony Eden.

The pride in receiving an honour could be tragically short lived. Able Seaman Hugh Hughson, of Greentoft, Eday, was awarded the British Empire Medal in 1941 for his efforts to save his ship that had been torpedoed. Six months later, he died on active service.

Captain George Swanson, who, as master of the *St Ola*, risked mines and enemy attacks as he continued the daily crossing of the Pentland Firth, was made an MBE in the 1941 King's Birthday Hours List, as was Mr George Thomson, secretary of Stromness lifeboat. Six months later, Orkney's Medical Officer of Health, Dr Walter Bannerman, a Cornishman who had been in the islands since 1924, became an OBE for his services to civil defence. At the start of World War Two, he had become responsible for arrangements for the treatment of civilian war casualties in Orkney. (In that same honours list, Gilbert Archer, chairman of R. Garden Ltd of Kirkwall, was knighted to become Sir Gilbert Archer).

Another military decoration saw Leading Seaman David Cusator of South Ronaldsay receive the Distinguished Service Medal for his work on HM submarine *Torbay* which sank two enemy ships in the Middle East. South Ronaldsay was well represented in the war at sea. Captain Alfred Cromarty, aged 35 and blind in one eye, from Banks, Herston, was made an OBE after one of the most astonishing feats of endurance of the war when, after his ship was torpedoed in 1941, he led his 49 officers and men to safety in the West Indies after 13 days and 900 miles in open boats.

It was in the Mediterranean that a Stromness civilian became part of military folklore in one of the most brutal theatres of war in Europe. John Chalmers, who served his apprenticeship with Spence's bakery in Stromness, became known as the "Brave Baker of Malta" where, as proprietor of Blackley's bakers and caterers in Valetta, he was at the centre of that heroic island's resistance through three years of siege conditions in which German and Italian bombs left a scene of devastation. "Mr Chalmers has helped to make history in Malta," General Sir William Dobbie was to say later. "Despite the worst blitzes to which the island has been subjected, he never failed to produce the foodstuffs so vitally needed."

Another hero of Malta was Group Captain William Satchell who later, at the end of war and stationed at Grimsetter, was to buy Lynnfield House in Kirkwall and convert it to an hotel. Group Captain Satchell was awarded the DSO for his part in the Battle of Malta. In one operation, he led a formation of four Hurricanes and three Spitfires against more than 100 enemy aircraft, of which 14 were shot down without any British losses. He himself shot down three German planes. (However his war record obviously cut no ice with those heroes of the Orkney County Licensing Court - when he first applied for a drinks licence for the Lynnfield, it was refused and he had to wait another six months before guests could drink with their meals.) In September, 1947, Group Captain Satchell returned to RAF duties as commanding officer of the RAF station in Ein Shemer, Palestine.

Vice-Admiral Lionel Wells, Flag Officer Commanding Orkney and Shetland, was made a Knight Commander of the Order of the Bath (KCB) in the New Year's Honours list of 1943, while Orkney's deputy Chief Constable, and later to be Chief Constable, Gathorne Cheyne, received the British Empire Medal.

As a turnout of thousands witnessed ceremonial parades to mark the third anniversary of the Orkney Home Guard units,

Anti-aircraft gunners prepare for action at their wartime emplacement in Stromness. (Picture from the files of *The Orcadian*)

two local Home Guard officers were honoured - Major Robert Scarth of Binscarth, Finstown, became an OBE while Lt John Dickson, in civilian life the Kirkwall Union Bank agent, was made an MBE.

Captain Ted Fresson, the pioneer of Orkney's civilian air services and managing director of Scottish Airways, now engaged in vital work for the domestic war effort, became an OBE, while Sergeant Major John Chalmers, Royal Artillery, of Brettovale, Harray, but stationed in Flotta, was made an MBE.

Harry Taylor, a salvage officer in Orkney for ten years and son-in-law of Thomas McKenzie, head of Metal Industries in Lyness, was made an MBE and diver James Thomson, of East Rinnigal, Hoy, received the British Empire Medal, while salvage boat skipper Donald McKay, son of the Longhope harbourmaster, was mentioned in dispatches after a feat of bravery reported as "without parallel in war."

Signalman William Sutherland of Graham Place, Stromness, was awarded the Military Medal for heroism in North Africa, where, throughout 48 hours of heavy and continuous shelling, he kept wireless communications open in an anti-tank ditch in which his battalion HQ was sited.

Back at home, Lady Wallace of Holodyke, Harray, formerly Miss Augusta Clouston, the only sister of county convener Storer Clouston, was made an OBE in the 1944 New Year Honours list. Her husband was Sir David Wallace, a leading Edinburgh surgeon. In 1946, she was further honoured with the CBE.

Private Bernard Edwards, 2nd Battalion Orkney Home Guard, who worked for Metal Industries at Lyness, was awarded the

BEM, as was William Kelly, foreman of the electrical branch, Lyness Naval Base. Papa Westray-born Merchant Navy Captain Thomas Harcus was made an MBE in recognition of his 46 years at sea.

Lt Magnus Work, Craigiefield House, St Ola, was awarded the Distinguished Service Cross for gallantry in the face of the enemy. Early in the war he was senior officer of a number of armed trawlers based in Orkney. Then for three years, he had been in command of HMS *Dahlia*, a corvette serving in Northern and Atlantic waters.

As Allied forces landed again in Europe, Bombardier Alex Wentworth, one of the original members of the Kirkwall Home Guard, was decorated with the Military Medal for bravery on the field in the D-day operations.

Lt Colonel Donald Robertson of the Seaforth Highlanders, the youngest son of the late county clerk of Orkney, Duncan J. Robertson, of Crantit House, St Ola, was killed in action in France. A qualified solicitor in his father's legal practice, he had served for 15 years in Bengal before joining the Army at the outbreak of World War Two.

The following month, his namesake, Lt Duncan J.T. Robertson, Royal Artillery, achieved a notable family double when he was awarded the Military Cross for gallantry in India, thus emulating his father, Major H.N. Robertson MC, of Woodwick, Evie.

And, in the air, Flying Officer George Clubley, then aged just 22, of Melsetter, Hoy, was awarded the Distinguished Flying Cross (DFC) for his service in the RAF. He was engaged to a Stromness Academy schoolteacher.

In the King's Birthday Honours list of 1944, Major Charles Calder, Royal Artillery, youngest son of Orkney vice-convener Alex Calder, of Sebay, Tankerness, was made an MBE. Petty Officer Robert Greig, of Alfred Street, Stromness, received the BEM, while Thomas Sutherland, of Melsetter, Hoy, was also awarded the BEM in recognition of his services to the Admiralty. And, back in Civvy Street, Miss Ann Tulloch, from North Ronaldsay, matron of Stobhill Hospital, Glasgow, for ten years, was made an OBE.

Mrs Mary Work, wife of Captain A.L. Work of Craigiefield House, St Ola, was made an MBE, in recognition of her wartime work as county organiser of the Women's Voluntary Service, as was Major Charles Hourston, Beaquoy Farm, Dounby, Officer Commanding B Company of the 1st Orkney Battalion of the Home Guard.

Meanwhile, at the start of 1945, Scapa Flow salvage expert Thomas McKenzie, whose family still lived in Lyness, and who had been made a CBE in 1941, was honoured again. Now Commodore McKenzie, he was made a Companion of the Order of the Bath (CB) for his distinguished service in organising salvage operations in liberated French ports after the Allied D-day invasion. Lt Colonel James Goodsir, a native of South Ronaldsay, and Assistant Director of Ordnance Supplies in the Orkney and Shetland Defences since 1944, became an OBE. John Dundas Neilson, Avonlea, Finstown, engineer in charge of the radio communication station at the top of Wideford Hill, was also awarded the British Empire Medal, the same decoration received by Chief Petty Officer Dan Kirkpatrick, Melsetter, Hoy, for "zeal and devotion to duty." Another to receive the BEM, at an investiture at Buckingham Palace, was Chief Petty Officer John Banks of Smiddy House, Burray.

Flt Lt Ronald Thomson, of Thoms Street, Kirkwall, was awarded the Distinguished Flying Cross for fortitude, courage and devotion to duty, while Merchant Navy Captain Charles Smith, of Franklin Road, Stromness, was made an OBE for the role he played in one of the most important meetings of World War Two. After a career of 40 years at sea, he was master of the ship that took Winston Churchill's party to the Yalta Conference with Stalin and Roosevelt in 1945.

Also in 1945, in Winston Churchill's resignation Honours list, the man who was MP for Orkney and Shetland throughout the war, Basil Neven-Spence, was knighted to become Sir Basil.

Another civilian honour a year later was that of Orkney county surgeon Mr Ian McClure who became an OBE. A veteran of the Royal Naval Air Service in World War One, Mr McClure had served as surgeon since 1928, the county's first appointment to that role.

* * *

One of the least likely and unsung heroes of World War Two - but, nonetheless, one who helped to save the lives of scores of Allied servicemen - was the Italian Constante Zanre who ran Kirkwall's Central Cafe in Albert Street for many pre-war years before handing over to his brother Livio.

Such was his contribution, it was revealed after the war, that Constante Zanre was sentenced by the Germans to be shot to death, although, fortunately, he lived to tell the tale.

At the outbreak of World War Two, Livio Zanre was still in this country and, as an Italian, he was interned for the duration of hostilities in the Isle of Man. But his brother Constante, and his wife, had returned to Italy for a summer holiday in 1939 and the outbreak of war prevented his return to Britain. The result was that he was regarded by the Italian fascist regime as a British sympathiser and he was placed under open arrest by the Italian authorities, his family's radio set confiscated and his liberty and movements severely restricted.

However, despite the watch kept on him, first by Mussolini's forces and then the Germans, Constante Zanre was able to link up with underground resistance movements of the Partisans to help soldiers, sailors and airmen of the British Commonwealth to escape from, or evade capture by the enemy, from the time of the invasion of Italy in 1943, through to the end of 1944. He aided escapees by guiding them through enemy

Mr Livio Zanre who ran Kirkwall's Central Cafe in Albert Street for several years, either side of the war.
(Picture courtesy of Orkney Library photographic archive)

lines to Allied units, hiding them in Italian "safe houses", feeding and clothing them and helping to provide money and documents.

Mr Zanre and his wife ran the risk of death if caught during the curfew imposed by Mussolini, and later by the Germans who occupied the north of Italy following the collapse of Mussolini's regime. For months he outwitted the enemy forces but one night he was caught in Borgotaro, Parma, and he was condemned by the Germans to be shot. His life was spared, it was reported, by the intervention of influential Italians but possibly also by the arrival of Allied forces, for the Allied victory swiftly followed.

At the end of the war, and the Zanres' return to Britain, his contribution was officially recognised with the presentation of a signed certificate from Field Marshall Harold Alexander, Supreme Allied Commander, Mediterranean Theatre. Alexander - who was the last officer to leave Dunkirk in 1940 - had fought in North Africa, Burma and Italy, and, in 1952, became Lord Alexander of Tunis before serving as the British Minister of Defence from 1952-54. His commendation read: "This certificate is awarded to Constante Zanre as a token of gratitude for, and appreciation of, the help given to the sailors, soldiers and airmen of the British Commonwealth of Nations, which enabled them to escape from, or evade capture by, the enemy - H.R. Alexander, Field Marshall". After the war, Constante Zanre continued in business in Forres, Morayshire, while his brother Livio and his wife ran the family business in Kirkwall, though Livio, who was said never to have forgiven the British authorities for his wartime internment, later returned to Italy to live.

(Incidentally, another Italian resident - in fact the son of an Italian father and a German mother - was Carlo "Charlie" Rigolo who had lived in Orkney for 40 years at the outbreak of World War Two and was spared internment on the account of his age. Charlie, who originally arrived in the county as a fairground worker and who figured at local fairs as a strongman, weight lifter and knife thrower, died at the age of 82 at Kirkwall's County Home in November, 1943.)

1943

1944

1945

Hollywood film star Greer Garson - who was the daughter of an Orcadian - won the 1943 Oscar for best actress for the film *Mrs Miniver*.

Although she was born in County Down, Ireland, she was the daughter of George Garson, whose family came from Orkney's West Mainland.

She moved to England with her mother following her father's death. She graduated from the University of London with honours before studying at the University of Grenoble in France.

Her theatrical career began at Birmingham Repertory Theatre at £4 a week. She rose to star with Laurence Olivier in the West End, and after starring in the film *Goodbye Mr Chips* she went to Hollywood, co-starring with Robert Taylor in *Remember* and then appearing with Laurence Olivier in the film of the Jane Austen classic *Pride and Prejudice*.

Mrs Miniver also won the Academy awards for best film and best director in 1943.

* * *

George Bernard Shaw, one of the great writers of the 20th century, wrote to *The Times*, following a visit to Orkney, urging that the power of the Pentland Firth should be harnessed in a massive hydro scheme to generate electricity for the nation.

* * *

The Wideford Hill race - from Kirkwall to the top of Wideford Hill and back - was revived again after last being run in 1895. The race of approximately five miles was won by Corporal Alec Munro in a time of 35 minutes 16 seconds - beating the record that had stood since 1893 when James Cormack, a Deerness man who later went to the USA, did 37 minutes 10 seconds.

* * *

The death of Miss Jessie Harper - joint owner of the Standing Stones Hotel, Stenness - was mourned by many distinguished friends including famous politicians, military leaders and the writer George Bernard Shaw.

She and her sister Christina took over the hotel in 1936, but the Orkney licensing authorities continually blocked their applications for a drinks licence. In 1946, the Standing Stones Hotel was purchased by the North of Scotland and Orkney and Shetland Steam Navigation Company - and granted a licence at the first time of asking.

* * *

A presentation was made to Miss Mary Stove, of Victoria Street, Kirkwall, who had taught at St Magnus Cathedral Sunday School for 50 years. Six months later, she was fatally injured in a road accident, aged 72.

A Christmas day fracas in Finstown led to one serviceman being killed and another appearing at Kirkwall Sheriff Court accused of murder, later reduced to culpable homicide. A 46 year old man from the London area was sentenced to six months.

* * *

Kirkwall Sheriff Court decided that it had jurisdiction to deal with offences committed in the USSR when a seaman from a British ship appeared, accused of being drunk in Murmansk. He was given 28 days jail after the court heard he had been locked up on board his ship and handed over to the civilian authorities on return to Kirkwall.

* * *

A total of 34 people died in accidents in Orkney in just the two years 1943-44. These included 14 fatalities in road accidents, 12 drownings and six fatal accidents at work.

* * *

Orkney's Sheriff Principal Sir John Watson - a former Solicitor General for Scotland under Ramsay MacDonald's government of 1929 - died at the age of 60 while travelling on an Edinburgh - London train.

A graduate of both Glasgow and Edinburgh Universities, he was called to the bar in 1909, and served in World War One in the Royal Artillery and, later, the Royal Flying Corps. He was knighted in 1931, when he became Orkney's Sheriff Principal.

* * *

Hundreds of people flocked to the Kirkwall pier when a school of 50 dolphins invaded the bay.

* * *

Orkney education committee agreed that notebooks and jotters could be provided for pupils "now that slates were so unsatisfactory and scarce".

* * *

Sir Robert Hamilton - Orkney's Liberal MP for 13 years 1922-1935, and a former Chief Justice of British East Africa - died at the age of 76. He was survived by Lady Hamilton - the former Miss Gertrude Williamson of Kirkwall.

* * *

Orkney's county convener, and popular novelist and historian, Joseph Storer Clouston, of Smoogro, Orphir, died at the age of 74. He was succeeded as convener by Alexander Calder, councillor for St Andrews and Deerness. Mr P.N. Sutherland Graeme CBE of Graemeshall - the retired Deputy Judge Advocate General who returned to Orkney on retirement - became the new vice-convener.

The freedom of the burgh of Kirkwall was bestowed on three of Orkney's most eminent men. They were:

Rev Andrew Campbell who in 1945 became the first active Orkney minister to preside over the Church of Scotland when he was chosen as Moderator of the General Assembly. He had served as minister for the parish of Evie since moving from Glasgow in 1936.

Mr John White, the retiring Sheriff Clerk of Orkney, former Provost of Kirkwall, chairman of Orkney education committee and Chief Air Raid Warden of the county in World War Two.

Mr John Mooney, retired secretary of R. Garden Ltd, but best known for his historical researches as author of books on St Magnus, the Cathedral and the burgh of Kirkwall.

* * *

Christmas Day saw a Woman's Ba' - the first time such a game for females had been staged - with between 20-30 women divided equally between Uppies and Doonies. There appeared to be male opposition to the game and, at one stage, the ba' was stolen. It was eventually recovered and the Uppies took the honours after 90 minutes with the ba' going to Miss Margaret Yule. Earlier it had been the briefest Boys' Ba' on record - just four minutes.

* * *

The promise of "cheap" electricity for most of the Orkney Mainland was revealed as the Hydro-Electric Development (Scotland) Act gave powers to the North of Scotland Hydro-Electric Board to extend the county's mains power network. The Hydro board would take over Kirkwall Town Council's municipal electricity scheme, which had functioned since 1923, and offer the chance of mains electricity to two thirds of the Mainland.

* * *

Canon Edward Kissack, Archdeacon of Orkney and Rector of St Olaf Episcopal Church, Kirkwall, retired after 21 years in Orkney. A native of the Isle of Man, and a founder of the Sea Cadets in Orkney, he was succeeded by Rev R. A. Whitton.

* * *

New efforts were begun by the Scottish Agricultural Organisation Society to revive the seaweed industry in the isles where islanders were promised £3 15s a ton for dried kelp. It was anticipated that Westray, Stronsay, Sanday and North Ronaldsay could, between them, raise nearly 1,000 tons over the winter.

* * *

Mr William Heddle retired as Kirkwall Town Clerk after 43 years - to be succeeded by Mr Edward Hendry from Stirlingshire.

Orcadians in the jungles of Burma

Tragically, some had no opportunity to be honoured for heroism, or public service. Mrs Archibald Sutherland, a 23 year old wife of a lighthouse keeper in Fair Isle, was killed, shot by an enemy aircraft that strafed the island in December, 1941, and seven men - including James Bracewell, proprietor of the Preston Salvage Company, and skipper George Oag - perished when their salvage vessel was lost in Orkney waters.

But a new concern by the end of 1941 was that Japan had entered the war, and Orcadians anxiously awaited news of loved ones known to be in the Far East. It was to be a traumatic wait for, in many cases, families received no news for months, even years; in one case three years. It was in July, 1942, that information reached Orkney that Captain Charles Shearer, from Kirkwall, was interned by the Japanese at Stanley Prison, Hong Kong - one of a number of civilian internees. It was November, 1943, when news arrived of Orkney's first woman prisoner of war, Nurse Alice Rossie, who had been taken prisoner by the Japanese 20 months earlier, on the fall of Singapore. Her sister was Nan Rossie of Stromness, the former international hockey player.

Another illustration of the part played by Orcadian women in the war came in February, 1944, when Nursing Sister Kathleen Hewison Walker, aged 24, of Meadowbank, Westray, whose father had been the island doctor for many years, was reported missing at sea. She was in the Queen Alexandra's Imperial Nursing Service and had served in East Africa during 1943.

Notification of casualties, and those taken prisoner, was by no means an exact science. Anguish could be turned to joy, and vice versa, within days. Driver Peter Leslie, of the Royal Corps of Signals, became the second Orcadian prisoner of war to escape from the enemy after a rescue operation mounted by British troops in Libya. In civil life, an ironmongery assistant with James Flett and Sons, he was reported missing in action from November 25, 1941. His wife Maggie was informed on January 23, 1942, that he was a prisoner in the hands of the enemy, and then, on January 26, she was officially notified of his rescue.

The family of Sapper Robert Sinclair, Brigend, Firth, were to learn that their son was injured, but alive, after wrongly being told by the War Office that he had been killed in action in Burma.

It's a far cry from temperate Orkney to the mountains and jungles of Burma but that's where many Orcadians were to fight their war. Many of the anti - aircraft gunners who originally joined the Territorial Army in Orkney, were sent abroad when the 226 Caithness and Orkney Anti-Aircraft Battery became part of the 101 Heavy Anti - Aircraft Regiment of the Royal Artillery. They arrived in India on July 1, 1943, and moved into Burma in October, 1944, coming under the command of Lt General Sir Montague Stopford's famous 33 Indian Corps. Remarkably, at least one Orcadian served throughout the war in the Far East in the French Foreign Legion - Leslie Smith, who ran a tobacconist's shop in Stromness.

It was not only overseas that Orcadians encountered other nationalities. The first Americans of war arrived at HMS *Sparrowhawk* at Hatston in early 1942 for training. Then in one of the most remarkable achievements of the war, the USS *Wasp* sailed from Scapa Flow, maintaining a speed of more than 20 knots throughout a memorable operation to take aid to the besieged island of Malta. Thirty Spitfires were delivered to Malta - but within 30 minutes 25 were bombed.

Orcadians of the 226 HAA Battery in Galinchee, India, in 1943. Back row, from Left: Jim Kelday, Thorfinn Keldie, Jim (Tiny) Leonard, Malcolm Rosie, John Wallace and Jim Ritchie. Front: Tommy Tait, Izat (Chuffy) Muir and William Marwick.

(Picture courtesy of Orkney Library photographic archive)

Stars of stage, screen and sport

Orkney played host to a "Who's Who" of stars during World War Two. It did not actually rival Broadway but, after a couple of years of war, Orkney could boast enough cinemas and theatres to accommodate more than 7,000 people in a single night.

All the major military bases had their own theatres - the pride of which was the Naval cinema in Lyness, not only the biggest in Orkney but one of the biggest in Britain, closely followed by the Fleet cinema in Flotta. HMS *Sparrowhawk* at Hatston had its Empire Theatre, and RAF Bignold Park could claim its New Theatre. There was a Garrison Theatre at Crocksness in Hoy and another, the biggest Army hall in the town, in Stromness, sited on the Market Green and accommodating 1,000 people. Lyness also had the Globe Theatre and Stromness the Craigmillar Theatre.

The Stromness Garrison Theatre opened in July, 1942. It was reported that it should have been ready months earlier - but vital construction materials were sent to Iceland by mistake!

In reality, they were giant prefabricated Nissen huts, but that did not detract from the calibre of the artists who appeared on stage. Throughout the war, a legion of international stars made the journey North to entertain the Forces and Orcadians too, if they were fortunate enough to be invited as a guest.

As well as regular shows organised by the Forces entertainments organisation ENSA, there were celebrity concerts starring musicians and entertainers as diverse as American violinist Yehudi Menuhin, comedians Flanagan and Allen, George Formby and Will Fyffe, theatre and music hall stars Evelyn Laye and Phyllis Monkman and, probably the greatest draw of them all, Gracie Fields. When the Lancashire singer and actress performed at Hatston, more than 5,000 servicemen and women paid 3d each to pack the cavernous converted hangar.

Some of the stars who came were in uniform - like the Hollywood actor Douglas Fairbanks Junior who spent some time in Scapa Flow aboard an American ship.

Not all the attractions were stars of stage and screen. In July, 1941, the Moderator of the General Assembly of the Church of Scotland, Rt Rev J. Hutchison Cockburn, minister of Dunblane Cathedral, held a service at the Lyness cinema, accompanied by a band of the Royal Marines.

An astonishing total of 10,000 people heard Miss Lai Po Kan, a graduate of both Hong Kong University and Oxford, who, in a lecture tour of Orkney organised by the British Ministry of Information, spoke on the subject of her native China at 71 engagements in 17 days. Another to visit Orkney on a lecture tour was *News of the World* sports writer Joe Binks, who in 1902 set the then world record for running the mile of 4 minutes 16 seconds. By the start of World War Two, the world mile record was down to 4 minutes 6.8 seconds, held by Sydney Wooderson.

Kirkwall, of course, already had the Albert Kinema (wartime matinee prices 3d, 6d and 1s according to seating) before the outbreak of war, but in June, 1943, a new picture house, seating 350, opened in Holm. The Strond cinema, built and owned by Mr John Marwick, provided entertainment for the hundreds of men engaged on building the Churchill Barriers, but after just 18 months, it was destroyed by fire in January, 1945. Another picture house was the Kirkwall Naval cinema, based in the Temperance Hall.

And it was in this building that the Kirkwall Arts Club was founded, an organisation that was to thrive until the end of the century, and hopefully will continue yet. A young Sub Lieutenant Donald Hewlett, then stationed at HMS *Sparrowhawk* at Hatston, but later to become a household name as a television actor with such series as "It Ain't Half Hot Mum," was the inspiration behind the club.

It was in October, 1943, that he first voiced the idea and became secretary of the organising committee. It quickly came to fruition and in February, 1944, it was officially opened by Vernon Bartlett, a well known broadcaster who was MP for Bridgwater in Somerset. One of the first speakers at the Arts Club was Dame Sybil Thorndyke. Others to visit the club were John Mills and Bernard Miles. Donald Hewlett even persuaded Sir John Geilgud to be club patron - and, in September, 1944, he welcomed Yehudi Menuhin who gave a public performance as part of an Orkney tour for units of the Fleet.

Donald Hewlett returned to Orkney, with his family, for the 40th anniversary celebrations of Kirkwall Arts Club, and later reminisced with *The Orcadian* about those early days. He recalled: "I wrote this rather pompous letter saying that if anyone was interested in the club they should get in touch with me. I got an amazing number of replies. I set a subscription of a penny a day, and arranged it so that we were able to wear civilian clothes."

He managed to secure the gift of a baby grand piano, and the loan of paintings to adorn the walls. "So there we were - we had about 200 members and we held exhibitions and play readings there and put on shows in the theatre above. It became very popular and eventually we were touring shows to the islands and places such as Twatt aerodrome and the Home Fleet. I wrote pantomimes and we toured with them as well."

When he was eventually transferred, Donald Hewlett's next port of call was Singapore and there he started a similar organisation which became the Singapore Stage Club. But setting up the Kirkwall Arts Club had been, he said, "one of the most worthwhile things I have ever done."

"It provided so much entertainment for people. We had a lot of fun, a terrific lot of fun, and we did some very good productions as well. I love the place very much and I love the people. I was shown immense kindness when I was here."

Astonishingly, in March, 1945, 1,000 people had to be turned away as 1,500 queued to see a concert by the band of the Queen's Own Cameron Highlanders at the Kirkwall Naval cinema.

The curtain came down on the Naval cinema four months later, but the Temperance Hall was later to be converted into the Kirkwall Arts Theatre. The last production at the New Theatre, Bignold Park, was the pantomime *Cinderella* in January, 1945, the last ENSA show to tour Orkney was in January, 1946, while the Garrison Theatres in Crocksness, Hoy, and Stromness both closed in July, 1946. The Stromness building was handed over to the town council and suggested as a possible swimming pool, but was demolished in 1947.

And by then Orkney was once again enjoying its fair share of civilian entertainment. In May, 1946, for example, top of the bill in Stromness was a musical revue act entitled, with not so much a thought of political correctness, the Alabama Coons. At the start of 1947, members of the Polish Army Choir - on tour in Orkney following an appearance at the Albert Hall, London - found themselves trapped in snowdrifts caused by blizzards in Holm, returning from a concert in St Margaret's Hope, and were rescued and entertained to a clapshot supper at the farm of Knockhall by Mr and Mrs Thomas Drever. And October, 1947, saw the opening of what was arguably the county's best known and most popular venue of the 20th century - the Cosmo ballroom in Junction Road, Kirkwall. The first Orkney-Shetland inter-county dancing competition was staged there on November 26, 1947, and won by Orkney.

But the biggest attendances in wartime Orkney were not for the stars of stage, screen and concert hall, but for football matches. The facilities for sport were extensive with some of the military bases having as many as six sports pitches, and they were graced by the top names of the day.

Sir Matt Busby, one of the giants of 20th century British football, was a physical training instructor, stationed on the island of Flotta. As a player with Liverpool and Manchester City he had already appeared in two FA Cup Finals in the 1930s when he was posted to Orkney where he helped to train several local players who took part in regimental matches throughout the islands. A wartime colleague of Busby was Joe Bruce of Shapinsay, himself one of Orkney's finest players, who credited the great man with having the hardest kick he ever witnessed. It was at the end of the war that Busby was appointed manager of Manchester United and laid the foundations for what was to become the biggest football club in the world.

But, in 1942, Busby was part of what was probably the finest football team to grace an Orkney pitch, the Scottish Command XI who played three teams of locally-based Service players at Haybrake Park, Hoy, Bignold Park, Kirkwall, and in Stromness, winning 7-0, 10-1 and 8-1 respectively.

The Scottish Command squad of players who toured Orkney that year were: goalkeeper John Moodie (Raith Rovers); backs Jimmy Carabine (Third Lanark), Jack Howe (Derby County), Alec Millar (East Fife); half backs Bobby Hardisty (Wolves), Alec Sharp and George Sutherland (both Partick Thistle), Jock

Thomson (Everton) and captain Matt Busby; forwards Bobby Campbell (Falkirk), Tommy Walker (Hearts), Peter Simpson (East Fife), Archie Gourlay (Partick Thistle), Albert Juliussen (Huddersfield) and Alec Herd (Manchester City).

A crowd of 6,500 saw the game at the Bignold Park, a game that Jimmy Carabine was excused so that he could go trout fishing at Stenness with Mr Douglas Bowie, president of the Scottish FA. The local Army teams also had some professional players including Tait (East Fife), Hickman (Aston Villa), Phil Watson (Blackpool) and Connelly (Bradford). The former Stromness Athletic and Orkney county winger Norman Robertson also played. Unfortunately, the Scottish Command XI were unable to play Orkney's Naval Base XI who were unbeaten at the time, underlined a week later when the Royal Navy beat the Army 4-2 at Haybrake Park, Hoy.

The Scottish Command team returned to Orkney the following year, this time captained by Tommy Walker of Hearts and Scotland, but including several of the squad of 1942. At Lyness, the visitors beat an Army Select XI 4-1, with Stevenson from Celtic playing for the Army team. At Stromness, Scottish Command beat an Orkney Services team 5-2, and at Hatston Farm, Kirkwall, a crowd of up to 3,000 saw Archie Gourlay of

Members of the Kirkwall Arts Club, founded by Lt Donald Hewlett, who is pictured on the right in the middle row.

(Picture courtesy of Orkney Library photographic archive)

Partick Thistle score all four goals as Scottish Command beat a Combined Services XI 4-0 in a match in which 18 of the 22 players had been professionals in pre-war civilian life.

Boxing was another sport enjoying its hey day at the time. Boxing greats Jimmy Wilde and Benny Lynch were just two of those who passed through Orkney in World War Two.

Regular boxing tournaments were staged at the recreation hall of Baldry, Yerburgh and Hutchinson at Lyness - including the first "Championship of Orkney." Gunner Jim Cowie, a former featherweight champion of Scotland, was one of the boxers who was locally based, but it was Aircraftman Bobby Marshall who was crowned featherweight champion of Orkney after beating Lance Corporal Bernard Stowe. Marshall and Stowe later boxed a draw in a £10-a-side return challenge match.

Representatives of other sports came and went. The Welsh international badminton and table tennis player Joan Morton was stationed with the WRNS in the county - in fact, she married Lt Desmond Brown, Royal Marines, in Orkney in 1942. Al Murray, who held the Scottish Amateur Weightlifting 11 stone title for three consecutive years up to the war, was stationed with the Royal Artillery in the islands in 1940. From Thornton in Fife, he was said to have performed the remarkable feat, which had never been equalled in the country, apparently, of tearing a pack of 52 playing cards into 16 parts in 59 seconds.

But despite the influx of sporting stars into the county, the final spotlight was to fall on a native Orcadian who achieved some of Orkney's highest sporting accolades of the 20th century.

Sanday wrestler Tom Ward, who represented Britain in the 1936 Olympic Games and Scotland in the 1938 Empire Games, returned to Orkney at the end of the war and took part in an exhibition bout at the Temperance Hall, Kirkwall, in aid of "Welcome Home" funds. His gallant opponent was Bill Langskaill, a drummer of the Orkney Home Guard Pipe Band!

The second barrier, from Lamb Holm, providing a road link to South Ronaldsay and Burray for the first time.

(Picture courtesy of Orkney Library photographic archive)

The tide of battle turns

Orkney's infantry regiment, the Seaforth Highlanders, fought at the Battle of E1 Alamein in North Africa in October, 1942, as many an Orcadian was to be laid to rest in foreign fields. Squadron Leader John Harrold from Kirkwall, who had served in World War One with the Royal Flying Corps, was to die in Port Sudan, while 21 year old Sergeant Pilot Leonard Sutherland from Stromness was killed on active service in the Mediterranean and his funeral held in Gibraltar. Pilot Officer Fred Buchanan of Kirkwall, an Orkney intercounty footballer before the war, was killed in an RAF bombing mission on Hamburg. His father had been Orkney's pre-war German vice-consul.

And, by the end of 1942, Orkney's 26th prisoner of war was reported.

British and Canadian troops who invaded Italy effectively signalled that country's exit from the war in 1943 - although 20 German divisions still controlled the North - and hopes were prompted for the release of Orkney prisoners of war. However, luckless Orcadian Gunner James Manson, one of 30,000 British POWs freed by the Italians, was captured a week later by the Germans and transferred to Stalag IVb in Germany, it was reported.

December, 1943, produced a footnote in history for the one mile long island of Auskerry when an Oxford trainer aircraft, on a flight from Aberdeenshire and piloted by a young Canadian, Sergeant Donald Franko, crash landed in a storm on the tiny isle, the first time there had been an aircraft on Auskerry. The pilot escaped injury but bad weather then marooned him there for 12 days, during which time he was looked after by local lighthouse keeper George Mainland and his wife - including being entertained to Christmas dinner. (In 1999, at the age of 73, Donald Franko made a sentimental return journey to the island to see the scene of his narrow escape.)

However, the tide of war was turning. When, in March, 1944, Orkney anti-aircraft gunners brought down a Junkers 88 aircraft - three of the German crew were picked up by RAF launch - it was the first time they had fired a shot in anger for four months. For the first time in the war, as service personnel moved away, the Ayre Hotel in Kirkwall, owned by Mr and Mrs Robert Matches, was able to reopen to the public.

In June, 1944, the security of the county was so assured that Orkney's "Foreign Legion" - the 2nd Orkney Battalion of the Home Guard, so nicknamed because of the many "South" civilian workers in its ranks, and the only Orkney battalion to be inspected by the King - was to be disbanded, said the War Office, as major civil engineering works in the islands came to an end.

In November, 1944, the entire Home Guard was stood down, but not before local members had first raised more than £4,100 in a Red Cross Week fundraising campaign. CQMS George Rosie and Lance Corporal Walter Haywood, both from Kirkwall, and Private David Hourston, Harray, represented Orkney at the "standing down" parade in London.

A parade of Orkney Home Guard members, past and present, was also held on December 3, 1944, in Kirkwall. A muster of 550 men in miserable weather marched from the Bignold Park, where they were inspected by Major General J.N. Slater, General Officer Commanding Orkney and Shetland Defences, to the Market Cross where Lord Lieutenant Alfred Baikie took the salute before the men gave up their weapons. Marching in the Harray platoon was former Local Defence Volunteer James Miller, a veteran of the Boer War, who was aged over 70.

The might of the Allied advance in Europe was to bring some consolation, at the start of 1945, for the news of casualties, and more Orcadian prisoners of war, in Burma and the Far East. In February, 1945, after four and a half years as a prisoner of the Germans, Driver Alfred Marwick, of the Royal Corps of Signals, arrived home in Kirkwall. He arrived in a week of heavy snow which blocked most Orkney roads, followed by floods in the streets of Kirkwall as a thaw set in, but was assured of "at least 42 days leave."

Gunner Frank Jackson, of the Royal Artillery, returned to his native Stronsay after four years as a POW and was immediatly collared to give a talk to the local SWRI. Captured by the Germans in Libya in 1941, he spent two years in Italian POW camps before, on Italy's capitulation, being loaded into railway trucks and sent to Poland where prisoners were put to work in coalmines. On being freed, they were sent by rail from Krakow to Odessa on the Black Sea and then repatriated by ship to Britain after a six week voyage through the Mediterranean.

Isles and parishes began to organise "Welcome Home" funds - in Westray, £389 was collected in door-to-door collections - and a public meeting was organised for Kirkwall Town Hall to discuss ways of commemorating Orkney's World War Two fallen.

Unfortunately, revelations of "wholesale plundering" of Army and RAF property, which had been vacated in Orkney, were made at Kirkwall Sheriff Court as ten local people, facing charges of theft and reset, received sentences of up to 12 weeks in jail. Generally, however, it was once again a peaceful, and more-or-less law abiding, Orkney population that received the news of Victory in Europe. A two day holiday was declared, with Tuesday, May 8, 1945, as VE Day - although there was a warning from Orkney's new Chief Constable Gathorne Cheyne (he had succeeded Colin Campbell who had been transferred to Wigtonshire) that Orkney still faced the danger of attacks from rogue U-boat commanders and "pirate" air raids. Orkney blackout precautions were finally cancelled on May 12, 1945.

Thanksgiving services were held in Orkney kirks, and a radio broadcast by Winston Churchill, confirming the ceasefire, was greeted with a heavy downpour of rain and the blast of ship's whistles in Kirkwall harbour. At the last moment, the Kirkwall VE day thanksgiving service was switched from St Magnus Cathedral to the East Kirk. Church bells rang in Stromness and *The Orcadian* reported: "Kirkwall, Stromness and villages made a plucky if somewhat pathetic show of flags and bunting." It was hardly a case, however, of thousands of people taking to the street in scenes of spontaneous celebrations. Many Orcadians still had men fighting in the Far East, where Japan, with all her treachery and greed, remained unsubdued, said Churchill. Also despite the victory in Europe, families were still being informed of the deaths of Orkney soldiers during the "final push" into Germany. Sergeant Pilot Wilson Campbell, son of the ex-Orkney Chief Constable Colin Campbell, was killed in a flying accident in Germany four days after VE day.

A total of 38 Orkney men - or men who gave their next-of-kin addresses as Orkney - had been held as POWs in the war in Europe, of which two, Lance Corporal James Spence and Private John Berston, died in captivity. In fact, there were many other Orcadian POWs, or with Orkney links, who had addresses outwith the county.

Orkney still held interned prisoners from enemy countries. The men of 558 Italian Working Company were still based at Bruna Camp, Stromness, at the time of VE day. In fact, 100 German prisoners were sent to Orkney on work duties as late as December, 1947, when they were put to work by the Ministry of Labour in clearing debris from the Market Green, Stromness, which during the war years had been the site of the town's Garrison Theatre.

Twelve surrendered German U-boats, captured in Norway, and with their German crews still on board, were brought into Scapa Flow in May, 1945, and three months later the captured 220ft German submarine *U776* was brought to Kirkwall and the public given guided tours to raise funds for the King George's Fund for Sailors.

Monument of war, symbol of peace

World War Two forever changed the face of Orkney. For, on May 12, 1945, just four days after VE day, the most tangible monument of Orkney's war years was officially opened - the Churchill Barriers, linking the Orkney Mainland and South Ronaldsay.

It was, said *The Orcadian*, "a ceremony rich in historical significance, closing an important chapter in the story of the 1939-45 European War, opening a bright and glowing page in the annals of Orkney's commercial and communal progress record.

"The ceremony was that of declaring open the most unique highway in the British Isles, a five miles thoroughfare that might well be titled Orkney's Great Eastern Road. Almost a third of this Orkney land route runs across salt water, laid upon causeways containing half a million cubic yards of quarried rock and more than 300,000 tons of concrete.

"Orkney's eastern South Isles are no longer islands; they are now districts of the Orkney Mainland. The causeways have linked to the Mainland, at the village of St Mary's, in the parish of Holm, the former islands of Lamb Holm, Glimps Holm, Burray and South Ronaldsay.

"United with Burray by another causeway, not included in the road scheme, is the island of Hunda. Closed to shipping are the eastern approaches to Scapa Flow, the channels of Kirk Sound, Holm Sound, Weddel Sound and Water Sound. Within the Flow, Hunda Sound is closed by the causeway founded upon Hunda Reef.

"Built for war defence of Scapa Flow, the causeways now begin to serve the needs of peace."

It had been one of the greatest civil engineering achievements in the world, the result of five years of work, about which Orcadians had been told nothing. Obviously, many on the Orkney Mainland would have seen the huge construction site, but for those in the North Isles, it was another world away. And, because of wartime censorship regulations, the announcement of the opening ceremony was the first time that *The Orcadian* had ever referred to the new barriers which had arisen from the sea in channels up to 55ft deep where the tide used to flow at ten knots.

The causeways had their origins, of course, in the disaster of HMS *Royal Oak*, sunk by the U-boat of Lt Gunther Prien which had penetrated the defences of Scapa Flow in October, 1939. It was a devastating blow just weeks into the war and, on Churchill's orders, the following Spring, work began to permanently seal the eastern approaches of the Flow.

Overall responsibility for the £2 million (nearer £100 million at 1999 prices) construction of the barriers fell on the Civil Engineer-in-Chief of the Admiralty Sir Arthur Whitaker, although the local mastermind behind the mammoth task was to be Admiralty Superintending Engineer, Mr Gordon Nicol, of Aberdeen, appointed in May, 1940. By then, hydraulic model experiments had been carried out by Professor A.H. Gibson, head of Manchester University engineering section. He had ascertained that concrete blocks of any shape were liable to drift considerable distances before reaching the seabed, but good results were obtained with rock, quarried locally, enclosed in steel wire cages, each holding approximately five tons of rock.

The main contractors appointed were Balfour, Beatty and Company - whose men were to remain in the islands for the next six years - but there were several firms of sub-contractors, including local Orkney companies. (The main representatives of Balfour, Beatty and Company throughout the construction were Mr J.B. Pettigrew and Mr A.B. Sharpe, under the supervision of the managing director Mr A.M. Taggart.)

There were several logistical problems to overcome - the first being accommodation for the 800 civilian workers engaged on the project. At the start, this was partly solved by using the 15,500 ton Royal Mail Lines ship *Almanzora* as a floating hostel, anchored off Holm, until contractors' camps were made ready at St Mary's village and Lamb Holm. The Rockworks Camp in St Mary's was to be the headquarters base while the Lamb Holm camp would eventually house 1,000 men.

The Moss quarry in Holm was taken over to provide the rock for the project and, before long, the site had not only its own power station but its own railway system. Giant overhead cableways were erected across the channels to carry, and drop, the rock and concrete blocks on which the causeways were founded. Several men were to be killed on the project, especially in cableway accidents. One of the worst tragedies was in October, 1941, when three "South" workers, aged 20, 27 and 34, died by drowning when a cable car crashed into the sea. Five others escaped.

In all, 650,000 tons of rock were carried by the cableways to the causeway sites, while a further 325,000 tons of concrete blocks were added. Within a year of starting work, the first barrier broke the surface of the sea, and within 18 months - although the project was by no means completed or permanent - the eastern approaches to the Flow were sealed.

In November, 1941, the workers of Balfour, Beatty and Company donated £800 to the Balfour Hospital in Kirkwall, but by 1942, the company and the sub-contractors were suffering a serious shortage of civilian labour. Conscription had taken most able bodied men, and the arduous and dangerous ten hour shifts were not popular with those who remained. This time the solution was provided by 1,000 Italian prisoners of war who were to stay in Orkney for just 1,000 days.

The first arrived in January, 1942. They came as defeated enemy soldiers - most were captured in the North Africa campaign - some still chanting defiant slogans in support of Mussolini, and were given uniforms with a bright red disc on the back, a target to be aimed at by marksmen in the event of their escape. One did abscond - he apparently intended to sail back to Italy in a dinghy he had stolen - but was recaptured, apparently, having gone into Leonards book shop in Kirkwall to buy an atlas.

However, at first, the new workforce refused to work. There were two Italian POW camps - No. 60 on Lamb Holm and No. 34 on Burray - and, in February, 1942, both found themselves on punishment rations of bread and water for 14 days after complaining that the barriers were "works of a warlike nature," contrary to the terms of the Geneva Convention.

The dispute was eventually resolved with the Italians being assured that the barriers were simply a civilian project to provide a road for the local islanders; which, eventually, of course, was true. And so the Italians played their part in Orkney's major civil engineering feat of the 20th century, although it could never be acknowledged at the time in their POW newspapers, printed weekly in Italian. Skilled prisoners were paid at 1s 6d a day and they too suffered the dangers of job. One Italian, a diesel locomotive driver, was killed in an accident and buried in St Olaf's cemetery.

After the capitulation of Mussolini in 1943, the prisoners were allowed greater freedom - the red target discs were removed - and a year later, with the barriers complete apart from the tarmacadam road, they were to leave Orkney, transferred to an agricultural work camp in Yorkshire.

The task of surfacing the roads across the barriers fell to Orkney County Council workmen. The war had seen massive public investment in Orkney's roads - imperative, of course, because in Hoy alone the highways had to carry 6,500 tons of traffic a day - and in 1944 the surfacing of the barriers was financed by government grants of more than £56,000 towards the total cost of under £60,000.

In fact, the barriers had been in use for several months when the First Lord of the Admiralty Mr A.V. Alexander arrived for the opening ceremony of May 12, 1945. It was an event to cause some local controversy because it was arranged so hastily that no official invitations were issued to Orkney councillors, the Lord Lieutenant or the MP - and local civic egoes were reported to be gravely offended - although county vice-convener Mr Patrick N. Sutherland Graeme, across whose land the construction work had taken place, the county roads surveyor John Robertson, and the Chief Constable Gathorne Cheyne did all attend the opening ceremony. MP Basil Neven Spence was said to be irked because he had wanted Winston Churchill to open the barriers and, no doubt, boost his campaign for the forthcoming General Election.

Whatever, the first offical cavalcade was to be a convoy of cars carrying the First Lord of the Admiralty, the Commander-in-Chief of the Home Fleet Admiral Sir Henry Moore, and the Flag Officer Orkney, Rear Admiral Patrick Macnamara. And the First Lord of the Admiralty received a "tumultuous" welcome from more than 1,000 shore workers who packed the Royal Naval Cinema at Lyness where Mr Alexander thanked them for six years of labour for the war effort.

Not long after, W.P. Swanney of Holm was to operate the first civilian bus service over the barriers between South Ronaldsay and Kirkwall. The fare was 3s 6d return and the journey took 90 minutes. It really was the road to the isles, although three years later, South Ronaldsay and Burray had to temporarily revert to island status - and rely on ferry transport - for six months in 1948 when the barriers were closed for work to be carried out to consolidate the foundations of the causeways. For several years after the war, the barriers were closed for one day per year to vehicles, as they belonged to the Admiralty, and were not on the list of highways.

The barriers were not the only monument of the war bequeathed to Orkney, however. The Italians who had worked on the barriers left behind on the island of Lamb Holm, watched over by a statue of St George slaying the dragon, the little building that was to become known throughout the world as, simply, the Italian Chapel.

Today it is the only visible reminder that this was once Camp 60, a symbol of peace and reconciliation after those years of conflict in World War Two. Yet, remarkably, it is based on a standard Nissen hut, enhanced only by items of apparently worthless scrap.

The man who must take the lion's share of the credit was the Italian prisoner Domenico Chiocchetti, an artist and sculptor. He recruited a squad of other craftsmen - plasterers, blacksmiths and electricians - from among his comrades and set to work. The corrugated iron was hidden by plasterboard, an altar constructed and a huge mural of the Madonna and Child painted. Ornate iron work created a sanctuary screen. The interior of the chapel was painted to resemble brickwork and then, outside, an impressive facade with a belfry was built to disguise the Nissen hut.

In fact, by the time the chapel was finished, all the other prisoners had already been transferred and Signor Chiocchetti was actually given leave to stay behind to complete the masterpiece.

Before he left, a special service was held with a recording of the bells and choir of St Peter's in Rome playing from the belfry.

At the end of the war, the chapel passed into the custody of Orkney vice-convenor Mr P.N. Sutherland, of Graemshall, the owner of the land on which it stood, and, in 1958, a chapel preservation committee - of which Signor Chiocchetti was later to be an honorary president - was formed to carry out repairs and maintain the building.

With the help of the BBC, who had broadcast programmes about the chapel in Italy, Signor Chiocchetti was traced living in the village of Moena and, in 1960 and again in 1963, he returned to Orkney and helped to restore some of the paintwork which his genius had created back in the 1940s. On Sunday, April 10, 1960, a service of rededication in the Chapel was attended by 200 Orcadians of all denominations. Signor Chiocchetti was the first to receive Holy Communion.

When he returned to Italy the following week, he left a moving message for Orcadians: "The chapel is yours - for you to love and preserve. I take with me to Italy the remembrance of your kindness and wonderful hospitality. I shall remember always, and my children shall learn from me to love you."

In the mid 1990s, under the supervision of local artist Mr Gary Gibson, further renovation work was carried out to ensure that the chapel will survive into the 21st century. And on May 7, 1999, Domenico Chiocchetti - three years after being honoured by Orkney County Council in a ceremony in Italy - died at the age of 88.

Italian prisoners of war are pictured around the statue of St George slaying the dragon at their internment camp on Lamb Holm.

(Picture courtesy of Orkney Library photographic archive)

A monument of war, a symbol of peace - the Italian Chapel on Lamb Holm. (Picture courtesy of Craig Taylor)

Domenico Chiocchetti, the Italian artist responsible for the decoration of the Italian Chapel, is pictured with his son and daughter-in-law when they made a return visit to the chapel after the war. (Picture courtesy of Orkney Library photographic archive)

Peace breaks out

Peacetime brought some swift changes. By the end of May, 1945, the 19th Battalion of the Royal Marines were preparing to take their leave of Orkney after six years, saying farewell at a special event at the battalion's Globe Theatre in Lyness. As hundreds of sailors, Wrens, Marines and soldiers bid farewell to the county, departing on the first stage of their journey back to Civvy Street, the daily steamer service from Lyness to Scrabster, to connect with the Jellicoe train south, was soon to be considered unnecessary and axed. The Toc H headquarters in Kirkwall would also close after six years of wartime service for the forces in Orkney, and Orkney's 147 auxiliary coastguards were demobilised.

But peacetime could not spare Orkney from further tragedy. And in June, 1945, the county suffered an ordeal which could have been a major disaster as four RAF men died when their plane, en route to Skeabrae aerodrome, crashed into a hut at Millfield Camp, Stromness, near the Garrison Theatre. Two men in the hut remarkably escaped injury. Fortunately, most of the soldiers in Millfield Camp were on pay parade at the time - otherwise casualties would have been much heavier.

And the men of Longhope lifeboat still had work to carry out that same month when they rescued 12 officers and 40 men - the crew included the world famous ex-professional boxer Benny Lynch - from the 7,000 ton Liberty ship *Fort La Prairie* which ran aground in dense fog on the Pentland Skerries, en route to the USA.

August 15-16, 1945, was declared a VJ holiday as the newly elected Prime Minister Clement Attlee announced the surrender of Japan. Street lamps were lit through the night as pipe music and dancing in the streets continued until 5am, *The Orcadian* reported. A further VJ holiday was celebrated in Kirkwall on August 24, with a fancy dress carnival parade.

The celebrations, of course, went ahead with many Orcadian soldiers still on duty in the Far East. There had been eleven prisoners of war from Orkney (again, there were others who had next-of-kin addresses elsewhere) who were held in Java, Shanghai, Borneo, Singapore, and Thailand. At least four died in Japanese POW camps - Captain Alistair Steele, Gunner George Partner and Signalman Thomas Walls, all from Kirkwall, and Trooper James Twatt, a private in the Cameron Highlanders, whose parents Mr and Mrs Thomas Twatt, of Breck in Eday, had to wait until December, 1945, to learn the dreadful news that he had died more than three years earlier.

The *Almanzora*, the ship that had been used as a floating hostel in Orkney for the contract workers engaged on the Churchill Barriers in 1940-41, collected 180 liberated POWs in Singapore to bring them home to Britain.

The evil of Belsen

Thousands of Orcadians saw the horrors of war. But one brave and skilled Orcadian woman had to witness the unspeakable evil of war - a nightmare scenario that had no place in what mankind called civilisation. Dr Rena Marwick had to endure the trauma of going into the infamous Nazi concentration camp of Belsen.

There she found the unbelievable and heart-rending sight of thousands of prisoners dying of starvation, disease - typhus, dysentery and TB - and brutal ill-treatment. Her accounts of the experience make up one of the most moving Orcadian documents of World War Two.

Dr Marwick had been the GP in the island of Sanday, but in July, 1944, with the rank of Captain, she was to be landed in Normandy and she spent the next six months giving blood transfusions to injured British troops in France, Belgium, Holland and, finally, Germany.

So by April, 1945, she had seen thousands of injured and dying men on the battlefield. But nothing could have prepared her for what was to follow in peacetime as the Allies liberated the notorious concentration camp in the German village of Belsen.

Alas, the Allies were too late to save many. One of the concentration camp's still-remembered victims was Anne Frank, the Jewish girl who was betrayed to the Nazis in Amsterdam and died at Belsen at the age of 15, her diary later becoming an immortalised story of courage.

Dr Marwick told the grim story of what she found in a series of letters home to her father, Provost James Marwick of Stromness.

"Wonder how you are to celebrate VE day in Stromness?" she asked in her first letter. "We are not exactly hilarious here, and I can scarcely imagine a less appropriate place for celebration than Belsen concentration camp - while living in tents on a windswept site and preparing to take in 4,000 ill patients."

A few days later and another letter: "We have been looking after one lot, and it is a soul-destroying job; though, after a week, apart from the hundreds of deaths, we can see an improvement in the others. The worst revealed in the papers, by the way, is a very mild account of the conditions. Not the least of our difficulties is the language problem and lack of interpreters - so many of the patients and helpers speak only Polish or Russian or Hungarian.

"It all seems hopeless at times but works out somehow."

Later, Dr Marwick wrote home: " The original camp has been burning bit by bit these last few days - and a good thing too. It has been completely emptied and the last hut is to be burned tomorrow. We can see the smoke for miles around.

"We are very glad to see an improvement in most of the patients. They are all civilians who are interned in this concentration camp - mine are all women. Their mental attitude is definitely better. For example, in the original camp, dead bodies meant nothing, or less than nothing - children played over them, other people had to walk over them, or sat and gossiped and cooked beside them, no matter who it was. Last week in one of my wards, one patient was very ill, and eventually died, and the others actually wept. So, at least, life is considered more valuable now."

And finally in June, 1945, she wrote: "The ceremonial burning of the last hut took place on Monday, and it was quite an impressive ceremony and well done. We all went down and watched it and were glad to see the end of such a place."

Her war service saw her mentioned in dispatches, and she later married Edinburgh barrister Mr Harald Leslie KC (later to be Lord Birsay) who stood as the Labour candidate in the 1950 General Election campaign in Orkney.

There have been many remarkable Orcadians, and many remarkable contributions made by Orcadians, in the 20th century. Dr Marwick surely deserves to take her place amongst that list.

Welcome home and does

Hostilities in all theatres of war had ceased only a month when a peacetime shambles led to the cancellation of the commemorative service planned for St Magnus Cathedral, Kirkwall, to mark the anniversary of the Battle of Britain.

The Forces had obtained the permission of Kirkwall Town Council, the guardians of the Cathedral, to stage the service on September 16, 1945, but then Cathedral minister Rev Arthur Fryer intervened to say that his consent was necessary. The RAF said that it asked for the Rev Fryer's endorsement and it was refused, leaving no alternative but to cancel the service. The Rev Fryer - who, as Captain Fryer, had only just returned to Orkney after being overseas as an Army chaplain - said it was a "slight misunderstanding" caused by communications problems and he shared the deep regret of Kirkwall people that the service was cancelled.

"Is this an example of the Christianity in the new world for which comrades fought so valiantly and won through?" asked an irate RAF airman in a letter of protest to *The Orcadian* the following week. It seemed to cause little surprise when, two years later, the Rev Fryer was soundly trounced in the elections when he sought a seat on Kirkwall Town Council.

On a happier note, Ernest Hood, a Londoner who came to Orkney to work with Balfour, Beatty and Company on the Scapa Flow defences, wrote "My Island Home," of which 5,000 copies were sold for Welcome Home funds, and Kirkwall branch of the British Legion, in abeyance since 1938, was revived.

The RAF had moved from the Bignold Park station in Kirkwall to Grimsetter in 1944. By 1946, only a small "care and maintenance" presence remained in charge at what would later become Orkney's civilian airport. With the transfer of HMS *Sparrowhawk* to Suffolk, Hatston had been in the control of a Naval care and maintenance party, but it was now to become the headquarters of the Orkney and Shetland Defences - the commander of which had been based at the Stromness Hotel - and a number of Army units in Stromness and district moved to Hatston, while the aerodrome would be handed over to the Ministry of Civil Aviation.

In Hoy, squads of Frenchmen arrived to dismantle hundreds of Orkney's wartime military huts which were to be sent to France to help solve that country's parlous accommodation crisis.

Also arriving in Orkney, based at camps at the Brig o' Waithe, Stenness, and South Ronaldsay, were 800 men from Polish units. They were to make a memorable impression, it seems. Within weeks of their arrival, 117 Orkney people - 76 of them women - enrolled for correspondence courses to learn the Polish language. The men certainly made an impression on the football field. The Polish Army XI won Orkney's 1946 Craigmyle Cup, beating Kirkwall Hotspur 2-1 in the final in front of a 1,000 crowd at the Bignold Park, having beaten Rovers, Dounby and Holm in previous rounds. When most of the Polish Army team left the islands in October, 1946, they were unbeaten in 31 games. Not all of the Poles left. The following year, a former Adjutant Polish Forces in Orkney, ex-Lieutenant Tadek "Ted" Zawadski, and his wife Catherine, from Perthshire, bought the Bu' Farm in Orphir, which included the Scapa Flow rock of the Barrel of Butter. The family were later to become owners of Balfour Castle in Shapinsay, and Ted Zawadski's son Christopher would stand as the Conservative candidate in Orkney's first election for the Scottish Parliament in 1999.

Gradually, through 1946, more tangible signs of peace, and efforts to rebuild a ravaged national economy, emerged. Civil

An all-action photograph shows a boxing tournament in progress as part of the regular sports days organised by the Italian prisoners of war in Burray.
(Picture courtesy of Orkney Library photographic archive)

anyone speak Polish?

aviation services would be nationalised, it was announced, and the Balfour Hospital, which under the wartime emergency, had been extended with the addition of two 42-bed wards in 1940, would later in 1948 become part of the new National Health Service. At a price of 1s 1d lb, but strictly rationed, Orkney had its first post-war distribution of bananas. During the war, a single banana, auctioned for charity at the Kirkwall Naval Cinema, had fetched 25 shillings.

The North of Scotland Milk Marketing Board announced plans to open a cheese factory at the former RAF Bignold Park camp - production would begin in July, 1946 - and the Kirkwall egg packing station, at the Ayre Mills in Kirkwall, handled 20 million eggs in eight months. An unusual legacy of the war, and the big increase in population, was that 10,000 rats were caught in three months by a team of four catchers. A similar number of rats were believed killed by gassing.

And there were still other echoes of war. A fleet of mine-sweepers arrived in Scapa Flow to begin the clearing of mines in Northern waters, but in March, 1946, two days after leaving Kirkwall, the 8,000 ton American liberty ship *Lord Delaware* struck a mine and sank in Swedish waters. Fortunately, the entire personnel, including women and children, travelling from New York, were rescued.

Kirkwall Town Council, meeting in April, 1946, reported public apathy over the plans for victory celebrations to be held on June 8. Just one suggestion had been received in two months. However, the celebrations eventually went ahead in most of the islands with the first post-war turnout of the Kirkwall City Pipe Band. Two Kirkwall men - Sergeant John Corse and PC Tom Mainland - marched in the June 8 Victory Day Parade in London.

The staff of Balfour, Beatty and Company prepared to leave Orkney after more than six years in the county engaged on defence works, including the Churchill Barriers. And, in April, 1946, Rear Admiral Patrick Macnamara, Flag Officer in Charge, Orkney, and Admiral Superintendent Orkney, and his American wife Ellen, said farewell to the county, also after six years in the islands. Rear Admiral Macnamara was to be knighted in the King's birthday honours list of 1946, and, with minimum fuss or ceremony, Kirkwall Naval Base closed at 5pm on Saturday, November 30, 1946, having been in operation since August, 1939.

A month later, a chapter of Orkney's history was brought to an end when a Ministry of Works sale of redundant military stock realised £45,900 - nearer £2 million at 1999 prices. Some of the sale was held at the former Royal Engineers Depot at Caldale, St Ola, but the main auction was held at Hatston, in the giant hangar where, during the war, 5,000 servicemen and women had paid 3d each to be entertained by Gracie Fields. Auctioneer Alex Beith of Glasgow disposed of 200 motor vehicles, 70 motorcycles and a vast array of diesel generating equipment that had served in Orkney's wartime military power stations. Buyers came from all over Britain with 11 special charter flights organised. Orkney buyers were able to purchase vehicles from £60, with six 27 hp Humbers, ex-Military staff cars, going under the hammer for £400 each.

The ghosts of war were not allowed to settle for long, however. On April 17, 1947, it was announced that recruiting had begun for the new Orkney unit of the Territorial Army, the 430 Coast Regiment of the Royal Artillery, which, covering Orkney and Shetland, would have an ultimate total strength of 600 all ranks. The Iron Curtain had descended. The Cold War had begun!

The Orkney XI of 1947 claimed to be the first team to fly to a football fixture in Britain when the players went from Kirkwall to Wick by air for the Archer Shield game against Caithness. The five men on the right of this line-up are, from the left, Robert Miller, Kenny McLeod, Russell Croy, Tommo Thomson and Bill Sim. Caithness won the game 5-3 after extra time. (Picture courtesy of Bill Sim)

Roll of honour

Mr Allan Taylor, of Kirkwall, has compiled the following list
of names inscribed on the war memorials of Orkney
to commemorate those who died in World War Two:

BIRSAY
Str John Delday RN
Edith Garson NAAFI
Str James Moar RN
Pte Sidney Phillips

BURRAY
Norman D. Bruce RNR
Alister Duncan MN
William Mills RN
Duncan Park

EDAY
Gillies Hercus, Royal Navy
Hugh Hughson, Merchant Navy
George Shearer, Royal Navy
James Tulloch, Gen Service Corps
James Twatt, Royal Armoured Corps

EGILSAY
James J. Mainland

FIRTH
Duncan G. Manson, Finstown
John Wilson, Ouraquay

FLOTTA
Pte James Flett

HARRAY
J.N.J. Flett, Woodwyn
F.D.P. Johnston, Breckan
J.R. Johnston, Yeldavale
J. Murray, Stoneyhill

HOLM
Frank Buchan, St Marys
Robert D. Firth, Netherbutton
Andrew Garson, St Marys
John W. Johnston, St Marys
John Louttit, Woodstock
John Norquoy, Howan

HOY
Isaac Watters Bremner, Seaforths
Spr Hugh Lyon, Royal Engineers
Annabella Sutherland, NAAFI

KIRKWALL
F/O Frederick Buchanan, RAF
R/O John A.P. Campbell, Merchant Navy
Sgt/Pilot Wilson Campbell, RAF
Cpl Thomas H. Chalmers, RAF
L/Bdr John A. Cooper, Royal Horse Artillery
Bdr Edwin Corsie, Royal Artillery
R/O John R. Firth, Merchant Navy
P/O James S.M. Flett, Royal Navy
O/S Robert R. Harcus, Royal Navy
F/O David B. Hume, RAF
Marine Norman Isbister, Royal Marines

KIRKWALL - continued
Pte Thomas Johnstone, Manchester Regiment
Seaman Jerry W. Kelday, Royal Navy
Spr David Linklater, Royal Engineers
Seaman George S. Morris, Royal Navy
Sgt John Norquoy, Royal Engineers
Gnr George Partner, Royal Artillery
Sgt F/Engr Norman J. Peace, RAF
Gnr James D. Rendall, New Zealand Artillery
Lieut/Col Donald Robertson, Seaforths
Ldg/Str George Robertson, Royal Navy
Gnr James Robinson, Royal Artillery
Pte Thomas Robinson, London Scottish
Lt Charles A. Shearer, Royal Field Artillery
Pte John Sinclair, Seaforths
Seaman James W. Sinclair, RNR
Major Alastair Steele, Royal Artillery
Signalman Thomas Walls, Royal Signals

NORTH RONALDSAY
Cpl Alexander D. Thomson, Howatoft

ORPHIR
L/Bdr Jack Bews, Outerdale
Pte J. Oliver Flett, Roadside
Seaman John Sutherland, Roadside

PAPA WESTRAY
Stewart Groat, Kimbland
William D. Groat, Ness
Capt Henry Groat
Capt Thomas Harcus MBE

ROUSAY
L/S John S. Gibson, Hullion
Signalman Thomas Walls, Store Cottage
LAM James S. Sutherland, Weyland

ST ANDREWS
John A. Foubister, Argyll and Sutherland Highlanders
Robert Harcus, RSF

SANDWICK
Pte Fraser A. Craigie, Rosemount
Pilot Offr James L. Harcus, Flotterston
L/Sgt Gordon W. Moar, Newhouse
Pte George Robertson, Roadside Cottage
L/Cpl James D.O. Spence, Brockan

SANDAY
Steward David King, MN HMS
Gunner William Muir, Royal Artillery

SHAPINSAY
Corpl William Allan, RE
Sgt William Skea, RAF

SOUTH RONALDSAY
Pte John S. Doull, Gordon HRS
Seaman John M. Gunn, RNVR
Seaman Magnus Henderson, MN
Sgt Robert M. Mathieson, Air Gnr RAF
Seaman William B. Rosie, MN
Second Officer William S. Rosie, MN
Seaman James Russell, RN
Dvr David Sinclair, Tank Corps
Seaman Walter Sinclair, MN
Capt Andrew Thomson, MN

STENNESS
William R. Coghill, Savedale
John R. Cursiter, Post Office
James W. Isbister, Brig o' Waithe
Samuel McKenzie, Neggheads

STROMNESS
W.G.M. Baker, RN
William Brown, RA
James Chalmers, RN
Queenie Donaldson, ATS
Stewart Guy, Guards
George Kirkpatrick, RN
Georgina H. Mason, WAAF
William Muir, RN
James Park, RN
John Smith, RN
James G. Spence, RA
John Sutherland, MN
Leonard Sutherland, RAF
William A. Swanson, MN
James Velzian, RAF
James Watson, RA

STRONSAY
James Chalmers, RN Patrol
William R. Grieve, Mines
Daniel Horne, Merchant Navy
Allan K. Smith, Fleet Air Arm
George Taylor, Merchant Navy

WALLS
Alexander Barnett, MN
George A. Groat, RASC
Harry Kirkpatrick, RNR
Thomas Kirkpatrick, RN

WESTRAY
Seaman John Foulis, Chapelbrae
Master Mariner Robert Gray, Gill
Master Mariner John M. Hewison, Trenabie
Cpl Georgina H. Mason, East Thorn
CPO George B. Reid, Links
James Reid, Rebuilding
Pte David Rendall, Glen
Pte William Rendall, Floss
James Swanney, Broughton
Lt Kathleen H. Walker, Meadowbank

End of the road for small schools

The biggest reorganisation in the history of Orkney education was set to lead to the closure of Orkney's tiniest schools and their merger with larger neighbours.

It also meant that a school hostel would be opened in Kirkwall for isles pupils.

The driving factor behind the changes was the raising of the school leaving age to 15 - which had been put in abeyance at the outbreak of World War Two but was now to be enforced with an expansion of secondary school education.

The victims over the next few years would be the host of small one teacher schools which dotted Orkney's isles and parishes. In 1940, the county had 28 one teacher schools and, in 1946, there were still four schools on each of Stronsay, Sanday, Hoy and South Ronaldsay, three each in both Westray and Rousay, two each in both Eday and Shapinsay, and five in the East Mainland - St Andrews, Deerness, Tankerness, Holm East and Holm West.

1946

At the same time, the statistics showed that depopulation was causing a sizeable reduction in Orkney's school roll which fell from 3,363 in February, 1928, to 2,845 in February, 1938. The biggest drop was at Stromness where the number of scholars had fallen from 398 to 305. Widewall school had fallen from 46 to 14, Frotoft in Rousay from 17 to five and Wyre from ten to three.

Nonetheless, by 1999 standards, the number of pupils was still quite healthy in the smaller isles with the schools of North Ronaldsay, Papa Westray, Eday, Rousay and Flotta having a total of 190 pupils. The smallest schools in 1945 were North Faray (4), Wyre (up to 8),

North Hoy (10), Graemsay (10) and Egilsay (10).

To allow island pupils to pursue their secondary education in Kirkwall, the first Kirkwall Grammar School hostel - providing accommodation for 36 island girls - was opened at the former Post Office hostel in Old Scapa Road.

The man who would have the responsibility of overseeing these changes in Orkney education was Mr John Shearer who, in 1946, was appointed the new county education director following the retiral of Dr Hugh Marwick OBE after 17 years in the post. Mr Shearer, formerly Stromness Academy principal science teacher, was appointed at a salary of £950 a year, rising to £1,100.

And - those were the days - the interviews by the 23 members of Orkney Education Committee of the three men on the shortlist for the job were carried out in public!

Beauty of the county

Chief Section Leader Evelyn Flett, from the Kirkwall Girls Training Corps, could claim to be the first "Miss Orkney" - although it did not actually carry that title - when she won a beauty contest, and £5 prize, organised by Kirkwall Hotspur FC who staged a series of heats through the

year with a grand final of ten finalists, in front of a crowd of 400 at Kirkwall Drill Hall.

A singing competition, run in conjunction, was won by Lance Corporal Zenon Lukawieki of the Polish Forces at Hatston who sang "Ave Maria" in Italian.

Men stop Women's Ba'

Violet Couper, a Kirkwall Grammar School pupil, won the 1946 New Year Women's Ba' for the Uppies - the last time the Women's Ba' was to be held before the end of the 20th century. Later in 1946, the Ba' committee announced that, after just two Ba' games exclusively for females, and, after much opposition had been voiced by men, the Women's Ba' would cease forthwith.

* * *

Tragedy in Scapa Flow saw the deaths of brothers-in-law William Sutherland (27) of Flotta and David Simison (31) of South Ronaldsay in a lobster fishing accident when they drowned in Pan Hope, Flotta.

* * *

Mr Ian MacIntyre, former Unionist MP, 1924-29, for West Edinburgh, and father of Marjorie Linklater, the wife of Orkney writer Eric Linklater, died. A lawyer, he played six times for Scotland at Rugby Union, and was president of the Scottish Rugby Union 1899-1901.

* * *

Orkney's first full-time county librarian Evan MacGillivray was appointed. A native of Kirkwall, he had worked for 18 years for a famous London firm of booksellers before joining the Royal Navy in 1941 and completing his war service as a Lieutenant on the minesweeper HMS *Elm*.

* * *

Sheriff George Brown - first appointed to Kirkwall 20 years earlier - died at the age of 74 in 1946. Captain David Keith of Caithness was appointed his successor.

Mystery of the 29 steps

The "Orkney mystery of the 29 steps" was revealed when excavations by Mr and Mrs J. W. Tait, Quoyburray, friends and neighbours, and Mr Alfred Harcus, KGS teacher, uncovered evidence of Orkney life 2,000 year earlier.

The discovery arose from stories of old folk who told how a cow had once disappeared into a hole at the site at Quoyburray. Excavations revealed first 15 steps and, eventually, 29 steps leading to an 18 feet square chamber with passages off it up to 40 feet long.

Mr R. Stevenson, Keeper of the Scottish Museum of Antiquities, believed that it could date to the Iron Age of 100 BC. Stone axes, knives, hammers and pieces of clay urn were brought to the surface.

Football team sent off

All eleven players of Thorfinn FC were sent off by referee David Walker of Kirkwall in the Garden Cup match against the Army team Hatston FC at the Bignold Park.

The Thorfinn players were ordered off

after they refused to restart the game unless the Hatston centre half was sent off following an off-the-ball clash with a Thorfinn forward. Thorfinn were fined three guineas by the Orkney FA and the match ordered to be replayed.

Best of British

Britain's best sea cadet was 19 year old Peter Leith, of Appiehouse, Stenness, a member of the Kirkwall Sea Cadets Corps, who, on a course for Petty Officers at HMS Foudroyant, Portsmouth, achieved 98 per

cent marks in general seamanship. He was reported by the Commanding Officer of Foudroyant to be the best candidate of several hundreds who had taken the course there.

1947

Orkney time

Stronsay National Farmers Union branch called for a separate time zone for Orkney.

Double Summer Time was still in operation in 1947 - a hangover from the war years - but there were protests from the NFU and Orkney County Council that it was unnecessary in Orkney and an inconvenience from which the islands should be exempted.

Music for all

The first Orkney Music Festival organised by the County Music Committee attracted contributions by 1,100 men, women and children, with more than 700 children taking part. Included in that number was Stromness Academy pupil William Turmeau, who played the saxophone, and who went on, 50 years later, after a distinguished university career in Edinburgh, to become head of the Scottish Environmental Protection Agency.

Cinema destroyed

The 400 seat Albert Kinema, Kirkwall, opened 18 years earlier, was completely gutted by fire. Film showings were switched to the Temperance Hall.

The great freeze!

A national crisis caused by fuel and power shortages was worsened by some of the worst weather of the 20th century. In Orkney, the snow continued for three weeks, with up to 15 degrees of frost at night.

Stromness lit up

Mains electricity and electric street lights came to Stromness, nearly a quarter of a century after Kirkwall. The official switch-on was at the town's Alfred Cafe.

* * *

Orkney's first school of dancing, mime and elocution was opened in the former ENSA building off New Scapa Road, Kirkwall, by two ex-RAF members Harold Mitchell and Norman Nicholson.

* * *

Orkney writer Edwin Muir became the first Briton to be made an honorary doctor of the Caroline University of Prague. Dr Muir was serving in Czechoslovakia with the British Council.

Mr Walter Grant, director of Highland Distillers Company Ltd, and son of James Grant of Highland Park, Kirkwall, died at the age of 61 at his home, Hillhead, Kirkwall. A keen historian - he helped Professor Gordon Childe with the excavations of Skara Brae in the late 1920s - he was also a president of Orkney Trout Fishing Association.

(Picture courtesy of Orkney Library photographic archive)

Ships are saved

The biggest ship ever to escape destruction after stranding on the Pentland Firth island of Stroma was the 7,176 ton 422 feet long American liberty ship *Art Young* which, in 1947, was pulled to safety by three tugs after running aground in dense fog.

A few days earlier the Norwegian oil tanker *Gundine*, bound for Copenhagen from Philadelphia, ran aground at Torness, Hoy, in dense fog - but refloated under her own power, and was later able to continue her voyage - after first discharging 1,450 tons of oil into the sea to lighten the vessel!

Death of an island - the evacuation of Faray

The "evacuation" of the island of North Faray would soon be complete, reported *The Orcadian*.

In 1911, the island had a population of 48 with a dozen children on the school roll. But, by 1947, the shortage of teachers had seen the local school closed and families had left rather than see their children billeted away from their homes in other parts of Orkney.

By April, 1947, only one family remained on Faray - the Wallace family of Ness who had been resident on the island for more than 60 years, but they were soon to take their departure, leaving all the holdings vacant and uninhabited, despite intensive advertising of the properties.

The chief difficulty of the island, said the departing families, was the lack of a regular boat service to maintain contact with the outside world.

Ammunition dump peril

North Walls children narrowly escaped a tragic disaster when they set fire to heather which threatened to engulf the Army ammunition magazine at Ore Camp. Steps were taken to turn the full available manpower of Lyness base - a total of more than 500 civilians plus service personnel - to the task of firefighting, but, fortunately, weather conditions favoured the fire engines and prevented the conflagration reaching the arms dump.

Stromness ends the ban on drink

The people of Stromness - "dry" since 1920 - went to the polls to vote in a referendum to decide whether to repeal the temperance legislation which had seen no pub licences granted for over a quarter of a century

The previous polls in 1923 and 1926 had seen majorities of 217 and 243 in favour of the continuance of prohibition. The Orkney Presbytery expressed their unanimous support for the continuance of the "dry" era.

But on the eve of the poll, Stromness Town Hall was full to hear Inverness lawyer Major J. Mitchell put the case for repeal of the ban. The "repeal" lobby claimed that Stromness had lost prosperity because of the drink ban, because ships and trawlers were now avoiding the town.

The vote took place on November 25, 1947, and among those who braved hail storms to vote was 89 year old Mrs C.G. Robertson.

The result was announced by her namesake, Provost George Robertson. For continuance 328, for repeal 405 - a majority of 77 for Stromness to go "wet."

Stromness had been Britain's northernmost "dry" town after Wick and Lerwick had both earlier repealed the temperance laws in their towns, and the vote in Stromness was to prove to be one of the final nails in the coffin of Scotland's controversial Temperance Act of 1913.

Even before the repeal of the temperance legislation, many Stromness people had been able to get a drink, for the preceding month had seen the British Legion create history when the organisation opened the burgh's first licensed club, which was permitted under different legislation.

But, even after the referendum vote, it would be another six months before licences were granted and the first bar in the town opened to the public. That honour fell to the Stromness Hotel which reopened its bar on Saturday, May 29, 1948. The previous legal drink sold over the bar in Stromness had been at noon on May 28, 1921, when the last licence lapsed.

The building in Victoria Street, Kirkwall, which served as the office of *The Orcadian* for all but the last three years of the 20th century.

(Picture courtesy of Orkney Library photographic archive)

Exotic visitor

A tarantula spider was found crawling amongst a bunch of bananas delivered to Birsay.

Royal holiday

Orkney schoolchildren were given a holiday on November 20 to mark the wedding of Princess Elizabeth and Lieutenant Philip Mountbatten, soon to be the Duke of Edinburgh. A full length film of the wedding was shown at Kirkwall Temperance Hall for two weeks.

Dockers jailed

Three Kirkwall dockers were jailed for income tax evasion. The three could be kept in prison for up to 12 months unless the payment of overdue taxes - said to run to hundreds of pounds - was made. In fact, they were released after three weeks having paid part of the arrears.

Old Man sale

North Hoy - including the Old Man of Hoy and the Dwarfie Stone - was purchased from Mr and Mrs Thomas Middleton of Melsetter, owners for the previous 50 years, by Mr Malcolm Stewart, of Buckinghamshire, who was stationed at Hatston Naval Air Station in World War Two. Mr and Mrs Stewart planned to make their home at Orgil Lodge.

Sir John dies

Sir John Flett, from Kirkwall, who from 1920-35 was director of the Geological Survey of Great Britain, died aged 77.

The Lord Lieutenant of Orkney and Shetland since 1930, Alfred Baikie of Tankerness, died at the age of 86.

Football revived

Inter-county football against Caithness was revived for the first time since 1938 when Orkney lost 8-5, after extra time, in the Archer Shield match in Wick.

Junior victory

The Orkney - Shetland junior inter-county competition for the Stuart Cup was held for the first time. Orkney won the athletics, hockey and football to secure the trophy.

Island laird

Cyril Kinmond, of Leamington Spa, Warwickshire, became owner of three islands at various times from the 1920s. His first was Cava, then Swona, and, in 1947, he purchased Copinsay from the estate of the late Thomas Reid.

A picture of health

The year of 1948 was to see the single biggest step forward in welfare provision that Britain witnessed in the 20th century - the introduction of the National Health Service. It was the guarantor of medical services for the people.

But, in many respects, Orkney had already led the way in establishing a county-wide infrastructure for health care and, in the 25 years prior to the NHS, major developments had seen the islands at the forefront of moves towards a caring and comprehensive network of hospitals and doctors, funded by benefactors, voluntary donations, insurance committees and council finance.

By the mid-1930s, every island and parish had access to a doctor, Kirkwall had its own hospital with a surgeon, the county was served not only by motor ambulance but also air ambulance, and schemes were in place to help the fight against such killers as Tuberculosis and Poliomyelitis. The statistics showed that the health and welfare of Orcadians was better than most, if not all, of the areas of Scotland at that time.

The Balfour family had been Orkney's main benefactors of health services in the 19th century, and, at the start of the 20th century, Kirkwall's hospital was still based in Main Street in what would later become the West End Hotel.

However, in 1914, new benefactors came forward, when the widow and family of the late Bailie Robert Garden, of Kirkwall, offered to build a new hospital in his memory. World War One then intervened, of course, and so it was 1927 before the Garden Memorial Building was opened on the site of what is still today the site of Kirkwall's Balfour Hospital.

The Balfour Hospital was handed over, on April 6, 1927, to trustees: Robert Scarth of Binscarth, Thomas Clouston of Gairsay, Sheriff George Brown, Dr Frank Peterkin, Dr William Sinclair and Provost John Slater of Kirkwall.

The revenue accounts for that first year of operation showed income of £1,954 18s 10d and expenditure of £1,968 10s 9d including "wines, medicines and surgical appliances" at £112 9s 2d.

In February, 1928, the hospital trustees proposed a consultant surgeon be appointed. If every householder in the county put aside 2d a week, it would provide all the money they needed, said the clerk and treasurer to the trustees, Duncan Robertson. The board proposed that an annual salary of £850 be offered to the surgeon, and the total annual cost of the service was estimated at £1,750.

By August that year, Orkney's first surgeon had been appointed - Ian McClure, aged 30, who had been working as an interim surgeon in County Cavan, Ireland. A World War One veteran of the Royal Naval Air Service, during which action he had been badly wounded to the extent that he lost a leg, Mr McClure now looked forward to the building of an enlarged operating theatre and hospital extension. Six months later, X-ray equipment was installed - and the first picture taken was of the right hand of the hospital treasurer.

Mr McClure soon learned the hazards of an Orkney winter. In February, 1929, when all the Mainland roads had been blocked by blizzard conditions, the new county surgeon was summoned to an emergency in Birsay. After two attempts, a car managed to get through the drifts from Kirkwall to Finstown, from where the surgeon - relying on an artificial leg - walked to the Dounby road where another car succeeded in getting the surgeon through to his destination without mishap.

Not so fortunate in that same storm was the principal keeper of the Pentland Skerries Lighthouse who was stranded seriously ill for 11 days when no vessel was able to land on the island due to heavy seas. A doctor was eventually landed and the sick man evacuated to St Margaret's Hope.

One of Mr McClure's contemporaries at this time was the county's Medical Officer of Health, Dr Walter Bannerman, a Cornishman who had been appointed in 1924. The number one scourge that he had to tackle was Tuberculosis. For instance, in the year 1928, a total of 28 cases had been reported in the county, of which 11 had died. The TB cases were kept in isolation at the Scapa Pavilion, which, in 1928, had to be extended to cope with the growing problem. Dr Bannerman reported: "The death rate from Tuberculosis is particularly high in the islands of Scotland. I am desirous of establishing a Tuberculosis clinic and it is my intention at an early date to devote one afternoon each week where examinations can be carried out and general advice and instruction given."

Mrs Marjorie Davies, who had been decorated by King George V for meritorious war service in France in World War One, was appointed the matron of Scapa TB hospital in 1932.

TB was not the only concern, however, as 1929 saw an epidemic of Poliomyelitis in Stronsay. Eventually, there were 17 cases, 11 in cases under the age of 15, and four young people died - a 14 year old girl and three males, aged 16, 21, and 26.

Another responsibility of the county council at this time was what *The Orcadian* used to inelegantly refer to as the "lunacy budget."

Under the headline "Maintenance cost of Orkney's lunatics," the newspaper reported that at January 1, 1928, there were 88 pauper lunatics (42 male, 46 female) in Orkney - 73 were in the County Home and other institutions, seven with relatives and eight boarded with strangers. Eleven patients from Orkney were admitted to the Royal Asylum, Edinburgh, in 1927. Birsay and Harray, alone, were responsible for nine patients in the Royal Edinburgh Hospital for Mental Disorders, and the Physician Superintendent reported to the parish council that "none of the patients is suitable for discharge or boarding out." The "lunacy budget" for Orkney for the year 1927-28, from the rates, was assessed at £2,750, and the cost of keeping each of Orkney's "pauper lunatics" in institutions was just a penny under 21 shillings a week.

In October, 1934, it was announced that the County Home was to be expanded with a new £1,000 five room bungalow for the governor and matron and a new £120 mortuary, as well as other improvements, to cope with what *The Orcadian* eloquently described, with no attempt at political correctness, as "an average nightly family of 46 inmates, excluding lunatic patients."

Astonishingly, the governor and matron constituted the total staff of the County Home at this time. In October, 1930, Orkney County Council agreed to increase the salary of Matron Bews from £70 to £80 per annum, with councillors underlining their magnanimity by pointing out that the cost of living had fallen by 35 per cent since 1921. (At the same time, the salary of the teacher of the blind, Mr Groat, was increased by £12 a year to £90 per annum.)

Mrs Bews was the widow of John Bews, a Stromness man who was appointed Governor of the County Home in 1911. He died in 1925 and was succeeded as Governor by his son Thomas. Mrs Bews, a recipient in 1935 of the King's Medal of the Royal Silver Jubilee, died in 1937, having been allowed, for the last year of her life, to recruit an assistant nurse to help care for the 55 patients at the home. Miss Grace Colvin, ward sister at the Balfour Hospital, was appointed as the new County Home matron.

The islands of Orkney could be grateful at this time to some long-serving stalwarts of the medical profession. These doctors were employed by the local parish councils, at an annual salary, to care for patients who were "on the panel." The rest of their income was made up by private practice patients.

Stronsay's medical officer Dr Robert Rosie, who died in 1928, had a salary from the parish council of just £130 a year. He served on Stronsay for nearly 30 years, caring for a population that grew by several thousands in the fishing season. However of Stronsay's population of 1,061, there were only 180 panel patients, so it seems that many hundreds had no medical cover at all.

On his death, his daughter Miss Irene Rosie was appointed interim medical officer and parochial vaccinator for the island, while the parish council sent a cable to Dr Rosie's son Captain Robert Rosie RAMC, then serving in the Sudan, offering him the job on a permanent basis.

South Ronaldsay and Burray offered an annual salary of only £105 but promised there was "a good private practice" when advertising for a replacement doctor following the retirement in 1928 of Dr David Dewar who had been the medical officer of the two islands for more than 56 years - an astonishing long service.

Dr F. L. Duncan, medical officer for the burgh of Stromness, reported on the cause of deaths in the population in the previous year: Senile Decay 5, Intestinal Obstruction 1, Bronchial 3, Heart Disease 6, Cancer 2, Tuberculosis 1, Disease of Arteries 2, Pleurisy 1, Violent Deaths 2, - total 23.

But Kirkwall Town Council was obviously quite satisfied with the well-being of the population of the Royal burgh for, in November, 1929, councillors decided to advertise Kirkwall as a health resort in conjunction with the LNE and LMS railway companies in the South, and to suggest that cheap travelling facilities be granted on certain days of the week.

The reorganisation of local government in 1930 saw the end of Kirkwall and St Ola parish council but Mr John D. Robertson, who had served since 1917 as the parish's Inspector of the Poor, became the new County Public Assistance officer.

The next crusade of county medical officer Dr Bannerman was, in December, 1930, against enlarged tonsils - and girls' sandals.

He warned that "enlarged tonsils are certainly a constant menace to the health of children so affected" and called for a system whereby operations to remove tonsils could be performed at the Balfour Hospital free of charge to parents. He also suggested it should be a punishable offence for parents not to get treatment for children suffering with enlarged tonsils. He added his complaint at girls wearing sandals. "This shoe is probably cheap, it is certainly nasty. Such footwear is but poor economy and it is not unfraught with dangerous consequences."

However by March, 1932, he had other concerns as the Balfour Hospital was placed in quarantine, with emergency admissions only, following a Scarlet Fever outbreak in Kirkwall. All out-patient clinics were cancelled and hospital visiting banned after two members of the nursing staff contracted the disease - and schools in Orphir and Holm as well as Kirkwall Grammar School were forced to close. By May, the situation was so bad that the Carness Isolation Hospital - the former Smallpox institution that had closed in 1926 - was reopened to cope because the fever hospital in Main Street was full with cases. To add to the problems, there was an outbreak of Whooping Cough and two cases of Diphtheria reported in the county. A year later, Orkney suffered two deaths as 14 cases of Para-Typhoid hit Papa Westray, Sanday and the Mainland.

In October, 1934, Orkney County Council had led the way in Britain by helping to finance the country's first air ambulance service, operated by Highland Airways, to cover Hoy and the North Isles. Doctors could use the service in cases where "transport by aeroplane is essential or, at least, eminently desirable" and payment would only be sought from those patients who could afford to pay. However, on the ground, the local branch of the St Andrews Ambulance Association warned in August, 1935, that "lack of support and apathy" could lead to the discontinuance of the motor ambulance service in Orkney. By 1938, ambulance services on the Orkney Mainland had been taken over by Orkney County Council and were operated by a new £430 Bedford vehicle, stationed in Kirkwall.

Other innovations were also unveiled. In September, 1936, it was announced that Orkney's new £13,000 Eastbank Hospital would be completed within a year, providing accommodation for 16 patients in the TB department, and 20 in the infectious diseases department. The existing TB hospital at the Scapa pavilion would be "destroyed" and the Balfour Hospital's infectious diseases ward in Main Street, Kirkwall would be vacated. The new TB wing of Eastbank Hospital was opened in June, 1937, when patients were transferred under the supervision of Matron Tantum.

Again, the Kirkwall fever hospital was fully occupied at the start of 1938 when an outbreak of Scarlet Fever swept the West Mainland, but by September that year the doors of the building in Main Street, owned by the Balfour Hospital trustees, were closed for the last time as a hospital, and all cases transferred to the Eastbank Hospital, which was owned by the county council. In 1940, the old hospital in Main Street was sold for £600 and, in March, 1943, the West End Hotel was opened by Mr D.J. Macrae, proprietor of the Stronsay Hotel.

It was also decided that the time had come to extend the Balfour Hospital. The number of in-patients had trebled since 1927 to 354 in 1935, as well as 490 out-patients treated that year. A public appeal was launched to raise £10,000 to pay for the extension.

Donations to the appeal fund were slow - it took two years to reach £1,718 - but, after the Department of Health for Scotland promised to provide 25 per cent of the cost, the trustees announced in August, 1939, that they would go ahead with the extension. A month later, war was declared and the whole project was shelved. However, the threat of wartime casualties meant that the hospital was indeed expanded - with two 42-bed wards built at government expense in 1940.

Wartime, and the huge influx of thousands of soldiers and civilian workers into the county, saw an epidemic of Meningitis in 1940, and the following year a mass innoculation of Orkney children against Diphtheria went ahead.

In May, 1941, Miss Louisa Gault, matron of the Balfour Hospital for nine years, left to take up a similar post in Haddington. She was succeeded by Miss J.M. Treasurer, a native of Inverness, who had been a ward sister at the Balfour. Five years later, Matron Treasurer resigned due to ill-health and was replaced, in 1946, by Miss Mary Brydie from Perthshire.

Matron Brydie arrived to find Orkney in remarkably good health. The county not only had the lowest rate of stillbirths in Scotland - just one tenth of the rate in Stirling - but also the lowest death rate of all the Scottish cities and counties, according to the annual report of the Registrar General for Scotland. The highest was Glasgow at 15.6 deaths per 1,000, the lowest Orkney at 9.3. However, it was reported that a drastic shortage of staff, at the end of the war, was threatening the future of the maternity service at the Balfour Hospital.

December, 1946, saw the retirement of another long-time stalwart of the Orkney health service - Dr William Sinclair, the Kirkwall GP for 25 years, who was the first doctor in Britain to fly on an air ambulance flight, from Sanday to Kirkwall, in 1933.

He was succeeded by a man who would become equally well known in the county with the dawn of the NHS: Dr James Gordon - a former Aberdeen University and Huntly FC goalkeeper - who had been demobbed from the Royal Army Medical Corps with the rank of Captain, after spending a year of his war service in the Faroe Islands with the South Staffordshire Regiment.

On Monday, July 5, 1948, the Balfour Hospital - founded 112 years earlier by John Balfour of Trenabie - passed into public ownership under the National Health Services (Scotland) Act.

But that year had already illustrated that disease was no respecter of legislation. Two girls, an 11 year old from Sandwick and a 12 year old from Rendall, were both treated for Poliomyeltis. It was the first outbreak of Polio in Orkney since before World War Two.

Tenants stage strike over rents of £15 a year

Rents starting at £15 a year were too much for 78 Kirkwall council house tenants - they staged a rent strike in protest!

Council house rents in Kirkwall varied from £15 a year for two apartment houses to £28 10s a year for five apartment houses. With rates included, a tenant of a two apartment house would pay 8s 6d a week.

But, under the banner of Kirkwall Citizens Association, tenants in 1948 complained that amounted to an increase, in rent and rates, of up to 60 per cent on the previous year. And they refused to pay up, claiming that they were being asked to subsidise the building of new houses.

After negotiations, and the intervention of MP Sir Basil Neven-Spence, the Kirkwall Town Council offered to halve the increases and the rent strike eventually ended after 12 weeks. In Stromness, the town council was accused of being dictatorial in ordering families to swap houses in order to make the most effective use of accommodation.

The end of war had seen the authorities facing a major housing crisis which, in Orkney, was partially solved by using former military buildings. In February, 1947, 24 local families were able to move into houses at the former Willowburn Camp in Kirkwall, and in 1948 families were assigned accommodation in the former "Wrennery" in Buttquoy Park.

But new houses were needed too, and, by the start of 1948, 13 houses in Earl Sigurd Street were about to receive their first tenants, and another 20 prefabricated Cruden houses were about to be erected at a cost of £1,650 each. When these 20 houses became available, Kirkwall Town Council was deluged with applications from 121 prospective tenants. Fortunately, by the end of 1948, Orkney had also been allocated 50 timber houses which were to be imported from Sweden - and which would become Laverock Road, Kirkwall.

And, whatever the Kirkwall tenants thought of 1948 rent levels, they would have been staggered by what followed. In the following 50 years, the burden of rents, plus rates, or community charge, would increase nearly 150-fold - that's six times the level of increase of the Retail Price Index over the same period.

Freedom for famous sons

Two of Kirkwall's most famous sons were awarded the freedom of the burgh: William Heddle, who was town clerk of Kirkwall for 43 years, and Stanley Cursiter, Orkney's best known artist of the 20th century.

William Heddle - he was aged 82 in 1948 - was town clerk from 1902-1945, and was the man given the credit for helping to preserve the future well-being of St Magnus Cathedral in the early years of the century when there was concern whether the Cathedral would be able to retain even a roof.

When restoration work on the Cathedral began, after a bequest from Sheriff George Thoms, Mr Heddle, a solicitor and partner in the law firm of Drever and Heddle, was the driving force behind the setting up of a permanent maintenance fund. He took his case to the Court of Session where it was agreed that £9,000 should be set aside for all time in a trust fund (this had grown to £16,000 by his retiral in 1945) and it gave the magistrates of Kirkwall special powers in their guardianship of the Cathedral.

It was a year of awards for Stanley Cursiter, who had been Director of the National Galleries of Scotland since 1930. Not only was he given the freedom of Kirkwall, but he was made a CBE in the New Year Honours List, and was appointed Painter and Limner to the King.

Stanley Cursiter was born at 15 East Road in Kirkwall in 1887 and, after leaving Kirkwall burgh school, moved to Edinburgh as an apprentice designer, developing his artistic talents at evening classes and at the Edinburgh School of Art. He won a scholarship at London's Royal College of Art, from where his career blossomed to one of national acclaim - his work was acquired for permanent collections as far afield as Munich - and he was a member of the Royal Scottish Academy.

During World War One, he was attached, with the rank of Captain, to the Field Survey Division of the Royal Engineers. He was twice mentioned in dispatches and was awarded the OBE.

In 1948, Cursiter retired as Director of the National Galleries and returned with his wife to Orkney, making his home at the former Stanger's boatyard at Ness, Stromness, which was converted into a family house. It was to allow him to spend more time painting Orkney scenes which were to become much sought after in the second half of the 20th century.

A year of tragedies

The weekly sailing races of Stromness Sailing Club were marred by tragedy in July, 1948, as two participants were drowned barely 200 yards from the South Pier.

The 14 feet dinghy of 28 year old lobster fisherman Magnus Bolt and 15 year old schoolboy George Waters capsized and threw them into the water. A motor boat raced to the scene but the two sailors had disappeared from view in a tragedy which was witnessed by hundreds, including Mrs Bolt and her two young daughters.

An appeal fund for the families raised over £600 within three weeks.

The following month, it was a tragedy on land which shocked the county when 14 year old William Scarth - the only son of Mr Henry Scarth of Skaill and Breckness - was killed in an accident with a horse at Skaill Farm, while at home on holiday from Eton College where he was a pupil. The boy's father was a member of the Allied Control Commission for Austria after being Depute District Commissioner for Civil Defence in Orkney during World War Two.

In September, 1948, the skipper was fatally injured and two crewmen washed overboard to their deaths, when the Aberdeen trawler *Kelvinway* ran into a storm off Orkney's west coast en route to the Faroes.

Shipping disasters

Eleven members of the mainly Greek crew were rescued by breeches buoy - and another 20 got off by boat - after the 3,500 ton Panama-registered ship *Bellavista* ran aground in thick fog near Mull Head, Papa Westray, in August, 1948. The vessel, carrying a cargo of iron ore, was abandoned as a total loss. A month earlier, the 9,414 ton American liberty ship *Thomas Jefferson*, was stranded on Seal Skerry, off Gairsay, carrying a cargo of iron ore from Sweden to Alabama. Over 1,000 tons of the cargo had to be jettisoned to allow the vessel to be refloated.

Nightmare in Scapa Flow

A schoolteacher Miss Jenny Wilson had an amazing escape after being caught in an open boat in a 60mph January gale in Scapa Flow. She "drifted helplessly for eight hours in pitch darkness buffeted by mountainous waves which threatened to swamp over her at any minute," *The Orcadian* reported.

Miss Wilson was being conveyed, with her possessions, from Longhope to St Margaret's Hope - where she had just started a teaching job - by St Margaret's Hope fisherman John Norquoy in his 18 feet yawl *Jessie*.

"It's a miracle we were not capsized," said Mr Norquoy after being caught in the gale which ripped away the sail before the boat's engine also failed.

The schoolteacher helped to steer the boat with an oar while Mr Norquoy worked on the engine, but, eventually, after drifting for miles, they were washed up on the shore at Deepdale, Holm. "But for Miss Wilson's courage, we would never have got out of that horrible nightmare. The waves were mountains high," said Mr Norquoy.

However, Mr J.R.F. Evans, district officer of Kirkwall Coastguard, said: "This was not merely an unfortunate and avoidable accident but a piece of crass stupidity which might have brought tragedy to two homes."

Orcadian killed in terror attack

Malayan gunmen fighting for independence from Britain killed George Swanson of Stromness - son of Captain George Swanson, the late master of the Pentland Firth steamer *St Ola* - in a terrorist attack on the rubber plantation where he worked.

Mr Swanson had worked in Malaya before World War Two and had been taken prisoner by the Japanese on the fall of Singapore, and was sent to work on the notorious "Railroad of Death" between Burma and Siam.

At the end of the war, he was repatriated to Orkney just in time to be reunited with his father before his death, but returned to Malaya in 1946.

Lord Lieutenant of Orkney

The first Lord Lieutenant of Orkney (previously the post covered Orkney and Shetland) was Patrick Sutherland Graeme, of Graemeshall, Holm, who was appointed in April, 1948, following the death the previous year of Alfred Baikie.

He had returned to his native Orkney ten years earlier on retirement after a distinguished legal career, and was already the vice convener of Orkney County Council.

Born in 1877, the eldest son of Alexander Sutherland Graeme, he trained as a barrister - during which time he gained a medal with Old Malvernians in the English Amateur Cup Final - and became secretary to Viscount Alverstone, Lord Chief Justice of England, from 1902-13.

In this role, he was present at many famous trials - including that of Dr Crippen, executed in 1910 for poisoning his wife, and the first criminal to be apprehended by the use of radiotelegraphy.

Mr Sutherland Graeme was made a CBE for his services as Judge Advocate at courts martial in Ireland, 1919-20, and served as the Deputy Judge Advocate General from 1932 until retiral in 1938.

Just a minute!

Emergency messages had to be broadcast on national BBC radio to tell Orcadians the correct time after *The Orcadian* caused a stir by announcing the end of British Summer Time a month early!

* * *

Stromness-born Police Sergeant James Groundwater (32), of Lyness Police Station, won £1,094 on the football pools.

Egilsay calling

A telephone exchange opened in Egilsay, for six subscribers. One of the first callers was Miss Mary Bews (90) of Victoria Street, Kirkwall, who telephoned her niece on her native island. It was the first time that Miss Bews had used - or even seen - a telephone. Orkney had 1,010 phone subscribers in 1948 - about one household in seven.

Orkney memory

The proprietor of the *Daily Express*, Lord Beaverbrook, erected a memorial to early settlers near his birthplace in New Brunswick, Canada, at Wilson's Point - named after an Orcadian Mr Robert Wilson who ran a ferry to Beaubear's Island a century earlier.

Merchant dies

Sir Gilbert Archer, chairman of the Kirkwall firm of merchants R. Garden Ltd, died aged 66, leaving £319,560 in his estate.

New rector

Stromness-born William Groundwater (42), senior English and History teacher at Kirkwall Grammar School, was appointed rector of Stromness Academy following the retiral of Mr J.R. Learmonth, Academy rector from 1927-48. Mr Groundwater was a former pupil of the school, going to Edinburgh University in 1923 to take an Honours degree in English.

Anniversary

Kirkwall's Highland Park Distillery, the world's most northerly distillery, celebrated its 150th anniversary.

Hotel sale

The Barony Hotel in Birsay was sold for £7,000. A bottle of whisky cost £1 13s 6d at the time.

Whaling work

Jack Smith (32) of Kirkwall was working on the *Empire Victory*, the world's largest whale factory vessel in 1948, with a mainly Norwegian crew. He earned £500 for nine months work - but £160 went in tax, he complained.

* * *

Sergeant William Mathieson, of St Margaret's Hope, but serving in the Malayan Police, earned the gratitude of jungle villagers by shooting dead a 15 feet long crocodile which had been terrorising the local population, and had killed at least one villager, reported *The Orcadian*.

Killer threatens ruin to Orkney

September 5, 1949, was a black day which threatened to decimate Orkney's biggest industry as a case of Fowl Pest was reported at Stromness.

Mr Alex Sutherland, of the Orkney office of the Ministry of Agriculture, said: "It is a very serious matter. If it became widespread, it would be ruinous."

The Orkney egg industry had grown to be worth £20 millions a year at 1999 prices. In the previous financial year, Orkney Egg Producers had handled nearly one million dozen eggs a week - a total of 42.5 million dozens valued at £890,000. (That was the equivalent of £40 for every man, woman and child in the county at a time when the average weekly wage was little over £5.) Orkney was acknowledged as the biggest egg producing county in Britain.

Within a fortnight, the Fowl Pest had

1949

spread as 2,500 hens were slaughtered in seven outbreaks around the county - and Orkney poultry farms were put in quarantine with a total standstill of stock.

By the first week of October, the disease had been confirmed in seven different islands, and 5,000 birds slaughtered in 14 cases.

Egg shipments were allowed to continue, as it was said that the infection was not carried in eggs, but there were increasing fears that Orkney would miss out on the Christmas poultry trade.

Investigations failed to produce a definite explanation of the outbreak, although

the eventual surmise was that it was spread by sea birds as many outbreaks were close to the shore, and the disease spread to the Hebrides and other coastal areas of Scotland.

Government compensation of around £1 a bird was paid to farmers who slaughtered poultry - although one unfortunate victim was Orkney's Garrison Commander at Hatston who lost his 50 hens.

Eventually, there was a total of 24 cases, stretching from Hoy and South Ronaldsay to the North Isles, but the ban on poultry movements was partially lifted on November 17, in time to save the Christmas trade, and, on December 22, all restrictions were lifted.

The county had got off lightly - and just one per cent of the county's estimated poultry population of nearly one million hens had been destroyed!

The dawn of an institution as Stromness Shopping Week becomes part of the Orkney social calendar.

(Picture courtesy of Orkney Library photographic archive)

Greatest day in 132 years

"Never in the 132 years of its existence as a burgh has there been such a day in Stromness as there was on Saturday. From morning until night the streets were thronged with people from all parts of the county," said *The Orcadian*.

And so began Stromness Shopping Week, the annual gala week which was to become a fixture of the Orkney Calendar in the second half of the 20th century.

The first Shopping Week was held from July 18-23, 1949, organised in just three weeks by the newly founded Stromness and West Mainland Chamber of Commerce to attract shoppers to the burgh. The credit, or otherwise, for the idea was given to Mr W.C. Howard who was said by *The Orcadian* to be the "inspiration" behind the suggestion which was "met with warm support."

There was no Shopping Week Queen

that first year when Provost George Robertson opened the event in front of a "Welcome to Stromness" banner across Victoria Street, but 4,000 people turned out for the closing fancy dress procession, led by Kirkwall City Pipe Band, with 900 flags bedecking the streets.

Mr W. Towers, chairman of the chamber of commerce, said members looked forward to holding "an annual event somewhat similar to this."

Orkney pioneers wind power trials

Orkney was chosen to lead the way in Britain as experiments went ahead to harness the power of island gales to drive wind generators and produce electricity.

A North of Scotland Hydro Electric Board delegation visited the county to consider suitable sites, and two 100 feet high masts were erected at Quoyloo and Costa Head to test wind velocities. Costa Head was adjudged, from the results, to be the most consistently windy place in Britain.

In the summer of 1949, the Hydro Electric Board placed a contract with the company of John Brown for the design and construction of the first experimental windmill of its kind in Britain - with 60 feet blades to generate 100 kilowatts of power.

But it was accepted that, for the immediate future, Orkney would rely on diesel-powered electricity as the firm of Orkney Builders was awarded the contract to build a new power station by the Peerie Sea in Kirkwall.

Football successes

It was the most successful year on record for Orkney's county footballers who, in front of 4,800 spectators at the Bignold Park, beat Shetland 6-1 and then crossed the Pentland Firth two weeks later to beat Caithness 6-0.

Earlier in the season, a crowd of 3,000 saw a visit to the Bignold Park by the players of first division Aberdeen who beat Hotspurs 5-0. Aberdeen's two internationalists Hamilton and Pearson were "outstanding," said *The Orcadian*.

Sobering facts on drink death

A Kirkwall jury heard that an Aberdeen trawler engineer had died on board his vessel - after drinking zinc chloride soldering fluid. It was stated that from the time the *Strathdee* left Aberdeen, until she arrived in Kirkwall, the crew had consumed eleven bottles of rum, some brandy and sherry, and an unknown quantity of beer.

Stalwart of Orkney good health

Mr Walter Bannerman, Orkney's Medical Officer of Health, announced his retiral after 25 years service to the county - and a career which stretched back to the Boer War.

A native of Cornwall, he was a medical officer with the 2nd Hampshire Regiment in South Africa at the start of the century, and in World War One he served, with the rank of Captain, with the Royal Army Medical Corps, in Belgium, France and Egypt.

He moved to Orkney in 1924 where he led the fight against the scourge of Tuberculosis, and at the outbreak of World War Two, he became responsible for arrangements for the treatment of all civilian war casualties in Orkney.

He was made an OBE in the 1942 New Year Honours List for services to civil defence.

His other great passion was the Orkney Trout Fishing Association, of which he was secretary for several years.

Troops called in

Eighty Kirkwall dockers - demanding extra "dirty money" for unloading coal, cement and fertilisers - walked out on strike when soldiers from Hatston were called to the pier to unload cement.

The North of Scotland shipping company said it was necessary to unload the *St Rognvald* to allow 1,000 boxes of eggs to be loaded for Leith.

The dockers were paid 2s 3d an hour, plus 3d when cargoes were designated as "dirty." The dispute was settled after six days following talks between the port employers and the Transport and General Workers' Union.

Tax hits tweed

The imposition of Purchase Tax threatened the future of the handweaving tweed business which employed 37 people in Orkney, MP Sir Basil Neven-Spence told the House of Commons.

In April, 1948, one Orkney firm sold 5,400 yards - but, after the introduction of the tax, they sold only 180 yards in eight months. The Mill Street, Kirkwall, factory of John Sclater and Company (Orkney) Ltd would probably have been the biggest Orkney tweed producer at this time.

Unperturbed by the problems of the tweed industry, the Kirkwall firm of R. Garden Ltd launched into tartan weaving, under the brandname Argarden.

Plane wreck

A BEA De Havilland Rapide aircraft - on a mercy mission to North Ronaldsay - nose-dived on landing and was written off, although the pilot escaped unhurt. The plane was answering a call in January, 1949, to take 37 year old Mary Muir to hospital in Kirkwall. After valuable engine parts had been retrieved, the fuselage of the plane was given as a gift to island headmaster Mr Alex Walker who planned to make it a playhouse for his children.

Relief at last

The Northern Lighthouse ship *Pole Star*, after being hit by bad weather, managed to get relief to the lighthousemen of Suleskerry who had been on the rock for three months.

For two of the lighthousemen, John Gillespie and William Learmonth, their Christmas and New Year celebrations were nearly six weeks overdue.

Harbour escape

Mr John Wood, the 68 year old retired Finstown sub postmaster, swam to safety after plunging more than 10 feet in his car into Kirkwall harbour. An hour later, the police found the car headlights still blazing under the water.

Ba' family double

For the first time in history, the Men's and Boys' Ba' games were won by a father and son on the same day as the 1949 New Year confrontations were won by Edgar Gibson, Main Street, Kirkwall, and his son Gary, for the Uppies.

* * *

Orkney Police Force had grown, by 1949, to 17 men, plus 60 special constables. The total mechanised strength of the force was one Wolseley car, one Morris van and a Sunbeam motorcycle.

* * *

Mr Croft Jackson, organist of St Magnus Cathedral, Kirkwall, for ten years, bid farewell to Orkney to move to Colchester, Essex. He was succeeded by Mr Hunter McBain, from Polmont, West Lothian.

They made their way in the world

Thousands of Orcadians left their island homes during the 19th and 20th centuries to make their way in the world - not only in Britain, but the New World and the colonies of Empire - Australia, New Zealand, Canada and the United States, South Africa and India. Many found fame if not fortune. This is just a random selection of those who featured in *The Orcadian* in the first half of the century.

Dr Charles Anderson, the youngest son of John Anderson, of Moa, Stenness, after graduating at Edinburgh University with both an MA and BSc, went to Australia, where, in 1921, he was appointed Director of the Australian Museum.

John Gerard Anderson, born in Orphir, the son of a clergyman, in 1836, and educated at Aberdeen University, he emigrated to Queensland, Australia, where he was appointed the first district inspector of schools in the colony - rising to the position of Under-Secretary for Public Instruction in the Queensland government in Brisbane. He retired in January, 1904.

David Balfour, one of eleven children of the Balfour family of Chalmersquoy, Westray, rose to become Registrar-General of Jamaica. Educated at Edinburgh University, he became a solicitor in 1888, going to Jamaica in 1891 where he practised at the Supreme Court of the Judiciary before becoming Clerk of Courts. In 1906, he was promoted to Stipendiary Magistrate and in 1908 appointed Registrar-General, a post he held until his death in 1922.

David Clouston, after teaching at the Kirkwall burgh school and a course at Edinburgh University, he joined the Indian Agricultural Service until 1929, during which time he became Director of the Agricultural Institute at Bihar. Mr Clouston died in 1948 at his home at Heathfield House, St Ola, at the age of 77.

Maribelle Cormack, the daughter of an Eday man, became a well known author in Providence, Rhode Island, USA, when her book *Wind of the Vikings* ran to seven editions when published in the 1930s.

Ralph Croy, born at the Brig o' Waithe, Stenness, completed 50 years in American banking as Vice-President of the Bank of Buffalo and the Marine Trust Company of Buffalo, in 1940. He had emigrated to the USA with his parents when he was eight.

Chief Drever - the descendant of a Westray man - was a chief of the Canadian Cree Indians for 55 years until his death, aged 85, in 1938. His ancestry could be traced back to James Drever who went to Canada with the Hudson's Bay Company and later married the daughter of the Cree tribal chief Mistowasis. Chief Drever - who was said to speak English with an Orcadian accent - had several first cousins in Westray, including Thomas Rendall, of Glen, Westray, who, in 1936, gave *The Orcadian* an account of the family history, James Drever having corresponded with his Orkney relatives right up to his death. In 1936, Chief Drever was one of the Native American chiefs who presided at a gathering in Saskatchewan of thousands of Canadian Indians to celebrate the 60th anniversary of a peace treaty by which the Crees and the Saulteaux tribe surrendered 140,000 square miles of territory to Queen Victoria. At the gathering, Chief Drever - who on his death was succeeded by his son Chief Joe Drever who later changed the spelling of his name to Dreaver - met Baron Tweedsmuir, Governor General of Canada, but better known as the novelist John Buchan.

George Drever, in 1935, had risen to become the first Orcadian to be Head Office Manager of the National Bank of Scotland in Edinburgh.

William Eunson - apparently from Fair Isle but invariably described as an Orcadian - went to Aberdeen at the turn of the century and revolutionised the fish trade. He is the man credited with discovering the suitability of a South American vegetable extract, Anatto, in the dying of cured fish. "Had he been less altruistic, he would have patented his discovery and become a millionaire. Instead in his zeal for the good of the trade, William Eunson broadcast the new treatment. Soon wholesale and retail traders throughout the country were preparing their goals in this attractive manner, and many who are millionaires in this business date their rise to fortune on the day this Orcadian came to Aberdeen," the *Daily Record* reported in 1929. In recognition of his contribution, the Aberdeen fish trade granted Mr Eunson a pension for life.

Sir John Flett, from Kirkwall, and a brother of Kirkwall's Provost Peter Flett, was from 1920-1935 director of the Geological Survey of Great Britain and the museum of Practical Geology. He died in January, 1947, aged 77, at his home in Ashdon, Essex. Lady Flett, his wife, was Mary Meason from Kirkwall. He received the OBE in 1918 and was knighted in 1925. He was educated at Kirkwall burgh school before proceeding to Edinburgh University, where he later became an assistant to Professor James Geikie. He joined HM Geological Survey in 1901 and was sent by the Royal Society to the West Indies to report on volcanic eruptions. From 1911-1920, he was assistant to the director of the Geological Survey and in charge of the Geological Survey of Scotland.

John Flett, originally from Orphir, for many years carried on the business of Flett, Smith and Company in Georgetown, British Guiana. He was an early benefactor of Kirkwall's Balfour Hospital and, on his death in 1931, he left a legacy of £500 to the hospital.

Captain Andrew Fotheringhame, born at Rusness, Sanday, emigrated to Canada where, in 1932, he was the inventor of a new magnetic compass - the first ship's compass to be adjusted without permanent magnets, - which successfully completed trials on vessels operating on the coasts of British Columbia.

Margaret Graham has a plaque in her memory in Kirkwall's St Magnus Cathedral: "Margaret Manson Graham, Nurse and Missionary, rescuer of children abandoned to die, devoted her life to Christian work in Nigeria, born Orphir 1860, died Arochuku 1933." After education at the Orphir School, she became a teacher before training to be a nurse in Glasgow where she volunteered to go to Nigeria. She became the first sister in charge of the new Calabar hospital helping to fight the ravages of tropical diseases. She returned to this country in 1919 but within two years she was back in Nigeria as a missionary nurse at the Slessor Memorial Home in Arochuku, where she died, aged 73.

They made their way in the world - continued

JOHN GUNN rose from butcher's boy to become one of Australia's most important politicians in the early years of the century. Born in 1885 in the mining town of Rheola, Victoria, the son of emigrants from Orkney, his Orcadian father died early, leaving his mother to bring up nine children. John Gunn became President of the Australian Drivers Union in 1910 and five years later was elected to the South Australian Parliament for Adelaide. He became leader of the South Australian Labour Party in 1918 at the age of 33.

ANNA M.B. GUTHRIE - a daughter of the Rev Thomas Wingate, minister of Stromness, was acclaimed as an artist, author and historian. She exhibited at the Royal Academy in 1902 and won praise in 1922 for her published collection of essays *Wordsworth and Tolstei and Other Papers.*

MAJOR HARRY HAMILTON HEBDEN MC, of Carrick House, Eday, inherited most of the island, as Laird of Carrick, after it had originally been purchased by his grandfather. After training at Sandhurst Military College, he joined the Royal Fusiliers, serving in Nigeria and India. In World War One, he served with his regiment in France and subsequently was with the Army of Occupation on the Rhine. A cousin of Orkney MP Basil Neven-Spence, he retired from the Army in 1936, and died at the age of only 52 in 1939.

DR JOHN HEPBURN, son of Col David Hepburn of Stromness, was recognised for his part in one of the major ground-breaking advances in medical science during the 20th century when he worked with three Nobel Prize winners in early research work on the treatment of Diabetes by Insulin. He emigrated to Canada in 1910 and, in World War One, served with the Canadian Highlanders in France before being wounded and repatriated to Canada where he completed his medical studies at Toronto University. It was there that Dr Hepburn collaborated with Professor John James Macleod, Sir Frederick Banting and Charles Best in clinical trials which proved that, with the discovery of Insulin, an efficient remedy for Diabetes had been found. Macleod, Banting and Best shared the 1923 Nobel Prize for their achievement.

JOHN HERCUS, from Faray, was the man who kept the "home fires burning" in Glasgow in World War One when he was Fuel Overseer for the city. He retired in 1937 after 47 years service with Glasgow Corporation.

SHERIFF COLIN INKSTER - an early pioneer of Manitoba - became one of the longest serving members of the Canadian judiciary. He was the son of an Orcadian stone mason John Inkster who had gone to Canada with the Hudson's Bay Company in 1821. Colin Inkster was Sheriff of Manitoba's eastern judicial district for 51 years, during which time, in 1930, he was honoured by Chief Red Dog at a special ceremony by the Cree Indians who presented the Sheriff with a ceremonial drum. The Sheriff replied in the Cree language. He died at the age of 91 in 1934.

WILLIAM INKSTER, born at Cogar, Rousay, rose to become Firemaster of the city of Aberdeen, after serving for several years in the London City Fire Brigade. He returned to Orkney and served on Kirkwall Town Council from 1924-29, during which time he helped to improve the local fire fighting facilities. He died at the age of 73 in 1933.

ANDREW KENNEDY, son of Kirkwall cabinet maker Mr T.S. Kennedy, invented and developed a system of portable lighting which helped to revolutionise the American film industry in 1920. Mr Kennedy, who had emigrated to Brooklyn, USA, named his invention "Orcadia." His new lighting system - capable of delivering two and a half million candle power - enabled film scenes to be shot outside of studios, thus paving the way for some of the great epic American films shot on location.

LORD KINROSS, the Lord Justice General of Scotland and Lord President of the Court of Session, as well as a former MP for Kinross and Clackmannan, who died in January, 1905, was born plain J.B. Balfour, the son of Rev Peter Balfour, a 19th century minister for Evie and Rendall.

J.J. KIRKNESS, born in Sandwick in 1858, went to South Africa in 1879 and set up in business as a builder - he actually built the Government buildings in Pretoria in 1888. He was elected to the city council and in 1906 was made Mayor of Pretoria. His wife was a daughter of Kirkwall architect Samuel Baikie.

SIR JOHN LATHAM, whose mother, then Miss Janet Scott, emigrated from Eday in 1852, rose to become, in the 1920s, Attorney-General of Australia and, later, leader of Australia's Nationalist party in opposition. In 1936 he was appointed Chief Justice of the High Court in Australia, at a salary of £3,500 a year.

A.J. LEARMONTH, son of Stronsay man Robert Learmonth, was appointed in 1948 as the engineer in charge of the construction of the biggest dam in the Southern hemisphere - the £9 million Warragamba Dam which, 400 feet high, would create a 36 mile long lake to supply water for the Australian city of Sydney.

COLONEL JOHN CECIL MACRAE DSO, born in 1881, the younger son of Orkney procurator fiscal John Macrae. Educated at Fettes College, Edinburgh, and Sandhurst, he received his first commission in 1900 as 2nd Lieutenant, Hampshire Regiment. In 1902, he was promoted to Lieutenant, Seaforth Highlanders. In 1904, he was seconded to the Indian Army, becoming Colonel in 1929. He served in Mesopotamia 1914-17 and for his war service received the DSO. In 1933, he represented the Indian Army at the Geneva Disarmament Conference - the same year he was appointed a Deputy Lieutenant of Orkney. Colonel Macrae retired in 1935 to make his permanent home at Rysa Lodge, Hoy - across Scapa Flow from his mother's home at Grindelay, Orphir. He became a Companion of the Bath in the 1935 Birthday Honours List. Recalled to service at the start of World War Two, he died in 1940.

THOMAS MOODIE, born at Melsetter, Orkney, was the central character in one of the most thrilling episodes in the history of the white pioneers in Southern Africa. He had led members of his family in the famous Moodie trek in 1892 when they made the nine month trek by ox wagon from Bethlehem in the Orange Free State to Southern Rhodesia where they founded the township of Melsetter. Thomas Moodie died in the first part of the 20th century, but other Moodies who survived the trek lived well in to the 20th century, including Malcolm Moodie, who died in the Transvaal at the age of 70 in 1948.

They made their way in the world - continued

BEATRICE NAIRNE, real name Scott, became a well known novelist in the 1930s. Born in Holm, the daughter of Jack Scott, and a second cousin of Stanley Cursiter, the Orcadian artist who became director of Scotland's National Galleries, she was sent as a child to the Riviera, following the death of her father, and later lived in Budapest. She also wrote a novel *The Last Spring* set in Switzerland.

GEORGE REID, born in Westray, was acknowledged as Australia's oldest Freemason when he died in Sydney at the age of 95 in 1933. He had been initiated in Kirkwall's Kilwinning Lodge in 1884, the year before he sailed to Australia.

COLONEL JAMES SCLATER DSO, born in Kirkwall in 1867, emigrated to Canada at the age of 21. A crack shot, he represented Canada at rifle shooting at the international competitions at Bisley in 1908 and 1912. After a distinguished war career - in which he went to France as the officer commanding the 29th Battalion of the Vancouver Regiment - he held both the Distinguished Service Order and the Croix de Guerre of France. After the war, he re-entered the service of the Canadian Pacific Railway Company, and transferred to run that company's operations in Australia. He died, aged 75, in British Columbia.

DR ALFRED SHEARER, born in Stronsay, became High Sheriff of Montgomeryshire in Wales in 1934. He had qualified as a physician at Edinburgh University before moving to Wales, and setting up a practice in Newton, in 1900.

JOHN AND DAVID SHEARER, from the East Mainland, who emigrated to Australia in 1852, along with their brothers Peter, William and James, established one of the first firms manufacturing agricultural machinery for the pioneer farmers in South Australia, and David Shearer is credited with building, in 1899, the first car in Australia, indeed the Southern hemisphere, a steam-powered vehicle capable of speeds up to 24mph. The brothers' main line of work, however, was the production of ploughs and harvesters - and it is said that Australian-built Shearer implements were even exported back to Orkney. John Shearer died in 1932 and his brother in 1936.

MAGNUS SINCLAIR, who left Orkney at the age of 19 to go to Canada with a few shillings in his pocket, became one of the top trades union figures in North America in 1935 when he was elected Dean of the Amalgamated Association of Street, Electric Railway and Motor Coach Employees of North America. Born in Burray in 1864, he had served on the association's executive board since 1903.

PETER SINCLAIR, from Kirkbreck, Holm, went on to become the champion hammer thrower of New South Wales, Australia, at the start of the century.

ALEXANDER SLATER, the son of Mr and Mrs Slater, Garra, Swanbister, Orphir, established a flourishing building business after emigrating to Australia before World War One. In 1936, his company won the £223,995 tender to build South Australia's new Parliament House.

GEORGE SPENCE, an Orcadian who was a gold miner in the Klondyke at the start of the century, became a cabinet minister in the provincial government of Saskatchewan as Minister of Railways, Labour, Industries and Highways. He was born in 1880 in Birsay and went to Canada as a teenager. He first was elected to the provincial parliament in 1917 and, in 1925, was elected to the Canadian Federal Parliament before returning to the Saskatchewan legislature in 1927.

WILLIAM SPENCE, born in Eday, emigrated to Australia where, after a spell as a gold prospector, he became one of the pioneers of the trades union movement, helping to organise the first miners' union, before becoming a leading Labour politician, culminating in his appointment as Postmaster General in the Federal government of 1914.

WILLIAM STRUTHERS, from St Margaret's Hope, was one of the pioneering electrical engineers at the dawn of the age of electricity at the start of the 20th century. In 1900, he was appointed manager in charge of the electricity power station serving the Argentinian seaport and city of Bahia Blanca.

JACK TAIT, later to return to his native Orkney and become the sub postmaster in Dounby, was the 1912 lightweight wrestling champion of Vancouver Island and runner-up in the All-Canada lightweight wrestling championships the same year.

JAMES THOMSON, from Quoys, South Ronaldsay, rose to become the Chief Factor of the Hudson's Bay Company in Canada before his death in 1933.

WILLIAM TRAILL, of Holland, Papa Westray, was a civil engineer by profession who worked on the Forth Bridge, the Manchester Ship Canal and the Vauxhall Bridge over the Thames. He also worked in Malaya for several years. In retirement, he returned to Orkney and died at the age of 80 in 1944.

JAMES WATT, born at the Bu of Rothiesholm, Stronsay, and a former tenant of Airy Farm, Stronsay, became Mayor of Hyde in Cheshire in 1939. He had moved to Cheshire 35 years earlier to start dairy farming.

JAMES AND THOMAS WATTS, two Stromness brothers, pioneered the development of cinema in London to the extent that they owned one of the biggest chains of picture houses in and around the capital in the years either side of World War One. They originally had a housebuilding business in the South London area before they turned to cinemas. At one time, up to ten picture houses, several attached to roller skating rinks, were under their control, and during the war years, some were temporarily converted into aircraft factories for the Sopwith company.

JAMES WILSON, of Melvin Place, Stromness, was one of the last surviving Orkney links with the 19th century whaling industry until his death, at the age of 83, in 1934. As a 16 year old boy he joined the famous old Hull whaler *True Love* in 1866, and went to the Davis Straits in Canada, later sailing on the Dundee whaling ships *Wildfire* and *Intrepid*.

JOHN M. YORSTON, the eldest son of Mr and Mrs Robert Yorston, Georth, Evie, left Orkney in 1890 to become a farmer in Canada, where he served three terms as a Liberal member of the British Columbia parliament, 1906-1909, 1916-24. He died at the age of 69 in 1937.

Mass suicide of whales

1950

The sands of the Bay of Holland in Stronsay were turned red with blood as 97 pilot whales died a pitiful lingering death after stranding ashore in what was described as a mass suicide.

The whales - from six feet to 20 feet long and up to seven tons in weight - came ashore on Saturday, April 22, 1950. One theory was that something had frightened them, possibly a large killer whale which had been sighted by boatmen near the Green Holms the week before.

A century earlier such a harvest of whales would have been regarded as a Godsend in the islands. In 1833, 25 Orkney ships, with crews of 20 men each, took part in whaling. As recently as the end of the 19th century, the islanders of Stronsay and Westray had organised whale hunts and deliberately shepherded pods of whales into sheltered bays to slaughter them for their meat and oil. Kirkwall had its own whale blubber industry - the Oilie House near the Peerie Sea - up until the start of the 20th century and the last whale oil produced in Kirkwall came from a number of whales which stranded in Sanday and were later towed to the town.

However, in 1950, although the whales were still potentially valuable to the Norwegian whaling industry, their arrival was regarded in Stronsay not as a Godsend but a public health menace.

Captain E.H. Clements, the Stronsay harbourmaster, appealed to whalers and trawlers to help remove the giant invaders before they became a major hygiene risk. "There is a little fortune lying out there which, if allowed to remain much longer, might well bring disease to Stronsay."

An endless procession of Stronsay folk went along to the beach, generally helpless to do anything but watch the slow death of the whales, 90 of which were concentrated in an area of just 100 yards of the two miles of white sands. A man who ventured too near one of the large whales was knocked off his feet by a flick of its powerful tail.

Mr W. Kelday, of Mount Pleasant, Stronsay, helped put four of the baby whales back in the sea. "They went out to different parts of the bay and played about for nearly half an hour. They then turned and charged the beach like speedboats, bringing a fifth one with them. They threw themselves among their dying parents heaped on the sand."

By the Sunday, only 30 of the whales remained alive, and the following day just 15 as the disposal of 450 tons of unexpected whale meat presented a massive headache for the county council. An appeal was sent to the Ministry of Health for help as Dr Walter Bannerman, the county medical officer of health, said : "I have never known the like of this in all my 25 years as medical officer of health here. We have had an odd whale or two washed up before but never anything like this."

County clerk Douglas Wood said : "We are going to face a critical situation if nothing is done pretty soon. With the warm weather coming, the carcases will start decomposing soon and this will be a serious menace to the health of the community."

But on Tuesday, April 25, warm weather seemed remote as Orkney was swept by blizzards with five inches of snow. On Stronsay, the last nine surviving whales were put out of their misery by butcher John Horn. "I just could not bear to see them suffer any longer," he said.

The heads of two of the whales were severed and island grocer Magnus Dennison arranged for them to be sent to the Natural History Section of the British Museum. Also, the lower jaw of a whale was dispatched to Edinburgh. It took four men to lift the heads on to a lorry.

A Norwegian whaling firm, based in Bergen, offered to collect the carcases, free of charge, but this plan collapsed when the veterinary authorities in Norway refused to sanction an import permit. The Norwegians did offer to dump them in the Atlantic - if Orkney County Council paid £2,000!

A move to bury the dead whales on Stronsay was rejected by the Medical Officer of Health on hygiene grounds, and, at one stage, it was considered calling in the War Office, with tank landing craft, to remove the mammals. Eventually, however, Mr A. Burgess, of Whitehall, Stronsay, offered to clean up what had been dubbed as "Suicide Bay" for £225, by mobilising the island's small fleet of lobster boats to tow the carcases out to sea.

The county council ordered that the whales should be dumped in the North Sea, at least three miles off the nearest land in Orkney. However, a week later, at least 18 dead whales were washed back on to the shores of Caithness and various parts of Orkney, including Deerness, Tankerness, Burray, Shapinsay, Gairsay and South Ronaldsay. It was suggested that they would have to be blown up with dynamite, but eventually the problem was solved with most of the carcases being burned.

The reasons for such mass strandings of whales still prompted controversy and debate amongst scientists at the end of the 20th century. But what was certain was that the year of 1950 was particularly remembered for the phenomenon. Just three weeks after the Stronsay stranding, another 147 whales came ashore at Dunbar.

Atom tests in Flow?

Government scientists were on the way to completing experiments on the first atomic magnetic mine - and, in September, 1950, it was suggested that tests on the new weapons could be started within months in Scapa Flow.

"Laboratory tests have shown that the atomic mine will be even more deadly than the atom bomb. When it explodes in the sea, it will not only render the air radioactive but also vast stretches of water," reported *The Orcadian.*

Although there was no suggestion that the mines would actually be exploded in the Flow, it is nevertheless astonishing, 50 years later, that the news did not appear to prompt a single letter of concern.

Such pragmatism certainly was not the case across the North Sea where German politicians - outraged that the British were using the island of Heligoland, a former wartime home of the German Navy, for target bombing practice - suggested that Orkney or Shetland should be used instead.

The British authorities had not allowed the former residents of Heligoland to return to their homes, and, in a strongly worded protest to British government minister Lord Henderson, the Germans said : "The British Government must realise it is time they stopped destroying and grabbing in Germany, and produce some proof that they desire an honest understanding with us.

"Lord Henderson's statement that there is no better bombing target than Heligoland cannot be accepted by any German of good faith. We venture to suggest to Lord Henderson that he uses the uninhabited Orkney, Shetland or Scilly isles for his bombs. Heligoland is German soil and no more bombs must fall there."

Accolades for Orcadians

Orcadians achieved success at home and abroad this year.

W.H. Traill was an Orcadian who became one of the foremost journalists in Australia as editor of the *Sydney Mail* and then *The Bulletin*, which celebrated its 70th anniversary in 1950.

The same month, Miss Edith Baikie, a daughter of William C. Baikie, of St Margaret's Hope, became chief of research and assistant professor for the institute of public affairs at the Iowa State University, USA.

Martin T. Flett, born in Orkney, the son of Sir John Flett, late Director of the Geological Survey of Great Britain, and a nephew of former Kirkwall Provost Peter Flett, became Under-Secretary at the Treasury at the age of 36. Three years later, in 1953, he was appointed to the British Embassy in Washington, USA.

Another Orcadian close to the power of government was W.G. Pottinger, son of a Burray minister Rev William Pottinger, who was appointed private secretary to Hector McNiel, Secretary of State for Scotland, in 1950.

Nearer home, Orkney's county convener Alex Calder was appointed a CBE in the New Year honours list. A farmer at Sebay,

Tankerness, he had been a member of the county council since the end of World War One, and a governor of the North of Scotland College of Agriculture since 1921. It marked a family double, for three years later - as the convener celebrated his 80th birthday - his oldest son, Dr Alexander Calder, who was Director of Pig Supplies at the Ministry of Food, was made an OBE in the New Year honours.

Dr David Marwick, born and raised in Rousay, became principal of Kersewell College, Lanarkshire. Educated in Kirkwall and with an honours BSc in agriculture from Aberdeen University in 1936, he had returned to a teaching career after war service in the RAF.

Another Orcadian was being acclaimed across the Atlantic in Canada. L.A. Learmonth, who left Orkney in 1911 at the age of 17, to emigrate to Canada, became a legendary figure in the Northern polar regions during his 39 years serving in the remotest reaches with the Hudson's Bay Company.

According to top Canadian museum officials, his contribution to man's knowledge of the Eskimo and the Arctic had been unmatched by any other Canadian, said the *Toronto Star Weekly* in 1950.

Learmonth was, at the time, said to be one of only four men in history to have travelled the Northwest Passage in both directions. Described as "Learmonth of the Arctic," he had collected, as an amateur scientist, a wealth of native artefacts which were on exhibition at the Royal Ontario Museum in Toronto and which were acknowledged as the most complete collection of the Thule Eskimo culture of 900-1300 AD. Learmonth's specimens came from remote Arctic regions which no other scientist had ever visited, said the *Toronto Star Weekly*.

In 1951, Learmonth was planning to embark on a new expedition of exploration to reach a remote island which, according to the newspaper, was not even known by Eskimos to exist until it was spotted by a recent aerial survey by the Royal Canadian Air Force.

Also across the Atlantic, David Laird, grandson of Stromness butcher Andrew Laird, was credited with teaching Hollywood movie star Alan Ladd to ride, and later he became trainer for Ladd's stable of racehorses. By 1950, David Laird had moved from California to Detroit where he operated a riding stable.

New ships for Orkney

An ambitious programme of ship building saw three new motor powered vessels introduced on to Orkney ferry routes in the years 1950-54 by the North of Scotland and Orkney and Shetland Steam Navigation Company.

In March, 1950, the 2,242 ton twin screw motor vessel *St Ninian* - the first North ship to be fitted with radar - was launched at Dundee after being built by Caledon Shipbuilding Company at a cost of £400,000.

The "luxury vessel" - which would replace the previous *St Ninian*, built in 1895 - could carry 162 first class passengers, 124 second class and 344 deck passengers.

Later in the year, plans were announced for the ship to be used for Kirkwall to Bergen cruises, price 40 guineas.

In March, 1951, the new motor vessel *St Ola* was launched at the Aberdeen yard of Alexander Hall and Company, ready to be fitted out for service on the Pentland Firth route between Stromness and Scrabster. The new single screw powered ship - which would replace her namesake *St Ola* which had been built in 1892 - had a speed of 13 knots and could take 20 cars and 360 passengers.

The new RMS *St Ola* made her maiden voyage across the Firth at the end of May, 1951. The 178 feet long diesel-driven vessel, with a beam of 33 feet and a crew of just 13, met up with her predecessor off Cantick Head before the old ship led her successor through Scapa Flow into Stromness where a big crowd had gathered at a pierhead bedecked in flags.

Captain William Banks took over as master of the new ship. He had been one of just four masters who had commanded the 135 feet long steamer which had been "Queen of the Pentland Firth" for the previous 59 years after being built at the yard of Hall, Russell and Company, Aberdeen.

Those four masters were Captain R. Robertson, 1892-1903; Captain Robert Swanney, 1903-11; Captain George Swanson, 1911-42; and Captain Banks, 1943-51.

Captain Banks died at the age of 67 in 1953 after 33 years service with the North of Scotland Company. He was succeeded as *St Ola* master by Captain John Stevenson, a Westray man.

The old *St Ola* was given a farewell visit by Mrs Asherola Sutherland, née Buchanan, aged 43, who in October, 1907, became the first baby to be born

on the *St Ola* - her christian name being an amalgam from Dr Asher, the Thurso doctor who tended her, and Ola.

The ship's bell from the old *St Ola* was to be presented to Stromness Museum.

One of the first passengers on the new ship was Captain Ted Fresson, home on holiday from Kenya, who would be forever remembered as the founder of Highland Airways and the pioneer of Orkney's civil air services throughout the 1930s and 1940s. He had flown over the Pentland Firth more than 3,000 times - but this was the first occasion he had ever crossed the Firth by ship.

The switch from steam power to diesel saw the North of Scotland company drop the reference to "Steam Navigation" from its name, and, in 1954, it was the North of Scotland and Orkney and Shetland Shipping Company which saw the new *St Rognvald* cargo ship - capable of carrying 280 cattle and 220 sheep - launched at the Aberdeen yard of Alexander Hall and Company.

The 246 feet vessel - the biggest ship ever built in the history of the yard - was capable of 13-14 knots, with a crew of 17 and accommodation for 12 passengers on services between Aberdeen and Orkney and Shetland.

America to Orkney in a day

The rapid development of international air services saw Orkney exile Sam Sinclair, of Portland, Oregon, leave New York on a Wednesday morning and take lunch at Kirkwall's Ayre Hotel on Thursday, at the start of a holiday with relatives in Sandwick in the summer of 1950.

Unfortunately, Orkney's local air services seemed to be going into a steep tailspin - with numerous complaints about the decline in the both standard and regularity of flights.

"Helicopters are the ultimate answer to the inter-island air service in Orkney," said Mr Frank Beswick MP, Parliamentary Secretary to the Ministry of Civil Aviation in the Labour Government of 1950, during a visit to Kirkwall.

However, it would be some years, he said, before they could be in general service as they were still largely in the experimental stage.

In the meantime, he would welcome any private company which wanted to operate an air service using the landing strips on North Ronaldsay, Westray, Sanday and Stronsay, he said. This was an offer which was echoed, and expanded, 18 months later by the new Conservative Government which went as far as to say that private enterprise air companies could provide services on all Scottish routes, alongside British European Airways.

It was no surprise that the Conservatives should attempt to offload the burden on the public purse. In 1951, BEA lost £1,062,000 - and it was estimated that between 75-80 per cent of this deficit was incurred on Scottish services.

Kirkwall Town Council protested that the 1951 summer service to Aberdeen had been halved, and, although a new £15,000 terminal building for Kirkwall Airport at Grimsetter was announced, concerns were expressed that the following winter service would see just two flights a day in each direction on the Kirkwall - Aberdeen service, compared with a total of 11 flights a day five years previously. BEA blamed a shortage of air crews due to the Government's policy of rearmament which saw pilots called up for military service.

The good news was that aircraft on the Orkney routes were being upgraded. It was announced that 17 of the 20 De Havilland Rapides, which had operated on Scottish services since 1936, would be withdrawn during 1952, with just three of the old planes retained for air ambulance work. Dakota Pioneers - or Pionairs - would replace the Rapides in most cases.

The first Pionair - with capacity for 32 passengers - to make a commercial flight on the Kirkwall route landed in April, 1951. With a crew of three - captain, assistant pilot and steward - the planes were now fitted out with British-made components whereas, previously, all parts and spares had to come from America.

The last De Havilland Rapide to fly from Orkney on a scheduled BEA flight was piloted by ex-RAF pilot, First Officer Ralph Landells, from Kirkwall to Wick, Inverness and Renfrew on Tuesday, September 30, 1952. It was the passing of an age - the Rapide had been the workhorse of Orkney's air age since the days of Captain Ted Fresson - and its demise seemed premature when the replacement 32 seater Pionair arrived on its first scheduled flight to Kirkwall with just two passengers on board.

It would have done little to encourage air traffic when, in February, 1952, BEA announced a ten per cent increase in air fares. Return fares were increased on the Kirkwall - Aberdeen service from £5 18s to £6 10s; Kirkwall - Glasgow £9 18s to £10 10s; and Kirkwall - London now cost £21 15s which was the equivalent of £420 at 1999 prices. Thankfully, BEA brought in 20 per cent reductions for the following winter schedule.

Orcadians were certainly playing their part in the development of the aviation industry.

And the most illustrious was, undoubtedly, Flotta-born James Simpson who had risen from the job of aircraft mechanic to become, in 1952, a vice-president of the world- renowned American Douglas Aircraft Company. He was also general manager of the Long Beach, California, division of Douglas. He still regularly visited his native Orkney on holidays, but sadly, at the relatively young age of 54, he died in 1953.

As the new Comet jet airliner came into service on the major air routes of the world, 24 year old Ruby Kemp, of Aden Cottage, Kirkwall, was working as a supervisor in the Ministry of Civil Aviation signals centre at London Airport. *The Orcadian* pointed out that teleprinter operators at the airport were earning from 68 shillings to 102 shillings a week in 1952, and there were vacancies!

Bill Baillie - one of Orkney's pioneer pilots, having flown with Allied Airways (Gandar Dower) in the 1930s - was, by now, BEA's chief flight captain and, in October, 1953, he was chosen to pilot a BEA Viscount turbo-prop in a 12,500 mile air race from England to New Zealand.

National Service calls

National Service had become a fact of life as young men faced a compulsory spell in uniform, and the first Orcadian to be demobbed after his 18 months serving King and Country was Gunner Robert Walls of 3 Earl Sigurd Street, Kirkwall, in June, 1950.

A baker by trade, he had been called up in January, 1949, and sent to Oswestry in Shropshire before completing his training as a coastal gunner at Dover Castle. He had served in Gibraltar, during which time he had seen the English matador Vincent Charles take part in a bullfight at La Linea in Spain, he told *The Orcadian*.

All National Servicemen had to join the local TA unit on their demob from the Regular Army.

Unfortunately, Orkney's fine reputation for the standard of education in the county received something of a knock when, during the four month period, May - August, 1952, 40 per cent of the National Servicemen from Orkney were classed by the Army authorities as "illiterate or backward."

In Orkney's defence, it must be pointed out that this involved just five men out of 12, but only two other counties - Anglesey and Caernarvon - had worse figures.

For the purposes of the Army's education centres, illiteracy was defined as inability to complete a simple form giving personal details, while sub-illiteracy or backwardness was failure to reach the minimum marks in elementary arithmetic and verbal tests.

Lucky escape

Two girls named as Cathleen (17) and Jeannie Macdonald (14) belonging to Stornoway, had a lucky escape from death after being found huddled together in the snow in ten degrees of frost, under a sledge near Saverock, near Kirkwall.

Their explanation was that their father was in hospital with a broken leg in Aberdeen and they had been sent to stay with an aunt in Thurso but, by mistake, had ended up on the steamer *St Magnus* to Kirkwall.

They were cared for at the County Home while arrangements were made for them to stay with relatives in the week before Christmas.

Kirkwall police said they had to talk to the girls through a Gaelic interpreter - although, curiously, their family insisted they were not Gaelic speakers.

A distinguished son

The year of 1950 saw the death at the age of 88 of distinguished Orkney historian and writer John Mooney - one of the men who has a memorial in the "poets' corner" of St Magnus Cathedral.

Educated at the old Glaitness school, which closed at the start of the 20th century, he was a director and secretary of the Kirkwall firm of R. Garden Ltd, a company he served for 66 years.

But he would be remembered for his historical researches which saw him publish several books on Orkney, especially the burgh of Kirkwall and St Magnus Cathedral. A fellow of the Society of Scottish Antiquaries, his mentor had been B.H. Hossack, author of *Kirkwall in the Orkneys*, and he was the last living person who had worked on the defunct newspaper, the *Orkney and Shetland Telegraph*.

His best known works included *Eynhallow - The Holy Island of the Orkneys* (1924), *St Magnus, Earl of Orkney* (1935), and *The Cathedral and Royal Burgh of Kirkwall* (1943).

A keen campaigner for the temperance cause, John Mooney, despite his undoubted repute as a historian, probably never received the national acclaim that was accorded to his son Erland who in 1921, was chosen as a 16 year old boy scout to accompany Sir Ernest Shackleton on his final expedition to the Antarctic.

Papay school strike

Parents of 19 children in Papa Westray staged a school strike - keeping the pupils away from classes - claiming that the youngsters were being beaten.

Eight parents were brought before Kirkwall Sheriff Court, in October, 1950, for withholding the children from school.

Their solicitor, Mr A. Buchan, told the court that parents were complaining at "excessive corporal punishment suffered by the children, punishment which apparently exceeded what was necessary to keep school children in order, and which was verging on assault."

The parents also complained that children over 12 were not obtaining a proper education so their futures were jeopardised. The parents considered that the only remedy was the removal of the present teacher, the court heard.

They complained that the Director of Education had failed to meet the parents whose children had suffered the most severe assaults, and the fact that no apparent effort was being made to remove the causes of their grievances led the parents to stage the school strike in protest, said Mr Buchan.

The parents were fined five shillings each and the court heard that all the children had returned to school while talks went ahead with the education authority to resolve the dispute.

However, the main cause of absence from Orkney schools during 1950 was illness. In March, more than 300 pupils were absent from Kirkwall Grammar School owing to a flu epidemic and schools at Firth and Graemsay were closed because of illness to teachers. In September, a measles epidemic kept 109 children away from Kirkwall infants school.

However, more seriously, 1950 saw four cases of Poliomyelitis. The first case hit a two year old Kirkwall boy, said Medical Officer of Health Dr Walter Bannerman. It was not an epidemic, he said, but he appealed to parents to take precautions to ensure it did not spread. Three more cases - a 14 year old girl in South Ronaldsay and two schoolboys in the East Mainland and South Ronaldsay - were confirmed in the following weeks.

It would be the last health scare with which Dr Bannerman had to deal. He had announced his retirement the previous year and in 1950, he was succeeded by Dr Cochran Cross, who had been Medical Officer of Health for Rutherglen for 15 years. Dr Cross would receive £1,400 a year salary and the occupancy of a house which the county council purchased in Glaitness Road, Kirkwall for £3,300.

Hollywood fame for bull

The fame of an Orkney bull spread as far as the world's film capital of Hollywood in 1950 as the pedigree Shorthorn Asereavie White Knight, the supreme champion of the West Mainland Show, also won the County Show cattle championship.

He was owned by Mr Peter Davidson, Skaill, Sandwick, and was the sire of another bull which had been recently bought at the Perth Bull Sale by Oscar-winning film star Greer Garson - the daughter of an Orcadian - for her ranch in America.

The Orkney bull went on to become the West Mainland and County Show cattle champion for three years running in both cases - a double hat-trick which rates as one of the major achievements in the 20th century history of Orkney's agricultural shows.

Jobs for all

Orkney enjoyed an unequalled boom in employment at the start of the second half of the 20th century - to the extent that, in 1950, it was suggested that foreign workers would have to be shipped to the county to fill jobs.

Problems in recruiting female staff for the Ayre egg grading station in Kirkwall led to the proposition that foreigners could be imported to help solve the problem.

At a meeting of the Orkney Local Employment Committee in June, 1950, it was agreed to ask the Ministry of Food about providing hostel accommodation to house girls from the islands and country districts. It was also agreed to "determine the question of the supply of female foreign workers."

It was reported at the meeting that Orkney had just 42 unemployed workers. A year later the situation was even rosier for jobs as, at September 6, 1951, Orkney had just 26 unemployed people on the register - the equivalent of one jobless person for every 500 adults in the county. Prospects were good and no problem of unemployment was anticipated, the local employment committee was told.

Full employment had been a major plank of the Labour government's policy, and Orkney still fared better than most areas under the Conservative administration that came to power in October, 1951.

By December, 1951, a total of 80 unemployed was reported in Orkney and "the prospect of placing these people in suitable jobs was less bright than in former years," reported *The Orcadian*. In March, 1954, Orkney had 108 unemployed - but that compared with 1,052 in Shetland!

Out of court

After being in existence for 113 years, the Stromness Small Debt Court closed on November 2, 1950, in Stromness Town Hall. A quarter of a century had elapsed since it had a case - although, in the early days of the century, it had handled as many as 15 cases in a day. In 1951, the court at St Margaret's Hope also closed.

Murder shocker

A 70 year old Stromness man, James Gibson, was beaten to death by raiders at his coal company office in Detroit, USA. Mr Gibson, the son of Mr and Mrs James Gibson, Burnside Farm, Stromness, had emigrated to the USA after serving his apprenticeship with Stromness blacksmith Alex Banks.

Football tragedy

Orkney football matches were postponed as a mark of respect after the death of 26 year old Rovers footballer Ronnie Park, who died after a collision during a game against Thorfinn B in May, 1950.

Shipping problems

The Orkney Steam Navigation Company - still an independent company in 1950, but later to evolve into the Orkney Islands Shipping Company and, eventually, Orkney Ferries - increased its cargo rates by 25 per cent, and passenger fares by five per cent, after requests by the company for a subsidy were rejected by the Government. The shipping company said it had operated at a loss for the previous three years.

"Exorbitant fares and freights" charged by the company were blamed for speeding up the depopulation of the isles. "At 32s return, the passenger service to Kirkwall must be the most expensive of its kind in Britain," complained one North Isles correspondent of *The Orcadian*. The fare was certainly the 1999 equivalent of well over £30.

Minister of action

A visiting American Kirk minister brought an "Action Man" image to the South Isles. The Rev Kenwood Bryant (26) from Indiana, USA, was acting as the temporary minister in Longhope for three months when he dived into the sea with a knife to cut free a rope which had fouled the propeller of the ferry *Orcadia* at Longhope pier. He had to rise to the surface eight times for air before he succeeded in his task, reported *The Orcadian* in July, 1950.

Rescue hero

Hugh MacKenzie of St Margaret's Hope was presented with a Royal Humane Society bravery award for saving the life of a three year old boy, James Wood, a visitor to the island, who fell in the sea at the pier. In 15 feet of water, he took the child under one arm, and swam back to the pier with the other. After seeing the boy safely ashore, Hugh climbed back on the pier, got on his bike and rode off home. The presentation of the bravery award was made by Orkney's Lord Lieutenant, Patrick Sutherland Graeme.

The Orkney poet and writer Edwin Muir was made a CBE in the Queen's Coronation Honours List of 1953.
(Picture courtesy of Orkney Library photographic archive)

Orkney crisps

Mr John W. Foulis introduced Orkney crisps to the market after setting up a small factory behind Kirkwall's Temperance Hall in the Spring of 1950.

The crisps had become so popular that the factory was coping with three to four hundredweights of potatoes every day, with a staff of two men and two girls.

Mr Foulis confidently expected production would involve hundreds of tons of Orkney potatoes every year. The crisps were being sold wholesale and so far, said Mr Foulis, he had been unable to cope with the demand for the new product.

Woman elected

Miss Thora Miller, of Hestivale, in September, 1950, became the first woman to be elected as an Orkney county councillor, in a by-election for Evie and Rendall, although female representatives of Kirkwall and Stromness burgh councils had sat on the county council previously.

Cathedral post

Mr T. Watson Forgie of Glasgow was appointed as organist and choirmaster of St Magnus Cathedral, to succeed Mr J. Hunter McBain who left to take up a school teaching post in Alloa.

Trawler drama

The Grimsby trawler *Daniel Quare*, with a crew of 21, ran aground immediately below Kirkwall Coastguard Station in Cromwell Road in a 66 mph northerly gale in April, 1950. At that time there was no Kirkwall lifeboat and the trawler was only refloated and towed to safety after Stromness lifeboat had made her way 60 miles in heavy weather through Scapa Flow and the Pentland Firth to Kirkwall.

Hill blaze havoc

A seven day hill blaze, in May 1950, destroyed up to 14 square miles of Hoy moorland after a five day heatwave left the undergrowth tinder dry. Over 1,400 acres of outrun at Melsetter was burnt out. The Admiralty had to take special precautions to protect the Naval fuel tanks at Lyness, and farmer Hugh Seatter managed to stem the blaze by ploughing fire breaks around his property. Fortunately, the fire was eventually dampened by the arrival of rain after a week.

* * *

Mr Archibald Jamieson (30) from Edinburgh was appointed county architect and planning officer for Orkney in 1950.

Not quite

A series of articles "looking to the future" in *The Orcadian* of 1950 predicted a Scottish Parliament within five years and an independent self-governing Orkney by 1962.

Capital service

An application by Magnus Spence, of St Margaret's Hope, to operate a fortnightly express bus service from Edinburgh to Orkney was refused by the Traffic Licensing Authority. Curiously, Mr Spence was licensed to operate a service in the opposite direction from Orkney to Edinburgh.

Seaweed harvest

Seaweed collectors in the North Isles - mainly on Westray and North Ronaldsay - collected and dried 340 tons of tangles, at £5 a ton, in 1950. The weed was sent to a processing factory at Loch Boisdale.

School meals

School kitchens were introduced, in 1950, at Sanday, North Walls, Pierowall, Firth, Shapinsay, Stromness and Dounby to allow school meals to be served to pupils.

* * *

The visiting Ross County team beat an Orkney Select XI 4-0 in a football match in front of nearly 2,000 spectators at the Bignold Park in June, 1950.

Epic rescue by lifeboat

One of the biggest sea rescues of the 20th century in Orkney waters - and one of the worst pollution incidents - saw the men of Longhope lifeboat acclaimed as heroes in April, 1951.

The lifeboat put to sea three times in 36 hours in a wild gale to bring to safety 40 men of the 8,683 ton Swedish tanker *Oljaren* which ran aground on the Pentland Skerries, homeward bound for Stockholm with a cargo of diesel oil from Curacao.

The vessel sent out a distress call after her midnight stranding and coxswain Fred Johnston - later to be awarded a RNLI gallantry medal for the rescue - and his crew of eight battled through 12 miles of seas to the crippled ship.

On being landed at Longhope, the first 24 survivors of the disaster were accommodated at the Lyness dockyard. Among them was a 33 year old Swedish barrister Stig Konigson who was returning from a pleasure cruise to the West Indies. The Longhope boat then returned to the *Oljaren* but the remaining 16 crewmen refused to be taken off until they were ordered to leave by the tanker owners the next day.

The tanker's master, Captain Alva Lottijer, had taken the vessel through the Pentland Firth 60 times since she was built four years earlier, and this was due to have been his final voyage before retiring after serving the same shipping company since 1913.

There was a total of five members of the Johnston family in the Longhope lifeboat crew - coxswain Fred Johnston, second cox Eric Mowat, bowman Jack Norquoy, mechanic Robert Johnston, second mechanic R. Johnston, Dan Kirkpatrick, Steve McFadyon, Freddie Johnston and Jimmy Johnston.

Miss Minnie Sutherland, the Longhope secretary, said: "I don't think any other lifeboat could have done the job they did. Their most hazardous moment came when they had to negotiate their boat between the rocks in the very bad seas to get the first survivors off. It was then that a wave lifted the bow and the lifeboat came down heavily on the tanker, damaging the lifeboat's stern. The second coxswain said he never expected to see Longhope again, so it must have been pretty bad then."

Unfortunately, despite the parlous state of the stricken vessel, looters still managed to get on board and strip the ship of valuables. The captain complained of "acts of piracy" after it had been abandoned by the crew.

Returning to the ship with some of the senior officers, he found that locked doors had been smashed open and the crew's

---

1951

personal possessions and valuables stolen. Police in both Orkney and Caithness were investigating after a haul of cameras, 50,000 American cigarettes and 25 lbs of tobacco was reported missing.

"I am very upset about this," said Captain Lottijer (63) who estimated his own loss of possessions at £400. "And it will make a poor impression at home in Sweden, which is a pity especially after the good job the lifeboat did."

Captain Lottijer actually had previous experience of real piracy for, in 1924, he and his ship were captured, and held to ransom, by pirates off the Chinese coast.

The pollution aspect of the disaster was scarcely mentioned in 1951, but 10,000 tons of the ship's 12,000 ton cargo of diesel oil was lost into the Pentland Firth before the *Orjaren* was refloated, by the Metal Industries salvage ship *Salveda*, commanded by Captain Herbert Sutherland of Kirkwall, in a remarkable salvage operation under the direction of the company's chief salvage officer Murray Taylor, and towed to Longhope Bay, and later to dry dock in Liverpool.

Sadly, Longhope lifeboat coxswain Fred Johnston suffered personal tragedy just weeks after the epic rescue when his youngest son Ian (15) died in a 100 feet cliff fall at Brims. Fred Johnston stepped down from the post of coxswain of the Longhope boat in December, 1954, to be succeeded by Dan Kirkpatrick, an employee of the Lyness Naval Base, and a member of the crew involved in the epic 1951 rescue of the *Oljaren*.

In January, 1951, it had been the men of Stromness lifeboat who had suffered one of their most arduous operations in their history. The Stromness boat was out at sea for 20 hours in an Atlantic gale to aid the 4,776 ton Norwegian ship *Tatra* which broke down 24 miles north west of Papa Westray, on passage to the USA with general cargo. In the end the lifeboat journey proved fruitless as she failed to locate the *Tatra* which had been taken in tow by an Icelandic trawler *Ingolfur Arnarson*.

"This has been one of my worst nights in 23 years," said coxswain William Sinclair when the lifeboat arrived back in Stromness 29 hours after being launched.

The *Tatra* was towed to Kirkwall and, after repairs, was able to continue her voyage to Boston, USA.

Population falls again

The first census in 20 years showed Orkney's population was down to 21,258 in 1951, a drop of 819 compared with the 1931 population of 22,077. The statistics also showed an increasing drift to Kirkwall with the population of Kirkwall and St Ola showing an increase from 4,398 to 5,519. The only other parishes to show a marginal increase were Sandwick, Evie and Rendall.

New community centre

Miss Margaret Herbison MP, Under Secretary of State for Scotland, opened the new £5,600 Sanday Community Centre. The islanders had decided to erect a new centre rather than accept the gift of Geramont House which had been offered for conversion into a community hall by Robert Tulloch, a Sanday exile who lived in Dundee.

Benefits increase

Retirement pensions for men over 70 and women over 65 were increased by four shillings to 30 shillings a week in 1951 A year later, in September, 1952, family allowances were increased from 5s to 8s a child and the standard old age pension was further increased to 32s 6d.

Police chief dies

John M. Tulloch, the last Chief Constable of the independent Orkney police force which was run by the county council until 1938, died at his home in Old Scapa Road, Kirkwall, aged 85, in October, 1951.

Isles phone link

Telephone services from the public kiosk at North Ronaldsay post office were available in 1951 for the first time thanks to a radio link to the Sanday telephone exchange. The link depended on battery power so a notice in the phone kiosk asked callers to keep their calls as brief as possible.

Bumper show

A crowd of 7,356 - a record attendance at the time - flocked to the 66th County Show at Kirkwall's Bignold Park.

A growing age of electricity

A new era in the electrical development of Orkney was born as Kirkwall's new power station was opened alongside the Peerie Sea as part of the local contribution to the Festival Of Britain celebrations in the Spring of 1951.

The new £280,000 7,000 kilowatt power station - built by Orkney Builders and officially opened on May, 15, 1951, by the wife of the former Secretary of State for Scotland, Arthur Woodburn - would be able to supply all the power needed for Orkney from three 1,540 hp diesel engines. It was proposed that Kirkwall could take advantage of the new power station to create a swimming pool at the Peerie Sea - with warm water coming from the power station's cooling plant.

By 1951, a total of 3,300 householders on the Orkney Mainland were connected to the North of Scotland Hydro-Electric Board mains supply. However, it is questionable just how many electrical appliances most consumers could afford. An exhibition by the hydro-electric board of the latest products included a refrigerator at £125 - the equivalent of £2,500 at 1999 prices.

The first island to be linked up to the mains electricity supply was, remarkably, one of the least populated - Gairsay. Mrs Lorna Coventry, an Englishwomen who had bought the 760 acre island for a reported £8,000 in 1949, lived with her daughter in the main house on the island which was reputed to incorporate part of the original banqueting hall of the 12th century Viking chief Sweyn Asliefsson. In July, 1951, Mrs Coventry paid for a private submarine cable to link her island to the mains power. Three years later, she sold the property to Orphir farmer Edward Wishart.

The switching on of 12 street lights in St Margaret's Hope, in November, 1954, marked the first publicly funded introduction of mains electrical power to the islands, with 400 consumers linked to the mains in South Ronaldsay and 150 in Burray. And plans were underway to make Shapinsay the next island to receive power.

Football highlights

Lord Morrison, president of the leading English football club Tottenham Hotspur FC, who was in the county, inspecting ancient monuments on behalf of the Ministry of Works, was presented with a book on Orkney by William Barrack, president of Kirkwall Hotspur FC. The Kirkwall club was formed in 1921 as a tribute to Tottenham Hotspur's FA Cup that year.

Dave Halliday became the new manager of Aberdeen FC in 1951. His son played for Wanderers in Orkney.

For the third successive season, the year of 1951 saw Orkney's footballers compete the "double" - beating both Shetland and Caithness - in the senior inter-county football matches.

Eight lost in air crash

An appeal for information from islanders was broadcast on the BBC Scottish Home Service after a four engined RAF Lancaster bomber, with a crew of eight, was reported missing off the west coast of Orkney on a flight from Kinloss in March, 1951. The last message received had given the plane's position over Suleskerry.

Boxing boom

Amateur boxing was a booming sport in Kirkwall in 1951 with more than 400 spectators packing the Boys' Brigade Hall to watch nine bouts, promoted by the Kirkwall Athletic Club.

Swimming rescue

The Kirkwall Athletic Club's 1951 swimming gala - which attracted a crowd of about 1,000 to watch the races in the Basin - saw local teenager Bruce Dunnett dive fully clothed into the sea to rescue ten year old Douglas Thomson, of Shore Street, Kirkwall, who had fallen in the sea.

An ill wind

A 90 year old Miss Anne Sinclair, of 22 Queen Street, Kirkwall was in hospital with a broken wrist and cuts, in November, 1951, after gale force winds caught her umbrella, lifted her off her feet and carried her several feet in the air before throwing her to the ground.

Centenarian dies

Orkney's oldest inhabitant of the time, Miss Margaret Seatter, of Vell, Westside, Westray, died in March, 1951, six months after her 101st birthday.

Tractor power

Sixteen horse-drawn and 24 tractor-drawn ploughs competed for the Orkney Agricultural Society county ploughing match in 1951 - the first time that mechanised horsepower had outnumbered the traditional in the competition.

Gas pioneer

Mr Thomas Gourlay, originally from Greenock, Renfrewshire, retired in May, 1951, after 39 years as works manager of Kirkwall Gas Works. Originally operated as a private company, the gas service was taken over by Kirkwall Town Council in 1923 and, in 1949, was nationalised under the Government controlled Scottish Gas Board.

Banks galore in Kirkwall

The Orkney branch of the Aberdeen Savings Bank (part of Lloyds TSB 50 years later) opened in 1951 in Bridge Street, Kirkwall, on the site of the first church built by Rognvald I in Kirkwall in 1040. Kirkwall had eight banks by 1953 - the National Bank of Scotland, the British Linen Bank, the Royal Bank of Scotland, the Union Bank, the Bank of Scotland, the Commercial Bank of Scotland, the Aberdeen Savings Bank, and the Clydesdale and North of Scotland Bank.

Radio features Stromness

Richard Dimbleby, the well known BBC commentator visited Stromness in November, 1951, to record a "Down Your Way" feature to be broadcast during Christmas week on the BBC radio Light Programme. Among those interviewed were retired county education director Dr Hugh Marwick, John Stevenson, the mate of the *St Ola* ferry, Provost George Robertson of Stromness, dancing teacher Florrie Tait and six of her pupils, as well as members of the farming and lighthouse communities.

Rugby honour

A.D. Cameron, the son of Mima Cameron, née Stockan, and nephew of Stromness boot and shoe merchant Alex Stockan, was selected to play for Scotland Rugby XV against France in Paris. Cameron, a trainee chartered accountant played as back for Hillhead High School Former Pupils.

Kirkwall Town Council ruled that people on the housing waiting list had to first accept accommodation in the former wartime huts at Hatston before they would be considered for permanent homes. (Picture courtesy of Orkney Library photographic archive)

Homes at Hatston camp

A new phase in the growth of Kirkwall saw the town council begin work to convert former Air Ministry huts at the wartime Hatston aerodrome into homes.

The ministry had originally proposed that the Hatston huts could be transferred to the county council - but that offer was rejected by county councillors.

Instead it was agreed that Kirkwall Town Council would take over the buildings and spend £500 on each hut to create temporary homes with an expected lifespan of ten years. In fact,

many of the huts remained as homes for nearly 25 years.

At that time, Hatston was outside the Kirkwall town boundary so it meant that Kirkwall Town Council would have to pay rates to the county council. At the same time, the town council was also campaigning to keep the Hatston Garrison Theatre for public use.

The first batch of 57 huts were ready for occupation within a year, maintaining Kirkwall's impressive record of housing development. The town council

had built 104 permanent homes between the end of World War Two and 1951. In addition, another 45 temporary homes had been created in ex-wartime buildings. It was still estimated that Kirkwall needed another 200 houses but the town council had already built one for every 40 head of population - whereas Stromness had built only one new house per 400 of population. Four new council houses at Grieveship Terrace, Stromness, prompted 44 applicants.

Tragedy led to new lifeboat

A series of tragic disasters at sea led to the restoration of a lifeboat in the North Isles in 1952.

An Icelandic ship *Eyfirdingur*, a 110 feet wooden lugger, was lost with all seven hands in a North Isles tragedy which saw the Stromness lifeboat out at sea for 24 hours as the stricken vessel went aground between Lashy Skerry and the Calf of Eday on February 11, and broke up in heavy seas.

One of the ship's boats was found by William Nicolson of Shapinsay in his motor boat *Sheena* off Tankerness while wreckage was washed ashore on several islands. The bodies of four men were found on the shores of Eday and Sanday.

Robert Clouston, of Headbanks, Sanday, had spotted distress flares, and men of the coast life saving corps on Eday and Sanday searched the shores all night for survivors while the Stromness lifeboat made the scene in a record four hours. She ploughed through a mass of wreckage, including the mast of the sunken vessel, in frequent snow showers, but, alas, could not save a life.

Coxswain William Sinclair said: "It was a terrible night having to look for something that was not there. The boat must have taken a terrible battering. Wreckage was floating like matchwood in the sea."

Lifeboatman Bob Greig stated: "We could have filled two boatloads with the wreckage we saw. She must have been pulverised. It was just like firewood."

In a poignant farewell, the bodies of the victims of the wrecked ship were returned to their home port of Akureyri in Northern Iceland.

The difficulties of covering the North Isles of Orkney from Stromness were illustrated five days later when the Stromness lifeboat was out for more than 18 hours for an all-night search between Stronsay and Auskerry. It was a false alarm but it meant that the lifeboat crew had been on duty for more than 42 hours in six days.

Calls for a lifeboat to be stationed in the North Isles intensified when all but one of 18 members of the crew of the German 447 ton trawler *Thor* were lost when their boat capsized and foundered in terrific seas off Orkney on Saturday morning, March 8, 1952.

The survivor was picked up in a ship's lifeboat after being adrift for 17 hours, 25 miles off Sanday, by another German trawler, the *Fladengrund*. The survivor was Willi Sunkiman - worn to the limit of his endurance by exposure, thirst and sea sickness - who said the *Thor*, built in Aberdeen in 1943, had sunk so quickly that no SOS radio message could be sent. There had been originally 11 survivors in the boat, or clinging to it, but they had been washed away.

The British authorities had been unaware of the disaster until the *Fladengrund* had sent a radio message revealing that Sunkiman, and a dead colleague, had been picked up from the drifting boat.

An RAF Shackleton aircraft was used to carry out an aerial search over two days - and Stromness lifeboat was again alerted - but no further survivors were found.

In May, 1952, for the fourth time in as many months, the Stromness lifeboat was involved in an all-night call-out to the North Isles after the Aberdeen trawler *Unitia*, homeward bound from Iceland with 500 boxes of fish, ran aground off Rousay. The Stromness boat was out for 30 hours, but all the trawler crew were safe.

As the incident renewed calls for a North Isles rescue boat, eleven fishermen and boatmen offered to operate a lifeboat from Rousay. However, within weeks, it was revealed that the RNLI was investigating re-opening the Stronsay lifeboat station that had closed at the start of World War One. In September, 1952, after a visit by two RNLI inspectors, it was announced that 15 island men had volunteered to crew the vessel and Stronsay would have a lifeboat within weeks. Eventually, a crew of eight, with ten reserves, was recruited and Westrayman Tom Carter was appointed coxswain.

The lifeboat allocated to Stronsay was the *Edward Z Dresden*, formerly stationed at Clacton. The vessel arrived in Stronsay on Tuesday, October 28, with the village of Whitehall bedecked with flags to welcome the boat which had made the 500 mile journey from East Anglia in five days. The next night, 240 people gathered at the public hall to show their appreciation of the re-establishment of the Stronsay lifeboat branch. Captain E.H. Clements, the Stronsay harbourmaster, became secretary of the Stronsay lifeboat station.

But one near-disaster brought Kirkwall an unexpected tourist boom in August, 1952, when the 11,672 ton Swedish liner *Anna Salen*, with 630 passengers and 190 crew on board, bound for America, spent six days in Scapa Flow undergoing emergency repairs after colliding in dense fog in the Pentland Firth with the Norwegian whale oil factory ship *Thorshovdi* (18,365 tons). Fires broke out on the two ships but were extinguished by the crews.

The *Anna Selen* was piloted into Scapa Flow by Longhope lifeboat coxswain Fred Johnston. Passengers on board included 370 Americans, many returning from the 1952 Helsinki Olympic Games, and 150 Germans emigrating to the USA. A scratch multi-national football team from the passengers and crew - five Italians, three Germans, a Swede, Frenchman and an American - played an Orkney Select XI, warming up for the forthcoming Shetland inter-county match, with the game resulting in an 11-0 win for Orkney.

In October, 1952, the waters of Orkney again proved a graveyard for the fishing fleet as the Aberdeen trawler *Strathelliot* had to be given up as a loss after the vessel went aground on rocks off Selwick, Hoy.

However, in a dramatic rescue operation, the 12 crewmen of the trawler were all saved as they were hauled 200 yards over stormy seas by breeches buoy.

The rescue was carried out by the Longhope life-saving company after a 20 mile dash by road to the scene, after Stromness lifeboat, under the command of coxswain William Sinclair, had been beaten back by terrific seas, with two lifeboatmen nearly swept overboard as they attempted to get alongside the stricken trawler.

Kirkwall Coastguard Officer James Clark was later awarded the British Empire Medal for his part in co-ordinating the three hour rescue operation which, remarkably, saw the fishermen all escape injury despite being dragged through the water for at least 200 yards. Another breeches buoy rescue had to be made four days later when the trawler skipper George Simpson, and two Hoy men, who had returned to the *Strathelliot* to assess refloating the vessel, found themselves cut off by huge seas.

Another rescue, however, saw the crew of Longhope lifeboat embroiled in a legal row in 1952. After towing the motor fishing vessel *Blenheim* to safety to Rackwick Bay, the lifeboat crew made a salvage claim of £1,000 - and even had the *Blenheim* placed under arrest in Thurso harbour where she lay for four months with a writ nailed to the mast. Sir David Robertson, Tory MP for Caithness and Sutherland, pleaded in Parliament for its release "in the interests of food production and full employment" and the dispute was eventually resolved, more or less amicably.

A line-up of vehicles from the first half of the century on Kirkwall's Harbour Street draws an interested crowd.

(Picture courtesy of Orkney Library photographic archive)

The King is dead, God save the Queen

King George VI died on February 6, 1952, having reigned as monarch since 1936. He had made several visits to Orkney during both world wars and messages of condolence were sent to the Royal family by Orkney's Lord Lieutenant, the county council and the burgh councils of Kirkwall and Stromness.

Princess Elizabeth and the Duke of Edinburgh had recently left for Kenya and the Princess was recalled to become Queen Elizabeth II. Sheriff D.B. Keith read the proclamation of her accession at the Mercat Cross in front of St Magnus Cathedral.

A memorial service was organised at the Cathedral for February 15 to coincide with the King's funeral service at Windsor Chapel. All of the secondary pupils of the Kirkwall Grammar School attended, along with civic dignitaries, councillors and clergy of all denominations, to hear the service conducted by the Rev Arthur Fryer to a congregation of 900.

Businesses were closed as a mark of respect, and the Cathedral's great bell tolled for an hour in a last farewell to the departed King as a large crowd gathered in Broad Street for the memorial service.

Sixteen months elapsed before the coronation of Queen Elizabeth II on June 2, 1953, remembered by thousands of Orkney schoolchildren who were given a three day school holiday for the occasion. Around 3,600 commemorative coronation spoons, beakers and other souvenirs were ordered for distribution to the children as celebration events were organised throughout the isles and parishes.

Sergeant James Leys, 1st Orkney Home Guard, was one of the Home Guard contingent which led the great coronation procession of the three services in London, while Sergeant James Towers (Harray) and L/Bdr James Scollie (St Ola) represented the 1st Orkney Cadet Regiment in the capital.

Back in Orkney, the day dawned with appalling weather conditions. There was still no television in the islands, so people had to listen to the radio commentary of the proceedings of the events at Westminster Abbey.

A service was also held in St Magnus Cathedral, followed by a fancy dress parade. The Queen broadcast on the radio at 9pm, and Kirkwall then staged a celebratory firework display.

A coronation day baby, Margaret Elizabeth Ireland, the 7lb daughter of Mr and Mrs George Ireland of the Stromness egg packing station, was presented with a special commemorative silver drinking mug at the Balfour Hospital, to mark her place in history. A total of 650 coronation trees, offered to Kirkwall Town Council, by ex-provost P.C. Flett, would be planted at Pickaquoy, it was decided.

The Orkney poet and writer Edwin Muir was made a CBE in the Queen's coronation honours list, and, a few days later, the Orcadian artist Stanley Cursiter - who held the title of Painter and Limner to the Queen in Scotland - left his Stromness home to travel to Edinburgh to record the scene in oils as the Queen visited St Giles Cathedral as part of her post-coronation state visit to Scotland.

Naval commander leaves

Commander C.E.L. Sclater DSO bid farewell to Orkney after five years as Resident Naval Officer, Orkney, the Queen's Harbour Master, Scapa Flow, and in command of Lyness Naval base.

Commander Sclater - a survivor of the *Royal Oak* disaster as a young lieutenant in 1939 - was the only son of Captain Guy Sclater, who died in command of HMS *Bulwark* in 1914, and a cousin of Lord Basing.

He won the DSO for shooting down six German aircraft in the Bay of Biscay in 1942 when commanding the destroyer HMS *Wild Swan*.

He was succeeded as senior Royal Navy officer in Orkney by Lt Commander Errol Bruce, a man who, in 1952, made national headlines as an international yachtsman when, at the age of 38, he won a trans-Atlantic race in the Royal Navy yacht *Samuel Pepys*.

Commander Bruce was to create a small piece of Orkney sailing history in 1954 when he took part in a race across the Pentland Firth in 14 feet dinghies - answering a challenge from 24 year old Caithness farmer's wife Rosemary Vickers. Mrs Vickers single-handedly crewed the *Hellespont* and Commander Bruce his

dinghy *Pomona* over 21 miles from Scrabster to Lyness. The race was judged a dead heat in a leisurely time of 5 hours 32 minutes.

It was believed to be the first time that such small craft had raced over the Firth - but they were, by no means, the smallest boats ever to cross that stretch of water.

In 1926, John Bremner - who was Kirkwall harbourmaster in the 1950s - and William Ritch had sailed a 12 feet 6 inch dinghy across the Firth from Brims to Armadale, near Bettyhill. They eventually continued to Stornoway - a journey which took 48 hours in total!

Orkney excavations underway

Professor Gordon Childe, Director of the Institute of Archaeology, London, best remembered for his discoveries during the excavation of Skara Brae in 1927-29, was appointed by the Ministry of Works in 1951 to undertake an excavation of the Stone Age burial mound at Quoyness in Sanday. It was thought to be between 3,000 - 4,000 years old. In 1954, Professor Childe returned to Orkney to research the neolithic chambered tomb of Maeshowe, which is pictured here. (Picture courtesy of Orkney Library photographic archive)

In 1960, there were just 380 working horses remaining in Orkney, compared with 1,100 tractors. This picture shows farmer Archie Learmonth of Hammerbrake, Sanday, with his four youngest children, from the left, Hazel, Myra, Vera and Archie junior.

(Picture courtesy of Myra Hazell)

The first Orkney football team to play Shetland after World War Two. The players travelled to Shetland in 1946 and came away with a 5-3 victory. Back row, from the left: Eddie Burns, Bill Sim, Bob Munro, Eric Robertson, Thorfinn Keldie and Arthur Dainty. Front: Easton Clark, Davie Fox, Angus McKenzie, Jim Owens and Billy Norquoy.

(Picture courtesy of Bill Sim)

Orkney schools chief condemns our dialect

Orkney's director of education Mr John Shearer used the annual Kirkwall Grammar School prizegiving of 1952 to launch an attack on his native Orcadian dialect in schools.

He upheld the BBC News as being a model of standard English pronunciation and now that pupils had the advantage of a radio service "we should discard our inborn prejudice in favour of our own dialect and make a serious effort in school to raise the level of spoken English."

It had been stated, he said, that the only class distinction in a modern state was the distinction of speech. "And I think that distinction should be eliminated in the schools," he said. It was doubtful that there had been any improvement in the use of formal English during the 20th century, said Mr Shearer.

His views were a complete contrast to what followed 40 years later when the policy of the Orkney education authority was to actively encourage the pres-

ervation of the Orkney dialect.

But Mr Shearer told the pupils of 1952: "The use of a dialect along with standard English imposes on our people the handicap of bi-lingualism - that is, they habitually use two languages. This is a real impediment to progress. Further, the dialects are not pretty and their literature is small."

Horror for school

The island of Hoy and the tiny school of Rackwick were hit by the most appalling tragedy in August, 1952, when brothers John (12) and Hugh Mowat (9) drowned while playing with a raft in Rackwick burn.

The impact of the disaster on the Rackwick school was measured by the fact that the two boys were the only pupils at the school, together with their 11 year old sister Ivy and brother James (5).

The school closed a year later.

International conference

A ground-breaking two week long Danish-Orcadian conference was held in Kirkwall in the Summer of 1952 with 100 delegates from both sides of the North Sea discussing mutual problems in agriculture and education. Speakers included Sir Patrick Laird, Secretary of the Department of Agriculture for

Scotland, as well as several of Scotland's top farming experts, the Orcadian writer Edwin Muir and the former Orkney education director and historian Dr Hugh Marwick. Government minister, the Earl of Home, attended some of the conference sessions while King Frederick of Denmark sent a goodwill message.

The motor age grows

There was one vehicle for every five people in Orkney by 1952.

By the end of the year, Orkney had 4,452 motor vehicles compared with 2,489 in 1947. The number of tractors had more than trebled from 450 to 1,462. In fact, in the six years up to 1952, Orkney had taken

delivery of 726 Ferguson tractors alone.

The number of private cars and goods vehicles had increased by 50 per cent in the same period. By 1953, Graemsay was the only island of any size without a registered motor car - it had just two motorcycles and two tractors!

TV traps conman

A 22 year old conman was trapped by a television appearance - and jailed for passing fraudulent cheques from the Kirkwall branch of the National Bank of Scotland.

He was arrested after bank officials spotted him on the TV programme

"What's My Line" on which he appeared as "a frogman from the Orkneys" - and for which he was paid a fee of three guineas, the London Sessions court heard.

The conman had told his victims that his father was the High Sheriff of Orkney.

Education pioneer

An Orcadian pioneer in the field of British education, Dr George Kenneth Sutherland, died in 1952. He was the son of Mr John K. Sutherland of Birsay and graduated at Aberdeen University with MA in 1909, BSc in 1911 and DSc in 1916. In

1912 he became Professor of Botany at University College, Southampton.

After war service, however, he joined HM Inspectorate of Schools which he served until retirement in 1946 when he was made a CBE.

Shopping Week Queen

The first Queen of Stromness Shopping Week was chosen in 1952.

The honour went to Ivy Flett (16) Beachview, Birsay, who was elected by pupils at Stromness Academy. Her attendants were Elizabeth Robertson of Sandwick and Nancy Linklater of Stromness.

Fish from the shop

William Jolly (39) opened his new fishmonger's shop in Willow Road, Kirkwall, helping to supply the shop from his own fishing boat *Marbeth*.

Fish from the tap

Kirkwall Town Council agreed to step up the analysis of the local water supply after complaints from householders that fish were coming out of the taps.

Ba' history

The two Ba' games on Christmas Day, 1952, made history - the Boys' event was the first to have a running commentary broadcast over the radio as part of the "Christmas Round Britain" programme, while the Men's Ba' was a runaway victory for the Doonies in the shortest time on record in less than five minutes from throw up to the basin. The photograph in *The Orcadian* showed there were scarcely 50 players in Broad Street for the start of the Men's Ba', and fewer spectators.

Royal neighbour

Queen Elizabeth, the Queen Mother, purchased the Castle of Mey on the North coast of Caithness, built in 1606 and with spectacular views of the Orkney Islands. In September, 1952, the Queen Mother and Princess Margaret made a flight over Orkney to see the Old Man of Hoy.

Veteran farmer

Orkney's oldest inhabitant of the time, Mr James Bremner, of Forswell Farm, Yesnaby, Sandwick, was working in the hayfield of his son's farm, just three months before his 100th birthday on November 24, 1952. He died, aged 100, in March, 1953.

New health chief

Orkney's Medical Officer Of Health Dr Cochran Cross resigned on the grounds of ill health after just two years in the post. He was succeeded by Dr Andrew Sinclair Brodie (34), previously depute medical officer for Dumfries.

Thirteen trawlermen die

1953

A total of 13 trawlermen died in two separate disasters in Orkney waters in 1953. And tragically, in the first incident, seven of the victims were claimed within yards of the shore, and safety.

The 411 ton trawler *Leicester City* grounded in thick fog in Hoy Sound on Sunday, March 22, 1953. The vessel had been at sea for 22 days and was returning to Grimsby from the Icelandic fishing grounds with 1,300 kits of fish valued at between £8,000 - £10,000.

The ship was equipped with the latest radar equipment but unfortunately the inquiry into the loss later heard that the radar was out of action, having broken down earlier on the voyage.

The result was that the Danish skipper Osman Johanson gave the order to abandon ship, believing that they were miles from land when they were in fact less than 200 yards from the shore - and well in range for a rescue by breeches buoy.

Seven men were to die from the effects of exhaustion and exposure after the cold waters of Hoy Sound took their toll as the trawler's lifeboat, carrying most of the crew, was overturned by the sea.

However, thankfully, another 11 were saved - partly due to the efforts of Miss Mary Ritch who was acclaimed in national newspaper headlines as "the lady with the lamp."

Of the 11 survivors, three owed their lives to the Stromness lifeboat which picked them up as they clung to a life raft. Ten others were able to reach the Hoy shore but two succumbed to their nightmare ordeal and died after the time spent in the water.

Mary Ritch, of The Head, Hoy, had given the alarm after seeing the *Leicester City* in distress, and the Stromness lifeboat, under coxswain William Sinclair, was launched in the early hours. The rescue operation was not helped by the original radio message from the *Leicester City* giving her position as 30 - 40 miles south-south-east of Suleskerry, instead of the correct east-south-east.

Mary Ritch, after alerting help, then went down to the shore with a lamp and with four other local women - Bella Sutherland, Mrs Mary Stewart, Mrs Bessie Moar and Mary Moar - joined the search for survivors.

Mary Ritch said : "The men all seemed to be in a daze and some were clinging to the boat. They did not seem to realise they had reached safety. We helped them up the rocks as best as we could. All we could get from the men were a few incoherent remarks."

Sixteen year old Archie Needham, the youngest member of the trawler crew, said: "The fog was all around us, and we had no idea where we were drifting. Then suddenly we found ourselves inshore. It was like a miracle. One minute I thought I was going to die - I couldn't have held on much longer - and the next we were safe."

Another rescuer, Mr Isaac Moar, on Hoy, said that the trawler mate, Edward Young, had died on the shore but most of the survivors were able to walk with assistance to the farm 500 yards away where they were revived and given emergency clothing. Chief engineer John Dye (45) was unconscious when brought ashore but recovered. The survivors were taken to Stromness later that day after being first attended by Dr Thomas Foubister.

Deckhand Alfred Jones - one of those saved by the lifeboat - said: "We must have been over an hour and a half on the raft before the lifeboat picked us up. Another 20 minutes and we would have had it. The worst part was the intense cold."

The Stromness and Thurso lifeboats retrieved further bodies from the sea.

A short but moving open air service was held in Stromness before the seven coffins of the victims, bedecked in flowers and wreaths, were conveyed on the *St Ola* ferry on the first leg of their return to Grimsby.

But the efforts of the Orcadian rescuers were not to be forgotten on Humberside. The five women who went to the shore to join in the search were given gifts of silver compacts by the trawler owners and insurers, while the men involved in the rescue effort were given wallets. The owners also presented £100 cheques to the lifeboat branches of Stromness and Thurso. But most moving were the letters sent to *The Orcadian* by bereaved widows, thanking the people of Orkney for their kindness.

The wrecked trawler eventually broke in half and at the later inquiry into the tragedy, Sheriff D.B. Keith said it was quite clear that the accident was not attributable to lack of care nor to negligence. It was unfortunate that the radar was not working but that was not anyone's fault.

The year ended with another tragedy for the fishing industry as six men, including the skipper, were lost when the Hull-registered, but Fleetwood-based, trawler *Hildina* foundered in heavy seas to the west of Orkney on December 1, 1953.

The *Hildina* was said to have turned over after her trawl gear caught fast, and Kirkwall Coastguards helped to coordinate a search for survivors. Nine of the 15 crew were saved by the Fleetwood trawler *Velia* which was fortunately fishing nearby.

The "great escape" of the year, however, came in June, 1953, when the 7,600 ton American cargo ship *Rutgers Victory* - loaded with motor lorries, on passage from Liverpool to Stavanger - was safely refloated after the vessel with 45 crew, ran aground in thick fog on the Pentland Skerries. She was taken into Longhope Bay to allow repairs to be carried out.

New KGS rector

Mr Alexander Leask retired in 1953 after 44 years service to the Kirkwall Grammar School, 24 of them as rector.

Mr Leask - who had been a pupil at the burgh school from 1894 -1904 - sadly died, aged 65, just five months after his retirement.

He was succeeded as rector by Mr Henry MacKerron (44), the second master at KGS and an elder of St Magnus Cathedral. Originally from Greenock, he had joined the KGS staff in 1947.

The raising of the school leaving age to 15 had seen Orkney's school population increase by ten per cent in the five years, 1948-53, to 3,488. It was Orkney's biggest school population for 30 years.

In 1953, there were still 49 schools in the county - the biggest being Kirkwall Grammar School with 1,111 pupils (that included 230 in the infants' department which was still part of KGS) and the smallest Graemsay with four.

Work started on the new infant school for Kirkwall, at Papdale, in April, 1954, at an estimated cost of £72,000.

The cost of education in Orkney in the 1953-54 financial year was £229,626 - the equivalent of £65 for every pupil.

New seaweed trade

A new factory for Moray Firth Seaweeds Products - manufacturing farm feedstuffs and fertilisers from seaweed - opened at Hatston with the company planning to employ 20 men. The first 112 ton shipment went from Kirkwall to Hull in March, 1953. The venture folded in 1959.

The Stromness lifeboat lands some of the 11 survivors from the wrecked Grimsby trawler *Leicester City* which grounded in Hoy Sound in 1953 with the loss of seven men.
(Picture courtesy of Orkney Library photographic archive)

Duke under fire

The *Daily Mirror* gave the story front page prominence as the Westray United Free Church of Scotland minister, Rev A. Small, launched a scathing attack on the Duke of Edinburgh for playing polo on a Sunday.

Mart take-over

Orkney farmers agreed in 1953 to set up a company to run the Kirkwall Auction Mart which had operated since 1928 under the ownership of Messrs T. Smith Peace. A total of 888 members subscribed to a share capital of £31,225.

Land for homes

Kirkwall Town Council paid £4,350, in November, 1953, to acquire the land of Quoybanks from the Church of Scotland trustees for 58 new homes to be built.

Eclipse of the sun

Fine weather conditions enabled Orcadians to witness a virtually total eclipse of the sun in the Summer of 1954. The eclipse was total in Unst in Shetland, but Orkney had to settle for about 95 per cent, sufficient for the temperature to fall two degrees.

Submarine visit

Sixteen submarines - said to be engaged in a "top secret" exercise off North Scotland - converged on Kirkwall Bay for a three day visit in July, 1953.

New hotel

The Royal Hotel, Stromness, opened on July 8, 1953 - owned by Messrs Frank Skinner and Company, the proprietors of Kirkwall's Royal Hotel.

Lifeboat hero

The coxswain of Stromness lifeboat William Sinclair retired in 1954 after a lifeboat career in which he helped save 62 lives. He was succeeded as coxswain by Stromness fisherman James Adam.

Mink farm

An experimental mink farm was started by David Balfour with 12 mink from Canada delivered to his Shapinsay estate. He hoped the animals would thrive in Orkney conditions and, in time, become a profitable industry serving the fur trade.

Salvage expert dies

Commodore Thomas McKenzie, for 14 years the chief salvage officer concerned with the raising of the German Fleet in Scapa Flow, died in 1954 at the age of 62.

Lurid tale of devil worshippers

Tales of devil worshippers in Orkney, a witches' sabbath and a virgin girl sacrificed on a devil's altar appeared in the national press. There's nothing like a good, accurate newspaper story - and this was nothing like a good, accurate newspaper story.

The *Empire News*, a Sunday newspaper with two million readers, told of secret happenings in Stenness, apparently related by a one-time RAF squadron leader who was stationed at Twatt - allegedly!

He claimed to have been taken at 2am to a midsummer ceremony at Maeshowe by a beautiful Orcadian blonde known familiarly as "Lollypop."

1954

The squadron leader claimed: "About 60 people were there, all with their faces hooded and wearing blankets. They held candles and incense was burning and it was so packed that some of them couldn't get in. One man with an Orkney accent read the Black Mass. And they all chanted, and I swear I can't remember it happening but certainly there was this brand mark on my leg - a burn but not

---

painful at all. There was another ceremony after this at the ring of stones. A girl was tied on the altar and a decorated white goat - pretty nasty all of it.

"Well I left the Orkneys two months after, but I couldn't get this thing out of my mind. Every midsummer night I have to walk about and think of it - sometimes all night."

The *Empire News* sent its own investigator "Fabian of the Yard" to Orkney where the reporter made "discreet inquiries talking to farmers, fisherfolk and local folklore authorities." Unsurprisingly, he failed to come up with a single fact to substantiate his newspaper's flight of fantasy.

Kirkwall jail break

Kirkwall Prison officially closed on March 1, 1954, and the building was taken over as the new headquarters of the Orkney Police Force.

The last principal officer in charge of Kirkwall Prison was Mr Robert Allison who had served in Orkney for five years. Despite the prison closure, the cells were retained for sentences of up to 30 days with the status of police cells.

However, within days of the changeover, a 21 year old prisoner took advantage of

the fact that there was no longer a jailer - and escaped.

He had placed a table by the 12 feet high wall of the exercise yard, a chair on top of the table, and two buckets on top of that, before using this precarious ladder to make for freedom.

He had a few hours out of captivity on a Saturday evening before police traced him to a house at Hatston. He had a further 30 days added to his 20 day sentence.

Council salaries

The salary of Orkney's county clerk and treasurer - the equivalent of the post of chief executive of Orkney Islands Council in 1999 - was increased from £1,450 to £1,500 a year in 1954.The director of social welfare (which was only a part-time post) had a salary increase from £572 10s to £650 a year, with the one part-time children's officer having a pay increase from £50 to £100 a year.

The town clerk of Kirkwall earned £800

a year for his duties in 1954.

Male manual workers, aged 20 and over, employed by the county council roads department, had been given a wage rise from £5 9s to £5 14s 6d a week in 1952, prompting a call for pay parity by Kirkwall's 30 burgh workmen who staged a lightning strike, leaving the town's rubbish uncollected, in demand of a wage increase of 3d an hour in 1953.

Blaze destroys town shop

The shop and stores of Messrs P.C. Flett, the well known Kirkwall firm of ironmongers and seedsmen in Albert Street, was completely destroyed by fire in January, 1954.

The alarm was raised in the early hours by Mrs Emily Celli, wife of the proprietor of the Pomona cafe, who saw flames leaping into the night sky. Damage was estimated at £15,000 but the Kirkwall fire brigade and firefighters from Kirkwall Airport succeeded in preventing the blaze spreading to the neighbouring premises of Cumming and Spence, grocers and bakers, and John Sclater, draper.

It was the worst fire since the loss of the Albert Kinema in 1947 and, before that, the loss of Messrs R. Garden's shops in Bridge Street in 1938.

The firm of P.C. Flett dated back to 1843 and the chairman of the company in 1954 was the former provost of Kirkwall, P.C. Flett, who had succeeded his father in business half a century earlier.

The firm reopened for business in temporary premises in Bridge Street, but within nine months the Albert Street premises were rebuilt and open to customers again.

Churchill salute for *The Orcadian*

Amongst messages of congratulation as *The Orcadian* celebrated its 100th anniversary as a newspaper in 1954 was one from the Prime Minister Sir Winston Churchill, who celebrated his 80th birthday the same month.

The Orcadian marked the occasion with a special centenary issue with contributions by Eric Linklater, Edwin Muir, Jo Grimond and Dr Hugh Marwick amongst others.

The man who headed the newspaper, and the company, at the start of the 20th century, was W.R. Mackintosh, an Ayrshire journalist who had married a daughter of James Anderson, one of the newspaper's original founding family.

He continued in control until his death in World War One when he was succeeded by his son James Anderson Mackintosh who ran the business until 1938. His daughter Elizabeth Miller, who had taken control of the firm by this time, set the presses rolling to print the centenary issue.

The circulation of the paper had increased from 3,600 in1914 to 6,000 in 1931 to just under 8,000 in 1954.

Also, in September, 1954, the old established firm of George Bain, painter and decorator, Broad Street, Kirkwall, celebrated its centenary with a commemorative party for staff and guests.

Freedom of Kirkwall

Kirkwall Town Council agreed to bestow the freedom of the burgh on Dr Hugh Marwick, retired county director of education and former headmaster of the Kirkwall school.

In addition to his services to education, Dr Marwick, a native of Rousay, was a distinguished scholar and historian. Among his many books and publications, he was the author of *Orkney*, generally acknowledged as the best general volume on the county published at the time.

Four minute mile

As a record-breaking run saw the athlete Roger Bannister credited with the first sub-four minute mile, a 71 year old Kirk minister claimed he had achieved the same feat 52 years earlier on the island of Rousay.

The Rev Alexander Spark, living in Glasgow, said he had achieved the same time as Bannister, running between two mile posts in Rousay in 1902.

"I was 19 at the time and a student at Edinburgh University. I had gone back to the Orkneys for a holiday - to the place where my father was parish minister for 30 years."

Rev Spark claimed he had made the run in his ordinary suit and shoes and timed himself with his pocket watch that "never lost a moment in 20 years."

Trees a crowd

The first Forestry Commission plantations in Orkney were laid out in Hoy in April, 1954.

The experiment was to assess both the rate of tree growth in the islands and also the potential for commercial timber production.

Four plots were chosen over a six mile area and fenced with rabbit-proof netting. The planting of 70,000 trees, about five feet apart, was carried out by a team of six men over three weeks.

The species planted were all coniferous with various types of pine, spruce and larch. It was expected that it would be three years before the growth rate could be assessed, but there was an immediate setback as many of the trees had their needles blasted from green to brown by a gale on April 3, 1954.

Killer rabbit plague

The disease Myxomatosis - which had been decimating Europe's rabbit population during the previous year - reached Orkney in the Summer of 1954.

The first local case was confirmed by Ministry of Agriculture vets at Burray - the furthest north that the disease had been reported. Reports from Burray said rabbits there were "dying by the hundred" and there were also unconfirmed reports of an outbreak in Sanday.

The Secretary of State for Scotland, Mr James Stuart, gave an assurance that there was no danger to humans from the virus. But within a couple of weeks, the disease had been confirmed in rabbits from South Ronaldsay, Hoy, the West Mainland and the North Isles.

New oil company

S.P. Robertson returned to his native Kirkwall in 1954 to take over the Shore Street oil storage depot as the authorised distributor of all BP and Shell products in the county. It was the birth of the company S. and J. Robertson which was to grow to become one of the biggest private companies in the North of Scotland in the ensuing four decades.

In World War Two, S.P. Robertson had reached the rank of major in the Royal Artillery, seeing active service in Europe, before joining the Anglo Iranian Oil Company in the Middle East.

He was a brother of county roads surveyor John Robertson and county director of social welfare Gordon Robertson.

Cathedral minister dies

After 18 years as minister of St Magnus Cathedral, Rev Arthur Fryer left Orkney in 1954 to take up an appointment with the Presbyterian Church in New Zealand. However, within months of his departure, members of his Kirkwall congregation were shocked to learn of his death in a motor accident in New Zealand.

When Rev Fryer first moved to Kirkwall, his congregation stood at 669. It had subsequently grown to 1,020.

He was succeeded as the minister of St Magnus Cathedral by the Rev John Rose who, like the Rev Fryer, had served as an Army chaplain during World War Two - being mentioned in dispatches with the King's African Rifles in East Africa and Ceylon, and serving throughout the Burma campaign.

The Rev Rose came to Orkney from Lady Glenorchy's North Church in Edinburgh where he had been minister since 1946. Also, in 1955, the Rev E.G. Chirgwin became minister of Kirkwall's East Kirk.

Harvest disaster

With six inches of rain in the first three weeks of October, 1954 was judged to be the worst harvest since 1923 which was credited with being one the most disastrous of the century.

Both the potato and grain harvests were said to be miserable. Orkney had 47 inches of rain in 1954 - compared with an annual average of 35 inches.

Dounreay plant

Plans were announced for a new atomic energy plant at Dounreay in Caithness in the Spring of 1954. A construction force of 2,000 men was expected to be employed on the building of the power station which, when running, would employ 300 locally recruited workers, said the Government.

Fishermen saved

The Aberdeen trawler *Koorah* was lost in stormy conditions in the Pentland Firth in March, 1954, but her 12 crewmen were rescued by a Thurso fishing boat.

Nine months later, the crew of six, including a sixteen year old, from the Swedish fishing vessel *Westfart* were landed safely at Stromness after their ship foundered in mountainous seas off Orkney.

War memorial

Kirkwall War Memorial, commemorating the victims of World War Two, was eventually unveiled - at a ceremony watched by nearly 2,000 people - nine years after the end of the war, and on the tenth anniversary of D-Day, June 6. The 28 names were unveiled by Mrs A.Tait, mother of two sons whose names were engraved on the roll of honour.

Hitler's barge

Captain William Dennison - who operated the mail, passenger and cargo shipping service between Kirkwall and Shapinsay - purchased a barge from Hitler's former luxury yacht, the *Grille*.

The 37 feet vessel was renamed the *Klydon III* and was used as a reserve vessel for the mv *Iona*. Captain Dennison acquired the barge, in 1954, from a Dumbarton man who had owned it since the end of World War Two.

Orkney honours

The Orkney writer Eric Linklater was made a CBE in the 1954 Queen's birthday honours list, while Inspector James Cormack, Depute Chief Constable of Orkney, who had served in the Orkney force since 1938, received the British Empire Medal.

Hurricane force twelve

The years of 1952 and 1953 saw Orkney rocked to its foundations as two great storms - with hurricane force winds well over 100 mph - left a trail of destruction that made front page headlines around the world.

The first storm, in the early morning of Tuesday, January 15, 1952, saw a 120 mph hurricane from the south west hit Orkney like a battering ram after the barometer had fallen 14 points in five hours.

£1 million damage was feared - this can be multiplied 20-fold to give the equivalent cost in 1999 - and dozens of families were homeless as a state of emergency was declared to give special powers to Orkney County Council to deal with the unprecedented crisis as the population was awoken to scenes of unimagined devastation.

The gale was at its height from 4.30 am - 7.30 am with the highest gusts at 6am when the average wind speed was 90 mph. The Met Office at Grimsetter airport registered the wind at up to 105 mph while gusts of 115 mph were recorded at the experimental wind generator at Costa Head. Both those, however, were the maximum readings of which the instruments were capable, and it was reliably estimated that wind speeds must have exceeded 120 mph.

"Many people were wakened during the storm by their beds being shaken as if by a small earthquake," reported *The Orcadian.* "When dawn broke, the two burghs looked as if they had been hit by an air raid. Wooden huts which had been converted into homes were hardest hit, and in many cases were completely flattened, their occupants being rendered homeless."

Remarkably, however, the occupants were all alive, although, in Sanday, one man had a terrifying experience when the wooden house in which he was sleeping was blown away for a considerable distance with him inside it. He luckily escaped with nothing more than a few bruises.

Orkney's Chief Constable Gathorne Cheyne - who two weeks earlier had been awarded the King's Police Medal in the New Year Honours List - had the task of assessing the damage, but communication was virtually impossible. Roads were blocked, with cars upended, the entire mains electricity system was out of action, telephone lines were down everywhere, the poles spreadeagled at grotesque angles, and the wireless station at the top of Wideford Hill was damaged.

The first result of the storm was that thousands of school-children had a holiday as their schools were closed. In Rousay, damage was estimated at £100,000, with the wooden recreation hall completely wrecked and the churches, shops and main school building damaged.

Eventually it was established that over 1,000 domestic buildings were wrecked or unroofed while well over 2,000 agricultural buildings were demolished or without a roof. The county convener Alex Calder said the total damage in the county would be £1 million. Experts estimated that it would take two years to recover from the storm which was said to have caused £500,000 damage to the farming industry alone.

The Orcadian reported: "Amongst the biggest sufferers were the hens, and Orkney's egg industry must have taken a severe setback. Henhouses were overturned, smashed and, in some cases, blown out to sea. Dead birds were strewn everywhere - across fields, on the roads, in the sea, and impaled on barbed wire fences. In Rousay they were being picked up by the barrow load. The survivors in many cases have been or will have to be killed off, as there is no accommodation or food left for them.

A scene of devastation in Shore Street, Kirkwall, the day after the 1953 storm of January 31. The street was filled by the debris of smashed concrete and tangled pipelines.
(Picture courtesy of Orkney Library photographic archive)

"Farm steadings lost their roofs in many instances and left the cattle exposed to the fury of the wind. In some cases, cattle were injured when their byres caved in, particularly at Melsetter, Hoy."

The loss of poultry and poultry houses at Sunnybrae, St Ola, was alone estimated at £2,000. Cattle were left without feed-stuffs as hay stacks were blown away, and an emergency meeting of the Orkney branch of the National Farmers Union called for help from the Department of Agriculture in getting speedy delivery of building materials for repairs.

It was not only the livestock population which was suffering however. Fourteen former Army huts erected during World War Two for the ATS - known as the "Attery" and later to become Grieveship Terrace, Stromness - were rendered uninhabitable, and the families and children living there were forced to seek shelter at St Peter's Manse.

Stromness Town Council sent a message to the Secretary of State for Scotland: "Storm damage situation desperate. Urgently requested top priority materials and feeding stuffs for farm stock. Financial assistance imperative for housing and farmers. Emergency measures necessary immediately to ensure earliest restoration of milk, egg and beef production."

Fortunately, the Balfour and Eastbank hospitals escaped with less than £1,000 worth of damage. St Magnus Cathedral also escaped serious harm but Tankerness House had a great hole torn in its roof. It was reported to Orkney Presbytery that every kirk in the county had suffered some damage with the kirk in Hoy unuseable and the Westray manse uninhabitable. Other kirks in Westray, South Ronaldsay, Walls, Sanday and Tankerness were temporarily out of commission. In Stromness churchyard, 49 tombstones were knocked down by the force of the wind; a fate also suffered in Eday where the war memorial was blown down and broken. The wooden Episcopal Kirk in Stronsay was flattened, while only six of the island's 150 farms had escaped damage.

The BEA garage near Bignold Park had its roof collapse on to the two buses inside while hundreds of trees were uprooted at Binscarth, Finstown. A three ton lorry owned by Mr Sam Bews was overturned when his garage situated on the Deerness road was blown down. A two hundredweight iron tank was blown half a mile from the farm of Millhouse, Tankerness, to the farm of Sebay.

Also on the East Mainland, Mr Peter Johnston of Gaitnip Farm told the story of Gaitnip's flying pig which was blown 50 yards through the air when the hut in which it was quartered blew over. The pig was missing for two days but was eventually found and reported to be "now doing fine."

A 26 inch long traditional stone roofing slate, weighing 35 lbs from Northbigging, Harray, was blown a mile in the storm, while corrugated asbestos from the Hoy community centre was blown nearly three miles to Graemsay. Wooden houses everywhere had collapsed "like a pack of cards" but brothers William and John Sabiston, of Arion Farm, Stromness, saw their tractor garage lifted by the wind and hurled a distance of more than 200 yards into Stenness Loch. Elsewhere, a ten feet yawl was lifted right over the top of a house - from the front garden to the back!

Such were the stories that were told as, for the first time, up-to-the-minute newsreel film from Orkney featured on national television news programmes which could be seen by viewers in the South.

The severity of the situation was underlined as the Lord Lieutenant of Orkney, Patrick Sutherland Graeme, set up an emergency relief fund and made a nationwide radio appeal for contributions.

He told listeners to the BBC Home Service: "In the early hours of Tuesday morning, a hurricane of violence unprecedented in our annals hurled itself upon us, bringing widespread devastation in its train. Our capital town of Kirkwall has suffered gravely, her sister burgh of Stromness in the west still more so. Throughout the county, buildings have been severely damaged and roofs torn off.

"Everywhere stacks of hay and grain crops have been laid low and scattered over countryside and sea. Beef and milk production of which we were so rightly proud has suffered a terrible disaster.

"The egg industry, an amazing triumph of achievement in recent years, has met with a dire calamity. In the course of a few hours, thousands of hen houses were reduced literally to matchwood, and the mortality among fowls has been at a rate impossible of computation. It may be weeks before electricity supplies can be fully restored or the miles of broken telephone wires repaired.

"We are faced with a human problem of immediate urgency. This disaster has overtaken many, both in town and country, for whom recovery will be difficult because even when materials are available, they have not the means to pay for them."

A separate relief fund was set up by the Lord Provosts of Glasgow, Edinburgh, Perth, Dundee and Aberdeen, appealing not only for cash contributions for Orkney but for Caithness and Sutherland which had been touched by the storm also.

The response of the British public was immediate and generous. Within days, donations of £6,000 were received by the Orkney fund.

King George VI sent the following message to Orkney's Lord Lieutenant Patrick Sutherland Graeme: "The Queen and I are much distressed to learn of the damage which has been caused to the people of Orkney by the recent storm. Please convey to them an expression of our sincerest sympathy." The King and Queen backed up their words with a donation to the relief fund. Princess Elizabeth, the Duke of Edinburgh and Queen Mary, the then Queen Mother, also contributed to the fund which, within two weeks had reached £16,000

Contributions also included donations from army units which had been based in the county in World War Two; the Scottish Football Association gave £500; the North of Scotland and Orkney and Shetland Shipping Company £1,000 and Orkney Egg Producers £1,000. Even the Labour Party - which had been defeated in the 1951 General Election - gave £776, most of it donated by trades union members.

The response from the Government - and the level of official financial aid for relief work to ease Orkney's plight - was condemned, however, as "niggardly."

The new Conservative Secretary of State for Scotland was James Stuart who arrived in Orkney, within 96 hours of the storm, to assess the damage with a party of Government officials. "I am much impressed by the courage of the people of Orkney and the way they are facing up to the disaster which threatened to overwhelm them," he told *The Orcadian*.

So impressed was the Minister with Orcadians' natural fortitude to overcome adversity that he announced that the Government would contribute a paltry £20,000 to the relief work. And even that would not go directly to Orkney - it would be given to the Scottish Lord Provosts' fund to be shared between Orkney, Caithness and Sutherland.

Orkney and Shetland MP Jo Grimond appealed in Parliament for more state aid but was rebuffed by the Secretary of State. The only concession that the MP wrung from the Government was that Orcadians doing National Service in this country could be released to return home and help repair the storm damage.

It is true that, in human terms, it was not the worst storm Orkney had ever suffered - the great gale of 1890, when most of the herring fleet had been caught 20 miles west of Hoy, had seen 85 lives lost as the fleet was devastated - but the miserly Government financial assistance caused widespread resentment as Orkney, and Orcadians, had to pick up the bill for 90 per cent of the damage that had been caused by the wrath of Nature.

And, although no one was killed or seriously injured in the 1952 hurricane, the disaster did lead to tragedy when William Gordon Grant (23) of Ayre Mills, Kirkwall, died in a fall while working on damaged overhead power lines at Swartabreck, Tankerness.

And relief work was not helped when ten days after the hurricane, Orkney suffered snow drifts up to four feet deep,

Front Road in St Margaret's Hope after the storm of 1953 washed away sea defences. (Picture courtesy of Orkney Library photographic archive)

and 17 degrees of frost were recorded on Monday, January 28, at Grimsetter airport.

In the midst of efforts to clear the ravages of the storm, two African chiefs arrived from the torrid heat of Kenya to see how Orkney farming was conducted. Chief Mukina Uku, father of nine, and Chief Paul Inda Enok Ndire (34) who lived near the shores of Lake Victoria, were both the elected heads of tribes of 20,000 people.

By February 21, the official figure of damage caused by the storm was £512,213, according to estimates compiled by the police. But Orcadian resilience was already beginning to piece together again the shattered landscape and economy. Electricity and telephone supplies were repaired and operational again within days in most parts of the Mainland, although some of the islands were without phones for two weeks.

And if a personification of Orkney grit was needed, one needed to look no further than 76 year old Mary Ann Stout who, for a week, refused to leave her roofless cottage on Fara, in Scapa Flow - dismissing a policeman and a social worker with a "hot reception" - although she did eventually agree to accept temporary hospitality at the County Home.

Two months after the 1952 storm, the total donated for relief work amounted to £57,000. The Scottish Lord Provosts' fund - which included the £20,000 from the Government - was divided up with £22,161 to Orkney, £14,750 for Caithness and £2,100 for Sutherland. The Orkney Lord Lieutenant's fund had reached £17,879 and the trustees had already dealt with 520 out of 630 applications for help, with grants ranging from £5 to £250.

The Orkney egg industry was wounded by the disaster - but reports of its death were overstated. Production at Orkney Egg Producers, following the great gale, was down by about £35,000 over the eight week peak period of the Spring of 1952, but recovered strongly in the following months.

A surprising number of the poultry population had actually survived. It was eventually accepted that around 30 per cent - about 250,000 out of 800,000 birds - had been lost, but, within a month, day old chicks were being delivered to Orkney in their thousands to help rebuild the industry.

By the end of the year, in spite of the hurricane, Orkney had suffered a decrease of just 12 per cent, or seven million eggs, over the year, and the county's annual egg income still totalled over £1 million.

It was just as well that Orkney had shown its resilience, for, on Saturday, January 31, 1953, the county was hit by the full force of Hurricane Number Two!

Kirkwall's waterfront was devastated as the northerly blast - recorded at a sustained 125 mph at Costa Head - inflicted widespread damage as gigantic seas tore open the sea front and, in little over three hours, washed away the sea wall and hundreds of yards of Shore Street and the Ayre Road, laying bare water, gas and oil pipes. In Stromness, the West Mainland Mart building was reduced to matchwood.

In this case, however, Orkney was not alone in suffering the might of the elements. Huge areas of North East Scotland, the East of England and the Netherlands were devastated by serious flooding affecting millions of people, with a national death toll feared in the hundreds.

And on this occasion, although Orkney again miraculously

escaped any local fatalities in the hurricane, the county was directly touched by tragedy as 14 Humberside fishermen on the Grimsby trawler *Sheldon* sailed from Kirkwall to their deaths in the teeth of the storm.

At 5am on January 31, all had been calm but the wind gradually increased in strength up to gale force by soon after 7am. It continued to rise in force and, between 10.20 and 10.30am, it averaged 80 mph with gusts registered at 107 mph at Grimsetter Airport Met Office, the highest level the instruments could reach.

Most of Kirkwall's damage was suffered either side of 11am as the hurricane force winds coincided with an abnormally high tide. Junction Road, Kirkwall, was flooded and the town's waterfront hotels - the Queen's, Kirkwall, St Ola and Ayre - were scenes of utter devastation as huge boulders and smashed concrete filled what had been the roadway. The wind gradually moderated by the evening but showers of sleet and snow added to the problems.

Trees around St Magnus Cathedral were blown down and at the North of Scotland Hydro Electric Board power station, the main front door, made of teak and weighing half a ton, was blown in. Amazingly, the electricity supply was maintained throughout the crisis but loud speaker vans had to tour Kirkwall warning householders of the risk of pollution to the water supply.

Hen houses had again suffered the hurricane blast but remarkably few hens were actually lost. However, it was a major blow to the newly formed West Mainland Mart Company - a co-operative of farmers which had been formed only four months earlier - with the mart buildings left in ruins. Corrugated iron roofing was simply blown away like pieces of paper.

But, unlike the storm of 1952, when most of the damage had been suffered on land, it was the sea which witnessed the greatest drama and tragedy in January, 1953.

The Grimsby trawler *Sheldon*, with a crew of 14, had sailed from Kirkwall on Friday, January 30. The skipper and mate were father and son and they were feared lost with the rest of the crew when no trace of the trawler was found in the following three weeks. An official inquiry later decided that the trawler had perished when she met the full force of the hurricane somewhere between Fair Isle and the Faroe islands.

The Dutch oil tanker *Marcella* broke loose from her moorings at the height of the storm and crashed against the top of Kirkwall's West Pier, leaving a gaping hole of 50 feet. The sea walls in St Margaret's Hope and Westray were also damaged. Three lighthouse keepers - Donald Felton, William Duell and Callum McIver - were isolated by the storms for eight days on Suleskerry before being relieved by the *Pole Star* lighthouse support ship. Felton and Duell had been on the island for two months without a break in duty.

But the abiding memory of the 1953 storm was the amazing story of the Orkney Steam Navigation Company vessel *Earl Thorfinn* - which had one of the most astonishing escapes in an epic voyage which stared potential disaster in the face.

The steamer, with her crew of 13 and ten passengers, was feared lost for several hours after failing to arrive on schedule in Westray. News had already come in of the loss of another ship, the *Princess Victoria* in the Irish Sea, with 83 passengers, and it was immediately dreaded that dire disaster had also overtaken the *Earl Thorfinn*.

In fact, what eventually emerged was a story of seldom matched heroism of the sea, as the 25 year old ship turned up safely 140 miles south in Aberdeen. The epic voyage of the *Earl Thorfinn*, under the command of her 32 year old master Captain Hamish Flett, would take an honoured place in the annals of Orkney seamanship, said *The Orcadian*.

The North Isles steamer - 150 feet long, 27 feet broad and with a top speed of 11 knots - had sailed from Kirkwall for Westray at 7am and, at 8.30am, was seen between Stronsay and Sanday. Thirty minutes later, as the full fury of the hurricane hit the ship, Captain Flett found it impossible to

The storm of January 31, 1953, saw the streets of Kirkwall turned into rivers. This was Junction Road. At high tide, it was said that the depth of water at the Kiln Corner was three feet.
(Picture courtesy of Orkney Library photographic archive)

reach shelter in either island, and took the decision that his only course of action was to turn the ship and run before the wind. With the engines kept at full speed to maintain steerage in the heavy seas, Captain Flett succeeded in turning the ship's head southwards.

Down in the saloon of the ship were ten passengers, including three women, varying in age from 18 to 73.

Captain Flett admitted later: "They didn't know just how bad things really were. I've never seen the like of it before. Visibility was nil and the gale was more than 100 mph. Twice we nearly went aground on Sanday."

Off Auskerry, the ship took three heavy seas in quick succession over the starboard side and, in the master's opinion, it was a miracle that the third sea did not roll the vessel completely over.

"With the wind behind us we were constantly being pooped by waves breaking over the stern. Lockers and seats aft were torn away and one lifeboat was swung out of her cradle. At one time the starboard lifeboat was buried in the sea as the *Earl* heeled over."

The shock of this was followed by a new crisis as the ship's steam steering gear was carried away - and the hand steering gear had to be engaged. At times, in a tremendous feat of endurance, it required five hands at the wheel to hold the vessel on her course. The master directed the steering from his position in the upper wheelhouse and passed his orders to the mate in the lower wheelhouse. Both the wheelhouses were being continually flooded as the seas broke aboard, Captain Flett recalled afterwards.

Back in Westray - eight of the crew belonged to the island - a mood of understandable despair was growing when 12 hours had passed with no reported sightings of the *Earl Thorfinn*. However, at midnight on that black Saturday night, came the heart-lifting news that the ship had reached Aberdeen.

Unfortunately, for the crew and passengers, their ordeal was not over. The port of Aberdeen was closed due to the weather and so the *Thorfinn* had to "dodge" around the bay for another 15 hours before being allowed to berth at 3pm on Sunday, February 1. The master and crew had been on duty continuously for over 30 hours with only one cup of lukewarm soup - which they had before the sea put out the galley fire - two cups of tea and a biscuit.

The passengers on the historic trip were Mr James Byers of Eday; Mr George Stuart, manager of the Kirkwall egg packing station; Mr T.W. Thomson of North Ronaldsay; Mr Inkster Thomson and his sister Miss Helen Thomson from Sanday; Mrs Margaret Peace and her son Thomas Peace, also from Sanday; Mrs Elizabeth Findlay of Kirkwall; Mr William Thomson of Stromness; and Mr William Meil, of Geramont House, Sanday. Ironically, Mr Meil had boarded the *Earl Thorfinn* to return home to Sanday after a visit to Aberdeen. Instead, he found himself back in Aberdeen.

Two other "passengers" on board - two cattle - were even more unfortunate. They could not be landed at Aberdeen because it was a "closed area" due to foot and mouth disease precautions.

On Monday, February 2, 1953, Mr Donald Bertram, secretary of the Orkney Steam Navigation Company, flew to Aberdeen to personally congratulate the master and crew on their achievement. The crew, under Captain Flett, were Ronald Vickery, a New Zealander and mate; Willie Rendall, boatswain from Westray; seaman David Hutchison, Westray; Harry Lovie, Kirkwall; John Burgher, Westray; Richie Rendall, Westray; and Willie Brown, Westray. The engine room staff were chief engineer Duncan Manson, who also lived in Westray, greaser Alexander Ross, Kirkwall, and fireman Malcolm Brown, Westray. Another Westrayman, Jackie Bain, was the steward, and Tommy Gray of Sanday was the cabin boy.

They returned to a heroes' welcome when they eventually sailed direct to Westray from Aberdeen. The people of Westray presented the master and crew a scroll in thankfulness for their return - and the shipping company, along with a letter of congratulations, gave each man an extra fortnight's pay. A big crowd also turned out to welcome the ship back to Kirkwall.

And the incident was to lead directly to improved safety conditions for the North Isles ships. Within months - in response to calls for wireless transmitting equipment to be fitted - both the *Earl Thorfinn* and the *Earl Sigurd* had radiotelephone sets fitted - and two years later radar was added to both vessels.

Captain Hamish Flett - he had survived a World War Two torpedo off the West coast of Ireland - went on to work with a yachting charter company in the South of England before returning to Orkney where he and his wife Ina took over the Kettletoft Hotel on Sanday. Later they moved to Peterhead to run the Union Bar before settling down to retirement in Aberdeen where Captain Flett still had a scrapbook of the worldwide publicity given to the ship which had survived the huge waves and 100 mph hurricane. And the epic voyage was immortalised in a painting by the artist Douglas Sinclair.

With the drama at sea thankfully over, thoughts turned back to repairing the damage on land. The first priority of the county surveyor and roads director John Robertson was to shore up the Kirkwall waterfront defences before the traditionally high Spring tides could wreak further havoc.

Jo Grimond MP admitted to the House of Commons that damage in Orkney and Shetland was small compared to the eastern counties of England, but said: "The island of Sanday was almost cut in half. Part of the shore where the mailboat from North Ronaldsay arrives has changed its character completely."

He pointed out that Orkney had to bear 90 per cent of the cost of repair and rebuilding work after the 1952 great storm, and he called for 100 per cent grants to help restore the Ayre Road.

Again Orkney resilience - and generosity to others in a crisis - came to the fore. The Lord Mayor of London had launched a national Flood and Tempest Distress Fund which was backed by the Lord Lieutenant, Patrick Sutherland Graeme, the county convener Alex Calder, and the provosts of Kirkwall and Stromness. Within weeks over £1,100 was raised in Orkney, and, within days, Orkney had sent south 30 cartons of clothing for the flood victims of England and the Netherlands, after a collection organised by the Kirkwall Chamber of Commerce.

Remarkably, within three months, by April 23, 1953, Jo Grimond had been invited to open the rebuilt saleroom of the West Mainland Mart, and the Ayre Road, after being shut to traffic for six months, re-opened in August, 1953, after repairs costing £14,289 - most of the cost being met by government grants.

Orkney, with few enough trees as it was, lost many hundreds in the storms of 1952 and 1953, with the Binscarth plantation - started by the grandfather of the then owner, Robert Scarth, in 1850 - worst hit. The 1952 storm destroyed about a third of the trees, uprooting several hundreds of sycamores, elms, ash, beech and alders.

It took William Johnstone, of Collingwood, Stromness, and his son Reynold, a year to clear the debris with a chain saw. A further 50 to 60 trees at Binscarth were laid low by the 1953 hurricane.

But to put an end to the myth that the great storms destroyed the Orkney egg industry, it should be pointed out that Orkney's two egg grading stations handled 61 million eggs between them in 1953 as the gross value of the county's egg exports exceeded £1.25 million - the 1999 equivalent of £25 millions - and output increased to over 66 million eggs in 1954.

On Thursday, November 11, 1954, Orkney was struck by Hurricane Number Three with wind speeds of 118 mph recorded at Costa Head between 5pm and 6pm, and a peak blast of 103 mph at Kirkwall Airport. The storm did considerable damage to the recently gathered grain harvest, with fields stripped bare of sheaves, and the telephone service was disrupted, but fortunately, on this occasion, the islands escaped any major structural damage. It meant, however, that Orkney had suffered three major hurricanes in the space of 34 months.

After the great blizzards of 1955 came the task of digging scores of stranded cars from snowdrifts up to ten feet deep.
(Picture courtesy of Orkney Library photographic archive)

Isles entombed by snow

Orkney was paralysed by the great freeze of January and February, 1955, as blizzard conditions left the county trapped beneath snow which drifted to ten feet deep.

The county was, in fact, hit by two blizzards - the first in mid January and the second a month later - both of which brought the islands to a standstill for ten days on each occasion.

More than 100 schoolchildren were trapped at their schools, power and telephone services were blacked out, all roads made impassable with the airport isolated, and emergency air drops of rations were necessary to save isolated communities.

Temperatures had been falling steadily, with frequent snow showers, for two days before, on January 12, Orkney was hit by Blizzard Number One. Temperatures had fallen to 25 degrees Fahrenheit as heavy snow fell all day driven by gusts of wind reaching 70 mph. By early afternoon, practically every road in Orkney was blocked and many were stranded, several having to abandon their cars in deep drifts - where they were to remain for nearly two weeks.

Schoolchildren were trapped. At Widewall schoolhouse, 14 pupils and two teachers had to stay the night, ten at North Walls School, seven at South Walls, and, in Westray, children from Rapness had to stay at Pierowall. Sixty pupils from country districts attending Stromness school were stranded in the town and had to be boarded out in private homes. By the following morning all 49 Orkney schools, with the exception of Kirkwall and Stromness, were closed.

Travel between the two main centres of population was impossible as the main Kirkwall - Stromness road became an early victim of the snow. Farms along the road had to offer hospitality to unexpected guests who had to stay for several days until the blizzard abated.

It meant a boom in business for the hotels in Kirkwall and Stromness which were all fully booked with people unable to return home. Among those trapped were members of a BBC radio team, who were in the county to record a programme on the population drift away from the isles.

Bus driver Jack Garson had to set off from Kirkwall to make the scheduled 2pm bus run to Stromness on the afternoon of January 12, but he and his passengers had to seek sanctuary at the farm of Barnhouse when they became trapped by snow at Stenness. One passenger, schoolteacher Archie Bevan, opted to trudge the remaining five miles home through the snow - eventually reaching his house at 11pm.

In the other direction, Arthur Johnson, Clay Loan, Kirkwall, and Dave Corse, Holm Branch Road, Kirkwall, walked to Kirkwall after being stranded in Stromness. It took them 24 hours to complete their arduous trek - and, at one stage, Mr Corse disappeared completely in a deep drift.

A wedding party returning to Stromness after the marriage of Captain Robert Sutherland and Elsie Collins were marooned for two days at the farm of Tormiston before eventually getting home by tractor.

The conditions led to several medical emergencies. A ten year old Dounby boy, Dennis Corrigall, who had taken off from Kirkwall airport to go to hospital in Aberdeen, found himself marooned at Wick when the blizzard trapped the BEA plane and 19 passengers on the runway there.

The Chief Constable of Orkney Gathorne Cheyne personally directed operations to get a Deerness woman in labour to the maternity hospital in Kirkwall. She was carried over fields on a stretcher until a snowplough cleared a way through the snow to allow an ambulance to complete her journey by road.

With roads blocked, virtually all transport had to be by sea. Stromness lifeboat was twice called out to take hospital cases to Scapa, and then had to take supplies by sea to Quoyloo after a SOS message that provisions were running low. Six of the county's seven Co-op grocery vans were trapped in various country districts.

For most of ten days, all contact between Kirkwall and Stromness was by sea. The fisheries cruiser *Longa* was sent to Orkney to keep the mail service operating between the two towns while the Stromness fishing boat *Ivy Lea*, owned by Alan Pirie, became a vital lifeline, making daily trips to Scapa with passengers and emergency cargo, a service she continued throughout the freeze-up, even bringing milk (frozen in the churn sometimes) from farms along the shores of Scapa Flow for the Kirkwall cheese factory.

The snow continued on January 13 as temperatures remained at nine degrees below freezing, which, with more snow, saw drifts ten feet deep by January 14. When, on January 15, the Kirkwall - Stromness road was cleared for an hour, there was just sufficient time to allow all the marooned schoolchildren to reach their homes for the first time in 72 hours before deep drifts again closed all roads in ten degrees of frost.

On January 16, another 14 inches of snow fell - causing drifts of mammoth proportions - and, with more snow on January 17, many areas of the West Mainland were without power for a week and outlying areas were running out of food and animal feed stuffs.

Emergency messages on BBC radio advised isolated communities to indicate their plight with smoke signals as a Naval aircraft made a reconnaissance flight over the islands. January 19 saw an RAF plane from Kinloss make the first air drops of animal fodder and other emergency rations over South Ronaldsay, while tractors had to be used to get funerals to the cemeteries.

Kirkwall's Peerie Sea had been frozen over for more than a week when, on Sunday, January 23, the Joint Under Secretary of State for Scotland, Mr J. Henderson Stewart arrived on the fisheries cruiser *Longa* to assess the situation. By now, only the side roads were impassable but he spoke of the idea of setting up "nerve control centres" for coping with similar emergencies in the future.

Thankfully, the temperature climbed up to 47 degrees on January 24 allowing the snow to clear, but the idea of a "nerve control centre" proved mere wistful thinking within three weeks as Orkney was hit by Blizzard Number Two which wiped out all communications.

It arrived during the night of February 16 after the weather had deteriorated all day with a 65 mph gale. This time, few people were caught away from home, but the weight of snow brought down power lines, cutting off electricity to all areas except Kirkwall, and the telephone service was dead.

Chief Constable Gathorne Cheyne said: "During last month's blizzard it was comparatively easy to know what was happening but this time, with the lack of communications, we are left in a complete state of uncertainty."

Mr Cheyne was given full powers to ask for any aircraft in cases of emergency and an RAF plane from Kinloss made a reconnaissance flight over the islands. Again all roads and the airport were closed - although, by this time, the county roads department had equipped snowploughs with two-way radio. It did not necessarily speed up clearing operations, but at least snow plough drivers could summon help when they became trapped in the huge drifts!

Two couples - Mr and Mrs Sandy Heddle and Mr and Mrs Tom Scullion - had to spend the night in their car, overwhelmed by snow, returning to Kirkwall from a dance in Stromness.

The roof of a warehouse at the Highland Park distillery caved in under the weight of three feet of snow, and came crashing down on the stock of 3,000 casks containing 230,000 gallons of whisky. A police constable was sent to mount guard over the precious stock.

Emergency teams of telephone and electricity engineers were flown in, but the Kirkwall - Stromness road was still impassable as more snow fell on February 20, and at least 11 of the local telephone exchanges were isolated until February 24. The Post Office director for Scotland, Mr A.G. Robertson, warned it would take two months to get all services back to normal.

With temperatures at ten degrees below freezing on February

Flooding was to prove a regular threat to Kirkwall's Junction Road. This was the scene as flood water lapped at the doors of the Phoenix Cinema in 1970. (Picture courtesy of Harry Russell)

22-23, fodder was dropped to sheep on the Pentland Skerries and animals in South Ronaldsay, Eday and Faray also got food by air. An emergency hospital case had to be brought from South Ronaldsay to Kirkwall by helicopter.

The snow prevented the opening of the annual drama performances staged by the Perth Repertory Company in Kirkwall, but a thaw through the first week of March eventually cleared the snow. Nonetheless, by then Orkney County Council had been saddled with a hefty bill - the equivalent of around a third of a million pounds at 1999 prices - for snow clearing operations.

The snow returned to Orkney in December, 1955, and, perversely, it claimed as one of its victims the Stromness fishing boat *Ivy Lea* which had provided such a valuable lifeline during the blizzards of January and February. Thankfully, however, four men reached safety in what was headlined as a miracle escape.

The *Ivy Lea*, a seine netter, ran aground in a blinding snow storm in Hoy Sound just before Christmas, 1955. The engine room and wheelhouse were quickly filled by water after being hit by heavy seas and the four men on board - the owner Alan Pirie with crewmen Ivan Breck, Alfred Sinclair and William Sutherland, all from Stromness - had to hang to the mast for two hours. Eventually, Ivan Breck managed to swim ashore - risking death from chilling temperatures and dangerous rocks - with a line round his waist. This enabled the other three men to clamber, or be hauled, to safety. Still their ordeal was not over, however, for they then had to stumble several miles through the snow to reach help at Orgill Farm in Hoy.

As is often the case, Orkney did get some compensation for the dreadful winter weather conditions with the county enjoying a heatwave during July which turned out to be the driest July of the century up until that time. The temperature reached 75 degrees at Grimsetter airport on July 13, 1955 - which was the highest temperature registered since records had started at the Met Office there.

Television reaches Orkney

Television pictures were witnessed in Orkney for the first time in October, 1955 - although it would be another three years before the county had its own TV transmitter.

Television reception became possible in Orkney when the new transmitter at Meldrum, Aberdeenshire, was opened on October 13, 1955. The authorities did not claim that the transmitter would cover Orkney, but the few early pioneers in the county who had purchased TV sets found they could get reception which varied in quality, according to weather conditions, from perfect to "like a snowstorm."

The first programme to be seen was coverage of the official opening ceremony of the Meldrum transmitter followed by a film entitled "Beyond the Grampians" and then a somewhat esoteric programme from London on the psychology of thumb sucking among young children.

Mr Robert Garden, of the Orkney Radio and Electrical Company, had a television set at his home in Berstane Road, Kirkwall, and several other people were trying out sets, it was reported. However, reception obviously did not prove sufficiently reliable for most people to venture to pay out the equivalent of two months wages on a TV set.

There were only 36 television licences in Orkney by the following June of 1956 when those who did have sets complained that reception was being disrupted by interference from a station in Russia.

Although the BBC had identified the site of the redundant radar masts at Netherbutton, Holm, as the base for Orkney's own television transmitter early in 1957, there were complaints that people, within sight of the station, would not be able to receive programmes because of delays in installing electricity supplies in parts of the Orkney Mainland.

However, with the announcement that TV transmissions for Orkney would start - on limited power - from the Netherbutton transmitter on December, 1958, there was a pre-Christmas rush to buy sets. They were not cheap at a time when the average farm wage was still below £10 a week. At the showroom of Orkney Builders in Great Western Road, Kirkwall, a 14 inch portable cost 56 guineas and a 17 inch set 67 guineas. However, hundreds of reconditioned second hand sets were imported from the South at prices from £25 upwards.

More than 600 people attended an open day at the Netherbutton transmitter station the following July and by December, 1959, when Netherbutton transmissions were increased to full power, there were nearly 2,000 licensed television sets in the county - about one in every four households. The arrival of TV led to a warning that the rural cinema scheme could be withdrawn from six areas of the Orkney Mainland where attendances had fallen, but, despite TV, borrowings of books from the county library were reported at a record level in 1959.

Shapinsay rumbles

Mystery underground rumblings below the farm of Newfield, Shapinsay, set a puzzle for Orcadians in 1955.

Earth tremors and underground explosions were reported and there was conjecture that they were caused by a reservoir of natural gas in a geological fault which runs under that part of Shapinsay.

The farm was owned by Mr James Bews who said his dog was particularly alert to the unexplained tremors which, he added, resembled the rumbling of a cartload of stones being emptied.

On November 18, 1955, he reported that there were three "rumblings" within 45 minutes and another six hours later. One was as loud as a clap of thunder, he said.

Thousands hear evangelist

More than 7,000 Orkney people turned out to listen to a week of broadcasts by the American evangelist Billy Graham, relayed from the Kelvin Hall in Glasgow, to Kirkwall's Paterson Kirk. However, the same month, it was announced that Orkney Church of Scotland membership was declining, then standing at 7,992, and one Orkney kirk in three was without a minister.

Another 63 whales die

A total of 63 pilot whales - averaging between 10-15 feet but some up to 22 feet long - died after beaching themselves near Pierowall in Westray, coming ashore on the rocks at the Point of Cott, and being stranded by a high Spring tide, in March, 1955.

It was the second mass stranding of whales in Orkney in five years - after more than 90 died in Stronsay in 1950 - and local boats were hired to tow the carcases out to sea.

Rev H.R.M. Fraser, the Church of Scotland minister for Westray, said: "It is very rocky and many of them have been cut to pieces. The sea all around them is dyed red and it is a very sad spectacle. Many of them are still alive."

In fact, two inspectors from the Scottish Society for the Prevention of Cruelty to Animals put the surviving whales out of their misery.

Just two months later, more whales threatened to strand in Longhope Bay when around 200 were seen in the bay in May, 1955.

However Longhope man James Wilson went out in his motorboat *Bluebird* and drove them safely into the open waters of the Pentland Firth.

New owner for hotels

The Kirkwall Hotel and Stromness Hotel had a new owner. They were among nine hotels owned by the North British hotel group - which had gone into liquidation - which was purchased for a total of £310,000 in 1955 by a Perth businessman Mr J. Gammick Clark, who already owned a chain of hotels as one of Scotland's major hoteliers.

Trawlermen rescued

A total of 24 Aberdeen fishermen were saved from tragedy in two separate disasters in Orkney waters within a week of each other in April, 1955.

The Aberdeen trawler *Gava* went aground in dense fog on the Pentland Skerries. The 12 crewmen took to their small boat but were thrown into the water when it capsized. Three managed to scramble back on board their stricken vessel while the other nine were rescued by the Wick fishing boat *Enterprise*.

The Longhope lifeboat was launched and helped to refloat the trawler.

Another trawler was in trouble a week later when the Aberdeen vessel *Doonie Braes* ran aground, again in thick fog, near the Old Man of Hoy. Again the 12 crew were all rescued - this time by a Lyness Naval vessel which spotted the trawler's distress flares - but the ship was a total loss.

Curtain up

A 650 seat cinema, a purpose-built infant school for Kirkwall, and the county's newest kirk were all opened in 1955.

Kirkwall provost James Flett performed the opening ceremony as the curtain went up on the new Phoenix cinema with a special showing of the film *Doctor in the House.*

Kirkwall's new infant school, with accommodation for 280 pupils, was officially opened at Papdale in November, 1955, by Mr Frank Young, who was Orkney's first county director of education after World War One.

The county's newest kirk, the Moncur Memorial Church, was opened and dedicated in Stronsay by the Moderator of the General Assembly of the Church of Scotland, Rt Rev Dr E.D. Jarvis, who described it as the most beautiful building he had opened.

The church was built from a legacy of the late Alexander Moncur of Dundee, whose grandfather, Rev James Mudie, had preached the sermon at the opening of the island's old church in 1858.

Age before duty

Age was obviously no barrier to public office in 1955 as 82 year old Alexander Calder was re-elected county convener with vice-convener being 79 year old Patrick Sutherland Graeme.

It was a year of apathy - or contentment with the status quo, perhaps - that saw only four seats contested at the county council elections. There were insufficient candidates for a poll for either Kirkwall or Stromness town councils.

Alexander Calder remained as county convener right up to his death at the age of 86 in 1959 after a council career of more than 40 years.

Patrick Sutherland Graeme of Graemeshall, Holm, who was Orkney's Lord Lieutenant as well as county vice-convener, died aged 81 in 1958. He had returned to his native Orkney prior to World War Two following a distinguished legal career.

He was succeeded as Lord Lieutenant by Lt Col Robert Scarth OBE, of Binscarth, Firth, aged 64, who had been Deputy Lieutenant of Orkney since 1944, and who had commanded Orkney Home Guard during World War Two. His grandfather - who had been the first agent of the Union Bank of Scotland in Kirkwall over a century earlier - had established the Binscarth estate in the 19th century.

When Alexander Calder died, he was succeeded as county convener by Col Henry Scarth, of Breckness, who represented North Ronaldsay on the county council, and who was a cousin of the new Lord Lieutenant.

Lifeboat ceremonies for isles

New lifeboats were officially named at Stromness and Stronsay in August, 1955. The two identical vessels, 52 feet long Barnett lifeboats each costing £36,000, could carry up to 145 people in an emergency.

The Stronsay boat was named *John Gallatly Hyndman* by Mrs Laura Grimond, while the Stromness vessel was christened the *Archibald and Alexander M. Paterson* by Miss Chris McKinnon, a cousin of the donor, Miss Margaret Paterson of Florida, USA, who named it after her brothers.

Police honour

Orkney's Chief Constable Gathorne Cheyne, aged 51 in 1955, was awarded the OBE in the Queen's birthday honours list. He already held the British Empire Medal and the King's Police Medal.

Mr Cheyne, who had served in Orkney since 1938, originally joining the force as sergeant, announced his retirement on health grounds in 1958. He was succeeded as Chief Constable by his deputy James Cormack.

Also honoured by the Queen in 1955 was ex-Kirkwall provost Robert Slater who, at the age of 78, was made an MBE. During a lifetime of public service, he had served on both Kirkwall and Stromness town councils.

The steamer *Earl Thorfinn*, the vessel which would be forever remembered for the epic 1953 trip to Aberdeen, driven 140 miles off course in the teeth of a hurricane, is seen here in the more peaceful surroundings of the pier at Papa Westray in 1950.

(Picture courtesy of Orkney Library photographic archive)

Sea rescue makes history

1956

A rescue at sea off Orkney made history when 41 members of the crew of the 9,800 ton Norwegian tanker *Dovrefjell* were snatched from danger by helicopters after the ship grounded on the Little Skerry in the Pentland Firth in a gale in the early hours.

The master of the *Dovrefjell* managed to send out a message "situation dangerous" before huge waves wiped out the ship's entire radio system in the disaster in February, 1956.

High seas made any approach by the Longhope lifeboat extremely hazardous but, by good fortune, the Mayday message from the tanker was picked up by the Naval frigate *Wizard*, carrying the Royal Navy Commander-in-Chief Scotland, Rear Admiral W.G.A. Robson. He was on his way to pay a farewell visit to the Scapa Flow Naval base before becoming Commander-in-Chief South Atlantic.

Admiral Robson called for helicopter support, and two from Lossiemouth, and a third from Leuchars, arrived at daybreak to begin airlifting the tanker crew to safety. They were taken off in relays and landed at John o' Groats.

The helicopters had to dart between waves throwing spray 100 feet high. Each rescue trip took 15 minutes and the helicopters made 19 trips altogether, carrying two or three survivors at a time. Last to leave the *Dovrefjell* - which fortunately was carrying no cargo - were the master and his nine officers.

Admiral Robson said: "In my experience this is the largest number of men ever rescued in such a short time by the use of helicopters. I consider their use, in conjunction with the lifeboat service, should be given the most serious thought in the future, especially after what we have seen today.

"Conditions were very bad round the wreck. I requested that a reconnaissance be made over it. The report came back that there were very bad spray conditions of 100-150 feet over the *Dovrefjell*, making it quite impossible for the lifeboats to operate. The weather at this stage was extreme."

The operation - which was to be seen as the fore-runner of a co-ordinated air - sea rescue service - led to helicopter pilots Jack Palmer and Harold Williams, from Lossiemouth, both being made MBEs, while helicopter crewmen Alexander Japp and Roy Moneypenny were commended for their bravery.

Coxswain Dan Kirkpatrick and the crew of the Longhope lifeboat were later presented with a silver medal from the King of Norway for their efforts in the rescue operation.

The following year, a Naval helicopter visited all three Orkney lifeboats and carried out a series of rescue exercises, for the first time, whereby casualties on stretchers were lifted off the lifeboats by the helicopter.

Unfortunately, the gratitude of the crew of the *Dovrefjell* for the rescue was diminished somewhat two weeks after the stranding when police from Orkney and Caithness had to board the tanker to investigate claims that the grounded ship had been looted.

Orkney's Chief Constable Gathorne Cheyne said: "It is a disgraceful state of affairs that the personal belongings of wrecked seamen should be looted like this. It casts a very grave reflection on the honesty and good name of people in the North, particularly from the point of view of foreign seamen wrecked on our shores."

The population of Stroma - the island still had 70 inhabitants in 1956 - was said to be indignant at suspicion being directed at islanders, especially when six police officers arrived on the island to investigate.

Donald Wares (68) said: "The plundering of the ship was not done by Stroma people and the stolen stuff, I feel certain, is not on the island. This apparent suspicion has given the Stroma people a sense of injustice."

Remarkably, after a skilled salvage job lasting three weeks, the *Dovrefjell* was refloated by the Metal Industries vessels *Metinda III* and *Salveda*, under the direction of Murray Taylor, and towed to Stockton-on-Tees for repairs.

Fortunately, 1956 was an year in which Orkney was spared any large-scale loss of life at sea, but it was not without incident. A New Year gale from the north west saw the Aberdeen trawler *Star of the East* ram the tanker *BP Transporter* at the Kirkwall Pier and, with her tanks holed, about 6,000 gallons of petrol gushed into the harbour which had to be sealed off while the fire risk was tackled. A sister ship of the trawler, *Star of Orkney*, ran aground at Hatston but managed to refloat herself.

Four months later, another north west gale led to two Norwegian shark fishing vessels *Leidulf* and *Astor* grounding on Vasa Skerry off Shapinsay. The Stronsay lifeboat went to their assistance and rescued the 14 crewmen. One of the boats was pulled off on the next tide but the other was stranded there for another two months.

It was the Stromness lifeboat which went into action in September, 1956, when seven crewmen were rescued when a Buckie seiner, the *Achieve*, ran aground on Graemsay in thick fog.

It was perhaps understandable that some were reluctant to go to sea. At Kirkwall Sheriff Court, in 1956, five fishermen off the Grimsby trawler *Conway* were fined £4 - or 28 days prison - for failing to obey the orders of their skipper when they refused to sail from Stromness.

They complained that, after steaming 1,000 miles, they had caught only 20 baskets of fish.

A monument to sacrifice

A solemn ceremony in June, 1956, witnessed the unveiling and dedication of the Cross of Sacrifice to servicemen of all nations who were buried in Orkney after losing their lives in either of the two world wars.

Erected in the St Olaf cemetery by the Imperial War Graves Commission, the simple white cross with a sword superimposed, looked across the waters of what had been the Scapa Flow Naval anchorage. The unveiling was performed by Rear Admiral Peter Skelton, then commanding Rosyth Naval Dockyard.

The following month, another ceremony saw a replica Mercat Cross unveiled outside St Magnus Cathedral by Orkney's Lord Lieutenant Mr Patrick Sutherland Graeme. The replica replaced the old cross which, after three centuries exposed to the Kirkwall weather, had been removed to the cover and safety of the North transept of the Cathedral.

It was an year of civic ceremony. The month of April, 1956, saw the dedication at St Magnus Cathedral of the £2,000 gold chain and badge of office for the Provost of Kirkwall which had been presented to the Royal burgh under the bequest of an Australian, Mrs Helen Gordon Gibson, as a memorial to her mother, Margaret Louttit, who was born in Kirkwall in 1847.

Brace invaders

The Doloughan family were awoken at their home in Great Western Road, Kirkwall, to find a scene of havoc - and a trail of peculiar footprints - left by two runaway racoons!

The animals had escaped from the fairground zoo further down Great Western Road.

International tensions rise

The Autumn of 1956 saw international tensions at fever pitch as Soviet troops invaded Hungary and British forces were on a war footing in the Suez crisis.

No wonder, some people threw themselves to the ground to take cover when three Vampire jet fighters flying at high speed and low level - estimated to be lower than the spire of St Magnus Cathedral - thundered across the skies of Kirkwall in a series of dramatic forays in November, 1956.

The summer had begun in a spirit of harmony. In response to a suggestion by the Scotland Soviet Friendship Society, Kirkwall Town Council agreed to send greetings to a town of similar size and standing in the Soviet Union.

Two months later however, there was international outrage as the Soviet Union invaded Hungary. Stromness Town Council had already rejected any suggestion of a twinning link behind the Iron Curtain, and Kirkwall councillors quickly rescinded their decision and agreed not to communicate with the Soviets.

A relief fund for the victims of the Hungarian invasion was started in Orkney and soon raised £1,500.

At the same time, however, the British Government, under the premiership of Anthony Eden, had contrived to trap itself in a political and military minefield by embarking on what proved to be an ill-judged adventure into the Middle East, and the Suez crisis.

The Egyptian president Nasser had nationalised the Suez canal, and tensions between Egypt and Israel had reached a state of war, when British and French forces invaded - only to be forced to withdraw after diplomatic pressure by the United States and USSR.

Orkney's MP Jo Grimond - who had just become leader of the British Liberal Party - was particularly critical of the Government on the British occupation of the canal zone.

Grimond condemned the bombing of Egypt while the events of Eastern Europe were going on. "An appeal should be made for all - party action to stop the war in the Middle East and try to give some help to Eastern Europe," he said. "The Government seem obsessed by the thirties when appeasement, as practised by Conservatives, proved so disastrous. But Nasser is not Hitler and the danger today comes essentially not from the Arabs but from the Russians."

As the British were forced to withdraw from Suez, amidst a certain atmosphere of humiliation, the Liberal leader said he did not think there had been anything like the Government action since "the grand old Duke of York marched his men

to the top of the hill and marched them down again."

He questioned whether the Government ministers who directed the operation could ever recapture the confidence of the nation. "Whether we like it or not, the fact is that one of the top three in the Cabinet must probably carry on, but behind them they must surely have people who are prepared to push new policies which are vital to this country and the western world."

Orkney Conservatives made a show in support of the beleagured Prime Minister Anthony Eden, sending a telegram saying: "Orkney Unionists pledge their support for your conduct of affairs and for your gallant efforts to secure peace with justice."

And there was some criticism of the Grimond stance elsewhere. The correspondent who wrote the Orkney notes, under the pen-name Loch Harray, for *The Scottish Farmer*, said: "Our local MP has been talking freely and openly disagreeing with the Government and making remarks of a kind which we never expected to hear coming from Mr Grimond in such an hour of crisis. We are honestly astounded. All the cross talk and adverse criticism is no credit to some of our leading politicians. It is nothing short of disgraceful at this momentous period."

The later consensus of history, however, probably tallied almost entirely with the Jo Grimond analysis of the situation.

And the jet aircraft which "strafed" Kirkwall proved to have no connection with the international tensions of the time. The RAF apologised for the low flying and the alarm it had caused. It had been an unauthorised operation and such low flying was contrary to instructions, said a senior officer. Those responsible faced disciplinary action.

A Royal occasion for Orkney

Queen Elizabeth the Queen Mother was acclaimed by *The Orcadian* as the first British queen to set foot on Orkney soil when she paid her first visit to the county in August, 1956.

The Queen Mother flew across the Pentland Firth by helicopter to officially open the new George V Playing Fields at Pickaquoy, amongst other engagements during a full day of events amidst blustery showers and sunny intervals.

The Royal visitor was greeted by a huge crowd of cheering people on Broad Street where she was shown around St Magnus Cathedral by Provost James Flett. "What a wonderful welcome - it's marvellous," she told the provost, surrounded by hundreds of flag waving children at the Kirk Green.

After lunch at the Kirkwall Hotel, the Queen Mother - then a mere 56 year old - proceeded to the opening ceremony at Pickaquoy where she was presented with a bouquet by six year old Alistair Gordon - the son of Dr J.B. Gordon, chairman of the town council parks committee. Young Alistair, of course, grew up to become a journalist with *The Orcadian* and later joined BBC Radio Orkney.

The Queen Mother told the crowds at Pickaquoy that, from her Caithness home at the Castle of Mey, her gaze was always drawn northward to the islands of Orkney. "Sometimes they lie shrouded in their mists and barely visible. Then the sun appears, the Pentland Firth sparkles and gleams, and the islands shine like jewels in their lovely setting. I always look at them with pleasure, and today it is a great happiness to set foot

upon the land which has beckoned to me so often."

The Queen Mother was presented with an Orkney Chair, specially made by the Kirkwall firm of D.M. Kirkness, then owned by Mr Reynold Eunson. The woodwork was supervised by retired chairmaker William Hay and the strawback was the work of Mr Thomas Groat from Kirbister, Longhope.

The Queen Mother inspected a detachment of the Orkney Territorials and visited the County Home to meet staff and residents. Harry Marwick - usually the Kirkwall Town Council digger driver - became Royal chauffeur for the day, at the wheel of a Daimler car lent by Mr D.G. Spence of Wideford.

The opening ceremony at Pickaquoy was followed by a drive through the beflagged streets of the burgh before the Royal visitor took tea with the Lord Lieutenant of Orkney, P.N. Sutherland Graeme, at Graemeshall, Holm, before returning across the Pentland Firth by Royal Navy helicopter again.

That evening, the Pickaquoy playing field was used for the first time since its official Royal opening when an Orkney football team beat the visiting Peterhead side 5-4.

New post office plan

Kirkwall head post office was part of the Kirkwall Town Hall at this time but, in 1956, the Post Office purchased the site of Peace's woodyard in Junction Road to build a new post office which would remain on the same site for the rest of the century.

New era for TA

Orkney's proud history of Volunteer soldiers which stretched back to the 19th century saw a new chapter begin with a new role for Orkney Territorials in 1956.

The 430 Coast Regiment Royal Artillery (TA), which had been commanded by Lt Col George Rouse, was to re-emerge under the guise of the 861 (Indep.) Light Anti-Aircraft Battery Royal Artillery (TA), under the command of Major S.P. Robertson.

The first official parade of the new 861 LAA Battery was the 1956 Remembrance Parade. The Pipes and Drums of the old 430 Coast Regiment RA TA would remain in Kirkwall and, thus, the Kirkwall battery was the only one in the British Army to have its own band.

In 1958, the Territorial Army celebrated the 50th anniversary of its formation with a parade to St Magnus Cathedral headed by 50 members of the "Old Brigade," comprising men from the old volunteers and the Territorial Force of 1908-14, led by Lt Col Fred Buchanan.

The newly formed Orkney anti-aircraft battery soon made its mark too. In successive years, 1958-59, the 861 Battery was the best in Britain, winning the *Sunday Times* trophy as Britain's premier LAA gunners.

Call to strengthen police

The Government demanded action to strengthen the Orkney county police force in 1956 - despite the fact that it had more than doubled its staffing level in the previous 20 years.

An inspection of the local constabulary revealed that members of the force were "seriously overworked," the North Isles were "virtually unpoliced" and the Kirkwall police headquarters was unmanned from 3am to 8am with the police cells unsupervised.

The Secretary of State for Scotland asked Orkney County Council to draw up proposals to increase the strength of the force which was then 18 men and one policewoman, Vera Gibson.

Vera Gibson, who had started as a civilian typist at the police station, was Orkney's first policewoman and, for the six years up to 1956, could also claim to be Britain's northernmost policewoman.

Viscount aircraft on the apron at Kirkwall Airport.

(Picture courtesy of Orkney Library photographic archive)

New age of air travel

A new step forward in the history of Orkney air travel was reached on May 29, 1956, when for the first time a 45 - seater Viscount airliner landed at Kirkwall airport on a proving flight from London.

The four engined Viscount - capable of 300 mph - was the biggest passenger aircraft ever to land in Orkney and was piloted by Captain Bill Baillie, chief BEA pilot, who had flown on Orkney routes in the pioneering days of the 1930s for Allied Airways (Gandar Dower) Ltd.

Also with him was another pioneer of Orkney services, Captain Eric Starling, BEA chief pilot in Scotland, who had been the pilot when the first ever passenger plane had landed at Stromness airport before World War Two.

In the five years, 1951-56, the number of air passengers from Kirkwall had increased by 50 per cent from 7,393 in 1951-52 to 11,352 in 1955-56, a fact that was recognised when BEA's new sales office was opened at 69 Albert Street, Kirkwall, in 1956.

Kirk condemns hanging

An end to hanging with the abolition of capital punishment was called for, by 14-2 votes, at a meeting of Orkney Presbytery in 1956. The Rev D. Sutherland (Sanday East) asked that his dissent to the motion be recorded.

Ba' in danger

Kirkwall's Christmas and New Year Ba' games were in danger of dying for want of support from the public, reported *The Orcadian* on December 20, 1956. A dance was organised at the Cosmo ballroom to raise necessary funds.

Football star in town

Willie Brown, who played full back for Preston North End and later Grimsby Town, and whose wife, née Kennedy, came from Stairolea, South Ronaldsay, spent six weeks coaching Orkney's young footballers during the summer of 1956.

Teacher honoured

Miss Margaret Sutherland (61) head teacher of the Costa primary school, Evie, was made an MBE in recognition of her 35 year teaching career in Orkney which began on the island of Cava.

Baby blues

Kirkwall police found themselves with a ten month old baby on their hands - found, apparently abandoned in a pram outside a shop in Victoria Street. It eventually transpired that a girl, who had taken the baby for a walk, had gone into the shop and become so preoccupied with her shopping that when she emerged from the shop she had forgotten all about the baby and gone home!

County show blues

The year of 1956 saw one of the worst County Show days on record as heavy rain kept the attendance to 2,500 and reduced the Bignold Park to a quagmire.

Golfers depart

Orkney lost two of its finest golfers in 1955. Wilfred Sinclair - who was Orkney golf champion on eight occasions - died in his home town of Stromness. He had taken up golf after harrowing experiences in which his ship was torpedoed in World War One. The same year, Orkney said farewell to local GP Dr D.M. Sibbald, who had won the Orkney championship three times, who moved to take over a rural medical practice in Gloucestershire.

Last sunset for Lyness

The strains of a lament, played by two Orkney pipers, drifted over the waters of Scapa Flow as the final act of the Lyness Naval Base - "probably the finest Naval base in the world" - was played out; a proud fortress of war reduced to a ghost town!

The base - a vital nerve centre in the two world wars - had been axed, without sentiment or great ceremony, by a government that had decided it was redundant for modern warfare in an atomic age.

The White Ensign was hauled down for the last time at the official close-down ceremony on March 29, 1957. HMS *Pomona* - the official name of Lyness - would be no more.

It was the end of a momentous era yet not one admiral was in attendance and the great harbour which had sheltered the pride of the Royal Navy through years of crisis had just one unarmed Navy vessel, HMS *Barleycorn*, a humble boom boat, to witness the final curtain.

The closure bombshell had been announced on June 6, 1956. It was true that the base had been running down since the end of World War Two but it was nonetheless an economic blow that would see not only the loss of most of the 200 jobs at Lyness but also many amenities, including ferry services, which the Navy had provided, and to which the islanders had become accustomed.

The Scapa Flow cutbacks were part of a £100 million package of economies in the government defence budget, announced by the Admiralty in a letter to Orkney MP Jo Grimond.

It was estimated that Hoy - and the 900 islanders - would be losing £112,000 a year in wages as the shutters went up at Lyness. Only a civilian staff of 26 would remain to supervise the oil depot which would remain open as Admiralty Oil Fuel Depot, Lyness.

On Hoy, the island post master and county councillor, Isaac Moar, said: "On the whole this is one of the most disastrous blows that the South Isles have ever received."

The news of the closure was given as a Stop Press item of *The Orcadian* of June 7, 1956.

The main bases in Scotland for the Home Fleet in future would be Rosyth and Invergordon.

"This means that Scapa Flow will revert to what it was in 1938," said Commander D.V. Morgan, Resident Naval Officer at Lyness. "The Admiralty state they cannot see any future use in peace or war for the establishments other than the oil fuel depot in Lyness. The question of finance demands that Scapa Flow be restricted to things that are vital."

Establishments affected by the closure included the boom defence depot and the South Walls radio station, and would involve the loss of more than 150 jobs.

Of those made redundant, about half were local residents of Hoy, estimated county convener Alex Calder who adopted a surprisingly optimistic tone. "They will feel it, there is no question, as a great hardship, but like good Orcadians I have no doubt but that they did not spend all they earned a week within that week, and have laid a good bit by. They will get over it perhaps. There is plenty of employment in the county if they care to shift to another job.

"It won't affect the economy of the islands in the slightest because the islands are entirely dependent on agriculture and commerce, and progress will go on just the same."

The Navy's ferry service had operated twice daily to Lyness at a cost of just two shillings. Jo Grimond warned that the loss of this facility could lead to further depopulation of the islands.

It certainly did force many men to seek work not only outwith Hoy but outwith Orkney. The government had suggested that shipbreaking could become an alternative industry at Lyness but nothing developed along these lines and, by the end of 1956, a fair number of the redundant workers had crossed the

Pentland Firth to find employment on the construction of the Dounreay atomic energy plant in Caithness.

Fortunately, as the county convener had stated, employment opportunities were fairly buoyant. All but 13 of Orkney's 250 school leavers in 1956 had found employment and, although the county unemployment register in March, 1957, had risen to 160 people, it included only seven of those made redundant at Lyness.

And so, at sunset on Friday, March 29, 1957, the White Ensign was lowered for the last time at HMS *Pomona*. Fewer than 200 local people were present for the ceremony, which was marked by a conspicuous absence of Royal Navy top brass.

The retired Rear Admiral Sir Patrick Macnamara - who commanded the base through much of World War Two - was prevented by ill health from attending but Lady Macnamara, his wife, made the nostalgic journey north.

There were two tankers berthed at the oil depot, the *Rowanol* and the *Black Ranger*, but HMS *Barleycorn* was the sole representative of Royal Navy sea power.

The official party was led by Captain A.J.M. Milne-Home, Chief of Staff to the Flag Officer, Scotland, Vice-Admiral Sir John Cuthbert, who was welcomed by Commander C.C.B. Mackenzie, who had become Resident Naval Officer, Scapa.

A detachment from the Territorial Army in Orkney paraded with a Naval guard of honour.

Commander Mackenzie told the gathering with a certain humour: "The formal dissolution of the Naval link with the Orkneys will not kill the affection in the hearts of two generations of the Royal Navy for Scapa - an affection which seems to grow warmer in retrospect than it did in those winter nights in the Flow."

Captain Milne-Home, who had served two 18 month spells of duty at Scapa, said he was torn between loyalty to government policy and his own personal feelings. The name Scapa had a kind of mystical meaning for the Fleet.

Conveying his respects to Rear Admiral Macnamara, Captain Milne-Home said: "All he has built is coming to pieces and it must be a cause of great regret to him."

"Without the wonderful understanding and co-operation of Orcadians this place would have been impossible," he said, adding that the people of Orkney had helped to make this probably the finest Naval base in the world.

Rev W.A. Simpson, minister of Hoy and Walls, led in prayer before the sad notes of "Sunset" were sounded by the bugles and the White Ensign was lowered by 19 year old Ordinary Seaman Ronald Henry, youngest member of the crew of HMS *Barleycorn*.

The Paying-off Pennant was lowered by Harry Berry, then a customs officer at Longhope after reaching the rank of chief petty officer in a 26 year Royal Navy career, before two pipers of the TA played the final lament.

There was more than a little poignancy to the occasion when Rear Admiral Sir Patrick Macnamara - the man credited with the making of Lyness as a modern fortress of war - died the week after the closure ceremony at his home in Ross-shire, aged 71.

In the following months however, the ghosts of Lyness were not allowed to settle. Orkney's renowned rumour factory produced a conveyer belt of fanciful stories of what the future held for the former Naval base - encouraged by reports that four "mysterious strangers," possibly from the UK Atomic Energy Authority, had arrived by special charter plane at Kirkwall and then visited Lyness.

This coincided with a NATO conference in Paris at which it was suggested that missile sites were needed in Scotland. This was all that was required to ignite a rumour that Hoy was to become a rocket station and the former Twatt airfield on Orkney's West

An aerial photograph illustrating the extent of the wartime base at **Lyness** which closed in March, 1957, after nearly half a century of service to the defence of Britain. Not one admiral attended the closure ceremony, and the only Royal Naval vessel in attendance was a humble boom boat, HMS *Barleycorn*. However, the wife of Rear Admiral Sir Patrick Macnamara, the man credited with making Lyness a modern fortress of war, did make the journey North for a poignant farewell. Sir Patrick died just one week after the closure of Lyness.

(Picture courtesy of Orkney Library photographic archive)

Mainland was to be taken over by the American Air Force.

Sufficient credence was given to the rumour that *The Scotsman* published an in-depth article which quoted Hoy's postmaster and county councillor, Isaac Moar, as saying: "If they were surveying our island for a rocket station, I can assure them they would be very welcome on Hoy. A £4 million building scheme is just what we are needing to revitalise our island and provide jobs for our men following the closing of the Admiralty base."

Local headmaster Robert Thorburn also backed the idea, apparently. He said: "The people here are conditioned to the hazards of service life and I am sure the possible dangers would not alarm them."

However, another teacher, Ian MacInnes - later to become rector of Stromness Academy - made clear his opposition. "Please allow me to go early on record that I do not want a rocket base in Orkney," he wrote to *The Orcadian*.

Fortunately it transpired fairly quickly that the four

"mysterious strangers" from the UK Atomic Energy Authority were simply checking whether any former Admiralty buildings at Lyness would be of use to Dounreay. It was decided that the buildings were unsuitable and there were no further visits to excite the imagination.

And to quell the notion that Orkney was to have an invasion of American airmen, the 560 acre Twatt airfield, which had been taken over by the Fleet Air Arm during World War Two, was sold back to local farmers at a total price of £8,300 at public auction in June, 1958.

That same month, however, the impact of the Lyness closure - and the migration of families away from Hoy - was felt when Orkney's education committee proposed that the school in North Hoy, which now had just three pupils, should be closed.

Hoy county councillor Isaac Moar forcefully argued that such a move would be a disaster for the island and, after his impassioned plea, it was finally decided that the school would remain open - for the time being!

Outrage at war grave 'desecration'

There were angry protests as it was learned that the Admiralty was seeking to make money by raising the warship *Royal Oak* in Scapa Flow.

It was announced in December, 1957, that the Admiralty had invited tenders for salvaging the 29,000 ton vessel, sunk by U-boat with the loss of 833 lives in 1939.

County convener Alex Calder apparently showed himself out of touch with public opinion when he said he did not think there would be any opposition. "Now we have no Naval base left here . . . this would be regarded as just another of the Flow's many salvage jobs," he was quoted as saying in *The Orcadian*.

Within days, however, the extent to which Mr Calder had misjudged the public mood was obvious, as military organisations and relatives of victims of the *Royal Oak* disaster expressed their outrage.

And, at the following meeting of the county council, councillors unanimously adopted a resolution protesting at the salvage plan and expressing "detestation and horror" that this "sea tomb should be desecrated."

The protests were led by the Lord Lieutenant of Orkney, and county vice-convener, Mr Patrick Sutherland Graeme who made an impassioned plea that steps be taken to prevent "this act of sacrilege" which was proposed for purely financial reasons.

"We, as Orcadians, have been the guardians of this sepulchre in the sea for 18 years and we have been proud to be so. To waver in any way in our guardianship would be quite unthinkable."

The tide of protest forced an immediate rethink by the powers in Whitehall. By January 23, 1958, the Admiralty agreed that there would be no salvage.

Curiously, however, all through 1957, salvage work had been going ahead on another tragic British warship which had suffered even greater loss of life than the *Royal Oak* - and there did not appear to be so much as a murmur of protest in this case.

The vessel in question was HMS *Vanguard*, the battleship which blew up and sank at anchor in Scapa Flow in July, 1917, with the deaths of around 1,000 men.

Despite the fact that there were literally thousands of close relatives of the victims still alive - wives, brothers and sisters, children and even parents - the Admiralty had sold the salvage rights on the 20,000 ton *Vanguard* to a Glasgow scrap metal firm. Unlike the *Royal Oak* controversy six months later, there did not appear to be a single letter of protest

1957

when *The Orcadian* revealed, in May, 1957, that divers had been down amongst the wreckage to prepare the salvaging of valuable metals. (Steel was fetching £10 a ton while copper and brass had reached as much as £200 a ton).

A converted steam drifter *Ocean Raleigh*, skippered by James Chalmers, was used to oversee the salvage work under the direction of Mr Arthur Nundy, a director of the Glasgow scrap firm, who had worked as a diver with Metal Industries in Scapa Flow more than 20 years earlier. "This is no fly-by-night, get-rich-quick scheme," said Mr Nundy.

The divers soon established that the *Vanguard* - a mile off Flotta at a depth of 16 fathoms - had been blown wide open when the boiler-room explosion had detonated the armaments carried aft, and it was anticipated by Mr Nundy that four

decades in this watery grave had removed all trace of the victims of the appalling tragedy.

Somehow, though, it gave a hollow ring to the Remembrance Day pledge: "We will remember them."

The year of 1957 produced a reminder of another Orkney wartime tragedy at sea with the death of Mr Cyril Kinmond, the last civilian to see alive many of the officers who died on the ill-fated voyage of HMS *Hampshire* which led to the death of War Minister Lord Kitchener in 1916.

Mr Kinmond, a lemonade factory owner from Leamington Spa, Warwickshire, owned the islands of Swona, Copinsay and Cava, and the *Hampshire* officers had lunched with him at his house on Cava on the day they sailed to their deaths.

Following the death of Mr Kinmond, Swona was purchased by James Rosie, who lived on the island, while Cava was bought by Lt Commander Erlend Clouston, son of the late Orkney writer and county convener J. Storer Clouston, of Smoogro, Orphir. Copinsay was purchased by Mr James Laughton of Toab.

Emergency airlift

An ex-RAF fighter pilot Robert Learmonth, a Ministry of Civil Aviation employee at Grimsetter airport, made a 55 mile mercy flight in the Orkney Flying Club Tiger Moth aircraft to take 28 year old assistant lightkeeper William Edwardson to hospital in Kirkwall from North Ronaldsay after he had been injured in a motorcycle accident.

The alternative trip by boat could have

taken seven hours, and the county council complained that the official air ambulance, operated by BEA, was based 250 miles away in Renfrew.

Unfortunately, soon after Mr Learmonth's mercy mission, Orkney Flying Club was forced to sell its Tiger Moth plane on economic grounds, threatening the end of the club's activities.

Orkney centenarians

Mr James Matches, of 51 Alfred Street, Stromness, became Orkney's only 100 year old of the time with the traditional telegram from the Queen and a celebration party at the Stromness Hotel in October, 1957.

Born in Deerness, he had worked in the engineering department of the Post Office from 1883 until his retirement and could recall laying cables in Burray with oxen.

Mr Matches died in June, 1959, aged 101.

The two Kirkwall firms of William Shearer, ironmonger, grocer and seedsman, of 71 Victoria Street, and William Slater, licensed grocer, 20 Bridge Street, both celebrated their centenaries in 1957. Records showed that both firms were established on the same day, June 11, 1857.

Police swoop on Golden Slipper

Orkney was abuzz with the news that police had raided one of the county's best known venues - the Golden Slipper establishment at the Brig o' Waithe in the West Mainland.

The police raid on the premises - also popularly known as Smokey Joe's - came

in the early hours of Sunday, October 20, 1957, when four policemen were led by the Chief Constable Gathorne Cheyne.

They questioned the eight or nine people present and took away more than 70 bottles of whisky and a number of empties.

Mirage mystery

People in Sanday reported a curious mirage as a village of white houses appeared where no houses existed.

The "vision" was seen by several people in the North Wall area of Lady parish on Monday, July 22, 1957, and Mr John D. Mackay, headmaster of the school, said it took the form of a large white building, or group of buildings, with smaller houses around it.

Weather conditions were suggested as the reason for the mirage - with the theory that it was the reflection of a Norwegian village.

Mr Mackay said the mirage had prompted memories of previous such experiences. "Shortly after World War One, a large town or village was seen in the Broughston area of Cross parish and this mirage lingered a whole afternoon," he said.

"Another islander assures me that, when he was a small boy, he saw a river and a clump of trees near his home in a field which, normally, is as treeless as the rest of our wind-swept islands. Then, again, there was that glorious day in September, 1940, when the mountains of Norway were seen lying along the eastern horizon, their snow capped peaks glistening in the sun."

The North Isles ferry *Orcadia* at Kirkwall Pier. (Picture courtesy of Myra Hazell)

A cabin of the *Orcadia* is converted into a Bank of Scotland sub-branch as an itinerant bank teller conducts business around the islands.

(Picture courtesy of Orkney Library photographic archive)

Chain gang

Orkney was to have its first national chain store.

In May, 1957, it was announced that F.W. Woolworth and Company had submitted a preliminary application to open a store at 31 Albert Street, Kirkwall.

Polio tragedy

A mass inoculation programme to treat the children of Orkney against the threat of Poliomyelitis had been put in train during 1957 - but it could not prevent four cases of the disease being reported in the county during the year.

Tragically, in July, Mrs Margaret Scott (29), the wife of the Birsay minister, Rev W.D. Scott, died after being flown to Aberdeen, having contracted the disease. Sadly, her premature baby, born 48 hours before her death, also died.

The first Miss Orkney

The Kirkwall branch of the British Legion decided in 1957 to launch a beauty contest to find "Miss Orkney" - with heats held in 24 districts of Orkney.

The first district winner, in December, 1957, was Miss Roberta Watt who became Miss South Ronaldsay.

The eventual overall winner and the first Miss Orkney - chosen at the grand final held at the Cosmo ballroom in May, 1958 - was 17 year old Miss Kirkwall, Elizabeth Davey.

Sea wall washed away

A February gale - which gusted to hurricane force 125 mph winds at Costa Head - washed away 50 yards of sea wall at Holm and shifted some of the five ton blocks of concrete on the first Churchill barrier.

Carry on drinking

In what was seen as a major liberalisation of drinking hours, both the Kirkwall licensing court and the county licensing court agreed that closing time in local pubs and hotel bars could be extended from 9pm to 9.30pm during the summer of 1957.

Home from home

The Eventide Home for old folk - at the former St Peter's Manse in Stromness - was officially opened by the Orcadian artist Stanley Cursiter in June, 1957, after a two year conversion costing £45,000. It could accommodate 30 residents.

Council prompts means test row

Hundreds of Kirkwall council house tenants were up in arms as the town council, in a glorious public relations faux pas, sent them a letter enquiring how much they earned.

What became headlined as the "great rent row" blew up as the Government announced cutbacks in housing subsidies, forcing an increase in council house rents.

Kirkwall Town Council decided on a system of rents based on incomes, which would require tenants to be means tested.

However, the decision provoked fury especially when tenants received the council questionnaire asking for details of their income.

Tenants - complaining that there was no guarantee of either accuracy or secrecy about the information - set up the Municipal Tenants Association, which soon had several hundred members, and refused to complete the questionnaires.

The dispute was not helped by the fact that three of the 12 councillors were barred from taking part in the debate because they were council tenants.

A crowded meeting at Kirkwall Town Hall saw 160 members of the tenants association put forward an alternative scheme whereby householders would only have to reveal their earnings if they were seeking a rent rebate. This compromise was eventually accepted by the council and, in the course of time, rent increases varying from two shillings to six shillings a week were introduced.

The dispute however, did serve to increase the level of interest in town council affairs and, after several years of apathy, nearly 1,000 people waited until 11pm to hear the results of the Kirkwall elections declared - the one new councillor being Mr Olaf Mooney, a member of the Municipal Tenants Association.

The new provost of Kirkwall was James Scott who succeeded James Flett, who stepped down on health grounds.

Lifeboat salute

Miss Minnie Sutherland - the only woman secretary of the lifeboats in the country - was given a VIP send-off after 11 years as secretary of the Longhope lifeboat.

She was moving South and she was carried across the Pentland Firth, on the first leg of her journey, by the lifeboat *Thomas McCunn*.

Foul pest panic

The Orkney poultry industry - the county's single biggest revenue earner at the time - was gripped by panic as the deadly disease of foul pest struck in the county for the second time in ten years.

Fortunately, after stringent precautions were put in place, it proved to be an isolated scare and just 1,100 birds had to be slaughtered at two neighbouring farms on the East Mainland. The source of the outbreak was traced to a farm in North East Scotland.

More council jobs

The number of people employed in Orkney in the national and local government had increased more than ten-fold in the previous 25 years.

By the mid 1950s, a total of 554 - 489 men and 65 women - were employed in council and government jobs. That compared with the figure for 1930 when the total was 44 - 39 men and five women.

Off to Paris

The age of foreign travel had arrived for Orkney schoolchildren by 1957 when 52 pupils from Kirkwall and Stromness left the county for a 2,000 mile round trip Easter excursion to Paris, via Aberdeen and London.

Girls on the trip outnumbered the boys by four to one.

Exodus from Fara

The population of the island of Fara in Scapa Flow had fallen from 70 at the start of the century to only five by 1957 - and the ages of those remaining ranged from 47 to 84!

Mrs Henrietta Mackay (67) who had just left the island to move to the Orkney Mainland, said: "We must face the fact that this type of life is ended."

Doctor at sea

Doctor Sydney Peace, who was out fishing, helped rescue the ten crew of the 480 ton coal ship *Mistley* which ran aground off North Ronaldsay. The ship became a total loss.

Prehistoric find

A prehistoric 31 inch long wooden sword from 700 BC - the like of which had not been previously seen in Scotland - was uncovered at a depth of seven feet from a peat bank in Tankerness by Mr Robert Petrie of Groatsetter. The National Museum of Scotland offered to buy it for £50.

We have lift-off

Orcadians were able to clearly see the Sputnik - the satellite which had been launched by the Soviet Union in 1957 - flash across the Orkney skies for several days, looking like a "red moon."

Archaeologist dies

Professor Gordon Childe, the distinguished archaeologist who had done much to excavate Orkney's history at Skara Brae, Maeshowe and other sites, died in a cliff fall in his native Australia in 1957.

Radio show

The famous radio show "Have A Go" with Wilfred and Mabel Pickles was broadcast from Kirkwall's Cosmo ballroom. Jack Walls, head waiter at the Kirkwall Hotel, was among those interviewed on the programme.

Unfortunately, weather conditions in Orkney made reception of the BBC Light Programme virtually impossible within the county.

Women elders

Orkney Presbytery voted in favour of allowing women as elders in the Kirk, but decided they would wish to seek the views of individual kirk sessions before making any firm proposals.

Dressed to chill

Eyebrows were raised at a meeting of Orkney education committee when Councillor Ben Grassick asked: "Is it absolutely necessary for girls to walk from Kirkwall Grammar School up Dundas Crescent for PT in the Bignold Park in their underclothes only?"

He argued that the girls should be able to change in the dressing rooms at the Pavilion, adding that their garb was often "more like bikinis."

Asked by committee chairman Mr Patrick Sutherland Graeme: "Do you watch these things?" Councillor Grassick replied: "Well, not having a car or an aeroplane, I have to walk down Dundas Crescent to get to the town and I meet them."

Cold War intrigue for Orkney

Orkney found itself caught up in the astonishing intrigue of the Cold War in an international diplomatic incident involving a defector from the Soviet Union.

In an atmosphere of "cloak and dagger" secrecy, an Estonian fisherman defected from the Russian fishing fleet off Shetland and sought political asylum in this country.

Thirty members of the communist bloc fishing fleet had landed in Shetland in pursuit of the man - prompting a major diplomatic incident as the British Government sent a strongly worded protest to the Soviet powers over their "unauthorised intrusion on British territory."

But, by that time, the defector - or "the man who made a dash for freedom" as he was dubbed by the National Press - had been spirited away from Shetland and brought to Orkney.

The Estonian, variously named as Erich Teayn or Klaub, had travelled down to Kirkwall overnight from Lerwick, locked in a second class cabin of the *St Ninian* ferry, with a police escort consisting of a sergeant from the Shetland force.

As the *St Ninian* berthed at 5.40am, the Kirkwall police car drew up alongside the gangway as soon as it was lowered. The "visitor" was taken to Kirkwall police station and then to Stromness as a security blackout was imposed.

The Orkney police officers - unprepared

for this role in the annals of the Cold War - admitted later that they did not have a "safe house" for such eventualities, so they had kept their guest at the Stromness police station for the day.

A specially chartered plane flew a party of national journalists north and, for a day, the great Orcadian public solemnly pronounced their views on subjects ranging from the KGB to the Siberian salt mines.

While this was going on, two officials from the Soviet Embassy in London were sitting quietly drinking tea in what was then called "the waiting room" at Kirkwall Airport. They had flown in on the first plane of the day.

Mr Konstantine Drobnitsa said: "We are not interested in the Estonian at the moment. We are going to see the commodore of the fishing fleet in Shetland."

But hundreds of Orcadians obviously were interested in the Estonian and, by 4pm, a big crowd had gathered at Kirkwall pier to see "the man who made a dash for freedom."

A few minutes before the *St Ninian* was due to sail for Aberdeen at 5pm, the police car drove up to the ship and inside, "heavily guarded," was a hooded figure in a purple striped blanket who was

quickly hustled up the gangway amidst the illumination of the flash bulbs of photographers.

But the man beneath the blanket was not the Estonian. While everyone's attention was distracted by this charade, the real man had made his way on board at the other end of the ship, unnoticed, having been driven from Stromness in the police van. The man under the blanket was a crew member of the *St Ninian*.

The Estonian was taken to Edinburgh for interrogation by immigration officials and, after two weeks in Saughton Prison, it was announced that Erich Teayn had been granted formal leave to stay in the UK and, accompanied by Home Office officials, he travelled down to London. Orkney's brush with the politics of the Cold War was over.

Sadly, the year of 1958 ended in real tragedy for the Soviet fishing fleet off Shetland with the loss of a large trawler and the deaths of 22 crewmen. For a few days, there was a brief thaw in the Cold War as Radio Moscow praised the "brilliant skill, the vast courage and the selfless heroism" of the Lerwick lifeboat crew.

Hospitals in staff crisis

The medical authorities in Orkney put out an urgent appeal for more hospital staff - warning that they were so desperately short of nurses that it was feared medical treatment in the county would have to be stopped.

Medical Officer of Health Dr A.S. Brodie warned: "So serious is the shortage of nurses that the medical staff have had to contemplate curtailing admissions to hospital, a step which so far we have only just avoided.

"The shortage in the rest of the country is so bad that in some cases hospitals have had to close down."

It was estimated that an extra 12 nurses were needed to cope with the 56 beds at the Balfour Hospital and 50 beds at Eastbank Hospital, and there were appeals for juniors to enrol for training.

In 1958, auxiliary nurses were paid from £263 a year at the age of 17 up to a maximum of £467.

The authorities were also having problems recruiting doctors. A Royal Commission, considering the future requirements of doctors and dentists, was told that doctors were demanding "inducement payments" ranging from £300-£1,200 a year to work in rural areas of the Highland and Islands.

Radioactive waste dumping

Limited quantities of radioactive waste material from the Dounreay atomic energy station in Caithness would be discharged into the Pentland Firth, *The Orcadian* revealed on September 18, 1958.

Twenty years later, any suggestion of radioactive dumping would prompt angry protests but the revelation in 1958 did not appear to raise a single voice of concern in *The Orcadian* of the following weeks.

The news of possible discharges was given at a conference in Geneva when it was revealed that a study of the coast had been made to assess the suitability. Samples of fish and shellfish had been taken "without finding any contamination, except once, when very slight contamination was found in the bones of certain white fish."

British scientist H.J. Dunster said that, because of the presence of lobster fishing, as a precaution the amount of radioactive waste discharged would be limited to one tenth of the maximum amount

considered safe. He admitted that there was a possibility of lobster creels becoming contaminated in the water and then spreading the radioactivity when brought ashore. Possible contamination of seafood destined for human consumption was one of the factors considered in the selection of dumping sites by the Government.

However, a Russian scientist E.M. Kreps warned the conference that deep sea dumping constituted a real menace in the very near future. There was not yet enough data to predict how much radioactivity could be dumped with safety into the sea, he said.

The news obviously did little to alarm the fish markets. A year later, Stromness Fishermen's Society was sending consignments of Orkney lobsters direct by specially chartered plane to Finisterre in France - the first of several consignments opening up new markets - while frozen Orkney lobsters were also on sale at Selfridges store in London.

The tomb of the eagles

A chance discovery one Thursday night in the summer of 1958 led to one of Orkney's most amazing archaeological treasures found in the 20th century - the "Tomb of the Eagles."

Discovered by local farmer and landowner Ronnie Simison, the chambered tomb at Isbister, at the south east tip of South Ronaldsay, takes its evocative name from the bones of sea eagles which were found within its walls.

But it was the remains of more than 300 people who lived 5,000 years ago that stirred even more interest in the site.

The tomb is set among dramatic landscape, alongside cliffs that were battered and eroded by the sea long before the Isbister folk decided to settle there.

One night in 1958 Mr Simison decided to uncover some flagstones that he had seen sticking out of his land.

Within ten minutes of digging he had reached the bottom of a wall and discovered a whole range of remarkable objects including a polished mace head made out of black and white stone, axe heads and a button made of jet.

The discoveries only added to his enthusiasm and a few days later he recruited some help and dug further, eventually breaking into one of the cells of the tomb.

First a lintel was exposed, and then after some more digging, the top of the entrance was uncovered. As the amateur archaeologists peered into the dark chamber - probably the first people to do so for thousands of years - a lighter was used to illuminate the interior.

The flickering light revealed a small chamber whose floor was covered with 30 human skulls.

"At that time we knew it was a burial chamber, but we were not expecting a whole room of skulls," recalled Mr Simison.

The bones were subsequently removed by archaeologists and the tomb was filled in with earth to await professional excavation.

But as the years went by nothing happened until 1972 when archaeologists in the county excavating another tomb agreed to investigate a mound on Mr Simison's farm.

The mound turned out to be a Bronze Age house and Mr Simison gained practical experience by helping the archaeologists. He learned about the correct methods to use during excavations and four years later, when there was no sign of archaeologists returning, he decided to thoroughly investigate the tomb himself.

"There was a burnt mound on the farm and excavations finished in 1975 so I knew a lot about what the archaeologists do, so I thought I would do the tomb the next year." he said.

Mr Simison uncovered the remains of 340 Stone Age tribal people - a total of 16,000 bones and he had to make use of 26 fish boxes on his farm to store the bones.

He meticulously recorded his findings, and his work, complemented by subsequent investigations by archaeologists, has provided a valuable insight into the life of people who lived in Orkney 5,000 years ago.

First Miss Orkney wins her crown

The first Miss Orkney! The Kirkwall branch of the British Legion decided in 1957 to launch a beauty contest to find "Miss Orkney" - with heats held in 24 districts of Orkney. The eventual overall winner and the first Miss Orkney - chosen at the grand final held at the Cosmo ballroom in May, 1958 - was 17 year old Miss Kirkwall, Elizabeth Davey, pictured alongside Brigadier S.P. Robertson. Margaret Bruce of St Ola became the 1969 Miss Orkney - the last time the competition would be organised by the Kirkwall branch of the British Legion before, the following year, it was taken over by the Orkney Tourist Organisation.
Since the launch of the competition in 1958, it had been won by Miss Kirkwall Elizabeth Davey (twice), two Miss Birsays Vera Cromarty and Bridget O'Malley, Miss Firth Norma Hourston, Miss St Ola Annette Russell, Miss Stenness Maureen Linklater, Miss South Ronaldsay Christine Scott, Miss Stronsay Catherine Maxwell (the first North Isles winner) and Kathleen Eunson from Deerness.

(Picture courtesy of Orkney Library photographic archive)

Cathedral campaign

The Society of Friends of St Magnus Cathedral was formally inaugurated at a public meeting in Kirkwall to collect funds for the preservation of the fabric of the Cathedral.

The society was formed, in September, 1958, just two days after a Cathedral service commemorating the 800th anniversary of the death of St Rognvald, the founder of the building.

The same month, Cathedral minister Rev John Rose preached before the Queen, Duke of Edinburgh, Prince Charles, Princess Anne and Princess Margaret at Crathie Church as he was invited to stay at Balmoral Castle for the weekend.

It was the first time an Orkney minister had officiated at Crathie while the Royal family was present at Balmoral.

Orkney trawler pioneer

The newest addition to the Hull trawler fleet, the 190 feet long *Northella*, which had achieved the greatest speeds ever recorded by a British trawler during trials, made her maiden voyage to the White Sea under the command of Westrayman William Drever.

The 21 day trip realised a catch of nearly £12,000 for the owners, J. Marr and Son. Mr Drever had sailed for the company since World War Two, while his son skippered another Marr company trawler *Bayella*.

Back in Orkney waters, two fishing vessels came to grief in 1958. The Stronsay lifeboat, under coxswain James Stout, rescued the six Banff crew of the Grimsby-registered *Tanana* in the Westray Firth before the vessel became a total loss, and both the Longhope and Wick lifeboats went to the aid of the North Shields-registered trawler *Ben Meidie* which went aground on the Pentland Skerries. The trawler's crew of 13 men, from Aberdeen, were all rescued.

Record traffic

A £71,000 South Pier extension was opened at Stromness to provide berthing up to a length of 230 feet. During June, July and August, 1958, 2,200 cars were carried on the Pentland Firth by the *St Ola* - a record number then.

In 1959, the North of Scotland Shipping Company started Sunday sailings of the *St Ola* for the first time to cope with the tourist rush of cars during the summer.

The new *Hoy Head* - a former Naval motor fishing vessel - came into service for Bremner and Company as the new ferry for the South Isles, replacing the *Orcadia*, in 1958.

Woman provost

Orkney had its first woman provost when Mrs Rosetta Groundwater became provost of Stromness Town Council in May, 1959. The wife of the rector of Stromness Academy, she had served three years on Kirkwall Town Council before moving to Stromness where she had been a councillor for 11 years.

Combine pioneer

There was something new in Orkney agriculture when the first combine harvester to be used in the county started work on the harvest at the farm of Quanterness, owned by Ted Zawadski.

The year of 1959 also saw Mr Zawadski purchase another of Orkney's big farms, the 830 acre Balfour Mains in Shapinsay from Mr David Balfour of Balfour Castle.

Soccer star

Stromness Shopping week, in 1958, was opened by international footballer George Young, the former captain of Rangers, regarded as "the greatest centre half ever to play for Scotland."

At a slightly lower level of ability, Orkney welcomed the visit of a Faroese football team from Klakksvik. The players arrived after a 36 hour journey by fishing boat to be greeted with a civic reception from Kirkwall Town Council. They lost 7-5 to an Orkney XI and 3-1 to a Kirkwall select team.

Trawler girl

A 22 year old girl who worked on the counters of a Woolworth's store in Edinburgh found herself in Kirkwall - after smuggling herself on board a deep sea trawler disguised as a man.

Teresa Scott had hitchhiked to Aberdeen where, dressed as a fisherman, she got on board the Grimsby trawler *Eroican*, on which she knew a crew member, and which promptly set sail for the Faroe islands.

After five days, sea sickness forced her to reveal herself to the skipper and, after being landed in the Faroes, she arrived in Kirkwall on her way home.

She told *The Orcadian*: "I am quite glad to get back. I'll be going back to my counter but one day I'll see the Faroes again. They're lovely. And next time I'll visit them properly."

Deadly invader

Orkney suffered an invasion of the Diamond Back Moth which caused havoc among the county's turnip and cabbage crops. Cabbages were left looking "more like a lace handkerchief than a vegetable."

Farmers and gardeners were forced to spray with DDT to destroy the pest and save their crops.

New hotel

The new Merkister Hotel in Harray was licensed in 1958. It had been converted from the house formerly owned by the Orkney writer Eric Linklater.

Record price for bull

The champion animal at the 1958 Orkney Bull Show, James Baillie's Aberdeen-Angus Edwin Eric of Sebay was sold at the Perth Bull Sales for 420 guineas - the highest figure for a single Orkney animal at the time.

Costly phones

The Postmaster-General Ernest Marples - later to become transport minister and the subject of millions of car stickers proclaiming "Marples Must Go" - visited Orkney in 1958.

He refused to agree to extend a 3d phone call scheme to all the North Isles. Although it cost 3d to phone Shapinsay from Kirkwall, the cost of a telephone call to North Ronaldsay was 1/6.

Emergency landing

Motorists on the Kirkwall-Stromness road got a shock when they saw an aeroplane coming along the road towards Kirkwall. It was on the back of a lorry with its wings extending right across the road, although cars could pass underneath.

It was the Auster plane owned by Mr Pat Sutherland who had made a forced landing on the Holm of Grimbister in the Bay of Firth. Returning from the North Isles he had engine failure and could not make the aerodrome at Hatston.

New town clerk

Mr E.J. Hendry - who had been Kirkwall's first full time town clerk - left the post after 13 years to take up a similar job in Helensburgh, Dumbartonshire. He was succeeded by Mr Andrew Buchan.

Through the hoop

The hula hoop craze reached Orkney and an Orkney championships was held in Kirkwall's Cosmo ballroom, with Michael Corsie of Kirkwall an easy winner.

Sacrifice at sea for fishermen

1959

Tragedy and heroic rescues marked a year of disasters for trawlers - and those involved in protecting them - during 1959.

The year began and ended with the loss of life. In January, three of the crew, including the master, Commander Gordon McLaren (56), were lost when the Scottish fishery protection cruiser *Freya*, a regular visitor to Orkney, capsized in a gale off Wick.

The other 17 crewmen, who spent five hours in a rubber dinghy, were saved by a Belgian trawler *St Jan Berchmans* and landed at Invergordon.

Two years earlier, the *Vaila* - a sister ship of the *Freya* - had foundered on the west coast of Scotland, also becoming a total loss.

It was a calamitous year for the Aberdeen trawler *George Robb* in Orkney waters. She began the year running aground in Deer Sound where she remained for two weeks before, eventually, being pulled free by the Orkney Steam Navigation Company vessel *Earl Sigurd*.

However far worse tragedy struck in December, 1959 when the *George Robb* was lost with all 12 members of her crew after striking on Duncansby Head on the Caithness side of the Pentland Firth.

The Longhope lifeboat - with her recently appointed secretary Dr Sydney Peace among the crew - attempted a rescue but was unable to locate the trawler under the cliffs in a wild easterly gale.

However, the Longhope crew did pull off a remarkable rescue of courage and seamanship that same year as the Aberdeen trawler *Strathcoe* ran ashore below 500 feet cliffs south of Rackwick on Hoy.

The 43 year old steam trawler was returning to Aberdeen with 1,500 stones of fish after a nine day trip. The public inquiry into the disaster later revealed

that a 15 year old apprentice, of three months experience, was at the wheel when the trawler went aground.

The vessel sent out a radio message that her position was desperate "and everything flooded." However, unfortunately, the trawler also gave an inaccurate position and it took a further 30 minutes to pinpoint her true situation. By the time the Longhope lifeboat, under coxswain Dan Kirkpatrick, reached the trawler, she was in darkness with her radio out of action.

In a gallant operation - for which Dan Kirkpatrick received the RNLI silver medal and the crew commendations on vellum - the lifeboat landed all 14 fishermen by breeches buoy in just one hour.

"Most of us thought our last moment had come," said the skipper. "The ship couldn't have stood much more. The lifeboat did a splendid job."

Unfortunately for the skipper, his ticket was later suspended for two years after the Ministry of Transport inquiry blamed the loss on his negligence, after going below leaving the 15 year old at the wheel.

The Belgian trawler *Lans* languishes ashore beneath the cliffs of Hoy in December, 1974. The nine crewmen were airlifted to safety in a dramatic rescue by an RAF Lossiemouth helicopter, with the rotor blades barely twenty yards from the cliff-face.

(Picture courtesy of Orkney Library photographic archive)

Costly electricity

The North of Scotland Hydro Electric Board pointed out that it operated at an annual loss of £100,000 a year in Orkney, as complaints grew that areas of the Orkney Mainland were still awaiting electricity. The island of Shapinsay had been waiting for a submarine power cable to be laid since 1954. Nonetheless, Robert Walls, manager of the Orkney section of the Hydro Board, was made an MBE in the Queen's birthday honours list.

Growing older

The number of people in Orkney aged 70 and over in 1959 was 1,886 - nearly one in ten of the population.

Creamery boost

A new £75,000 creamery for the Milk Marketing Board reached full production in Deerness Road, Kirkwall. It would handle 10,000 tons of milk a year, producing butter and milk powder.

Kirk anniversary

Shapinsay church celebrated 400 years of public worship on the island with a special commemorative service in 1959.

Bertie Stockan is pictured in the projection room of the Phoenix Cinema in Kirkwall.
(Picture courtesy of Orkney Library photographic archive)

Atlantic dream laid to rest

A three man documentary film team arrived in Stromness in a thirty year old, battered looking 28 feet Bermuda-rigged cutter - and announced plans to sail to America.

Film maker Leslie Sheppard (42), journalist David Regan (42) and Cambridge engineering graduate Jon Field (22) planned to cross the Atlantic by the so-called Viking route via the Faroes, Iceland and Greenland.

The boat, called the *Maid Nellie*, and relying on the emergency power of a 7hp engine, had set off from the Thames in London in May, 1959, and had taken two months to get as far as Stromness.

Undeterred, they set off from Stromness on August 1 but, as many local people predicted, they ran into immediate trouble and the boat was leaking by the time the hills of Hoy had faded from view.

The hopeful sailors had to make for Pierowall in Westray - the nearest to America the boat ever got. It was brought back to Kirkwall and laid up at Hatston as the idea of an Atlantic crossing was quietly laid to rest.

Strike stops the papers

The June 18, 1959, issue of *The Orcadian* was the last printed edition of the paper until August 13, as the newspaper's printers, as part of a national printing dispute, staged a seven week strike.

Emergency editions of type-written and duplicated news-sheets were produced and distributed instead. It was the first time in 104 years that *The Orcadian* failed to appear in conventional printed form.

Goals galore

The annual inter-county football fixture between Orkney and Caithness for the Archer Shield became a two-legged affair in the 1950s with matches played both at home and away each year.

From 1953-59, the 14 games played between the two counties produced a total of 94 goals - an average of nearly seven a game. The highest scoring game in 1959 saw Caithness beat Orkney 7-5.

Mini mania

Kirkwall motor dealers J. and W. Tait took delivery of the car which was to revolutionise vehicle design - the Mini. The price, in October, 1959, for the basic model, including Purchase Tax, was £496/19/2.

Meanwhile, along the road, at John G. Nicolson, a Vauxhall Victor car cost £498 plus £250 Purchase Tax - a total of £748. The Vauxhall Cresta cost £1,073 total.

Orkney heroine scales heights

Nursing sister J. Rendall, the youngest daughter of Mr and Mrs W. Rendall of Sandihall, Westray, was acclaimed a heroine after she climbed to a height of 175 feet to the top of the tallest crane on the Clyde.

Sister Rendall was in charge of the port medical centre in Glasgow and she was called into action to aid an injured engineer, James Cecil, who had been trapped in the crane machinery at Stobcross Quay.

In freezing temperatures, she had to climb ice-covered ladders inside the structure of the crane to help release the man and lower the patient to the ground on a stretcher.

Death of a literary giant

The death of one of the great literary figures of the century, Edwin Muir, a distinguished son of Orkney who was acknowledged as a poet, scholar and critic, occurred in January, 1959.

He was buried at the Cambridgeshire village of Swaffham Prior, near Newmarket, where he had been living in retirement since a year's appointment as Professor of Poetry at Harvard University, USA.

Farmers rocked by disease crisis

The stench of burning animals hung in the air over Kirkwall as Orkney reeled under "a crisis that could be catastrophic to its whole agricultural ecomomy."

For the first time in 100 years, the county had been hit by the scourge of the dreaded Foot and Mouth disease.

"The plight of Orkney's farming industry was brought home to town dwellers at the weekend when a great pall of grey smoke hung over parts of Kirkwall's south west outskirts from the vast funeral pyre at Pickaquoy where the carcases of close on 100 animals were burned," *The Orcadian* reported in November, 1960.

Orkney farmers had been praying for weeks that they would be spared the disease. It had been raging in the South and had spread rapidly in Aberdeenshire. Eventually it reached Orkney.

It first struck at the 260 acre farm of Roeberry in South Ronaldsay, owned by John Scott, one of Orkney's best known and most progressive farmers. Within hours of being diagnosed, 160 head of cattle - including a pedigree dairy herd of 80 Friesians - and 297 sheep were slaughtered. The value was estimated at £15,000.

"This is a lifetime's work gone," said Mr Scott.

A team of ten Ministry of Agriculture vets were flown in, and set up a "battle HQ" at the Kirkwall Hotel to cope with the disease and introduce stringent precautions to prevent its spread.

However two outbreaks in Tankerness were followed by another at Saverock, St Ola, and then farms in Evie, Stromness and Orphir all fell victim. Five outbreaks were confirmed in five days.

Orkney was "in a state of siege," reported *The Orcadian* as a standstill order was imposed to forbid all movement of cattle and livestock within, or out of, the county. All the cattle that were at the mart had to be slaughtered.

Farms were barricaded against visitors, tubs of disinfectant appeared at gateways and road-ends. Orkney social life was brought to a halt as virtually all functions were cancelled.

It was a dreadful blow to the farming community which had been enjoying a certain prosperity. The year had begun with *The Orcadian* carrying an article which stated: "The general aspect of the farming landscape is one of great prosperity: every farmer has a car, often his son has too. The Mainland forms part of the most highly mechanised community in Europe."

But it was so different by the end of November, 1960, when 3,000 animals had been slaughtered and buried. The

1960

total cost had risen within two weeks to £70,000 or more.

One hundred animals were burned in the huge pyre at the Peerie Sea on November 26-27. Pickaquoy Road was closed to traffic as the carcases were burned in a trench along with 20 tons of coal, wood, straw and oil. The gruesome task of burying hundreds of carcases fell to the workmen of the county and burgh councils and local contractors.

The whole of the Orkney Mainland - including the linked islands of South Ronaldsay and Burray - was designated an infected area, while the rest of the county, under strict precautions to prevent the disease spreading to the North Isles, was declared a controlled area.

The East Mainland farm of Sebay became a victim and many fine animals had to be slaughtered including that year's East Mainland Show cattle champion and several bulls destined for the 1961 bull sales.

By the time Orkney suffered its 13th outbreak in Tankerness, one of the worst affected areas, animals valued at £82,000 had been slaughtered - 987 cattle, 1,951 sheep and 297 pigs.

And then, thankfully, came the respite. Three weeks without a new case saw the Ministry vets partially lift the restrictions the week before Christmas to allow more than 700 lambs from Westray to be shipped direct to Aberdeen for the Fatstock Marketing Corporation.

On December 28, 1960, Orkney was judged to be officially free of the disease. All the Foot and Mouth restrictions were lifted and all livestock could move freely again. It had been a crisis - but the islands had survived.

Seal wars break out

A controversy which was to rage with increasing fervour for the next two decades broke out in the Autumn of 1960 as more than 100 seals were killed.

More than 20 years later, Margaret Thatcher was to comment that the welfare of seals was one of the major topics of the Downing Street postbag during her tenure as Prime Minister. Until 1960, however, it was a subject that had scarcely raised its head in Orkney.

The controversy arose in October, 1960, when first of all a team of four from the Nature Conservancy, headed by research officer Mr A.E. Smith, came North to tag grey seals. They spent several days on the Green Holms, tagging over 700 seal pups which were later tracked as far away as the Faroes. Four grey seal pups were taken south by Mr Smith to be taken to the Zoos in Edinburgh and London.

But at the same time, another Government-sponsored party, headed by Dr Bennet Rae, of the Marine Laboratory in Aberdeen, came to Orkney to "cull" a number of seals. The group left after killing 140 grey seals.

In the House of Commons, Orkney MP Jo Grimond was told that the experimental cull was undertaken in view of widespread complaints of damage done by seals to salmon and marine fisheries. It was to establish the most humane and practical methods of controlling the grey seal population.

However, Orkney Field Club condemned the killing of seals. A party of Field Club members found 35 skins of grey seal pups which, they said, had been clubbed to death on the Muckle Green Holm. Mr Grimond was told by the Government that permits had been granted for seals to be killed in a number of parts of Orkney but no permit allowed the clubbing of seals.

In Orkney however it prompted the question: Was it not strange for the Government to finance the tagging of over 700 seals for study purposes and then issue permits to hunters to kill them?

The following year, 1961, it was officially stated that 323 grey seals had been slaughtered under veterinary supervision during the culling "season" while another 900 had been tagged.

By 1962, six licences had been granted to seal hunters in Orkney and 750 grey seals could be killed in that year's cull, said the Secretary of State for Scotland. Three seals were airlifted by Royal Navy helicopter from the Green Holms to Hatston, en route to London Zoo, raising another question in Orkney: Why do seals get helicopter airlifts while human ambulance cases do not?

It would be another five years before the arrival of Loganair - and the return of a locally-based air ambulance service for the islands - but the row over the killing of seals would continue for much longer than that.

Queen visits on 'glorious twelfth'

Crowds turned out in their thousands for the visit of the Queen and the Duke of Edinburgh to Orkney on August 12, 1960. The last time Scapa Flow had seen a reigning monarch was during World War Two when the Queen's father, George VI, had visited the Home Fleet.

Now Broad Street was packed with an estimated 5,000 people as the Queen visited St Magnus Cathedral - the first reigning British monarch to do so.

The people of Orkney had been waiting for more than a year for the Royal visit which had originally been scheduled for 12 months earlier in 1959. Then the Queen had been scheduled to arrive on the Royal Yacht *Britannia*, homeward bound from a tour of Canada.

However, after being ill in Canada, the Queen instead returned to Britain by jet aircraft and just four days before her planned visit, the Orkney trip was cancelled as it was announced that the Queen was pregnant.

The 1959 cancellation "was received with a mixture of dismay, irritation and disappointment. Many people felt that Orkney could well have been given longer warning in order to save both private and public expense," wrote *The Orcadian*.

However that disappointment was forgotten when the Queen arrived in August, 1960. (All Orkney schoolchild-ren had been given a holiday on Friday, February 26, to celebrate the birth of Prince Andrew).

The Queen and Duke arrived by royal barge off *Britannia* at Stromness, to be accompanied by the Secretary of State for Scotland Mr J.S. Maclay, and welcomed by a contingent of Orkney TA, before visiting Skara Brae and Binscarth, the home of the Lord Lieutenant Colonel Robert Scarth, before reaching Kirkwall.

Among those presented to the Queen was 84 year old Burray county council-lor Eric Sutherland who had attended the funeral of the Queen's great-great grand-mother, Queen Victoria. In St Magnus Cathedral, the organist T. Watson Forgie (70) played Mendelssohn's Sixth Sonata - a VIP farewell recital before his retire-ment that week after ten years as the Cathedral organist.

While the Queen and Duke carried out their official engagements, their two eldest children Prince Charles and Princess Anne enjoyed a picnic on the Holm of Houton in Scapa Flow - dressed infor-mally in jeans and sweaters - with Princess Alexandra and Prince Michael.

They were taken there by Stromness fishermen Angus Brown, and his son George, and Tom Clouston in their fishing boat *Victory 2*, along with Colonel Robert Macrae, Deputy Lieutenant of Orkney, who planned the outing. They lifted Mr Clouston's lobster pots - which yielded four lobsters - and remained for two hours on the holm.

After lunch at the Kirkwall Hotel, the Royal party embarked on *Britannia* for Stronsay where they inspected the lifeboat and crew - as they had done in Stromness where both the local crew and the Longhope crew were on parade - before visiting the small Stronsay shop of John and Pat Dennison and their sons Magnus, Roy and Keith - later to become one of Orkney's best known families of hoteliers. Shown round the shop by Mrs Dennison, the Queen purchased a 11d packet of oat-cakes and a 10d pack of Orkney fudge.

Continuing on to Westray, the Duke of Edinburgh drove the party in the island's new school bus to Pierowall, where the Queen was given a guided tour of the recently reconstructed school by head-master Norman Cooper.

By the time *Britannia* and the Royal party sailed from Westray for Aberdeen that evening, a total 126 Orkney people had been presented to the Queen.

The Orkney artist Stanley Cursiter - official Limner to the Queen - had painted a picture of the scene outside St Magnus Cathedral when the Queen arrived. It was later presented to Kirkwall Town Council.

The Queen made three official visits to Orkney in the years between 1960 and 1987. She is seen here in August, 1987, when she visited Kirkwall as part of the 850th anniversary celebrations of St Magnus Cathedral. (Picture courtesy of Orkney Library photographic archive)

Mercy dash saves baby

An epic life-saving mission saw six Sanday men and a nurse hailed for their heroism as they defied gale force winds and heavy seas in a small boat to get emergency equipment to a premature baby.

Baby Andrew Allan, the son of Mr and Mrs James Allan, the depute headmaster of Sanday school, weighed just three and a half pounds and island GP Dr A.J. Blair called for an oxygen tent and other specialist equipment from Kirkwall to help ensure his survival.

However when nursing sister Helen Stott tried to reach Sanday on the steamer *Earl Sigurd*, the weather conditions prevented the ship from landing and it was forced to return to Kirkwall. A fresh attempt was made the next day and again the ship was unable to reach Kettletoft pier.

This time though, the *Earl Sigurd* found some shelter in the Bay of Brough and Mr James Sinclair, owner of the 13 feet motor boat *Janet*, launched his small boat, along with five other local men - W. Muir, T. Dearness, John Dearness, William Cooper and David Sinclair - to go out to meet the ship and pick up the nurse and equipment.

At times, reported *The Orcadian*, their little boat disappeared in ten feet waves and the sea flooded the outboard motor. The men rowed until the rowlocks broke, but they were eventually successful in their errand of mercy.

The great trek south

Orcadian Tom Anderson, a 29 year old farmer from Graemsay, had never previously been further south than Inverness. That was all to change, however, in March, 1960, when he set out to walk 1,000 miles from John o' Groats to Land's End.

He was Orkney's only representative in the Butlin Walk - sponsored by holiday camp king Billy Butlin - which was to see hundreds set out on the great trek south.

For some it was a professionally organised expedition. They had back-up vehicles to provide regular refreshments and overnight accommodation. Tom Anderson was on his own; he had no support crew and, at the end of a day's walking, he then had to find a bed and breakfast establishment to stay.

Despite such obstacles, he completed the walk - footslogging up to 64 miles a day - in just 21 days, finishing the event in 32nd position, with well over 100 other walkers following him.

Battle over Iron Curtain trawler

The rescue of an East German trawler in Orkney waters led to a war of words across the Iron Curtain in June, 1960.

The Longhope lifeboat towed the fishing boat *Adolphe Hennecke* off Swona, after she had grounded with 15 men on board, and took her to Longhope. The following day she was joined by another East German trawler *Karl Marx*.

And that might have been the end of the incident - but for the fact that the eight lifeboatmen, through Kirkwall solicitor Mr Frank McGinn, then claimed a £16,000 salvage bounty from the German owners, and a writ of arrestment was pinned to the mast of the *Adolphe Hennecke*.

Dr Sydney Peace, honorary secretary of the Longhope lifeboat, made it clear that the RNLI was not party to the salvage claim. "The position of the lifeboat crew is that of a salvage party operating on their own behalf. The institution does not stand to gain one penny from this."

Dan Kirkpatrick (50), the Longhope coxswain, denied the East Germans were being held to ransom. He was quoted in the *Scottish Daily Express* as saying: "She would have been a goner had we not lent a hand after the German skipper had sought our help.

"We are entitled to something. After all we risked everything. Had anything gone wrong we would have been held responsible - not the RNLI."

The East German skipper told the newspaper: "They never asked for money at first. They took us in, and then it comes. The whole thing is crazy. It is not good for international feelings."

A week later, the East German Government-owned trawler company lodged the money in a London bank to allow the *Adolphe Hennecke* to sail from Longhope, being towed by the *Karl Marx* back to Germany.

Olympic visitors

Star attraction of the 1960 Stromness Shopping Week was the team of Olympic Games boxers who would represent Britain at the 1960 Rome Olympics - including lightweight champion Dick McTaggart, the 1956 gold medal winner at the Melbourne Olympics.

Escape at sea

Nineteen people, including a woman and child, had a narrow escape from disaster when the 620 ton Icelandic ship *Drangajokull* turned turtle and sank in the Pentland Firth in June, 1960.

The 19 people on board, including the wife of the Icelandic captain, Hantour Gudmundsson, and their four year old son, were all picked up by the nearby trawler *Mount Eden* and landed at Aberdeen.

Art gift to nation

One of the finest collections of post-impressionist art in Britain, valued at £500,000 in 1960, including paintings by Van Gogh, Renoir, Picasso, Cezanne, Gauguin and Degas, was gifted to the National Gallery of Scotland by Alexander Maitland (83), who had been Sheriff of Orkney from 1929-31, in memory of his late wife.

Football setback

Orkney lost the annual junior inter-county football match with Shetland by a record 11-2 defeat. "Never in Orkney's football history has such a dismal display ever been witnessed, and never again will such a humiliating defeat be inflicted upon a representative team," wrote Corinthian in *The Orcadian*.

Kirk history

The first Deaconess of the Church of Scotland to come to Orkney took up her post in North Ronaldsay in 1960. She was Miss Agnes Currie who made history in another way by arriving in the new air taxi service which was being operated on a trial basis by Mr John Swanson (32) of Glasgow-based Caledonian Flying Services. Charters cost ten guineas a trip, but, unfortunately, the service did not prove a viable proposition in the long term.

Farewell to horses

The number of working horses in Orkney had fallen to less than ten per cent of the level of 20 years earlier. By 1960, there were only 380 working horses - compared to 1,100 tractors.

There was just one Clydesdale foal forward at the 1960 annual foal show at Kirkwall Auction Mart.

Water for isles

Orkney County Council decided that Westray would be the first island to get a piped water supply.

Birth of an industry

The decade of the 1960s witnessed the embryonic beginnings of a new industry for Orkney - the first of what would grow into an impressive fleet of white fish boats.

But in 1960, Orkney had only three fishing boats over 40 feet - all based at Stromness. By comparison, Shetland had 65 vessels over 40 feet.

In the year 1959-60, Orkney shellfish landings totalled 4,881 hundredweights valued £73,714 and 1,027 hundredweights of white fish worth £3,543 - giving a total value of Orkney fishing of just over £77,000. (Thirty five years later, the estimated value of Orkney fishing reached £15 millions.)

Orkney had a total of 510 fishermen in 1960 - but 334 of these were part-time "crofter fishermen" - and most were still based in the isles. Westray had 43 boats, 65 fishermen; Sanday 48 boats, 73 fishermen; Eday 26 boats, 33 men; Stronsay 26 boats, 42 men; Hoy and Walls 55 boats, 64 men; South Ronaldsay 33 boats, 38 men; while Kirkwall had just 15 boats and 40 fishermen.

Much of the fishing effort at this time was devoted to creel fishing for crabs and lobsters and, in 1963, Joe Malloch, manager of the Orkney Fishermen's Society, called for the introduction of lobster nurseries to restock areas of sea around the county. A small boat could no longer fill its creels off the Kame of Hoy, he said, and local fishermen were having to go further afield, as far as Loch Eriboll.

By 1964, the value of Orkney catches had nearly doubled in four years, as figures showed that landings that year were worth £157,000. And when John Davidson of Shapinsay bought the 72 feet long fishing boat *Argonaut* in 1965, it was the biggest fishing boat in Orkney at the time.

The first suggestion of official support for a white fish industry in Orkney came in 1966 in a report backed by the newly formed Highland Development Board. It was certainly time for Orcadians to exploit the resources in local waters before others stepped in and took advantage.

Danish fishing boats from Esbjerg were already crossing the North Sea to the fishing grounds and, in 1966, there were as many as 32 Danish boats sheltering in Kirkwall at any one time.

Jo is rector

Orkney MP Jo Grimond was elected rector of Edinburgh University in 1960 - gaining 1,907 votes to 847 achieved by newspaper proprietor Roy Thomson.

Open days

A new theatre block for the Balfour Hospital was officially opened in 1960 by Mr T.D. Haddow of the Department of Health for Scotland as part of an £88,000 programme of improvements.

Also, the new Salvation Army hall in Junction Road, Kirkwall, was opened by Mr Harold Leslie QC, later to become Lord Birsay.

'Ban the Bomb' protests

The tension of the Cold War was illustrated as work began to construct three Royal Observer Corps posts in Orkney to observe radioactive fall-out in the event of a nuclear bomb being dropped on Scotland.

They would be sited near Kirkwall, Stromness and in Deerness. Recruiting began to find 40 Orkney men and women to staff the posts which would be built of three feet thick concrete.

The following year, an Orkney branch of CND, the Campaign for Nuclear Disarmament, was formed in Stromness with Ian MacInnes as chairman.

In April, 1962, coinciding with the famous Easter march from Aldermaston to London, Orkney CND supporters staged their own "Ban the Bomb" march from Kirkwall to Stromness. About 20 marchers, led by Mr MacInnes, started from Broad Street, watched by a sizeable 400 crowd, and the number of walkers had grown to about 30 by the time the procession reached Stromness pierhead where a rally was held in front of 300 people.

Strike up the band

Orkney's newest dance band, Norman Brass and his Ballroom Orchestra, made its debut in 1960 - Norman Brass, alto sax / clarinet / viola; Jack Wood, tenor sax / clarinet; Bill McDougall, trumpet; Douglas Shearer, violin / vibes; Bert Finlayson, piano / accordion; Bob Park, double bass; Douglas Cooper, guitar; and Louis Macdonald, drums.

Death of provosts

The year of 1960 saw the deaths of three former Orkney provosts - Peter Flett (82) and James Flett (79) of Kirkwall, and James Marwick (84) of Stromness. Mr Marwick's work had appeared in *The Orcadian* for more than 50 years as the newspaper's Stromness correspondent.

The same year saw the death of Lady Wallace - born Augusta Clouston, the daughter of Sir Thomas Clouston and brother of the Orkney writer J. Storer Clouston - who died at the age of 88. She was the widow of the noted surgeon Sir David Wallace, and had a family home at Holodyke, Dounby.

Town protests

There was a row in Stromness as 200 people signed a petition complaining at Stromness Town Council plans to buy the former Commercial Bank house near the head of the pier for use as municipal offices. The purchase went ahead, and it became known as the Town House.

New owners for shipping company

The company which provided most of Orkney's external shipping services throughout the 20th century began a new chapter in its history after a £1,146,000 take-over bid.

The North of Scotland and Orkney and Shetland Shipping Company - which could trace its roots back to 1790 - owned seven ships operating on routes to the Northern Isles, the *St Ola, St Clair, St Ninian, St Rognvald, St Clement,* *St Magnus* and the *Earl of Zetland.*

The take-over bid in 1960 came from the Liverpool-based Coast Lines, which was valued at £13 millions with around 100 ships already under its control. The North company shareholders were advised to accept the offer and the deal went through in February, 1961.

The North company, which continued to operate under its old name, later evolved into P&O Scottish Ferries.

Century not out

Mother of eight Mrs Frances Corrigall of Whitecleat, Birsay, was Orkney's oldest inhabitant in 1960 when she celebrated her 100th birthday.

She was born in Oban of Orkney parents but had been raised in Orkney, after her mother died when she was three, and had never left the county since. She died in 1962, aged 101.

Population slumps to new low

1961

As a volcano erupted on the South Atlantic island of Tristan da Cunha - forcing the 264 inhabitants of the rocky outpost to flee to Britain - it was suggested that the exiled islanders could be accommodated in Orkney to help reverse the county's serious population decline.

The 1961 census showed that Orkney's population had virtually halved in 100 years, now standing at just 18,743 - a decline of 11.8 per cent, or 2,512 people, in the previous ten years.

Every burgh, parish and island in Orkney had shown a decrease in population since the 1951 census. Kirkwall had 33 fewer people, down to 4,315, while the population of Stromness fell by 26 to 1,477.

The biggest exodus was from Hoy and Walls where the population was 590 fewer at 685. In the North Isles, the biggest drop was in Westray which had 263 fewer people with a population of 1,012.

Hardest hit in the North Isles were the smaller islands like North Ronaldsay which, in ten years, had lost 28 per cent of its population (63 people) with a 1961 population of 161, and Eday which had lost 110 people, a drop of more than 30 per cent, to have a 1961 population of 198.

Rousay's population was 338 (a drop of 107 since 1951), Sanday 669 (197 fewer), Shapinsay 421 (66 fewer), South Ronaldsay 1,247 (265 fewer) and Stronsay 504 (a decrease of 146 in ten years).

It was understandable therefore that Orkney should offer a new home to the islanders of Tristan da Cunha who, it was suggested, could reverse the depopulation of areas like Rackwick which were now almost denuded of people.

Orkney MP Jo Grimond said the South Atlantic islanders could perhaps revive the fishing in Stronsay or in Scapa Flow. And Hoy county councillor Isaac Moar said: "We would welcome them with open arms. Since the war, we have seen Hoy's population drop from over 1,000 to 500. If Orkney could accommodate 80,000 servicemen during the war, surely it can offer help to 300 of these unfortunate people. It might be their salvation and ours too."

As it was, the islanders of Tristan da Cunha never came to Orkney and the county's population continued to spiral downwards for another ten years. Many Orcadians were still looking to new opportunities in countries like Canada and Australia.

By now, the Australian Government was offering emigrants assisted passages Down Under for just £10. And the one month of March, 1957, saw nine people leave Dounby to emigrate to Canada.

In 1966, the last two inhabitants of Fara in Scapa Flow, Mr and Mrs Gordon Watters, left the island to live on Hoy. At the start of the century there was a population of 70 but now the island was uninhabited.

But many people were going even further afield as they left Orkney. In April, 1965, *The Orcadian* reported that at least 60 people - of whom 44 were going abroad - were due to leave Orkney within the forthcoming few weeks. As many as 26 were leaving the parish of Holm as the population drift was becoming increasingly like a torrent. Opportunities in Orkney were too limited, said many of the Orcadians who were leaving.

Such was the level of emigration from Orkney that it became a story when people actually moved to the islands. In 1962, *The Orcadian* reported that Mr Ronald Corkett (40), his wife Ruth and two children, aged 17 and four, had moved from Hampshire to settle on the 15 acre croft of Blackhamar, Rousay.

"Having seen how friendly and helpful the Orkney people are, we are more convinced than ever we are doing the right thing," said Mr Corkett. Unfortunately, the family left a year later.

Bob and John Inkster with Bill Mainland unloading fish at Rousay pier in the early 1970s.
(Picture courtesy of Orkney Library photographic archive)

The Bard of Ballarat

The year of 1961 saw the death of George Corrigall, of West Ballarat, Harray, who was well known for his comic and topical ballads which he had performed at concerts all over the county.

Born in 1904, it was his talent and ability to make verse and set it to music that made him so renowned in his home county. He was initially shy of airing this talent and it was many years before he could be persuaded to perform in public.

Then, however, he became instantly popular and there was not a hall on the Mainland in which he had not appeared; and many in the isles had witnessed his shows too.

Making full use of Orkney dialect and idiom, he put into verse many features of the daily life of Orcadians, and tapes of his work were sent to Orkney exiles around the world.

Orkney Sheriff

Harald Leslie QC - an Orcadian whose family came from Stromness - was officially installed, at Kirkwall Sheriff Court, as Sheriff Principal of Orkney, Shetland, Caithness and Sutherland.

Sheriff Leslie - he had stood as the Labour candidate for the Orkney and Shetland constituency in the 1950 General Election - was still destined for higher office yet.

In 1965, at the age of 59, he was appointed to the £5,500 a year post of chairman of the Land Court and elevated to the peerage as Lord Birsay. His wife, and the new Lady Birsay, was the daughter of the late Provost James Marwick of Stromness.

Shop blaze

The shop owned by Mr David Sinclair of the Smithy, Flotta - it was one of three shops on the island in 1961 - was gutted by fire.

The building was destroyed with all its contents - groceries, clothing and hardware - but, more devastatingly, documents and records covering the island's history, over two or three centuries, were also lost in the fire.

Cinema blackout

The Mainland circuit of the Rural Cinema Scheme had to close through lack of support, a victim of television. There were nearly 3,000 TV licences in the county by 1961.

The death of a newspaper

Just eight months after the newspaper had celebrated its 100th anniversary, the editor of the *Orkney Herald* Jack Twatt announced in its edition of Tuesday, January 10, 1961, that it would be the final issue.

Staffing shortages had led "to the point where the production of the newspaper is no longer technically possible." The paper, after more than 5,000 editions, was no more.

The paper had first appeared on April 17, 1860, under the editorship of James Tait, with William Peace as secretary and treasurer. Mr Peace became sole propietor ten years later - and the Peace family ran the paper for the next half century until, in 1921, the business was purchased by Mr George Leonard and his brother-in-law James Twatt, who became editor. Mr Twatt became the sole owner in May, 1935, and his son John became the paper's final editor.

The *Orkney Herald* - a stalwart supporter of the Liberal cause - featured many well known writers including Bob Johnston who, as well as his regular feature from the imaginary parish of Stenwick, also produced weekly cartoons under the name of Spike; Ernest Marwick, with a weekly column "Sooan Sids"; David Horne who wrote sport under the name Cubbie Roo; and George Mackay Brown who wrote as Islandman.

The Germans return

A West German Naval squadron of three frigates visited Kirkwall in 1961 - the first German military craft to enter Orkney waters since World War Two.

Members of the crews took part in an "international" football match in the Bignold Park, and were beaten 7-0 by an Orkney team.

On July 17 the squadron sailed through Scapa Flow to attend Stromness Shopping Week, thus becoming the first German Naval unit to enter the Flow since the Kaiser's Fleet was scuttled there in 1919.

Sadly their visit was marked by tragedy when Kirkwall solicitor James Flett died on Kirkwall Pier while waiting to board the German flagship.

There was another distinguished visitor arriving by sea for Shopping Week in 1961 - the new £500,000 lighthouse support ship *Pole Star*, under the command of Captain A.W. Walker, which, like her predecessors, would be based in Stromness.

Moderator visits

The Moderator of the General Assembly of the Church of Scotland, Dr A.C. Craig, paid a ten day visit to Orkney in 1961. He toured the North Isles and was present at the induction of Rev I. G. Ramsay, who was the first minister of the whole island of Sanday. Previously the island had been divided into two, or even three, parishes.

Suleskerry rule OK

During investigations which followed the tragic death of a lightkeeper on Suleskerry, it was discovered that the 35 acre island of rock was in administrative limbo - it did not belong to Orkney, Caithness or Sutherland.

In December, 1961, it was announced that Orkney had laid a claim to it so that it might officially be part of the Orkney islands.

Golf record

Nairn golf professional Gregor McIntosh set a new record for the time when he completed the 18 holes of the Kirkwall golf course in a round of 66.

New bus station

The Kirkwall bus station on Great Western Road opened in 1961 with criticism that it was too far from the centre of town.

Veteran of the sea

Orkney bid a fond farewell to Captain William Moodie, for years the master of the *Amelia* which, in war and peace, made the weekly trip between Kirkwall and Leith, who died in 1961, aged 82.

Captain Moodie, who was awarded the DSC for his wartime sinking of a German U-boat, retired at the age of 74, but still made trips as relief master after that.

Royal message for TA

The Queen sent a message of welcome to the new TA unit in Orkney as the 861 LAA Battery amalgamated with the 540 LAA Regiment of the Lovat Scouts. In the 1962 New Year honours list, Major S. P. Robertson, Officer Commanding the Orkney and Shetland Battery of the Lovat Scouts, and head of the S. & J. Robertson oil company, was made an MBE.

Bigger Kirkwall

The boundaries of Kirkwall were extended, in April, 1961, to take in Hatston and Weyland Bay, thus bringing Kirkwall town council housing schemes within the boundary of the burgh.

Marathon effort to save crew

The loss of the Peterhead fishing boat *Daisy* 40 miles off Stronsay saw the Longhope lifeboat cover a marathon 240 miles with the crew on duty for nearly 30 hours.

The skipper of the *Daisy*, James Bruce, managed to send out a Mayday message which was fortunately picked up by another Peterhead vessel which raised the alarm.

Mr Jackie Groat - who had become secretary of the Longhope lifeboat, a role he was to continue until the 1990s - gave the call for the lifeboat to be launched. The Stronsay lifeboat was also launched and a relay of RAF Shackletons began an air search.

The ten crew of the *Daisy* were in their life raft for 20 hours before being picked up by the Danish passenger and cargo vessel, the *Mella Dam* which transferred the survivors to the Longhope lifeboat which had covered 95 miles to reach the scene.

It was the first operational mission of the new Longhope lifeboat *TGB* which arrived in Hoy in April, 1962, to continue the distinguished service of Longhope lifeboats which had saved 498 lives since 1884.

The new £37,000 *TGB* - sadly to be lost with her crew in Orkney's worst ever lifeboat disaster in 1969 - was 47 feet long, with a beam of 13 feet and a draught of 4 feet 4 inches, with twin 60hp diesel engines. She was divided into ten water-tight compartments and the engine room had a double bottom for maximum protection. As well as a radio telephone, she had a VHF link to enable communication with aircraft.

Her arrival at Longhope meant a farewell to the *Thomas McCunn*, the pre-vious lifeboat which had given such yeoman service in the Pentland Firth over the years. Her biggest rescues had been in World War Two when she saved 76 people from the ss *Chas D. McIver* in 1944, and 52 from the ss *Fort La Prairie* in 1945. The *Thomas McCunn* was to be transferred to Buckie.

The new *TGB*, having picked up the crew of the *Daisy*, landed them at Wick before returning to Longhope and the end of the 240 mile marathon.

Orkney witnessed another fishing boat disaster in the week before Christmas, 1962, when the Belgian trawler *Prince de Liege* ran aground on the Corn Holm between Copinsay and Deerness.

The 36 year old, 400 ton vessel was to become a total loss but all her crew of 13 were saved. They got off on liferafts and landed on the holm where they sheltered until picked up by the Stronsay lifeboat.

"We mistook Copinsay for Auskerry," explained the 61 year old Belgian skipper Frederik Vanderwal-Willems. He had retired but had agreed to do a trip to allow the regular skipper to have Christmas at home.

It was a sad end to the career of skipper Vanderwal-Willems, a man who had displayed his seamanship in World War Two when he sailed from Belgium in 1940 with 159 refugees on his trawler, many of them children, to escape the advancing Germans and then picked up troops from the inferno of the Dunkirk beaches, before bringing them all safely through to Britain. He had remained in Britain, based in Fleetwood, for the remainder of the war before returning to Belgium in 1945.

The rescued crew of the *Prince de Liege* were flown home in time to enjoy Christmas back in Belgium.

But the rescue which captured the public imagination in 1962 was that of the 70 year old William Fergus - a 20 stone bachelor - who was saved by Stronsay lifeboat after being carried out to sea, and adrift for four hours in the Atlantic, while lifting creels.

Fortunately his plight was spotted by lightkeepers at Noup Head who sounded the alarm for an air and sea search to be launched for Mr Fergus - described as "a tough nut who knows no fear" - who had returned to live with relatives at Noup Farm, Westray, after 50 years in the United States.

After the rescue, he calmly told reporters: "I whiled away the time chewing tobacco."

The Stronsay lifeboat landed him back at Pierowall Pier, where he delighted in telling the waiting undertaker George Sandison: "You won't have any coffin to make this time."

Twist champions

The dancing craze, the Twist, hit Orkney and the county's first Twist championship was decided at a dance in Kirkwall, judged by BBC compere Jameson Clark who was in the county to record the variety show "On Tour." The winners were J. Muir and Miss E. Pottinger of Stromness.

It was a time of swiftly changing cultures. Advertisements for concerts by Jimmy Shand now appeared alongside adverts for films starring pop stars like Chubby Checker and Billy Fury, and dances featuring chart toppers like Crispian St Peters and the Four Pennies.

Heavy duty power

It took 40 men to haul a new 33,000 volt power cable from the power station in Kirkwall to feed the new overhead electricity line between Kirkwall and Stromness, replacing two 11,000 volt cables which had been in use.

Record year for mart

The financial year 1961-62 was the best year, up until that time, in the history of Kirkwall Auction Mart with a turnover of £1,250,000 during the year, handling 17,000 cattle and 33,000 sheep.

New schools for Orkney

Kirkwall's new £110,000 Papdale Primary School, designed to take up to 500 pupils, was opened in 1962, having been built in the previous 18 months by Orkney Builders.

The official opening ceremony was performed by Mr John Shearer, who had retired the previous year after 15 years as the county education director, to be succeeded by Mr Robert Mack (50), who had been headmaster of Shapinsay school.

Plans were also announced to build a new Kirkwall Grammar School, near to the Papdale School, abandoning plans to convert the old school building in School Place. Instead it was proposed that the old school would become the site of new offices for Orkney County Council.

This immediately prompted opposition from Kirkwall Town Council members who dismissed any suggestion that the old school should be demolished.

The next new school to be opened was the £114,000 Sanday Junior Secondary School where there were 106 pupils under the headship of Mr John D. MacKay when the official opening ceremony was performed by Sheriff Harald Leslie in December, 1964.

There was a price to be paid for new buildings however when in March, 1962, the education committee announced the closure of three Orkney schools - Hundland, Grimness in South Ronaldsay and Kirbister in Orphir - and warned that several other small schools were earmarked for eventual closure.

New era for isles shipping

Travel to the North Isles had at last come into "the luxury class," reported *The Orcadian* as the new 895 ton, 150 feet long *Orcadia* arrived in Orkney to start a fresh chapter in the annals of island shipping in the 20th century.

The £230,000 motor vessel - launched at Aberdeen shipyard of Hall Russell in April, 1962 - was designed to carry 250 passengers and 100 cattle, and would serve the North Isles into the 1990s.

It was the first vessel to be built for the newly formed Orkney Islands Shipping Company which had been established, with Government support, to take over the services of the Orkney Steam Navigation Company.

The old company had been floundering for a dozen years or more. As early as 1955, the directors had declared that both their steamers, the *Earl Thorfinn* and the *Earl Sigurd,* were approaching the end of their economic life and the time had come for replacement vessels. A report, in 1957, by shipping expert William MacGillivray said it would cost £375,000 for new boats to replace the ageing North Isles ships. It would either require closer co-operation with the North of Scotland company, or money from the Government, he said.

The Secretary of State for Scotland said he was prepared to consider any proposals but, in 1959, when it came to producing the money, the Government announced assistance of just £250,000 for the provision of two new vessels, a figure derided by MP Jo Grimond as totally inadequate. Isles shipping, he said, had to be returned to a situation in which it was economic for islanders to use, citing the fact that it cost 36 shillings to transport a beast from the North Isles to Kirkwall.

By June, 1961, the end was nigh for the Orkney Steam Navigation Company - the firm which had served most of the North Isles throughout the century. The company could not raise enough capital locally to supplement the Government cash to replace the *Sigurd* and *Thorfinn*, both over 30 years old.

And so, on June 29, 1961, it was announced that, at the invitation of the Secretary of State for Scotland, Orkney's county convener Henry Scarth had formed a new company to run the service with ships which would be built by the Government and chartered to the new Orkney Islands Shipping Company, which would also take over the assets of the old Orkney Steam Navigation Company for the princely sum of £26,500.

Within weeks, the order had been placed with Hall Russell and Company for the new diesel-powered *Orcadia*. Previous vessels of that name had operated in the North Isles but the last *Orcadia* had, in fact, been operated not by the Orkney Steam Navigation Company but by the Stromness-based Bremner and Company which plied between Stromness and the South Isles. Bremner and Company had also warned that those services were under threat unless financial aid was forthcoming, and, in 1963, the Government agreed a £10,000 grant to subsidise the South Isles routes, now operated by Bremner and Company in the former Naval vessel *Hoy Head.*

The first master of the new *Orcadia* in 1962 was Captain George Harcus, who had previously, for ten years, been master of the *Earl Sigurd.*

But, in 1963, it was not the *Earl Sigurd* but the *Earl Thorfinn* which was withdrawn from service. On February 18, 1963, the veteran of the 1953 gale sailed from Kirkwall pier for the last time to the sound of wailing sirens and watched by a crowd of several hundreds. The ss *Earl Thorfinn* was on her way to a breakers yard at Bo'ness after 35 years of service to the North Isles.

It was soon announced that the Orkney Islands Shipping Company would investigate the possibility of using 40 seater hydrofoil craft - capable of speeds of up to 40mph - to operate a passenger service on the North Isles routes.

In fact it was 1964 before the hydrofoil, Shadowfax, arrived in the county to begin trials. Unfortunately, mechanical problems kept the vessel tied up at Kirkwall pier for six weeks. However, on September 5, an experimental regular service to the isles was commenced and proved "very speedy and comfortable" according to passengers.

A round trip to Papa Westray for an ambulance case took just 2 hours 20 minutes.

But, on September 22, 1964, the hydrofoil caught fire after leaving Kirkwall pier, and ten passengers had to be taken off. The vessel was out of action again - and, on October 1, it went back to Holland.

Six weeks later, Orkney had to say farewell to another vessel which had proved a much more reliable servant of the county. In November, 1964, the 72 year old mv *Iona,* operated by the Dennison Shipping Company, which had served the island of Shapinsay for so long, sank at her moorings off Balfour Village as a gale swept the county.

The standard of Orkney's transport services - the story that refused to go away for the remainder of the century - was an issue throughout the 1960s.

MP Jo Grimond dismissed the BEA air services in 1962 as "quite unsatisfactory." In response, BEA complained it had lost £1.75millions on its Scottish routes in five years, and a £500,000 a year Government subsidy was needed simply to sustain the Highlands and Islands services.

The airline even warned that it might be forced to withdraw from non-profitable routes to the North of Scotland if other airlines were allowed to cream off the lucrative trade on routes from London.

Although four engined Viscount aircraft would be introduced on Orkney routes, flights were cut from three to two a day, with mail and newspapers not arriving in the county until the afternoon.

"It would be appalling if we were driven back 30 or 40 years and become entirely dependent on sea communications in the islands - but this does not look impossible," said Mr Grimond.

Anthony Milward, BEA chief executive of the time, said the company could vastly improve Highlands and Islands services if it was given £1million annual grant. If there was no subsidy to cover losses in Scotland "then eventually we'll have to withdraw the services."

BEA then increased fares by 20 per cent in February, 1963. The Orkney-Aberdeen excursion return increased from £6 5s to £7 12s while Orkney to Glasgow or Edinburgh now cost £12 12s return. The cost of a return ticket from Orkney to London ranged from £24 off peak to £32 10s first class.

It was not much more encouraging for those who travelled by sea as, in 1962, the North of Scotland shipping company increased passenger and freight charges by ten per cent. A return passenger fare on the *St Ola* went up from 35 shillings to 39 shillings while Kirkwall to Aberdeen increased from 85 shillings to 93 shillings return.

The term "customer care" had still not entered the vocabulary however and the North company refused to introduce a booking system for motorists on the *St Ola,* but promised the ship would make a double trip if there were five cars left waiting at Scrabster. The shipping company eventually relented and introduced a booking system in 1965 - but only after a shambles that saw as many as 55 cars stranded at Scrabster.

However, we did get our "own" train! Or to more precise, the train, which made the daily four hour run from Inverness to Thurso was renamed "The Orcadian" in 1962.

The *Earl Thorfinn* and the *Earl Sigurd* at Kirkwall pier.

(Picture courtesy of Myra Hazell)

Passenger conditions were hardly luxurious on the *Earl Sigurd*. Pictured here are the Learmonth sisters, Ann and Jean, travelling to their home island of Sanday in 1956.

(Picture courtesy of Myra Hazell)

Castle's new owners

Balfour Castle was bought by Mr and Mrs Ted Zawadski, who already owned Balfour Mains, following the death of Mr David Balfour.

Balfour Castle had been built in 1847 on the site of a house which dated back another three centuries, and the Balfour family records, dating back 500 years, were donated to Kirkwall Library.

Legion club opens

Members of the Kirkwall branch of the British Legion opened their new club premises in the old community centre in Great Western Road, Kirkwall, in 1962.

The new community centre had been opened in Kirkwall Town Hall where, Orkney education committee ruled, no youth club dances would be permitted on Sundays.

Memorial protest

Visiting Australian war veteran Archie McLauchlan (65) started a storm by criticising the "absolutely disgusting" state of the Kitchener memorial at Marwick Head. It was "an insult to a very great man," he complained. The county council agreed to give the monument a clean-up.

Barriers chief retires

Mr John Robertson (63) who, as county surveyor, had become responsible for the upkeep of the Churchill barriers after World War Two, retired in 1962 after 43 years of public service. He was succeeded by Mr James Melrose, who had been assistant surveyor for the previous 20 years.

New surgeon

Orkney's first ever county surgeon Mr Ian McClure retired in 1962 after 34 years service to the county. In a packed Phoenix cinema, he was presented with a cheque for £2,500 collected by the people of Orkney.

Mr Peter Konstam (54), who had been working in Nigeria, was appointed as the new county surgeon. Peter Konstam had qualified in Frankfurt in 1933, and was made a Fellow of the Royal College of Surgeons at Edinburgh University two years later.

Tragic minister

Hoy and Walls was hit by tragedy in April, 1962, when - after being without a permanent minister for five years - the Rev H.T. Cartwright collapsed and died just a week after being inducted to the charge at Longhope. He had moved to the island from Kirkpatrick Fleming, near Lockerbie, to become minister of Hoy and Flotta.

Banking on success

A new banking venture - unique in the world - started when the motor boat *Otter Bank* did its first trip round the North Isles in 1962. The boat was a floating branch of the National Commercial Bank of Scotland, visiting the various North Isles to do business each week. Willie Groat was the accountant and David Irvine the skipper. (Picture from the files of *The Orcadian*)

Sisters follow U-boat father

The ghosts of the past were stirred as two daughters of the U-boat commander who sank the *Royal Oak* travelled to Scapa Flow to see the spot where the tragic warship lay.

The daughters had been very young children when their father Gunther Prien - commander of the German U-boat 47 - had infiltrated the defences of Scapa Flow in October, 1939, to destroy the *Royal Oak* with the loss of 833 lives.

And the girls were to scarcely know their father for, 18 months after his Scapa Flow mission, Commander Prien died on board the *U47* when she was sunk by HMS *Wolverine* off the Faroes in March,1941.

Prien's daughters Birgit (25) and Dagmar(23) came from Offenbach, near Frankfurt, where they had been raised by their mother who had remarried in 1944. They travelled to Orkney on the ferry *St Ola* as part of a three week motoring holiday in Britain.

In their short time in the county, they visited the Churchill barriers and saw the scene of their father's daring exploit and the spot where the *Royal Oak* lay.

Dagmar Prien, a schoolteacher, said: "My sister and I are profoundly moved to be here and to relive the emotions our father must have felt on that dark October

1963

night when he accomplished his feat. We feel he could just as easily have died here. I have never felt so near to my father as now.

"My sister was only two and a half and I was one year old when this happened. We cannot remember him but he is very much alive in our hearts. It is depressing to think that where father performed such a great deed, so many people had to die. Scapa Flow looks much bigger than we visualised."

They were not the only German visitors to Orkney to make news in 1963, but the arrival of 50 year old Henri Starke from Berlin had equally sad undertones for he was pursuing a legend which he hoped could spare him from the death sentence of a degenerative brain disorder.

Herr Starke had opposed the Nazis and had operated an underground escape organisation in Germany through the Hitler years. He blamed his treatment at the hands of the Nazis for the onset of a form of Parkinson's Disease.

Conventional medicine had failed to bring any relief when he heard of the legendary curative properties of a well on the island of Stronsay which he believed could restore him to health.

The legend was mentioned in Sir Walter Scott's book *The Pirate* and Herr Starke put his faith in an ancient Orkney quotation that said: "He who drinks of the wells of Kildinguie and eats of the dulse of Guiydin can be cured of anything but the black death."

Herr Starke travelled to Stronsay where three well known local men - John Dennison, who then owned the Stronsay Hotel, William Work of Holland House, and Robert Miller of Hunton - showed him the old well on the shore not far from where a monastery once stood. He filled bottles with the water and collected the nearby seaweed.

He said: "I know that no operation can cure me. It is a miracle, I feel, to have found the source of the legend. I am going to get the spring water analysed and only hope it can help me. I am delighted with my visit. I found everybody so helpful and friendly."

John Dennison said: "Nobody nowadays ever uses the well but I know of one man, a diabetic case, who said it was the only water that could quench his thirst."

TV honour for lifeboatman

Dan Kirkpatrick, one of the most decorated men of Britain's lifeboat service, featured as the subject of a special New Year edition of the television programme "This is your Life."

The 53 year old coxswain of the Longhope lifeboat had been lured to television studios in Glasgow where he was confronted by compere Eamonn Andrews with the famous red book to record the programme which catalogued his many exploits and rescues in the seas of Orkney.

MP Jo Grimond was among the guests interviewed and Dan Kirkpatrick's brother James was flown 12,000 miles from Melbourne, Australia, to appear. "Like all men of action, Dan said very little. But his exploits spoke volumes. It was a proud moment for Orkney," said *The Orcadian.*

Ironically, "action man" Dan had to watch the New Year screening of the programme from a bed in the Balfour Hospital, where he was recovering from illness.

But the year which began with nationwide television coverage ended with Dan Kirkpatrick back in the lifeboat in the

more familiar surroundings of the Pentland Firth - as it was feared that his two sons, Ray and Jack had been lost at sea in December, 1963.

The Longhope lifeboat was just one of the vessels called to join the search when the brothers were adrift for 17 hours in their fishing boat in the Pentland Firth. Fortunately, they were found safe and well the next day, having made the shelter of the Caithness coast.

But the biggest rescue in Orkney waters in 1963 was pulled off not by the Longhope lifeboat but the Stronsay lifeboat, which rescued 13 crewmen of the trawler *Aberdeen City* which grounded on Start Point, Sanday, in a westerly gale in September.

The trawler became a total loss but the rescued men were safely landed at Kettletoft, Sanday. Captain Edward Clements, the secretary of the Stronsay lifeboat, praised the efforts of the Stronsay men. "They did a very fine job in rescuing the 13 men - this is the best service we've had since the lifeboat station was reopened in 1952."

However, another mission by Stronsay lifeboat in March, 1963, was to remain a mystery of the sea. The lifeboat was launched after reports that a 35 feet long vessel - conjectured to be a Dutch or Swedish fishing boat - had been seen to founder, in a gale and poor visibility, just 200 yards from the shore of Wyre. No trace was ever found.

Betting shop refused

An application for a licence to open Orkney's first betting shop - at premises in the Strynd, Kirkwall - was rejected by the local licensing court in 1963.

The application was by the Thurso firm of William Arif, and was supported by a petition of 100 names in favour. However

the Chief Constable led the objections to the scheme.

After a two hour hearing, the reasons given for the rejection of the application was the proximity of Kirkwall Grammar School and the fact the proposed premises were within the Cathedral precincts.

Drama triumph for Kirkwall

There was as much drama behind the scenes as there was on stage as a team from Kirkwall Arts Club won the top honours in Scotland in the annual drama festival.

The arts club team won the All-Scotland finals of the Scottish Community Drama Association festival in Aberdeen with their production of an excerpt from the Willis Hall play *The Long and the Short and the Tall*, produced by John McDonald.

But it had been a race against time to even reach the final for the play cast of James Cruickshank, Ian Fleming, Billy Dass, Keith Donaldson, Mike Sweeney, John McDonald, Harry Cordock and Billy Jolly.

They had been due to fly to Aberdeen but fog cancelled all the planes so, with just 24 hours before they were due on stage, they had to charter the Stromness fishing boat *Venture* to take them across the Pentland Firth from where they made a night-time dash by Highland Omnibus coach to compete in Aberdeen, where they arrived at 4am.

Their success was marked back in Kirkwall with a civic reception before the cast set off again to compete in the All-Britain finals at Stirling. The founder of the club back in wartime days, the actor Donald Hewlett, flew to Orkney to join the celebrations.

Unfortunately, the members of the cast could not repeat their triumph at the All-Britain finals.

Viking anniversary

Kirkwall played host to 50 distinguished scholars and historians from Norway, Sweden, Denmark and Britain who came for a special conference to mark the 700th anniversary of the visit to Orkney by King Haakonsson before and after the Battle of Largs in 1263.

The Bishop of Stavangar preached at St Magnus Cathedral and a series of lectures and visits to archaeological sites were arranged as Kirkwall was bedecked with international flags.

The last act in the commemoration of Haakon Haakonsson - and his subsequent death in Bishop's Palace - took place on December 15, 1963, the anniversary of his death.

Mr Dagfinn Austad, from the Norwegian embassy, flew north to hand over an inscribed marble memorial tablet from the Norwegian government. It was to be placed where Haakon was buried before his body was taken back to Norway.

Rousay treasures found

A remarkable archaeological find at Westness, Rousay, saw the discovery of a Viking woman's grave by local grieve John Flett. The discovery was to lead to further finds which saw the Westness site being acclaimed as one of the most important in Western Europe.

The grave contained a fine brooch thought to date from 750 AD and of Celtic origin. The brooch was said to be one of the finest ever found in Scotland. All the items - including tortoise brooches, beads and knives - were sent to the National Museum of Antiquities of Scotland for analysis.

However, in the summer of 1968, a party of Norwegian students came to Orkney to carry out further excavations. By the time they had left, the party had uncovered "the most important grave to be excavated in Western Europe since the War."

The grave was probably that of a chieftain who had been buried with his shield and other objects dating back to the tenth century.

Mains gas dries up

The end was approaching for mains gas supplies as, in April 1963, the Scottish Gas Board said it would accept no more consumers in Kirkwall. Production had risen by 50 per cent and the local gas plant had reached full capacity.

It was a blow for Kirkwall Town Council. The burgh had enjoyed the benefits of a mains gas supply since 1838 and the council had intended to install gas central heating in all its new council houses.

However the news was worse in the West Mainland where it was announced that the 90 year old works in Stromness would close down. The plant was uneconomic and it would be too costly to update. Instead the Scottish Gas Board would supply consumers by means of bottled gas.

Air pioneer dies

The pioneer of Orkney's air services - and undoubtedly one of the county's "men of the century" - Captain Ted Fresson died, aged 71, in Inverness, in September, 1963.

The founder of Highland Airways, he had helped put Orkney at the very forefront of the aviation age in 1933 when he began scheduled services between Kirkwall and Inverness. He had given Orkney an air ambulance service and air mail.

He had remained a central figure in developing the county's transport links - flying over the Pentland Firth more than 3,000 times - for the next 15 years until he had become one of the first victims of the newly nationalised British aviation industry when he was made redundant from his post of North of Scotland manager of BEA.

Orkney's winter break

The winter of 1963 went down in history as one of the worst in Britain this century with most of the country paralysed by snow for most of January and February. However, for once, Orkney escaped the worst of it - although many of the lochs were frozen over for a time as the county suffered Arctic temperatures.

Warning signs for council

A Government White Paper on Local Government recommended the amalgamation of councils into larger authorities. This was welcomed by Orkney County Council but greeted with misgivings by Kirkwall Town Council which feared that its powers would be lost. It was a decade later that Orkney Islands Council came into being.

There were changes before that at Stromness where the town clerk for nearly 40 years, solicitor Mr J.E.P. Robertson retired in 1963 at the age of 81.

President assassinated

As the world reeled at the shocking news of the assassination of the American President John F. Kennedy, the Roman Catholic community in Orkney sent a letter of condolence to his widow, Jackie Kennedy.

They received a reply of acknowledgement from Mrs Kennedy with a photograph of the late president.

Charolais cattle arrive

February, 1963, witnessed the arrival in Orkney of the first Charolais cattle - a three week old heifer calf bought by D.A. Sinclair of How, Sanday. Within a month, a second calf was bought by John Traill Thomson of Nether Onston, Stenness.

Whirlwind Jim

Orcadian Jim Baikie - later to become a cartoonist with an international reputation - was, in 1963, a 22 year old corporal in the RAF in Cyprus where he was the bass guitarist of the Whirlwinds - "the most popular rhythm group on the island."

Blazing a trail

Orkney's Sheriff Principal Harold Leslie became a CBE and Mrs Eliza Isabella Leask (72) of Glaitness House, Kirkwall, the Orkney organiser of the WVS Clothing for Refugees scheme and a tireless worker for charity, was made an MBE in the 1963 Queen's birthday honours list.

Rousay ferryman Mansie Flaws (left) is interviewed by Robbie Shepherd for the television programme Out and About. (Picture courtesy of Grampian Television)

April, 1962, saw Orkney's first Ban the Bomb march after the formation of a local branch of the Campaign for Nuclear Disarmament. Chairman Ian MacInnes led the march from Kirkwall to Stromness. (Picture courtesy of Orkney Library photographic archive)

Trawler tragedies leave their mark

1964

The years of 1964 and 1965 were remembered for three major trawler disasters in Orkney waters as the sea took its relentless toll of the fishing industry.

In January, 1964, Longhope lifeboat helped to rescue the 14 crew of the Aberdeen trawler *Ben Barvas* which went aground on the Pentland Skerries, en route to Iceland.

It was a perilous operation as the fuel tanks of the trawler burst and diesel oil covered the water. Five of the crew, including the youngest member, 15 year old James Simpson of Aberdeen, managed to take to a life raft and they were picked up by the trawler *Ben Screel*.

However the remaining nine crewmen were still in a life-threatening situation as they remained on the stricken *Ben Barvas*. Fortunately, the Longhope lifeboat, under coxswain Dan Kirkpatrick, was able to fire a rocket line on to the trawler and the remaining men were dragged to safety by surf buoy.

"The sea was covered with fishboards, wreckage and diesel oil. We could hardly get hold of the men," said Dan Kirkpatrick. "One old man of about 60 seemed to have swallowed a lot of oil. We got them off in little over an hour. They had to be dragged through the surf. At times the sea broke over them and they were under water. It was one of the trickiest jobs we have had."

The five survivors on the *Ben Screel* were transferred to the lifeboat and all 14 crewmen were landed at St Margaret's Hope.

The Longhope lifeboat crew included Dan Kirkpatrick's two sons Jack and Ray, and four members of the Johnston family. They all later received gallantry awards for their part in the rescue, and Dan Kirkpatrick was honoured with his second RNLI silver medal.

The wreck of the *Ben Barvas* - which had only been built in 1957 - was bought by local fisherman William Mowat of School House, South Parish, South Ronaldsay.

A year later, it was the turn of Stromness lifeboat, under coxswain Alfie Sinclair, which was in action when the ten year old, 800 ton Hull trawler *Kingston Turquoise* sank in four minutes after hitting the North Shoal - a reef which had been the graveyard of so many ships - nine miles off the Brough of Birsay.

One man was lost but 19 other crewmen - including the youngest, 15 year old galley boy Ralph Bennett - who had been drifting for three hours in two life rafts were picked up safely after an RAF Shackleton had helped guide Stromness lifeboat to the scene.

The trawler had been returning home from Iceland with 1,400 kits of fish, on Monday, January 25, 1965, when the starboard side of the vessel was ripped open, giving the radio operator Eric Stansfield only precious seconds to send out a Mayday message.

Skipper Colin Cross (32) said: "Everything happened so suddenly that we were in the water before we realised we had struck something." Another crewman said: "She went down like a rocket. We hardly had time to think."

Missing was deckhand Walter Denton (50), a veteran of wartime convoys, who had jumped into the water with his pet dog. The skipper said: "We heard his cries for about an hour. We lost sight of him and no more was heard."

The survivors were landed at Stromness and flown South the next day.

Just months later, the same North Shoal which had swallowed up the *Kingston Turquoise* claimed another victim when in May, 1966, the Norwegian coaster *King's Star*, just eight months old and carrying a crew of 16 with a cargo of coal, struck the reef. Although badly holed, she managed to refloat and, in a race against time, the ship made the safety of Stromness before she sank.

A week after the loss of the *Kingston Turquoise,* a worst disaster struck - with 13 Aberdeen fishermen being lost to an unknown grave.

The Aberdeen trawler *Blue Crusader* had been overwhelmed by heavy seas somewhere off Orkney - the last contact with her was off North Ronaldsay - on her way to the Faroese fishing grounds.

The *Blue Crusader* was assumed lost, with her 13 crew, after being reported missing for more than two weeks. The only trace was a lifebuoy washed up on Auskerry on February 5, 1965, found by Stronsay fisherman John Stevenson in his boat *Guiding Star.* A fruitless air, land and sea search found nothing else.

Others were more fortunate. The Aberdeen trawler *Loch Kildonan* ran aground in the Bay of Holland, Stronsay, in March, 1965. She was refloated by Stronsay lifeboat but a court of inquiry later censured the trawler skipper for being drunk.

It was not only British fishermen who suffered the wrath of Orkney waters.

In April, 1965, a small Norwegian whaler *Jerv* grounded in Hoy Sound. The crew of four safely landed ashore after taking to their rubber dinghy - and then walked the three miles into Stromness, carrying their life raft with them.

The following month a "ghost ship" was towed into Holm Sound. She was the Norwegian fishing vessel *Judy* which had been abandoned by her crew in a North Sea Gale.

And it was another Norwegian fishing boat, the *Norholmen* which ran aground in Hoy Sound in November, 1966. Fortunately, the crew of nine managed to get away by life raft before the vessel became a total loss.

Remembered by generations of Kirkwall schoolchildren is the old Rocky Shop at the top of the Strynd. (Picture courtesy of Orkney Library photographic archive)

Typhoid city under siege

Public concern - verging on panic - gripped Orkney as a Typhoid outbreak in Aberdeen reached alarming proportions.

Many Orkney students were studying in the city and they were due to return home to Orkney for their summer holidays in June, 1964.

Orkney's Medical Officer of Health, Dr A.S. Brodie, introduced strict precautions to guard against the disease spreading to the islands - having to balance the need for vigilance against the danger of public hysteria.

The North of Scotland shipping company - "in response to public concern" - altered the sailing arrangements of the *St Ninian* and *St Magnus* to bypass Aberdeen and sail direct to Leith.

Dr Brodie said: "It is important that we in Orkney realise that, because of our close connections, both in commerce and in travel, with Aberdeen, we should consider ourselves very susceptible to the import of the infection."

At the moment there was no question of limiting public movement, but he added: "Arrangements have been made by the local hospitals for the isolation and treatment of any cases that may arise."

Plans were introduced for the inoculation of hospital and local authority staff who would have to deal with any local outbreak, and Dr Brodie gave the assurance: "Medical treatment has gone a long way since the last case of Typhoid fever was notified in Orkney 20 years ago. Powerful drugs are now available, highly effective in the treatment of this illness."

It was the last health crisis that Dr Brodie would face in Orkney. A few months later he moved to become Medical Superintendent of 17 hospitals in the Borders. Dr Roderick MacLennan (47), who was working in Sussex but originally from Edinburgh, was appointed as the new Medical Officer of Health for Orkney.

Kirkwall international airport

Kirkwall became Britain's smallest international airport in April, 1964, as the Danish air company Scanfly opened an air service between Scandinavia and the Faroes, via Orkney.

The service was expanded the following year by Faroe Airways, allowing Orcadians to fly direct from Kirkwall to Denmark and Norway.

Unfortunately, it was not to last and, in September, 1967, the airline announced the service was to be axed.

Orkney theatre

Fund-raising was underway as plans were announced by a federation of local clubs and societies to convert Kirkwall's Temperance Hall into a theatre. It was estimated that the theatre scheme would cost £16,000.

Within three years the target had been met and the Orkney Arts Theatre was officially opened on Friday, October 13, 1967, by Mr D. Mathers, depute director of the Arts Council in Scotland. The first professional performance, the following week, was the Pitlochry Festival Theatre Company's production of *School for Scandal.*

Monster landing

An Edinburgh man Mr Douglas Blyth, who was on holiday at the Merkister Hotel, landed a 17lb female brown trout while fishing in the Harray Loch.

It was over 34 inches long with a girth of more than 19 inches. It was estimated to be 14 years old.

It was believed to be the largest trout to be caught by rod in Orkney. Orkney's all-time record, a trout taken from the Stenness Loch in March, 1889, and weighing more than 29lbs, was caught with a set line.

Monster attack

A helicopter, which was chartered by the county council to carry equipment for a new water scheme in Hoy inaccessible by road, received a hostile reception from the native population. The helicopter was attacked by hordes of bonxies, or great skuas, enraged at the invasion of their air space.

Council buys farm

Orkney County Council paid £26,000 in 1964 to buy 230 acres of the farms of Weyland and Watersfield, near Kirkwall, to be used for further education, with the farm leased to the North of Scotland College of Agriculture.

Solo taxi service

Orkney had just one registered taxi in 1964 - operated by James Donaldson (45) of George Street, Kirkwall. He parked at a taxi stance at the head of Kirkwall pier and he guaranteed to get his cab anywhere in Kirkwall within three minutes of a call, offering a 24 hour day and night service.

Also in 1964, Mrs Thora Spence of the Mistra, Evie, was granted a licence for what was then Orkney's only public house. All the other bars in the county had either hotel or club licences.

All 47 passengers and four crew had a lucky escape in October, 1979, when this Guernsey Airways Viscount aircraft, operating on a charter to Alidair, crash landed at Kirkwall Airport. (Picture courtesy of Orkney Library photographic archive)

Fifty escape ship disaster

Fifty people - including nine women and a ten year old boy - were saved from disaster as an 8,000 ton East German cargo ship was lost on the Pentland Skerries just months after being launched.

The *Kathe Niederkirchner*, built in 1964, was bound for her home port of Rostock with a cargo of sugar from Havana, Cuba, when she grounded on the skerries and subsequently sank in August, 1965.

Most of the ship's company had been asleep when the ship struck in the early morning.

The crew and passengers, including the ten year old, managed to get away in their own lifeboats - along with the ship's Alsatian dog Ajax - but were forced to

1965

leave behind all their personal possessions which, nine hours later, disappeared into the sea as the ship sunk.

Fortunately calm sea conditions, despite poor visibility, allowed the survivors to land on the skerry and seek the hospitality of the only inhabitants - the three lightkeepers David Leslie, Eric Malcolm and Calum MacAulay. "They ate practically everything in the lighthouse," Mr Leslie commented later.

The marooned East Germans were later taken to St Margaret's Hope by the Longhope lifeboat, and then driven to Kirkwall where the shipwrecked men and women were kitted out in new clothing by William Jolly of the Shipwrecked Mariners benevolent society. The women even got the luxury of British cosmetics.

As the survivors were later airlifted to London on the first leg of their journey home, the ship's master Captain Horst Wentzel (44) said: "We are eternally grateful to the lightkeepers for everything they did for us. We are also deeply touched by all the wonderful kindness shown by the people of Orkney after the rescue of the ship's crew and passengers."

THE ORCADIAN, THURSDAY, MARCH 3, 1966

E £5 | **SHE WON'T MAKE IT FOR SHOPPING WEEK . . .**

vice | **"MISS WORLD 1965"**

Orkney's own Miss World as Lesley wins top beauty contest

Orkney could share the glamour and glitter of the 1965 Miss World contest as the title was won by Stromness-born Lesley Langley.

The 21 year old blonde model and typist, whose home was in Weymouth, Dorset, and who already held the Miss United Kingdom title, received a £2,500 prize for the Miss World success.

Langley was her stage name and she was, in fact, born Lesley Hill at 5 Alfred Terrace, Stromness, on March 26, 1944 - safely delivered by Stromness medical officer Dr Cromarty.

She was the daughter of Captain Ormonde Hill - a master of one of the wartime boats in the Flow - and his wife Doreen, who reminisced with *The Orcadian* in 1965: "What a happy time it was, in spite of it being wartime."

And commenting on her daughter's success, she said: "It seems to me that she must have taken away a little of the magic from your wonderful islands when we left."

Sadly, it was understood that Captain Hill had died later in the war.

Lesley Langley was estimated to have reaped £30,000 in personal appearances during her year as Miss World but her busy schedule prevented her from accepting an invitation to open the 1966 Stromness Shopping Week.

" Miss World 1965," Stromness-born Lesley Langley, has sent us this picture of herself addressed " To the people of Orkney, with very best affectionate wishes." Lesley was very anxious to come to Orkney this summer to open the annual " Shopping Week " in Stromness. Unfortunately, she informs us, she will be on a world tour at the time of the gala week. But she hopes to be able to arrange a visit

Churchill funeral

The death of Sir Winston Churchill - the man whose order to build the Churchill barriers literally changed the shape of Orkney - brought forth a eulogy of tributes in the county.

The wartime leader had been a frequent visitor to Scapa Flow in two world wars as First Sea Lord and later Prime Minister.

It was, to a large extent, his decision that the causeways, linking the Orkney Mainland to Burray and South Ronaldsay, should be built to protect Scapa Flow after the 1939 *Royal Oak* disaster.

"The death of Sir Winston Churchill puts an end to a career the like of which we shall not see again," said Orkney MP Jo Grimond. "He was one of the great leaders in the last great conventional war. He was the last politician who was able to carve out his own part among the political parties."

Sheriff D.B. Keith, before commencing the business at Kirkwall Sheriff Court, said: "The old warrior has died. And with his passing much virtue has gone . . . the world will never be the same again. To the end he held the stage and the limelight never flickered from his face."

Angus Findlater who, in May, 1965, recorded one of Orkney's best known songs of the 20th century "Lonely Scapa Flow," written by Allie Windwick. The song was one of four Allie Windwick compositions on the record Owre the Ferry, which Angus recorded with Allie's nephew Sandy Windwick.

(Picture courtesy of Orkney Library photographic archive)

Sporting heroes

Kirkwall-born Eric Thompson (27), a former Kirkwall Grammar School pupil and son of Mr and Mrs D.E. Thompson of Weyland Terrace, Kirkwall, was Orkney's first international cricketer of the 20th century.

He was a member of the 1965 Scotland cricket team which beat Ireland by an innings and 22 runs in Dublin. A fast bowler and useful bat, it was his first cap as he took five Irish wickets for only 11 runs in 11 overs.

Kirkwall could boast another sports star that year as Colin Wooldrage (24) of The Quadrant, Kirkwall, held four Scottish records for weightlifting in the 12 stone class in 1965.

He came from a sporting family. His father held the record of 17 appearances in Orkney-Shetland inter-county football matches.

But Colin went even better in 1966 when he became the British light-heavy-weight- weight-lifting champion.

Competing in the tournament at Doncaster, he broke no fewer than nine Scottish records - lifting up to 370lbs.

Independent TV

June 25, 1965, saw the arrival in Orkney of independent commercial television as programmes from Grampian TV came on the air in the islands for the first time, thanks to a new transmitter at Rumster Forest, Caithness.

The number of licensed TV sets in Orkney increased to 4,071 that year. Amongst them would have been TV viewers in Shapinsay who, after a ten year wait, were connected to mains electricity when a submarine power cable was laid across the String to the island.

A cable was also laid to Rousay but islanders there had to wait until 1966 for the big "switch on."

The Oil Age looms

Orkney was on the verge of an industrial revolution which would herald the Oil Age, and an era of some prosperity, as the Government announced in 1965 that areas of sea around Orkney and Shetland would be opened up for exploration by oil and gas prospecting companies.

However, workmen nearer home, working on the new £120,000 pier for Papa Westray thought they had struck oil already - or, at least, they had found rock which seemed to contain oil and which certainly ignited when put to a match.

There was speculation - with trial North Sea drillings already underway further south - that Orkney could strike it rich.

Air veteran

BEA pilot Captain David Barclay retired in April, 1965, after 35 years flying during which he had carried out 2,000 mercy ambulance flights, mostly to the islands. He had first flown to Orkney in the 1930s when he worked with Captain Ted Fresson, the pioneer of island aviation.

Loss of an Orkney scholar

Orkney mourned the death in 1965 of one of the county's most distinguished sons. Dr Hugh Marwick, historian, teacher, archaeologist and scholar, died at the age of 83 after a career which had seen him serve both as headmaster of Kirkwall Grammar School and Orkney's county education director.

Just a year before his death, he was honoured as the first scholar from outside Norway to receive an honorary doctorate from Bergen University. With his death, his valuable collection of Orkney books was gifted to the town of Kirkwall.

Pop pioneers

The Orkney group the Nomads were credited with being the first group from the county to cut a "pop" record. The group - Ian Farquhar, Ken Ross, Brian Peace and Roy Wood - made the recording at the Grampian studio in Wick in 1965.

Both songs on the disc - "I'm Coming Home" and "Hey Little Girl" - were written by Roy Wood.

Silence is broken

Two Orcadian brothers John Tulloch (85) of Yorkton, Saskatchewan, Canada, and Robert Tulloch (75) of Hornsby, New South Wales, Australia, broke a 55 year silence when they spoke to each other over the telephone in 1965.

Although they had regularly corresponded by letter, the last time they had heard each other's voice was in 1909 when the two brothers, both born in Eday, parted in Orkney - John to go to Canada and Robert to Australia.

Strike holds Orkney to ransom

1966

Islanders are always at the mercy of the sea but a six week shipping strike in 1966 left Orcadians as virtual hostages in their own land.

A state of siege imposed by striking seamen brought Orkney's economy almost to its knees - with the islands having to stockpile two million eggs and tons of butter and cheese on one side of the Pentland Firth while tourists, cars and essential commodities built up at the other side.

The strike by members of the National Union of Seamen had been threatening for weeks before it began in May. The impact on Orkney was immediate as the North of Scotland shipping company vessels - including the *St Ola* - and the Orkney Islands Shipping Company ferries *Orcadia* and *Earl Sigurd* were tied up.

Sanday District Council, under the chairmanship of county councillor Mrs Christine Muir, held an emergency meeting at which it was decided to telegraph the Prime Minister Harold Wilson appealing for a state of emergency to be declared in the isles. Supplies of fuel and animal feedstuffs were urgently required. "We are very angry as we feel we are being held to ransom," said the island headmaster Mr John D. MacKay.

There were complaints that the Western Isles were getting a lifeline service from Naval ships while Orkney was left at the mercy of the dictatorial powers of members of the seamen's strike committee in Aberdeen.

An ad hoc emergency committee under the chairmanship of the county convener Henry Scarth was set up to negotiate with the strikers, over the shipment of essential supplies, but there was criticism that the committee was following a policy of appeasement as the convener appealed to local boats not to offend the unions by attempting to break the strike.

Any sympathy for the seamen's wage claim soon evaporated in most quarters as it became obvious that island communities were much worse hit than the real power-brokers in the major cities of the South. In fact, it was felt that Orkney was condemned to take the role of the "sacrificial lamb" in what was meant to be a nationwide strike.

Some items were scarce in the shops before the Aberdeen strike committee relented to the extent of allowing special sailings of the cargo vessel *St Rognvald* to bring vital and essential goods to Orkney, while the *Earl Sigurd* could go out to the North Isles which were worst affected.

By this time, most in Orkney had abandoned any concern about offending the strikers - and a small "pirate fleet" of Orkney fishing boats was operating a clandestine shuttle service across the Pentland Firth, bringing in supplies and taking out eggs.

Nevertheless, Orkney Egg Producers Ltd had to hire a hangar at Hatston to stockpile two million eggs which it was feared would have to be dumped.

By June 9, petrol and fuel oil were running short and men would soon be thrown out of work. Both the Kirkwall Creamery and the Scapa distillery were forced to temporarily stop production because of lack of fuel.

Although air transport continued, large parts of the Orkney tourist industry were brought to a standstill, and new cars, valued at £50,000 - £60,000 were left languishing at Scrabster. The shipment out of Orkney of around 1,000 cattle was held up.

On June 14, the *St Rognvald* arrived with what the Aberdeen strikers warned would be her last "mercy cargo." A member of the strike committee said the strikers were no longer prepared to act as wholesale grocers for the islands - a remark that caused bitter resentment in Orkney.

On June 24, after increasing protests to the Government, it was agreed that two landing craft manned by the Army and Navy would be sent North to supply the islands. Thankfully, they were not to be needed for long as, on June 29, a peace deal was agreed nationally to settle the strike.

It was just in time to allow Orkney's stockpiled two million eggs to be saved by being processed for manufacturing purposes.

The North of Scotland, Orkney and Shetland Shipping Company came under the ownership of the shipping giant P&O at the start of the 1970s. P&O immediately announced the building of a new *St Ola*, a £1.4 millions roll-on, roll-off vehicle ferry, which came into service on the Pentland Firth route in 1974. (Picture courtesy of Orkney Library photographic archive)

Old Man is conquered

Three mountaineers scaled the heights as they conquered the 450 feet high stack of the Old Man of Hoy in a record-breaking 28 hour climb in July, 1966.

The climbers were Chris Bonington (31), Tom Patey (34) and the Rhodesian Rusty Baillie (25). Bonington and Baillie had previously conquered the North Face of the Eiger.

Chris Bonington told *The Orcadian:* "The Old Man of Hoy presents a great challenge, one of the few left in Britain today. There is nothing like this rock anywhere else in the country."

The climb began on July 16 and the trio enjoyed three sunny days, with only a breeze, as they completed the ascent in 28 hours climbing time. They celebrated reaching the top by lighting a bonfire and building a cairn on the summit.

The main hazard, they said, had proved to be the nesting fulmars which constantly vomited over the climbers.

"I feel the same satisfaction as on reaching the summit of a Himalayan peak," said Chris Bonington afterwards. "It seemed unbelievable that we could be standing on a virgin top in the British Isles."

The following year, Bonington, Patey and Baillie all returned to climb the Old Man again - but this time the ascent was to occupy the screens of millions of TV viewers all over the country as it was part of a major television outside broadcast, costing nearly £50,000 to produce.

The climbers climbed the Yesnaby Castle by way of a curtain-raiser for the TV coverage on July 8-9 which, with commentary by Chris Brasher, was to see six climbers make the ascent of the Old Man: Chris Bonington, Tom Patey, Ian McNaught-Davis, Pete Crew, Dougal Haston and Joe Brown. (Joe Brown was to return 15 years later for another live TV spectacular, climbing the Old Man with his teenage daughter Zoe).

However, as well as the six televised climbers in 1967, another four men also had to make the ascent, and their job was even more arduous for Rusty Baillie, John Cleare, Ian Clough and Hamish McInnes had to carry the TV cameras and transmitter equipment.

The television coverage was later to win the TV award for the most spectacular outside broadcast of the year.

It certainly made dramatic television, but it soon became apparent that the Old Man of Hoy, which had previously been regarded as impossible to climb, was, in fact, within the capabilities of most competent enthusiasts.

This was illustrated in August, 1967, when three young weekend climbers from Sheffield - John Hadfield (22), John Whitley (22) and Bob Turner (17) - climbed the Old Man, with virtually no publicity, and built their own cairn at the top. Another group of English climbers followed suit the next month.

By May, 1968, the stack had been conquered by the first woman, 23 year old Christine Crawshaw from Yorkshire who climbed it with her husband, and in July, 1968, it was rush hour traffic for the Old Man as a team of Territorial Army signallers not only reached the top but set up a radio station on the summit.

And, on September 4, 1968, Orkney's most famous landmark was climbed by a seven year old boy, Roy Clarkson, from Lancashire, who scaled it, roped to his father Arthur, a friend of Chris Bonington. Suddenly, the Old Man did not seem so invincible.

Rugby debut

What was to become Orkney Rugby Club took shape in 1966 when, for what was said to be the first time this century, enthusiasts got together in the county to organise some trial games.

The first rugby inter-county match of the modern era was played on April 1, 1967, and saw Orkney beat Caithness by 20 points to five. It was the first time in 70 years that the two counties had met on the rugby field. The next match, in October, 1967, saw Caithness gain revenge with a 5-3 victory.

Lord Lieutenant dies

The death of Orkney's Lord Lieutenant Lt Col Robert Scarth (71) of Binscarth occurred in May, 1966. He had been the Queen's representative in Orkney since 1958. He was succeeded as Lord Lieutenant by his cousin, Col Henry Scarth.

Giant lobster

An 11lb lobster, 32 inches long and estimated to be half a century old, was found by 32 year old John Drever of Mount Drive, Kirkwall, in Kirkwall Bay.

It was sent to the Orkney Fishermen's Society in Stromness and presented to the town's museum.

However, the monster find still did not match the previous biggest specimen recorded by *The Orcadian* - a 12lb lobster, measuring nearly a yard, found by Finstown garage proprietor Leslie Esson.

New arrival

A new £67,000 maternity unit at the Balfour Hospital was opened by Mrs Laura Grimond in July, 1966. The first baby born there was 5lb 7oz Stuart Balfour Laing, the son of Mr and Mrs Albert Laing of Old Scapa Road, Kirkwall, who actually arrived in this world a couple of days before the official opening.

Canadian century

Westray-born Miss Mina Ingram, née Rendall, who had emigrated 80 years earlier, celebrated her 101st birthday in Winnipeg, Canada. Nearer home, Miss Margaret Scott, born at Thorness, Sanday, celebrated her 100th birthday at an old folk's home in Arbroath.

Cathedral minister

The minister of St Magnus Cathedral Rev John Rose left Orkney to move to the charge of West St Giles in Edinburgh in October, 1966. He was replaced by a locum minister Dr Alexander White (71) who sadly died on December 31, 1966. The Rev Bill Cant - who had been minister of St Thomas Church, Leith, since 1960 - was eventually confirmed as the new Cathedral minister on August, 1968.

Long serving vet

When Kirkwall veterinary surgeon George Johnson retired in 1966, he had devoted more than 37 years to animal welfare in the county.

Front page news

News returned to the front page of *The Orcadian* on November 3, 1966, for the first time since World War One. Front page news had been carried from December 12, 1908, until March 11, 1916, when newsprint shortages forced the size of the newspaper to be reduced with advertisements filling the front page instead.

Orkney seethes in ferment

An increasingly angry mood of protest and frustration which had been growing for a year in Orkney manifested itself in a bitter demonstration as a Government minister visited the county.

Secretary of State for Scotland Mr Willie Ross arrived to be greeted by a poster campaign demanding Orkney's return to Denmark (Orkney had been part of the Kingdom of Denmark until 1468) and an effigy of the minister hanging at Stromness pierhead.

Orkney was certainly in ferment if not ready for outright rebellion. There was still a lingering bitterness that the county and its population had been the "sacrificial lamb" in the previous year's shipping strike.

And in 1967 a series of grievances accumulated as fears mounted that the Labour Government - in the guise of the Scottish Office at St Andrew's House in Edinburgh - was set to steamroller through proposals which would destroy Orkney's separate identity.

The Government had ordered that talks should begin on proposals for Orkney, Shetland and Caithness police forces to be merged. It then produced legislation to combine the water authorities of Orkney, Shetland, Caithness and Sutherland - pushing the merger through the House of Commons despite a major revolt by peers in the House of Lords, with eight peers writing to *The Times* in support of Orkney's case.

A Royal Commission on local government visited the county and it was feared that the next step would be that Orkney would be swallowed up by a huge local authority covering all the Highlands and Islands.

Orkney MP Jo Grimond complained that Harold Wilson's government was pursuing a policy of "bureaucracy and uniformity gone mad." He hit out at the "rigid and over-centralised government" accusing the Scottish Office of acting as "colonial administrators for London."

Lord Birsay - formerly Sheriff Harald Leslie, and an Orcadian himself - took a verbal swipe at the bureaucratic stranglehold from the South which was dragging Orkney down. But then a report, produced under his chairmanship, proposed that Orkney health matters should be controlled by a Highlands and Islands body, and recommended the withdrawal of permanent doctors from Flotta and Papa Westray.

At the same time, there was a growing unease in Orkney at the fragile state of the economy which was being seriously rocked by increased air and shipping fares. Unemployment had increased by two per cent - to be above the Scottish

1967

average - and Orkney seemed to have gained little from the newly formed Highlands and Islands Development Board. In the first year, Orkney had received just £3,690 out of a total £129,652 in HIDB grants, and only £12,900 out of £708,635 in loans (whereas Shetland got £78,000). British Airways had wanted to increase fares by as much as 50 per cent.

There were complaints too that the government's Selective Employment Tax was costing Orkney £180,000 a year - with nothing in return.

And so it was that a poster campaign began in the Summer of 1967 demanding "Back to Denmark." A typical poster proclaimed: "Harold Wilson talks but does nothing. Orkney is dying under British rule. Re-unite with Denmark now."

Kirkwall town councillor Edwin Eunson said: " No doubt it will be considered a prank but at the same time it shows the underlying dissatisfaction in Orkney with Whitehall and St Andrew's House for the way they completely ignore our wishes and protests."

The Scots Secretary Mr Willie Ross arrived at Kirkwall pier by fishery cruiser to be welcomed by the posters and slogans, and to be told by county convener Henry Scarth of the "widespread feelings of resentment and frustration permeating the community resulting from the actions of St Andrew's House in the last 12 months."

The next day Mr Ross went to Stromness where he met a barrage of protest banners including "Willie Ross -

Dead Loss." The St Andrew's Cross was at half mast and an effigy of the minister hung from a lamp post. Stromness was particularly aggrieved because the Government had failed to back new pier developments for the town and the fishing industry.

The Scots Secretary dismissed the posters as the "work of 14 year olds," but even Orkney Presbytery condemned the Government for "destroying the soul of Orkney."

A publication advocating independence for Orkney was distributed by an organisation calling itself the Independent Orkney Party. No one put a head over the parapet to claim responsibility, but within months a newly formed Orkney branch of the Scottish National Party claimed more than 200 members in the county.

Shetland went a step further with plans to petition the Queen, asking for a larger measure of self government and control. Stromness Town Council agreed to support the petition but Kirkwall town councillors and Orkney County Council decided not to add their weight.

But Orkney did go ahead with a petition of its own and Jo Grimond MP handed a petition, signed by 6,000 people, to Downing Street, calling on Harold Wilson to ensure that, in any reorganisation of councils, Orkney would retain its own local authority and not be part of a pan-North of Scotland authority. The petition was passed on to Scots Secretary Willie Ross.

Orkney's case was certainly helped when, in January, 1968, the first meeting of the new North of Scotland Water Authority had to be cancelled because the weather prevented Orkney and Shetland members from reaching Wick. An Orcadian chorus of "Told You So" reached government ears.

Uranium discovered

Orcadians got the first inkling of what was to be a major controversy a decade later when deposits of ore containing uranium were discovered on Stroma in the Pentland Firth.

The discovery was made by Mr Jack Saxon, who worked for the UK Atomic Energy Authority at Dounreay. It was found in the rocks, up to 350 million years old, that make up the island.

Although the proportion of uranium oxide was small, it was higher than any other known deposits in Britain. All Britain's uranium was imported and world reserves were said to be low.

Mr Saxon said that while it might not prove economically worthwhile to mine the ore, it should not be written off as valueless to the country.

Hovercrafts ahoy

Caithness County Council authorised that county's development officer Mr A.V. Levens to "give all assistance in his power" to promote a proposed hovercraft link between John o' Groats and South

Ronaldsay. Mr Anthony Wedgwood-Benn, Minister of Technology, (later just plain Tony Benn) said he believed the future of the hovercraft to be at least as great as that of aircraft. We're still waiting, of course.

Return of isles air service

For the first time since the outbreak of World War Two, the North Isles of Orkney could enjoy the "luxury" of a regular scheduled air service as the county welcomed the arrival of Loganair.

Curiously, the services, when they began in September, 1967, were under the auspices not of the airline but Orkney Islands Shipping Company which chartered Loganair to operate the flights.

It had been a long wait. The start of the isles air link had been announced back in 1965 and Loganair formally applied for the licence to operate the service - using a £17,500 two engined Britten Norman Islander aircraft - on November 17, 1965.

At first, it was announced that the starting date would be June, 1966, but that year came and went without a plane to be seen on a scheduled flight.

The Renfrew-based Loganair had been started by the civil engineering magnate Mr William Logan but, sadly, Mr Logan (52) was to be killed in an air crash near Inverness before the Orkney service got off the ground. (Loganair was later taken over by the National Bank of Scotland in October, 1968).

Eventually, August 16, 1967, was announced as the start-up date but this was to prove an embarrassing anti-climax as - with VIPs and a party of 30 journalists waiting for take-off - it was revealed that the Air Registration Board had not granted the company the necessary licence to land on the five North Isles airstrips with scheduled flights. Charter flights and flights for "test purposes" were still permitted however so the Islander aircraft - specially named "Captain E.E. Fresson" after the pioneer of Orkney aviation - was able to give members of the waiting party a joy ride to Sanday and Stronsay.

The legislation also allowed the plane to make emergency flights for air ambulance cases and the first was made on September 23, 1967, to Papa Westray to fly 64 year old farmer William Mackay to the Balfour Hospital.

Mr Bob Tullock, who became the Loganair manager, was later to claim, with justification, that the Loganair service, and especially the air ambulance, was to be the single biggest factor in helping to stem the tide of depopulation in the North Isles in the 1970s and 1980s.

The perils of island life, in the event of illness, had been clearly illustrated in January, 1967, when the Stronsay lifeboat was out for a total of eight hours to make a 60 mile dash to take four year old Jean Tulloch, of Purtabreck, North Ronaldsay, to the Balfour Hospital with suspected appendicitis.

At last the Board of Trade gave the necessary approval for the scheduled inter-island air service to go ahead. After the anti-climax of the non-start of the flights in August, it began without ceremony with nine passengers on a plane, piloted by Captain Jim Lee, from Kirkwall to Stronsay, Sanday and North Ronaldsay on Wednesday, September 27.

The service carried 70 people in its first week, including another mercy trip to Stronsay to bring a patient to hospital in Kirkwall. In the first two months, the Loganair Islander carried 836 passengers, although services to North Ronaldsay had to be suspended for a time due to a waterlogged airfield.

Loganair - under a variety of ownerships - would continue its link with Orkney for the remainder of the century.

The Loganair Islander comes into land at Sanday.

(Picture courtesy of Kenneth H.S. Foubister)

Tributes for an Orkney poet

Robert Rendall, poet, historian and naturalist, died in 1967 at the age of 69. "In the judgement of many, Robert Rendall was the most outstanding man of his time reared and brought up in these islands," said Sheriff D.B. Keith in a tribute.

Just before his death, the Queen had honoured his poetry by awarding Robert Rendall a pension on the Civil List. "This meant recognition of his life's work," said Sheriff Keith.

Robert Rendall was born in Glasgow, son of a master mariner from Westray. He was seven years old when the family came back to Orkney and he was educated at the Kirkwall burgh school. He then joined the staff of the Kirkwall drapers George Rendall and Company, a firm with which he was connected for the rest of his life.

"Robert Rendall was a poet of distinction whose deeply sincere verse conveyed the atmosphere of his native Orkney in a unique way. Its simplicity of style could not hide the craftsmanship which was the result of long study and genuine inspiration," said *The Orcadian*.

Although he never saw the national or international acclaim achieved by fellow Orkney men of letters like Edwin Muir,

Eric Linklater and George Mackay Brown, he had the great satisfaction during the last few months of his life of seeing two of his poems included in *The Oxford Book of Scottish Verse*.

Although he would be remembered primarily as a poet, his first book of poems *Country Sonnets* did not appear until he was nearly 50.

In the last 20 years of his life, he published three further collections of poetry, *Orkney Variants*, *Shore Poems* and *The Hidden Land*.

Also published were his *Mollusca Orcadensia* - accepted as the standard work on Orkney marine shells - and the semi-autobiographical *Orkney Shore*.

He was a devout worshipper with the Christian Brethren and he published two volumes of theology - *History, Prophecy and God* and *The Greatness and Glory of Christ*.

Orkney was to lose another locally respected writer in 1967. David Towers (63), an outstanding amateur actor and entertainer as well as playwright - who had national headlines in 1934 when the Lord Chamberlain banned one of his plays - was killed in a tragic accident as he crossed the Kirkwall-Stromness road.

Record breakers at sea

The annual Orkney sea angling festival at Stromness in 1967 saw Mr Jack Scott of Kirkwall - fishing in George Sinclair's boat *Delightful* - haul in a 70lb halibut in Rackwick Bay. It was a new British record and possibly a European record, said *The Orcadian*.

However, a year later, that was a mere minnow as Stromness Provost W.E. Knight landed a halibut of 162lbs off Marwick Head. That was definitely a European record.

All of this however was to seem small fry in July, 1968, when a Swedish sea angler Jan Olsson, from Gothenburg, landed a 214lb skate off Graemsay - just seven pounds short of a world record for a skate caught with rod and line at the time.

Stromness anniversary

Stromness celebrated the 150th anniversary of the burgh in 1967 with a commemorative service, a pageant written by George Mackay Brown and a book telling the history of the town, written by James Troup and Frank Eunson. The same year, Stromness celebrated the 100th anniversary of the lifeboat station in the town. Stromness had a lifeboat for a century before Kirkwall welcomed its first lifeboat, the *Grace Paterson Ritchie*.

Earl's Cathedral wedding

Miss Ann Augusta Wallace (24) of Holodyke, Dounby - whose forebearers included Sir Thomas Clouston, the Orcadian pioneer of the treatment of mental illness; the Orkney writer and historian J. Storer Clouston; and the eminent Edinburgh surgeon Sir David Wallace - married the Earl of Dunmore (28) at St Magnus Cathedral. Seventy wedding guests missed the service because of the disruption of air services.

Father Herbert Bamber, Kirkwall's long-serving Roman Catholic priest, is pictured outside his church during the snow of December, 1981.

(Picture courtesy of Orkney Library photographic archive)

Eyes down

Kirkwall's Phoenix Cinema, like picture houses throughout the country, was suffering falling attendances. In September, 1967, Kirkwall Town Council gave permission for the cinema to hold bingo sessions to increase revenue.

Rotary Club charter

The newly formed Rotary Club of Kirkwall received its charter at an official dinner at the Ayre Hotel on February 24, 1967. The first president was Mr Andrew Buchan.

Champion dies

Kirkwall weightlifter Lionel Laird emulated his fellow Orcadian Colin Wooldrage by winning the Scottish heavyweight weightlifting championship in September, 1967. However, tragically, Lionel died suddenly before the end of the year.

Rain reigns

In the 153 days up to January 31, 1967, Orkney had only five completely dry days, according to the records of the Met Office at Kirkwall Airport.

Minister's rescue

The Minister of Hoy, Rev Charles Abel, dived fully clothed into the sea to rescue nine year old non swimmer Elaine Grieve who had stumbled and fallen nine feet into 15 feet of water at Longhope Pier. "That's the first dip I've had since I came to Orkney," said Mr Abel, a Dundonian who had been island minister for four years.

New solicitor

Miss Helen Nicolson (28), Kirkwall's depute town clerk, was admitted by the Law Society as a solicitor. She had completed a law degree after joining the Kirkwall town clerk's department after leaving Kirkwall Grammar School and was acknowledged as the first person to complete her solicitor's training entirely in Orkney.

No smoking

A sign of the times in 1967 as Orkney County Council agreed that there should be a ban on smoking at its general meetings - although councillors could still smoke at committee meetings.

Nautical college

Orkney education committee bought the old Anderson's boat-building yard at Stromness to set up a nautical training college as part of Stromness Academy, and announced that a new school hostel in Kirkwall, to house 200 isles pupils, would cost over £500,000.

Fifteen men plucked from death

Dan Kirkpatrick, the coxswain of the Longhope lifeboat, became the only man alive to hold three RNLI silver medals after he led the perilous operation in which 15 trawlermen "were plucked from certain death."

The crew of the Grimsby trawler *Ross Puma* were saved in a dramatic rescue in the early hours of Monday, April 1,1968, after their vessel ran aground on a reef south of Little Rackwick, Hoy, in a blizzard which reduced visibility to nil.

Returning home after 11 days at sea, the skipper Denis Speck (41) managed to send out a Mayday message as his vessel rocked precariously like a pendulum on the rocks. Two other Humberside trawlers, the *Ross Renown* and the *William Wilberforce* stood by but were helpless to get close enough to offer a realistic chance of rescue.

The lifeboat reached the scene in just over an hour as the *Ross Puma* languished beneath the cliffs. The lifeboat had to make two attempts to secure her anchor to allow a rocket line to be fired aboard the stricken trawler and attached to a life raft.

The first seven members of the *Ross Puma* crew got into the raft which was hauled across to the lifeboat hand-over-hand by Dan Kirkpatrick, the second coxswain James Johnston and his brother Robbie Johnston. Although the raft was swamped by a wave, they managed to get the seven men aboard the lifeboat *TGB*.

The raft was then pulled back to the trawler for the remaining eight men and all 15 survivors were on board the lifeboat within two hours of sending their Mayday. They were landed at Longhope and taken to the Longhope Hotel to recover. Bosun Charles Bendell said: "We knew there was absolutely no hope of help from the shore, and our lives hung entirely on the lifeboat. If the tide had been flowing we would have been crushed against the cliff. As it was, the lifeboat arrived in the nick of time. I cannot speak too highly of the courage and skill of the lifeboatmen in those conditions."

Galley boy Ernest Spencer, who was just 16, said: "Because of the tremendous swell it was no joke jumping from the heaving ship on to the liferaft alongside."

And Colin Pearce (17) said: "Water was pouring into the engine room. I thought we might heel over at any moment."

Dan Kirkpatrick congratulated the trawler skipper Denis Speck on the calm and excellent discipline maintained by his crew throughout the rescue. "There was no sign of any panic whatsoever," said the lifeboat coxswain.

His crew on the rescue mission - also honoured with the RNLI inscriptions on

1968

vellum - were second coxswain James Johnston, bowman Ray Kirkpatrick, mechanic Robert R. Johnston, assistant mechanic James Swanson and emergency mechanic Robbie Johnston. The *Ross Puma* became a total loss.

Another Orcadian to be honoured that year was the coxswain of the Stronsay lifeboat, Jim Stout, for a rescue he made in his fishing boat *Ocean Gift* in January, 1968.

The fishing vessel *Flourish*, with Shapinsay skipper John Davidson and three crewmen aboard, had been hit by a heavy sea which washed more than 100 creels overboard, fouling the propeller and threatening to smash the vessel on rocks in Eynhallow Sound.

Jim Stout managed to secure a line to the stricken vessel and the *Ocean Gift* hauled the *Flourish* to safety; an operation for which Mr Stout was given a Board of Trade award for his skill and seamanship.

Unfortunately, just one week after the *Ross Puma* disaster, nine men were lost in another drama in Orkney waters as the 1,333 ton Greek cargo ship *Manina* struck Stack Skerry, near Suleskerry, and foundered.

The *Manina* was able to send an SOS and Stromness lifeboat was launched. Also, for the first time, a lifeboat sailed from Kirkwall to join the air and sea search. Although the *Grace Paterson Ritchie* had not yet been officially allocated to Kirkwall, she was based in the harbour to take part in winter trials in Northern waters.

Thankfully, a Swedish tanker was able to pick up the only five survivors in winds gusting to gale force. Another five crewmen were found dead, hanging to an upturned lifeboat, and Stromness lifeboat found two more bodies. As well as the seven men known to be drowned, another two were missing, believed lost.

The second mate of the *Manina*, Vasilios Kyriacou, who with the rest of the survivors was landed at Stornoway, said: "We abandoned ship and seconds later she keeled over and broke up. Every time a wave came we thought we would capsize."

Soviets target Papa Westray

The islanders of Papa Westray were left baffled as to why they had become the focus of attention from war ships of the Russian fleet in a strange cat and mouse game of Cold War manoeuvres in 1968.

"What are the Russians doing here?" asked the front page headline in *The Orcadian* as up to ten Soviet warships and support vessels suddenly became a common sight in the North Isles.

Soviet vessels had seldom been seen in Orkney waters until, in October, 1968, a large oil slick seen off Sanday was blamed on Russian warships believed to be snooping on a NATO Naval exercise off the islands.

A Royal Navy anti-submarine frigate HMS *Malcolm* was sent North from Rosyth and RAF Shackletons kept the Red fleet under surveillance as by November 22 there were as many as six Russian warships including a destroyer and a guided missile cruiser. "They always return to the same location in the North Isles, usually in the Papa Westray area," said *The Orcadian*.

A Royal Navy spokesman could offer no suggestion why Papay deserved such attention. However, there was no real concern as the Soviet ships were not breaking any regulations, he said.

Royal honour for shop

The Kirkwall company of Mr Sid Watson, a past president of the Kirkwall Chamber of Commerce, became the first Orkney business to be granted a royal warrant - as a royal coat of arms, resplendent in red, blue and gold, was erected over the company's Scott's Fish Shop in Bridge Street, Kirkwall.

Although Mr Watson was renowned as a fish-curing specialist, he in fact gained the warrant for supplying Orkney cheese.

Apparently Queen Elizabeth the Queen

Mother had been buying the traditional farmhouse delicacy since first being introduced to it following the visit of the Queen and Duke of Edinburgh to Orkney in 1960.

The document conveying the royal honour said: "This is to certify that by command of Queen Elizabeth the Queen Mother, I have appointed Scott's Fish Shop into the place and quality of cheesemonger to Her Majesty. Signed Lord Dalhouse, Chamberlain.

Scots anniversary

Orcadians marked the 500th anniversary of the islands coming under Scottish rule with a international conference in 1968.

The islands had been part of the Kingdom of Denmark until 1468 when they were pledged by Christian I of Denmark and Norway as a dowry for his daughter Margaret when she married James III of Scotland.

Historians from Norway, Denmark, Sweden and the UK came to Orkney for the 1968 conference, under the chairmanship of Lord Birsay.

Mrs Thelma Jexley, of the Danish National Archives, caused a major surprise when she produced a copy of the Marriage Treaty which was thought to have been destroyed centuries earlier.

Ships of the Danish and Norwegian Navies made courtesy calls at Kirkwall as Orcadians appeared to commemorate 500 years of their lost Norse heritage rather than 500 years of being Scottish.

There was a sequel to the celebrations when Orkney's county librarian Evan MacGillivray, who organised the conference, was honoured with the presentation by the Norwegian Consul-General for Scotland of the award of the Knight's Cross of St Olav.

Golden Slipper memories

The month of April, 1968, saw the death of one of Orkney's best known characters, Willie Farquhar, at the age of 74.

Before World War Two, he had a cobblers business at the Brig o' Waithe in Stenness and he was injured when the Germans bombed the hamlet in 1940.

He later developed a tea shop at the site, selling cups of tea and lemonade, which was especially patronised by wartime servicemen.

The premises - with the nickname the Golden Slipper - continued after the war and became a well known rendezvous amongst the youth of the county.

Willie Farquhar died in retirement in Aberdeenshire, where he had moved in 1967.

George Burgher, who became secretary of Orkney NFU in 1969.
(Picture from the files of The Orcadian)

New Legion club

Kirkwall branch of the British Legion, which had been based at the former community centre in Great Western Road, moved into new permanent club premises in Junction Road. The club was opened by Lord Birsay who described it as a "credit to the town."

Boatbuilding milestone

The Duncan family boatyard in Burray - which had been run by five generations of the family - produced its 400th boat since World War Two, a 36 feet long vessel destined for the Western Isles.

Seal sanctuary

The animal welfare organisation, the Ferne Trust, bought Little Linga Holm, off Stronsay, for £1,450, to be used as a seal sanctuary.

Second class mail

The Government introduced a two-tier postal service which meant that second class mail (a 4d stamp) to and from Orkney would now go by sea instead of air. Jo Grimond MP described it as organised chaos!

Powering ahead

By 1968 - the 25th anniversary of the formation of the North of Scotland Hydro-Electric Board - there were 6,257 electricity consumers in Orkney.

Museum opens

Tankerness House in Kirkwall - which had been saved from demolition and restored - was officially opened as a museum by the Keeper of the National Museum of Antiquities for Scotland, Mr R.B.K. Stevenson, in May, 1968.

Blizzard ordeal

March, 1968, went out like a lion as sudden blizzards created chaos with deep snowdrifts which trapped a family in their car for 16 hours.

Stromness headteacher John Finlayson, his wife Morag and children Christina (6) and George (10) were stranded after their car ran into a drift at Rennibister on the Kirkwall - Stromness road as the blizzard raged in 70 mph northerly gusts.

They were eventually found by a snow plough the next morning.

Westray venture

Westray folk put up £5,000 of the necessary capital to launch Westray Crab Processors Ltd. Crabmeat would be cooked and blast frozen for markets not only in Orkney but the rest of the UK and Europe.

Within weeks, 25 full-time and part-time workers were employed handling nearly 2,000 stones of partans a week - with 75 per cent of production going to the Continent.

Kirks unite

The Paterson Church and the King Street Church in Kirkwall were united as the East Kirk under the ministry of Rev G.L. Parkinson. The Paterson Kirk pulpit had been vacant since the death of Rev E.G. Chirgwin.

School is shut

The year of 1968 saw the closure of Tomison's Academy - which had served South Ronaldsay's South Parish for over a century - as part of a scheme for the centralisation of Orkney primary schools.

The school was named after William Tomison of South Ronaldsay, an early Orcadian pioneer who rose to become Governor of the Hudson's Bay Company after going to Canada in the 18th century, and who bequeathed the money for the school to be built in his native island.

North Atlantic Cup

A football trophy to be competed for by Orkney, Faroe and Shetland - the North Atlantic Cup - was brought home to Orkney in 1968 after the Orkney team went to Thorshavn and won 2-0 and drew 1-1.

New Sheriff

Sheriff David Keith, a native of Thurso, who had sat on the bench at Kirkwall Sheriff Court for 22 years, retired in 1968.

In future, Orkney would share a Sheriff with Shetland and Sheriff Alastair MacDonald, who had been Sheriff of Shetland for seven years, was given the task of covering all the Northern Isles.

The heroes of Longhope

In the worst tragedy to strike Orkney in a generation, the Longhope lifeboat was lost with all hands in the Pentland Firth. The eight men who lost their lives included two fathers, each with two sons on board. They would forever be remembered as the heroes of Longhope.

They left behind seven widows and ten fatherless children. It was a calamitous disaster which touched the consciousness of all of Britain - but nowhere with such catastrophic consequences as for the small township of 30 people at Brims, Longhope, which was home for the lifeboat and her crew.

The Longhope lifeboat *TGB* was launched just before 8pm on the night of Monday, March 17, 1969. The *TGB*, under the capable and experienced control of coxswain Dan Kirkpatrick, a name honoured amongst lifeboatmen throughout the country, had been called to go to the assistance of the 2,000 ton Liberian cargo ship *Irene* in trouble off South Ronaldsay.

The lifeboat was seen by the keepers of the Pentland Skerries lighthouse at 9.30pm. After that, there was a night of silence. The *TGB* was never seen again until, at 1.15pm on Tuesday, March 18, the Thurso lifeboat made the tragic discovery of the upturned vessel.

At some dreadful unspecified moment between 9.30pm on March 17 and 1.15pm the next day, the Longhope lifeboat had capsized and her crew had died.

In a front page comment, *The Orcadian* wrote: "All Orkney this week mourns over the tragic loss of the Longhope lifeboat with its crew of eight fine men.

"Right up until the last minute, everyone was hoping against hope that the lifeboat crew who had so often snatched others from what looked like certain death might still themselves have a chance.

"Then came the sad, final messages. There was no hope. The crew of the Longhope lifeboat were dead.

"A wave of sorrow swept through Orkney as Orcadians everywhere realised the magnitude of the disaster. Their hearts went out to those who had waited in the little houses of Brims, and who had waited in vain. With a population of only about 30, a quarter of them, the ablest and most experienced in the ways of the sea, had been taken away in one bitter blow.

"The whole of Orkney sorrows over this terrible calamity, but only in Brims itself and Longhope can the utter tragedy of it be felt."

The eight men who died were led by Dan Kirkpatrick, the 59 year old coxswain, who worked at the Lyness Naval base and who had been honoured with the British Empire Medal back in the days of World War Two. But it would be for his lifeboat service that he would always be remembered.

On the very day of the tragedy it was officially announced that he was to go to London a week later to receive his third RNLI silver medal for his hazardous service the previous year when the lifeboat saved 15 men from the Grimsby trawler *Ross Puma*.

Also on the lifeboat on that fateful night were two of Dan Kirkpatrick's sons, the bowman, Ray Kirkpatrick (29), and crewman Jack Kirkpatrick (26). They worked together and both were married with a child.

Another family was also devastated by the loss of a father and two sons.

Engineer was Robert R. Johnston (61) and he was accompanied by his sons James, the second coxswain, a 34 year old married man with two children, and crewman Robbie Johnston (31), also married with two children.

The other two crewmen on the final voyage were assistant mechanic Jim Swanson, who left a wife, and 24 year old single man Eric McFadyen. He had volunteered to go at the last minute although the lifeboat could have sailed with just seven crew.

Dan Kirkpatrick had been coxswain at Longhope since 1954 and the 47 feet long *TGB* had been stationed there since 1962. Their exploits together had been chronicled around the world as a series of daring rescues made national headlines. The *TGB* had saved 24 lives in the previous seven years.

As it turned out - in one of those perverse twists of fate - the *TGB* was not required to save any lives when she set out on that last mission.

The reason for the call-out of the Longhope lifeboat was a request for help from the Liberian ship *Irene* which radioed that she was in difficulty off the east side of Orkney and apparently out of control, drifting before a south easterly force nine gale. The gale had been blowing for several days and had whipped up huge waves which were thrashing Orkney's east coast.

The *Irene,* with a crew of 17 and outward bound from Granton to Norway, without a cargo, also fired red flares which were sighted in South Ronaldsay.

The Broughness lifesaving company - later to be joined by the Deerness company - was called out and rescuers were actually on the shore at Grimness when the *Irene* grounded.

A rocket was fired on to the stricken vessel and the crew, mainly Greeks, Algerians and Portuguese, were brought safely ashore very quickly, most of them apparently not even getting wet, although the master was temporarily knocked unconscious after going in the sea.

The men of the Broughness and Deerness companies were later honoured for their rescue. And that might have been the story of the night - another efficient operation had saved 17 lives in the stormy waters of Orkney.

However, by the time the crew of the *Irene* had been delivered to the comfort of Kirkwall, concerns were mounting for the Longhope lifeboat.

At first it was hoped that radio problems were to blame as communication ceased between the lifeboat and Coastguards. But as the night wore on, and the silence grew longer, anxiety grew for her safety.

A massive land, air and sea search swung into operation. Several coast rescue companies were called out, along with the lifeboats from Kirkwall, Stronsay, Thurso and Stromness. Three aircraft and a helicopter joined in.

The 70ft lifeboat *Grace Paterson Ritchie* - not yet officially assigned to Kirkwall but spending a second winter there undergoing trials - had been launched at the same time as the Longhope lifeboat in answer to the Mayday from the *Irene*.

Seas were reported to be mountainous with waves of up to 60 feet and, by the time the *Grace Paterson Ritchie* reached the area of the casualty, Coastguards were reporting "conditions alongside the *Irene* almost impossible."

Continuous attempts to raise the Longhope lifeboat on her radio still proved fruitless and the big lifeboat was instructed to proceed southward down the shore of South Ronaldsay in search of her. The Kirkwall vessel reported heavy seas but she could see nothing on her radar to account for the *TGB*.

The search continued until at 1.15pm on Tuesday, March 18, the Thurso lifeboat sent the grim radio message that she had found the missing Longhope boat upturned, four miles west of Torness, Hoy.

Then began the long haul to tow the capsized lifeboat across the Pentland Firth. She was towed by the Thurso boat, with the Stromness lifeboat escorting her, into Scrabster harbour where a crowd of hundreds of people had gathered.

There, for the first time, the Longhope vessel was turned over into her proper position. The body of coxswain Dan Kirkpatrick could be seen in the wheelhouse. Other crewmen - all wearing their yellow oilskins, seaboots and headgear - were down below.

The Longhope lifeboat crew of 1962 with the lifeboat *Thomas McCunn*. Five of these men would perish in the 1969 disaster. Back row, from the left: coxswain Dan Kirkpatrick, James Johnston, engineer Robert R. Johnston, Jack Norquoy, and Ray Kirkpatrick. Front: Robbie Johnston, Robert Johnston and J. Nicolson. (Picture courtesy of Orkney Library photographic archive)

At 9.50pm came the official confirmation that all on board were dead. One man, second mechanic Jim Swanson, was missing.

The magnitude and impact of the disaster in such a small, remote community tugged at the heartstrings of the nation.

The Queen sent a telegram of sympathy to Mr Jackie Groat, the honorary secretary of the Longhope lifeboat and the man who had passed on the message which saw the launch of the lifeboat on her last tragic mission.

The telegram read: "I am greatly distressed to learn of the tragic loss of the coxswain and crew of the Longhope lifeboat. Please convey my deepest sympathies - Elizabeth R."

The Secretary of State for Scotland, Mr Willie Ross, said: "I am appalled to learn of this terrible tragedy. The loss of such brave men will be felt deeply by the people of Scotland. The gallantry of the men of the lifeboat service is known to us all. The Longhope crew made the supreme sacrifice in the service of those whose life is on the sea. My deepest sympathy goes to their families and to Orkney at this sad time."

The Duke of Atholl, chairman of the Scottish Lifeboat Council, chartered a plane to fly to Orkney and, with Jackie Groat, visited the next of kin of those who perished.

Orkney MP Jo Grimond knew Dan Kirkpatrick, his family, and his crew. He said: "I feel very strongly that the RNLI should look closely into the question of father and sons going out in the same lifeboat on such operations."

A House of Commons motion expressing deep admiration for the courage of the crew of the Longhope lifeboat was signed by MPs of all parties. Mr Bill Rodgers, Minister of State of the Board of Trade, said the waters where the Liberian cargo ship *Irene* ran aground off South Ronaldsay were one of the worst stretches in the world. It was an act of singular courage for the Longhope lifeboat to have put out in such conditions as those she encountered that night. A message of sympathy was even received from Tristan da Cunha.

The degree to which the tragedy touched the nation was illustrated when an appeal fund for the families, set up by the Lord Lieutenant, topped £100,000 in a matter of weeks.

On Saturday, March 22, the funeral of the seven lifeboatmen whose bodies had been recovered took place at Longhope at a service conducted by the Rev Charles Abel. The Stromness lifeboat - with second coxswain Jack Leslie in charge - had volunteered to undertake the sad task of bringing the bodies back from Scrabster, but it was found that the hatches were too small to take the seven wreath-covered coffins, so they were carried by the *Grace Paterson Ritchie,* with the Stromness vessel as escort, back to Longhope.

More than 100 people stood silently on the pier at Longhope with the RNLI flag flying at half mast as the coffins were gently lifted ashore. Among those there to express their sympathy was Lord Saltoun whose daughter had travelled to Longhope to name the *TGB* in 1962.

The coffins were taken to the Walls parish church. "We know their lives were not given in vain," said Rev Abel. "They could have given them in no more worthy cause. They died that may help save their fellow men."

The Rev Abel had left Hoy the previous year to move to Sutherland, but he had immediately flown to Orkney as soon as he heard of the cruel blow suffered by the little community of Brims, where he had so many close friends. He had conducted the wedding ceremonies of Robbie Johnston, Ray and Jack Kirkpatrick.

The funeral was attended by an estimated 1,000 people, and

The Longhope lifeboat *TGB* served in Orkney from 1962-1969 and made 34 launches, saving 24 lives, before the fateful night in March, 1969, when she was lost with her crew of eight. (Picture courtesy of Orkney Library photographic archive)

to accommodate so many mourners, the service was relayed to the overflow congregation in the community centre opposite.

Below the pulpit lay the seven coffins draped in RNLI flags. On the coxswain's coffin lay his decorations - his BEM and his lifeboat silver medal with two clasps.

After the Benediction, Bugler Brian Farley (21) of the Royal Marines, HMS *Condor*, Arbroath, sounded the "Last Post" and "Reveille" and 14 year old Gary Kirkpatrick, the only surviving son of the coxswain, carried his father's medals on a cushion as he followed the coffins from the kirk.

They were carried to Osmondwall, where, overlooking the Pentland Firth and Scapa Flow, they were buried amidst hundreds upon hundreds of wreaths. Pipe Major Albert Sim of the Kirkwall City Pipe Band played "Flowers of the Forest" as the committal service concluded.

The presence of one mourner had a special poignancy. He was Denis Speck, the skipper of the Grimsby trawler *Ross Puma*, who had returned to Hoy to pay tribute to the men who had saved his life in a dramatic rescue the previous year. It was the rescue for which Dan Kirkpatrick was awarded his third RNLI silver medal.

The ever-present dangers of the sea were brought home when - even during the funeral service - the lifeboat *Grace Paterson Ritchie* was called away from Longhope to answer a Mayday call in the Pentland Firth.

Mrs Margaret Kirkpatrick, who had been married to Dan Kirkpatrick for 29 years, said: "They were good years and I was grateful to my husband for the happiness we shared together."

There was no recrimination or bitterness from anyone who had lost their menfolk, she said. "I have no regret about the boat being lost on its way to help others, because that is why it was there. I am happy that the lives of the crew of the *Irene* have been saved." Mrs Kirkpatrick later that year travelled to Glasgow to be honoured by the Glasgow *Evening Times* as "Scotswoman of the Year."

Dr Sydney Peace, who was the doctor in Longhope for seven years and a former secretary of the lifeboat who, on occasion, sailed as a crew member, paid tribute to all the crewmen he knew personally.

"No man knew the iron challenge of the sea better than Dan Kirkpatrick. If it is possible to know the ways of a boat in a sea, he did. If it is possible to know the Pentland Firth, he did. While his limitations were less than those of most men, Dan knew himself and always had himself under control. Had he been a rash man, he, and others of us, would have perished long ago.

"People so easily forget or fail to realise that Dan's greatest achievement was not doing what he did, but doing it and remaining alive as long as he did."

The day after the funeral in Longhope, 1,200 people packed St Magnus Cathedral for a memorial service conducted by the Rev Bill Cant. Human words were totally inadequate, he said, to record the sense of shock that had seized Orkney at the sudden loss of such men, and utterly inadequate too to express the genuine and deep sympathy that Orcadians felt for their loved ones and dependants.

Likening the courage of Dan Kirkpatrick and his crew to that of Captain Scott and his comrades during the last days in the Antarctic, Rev Cant said: "They were men who knew the meaning of real brotherhood and teamwork. In many a situation of hazard and stress they had learned to rely on one another and to trust one another. No one was spare; each one had his job to do.

"They combined to snatch human lives from tempestuous seas and to bring them to safety. And in this hard task, each was glad to have comrades standing by him and working with him - volunteers for the dangerous life, with the courage to stick to it; men experienced in brotherhood and teamwork; and men who were prepared to sacrifice their lives in seeking to save others."

Orkney's Lord Lieutenant Colonel Henry Scarth launched a disaster fund which received £5,000 in its first two days. "Now that the last tributes have been paid with reverence to the memory of those who lost their lives, it is time to consider those who remain to mourn in homes bereft not only of their loved ones but of the family breadwinners. I earnestly urge all members of the public to recognise the deep debt we all owe to such brave men by contributing as generously as possible to a fund for the benefit of their bereaved families," said Col Scarth.

In the wake of the loss of the Longhope lifeboat, the RNLI

decided that to ensure that the Pentland Firth was adequately covered, the lifeboat *Grace Paterson Ritchie* would move to a temporary station at Scapa.

Over the whole period of the grounding of the *Irene* and the Longhope lifeboat loss, the *Grace Paterson Ritchie* had been at sea for a total of 61 hours. The boat was under the command of RNLI staff coxswain Ian Ives (39) from Whitley Bay, Northumberland who said: "We encountered our worst seas off Mull Head. We hit one heavy sea which was about 60 feet high. The boat behaved beautifully and we have every confidence in her."

Kirkwall harbourmaster Bill Sinclair was second coxswain and other local men on the *Grace Paterson Ritchie* that night were Dan Grieve, Ian Thompson, James Craigie and Norman Cooper, along with mechanic William Pyke from Ullapool.

The new Scapa-based boat was soon in action again when on Thursday, March 27, she was called out to the Hull trawler *James Barrie,* with 21 men on board, which ran aground on the Pentland Skerries. All the trawler crew were safely taken off in life rafts and landed by the Wick lifeboat.

Meanwhile, the Longhope lifeboat *TGB,* saved from the sea, was taken on a 650 mile road journey from Scrabster to go South. The RNLI proposed that the vessel be repaired and returned to service - but not in Longhope or any other North of Scotland station.

However, Admiral Sir Wilfrid Woods, chairman of the RNLI, said eight volunteers - five of them relatives of the lost lifeboatmen - had already come forward, offering to crew a new Longhope lifeboat which he hoped would be on station in the foreseeable future.

Sir Wilfrid said: "All the people of Longhope, including the widows, definitely do not like the idea of no boat being there, when fishermen or any other persons might be in danger and in need of rescue. An empty lifeboat shed is a very sad reminder."

Exactly how, when or why the Longhope lifeboat was lost will never be known. However, a probable cause of the disaster was given in evidence to a Fatal Accident Inquiry before Sheriff Alastair MacDonald at Kirkwall Sheriff Court on June 10, 1969.

Mr Richard Oakley, Consulting Naval Architect to the RNLI, said it appeared that tremendous seas broke two windows in the front of the wheelhouse. The sudden inrush of water through this gap would have resulted in the coxswain being swept from the wheel and so losing control of the boat, which, he surmised, then went broadside on to the sea and finally turned over.

This opinion was supported by Commander Wilfred Dutton, Chief Inspector of Lifeboats, who had high praise for the qualities of the coxswain and crew. "There was no better in the service," he said.

Sheriff MacDonald said there was no evidence of negligence nor lack of precautions, which had they been taken might have saved the crew. Nor had there been evidence of defects in the boat.

The jury of four men and three women returned a formal verdict that the eight men had died by drowning.

That week, Mr Bill Rodgers, Minister of State at the Board of Trade, flew to Orkney to honour the men of the Broughness and Deerness coastguard rescue companies who had saved the 17 crew of the stricken *Irene* on the night the Longhope lifeboat made her last launch.

It had been a rescue worthy of great tradition, said Mr Rodgers as he presented the two Orkney companies with the shield for the most meritorious wreck service of 1968-69 at a ceremony in Kirkwall. The rescue would be long remembered - "not only by those who go down to the sea but also by those who stand

A line-up of the crew of the Longhope lifeboat in 1963, including Dan Kirkpatrick, back row, second from left, and Dr Sydney Peace, who served as secretary and medical officer of the Longhope lifeboat, who is pictured standing on the extreme right.

(Picture courtesy of Orkney Library photographic archive)

afar and admire the courage and heroism of the men who do," said the Minister.

It was an occasion of both heroism and tragedy. "For while we are here to do honour to those who took part in this gallant and memorable rescue we are also, all of us, remembering the tragedy that occurred on that night - the loss of the Longhope lifeboat and her crew."

The shield was formally presented to the two Auxiliaries who had been in charge that night - Mr G.S. Manson for Broughness and Mr D. Foubister for Deerness.

(Orkney was touched again by a lifeboat tragedy in January, 1970, when the Fraserburgh lifeboat *Duchess of Kent* was lost with five of her crew - including the boat's mechanic Fred Kirkness who spent his early life in Rousay.)

Orkney MP Jo Grimond had called for a full inquiry into the loss of the Liberian cargo vessel *Irene* - but, by the time of the first anniversary of the Longhope lifeboat disaster, the only report that had been published was issued by the Liberian government.

It suggested that the *Irene*, a 22 year old ship with a single screw, ran out of fuel only two days after leaving Granton for Norway. It also showed that the ship's officers had no accurate idea of their position. The captain thought they were off the Norwegian coast when they were, in fact, almost 300 miles away. However, none of the ship's papers, bridge log or engine telegraph book was ever recovered, making an accurate assessment of the master's actions extremely difficult.

But Prince Abraham Massaquoi, Commissioner of Maritime Affairs of the Republic of Liberia, found that the *Irene* captain was not incompetent and blamed the heavy weather encountered by the ship as the primary factor "in this most regrettable loss."

However in his conclusions he stated: "The master's continuance of the voyage in the face of a rather pronounced drift and his failure to see that proper steps were taken to check the vessel's position with available coastal stations may be ground for criticism and, in my judgement, warrants some action on our part."

As a result, the Greek master of the *Irene*, Stavros Giannakis (44) had his licence suspended for six months from November 10, 1969, said the report.

Of the attempted rescue, the Liberian government report said: "A valiant effort to rescue the 17 officers and men aboard the *Irene*, made by a crew from the lifeboat station at Longhope, ended in disaster when the boat capsized in the heavy seas and all aboard were lost. The loss of these gallant men, who were acting in the best tradition of the sea, is the supreme tragedy of this most unfortunate disaster."

On March 22, 1970, over 200 people packed Walls Old Parish Church in Longhope for a 45 minute remembrance service, conducted by the Rev Ewan Traill. The minister read the names of those who had been lost and this was followed by two minutes silence.

While Longhope waited for a new lifeboat to be permanently assigned, the RNLI announced that the 52 feet *Hilton Briggs* would come North for the summer of 1970.

The new full time coxswain to succeed Dan Kirkpatrick would be Jack Leslie (39), previously second coxswain of the Stromness lifeboat. The new mechanic would be Ian McFadyen (23), whose brother Eric was lost in the 1969 disaster. The crew would be made up from a pool of 12 volunteers.

Lifeboat secretary Jackie Groat said: "The arrival of another boat is what we have been working and waiting for. It is already bringing a new outlook to the community and a much needed uplift. With no lifeboat here we have felt something vital missing in our midst."

In August, 1970, 17 months after her fatal capsize, the *TGB* returned to duty - taking up a new station at Arranmore, County Donegal, after being refitted at Littlehampton, Sussex.

That same week, Orkney relived the darkest hour of the *TGB* as Queen Elizabeth the Queen Mother travelled to Orkney to unveil a memorial to the eight men of the Longhope lifeboat who died.

The memorial to the heroes of Longhope - a life-sized statue of a lifeboatman, sculpted by Ian Scott of North Ronaldsay, on a plinth of Orkney stone - at Osmondwall Cemetery.

(Picture courtesy of Craig Taylor)

The Queen Mother arrived by helicopter and, in the course of a three hour visit, she unveiled, first, a plaque presented by Coastguard members in Orkney, and then a six feet high bronze statue of a lifeboatman looking out to sea which had been sculpted by Ian Scott of North Ronaldsay.

With an overflow of several hundred people outside the Walls Old Kirk, who heard the service relayed by loudspeakers, the Rev Ewan Traill painted a vivid picture of the disaster and its victims.

"These men were not saints but essentially they were good men. They had qualities which constituted greatness. They had splendid courage, not rash impulsiveness. As a crew, they were unsurpassed anywhere in the world for efficiency, judgement, for loyalty and for courage."

The Queen Mother - she had celebrated her 70th birthday the week before - then joined the congregation outside to unveil the granite plaque, set into the west wall of the kirk, which had been presented by companies of Orkney Coastguard, who played such a vital role in the events of that black night in March, 1969.

The Queen Mother walked to the wooden community centre across the road where she talked with the widows and their families. "Her charm, as always, was to win on that day the hearts of all who saw," said *The Orcadian*.

The ceremony then moved three miles along the road to Osmondwall Cemetery, where seven of the crew were buried. (The body of Jim Swanson had not been found). There the Queen Mother unveiled the life sized statue of a lifeboatman on a plinth partly built from coloured sandstone boulders from the beach at Brims beside the shed of the lifeboat.

Inscribed on the pedestal were the names of the eight heroes of Longhope and the inscription: "Greater love hath no man than this, that he lays down his life for his fellowmen."

On October 16, 1970, 19 months after her predecessor was lost with all hands, the new Longhope lifeboat *Hilton Briggs* successfully carried out her first mission as she went to the aid of the Buckie fishing vessel *Capella*. By a grim twist of fate, the *Capella* was held fast on rocks just one mile south of Grimness, where the hulk of the *Irene* was laid still.

The *Hilton Briggs* and the *Grace Paterson Ritchie* succeeded in refloating the stricken fishing boat, with her five crewmen all safe.

In December, 1970, a line - however fragile - could be drawn under the tragic chapter in the history of the Longhope lifeboat as the station became fully operational with its own new permanently-based lifeboat once more.

The new £70,000 self-righting, steel-hulled vessel, named the *David and Elizabeth King and EB*, arrived at Longhope - with an aerial salute from a Nimrod and Shackleton aircraft - to be greeted by 100 islanders, including the island schoolchildren who had been given the morning off.

Longhope's proud record of lifeboat service would continue. The island had endured tragedy of numbing magnitude but, once again, stood ready to help those in peril on the sea!

Jack Leslie, previously second coxswain of the Stromness lifeboat, was appointed as the coxswain of the newly recruited crew for the replacement Longhope lifeboat in 1970.

(Picture from the files of *The Orcadian*)

The Longhope lifeboat station became fully operational again in December, 1970, with its new permanently-based lifeboat *David and Elizabeth King and EB*.

(Picture courtesy of Orkney Library photographic archive)

Last beat for Orkney police

1969

For the first time in the 20th century, Orkney was without its own police force. The Orkney constabulary was merged - at Government insistence - with the forces of Shetland and Caithness in what was to become Northern Constabulary.

The final days of the independent Orkney force, at the start of 1969, had seen Orkney's Chief Constable James Cormack (52) awarded the Queen's Police Medal for distinguished service, while his deputy Inspector Samuel Bews (48) received the Police Long Service and Good Conduct Medal.

Mr Cormack had joined the Orkney Police in 1938 - the year that the force came under the control of the Scottish Office for the first time. (Until then, the force was run and paid for by the county council).

In the previous 30 years up to 1969, there had been just three Orkney Chief Constables - Colin Campbell, Gathorne Cheyne and Mr Cormack. Until the months before World War Two, Mr Campbell had policed the county with just half a dozen constables and, with that small force, had been responsible for preparing precautions for the defence of the county's civilians and the upholding of law and order as the islands experienced an invasion of contract workers and troops which trebled the population.

Mr Cormack was on the short list for the post of Chief Constable for the new combined Northern force but the job was given to Chief Superintendent Robert McNeill (48), formerly of the Lanarkshire Constabulary, and Mr Cormack decided to retire from the new force - which covered an area stretching 200 miles and including 170 islands - in August, 1969.

The last serious case of the Orkney force came in March, 1969, when three detectives were flown North from Glasgow to investigate a suspected murder as a 74 year old retired and widowed Burray crofter was shot dead at his home.

An 18 year old man later appeared in court accused of the killing. However the teenager walked free from Aberdeen High Court, in June, 1969, after a verdict of not proven to a charge of culpable homicide. He had lodged a special defence that, at the time of the shooting, he was insane and therefore not responsible for his actions.

There was criticism by the trial judge, Lord Walker, that the police had taken the accused man from his home for questioning at the "Gestapo hour" of 3am.

Whether the Northern Constabulary would prove to be more efficient in its operations remained to be seen. However, it was soon seen that it would not be more economic as the cost of the new force immediately went up.

In the last year of the independent Orkney force, the cost to the county was £30,000. Orkney's share of financing the new organisation would be £35,440 - an 18 per cent increase. Still, if it was any consolation, Shetland would have to pay 66 per cent more.

In a couple of years, Orkney had lost control of its own water authority and police force, and there were danger signs that it would lose its own local authority as the Wheatley Report on the future of local government proposed that the county should come under the control of a council covering all the Highlands and Islands.

But the most outrageous suggestion for the centralisation of services came from the Scottish Home and Health Department. At that time, there were ten resident doctors in various outer isles, but officials in Edinburgh now suggested that the islands could be served by a flying doctor service with a group of doctors, based in Kirkwall, visiting isles patients by aircraft.

Orkney MP Jo Grimond said: "Any removal of the resident doctors on the outer islands of Orkney and Shetland will be disastrous. It will be bitterly and rightly resented and I can imagine few things more calculated to hasten depopulation. I hope any such project will be dropped."

Fortunately, the idea was to fade away. (As was the proposal that Orkney should be part of a Highlands and Islands council).

And to press home the point that Orkney was quite capable of governing itself, the county council rejected a recommendation that the salary of the director of education be increased to £3,965 a year!

Woman provost

For the first time in its long history, the Royal burgh of Kirkwall had a woman provost, Mrs Georgina Leitch, a member of the town council for 20 years who, in 1969, succeeded Provost James Scott who stood down from the position after 11 years.

Mrs Leitch, the widow of Kirkwall nurseryman Robert Leitch, had come to Orkney from her native Edinburgh after her marriage in 1933. She was Kirkwall's eleventh provost of the 20th century, and, in 1970, created another footnote in the history of the county when she was named as Orkney's first woman Deputy Lieutenant.

Blockbuster film

More than 4,000 people saw the film *The Sound of Music* during a two week run at Kirkwall's Phoenix Cinema in 1969.

Airport facelift

A new £45,000 terminal building was officially opened by Jo Grimond at Kirkwall Airport - replacing the old terminal which had consisted of wartime Nissen huts. In the previous eight years, the number of passengers using the airport had nearly doubled from 27,000 a year to 52,000.

Climbing triumphs and tragedy

Britain's highest vertical cliff, the 1,140 feet high St John's Head in Hoy, was conquered by five climbers from the North of England - Edwin Ward-Drummond, Jack Street, Alan Evans, Ben Campbell-Kelly and Leo Dickinson.

It took them three days, including two nights, on a route which involved 2,000 feet of climbing, with 15 pitches, on the red sandstone headland, two miles north of the Old Man of Hoy.

"The climb was quite Alpine with no hope of rescue and we encountered very precarious rock in some places," said Ward-Drummond.

However, also in 1969, Orkney was shocked to learn of the death of eight year old Roy Clarkson with his father while climbing the Matterhorn, some 700 feet from the summit of the 13,500 feet Swiss mountain, just a year after they had scaled the Old Man of Hoy when Roy was aged just seven.

In May, 1970, Dr Tom Patey (38) from Ullapool - who was one of the first three men to conquer the Old Man - died in a climbing accident in Sutherland, thus becoming the third fatality involving climbers who had reached the top of the Orkney landmark.

On a happier note, in 1970, Leo Dickinson (24), who had conquered St John's Head the year before, returned with three colleagues from North Wales and the North of England - Pete Minks (22), Clifford Phillips (25) and Peter Crew (28) - to climb the previously unscaled 150 feet high rock pinnacle of North Galton Castle on Orkney's west coast.

A power in the sea

The biggest fishing boat ever to be launched for Orkney owners made its debut as the Reid brothers from Stronsay pioneered the rebirth of a white fishing industry for Orkney.

The £56,000 *Bountiful* (K67) was launched by Mrs Peggy Reid for her sons David, Albert and James at the yard of J. and G. Forbes at Sandhaven, near Fraserburgh. The new vessel was 72 feet, with a beam of 21 feet, equipped for side trawling or seining.

Skipper would be David Reid (29) who had spent seven years in the Merchant Navy, which included a winter in the Antarctic in the research ship *Shackleton*, as well as service in tankers and with the Blue Star Line, before returning to Orkney to fish. He had already owned four smaller fishing vessels - *Our Queen*, *Radiant Queen*, *Millburn* and the *Michael J.*

The mate would be 23 year old Albert Reid who had seen service round the world before he was 17, working with the Shaw Savil Line before returning to Orkney.

The chief engineer was 41 year old James who had served in Aberdeen trawlers for 16 years and who held the distinction of having been the engineer on the last of the steam trawlers to sail out of Aberdeen, the *Souvenir*.

The *Bountiful* would sail with a crew of seven or eight, all of whom would eventually come from Orkney. She certainly lived up to her name when she landed her maiden catch at Aberdeen in June, 1969 - making £1,102 for 330 boxes from the Bergen Bank. The first box of haddock was auctioned off for Stronsay lifeboat funds.

The earnings of the *Bountiful* in her first 21 days of fishing totalled £4,200, and, in her first four months, she grossed £25,809. It was the start of an era of enterprise for a new breed of Orkney fishermen.

With the help of the Highlands and Islands Development Board fisheries scheme, the biggest boat to be built in Orkney for 50 years - the 50 feet stern trawler *Kildinguie* - was also launched in 1969 at a cost of £25,000 at Anderson's boatyard in Stromness for Stronsay fishermen John Dennison and his son Magnus. The vessel was equipped both to trawl for white fish and dredge for scallops.

The Reid brothers were to progress to bigger and more modern trawlers in the following 25 years with vessels like the *Mount Royal* and *River Dee* while a complete new industry would develop in Westray as a generation of trawler skippers grew up on that island - people like Malcolm Brown, George Costie and the Bain brothers, Tam, Kenny and Balfour.

By 1988, it was estimated that the gross value of the catches of Westray boats - mostly landed at Aberdeen or Peterhead - was about £2 million for the year.

Malcolm Brown - who, in partnership with Jimmy Moodie, George Costie and Raymond Leslie, took delivery of the £900,000 *Vestrfjordr* in 1986 - was quoted at the time as saying: "My first boat was a floating scrapheap compared to what we've got now. We've just worked our way up the ladder, getting a better boat each time. If the reward is there at the end, you don't mind the hard work."

Power blast

The most powerful ground-level gust ever experienced in Britain, up until that time, was recorded at 136mph at Kirkwall Airport at 9.15am on Friday, February 7, 1969, as gales and blizzards paralysed Orkney for three days.

Banks join forces

The National Commercial Bank and the Royal Bank, both of which had branches in Kirkwall, merged in 1969 to become the Royal Bank of Scotland.

Stromness in the swim

The highlight of the 21st Stromness Shopping Week was the official opening by Lord Birsay of the new £22,000 indoor heated swimming pool for the town. Over 1,000 swimmers used the pool in the first week.

NFU secretary

Mr George Burgher (31) from Westray became the secretary of the Orkney NFU area, based at the offices in Junction Road, Kirkwall. The former assistant headteacher at Dounby School, he succeeded Mr John Riddell who had bought the farm of Balaclava, Shapinsay.

New ship for isles

It was the end of a 38 year old career for the coal-burning steamer *Earl Sigurd* as the Orkney Islands Shipping Company took delivery of the new 132 feet long cargo vessel, the *Islander*, to support the *Orcadia* on the North Isles shipping services.

The 250 ton *Islander*, equipped to carry both cargo and cattle, as well as 12 passengers, was launched at the Aberdeen yard of John Lewis and Sons and began her Orkney service in July, 1969.

The following year, the Orkney Islands Shipping Company, also took over the Shapinsay service, from the Dennison company, using the 52 feet *Clytus*.

Tourism takes off

Roy Learmonth (38) of Kirriemuir, Angus, was appointed Orkney's first full-time tourist officer by the Orkney Tourist Organisation which, in 1969, claimed tourism as Orkney's second most important industry.

In 1972, Josh Gourlay - then studying for his honours degree in business administration at the University of Strathclyde - became the tourist officer for Orkney. He would remain in the job for the next 20 years.

A Legion of beauty queens

Margaret Bruce of St Ola became the 1969 Miss Orkney - the last time the competition would be organised by the Kirkwall branch of the British Legion before, the following year, it was taken over by the Orkney Tourist Organisation.

Since the launch of the competition in 1958, it had been won by Miss Kirkwall Elizabeth Davey (twice), two Miss Birsays Vera Cromarty and Bridget O'Malley, Miss Firth Norma Hourston, Miss St Ola Annette Russell, Miss Stenness Maureen Linklater, Miss South Ronaldsay Christine Scott, Miss Stronsay Catherine Maxwell (the first North Isles winner) and Kathleen Eunson from Deerness.

Centenary for firm

The Kirkwall firm of J.&W. Tait celebrated its centenary in 1970 after serving the Orkney farming community for 100 years. Taits could also claim to have opened the first self-service shop in Orkney.

Uproar as pilot is sacked

For the second time in 25 years, Orkney was in uproar over the sacking of a pioneer of island air services.

It was almost an echo of the storm of protests when Captain Ted Fresson was made redundant by the nationalised BEA airline in 1948, as Orcadians complained long and loudly as Captain Jim Lee (33), the chief pilot for Loganair in Orkney, was sacked in 1970.

The bearded pilot from County Wicklow, Ireland, was on first name terms with most of his North Isles passengers after making 6,000 landings in 1,000 flying hours during the previous two and a half years.

In the first two years, the inter-isles service had carried 14,000 passengers, covering 175,000 miles, in the eight seater Islander piloted by Captain Lee and his fellow pilot Andy Alsop.

Captain Lee, a veteran of flying Shackletons in the RAF, and Captain Alsop, who had flown Buccaneers in the Royal Navy before joining Loganair, were already well on the way to clocking up 100 emergency air ambulance flights between them.

All this appeared to matter little when Captain Lee was sacked by Loganair on January 9, 1970, after being suspended for the previous eleven days for breaking into a BEA store at Kirkwall Airport in order to fly a two day load of newspapers from Orkney to Shetland.

Captain Lee said he had forced the door only because BEA staff had not turned up to open it. "I pointed out that my action was to provide a service, not an act of hooliganism."

BEA had reported the incident to Loganair, and Captain Duncan McIntosh, the Loganair managing director, said the resulting dismissal was a matter of company discipline.

However, Captain Lee said: "I feel the real reason for my dismissal is due to a series of differences of opinion I have had with the company on the priority Orkney should have within the Loganair operations."

A letter signed by 26 Orkney doctors and dentists was sent to Loganair expressing "profound admiration" for Jim Lee's work in initiating the air ambulance service and saying it was insupportable that he be sacked for an "apparently trivial charge."

Dr Derrick Johnstone, chairman of the Orkney Medical Committee, said: "We are appalled by the news. We know Captain Lee's skill and devotion to duty have been responsible for saving the lives of many Orcadians."

County councillor Christine Muir in Sanday added: "I have never seen such unanimity of opinion in the North Isles, and such distress. There have been petitions from all the islands."

However, Captain McIntosh said: "Our decision is final." And that was that!

Jim Lee was still to leave his mark on Orkney, however, for his next venture was to open the Torvhaug Inn in Kirkwall.

Then, in 1972, he went to college in Aberdeen to obtain entry qualifications for a medical career. After five years study, he graduated MB,ChB at the Royal College of Surgeons in Dublin in 1978.

And the new inter-island service would continue, albeit without its first pilot. By 1970, Loganair was operating the world's shortest scheduled air service - just two minutes or 1.3 statute miles - between Westray and Papa Westray. Also the island of Eday could boast its own London Airport (named after the neighbouring Bay of London) and, for the first time since the days of Ted Fresson, there was now an air mail service for the North Isles. Loganair even operated a special charter flight on Christmas Day, 1970, to bring the national newspapers to Orkney.

By 1970, the popularity of the air link was illustrated by the fact that, in the winter months, the aircraft was already carrying more passengers than the *Orcadia* ferry - although this was reversed in the summer.

The financial deficit of the service was, at this stage, underwritten by the Scottish Office. However, in May, 1971, the Government - in a bid to stem the losses of the Orkney Islands Shipping Company - announced increases of 20 per cent on the air service, with the return fare to the isles going up to £6.

The increase did not seem to have an adverse impact on the numbers flying. In 1971, Loganair carried 12,940 passengers in Orkney and carried out 48 ambulance flights in 12 months. When, Loganair celebrated its fifth anniversary of the service in 1972, the company had flown 60,000 passengers in Orkney, and made 245 ambulance flights.

The company had also survived its first serious mishap in August, 1970, when the eight seater Islander crashed into a stone dyke after landing at Stronsay. The plane was badly damaged but the pilot, Captain Arthur Kerr, and six passengers were all unharmed. A replacement plane allowed services to resume after a week.

The county was touched by another air tragedy in 1970. BEA Captain Ronald Roberts, a well known pilot in Orkney, and his son Tony were killed in a crash at Kincardine when the private Cessna plane they were flying burst into flames as it hit the ground. Just 24 hours earlier, Captain Roberts had flown the last Viscount of the day from Orkney to Aberdeen.

Superstar visitor

Beatle Paul McCartney, his wife Linda, and children Heather and Linda, spent a few hours in Orkney, in 1970, en route to a holiday in Shetland.

They arrived virtually unrecognised, with their Old English Sheepdog, after they crossed from Scrabster to Stromness in the Wick fishing boat *Enterprise*.

The family were driven by Steve Omand in a hire car to Kirkwall Airport from where a chartered Loganair plane - booked under the name of Mr P. Martin - took them to Shetland.

Another visitor to Orkney in 1970 was the round-the-world yachtsman Sir Alec Rose who travelled North to take part in the Scapa '70 festival of the sea.

Happy hundred

Mrs Margaret Skea of North Myre, Sanday - the birthplace of the 19th century Orkney writer Walter Traill Dennison - celebrated her 100th birthday as the only centenarian living in Orkney in 1970. She died three years later at 103.

Marooned lightkeepers airlifted

Lightkeeper Angus Hutchison (32) was reunited with his family after 64 days when, for the first time in its history, Suleskerry lighthouse was relieved by air.

The lighthouse, 30 miles west of the Orkney Mainland, had been cut off by storms - with the lighthouse support ship *Pole Star* unable to land - and the three lightkeepers had already broken into emergency rations, with only two tins of corned beef and a few packets of biscuits remaining, when a Whirlwind helicopter from RAF Leuchars managed to lift off the marooned men.

The principal keeper Robert Wood had been taken off by helicopter earlier when he was taken ill.

Then the helicopter made two further trips - the first with fresh supplies and the second to make the transfer of keepers.

Angus Hutchison, who had been on the rock for more than two months, had been born at the Stromness shore station and had followed his father into the lighthouse service. His two fellow lightkeepers who were flown off were David McLeod (25) and James Leask (27).

Death of a 'legend'

The death of John D. Mackay - headmaster of the Sanday School - saw the loss to Orkney of one of its best known and most remarkable personalities.

"With John Mackay's passing, something unique and irreplaceable has been taken from Orkney life, for he was the complete original, brimming over with an expansive personality, partly natural, partly self-created, which became richer and more idiosyncratic as the years went on," wrote *The Orcadian* after his death in December, 1970.

"He was happy that he should become almost a legend, noted for his strongly individual views on local and national affairs; noted too, and greatly liked, for his sense of humour and for his incomparable gifts as a story teller."

Born in Papa Westray, he had worked long and hard in his own time to gain the qualifications which eventually led him to gain his MA at Edinburgh University and to become director of correspondence tuition in the early years of World War Two - operating lessons by post for pupils in those smaller islands where schools were forced, by the strictures of wartime, to close.

He had been one of the most ardent correspondents to the letters pages of *The Orcadian*, and had been co-editor of *The New Orkney Book*, published in 1966. He had also taught at Kirkwall Grammar School and in North Ronaldsay before moving to Sanday.

Orkney schoolchildren could again enjoy the delights of a double decker bus as a 17 year old, 53 seater Leyland bus was brought to the county in 1970 by James D. Peace. The first double decker bus came to Orkney in 1906, and the BEA airline brought another to the county after World War Two. *(Picture from the files of The Orcadian)*

Leith link is axed

"This is the worst thing that could happen to Stromness in half a century," said Provost W.E. Knight at an emergency meeting of Stromness Town Council as the North of Scotland, Orkney and Shetland Shipping Company confirmed its intention to terminate the weekly service to Stromness from Leith and Aberdeen.

It was feared that the loss of the shipping route would threaten the future of the West Mainland Mart. The Kirkwall service with Leith would also be axed - ending a 21 year link with Orkney for the ferry *St Ninian* which had first called at Kirkwall in May, 1950.

The *St Ninian* went to Canada to serve as a cruise liner.

New convener

Colonel Henry Scarth of Breckness - Orkney county convener for 11 years - announced his retirement from the county council in 1970.

He was succeeded as convener by Councillor Donald Brown of Stromness, who had been vice-convener. George Marwick of Birsay became the new vice-convener.

Colonel Scarth - who was also Lord Lieutenant of Orkney - died in 1972, at the age of 72. He was succeeded as the Queen's representative in the county by Colonel Robert Macrae.

Island birth

The first baby - an 8lb boy - to be born in Gairsay for 50 years was safely delivered to Valerie and David McGill who had settled on the island in 1969 with their three children after moving from Cornwall.

The mother was attended by Dr Donald Fairley of Rousay who was ferried across to the island by boatman Charlie Craigie from Wyre.

The baby was born in the mansion house of Laingskaill, the history of which could be traced back to the Norse chieftain Sweyn Asleifsson.

Faroese football

The month of July, 1970, saw the first official visit to Orkney of a football team from the Faroese Sports Association.

Less than 25 years later, the Faroese Islands would be competing as a nation in the qualifying rounds of the World Cup.

The team, which came to Orkney to compete in the North Atlantic Cup, was delayed for 24 hours as the weather disrupted flights to Kirkwall, so the players missed out on a civic reception from Kirkwall Town Council. But they were still good enough to beat Orkney 4-3.

Race to save Cathedral from ruin

Orcadians were shocked to be told that a worldwide appeal was necessary to save the county's proudest possession - St Magnus Cathedral - from ruin.

The first warning of the impending threat to the Cathedral came in September, 1970, when consultant architect Alexander Heward said the condition of the vaulted roof of the nave was serious and needed to be remedied with reinforced beams.

He suggested that the earth tremor, experienced in Kirkwall in January, 1927, had caused movement in the Cathedral which, over the years, had led to cracks in the masonry and vaulting.

"Your Cathedral is a wonderful building historically, and architecturally a gem," he said, but work needed to go ahead uninterrupted if the building was to maintain that proud boast.

A few days later, the architect's warning could have been totally irrelevant - as the Cathedral came close to being burned down!

The drama happened on September 29, 1970, as firemen were called out at midnight to deal with a blaze in the north east corner of the roof closest to the great east window. It was thought to have been caused by a dislodged floodlight which ignited timbers.

Passer-by Robert Wood had spotted flames and alerted the emergency services. By the time the fire brigade arrived, the fire had already got a good hold and

1971

was burning fiercely under the slates.

When Cathedral minister Rev Bill Cant arrived, the whole building was filled with smoke.

The blaze could have been disastrous if it had spread any further along the roof. As it was, the fire was so fierce that charred beams had to be removed, but the quick action by the firemen limited the damage to an area of just 200 square feet of roof.

However, it was soon obvious that the fire damage was almost a minor concern for the guardians of the Cathedral as it was revealed in December, 1971, that, if the 800 year old building was to be preserved for future generations, a worldwide appeal for funds was essential.

"St Magnus Cathedral is urgently in need of funds unless it is to become a ruin," said Colonel Robert Macrae.

The appeal fund was set up with an initial target of £50,000 but the eventual aim of raising £300,000. The guardians of the Cathedral had used up all available funds on a £12,000 renovation of the Cathedral organ - "unaware that a major catastrophe was facing them in the structure of the Cathedral itself," said Colonel Macrae.

"The Cathedral is now in a dangerous state, movement is still taking place and, if allowed to continue, the roof would undoubtedly collapse."

The Society of Friends of St Magnus Cathedral was to liquidise all its assets to put to the Save St Magnus Cathedral Fund, and what was to become the annual St Magnus Fair was launched in 1972 to further boost fund-raising.

Colonel Macrae added: "The Cathedral is part of our Viking heritage. It is over 800 years old and still a place of worship, and at this point in its history, it is in our keeping. It is clearly our duty to see that we hand it down to posterity in good order."

Kirkwall Town Council immediately announced that the main part of the Cathedral would be closed for repairs for a year to allow work to go ahead, while services would continue using the Choir and St Rognvald Chapel.

The Appeal fund was officially launched in January, 1972, by Lord Birsay. One of the first gifts came from Queen Elizabeth, the Queen Mother. Within six weeks, £20,000 had been raised and the initial target of £50,000 was reached by May, 1972, as the Government contributed £15,000.

Drought hits the isles

A drought saw island wells dry up in 1971. Two emergency 400 gallon tanks were installed on North Ronaldsay by the North of Scotland Water Board.

Mrs Catherine Zawadski, of Balfour Castle, Shapinsay, said: "There is not a drop of water left in the Castle well - it has never been dry for 130 years. All the big farms on the island have also run out and the situation is becoming critical. What is annoying us is that we have been promised, for long enough, a mains water supply."

As the isles bemoaned a lack of water, it was the gas supply which was drying up in Kirkwall.

Gas production was to stop in the town, a new £75,000 gasholder would be demolished and the site would be cleared for redevelopment, announced the Scottish Gas Board. Around 550 Kirkwall consumers would be offered compensation to switch to other fuels.

Smoking room for pupils

As a new hostel opened in Kirkwall to house 200 isles pupils attending Kirkwall Grammar School, a row broke out as it was decided to provide a smoking room for pupils.

The hostel sub-committee decided the room would be set aside for those pupils whose parents did not object to their smoking. (Fourteen pupils were said to have such permission).

The decision caused raised eyebrows, if not raised blood pressure, at the following meeting of Orkney Education Committee.

"It is our duty and responsibility to make absolutely no provision whatso-

ever to encourage smoking or even to make it comfortable or socially respectable," said Mr Ian MacInnes, depute rector of Stromness Academy. The education committee voted by just one vote, by 12-11, to block the smoking room.

However, a month later the committee reversed its decision, by 18 votes to six, after an appeal by hostel warden Mr J. Merriman. He was not promoting smoking, but pointed out that those over the age of 16 would be legally entitled to smoke outwith school, and warning of the fire risk that would be created in the hostel by clandestine smoking.

Decimal Day

A national strike of Post Office workers lasted 47 days at the start of 1971, with no postal deliveries from Tuesday, January 19.

During the middle of the strike came Decimal Day on February 15, 1971, as

we said farewell to shillings and pennies and "welcomed" the new pence, of which there were 100 to the pound. Curiously, the word "inflation" entered the vocabulary of the nation at about the same time.

From Persia to Hoy

December, 1971, saw the death in the Balfour Hospital of Lady Doris Skrine - the widow of Sir Clarmont Skrine, a former British Ambassador to Persia - who had retired to Rysa Lodge in Hoy in 1949.

A loyal servant to the North Isles of Orkney for a quarter of a century, the *Islander*, is seen here at Fair Isle. *(Picture from the files of The Orcadian)*

Two for one at council

Mr Douglas Wood - who had been only Orkney's second county clerk of the century - retired after 30 years service as clerk and treasurer. The county council decided to split the post and appointed a new clerk, Graeme Lapsley (46), formerly director of the Scottish Federation of Building Trades Employers, and a new treasurer, Ron Gilbert (34), originally from Derbyshire but who had been working as depute treasurer with Caithness County Council.

At the same time, Alex Bain was appointed to succeed the retiring Robert Mack as director of education. Also, the year of 1971 saw the death of Kirkwall Grammar School rector Henry MacKerron, aged 63. He had been rector for 18 years after originally joining the KGS staff as principal teacher of science in 1947. He was succeeded as rector by Mr William Thomson (38) from the Anderson High School in Lerwick, where he was depute headmaster. Mr Donald McInnes, a former headteacher in Shapinsay, became the first headmaster of Kirkwall Primary School, which was now administered separately from the grammar school.

It was agreed that offices for the new Orkney Islands Council would be created at the old Kirkwall Grammar School building which was soon to be vacated as pupils moved to the new school building at Papdale.

Ron Gilbert - later to become chief executive of Orkney Islands Council - joined the Orkney County Council in 1971.

Bird reserve

Orkney's first bird reserve at the 300 acre Dale of Cottascarth was formally inaugurated by Mr George Waterson, deputy director of the Royal Society for the Protection of Birds, in October, 1971.

Great exodus goes on

The 1971 census showed that Orkney's population had fallen to 17,254 - a further drop of 1,500 compared with 1961.

Although Kirkwall's population had increased by 300 to 4,638 and Stromness by 200 to 1,674, there had been a fall in the rest of the Mainland from 7,764 in 1961 to 6,535 in 1971.

Tragedies at sea

There was tragedy for Sanday in November, 1971, as two men were lost in a fishing accident. Leslie Wilson (18) was saved but Henry Thomson (38) and Thomas Harcus (19) died as the fishing boat *Northern Isle* was lost off her home island while creeling. An appeal fund raised more than £2,000 for the families.

Six months later, the provost of Stromness opened a fund for the families of two fishermen - Jim Pratt (33) and Greig Pirie (31) - who were lost, leaving six children fatherless, after their lobster boat *Mayflower* was swamped by heavy seas south of Marwick Head.

In 1977, there was a tragic repeat of history as Sanday and Stromness mourned the loss of four men. In June, 1977, Ian Slater (34) and Brian Peace (29) were lost as they capsized as they came ashore from the lobster boat *Burness Queen* in Sanday.

In October, two men were lost - James Thorpe (37) and Norbert Kunkel (26), both living in Stromness - when the 28ft fishing boat *Delightful* broke up off Hoy in a gale. An air and sea search was launched as wreckage came ashore.

Westray's population had fallen from 1,012 to 866; South Ronaldsay from 1,247 to 1,006; and Rousay from 338 to 256.

It meant that, in the first 70 years of the 20th century, the population in Orkney had declined by more than 10,000 - from a total of 27,723 in 1901.

Success? We had it cracked!

For half a century or more, Orkney's economy was built on the golden egg! Or, to be exact, over three billion eggs!

For that is a very approximate estimate of the number of eggs produced by the county's poultry industry during the years 1900-1970, the 70 years which saw the rise and fall of a business that earned millions of pounds in real terms - or the equivalent of hundreds of millions at 1999 prices.

Orcadian egg producers could truly boast that they fed the nation as Orkney became the biggest egg-producing county in Britain. In 1950, Orkney could claim ten per cent of Scotland's total egg output as Orkney Egg Producers handled over one and a half million eggs a week. The motor vessel *Shapinsay*, bought by Captain Bill Dennison in 1950, carried 36 million eggs from Kirkwall to Glasgow in her first three years in Orkney - the equivalent of three dozen eggs for every head of population in Glasgow.

It was already an established industry at the start of the 20th century with Orkney egg production at 21 millions a year. It was to almost double in the next three decades and, by 1935, it had increased to nearly 40 millions.

That was mere chickenfeed compared to what was to follow. By 1950, Orkney's poultry population was up to 810,000 - that's 40 hens for each man, woman and child in the county - and, for the first time, the annual turnover at Orkney Egg Producers topped the £1 million mark at £1,080,000 for the 1949 financial year.

Incidentally, there were 3,200 agricultural holdings in Orkney in 1950 - but only 162 were over 100 acres, with the average being just 34 acres, although the majority of land-holders - 2,019 - were owner occupiers.

Half of Orkney's acreage was under crops or grass - compared with only three per cent in Shetland, and an average of eight per cent in the rest of the crofting counties. Cattle stocks in Orkney in 1950 totalled 48,598, while there were 61,290 sheep. And milk production for the year reached 1,224,333 gallons.

Nationally, of course, we were still in the grip of food rationing introduced during the war. Aggravating as this obviously was for millions of consumers, it has to be accepted that Orkney benefited enormously from this regimented system of government intervention. Not only did various marketing boards ensure that there was a ready market for everything that Orkney could produce, there was also the added advantage of guaranteed prices.

The result was that Orkney's agricultural exports in 1950 were valued at over £2 millions for the first time - the equivalent of £40 millions at 1999 prices - half of which could be attributed to eggs.

Sixty million eggs were exported from Orkney in 1950, with an estimated gross income to the county of £1,110,000. Most of these eggs, just under 50 million, were handled at the Ayre grading station at Kirkwall.

At the same time, Kirkwall poultry dealer James Sclater was able, via BEA air services, to have Orkney-produced poultry delivered to Smithfield meat market in London within 36 hours of being slaughtered.

Such prosperity more than compensated for the fact that, in November, 1951, local farmers had to suffer Orkney's wettest November for 85 years with a fraction under eight inches of rain that month.

In fact, by the time the new Conservative government announced at the start of 1953 that eggs would no longer be rationed to the public, and the production and marketing of eggs would be de-controlled, Orkney's industry was in strong enough shape to survive the relaxation of intervention policies.

But, nonetheless, there were already warning signs for the future. The new free market would mean the end of egg subsidies which had nationally totalled £20 millions, or a penny an egg, and there were fears that rural areas like Orkney would be penalised by having to pick up the bill for transport to the major population areas. Another blow was the rise of £2/7/6 a ton in the cost of animal feedstuffs.

However, Orkney producers were hardly complaining in August, 1953, when Orkney egg packing stations were paying 5/3 dozen for top quality hen eggs - the 1999 equivalent of around £5 a dozen, or the price of a pound of sirloin steak at the end of the century.

And they were still expansionist times. The Edinburgh City Egg Packing Station on the Market Green, Stromness - in what was the wartime Church of Scotland canteen - was converted to produce oven-ready poultry for South markets. The plant could produce 1,000 birds a day.

To Orkney's eternal credit - and a tribute to Orcadian resilience - the two great storms of 1952 and 1953 proved nothing more than a mere hiccup in the continued development of the county egg industry, despite the fact that a quarter of a million hens were literally blown away to oblivion.

Despite the disruption of the storms, Orkney's two egg grading stations in Kirkwall and Stromness handled 61 million eggs in 1953 (valued at £1,250,000) and 66 millions a year later.

Business was good enough to encourage a new venture, the Pomona Egg and Poultry Packing Station, opened at Hatston by Maurice Leask and Edwin Rendall, who was still completing his National Service. The company handled eight million eggs in its first 16 months.

There certainly seemed to be enough business for everyone. In the year 1955, Orkney Egg Producers made a profit of £36,714 with a throughput of 54 million eggs. Orkney's total egg production was estimated to be 67 millions with a gross value of £1,200,000. A year later, Orkney's total egg exports had grown to 72 millions.

The man who had overseen this post-war growth in the Orkney egg industry was George Stuart, manager of the Ayre egg packing station for 12 years. He originally came to Orkney to open the Lipton's branch in Albert Street, Kirkwall, of which he was manager for 15 years. The number of staff at the egg packing station had nearly doubled to 60 during his time when the firm grew to have an annual turnover of £1 million. George Stuart left Orkney, to be succeeded as manager by Mr James Sutherland, at the end of 1957.

That year, coincidentally, proved to be the peak of the industry in the county - an economic summit which would never be regained - as egg production in Orkney reached 78 millions, producing an estimated income of £1,400,000 for the county, the equivalent of around £25 millions at 1999 prices.

It was a statistic to savour for, perversely, it was to prove to be the beginning of the end. There was always a danger - with Orkney's reliance on sea transport and its associated costs - that there was a flaw in the economics of the operation that saw thousands of tons of feedstuffs shipped in, and millions of eggs shipped out.

It was not a sudden death by any means, rather a lingering demise over the following 15 years.

Egg production was still 77 million eggs in 1958 and, despite a warning from the British Egg Marketing Board that farmers were over-producing at a rate with which sales could not keep pace, exports were still over 76 millions in 1959.

The first sign of a rationalisation of the industry came in 1960 when Orkney Egg Producers took over the Stromness egg packing station that had been run by Edinburgh City Egg Packers Ltd.

The value of Orkney egg production continued at over £1 million until, in 1962, it fell below that level for the first time since the immediate post-war days of the 1940s - the 1962 value being estimated at £976,400 for just over 66 million eggs. A bright spot, however, saw the Stromness station handle over 500,000lbs of poultry - a 45 per cent increase on the year.

As has already been stated, Orkney agriculture had benefited from the marketing boards throughout the 1950s. September, 1959, saw the first warning signs that this would not continue for ever and it meant a crisis for the county's pig producers.

Messrs Lawsons in Dyce - where most of the Orkney pigs went - pulled out of the Fatstock Marketing Corporation to deal directly with producers. In reality, this meant that Orkney pigs were worth £1 less to the producer than their counterparts further south, owing to the transport charges which would now fall on the local producers.

A similar situation hit the egg industry in 1962 as the guaranteed price of eggs was reduced by the government by a penny ha'penny a dozen. The price being paid in 1962 had fallen below 3/- dozen for large eggs, compared with a peak of 5/3 dozen a few years earlier.

Mr Rupert Chalmers Watson, of the British Egg Marketing Board's National Advisory Committee for Scotland, warned that many small producers would be unable to continue in egg production at that level of prices.

He was soon proved correct. By 1964, the egg trade in Orkney was on the downward spiral. Production for the year was still at a commendable 65 millions but the value was down to £833,000 gross - nearly 40 per cent down on the figures seven or eight years earlier.

By 1966, it was obvious, reported *The Orcadian*, that eggs had ceased to be the money spinner they once were. Production was down from its peak of 78 millions to 50 millions, with a value of £624,000. A year later, the value had fallen even further to £484,000 as David Smith, the egg board's chief information officer, visited Orkney to explain the impact of a further reorganisation of the industry. The blueprint for a freer market would spell ruin for local producers, it was feared.

It was suggested that one solution would be a merger of the egg producing company with the two marts in the county so there would be just one organisation handling the marketing of Orkney meat and eggs. Orkney Egg Producers Ltd agreed to a merger proposal with the West Mainland Mart, but Kirkwall Mart members rejected the idea.

By now, the egg industry had probably gone past the point of no return. For the first time in its history, Orkney Egg Producers Ltd had a net trading loss - amounting to £2,433 - for the 1968 financial year as the county's egg output fell to 33 millions valued at £367,000, virtually a quarter of the value ten years earlier. It was the lowest level of egg production in 40 years.

Orkney Egg Producers' balance sheet for 1969 showed a total deficit of £7,661. The number of eggs produced in the year was down to 25 millions, worth just £286,000. The future was none too bright, said chairman Mr R.J. Paterson. Producers were getting out of the industry at a fast rate and there was a need to cut overheads. It was not enough to stop the decline - by 1970, production levels were down to their lowest level of the century. The industry would struggle on for a few more years, but the epitaphs had already been written.

The impact of the collapse of the egg industry was reflected in the gross earning of Orkney's agricultural sector in the years 1957-1969.

The gross value of Orkney agriculture (cattle, sheep, pigs, eggs and milk) in 1957 was £2,857,410 - of which half came from the egg industry. By 1969, the value of agriculture had grown by only ten per cent to £2,917,500, but farmers had compensated for the decline in eggs by building a sturdy beef industry. Store cattle were topping the £90 mark on average, the equivalent of around £1,000 each at 1999 prices.

The emergence of beef cattle as the mainstay of Orkney agriculture was a gradual process over the 25 years after World War Two.

Progressive Orkney farmers had invested in new breeding stock and the annual bull show at Kirkwall Mart, in January, 1953, saw a new record high price for the time when the reserve champion, an Aberdeen-Angus, Earl of Weddell, shown by Eric Laird of Weddell, Burray, was sold for a few shillings over 173 guineas - an equivalent approaching £4,000 at 1999 prices.

The following year, for the first time, the Kirkwall Mart spring sale saw the price of steers reach £100 as 708 cattle were sold over three days.

The highest price in Orkney for any animal, up until that time, was also achieved that year, as a total of £600 was paid for two Aberdeen-Angus cows from the Flett brothers at Kingshouse, Harray. They were bought on behalf of an American purchaser.

After nearly 15 years of meat rationing, government controls were lifted in July, 1954, and up to 700 spectators attended the first "de-controlled" sale of cattle as Kirkwall Auction Mart returned to a "free market."

The lifting of restrictions did nothing to slow the demand for good bulls - in fact, it probably encouraged the demand as, in January, 1955, bulls again went for record prices at the annual show and sale in Kirkwall.

The champion, an Aberdeen-Angus from James Baillie of Sebay fetched 232 guineas, paid by Mr J. Brown of Westray. In all four bulls fetched over 200 guineas, all purchased by North Isles buyers.

That year ended with many of the animals at the annual Christmas fatstock show in Kirkwall topping £100. The West Mainland Mart saw similar prices with 11 steers fetching over £100.

The year of 1957 saw the formation of Orkney Sheepbreeders Association, marking an increased interest in sheep in the county as, at its first lamb sale in August, there were 1,741 lambs forward making prices up to £12 12s 6d.

But it was back in the cattle ring that the next Orkney record was made as the champion at the Orkney Bull Show, James Baillie's Aberdeen-Angus Edwin Eric of Sebay was sold at the Perth Bull Sales for 420 guineas - the highest figure paid for a single Orkney animal at the time.

A certain affluence amongst Orkney farmers was illustrated as small farms coming on the market in 1958, with an upset price of £1,000, were selling for over £2,000 - or more than £50 an acre.

The 1959 Kirkwall Christmas fatstock show saw a record high price of £201 - the equivalent of around £3,000 at 1999 prices - for the champion animal from Alfie Learmonth of Shapinsay, which was purchased by Kirkwall butcher Walter Lobban.

In 1967, Orkney farmers R. Allen, of Leafea, Stromness, and D.W. Sinclair, Unigarth, Sandwick, joined forces at the Perth bull sales to buy what was then probably the costliest animal ever to come to the county - a year old Aberdeen-Angus bull costing 900 guineas.

Although the number of people working in farming in Orkney had fallen by 400 during the previous ten years, Orkney NFU could still boast 1,168 members in 1968, and the county had a total of 1,748 tractors. And another indication of the reasonable prosperity of the time came when, for the first time, Kirkwall Auction Mart reached a turnover of over £2 million (£2,113,567) in the 1971-72 financial year.

It may not have been a land of milk and honey, but compared to the crisis-ridden last dozen years of the 20th century, that is how we will probably remember it.

Men of mark - and literature

Orkney can look back with pride at the literary achievements of some of her most famous sons during the 20th century.

But four writers stand apart as having achieved national, if not international, status during their careers - J. Storer Clouston, Edwin Muir, Eric Linklater and George Mackay Brown.

There have been others, of course. George Mackay Brown regarded Duncan Robertson as one of Orkney's most under-rated poets, but the solicitor who was Orkney's county clerk from 1890-1940 would not have claimed literature as his primary career by other means. The same applied to John Mooney, who is probably regarded more as a historian than for quality of writing, and Robert Rendall, although an acclaimed poet in Orkney, could not enjoy the same level of recognition nationally.

In the last decade of the 20th century, two men who made their homes in Orkney - the novelist and short story writer Duncan MacLean, who settled in Stromness, and the Rev Ron Ferguson, minister of St Magnus Cathedral - have achieved national recognition for their work, but they are still comparatively young and there is still time for the 21st century to provide an assessment of their literary contribution.

J. Storer Clouston could claim to be the first Orkney writer of the 20th century to achieve any degree of prominence and, somewhat oddly, considering he probably had the more privileged upbringing compared to those fellow Orcadian writers who followed, he had the most populist style of them all.

Born in Cumberland, the eldest son of the Orcadian pioneer of mental health treatment Thomas Clouston (later to be Sir Thomas), Joseph Storer Clouston was educated at Merchiston Castle, Edinburgh, and Magdalen College, Oxford, before he was called to the bar in 1895.

By the 20th century, his novels were written at an impressive rate - he often had books published at the rate of one or even two a year - but, to be fair, his work was better known outside the county than in Orkney until he returned to Orphir to live.

The literary merit of some of his novels - generally, a mixture of thrillers and comedies - is questionable. Some of them were perhaps no more that "penny dreadfuls" (George Mackay Brown certainly admired him more as a historian than a prose writer) but, undoubtedly his books were popular and sold in their many thousands. And his expertise in story-telling saw at least three cinema films based on his books.

Storer Clouston also wrote some plays, including *The Pocket Miss Hercules* (1907), but it would be his novels - more than 20 of them - for which he would be best remembered, including *The Lunatic at Large, Lunatic at Large Again, Lunatic Still at Large, Lunatic in Charge, The Duke, A County Family, The Prodigal Father, The Peer's Progress, His First Offence, Two's Two, The Spy in Black, The Virtuous Vamp* and *The Best Story Ever*.

The Lunatic at Large was made into a film in 1928, and *The Spy in Black* in 1938 - its world premiere being held at the Albert Kinema in Kirkwall. Another film of his work was made in France after World War Two.

And his value as a historian was shown when his book *A History of Orkney* appeared in 1932.

It was a prolific output from a man who still found time to be county convener from 1930, and who became an OBE in the 1935 birthday honours list. J. Storer Clouston died in June, 1944.

Edwin Muir was born on May 15, 1887, at the farm of Folly in Deerness. He was the son of a Sanday man, James Muir, from Colligarth, and a Deerness mother, Elizabeth Cormack.

When he was two, the family left Deerness to go to Wyre - first to the farm of Bu and then Helziegetha - before returning

to the Orkney Mainland and the farm of Garth, near Kirkwall, when Muir was eight.

He had three brothers and two sisters, but Muir later portrayed himself in his autobiography as a sad, timid, withdrawn little boy who did not go to school until the age of seven because of ill health. According to Muir himself, he was backward, good at nothing but singing and disliked school.

He was 14 when his parents decided on a fresh start in Glasgow. It was a black period in Edwin Muir's life - by the time he was 18, death through illness had claimed the lives of his mother, father and two brothers.

At 21 he was converted to Socialism and joined the Independent Labour Party. His first job was an office boy in Glasgow at 4s 2d a week, then a junior clerk in a beer-bottling factory before two soul destroying years in a bone factory.

However, in 1919, at the age of 32, he married Willa Anderson from Unst in Shetland and the literary chapter of his life began. He began to write poetry, and his wife achieved fame as a novelist.

Suddenly he was transformed. He learned German - and was responsible with his wife for notable translations of the work of the Czech novelist Franz Kafka - and he discovered Europe, living in Prague, Vienna, Rome, and cities of France and Germany.

His autobiography was first published as *The Story and the Fable* in 1940 and then updated as *An Autobiography* in 1954.

After seeing the rise of Nazi-ism in Germany, he saw the growth of Communism after World War Two in Prague where he worked for the British Council, before returning to Scotland in October, 1950, as warden of the adult education college at Newbattle Abbey, Dalkeith, where both George Mackay Brown and Robert Rendall studied.

In his autobiography published by the Hogarth Press, Muir wrote: "When I began to write poetry - I was in Germany at the time - I wrote in baffling ignorance, blundering and perpetually making mistakes. I must have been influenced by something, since we all are, but when I try to find out what it was that influenced me, I can only think of the years of childhood which I spent on my father's farm in the little island of Wyre in Orkney, and the beauty I apprehended then, before I knew there was beauty."

Ironically, it was not an original work but his translation of the novel *Jew Suss* by the German author Feuchtwanger, which he translated with his wife, that made him world famous. He followed with a biography of John Knox - published to favourable reviews in 1929 - and novels like *The Three Brothers*.

The Orkney poet Robert Rendall in an appreciation said that his poetry had achieved international stature. "His poetry, without noise and tumult, quietly found a niche for itself in contemporary literature. Reviews, if sometimes slightly puzzled in tone, were always respectful, as if the reviewer realised that this poet had something to say which, if not fully understood at first, would in time come into its own. This expectation was met by the increasing clarity of his later poems, which have in them a spontaneous release of feeling, expressive of his growing comprehension of the mystery of life. For, from the first, Edwin Muir's poetry was a search for the ultimate spiritual values that give meaning to human existence. In the future, his work will almost certainly be seen in perspective from this standpoint and its values duly assessed by those competent to do so: the poems themselves have their own immortality."

Rendall added: "Though an exile from his native Orkney he retained a deep and abiding love for the islands. This was not nostalgic romanticism: he was too clear-sighted not to see things as they are; but he valued the simplicities of life that often find place in an island community."

Eric and Marjorie Linklater with young members of the family.　　(Picture courtesy of Orkney Library photographic archive)

He was buried in the Cambridgeshire village of Swaffham Prior, near Newmarket, where he lived in retirement following a year's appointment as Professor of Poetry at Harvard University, USA. He died aged 71, on January 3, 1959, leaving his wife and a son. His memorial at Swaffham Prior read: "His unblinded eyes saw far and near fields of paradise".

George Mackay Brown wrote: "Only time will tell but I think Edwin Muir was the greatest of Orkney poets.

"Edwin Muir's poetry was a new kind of poetry; we will get used to it in time. Even today, what intelligent Orkney reader could fail to be moved by a poem like "Horses," "The Transfiguration" or "For Ann Scott-Moncrieff?"

"As a prose writer he had few equals in the literary world of the 20th century. His style was absolutely pure and crystalline; nothing was forced or affected, but the still waters of his prose ran very deep and flowed around the roots of life and creation. The beauty and pattern and purpose of life, under all the shifting complexities, were always actual to him. That was why he loved Orkney so much, because the good primeval patterns were everywhere around."

People tended to think of Muir as a quiet gentle writer, but George Mackay Brown said: "He could be angrier than the angriest young man." There was no more bitter and crushing denunciation of the worst evils of industrialism than his book *Scottish Journey* published in 1935.

George Mackay Brown, who knew Muir personally from his time at Newbattle Abbey, said: "To say in the 20th century, that a man is a Saint is to invite immediate ridicule. Yet he had those saint-like qualities, and anyone who has been in his company for an hour will know what I mean. He had, in addition, boundless generosity and much quiet humour."

"Without the great courage and love and sympathy of Willa Muir, it is unlikely that he would have produced such lasting literature in such quantity," said George Mackay Brown.

Edwin Muir was in the same class at school as the Orkney artist Stanley Cursiter for a couple of years. When Edwin Muir

and his wife Willa visited Cursiter in Stromness in 1951, it was Muir's first visit to his home county in 15 years. Cursiter - according to *The Orcadian* - described his lifelong friend as "the loveliest mind that ever left Orkney." One is left wondering whether that should be "liveliest" but, whatever, it's a powerful tribute.

A memorial service for Edwin Muir was held in St Giles Cathedral, Edinburgh on January 17, 1953, where those taking part included Douglas Young, the St Andrews professor and poet, and Dr Charles Warr, the minister of St Giles. Stanley Cursiter attended.

The poet Norman McCaig, a friend of Muir, made the memorial oration while actor Tom Fleming read what many consider to be Muir's finest poem, "The Transfiguration."

"Rarely can the poem have sounded so moving as under the dim arches of Edinburgh's High Kirk, spoken in the grave priest-like tones of one of Scotland's finest contemporary actors," wrote George Mackay Brown.

In 1999, Alan Taylor, managing editor of Scotsman Publications Ltd and a former Booker prize judge, compiled his list of Scotland's 100 best books ever written in a personal view for *Scotland on Sunday* magazine. He chose three works by Muir - *Scottish Journey* (number 22), *Collected Poems* (number 42) and *Scott and Scotland* (number 80) to prove the enduring appeal of his work.

Edwin Muir's rise to literary acclaim coincided with that of another Orkney writer, Eric Linklater. And, unlike Muir, who left Orkney as a boy and completed virtually all his work outside the county, Linklater was to spend a significant part of his life in the islands.

Eric Robert Linklater was born in Glamorgan, South Wales, on March 8, 1899. His father, Robert Linklater, was a master mariner whose family came from Mossetter, Harray, while his mother, Elizabeth Young, was the daughter of a Swedish sea captain.

In 1917 he joined the Black Watch, rising in the ranks to Corporal by the end of the year when he was posted to the front line where he served as a marksman. He saw action at Passchendale and the Somme but at Ypres he was badly wounded by a German bullet that passed through his helmet and blew away part of his skull in a near fatal injury. He would always bear the scar in the back of his head.

Eric Linklater had been studying medicine at Aberdeen University before the war but at the conclusion of hostilities, he transferred to Kings College, Aberdeen, to study English Literature.

After graduating from university he worked in the offices of the *Press & Journal* before taking a post as assistant editor of the *Times of India* in 1925. After two years, he set off with a friend to travel home through Persia, Russia, Turkey and Austria before reaching Britain, where, at the end of 1927, he took a teaching post at Aberdeen University. Nearly 20 years later, he would return to the university as rector.

He finished his first novel in 1928, *White-Maa's Saga*, a semi-autobiographical story about an Orcadian medical student at the fictional Inverdoon University.

He later went to the USA and studied at Cornell, before transferring to Berkeley in California, and when he returned to Britain in 1930, his second novel *Poet's Pub* had been published and he was working on another. *Juan in America* was based on his experiences there, and proved to be a great success. Published in 1931, it was reprinted nine times by the end of the year. It made the name Eric Linklater famous.

The regard in which he was held in literary circles was clearly shown in 1935 when the first ten books ever published by Penguin included *Poet's Pub*. The 12th impression of the book was published (again by Penguin) in 1951.

His following novel *The Men of Ness* was the story of Orkney Vikings told in a saga style.

But his next move was a temporary excursion into politics. The Scottish National Party approached him to stand in the East Fife by-election of 1933. When polling day arrived, he finished bottom of the poll.

Although an advocate of Scottish self-determination, Linklater was certainly not of the republican wing of the SNP - in fact his views were probably not far removed from those of many people who were to call for increased devolution of power later in the century.

In 1950, the Scottish Covenant, a petition calling for a greater say for Scotland in government, was signed by around 800 people in Orkney. But Eric Linklater asked for his signature to be removed after several of the leading people behind the campaign sought financial and political support in the USA.

"Heaven forbid that Scotland should ever take Ireland's path of self-determination," he said. "I signed the covenant because I am deeply interested in the fortunes of Scotland and hope to see it play a larger and better part for its own sake and that of the United Kingdom, under the Sovereign of the United Kingdom. I cannot, however, remain a signatory of the covenant if it is to become a weapon loaded with American dollars, aimed from without at the structure of the United Kingdom."

In fact, in the 1955 General Election, one of the few highlights of a lacklustre campaign in Orkney was the so-called Linklater Letter when Eric Linklater wrote a letter of support for Orkney's Liberal MP Jo Grimond, saying that, although he was not in the process of becoming a Liberal, he felt that Grimond was the best man to represent Orkney in Parliament.

In October, 1932, Eric Linklater had met his future wife, Marjorie MacIntyre, the daughter of Ian MacIntyre, a Conservative MP. They were married at Old St Paul's, Edinburgh, in 1933 and moved to Orkney where his mother offered them the house of Ingleneuk. Work started to enlarge the property, which was renamed Merkister, and they moved there in the summer of 1935.

Magnus Merriman was published in January, 1934, and became another best seller but Eric Linklater's outspoken condemnation of Hitler and the Nazi party had led to his books being banned, and publicly burned, in Germany. He was officially informed that he was not welcome in that country.

He was serving as captain in the Orkney Territorial Army when war was declared in 1939. In November he was promoted to Major in the Orkney (Fortress) Royal Engineers, but, nonetheless, found the time to write an autobiography called *The Man on my Back*, which was published in 1941. Also in Orkney he edited the first issue of the newspaper for the troops, the *Orkney Blast*, published for the first time on January 17, 1941, before handing over to Gerry Meyer (later editor of *The Orcadian*).

In 1943, Linklater was sent to Italy to write a history of the Italian Campaign. He also met the BBC war correspondent Wynford Vaughan Thomas in Rome. Together they discovered a collection of art treasures that had been removed from Florence for safety, but were now only yards from the German lines, stored in an old castle. Their value was impossible to price.

Two books resulted from these visits: *The Italian Campaign* published in 1951, and the novel *Private Angelo* published in 1944 and later turned into a film by Peter Ustinov, who produced, directed and starred in the film.

In 1947, the Linklaters left Orkney when they moved to Nigg in Ross-shire. But Eric Linklater was never again to achieve the status as a novelist which he enjoyed in the previous two decades. And after his final novel, *A Terrible Freedom*, was published in 1966, to a lack of critical acclaim, he published no more fiction.

However, in 1970, his history *The Royal House of Scotland* was published. He sent a copy to the Duke of Edinburgh who was apparently so delighted with it that he invited Eric and Marjorie Linklater to spend a weekend at Balmoral.

In 1970, his third autobiography *Fanfare for a Tin Hat* was also published while September, 1972, saw the publication of his last book, a history of the scientific expedition *The Voyage of the Challenger*.

Eric Linklater died on November 7, 1974. His funeral was held at St Olaf's Episcopal Church, Kirkwall, and he was buried at St Michael's Churchyard, Harray.

He could have had no better epitaph than the tribute that George Mackay Brown paid him in *The Orcadian* of February 11, 1954: "Eric Linklater is not primarily a novelist, or an essayist or a dramatist. He is above all else an enchanting prose poet. These fragments of wonderful singing prose are scattered all over his books, and through them English literature is permanently enriched."

After his death, Marjorie Linklater moved back to Orkney, living in Main Street, Kirkwall. She donated 12 of the paintings that her husband had bought during his life to Aberdeen University.

Both Edwin Muir and Eric Linklater had seen the world, enjoying a cosmopolitan lifestyle. By contrast, George Mackay Brown, the man who was to follow as Orkney's most acclaimed writer in the second half of the century, was truly a man of Orkney. He was born in Stromness and, apart from a spell in the 1950s when he went south to study, he seldom ventured far from his native islands or his home town.

And yet George Mackay Brown, or GMB as he was simply known to most, still achieved an international reputation as a poet, dramatist and novelist - culminating in 1994 with his novel *Beside the Ocean of Time* being short-listed for the Booker Prize.

Born October 17, 1921, George Mackay Brown was brought up and schooled in Stromness, the son of a part time postman and tailor, John Brown, and his wife Mary Jane Mackay, a Gaelic speaking Highlander. He appeared to have enjoyed his schooling at the Old Stromness Academy, showing an early gift for writing, and he obviously followed an artistic temperament.

Tragically, in 1941 he suffered an attack of that scourge of the time, Tuberculosis, which kept him out of work for 10 years - but it was to be a period he used to the full in reading and writing.

And one of his first literary successes came with his play *Spoils of the Sea*, which was performed by Stromness Amateur Dramatic Society in the Scottish Community Drama Association festival of 1949. He followed this in 1950 with *The Wheel o' Fortune*.

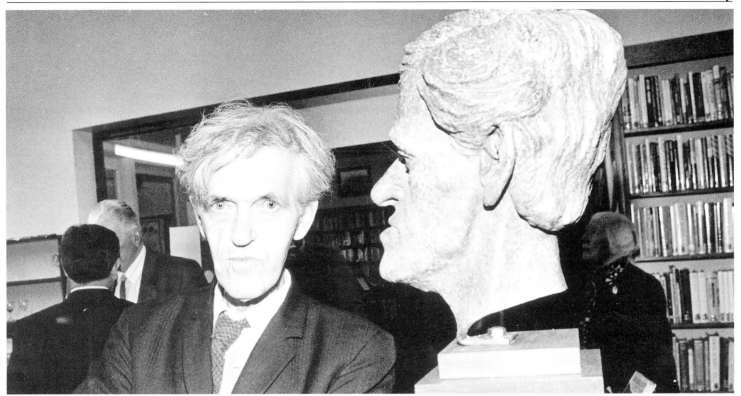

George Mackay Brown, pictured alongside a bust sculpted by Ian Scott of North Ronaldsay which was unveiled at the Kirkwall library to mark the 70th birthday of the poet and author. (Picture courtesy of Orkney Photographic)

But the most important stage of his life was to follow from 1951-52 when he attended Newbattle Abbey College, then run by fellow Orcadian and poet Edwin Muir who was warden at the time.

Muir encouraged GMB's interests and became a friend and mentor for the Stromnessian. "He has the gift of imagination and the gift of words: the poet's endowment," said Muir.

Later, he went to Edinburgh University from where he graduated MA with honours.

George's early works included a book of poems *The Storm* in 1954 and *Loaves and Fishes* (1959) and *The Year of the Whale* (1965), but publication of *Calendar of Love* in 1967 took him to a new position as an eminent writer of short stories.

George Mackay Brown's prodigious output spanned over 30 years, from his early, local publication of the poetry collection, *The Storm* to the 1994 release of *Winter Tales*.

Most of his output dated from his time at Mayburn Court, Stromness, where he stayed from 1967 until his death on Saturday, April 13, 1996. His funeral was on April 16 - St Magnus Day - the day commemorating Orkney's saint.

During this period, his work received many accolades, including the 1994 Saltire Scotsman Award for Scottish book of the Year with *Beside the Ocean of Time* which was also nominated that year for the Booker Prize. In 1988 he was awarded the James Tait Black Prize for *The Golden Bird*.

Both within and outwith Orkney, George Mackay Brown's work was also read every week by thousands in his hugely popular weekly column "Under Brinkie's Brae" in *The Orcadian*, after originally writing for the *Orkney Herald*.

George received many honours during his life, being awarded an OBE in 1974 and becoming a Fellow of the Royal Society of Literature in 1977. Honorary doctorates came from the Open University, Hon MA in 1976; Hon LL.D from Dundee University in 1977 and an Hon D. Litt from Glasgow University in 1985.

GMB also helped open a rich artistic vein in the islands in 1976, with the first St Magnus Festival. As a co-founder, he collaborated closely with Orkney-based composer Sir Peter Maxwell Davies.

In his tribute to George Mackay Brown Sir Peter spoke of the debt he owed to his friend.

Writing from his Rackwick home on Hoy, a place of magic for many Orcadians and a place to which George returned time and again, Sir Peter spoke of his early memories of the poet and writer.

"One sleepless night in 1970, while on holiday on Orkney, I sat up spellbound, reading George Mackay's *Orkney Tapestry* - still, I would think, the most evocative and poetic initiation into the county. The next day I visited Hoy, and by one of those rare happy chances, met George in Rackwick. It was an epiphany which determined my future - I was bowled over by the place and the people, and soon settled in Rackwick, renovating the smallest and most remote of the roofless cottages - the one recommended by George.

"Since then I have written all my music here. Not only did I feel the place blessed by George's Rackwick poems, but I myself felt blessed by his approval of my move.

"He and his work effected a magic which informed and transformed my own creation. I have set many of his poems and we collaborated on several projects, perhaps the most ambitious of which was the opera *The Martyrdom of St Magnus*, with which the first St Magnus Festival opened, in the Cathedral, in 1977.

"George was a staunchly supportive friend and the most modest and unassuming of men, and an exemplary creator, whose work has defined and refined for me, over a quarter of a century, my perceptions of Orkney, as expressed in my music: he must be the most positive and benign influence ever on my own efforts at creation.

"I finished my sixth symphony, for the 1996 St Magnus Festival, on the day George died. The least I can do is to dedicate it to his memory."

George's popularity as a writer and inspiration to others has not diminished though, with three of his books being published posthumously within months of his death, including a selection of his late poems, *Following a Lark*.

George's first published novel, *Greenvoe*, telling the story of a week of summer in the fictional Orcadian community on the island of Hellya, has frequently been suggested as a possible film.

But whatever, George Mackay Brown's name joined those of his other eminent fellow Orcadian writers when a plaque in his memory was erected in the east nave of St Magnus Cathedral in Kirkwall - a building he returned to often.

Are you the man who drooned?

Diver Malcolm Waddilove (37) was washed ashore in Shapinsay after being lost at sea for seven hours.

He made his way the 500 yards to the farm of Harroldsgarth where he was greeted by the farmer Edwin Sinclair with the question: "Are you the man who got drooned this afternoon?"

A full scale search for Mr Waddilove had been started when he failed to reappear after diving from the fishing boat *Hildona*.

The Kirkwall lifeboat had called off the search for the night when Mr Waddilove made his remarkable reappearance.

1972

"We were surprised to find on our doorstop a man in a frogman suit. It was like greeting someone from outer space," said Mr Sinclair's wife.

The *Hildona*, the boat from which Mr Waddilove was diving, had made history earlier that year - it was the first glass fibre boat in Britain designed and built specif-

ically for commercial fishing when it was launched at Burray in February, 1972.

The 36 feet *Hildona* was constructed by the company of Halmatic (Scotland) Ltd at Hatston and fitted out at Duncan's boatyard in Burray, for Mr William Rendall of Holm.

It was the first vessel to come off the production line at Halmatic's Hatston factory since it opened the previous year. The factory employed ten men, under the managership of designer Pierce Webb, an Ipswich man married to a Kirkwall woman.

Strike stranglehold for Orkney

A three day airlift of emergency supplies - delivered by two RAF Hercules aircraft - saved Orkney from a crisis as the county again found itself in the front line of an industrial dispute when a dock strike strangled the lifeline shipping link with Aberdeen.

It was the third docks strike at Aberdeen in three years to impact on the county. The first in 1970 lasted two weeks but was settled before desperate shortages were caused, and a week-long dispute in 1971 was also resolved within a week.

But the strike in July, 1972, soon saw Orkney as a hostage to fortune once again - bringing back memories of the 1966 seamen's strike - as the Aberdeen dockers decided to ban all emergency cargoes to Orkney and Shetland.

In the two previous strikes, the dockers had agreed to handle such emergency shipments of essential goods. But they now imposed a ban in protest at a government decision to curb social security payments to their families.

County convener Donald Brown said: "Let there be no misunderstanding. The Government has a responsibility to

ensure that this island community does not suffer disproportionately compared to other parts of the kingdom."

Cargoes of beer were brought into the county by fishing boat but supplies of animal feedstuffs were becoming desperately scarce - and it was only a fortnight before thousands of cattle were due to leave the county at the start of the annual shipment of livestock.

Eventually, as the strike lasted three weeks, the Government gave the orders for the two RAF Hercules aircraft of Transport Command to start the emergency airlift. A total of 17 flights were made from RAF Kinloss to Orkney and Shetland, while Loganair made 40 round trips across the Pentland Firth to bring in animal feedstuffs.

As the dispute was resolved, Orkney received its first full cargo by sea as the *St Rognvald* arrived with a 360 ton consignment of goods. But a week later, Aberdeen dockers walked out again for two days, although they agreed to disembark 600 cattle and 160 sheep from the *St Rognvald* and *St Magnus* before again settling their differences and returning to work.

Stronsay lifeboat farewell

There were bitter protests in Stronsay when it was announced, for the second time this century, that the island was to lose its lifeboat.

A lifeboat was based in Stronsay for a decade before World War One, but the station was then closed until 1952. Now the 52 feet boat *John Gallatly Hyndman* was to be withdrawn from May 30, 1972, said the RNLI.

The lifeboat organisation felt that the area could be adequately covered by the *Grace Paterson Ritchie,* the lifeboat then permanently stationed at Kirkwall.

But the secretary of the Stronsay lifeboat Andrew Burgess said: "We are not at all happy about the way all this had been handled. It has caused consternation in the island. We are in the best position now since the lifeboat came to Stronsay 20 years ago as regards mustering a crew."

There were 20 to 30 young men available on the island - eight of them with skipper's tickets - and there were complaints that, with a new fish processing factory opening in Stronsay, the lifeboat would be needed more than ever.

Protests were in vain, however, and the last mission of the Stronsay lifeboat was on May 28, 1972, to take local farmer Tom Stevenson to hospital with a feared fracture of the skull.

Terror bomb brings Orkney grief

The troubles of Northern Ireland were brought home to Orkney as a 26 year old Kirkwall soldier, Lance Corporal Colin Leslie, 1st Battalion of the Gordon Highlanders, was killed by a terrorist bomb.

He was one of a ten man patrol searching a house in County Armagh when the explosion killed three men and seriously wounded five others.

A soldier for the previous six years who had seen service in Cyprus and West Germany, Colin Leslie became the first Orcadian to lose his life in the Northern Ireland troubles.

Gordon Highlanders Adjutant Captain

George Kennedy said: "It was a deliberate booby trap. It was aimed at murdering whichever of the security forces went to that house. It was designed to murder."

Lance Corporal Leslie was buried with full military honours in St Olaf's cemetery following a moving service in the St Rognvald Chapel of St Magnus Cathedral. The escort party of ten riflemen fired three volleys over the grave as a pipe major, who had also flown from Northern Ireland, played the lament.

The wreaths included tributes from both the Roman Catholic and Protestant communities living in the area where Colin Leslie was killed.

Council homes for sale

Kirkwall Town Council agreed that the 740 tenants of council houses in the town were entitled to buy their homes, with the proviso that they had to be offered back to the council if sold within five years.

It was expected that prices of the council houses would be in the region of £3,000 each.

Blaze hits newspaper

In the worst calamity to hit the newspaper in its 118 years existence, the printing works of *The Orcadian* in Victoria Street, Kirkwall, was destroyed by fire on March 17, 1972.

The fire brigade tackled the blaze for five hours while a human chain of staff and neighbours saved valuable records including all the files of past issues of *The Orcadian.*

Fortunately, the newspaper press at the back of the building was saved and, with offers of help from the newspapers in Wick and Shetland, and printers Messrs W.B. Peace and Son in Kirkwall, *The Orcadian* was published as usual five days later.

Within six months, the construction of temporary premises allowed a full resumption of printing services.

Short sea sailing

Captain Bill Banks (29) from St Margaret's Hope started a short sea passenger service across the Pentland Firth between John o' Groats and St Margaret's Hope, charging £1 a head for the 16 mile, one hour trip in his launch, the *Pentalina.*

In the first three weeks of the service in the Summer of 1972, he carried over 1,000 passengers.

Russian ship arrested

The 700 ton Russian fishing vessel *Yubileiny* was arrested by the Royal Navy fishery protection minesweeper HMS *Chawton* inside British fishing limits, off Copinsay, in September, 1972. She was escorted to Aberdeen.

Long serving fiscal

Kirkwall lawyer Mr Frank McGinn, who served as Orkney's Procurator Fiscal for nearly a quarter of a century, died at the age of 60. He was succeeded as fiscal, in 1972, by Mr Bill Wright.

P&O take-over

Shipping giant P&O became the parent company of the North of Scotland, Orkney and Shetland Shipping Company, and announced the building of a new £1.4 million roll-on, roll-off vehicle ferry for the Pentland Firth service.

The 230 feet ship, which would carry 400 passengers and 85 cars, was being built by Hall, Russell and Company, Aberdeen, to replace the 750 ton mv *St Ola* which had served the Stromness - Scrabster route since 1951. The new vessel would come into service in 1974.

A scene of devastation after "the worst calamity" to hit *The Orcadian* newspaper in 118 years as the printing works was destroyed by fire in March, 1972.

(Picture from the files of *The Orcadian*)

New surgeon comes home

One of the cornerstones of Orkney's health service in the 20th century has been the fact that, for the period 1927-99, the county was served by just three surgeons.

In 1972, Bill Groundwater (36), then working as a surgeon in Thunder Bay, Ontario, Canada, was appointed to succeed the retiring Peter Konstam, who had held the post since taking over from Orkney's first ever county surgeon Mr Ian McClure. Peter Konstam was made an OBE in the 1973 New Year honours list.

Bill Groundwater, who qualified in medicine in 1960 in Edinburgh, before going to Canada, was the son of former Stromness Academy rector William Groundwater. His mother was the first woman provost of Stromness.

Mr Groundwater senior retired in 1969 after 21 years as rector of Stromness Academy. A former principal teacher of English at Kirkwall Grammar School, he had given 40 years service to Orkney education. He was succeeded as Stromness rector by Mr John MacLean.

Nurse is rescue heroine

Young Kirkwall nurse Ingrid Taylor was hailed as a heroine as she dived fully clothed into Kirkwall harbour in the middle of the night to rescue an unconscious man.

Crewman John Mowat (64) had slipped and fallen overboard from the vessel *Watchful* as it berthed, returning from a

dance in Shapinsay with a party of young farmers. Miss Taylor had recently been awarded the title of "Nurse of the Year."

"She never hesitated one minute to go over the side, even though she was in her dancing clothes, into the icy water in the darkness," said Captain John Gray of the *Watchful.*

Longhope lifeboat back in action

1973

The proud history of gallantry and seamanship displayed over a century by the crews of the Longhope lifeboat was continued as the new Longhope lifeboat carried out its first major rescue with the volunteer crewmen who were recruited after the 1969 disaster.

The rescue mission by the *Elizabeth and David King and EB* saved the 11 man crew of the Grimsby-registered, but Aberdeen based, trawler *Ross Tern* after she had grounded on Swona in snow showers and darkness in the early hours of the morning of February 9, 1973.

"In a skilful and precise operation involving seamanship of the highest order, the lifeboat, under the charge of coxswain Jackie Leslie, picked up six survivors off a liferaft, then went on to snatch five other men from the trawler itself, which was held fast on Little Windy Skerry on the south east coast corner of Swona. With her bows on the shore, she lay helpless on her starboard side, with the funnel nearly in the water, and a heavy swell rising and falling 12 feet," said *The Orcadian*.

From the time of the launch, it took just one hour to save all 11 of the crew of the trawler which was on her way to the Icelandic fishing grounds when the stranding occurred. The rescue was watched by Jim Rosie, one of Swona's remaining population of just three people. "The lifeboat did a wonderful rescue," he said.

The praise was echoed by the trawler skipper William Gardner and chief engineer Teddy Wiseman. "They were truly magnificent - they really were. The seamanship of the coxswain who handled the boat was out of this world. He brought the boat up to us after we had put up flares to show him the way in. Our entire crew owe their lives to them."

Another hero was *Ross Tern* deckhand John Calder, from Peterhead, who was praised for his bravery when he dived into the water to help a man without a life jacket and another who was trapped under the liferaft. George Booth (25) of Aberdeen said: "I am lucky to be alive and I owe it all to John."

The trawler subsequently had to be abandoned as a total loss but the rescue earned coxswain Jack Leslie the RNLI bronze medal, and the lifeboat crew of Ian McFadyen, Bill Budge, John Budge, James Swanson and Ian Williamson received commendations on vellum.

Ten months later, Orkney witnessed another epic rescue of a trawler crew - this time from the air.

A British Airways Sikorski helicopter from Aberdeen - piloted by Captain Mike Evans and Captain Tom Price - lifted to safety the crew of 12 of the 323 ton Aberdeen trawler *Navena*.

She had run aground in storm-lashed seas on a reef 300 yards north of Copinsay as she sought shelter from the weather on her way to the fishing grounds.

Kirkwall lifeboat stood by, but with winds reaching hurricane force, it prevented the lifeboat getting close enough for a rescue and the helicopter was alerted.

For 25 minutes, the helicopter hovered over the holed trawler as winchman Ted Clarke, blinded by the billowing spray and buffeted by the gale, was lowered 30 feet down on to the trawler to successfully lift the men, one by one, from the wheelhouse, where the crew were forced to take refuge as the vessel began to take in water. The mate on the trawler was Kirkwall man Derek Watt.

The three helicopter crewmen were all later honoured for their skill and bravery in the appalling weather conditions. "It was about as bad as I have seen," said the trawler skipper Jim Clarke (48). "My worst moment was when I was the last man on board. It was a very sad moment - I have never lost a ship before."

A week later, a similar disaster was averted when, in winds gusting to force ten in heavy sleet, Orkney trawler skippers and brothers, Albert Reid, of the *Bountiful*, and David Reid, of the *Norseman's Bride*, carried out a superb rescue operation in Kirkwall Bay in the early hours of the morning to save the Aberdeen fishing vessel *Alexander Bruce* which was drifting helplessly with no power.

The *Bountiful* managed, at the very last moment, to prevent the stricken vessel from stranding at Weyland, and then, with the *Norseman's Bride*, succeeded in getting the disabled trawler to Kirkwall pier.

Unfortunately, just 13 months after her part in that rescue, the *Norseman's Bride* met disaster herself as she was driven

Captain Billy Sinclair who became coxswain of the Kirkwall lifeboat *Grace Paterson Ritchie*.

(Picture courtesy of Orkney Photographic)

aground on Fair Isle as she attempted to dodge the weather.

The *Norseman's Bride* was holed and breaking up, but all six members of the crew of the Kirkwall-registered vessel were rescued - although only after another moment of drama.

The Aberdeen trawler *Summerlee* had arrived on the scene and the mate, Ronnie Sim, launched an inflatable liferaft to take off three of the crew. However when he returned for the other three, the dinghy capsized and the 46 year old father of four, who had an artificial leg, was thrown into the sea, where he managed to stay afloat for ten minutes before being hauled back on board the *Summerlee*.

Eventually the remaining three men on the *Norseman's Bride*, including the skipper, were taken off by the yawl of the Fair Isle mail boat *Good Shepherd*.

Detective honoured

Detective Constable Bill Miller from Stronsay, who had served in the Metropolitan Police for ten years, was commended by the Commissioner of the London force, Sir Robert Mark, for his outstanding courage when - despite having ammonia squirted in his face - he tackled two men who were armed with a sawn-off shotgun. Bill Miller was to retire to his native island 20 years later.

£250,000 plea to save Hoy

An ambitious £250,000 appeal fund was launched to help preserve the 20,000 acre estate of North Hoy as a living community.

Mr Malcolm Stewart, of Hoy Lodge, had originally offered the estate - comprising most of the north of the island, including the Old Man of Hoy, St John's Head and Rackwick - to the National Trust in 1970.

However, partly due to Hoy's remoteness from the trust's main centres, the offer had been declined by the National Trust.

Undaunted, Malcolm Stewart decided to set up a charitable trust to own and manage the estate for the benefit of the nation and "the inhabitants of the island of Hoy as a community."

Laura Grimond, who became one of the trustees along with Lord Birsay and others, said: "His gesture is a generous one. Land is a commodity of increasing value in an inflationary world, and the estate could have found a ready market."

The new Hoy Trust immediately launched a £250,000 appeal to protect the estate. The population of North Hoy had shrunk to 30 with Mr Jack Rendall the sole remaining inhabitant of Rackwick.

"This is the aspect of Hoy's future that gives us much greater cause for anxiety than the threat of oil developments, pollution or any other threat," said Laura Grimond. "The major task of the Hoy Trust is to ensure that Hoy is a place where young and old live happy and prosperous lives."

Busy Pentland Firth

Former Dounreay workers Ian Thomas and Donald Bews went into partnership to operate a summer short sea passenger service between John o' Groats and Burwick in South Ronaldsay in a former 40 feet RAF launch they called the *Pentland Spray*. They later upgraded to a bigger vessel, the *Souter's Lass*. The rival summer passenger service operated by Captain Bill Banks between John o' Groats and St Margaret's Hope in the *Pentalina* had carried 10,000 passengers in its first year of operation.

Baby born in Orkney skies

Little Katy Devin arrived in this world to claim her own place in history.

She was born 2,000 feet over Kirkwall on August 2, 1973, as mother Mrs Freida Devin (24) was being flown, in labour, from Stronsay to Kirkwall in a Loganair ambulance flight piloted by Captain Jamie Bayley.

Captain Bayley was trying to land his plane at Kirkwall but thick fog was preventing an approach to the airport when the baby was delivered in the plane by Stronsay GP Dr G.M. Ferguson, assisted by a nurse from the Balfour Hospital.

The fog forced Captain Bayley to fly on to Aberdeen where mother and 9lb 2oz baby were admitted to maternity hospital.

Mrs Devin, the Stronsay sub-postmistress who already had two children, christened the new arrival Katy Ferguson Leynair. Her husband Mr Charlie Devin said: "The pilot made three attempts to land in Kirkwall. He did a wonderful job and we are very grateful to him."

He was unsure where he would register the place of birth. It was eventually registered simply as Stronsay.

Cargo ship is high and dry

Orkney's main cargo ship, the 1,024 ton mv *St Rognvald* - operated by the North of Scotland, Orkney and Shetland Shipping Company - was left high and dry for two weeks after she ran aground on Thieves Holm, at the entrance to Kirkwall bay in May, 1973.

The vessel - carrying five passengers, a consignment of Orkney whisky, 204 cattle and 80 sheep - had been forced by bad weather to return to Kirkwall after earlier setting sail for Aberdeen.

Kirkwall lifeboat *Grace Paterson Ritchie* was called out to take off the passengers, including a child.

The master, Captain Andrew Moncrieff, and his crew of 14, remained on board to help transfer the livestock, via a landing barge, to the Orkney Islands Shipping Company vessel *Islander*.

The *St Rognvald* was eventually refloated after two weeks by the Dutch salvage vessel *Bever*, and was able to berth at Kirkwall Pier.

New health centre

Brigadier S.P. Robertson MBE was appointed chairman of the new Orkney Health Board which was set up under the National Health Service (Scotland) Act of 1972.

Kirkwall's new £99,000 health centre - which would house all the town's family doctors, beside the Balfour Hospital - was opened on April 4, 1973, by Sir John Brotherton, Chief Medical Officer for Scotland.

Yellow peril

Yellow lines appeared on the streets of Kirkwall and Stromness for the first time in 1973 as the town councils introduced new traffic schemes to restrict parking.

Shipping merger

The firm of Bremner and Company of Stromness, which had provided the South Isles shipping services, was to be merged into the Orkney Islands Shipping Company, which would now be responsible for serving the North and South Isles, it was announced.

Cup of cheer

One thousand spectators saw the Orkney county football team defeat Faroe 2-1 to win the North Atlantic Cup at the Bignold Park, Kirkwall, in June, 1973. Twenty five years later, Faroe would succeed in holding the Scotland national team to a draw.

Colour television

The first colour television test transmissions on the BBC and Grampian TV channels were started from Rumster Forest transmitter in Caithness in December, 1973. It would be 1975 before colour transmissions started from Keelylang in Orkney.

Copinsay reserve

The 210 acre island of Copinsay was officially inaugurated, in July, 1973, as a nature reserve and memorial to the late James Fisher, the nationally respected naturalist, ornithologist and author, who had died in a car crash. The island would be administered by Royal Society for the Protection of Birds officer David Lea.

Sweet success

The Stromness confectionery manufacturer Mr James Robertson, whose Orkney fudge was one of the county's best known products and exported all over Britain, announced a new £170,000 factory as his staff of 25 full and part-time workers were producing four tons a week of the sweet delicacy.

Jail shame for civil servant

A man who was regarded as one of the most distinguished sons of Orkney, having reached the top of the Civil Service in Scotland, was led away in shame to begin a five year prison sentence.

Mr George Pottinger (56) - the oldest son of the late Rev William Pottinger of Stromness, a one time minister of Burray - had risen to the £10,750 a year post of Secretary to the Department of Agriculture and Fisheries for Scotland.

However his position at the centre of power came to an end when he was suspended, on full pay, in July, 1972, having been implicated in a cash-for-favours

1974

scandal involving the Yorkshire architect John Poulson.

A year later Pottinger was remanded on £30,000 bail when he appeared in court at Leeds, alongside Poulson, facing conspiracy and corruption charges. In 1974, after a 52 day trial at Leeds Crown Court, Pottinger and Poulson were each jailed for a total of five years.

The jury took four hours to decide that £30,000 worth of gifts from Poulson to Pottinger were corrupt and designed to influence Pottinger's conduct as a civil servant.

The Judge, Mr Justice Waller, commenting on the "magnitude and evil nature" of the offences, said: "To offer corrupt gifts in these circumstances strikes at the very foundation of our governmental system. To accept them is a betrayal of trust."

Ro-ro age reaches Orkney

The age of the roll-on, roll-off vehicle ferry finally reached Orkney in November, 1974, when the new £1.4million, 230 feet long, 1,344 ton *St Ola* berthed at Stromness, under the command of Captain David Pottinger.

A new 350 feet access bridge and loading ramp had been built at Stromness to accommodate the new vessel which was only the third *St Ola* to operate the Pentland Firth route to Scrabster during the 20th century.

The first - which operated for 57 years - had cost only £11,000 when she was built in 1892.

The maiden voyage of the new *St Ola* was not made until January 29, 1975. By now, the North of Scotland Shipping

Company - the operators of the service throughout the century - had come under the ownership of P&O.

The North Company general manager Herbert Scott said: "The old North Company had good intentions but we had no money - now P&O can do what we could never have done ourselves before."

The old *St Ola* was to be sold to a company for oil-related work in the North Sea. At the same time, Westray-born Captain John Stevenson (63), who had been her master for 21 years, retired after a career in which he had made 20,000 crossings of the Pentland Firth.

He could claim to have passed the Old Man of Hoy more times than any other living sea captain.

Pirate radio job

Kirkwall-born John Mair (24) achieved an ambition by becoming a disc jockey with his own programme on the one-time pirate Radio Caroline, broadcasting from the ship *Mi Amigo* anchored six miles off the Dutch coast. His father had served in the Orkney police force for 30 years.

£500,000 study

A £500,000 study was launched by Scottish and American medical teams in Orkney, Shetland and Caithness to discover clues to the prevalence of Multiple Sclerosis in the North, which was higher than in any other part of the world.

Strike hits schools

Nearly 3,300 pupils and 200 teachers were effected as a strike closed most of the Orkney Mainland schools in December, 1974. By 11 votes to six, members of Orkney Education Committee decided to inform the Secretary of State for Scotland that they supported the teachers in their demand for improved pay.

Glittering future

Plans were presented to Kirkwall Town Council for a £54,000 silvercraft factory and showroom, at Hatston, for the Ortak company, owned by Malcolm Gray and his family. The new unit - the biggest of its kind in Scotland when it was opened in 1976 - was expected to employ 30 people.

At the same time, it was announced that the firm of Ola Gorie planned to expand its silvercraft premises in Broad Street, Kirkwall, which employed nine full-time craftsmen and women with up to ten part-timers. Arnold Tait, one of the partners in the company, was about to embark on a sales mission to the USA.

Coastguard honour

Shapinsay man James Bews (61) was acknowledged as Britain's longest serving coastguard as he completed 34 years service at the Coastguard District Rescue Headquarters in Aberdeen, where he now lived. He had started his coastguard career as an auxiliary in Kirkwall and at Broughness, South Ronaldsay, in 1941.

New council elected

In the most far-reaching local government reform in the county since 1929, the first election of members for the new Orkney Islands Council - which would take over the duties of the former county council and Kirkwall and Stromness town councils - was on May 7, 1974.

The new council would have 23 members and 15 seats were contested as 49 candidates came forward. Among those successful was Laura Grimond, the wife of Jo Grimond MP.

However, the two provosts of the old

town councils - Georgina Leitch in Kirkwall and J.R.T. Robertson in Stromness - were both defeated.

The new council would take over its official duties in 1975. The county clerk Mr Graeme Lapsley became the first chief executive of the new organisation, and the first convener was Councillor George Marwick (42) from Birsay. It was reported that 60 per cent of the new Orkney Islands Council's annual revenue budget of £4,573,000 would go on staff costs.

Higher wages

The national average salary for men in 1974 was £2,480 per year. The average female salary was just £1,400. Twenty five years later, in 1999, the national average earnings, according to Income Data Services, reached £20,265.

Orkney's main cargo vessel of the day, the *St Rognvald*, was left high and dry for two weeks after she ran aground on Thieves Holm, at the entrance to Kirkwall Bay, in May, 1973. (Picture courtesy of Orkney Library photographic archive)

The dawn of a new era! The 72 feet long *Bountiful* was the biggest fishing vessel ever to be built for Orkney owners when it was launched by Mrs Peggy Reid for her sons, the Reid brothers, David, Albert and James, originally from Stronsay, in 1969. The £56,000 vessel would pioneer a new whitefish industry for Orkney. (Picture courtesy of Albert and Christine Reid)

Helicopter rescues help save 29

Queen Elizabeth, the Queen Mother, made eight official visits to Orkney in the second half of the 20th century. She is pictured here with the Lord Lieutenant of the day, Colonel Robert Macrae, after arriving at Kirkwall Airport. (Picture courtesy of Harry Russell)

Two dramatic air and sea rescue operations saw 29 foreign trawlermen saved after separate disasters within weeks of each other in Orkney waters.

The first, in December, 1974 saw the 418 ton Belgian stern trawler *Lans* run aground under the 600 feet high cliffs of the Berry, Hoy, as she returned to her home port of Ostend with 55 tons of fish from Icelandic waters.

Both the Stromness and Longhope lifeboats were launched in response to the trawler's Mayday call, but the weather and sea conditions prevented the Longhope vessel from attaching a line for a breeches buoy rescue.

However, with her rotor blades barely 20 yards from the cliff face, an RAF helicopter from Lossiemouth carried out a daring rescue in the gale to airlift the nine crew to safety from the storm-lashed sea.

It was "a brilliant and hazardous operation" lasting 50 minutes, said *The Orcadian* as the helicopter crew of Flt Lt Dave Cosby, Flt Lt J. Taylor and Master Air Loader Peter Barwell hoisted the trawler crew, three at a time, and landed them on the Longhope lifeboat.

Six weeks later, on January 31, 1975, another operation saw the rescue of 20 crewmen from a German trawler which sank within minutes on the Pentland Skerries.

The sighting of red flares from the 824 ton *Thunfisch* was the prelude to the rescue which was to involve three lifeboats, two helicopters from Lossiemouth, an RAF Nimrod aircraft from Kinloss, a German military plane and shore rescue parties.

Longhope lifeboat, under coxswain Jack Leslie, was launched and quickly picked up three survivors from an inflatable life raft near Swona. The trawler had been en route to Iceland and most of the crew had been in their bunks at the time she struck.

The other 17 men in three rafts - including the ship's 20 stone skipper, Captain Gunther Jauchuk, who had been injured in the drama - were swept ashore on Swona, where they sought shelter in the deserted houses. Some of the survivors had been in the water for two hours.

Ten were airlifted off by helicopter in three separate operations, while the remaining seven were picked up from the island by Longhope lifeboat and landed at St Margaret's Hope.

Coastguards recruited Mr John Marshall, principal teacher of German at Kirkwall Grammar School, to act as interpreter.

Helicopter pilot Flt Lt Ron Scott said: "It is fantastic that they all survived and that so many finished up on the island."

Royal visitors

Queen Elizabeth the Queen Mother spent five hours in Kirkwall, on August 7, 1974, to attend a Thanksgiving Service, attended by 700 people, to celebrate the saving of St Magnus Cathedral from collapse.

The Cathedral restoration fund had already raised over £100,000, most of which

had already been spent, said Cathedral minister Rev Bill Cant.

A week earlier, the Queen Mother's grandson, Prince Charles, visited Orkney informally for a few hours when he came ashore from HMS *Jupiter*, which was in Scapa Flow with a fleet of NATO vessels.

Hollywood star's name in lights

International film star Robert Shaw - the son of a former Stromness doctor - could share the plaudits as he starred with Robert Redford and Paul Newman in the film *The Sting* which won seven Oscars in the Motion Picture Academy Awards in 1974.

It was just one of a string of blockbuster hits achieved by the actor who received several years of his education at the Stromness school. Young Robert was aged six or seven when his father, Dr Tom Shaw, moved to Orkney in 1933 to take over the Stromness medical practice. The family left the town after a stay of five years.

Robert Shaw grew up to become a respected actor on both sides of the Atlantic. His credits included *Battle of Britain*, *Battle of the Bulge*, *Young Winston*, *Force Ten from Navarone*, *From Russia With Love* and *Man For All Seasons*.

And he was also to make a name for himself in Hollywood. In 1968, he starred in *Custer of the West* and went on to share the billing in *The Sting* before, perhaps the biggest blockbuster of all, the box office record breaker *Jaws* - a film which attracted 4,000 people to the Phoenix Cinema in Kirkwall in April, 1977.

It was said that Robert Shaw had been offered a share of the profits in *Jaws*, which could have made him a multi-millionaire overnight, but, unwisely as it turned out, he instead opted for a guaranteed fee for his appearance in the film.

The actor returned to Orkney on holiday visits in 1959-60 and 1963; the latter occasion immediately after filming the James Bond spectacular *From Russia With Love*, when he met up with local teacher Archie Bevan, a pal from his schooldays. He was interested in buying a property in Orkney, in which to stay, but eventually opted for the tax advantages of settling in Ireland.

And it was in Ireland that Robert Shaw died suddenly of a heart attack in 1978. He was a talented writer and had also written several novels, including the first of a trilogy, which his death never allowed him to finish.

Twenty years after his death, however, a new link was forged between the Shaw family and Orkney when Dr A.M. Shaw, a nephew of the actor, moved to the county to join a local medical practice.

Robert Shaw's success meant that Orkney can claim links with two giants of 20th century cinema.

The first great Hollywood star with Orkney roots - as has already been recorded - was Greer Garson, the daughter of a West Mainland man, who won the Oscar as best actress in 1943 for the film *Mrs Miniver*.

Former Prime Minister Edward Heath twice visited Orkney - but never during his tenure of 10 Downing Street. He is pictured here walking along Kirkwall's Albert Street with local Conservative official Jim Moar in May, 1984.

(Picture courtesy of Orkney Library photographic archive)

Westray brothers, from the left, Tam, Kenny and Balfour Bain, who were driving forces behind the development of Orkney's fishing industry from the 1980s into the 1990s, are pictured at Kirkwall where they would all skipper their own fishing vessels. Tragically, Kenny Bain was later to be killed in a road accident.

(Picture courtesy of Orkney Library photographic archive)

The Grimond years –

One man dominates the story of Orkney politics in the 20th century: Jo Grimond. For 33 years his name was synonymous with that of Orkney as he became a household name in Britain, not just as MP for Orkney and Shetland but, for ten years, as leader of the Liberal Party.

As others came and went, Jo Grimond remained a constant. In ten successive General Election victories, he was returned as an MP to a House of Commons which saw nine different Prime Ministers during his Westminster career.

With hindsight he realised that he could have won the Orkney and Shetland seat in the 1945 General Election. The young Major Grimond, as he was then, was able to devote only a matter of days to the task of electioneering but still reduced the majority of the Conservative Sir Basil Neven-Spence to just 329.

He returned to the fray in the 1950 General Election when, at the age of 36, he gave up his job as Secretary to the National Trust for Scotland to contest the seat again as the Liberal candidate.

There had been some conjecture over whether Sir Basil Neven-Spence would defend the seat he had held since 1935. In 1948, it was reported that on health grounds he and Lady Neven-Spence were advised to take a long sea voyage, and they had arranged a three month trip to Malaya and the Far East. But, when it came to the General Election on February 23, 1950, Neven-Spence, then aged 61, was still the Tory standard-bearer.

The Labour candidate was the Edinburgh-based barrister Mr Harold Leslie KC, a man of strong Orcadian roots as the son of Mr Robert Leslie from Stromness, and married to Rena Marwick, the daughter of Stromness Provost James Marwick.

Polling day had seen snow showers, but the following day there was a heavy fall of snow with North Ronaldsay, and its ballot box, isolated by heavy seas, prompting fears that the count would have to be postponed. However, the box was eventually delivered to Sanday and later collected from there on Sunday, February 26 - three days after the poll.

After criticism in previous elections over the difficulty of reaching polling stations for Orcadians in remote areas, electors who had to make a sea journey to a polling station were granted a postal vote in the 1950 General Election.

The electors were treated to quite a high profile campaign. Lady Violet Bonham Carter, daughter of former Prime Minister Herbert Asquith, and Jo Grimond's mother-in-law, came to Orkney to speak for the Liberal cause, while *The Orcadian* carried a message from Winston Churchill asking the electorate to vote for Neven-Spence, who had been one of Churchill's closest lieutenants during World War Two.

The Orcadian devoted a full page, headlined "The man who gets things done" to the achievements of Neven-Spence, while the *Orkney Herald* carried a four page election address from Grimond as the papers divided on partisan political lines.

For the first time in British election history, ballot boxes were flown from Shetland to Orkney by BEA for the count to take place. Nevertheless, it was Monday, February 27, before the vote was announced - one of the last three results in the country to be declared.

Jo Grimond was returned with a majority of 2,956 as he increased his 1945 vote by 3,262 in a 67.86 per cent turn-out. Result: Grimond 9,237; Neven-Spence 6,281; Leslie 4,198.

A young Jo Grimond addresses a campaign meeting in Rousay in the early days of his political career which saw him win ten successive General Election victories in the Orkney and Shetland constituency. (Picture courtesy of Orkney Library photographic archive)

ten times a winner

Nationally, Labour scraped home with an overall majority in single figures. Most Liberal candidates in the country had lost their deposits and Jo Grimond was one of only nine Liberal MPs returned to Parliament.

With such a small Liberal representation, early Parliamentary recognition came the way of Jo Grimond as he was appointed Chief Whip to the Liberals. In his maiden speech in the House of Commons, he called for Scottish devolution.

Within weeks of his defeat, Sir Basil Neven-Spence announced he would not contest the seat again for the Tories, and in June, 1950, 42 year old Archibald Tennant - a barrister like Grimond - was adopted by Orkney Unionist Association as the Prospective Parliamentary Candidate for the Tories.

Tennant was the son of Herbert Asquith's brother-in-law, while Grimond was married to Asquith's grand-daughter.

Sir Basil Neven-Spence would continue to play a role in public life, however, for, in 1952 he became Lord Lieutenant of Shetland.

The Labour candidate in 1950, Harald Leslie, also stood down but he too would remain in public life during a distinguished legal career which culminated in his award of a peerage - taking the title Lord Birsay - in 1966.

Within six months of his election victory, Jo Grimond paid £3,020 to buy the Old Manse in Finstown - which was to remain his home for the rest of his life.

But in the autumn of 1951, the Labour government returned to the country for another General Election. Grimond would defend the Orkney and Shetland seat against Archibald Tennant (Conservative) and Magnus Fairnie, of the Scottish Miners, who had been hastily recruited by Labour.

The result was that Jo Grimond romped home with a 6,391 majority from a 69 per cent turn-out. He had virtually doubled his vote between 1945-51, the result being: Grimond 11,745; Tennant 5,354; Fairnie 3,335.

It was conjectured that, if the Liberals had linked up with the Tories, Grimond would have been given a cabinet post by Winston Churchill who returned as Prime Minister in a Conservative victory, ending Clement Atlee's six year tenure. The Conservatives would rule nationally for the next 13 years under, successively, Churchill, Anthony Eden (1955-57), Harold Macmillan (1957-63) and Alec Douglas-Home (1963-64).

Archibald Tennant quickly announced that he would not stand again, and, in 1952, Lt Col Magnus Shearer (61) from Lerwick, a former convener of Shetland County Council, and a man who had served in Orkney for a time in World War Two as Commander of the Headquarters Company of the 5th/7th Gordon Highlanders, was adopted as the Conservative Prospective Parliamentary Candidate. However, he was forced to resign, through ill health, a year later.

It was 1954 before John Eunson (34), a Shetlander and Lerwick town councillor, was adopted as the new prospective candidate for the Tories. A former RAF man, he was employed by the North of Scotland Hydro Electric Board after losing a leg in an air crash in 1943.

Edgar Ramsay, a Stromness-born insurance agent living in Edinburgh, became the Labour candidate as the 1955 General Election was called for May 26.

The so-called "Linklater Letter" was one of the few highlights of a lucklustre campaign, as a letter from the Orkney writer Eric Linklater was produced saying that, although he was not in the process of becoming a Liberal, he thought Jo Grimond was the best man to represent Orkney in Parliament.

The other two parties reacted strongly to this intervention, with Ramsay denouncing it as a "grotesque intrusion."

The Orcadian called on the electorate to vote Conservative, saying: "Mr Grimond represents a dying party. He was the sole Liberal MP in Scotland in the last Parliament."

So much for the power of the Press! When the result was announced on May 28 - after the Shetland ballot boxes were again flown to Orkney - Jo Grimond was returned with a record majority for the constituency of 7,993 votes, in a turn-out of 66.12 per cent.

The result was: Grimond 11,753; Eunson 3,760; Ramsay 2,914. Nationally, the Conservatives were returned to power again.

A recurring concern for Jo Grimond throughout his 33 years as MP for the Northern Isles was the problem of de-population which saw the electorate shrink almost by the month. It was already one of the smallest constituencies in Britain, and there were fears that if the population continued to leave, Orkney and Shetland could even lose its own separate representation.

Grimond was a stalwart supporter when six islands - Westray, Papa Westray, Eday, Stronsay, North Ronaldsay and Sanday - formed the North Isles Association to present a petition to the county council to be sent to the Secretary of State of Scotland. It was signed by 1,706 people, or 98 per cent of those approached, said the organisers.

They demanded a public and independent commission to investigate such issues as transport and freight, postal and health services, education, agriculture and electricity.

The petition stated: "While at the present moment, we are making a worthwhile contribution to the national economy, there are factors which cause us grave concern - and which call for expert examination - if this contribution is to be maintained and developed."

Jo Grimond told the House of Commons in 1955: "This is a matter of urgency. People are leaving the more remote islands of my constituency month by month. We shall be wasting our money and our effort if we do not reverse that trend very soon."

However, whatever the population problems of Orkney, Grimond had established himself as a major political figure and it was no surprise when, after six years as Chief Whip, he was elected, at the age of 43, as the new leader of the Liberal Party in succession to Clement Davies (72) who announced his resignation at the party's annual conference in 1956.

The appointment was made by the Parliamentary Liberal Group which, it has to be admitted, consisted at the time of just five MPs. If Orkney's problems were difficult, those of the Liberal Party in 1956 were dire!

The news of the Grimond leadership victory was celebrated in Orkney by Lady Violet Bonham Carter who was holidaying in Finstown with her daughter Laura.

So how was the new leader assessed? *The Scotsman* said: "Behind a deceptively lazy manner lurks a very keen brain and a certain amount of political ambition.

"He is very popular with his women constituents in Orkney and Shetland. He is a fluent speaker and can at times be vigorously eloquent and pleasantly humorous. Whether all that is enough to breathe a new life into the faintly glowing embers of Liberalism is, of course, another question."

Back on the home front, John Eunson was re-adopted as the prospective Conservative candidate for the constituency but he resigned a year later and, in 1958, was replaced by Mr Robert Bruce (50) a land owner who had returned to Shetland after a career in railways and with the Rio Tinto Zinc mining company in Africa.

Mick Cornish, a 21 year old Cambridge undergraduate, was set to be the new Labour standard bearer but he withdrew his interest within months, to be replaced by Robert McGowan, a 34 year old Canadian living in Edinburgh, where he was a lecturer in philosophy at the university.

The General Election of October 8, 1959, was notable for the fact that it was probably the first election of the modern era that *The Orcadian* did not use its editorial columns to urge people to vote Conservative. The newspaper obviously had to accept that, whatever its political leanings, it was out of step with the voters if it appeared hostile to the man who could now campaign on the slogan "Vote for Jo - the man you know." By now, *The Orcadian* referred to him simply as "Jo" in headlines.

The Tories, who campaigned under the somewhat tortuous slogan "Don't fiddle, Ban-Jo," brought some big names North, including Lord Forbes, a former Scots Secretary, and Lady Tweedsmuir.

It was to do them no good as Jo Grimond was returned with a record vote and a record majority of 8,612 in a 71.3 per cent turnout. The result was Grimond 12,099; Bruce (Conservative) 3,487; McGowan (Labour) 3,275.

Nationally, the Tory government of Harold Macmillan was returned to power, but it was a good year for the Grimond family as they could celebrate the birth of their fourth child Magnus, joining Andrew (20), Griselda (17) and John (12). And another success, in 1960, saw Jo Grimond elected rector of Edinburgh University, gaining 1,907 votes to 847 achieved by newspaper magnate Roy Thomson.

Neither Robert Bruce nor Robert McGowan were to contest the Orkney and Shetland constituency again.

Stromness teacher Ian MacInnes (40) was adopted as the new prospective Labour candidate, while the Conservatives opted for Michael Forsyth-Grant (41), a farmer and land owner from Montrose.

It was a decision which was to leave the Tories in local disarray and bitter recrimination. The row exploded at the end of 1963 when newspaper reports appeared of an action taken by Forsyth-Grant to evict a 71 year old tenant on his estate.

Local Unionist supporter Mr John Sanderson said: "Unionists throughout the constituency must take this opportunity of openly dissociating themselves from Mr Forsyth-Grant and make haste to find a more suitable candidate."

The local Tories were obviously divided as the candidate came North to explain his actions as an extraordinary general meeting of the Orkney Unionist Association was held.

Eventually, on January 15, 1964, the Conservative executive in Orkney, by eight votes to two, gave a vote of confidence to their man. However, the next day came the announcement that Michael Forsyth-Grant was standing down as a candidate in the interests of party unity. A few days later, seven of the Orkney Conservative executive resigned.

Those who remained quickly selected a replacement Tory candidate - Dr John Firth (27), a house surgeon at a London hospital, whose family lived on Rousay. John Firth would actually go on to contest four General Elections as the Conservative standard bearer in the constituency.

He did not have to wait long for the first contest which was the General Election of October 15, 1964.

There had been suggestions, nationally, that Jo Grimond should abandon Orkney and Shetland to fight a seat nearer London in a bid to give the Liberals a higher profile. The Liberal leader had rejected this out of hand, and so he was now contesting the constituency for the sixth time.

This was the first election since the demise of the *Orkney Herald*. The *Herald* had traditionally been the mouthpiece of Liberalism in the county while *The Orcadian* had supported the Conservative cause. Now the policy of *The Orcadian* throughout the campaign "was one of editorial impartiality, owing no allegiance to any of the parties," said the newspaper.

Jo Grimond was returned with a slightly reduced majority of 7,900 from a turn-out of 72.5 per cent. The result was: Grimond 11,604; John Firth (Conservative) 3,704; Ian MacInnes (Labour) 3,232.

Nationally a Labour government was returned to power with a narrow majority for Prime Minister Harold Wilson. By 1965, the Conservatives had a new national leader in the shape of Ted Heath who made what was literally a flying visit to Orkney in September that year, spending an hour or so in Kirkwall.

John Firth was re-adopted as the Conservative candidate

Jo Grimond with a young Magnus Grimond.
(Picture courtesy of Orkney Library photographic archive)

but Ian MacInnes announced that he would not be standing again in the Labour colours. He was followed by Hugh Lynch, a 24 year old college lecturer, who was selected as the Labour candidate just three weeks before the General Election of March 31, 1966.

It was a sad and difficult time for the Grimond family as they were struck by tragedy during the campaign when their eldest son Andrew was found dead in his flat in Edinburgh.

The turn-out was down to 65.2 per cent as Jo Grimond was returned with a reduced majority of 5,975, although the votes of both the Conservative and Labour candidates were down on 1964.

The result was: Grimond 9,605; Firth (Conservative) 3,630; Lynch (Labour) 3,021.

The following year, after ten years in the post, Jo Grimond, now aged 53, resigned as leader of the Liberal Party in January, 1967 - although he would continue as MP for Orkney and Shetland for another 16 years. Jeremy Thorpe took over as leader of a Liberal party which could well have been extinct as a parliamentary entity but for the efforts of Jo Grimond during the black days of Liberalism in the 1950s.

And Grimond was obviously still in the public eye. In 1969, he was elected as rector of Aberdeen University - defeating other candidates who included Willie Rushton and Clement Freud.

The General Election of June, 1970, was to see the Grimond family fighting three constituencies. Jo would defend his seat, while Mrs Laura Grimond was adopted as the Liberal candidate for West Aberdeenshire and their son Johnny was selected as the Liberal candidate for North Angus and Mearns.

It was to mark the lowest point in Grimond's association with the constituency since he was first elected 20 years earlier as, with a turn-out of just 65 per cent, his majority fell by 3,443 to just 2,532, compared to 8,612 in 1959.

A major reason was that this was the era when Britain's potential membership of the European Common Market was a major issue. The Liberal party had long championed such a cause whereas Orkney, generally speaking, was distinctly luke warm to the idea. The result was that several Grimond voters obviously stayed at home. Nonetheless, the Conservative candidate, John Firth, still managed to increase his vote by 1,700 compared with the previous election.

The result was: Grimond 7,896; Firth 5,364; William Reid (Labour) 3,552.

Nationally, Ted Heath's Conservative government was returned to power - and he was to lead Britain in to Europe within a couple of years.

The year of 1974 was to see two General Elections within eight months of each other.

Jonathan Wills (25) from Shetland had been adopted as the Labour candidate, and it was anticipated that, for the first time, there would be a challenger from the Scottish National Party.

However, in February, 1974, Jo Grimond attempted to introduce a Scottish Home Rule Bill in the House of Commons. Mr Grimond said the proposed legislation was the "first and essential step" towards the establishment of a Scots parliament.

In the event, the bill ran out of debating time and was "talked out" but, as a result of his efforts, the Orkney and Shetland branches of the SNP said they would not contest the following election in the constituency.

In the General Election of February 28, 1974, Jo Grimond was almost back to his halcyon days of 1959 as, with a turn-out of 71 per cent, he increased his majority back to 7,305 - destroying any hopes of the Tories that it had become a marginal seat.

The result was: Grimond 11,491; Firth 4,186; Wills 2,865. It was Jo Grimond's eighth success in the constituency.

Nationally, the Liberals secured six million votes but returned just 14 MPs as the Ted Heath administration was defeated and Harold Wilson returned to power in a minority government.

The result was that another General Election was called for October 10, 1974.

And this time the SNP would contest the constituency in what would be the first ever four-cornered contest in Orkney and Shetland. The SNP candidate was 29 year old Orkney teacher Howie Firth, son of Stromness chemist and optician Nicol Firth.

Jonathan Wills would stand again for Labour but John Firth, after contesting the seat four times for the Tories, was replaced by a new Conservative standard bearer, Edinburgh advocate Raymond Fraser.

Jo Grimond's vote went down but he still received 56 per cent of all the votes cast as he was returned with a majority of 6,852 from a 66.6 per cent turn-out of the electorate.

The result saw the SNP finish in second place as support slumped for both the Conservatives and Labour. It was the lowest ever Labour vote in the constituency at the time as Jonathan Wills lost his deposit.

The result was: Grimond 9,877; Firth 3,025; Fraser 2,495; Wills 2,175. Nationally, the Labour government was returned to power.

Neither Howie Firth nor Jonathan Wills would return as candidates for their respective parties at the next election as, by coincidence, both began new careers in radio as the senior producers of the newly launched BBC stations that began broadcasting in Orkney and Shetland in 1977.

Robina Goodlad, from Shetland, was adopted as the new Labour candidate - thus becoming the first woman to contest the constituency - while Michael Spens was selected for the SNP.

An Edinburgh architect, Charles Donaldson (42) was named as the Conservative challenger.

Before this, however, Jo Grimond had stepped temporarily back into the national spotlight as he was restored to the leadership of the Liberal Party after the crisis, surrounded by

The Freedom of Orkney for Jo and Laura Grimond in April, 1987.
(Picture courtesy of Orkney Library photographic archive)

scandal, following the withdrawal of Jeremy Thorpe in May, 1976. Jo, then aged 62, would remain at the helm until David Steel's election as the party's new permanent leader.

And so we came to Jo Grimond's final General Election on May 3, 1979, and the commencement of his last four years in the House of Commons. (He would be nearly 70 by the time the 1983 General Election came along).

It was "the quietest campaign of the century," proclaimed *The Orcadian*. However Jo Grimond again romped home a comfortable winner with a majority of 6,810 as again he got more votes than all the other candidates put together in a poll which saw a 67.35 per cent turn-out of voters.

The result was: Grimond 10,950; Donaldson (Conservative) 4,140; Goodlad (Labour) 3,385; Spens (SNP) 935. The SNP candidate lost his deposit.

It was Jo Grimond's 11th General Election contest since 1945 - and his 10th successive victory. Nationally, the Labour government of James Callaghan was defeated and Margaret Thatcher was returned for the Conservatives as Britain's first woman Prime Minister.

In 1983, another young barrister, Jim Wallace, would come North to take over the Liberal mantle in Orkney and Shetland. He would remain as our man at Westminster until the end of the century. It would mean that, apart from just a few weeks at the start of 1950 before Sir Basil Neven-Spence was defeated, Orkney had just two MPs in 50 years as it became the most powerful Liberal stronghold in Britain.

It was not the end of public life for Jo Grimond when he stood down as MP in 1983. He was given a peerage to become Lord Grimond and the great older statesman - once described as the "greatest politician never to become Prime Minister" - remained a powerful voice of Liberal thinking.

The regard with which he was held in Orkney was shown after his death in 1993 when hundreds attended his funeral service at St Magnus Cathedral before he was laid to rest at the Finstown cemetery not far from the Old Manse that had been his home for 43 years.

Sober parish lifts drink ban

It was the end of an era - and the end of 55 years without being able to enjoy a drink in public - as residents went to the polls to end a legal anachronism which made Holm the only "dry" parish in Orkney.

The 500 population had never got round to lifting a ban on licensed premises selling drink in the parish, under legislation dating back to World War One.

In the 1920s, several towns and parishes - including both Kirkwall and

1975

Stromness - had voted either to go "dry" or to restrict the number of drinks licences; a situation which continued for 27 years in Stromness which was "dry" until 1947 when the residents of the town voted to lift the ban on drinks licences.

Only Holm had remained with the ban in place and the poll, on November 28, 1975, was likely to be the last in Scotland before the archaic legislation was scrapped, said the Scottish Office.

Over 52 per cent of the Holm electorate turned out to vote and they voted by 136 - 79 to go "wet."

It meant that Holm Community Association could now legally apply for drinks licences for functions such as weddings and harvest homes.

Kirkwall freedom honour

For the last time before it was abolished by the reorganisation of local government, Kirkwall Town Council honoured two of its most distinguished citizens with the freedom of the burgh at a ceremony in St Magnus Cathedral.

They were Sanday-born ex-Provost James Scott, who served on the council for 29 years, and writer, historian and broadcaster Ernest Marwick, whose work as a past chairman of the Orkney Heritage Society had helped to preserve much of Orkney's history and folklore.

Mr Marwick's work had appeared in both the *Orkney Herald* and *The Orcadian* and his voice was one of the first to be heard on BBC radio broadcasts from Orkney. He had also gathered together some of the county's finest poetry in his *Anthology of Orkney Verse.*

Top man on road project

A £130 million upgrading scheme to modernise 137 miles of the A9 trunk road from Perth to the Cromarty Firth was given the go-ahead with an Orcadian, Mr Garson Miller (54) as the superintending engineer. Educated at Kirkwall Grammar School and Edinburgh University, he had spent ten years in Nigeria before returning to Scotland and joining the Scottish Office. He was made an OBE in 1980.

Police force merger

Helicopter rescues aircraft

A helicopter came to the rescue when this Loganair Islander aircraft was disabled in the North Isles. The helicopter airlifted the plane back to Kirkwall Airport where repair work could be carried out by engineers. (Picture courtesy of Orkney Library photographic archive)

The Northern Constabulary - consisting of Orkney, Shetland and Caithness - was extended in 1975 to take in Ross-shire, Sutherland, Inverness-shire, the Western Isles and North Argyllshire. The new headquarters would be at Inverness.

Vote on Europe

After three years membership of the Common Market, a national referendum to decide whether or not Britain was to remain in the European Community took place on June 5, 1975.

Nationally, the result was a comfortable majority in favour and Orkney also voted for continued membership with 3,911 (61.8 per cent) in favour and 2,419 (38.2 per cent) against.

Shetland and the Western Isles were the only two areas of the country to vote against.

Flying milestone

Travelling Orkney schoolteacher Mrs Harriet Kirkness became the 100,000th passenger to use Orkney's internal air service operated by Loganair. She was presented with a commemorative bracelet before she made one of her regular trips to the isles to teach.

End of school

Pupils left the old Kirkwall Grammar School in School Place for the last time as they started their 1975 Summer holidays. After the holiday, lessons would resume at the new £1.2 million KGS at Papdale and the old building would be converted into offices for Orkney Islands Council.

The new Kirkwall Grammar School was officially opened in March, 1976, by Donald Brown, the last convener of the now defunct Orkney County Council.

The price of the new school - which included a gymnasium and Kirkwall's first indoor public swimming pool - indicated the increase in building costs over the previous 20 years. The Kirkwall infant school in 1955 cost just £64,000 to build, while the primary school in 1962 cost £110,000.

Cathedral visitor

The Poet Laureate Sir John Betjeman came North to open the 1975 St Magnus Fair, in aid of Cathedral funds. It raised £2,000 to further boost the Cathedral appeal fund which had reached £104,000 towards its £300,000 target.

Lifeboat rescue

The Kirkwall lifeboat *Grace Paterson Ritchie* took off eight members of the crew of the Aberdeen trawler *Kinellan* - and then helped refloat the vessel - after it ran aground on Sanday.

Oldest person

A stream of well wishers visited Mrs Margaret Lennie of Stronsay as she celebrated her 102nd birthday as the oldest person living in Orkney in August, 1975.

Home rule threat from Orkney

Orkney MP Jo Grimond issued a warning that if the United Kingdom were to break up, Orkney and Shetland would demand greater independence and could even return to Scandinavia, of which the two island groups were a part up to 1468.

"I am pleased that the Government recognises the right of Orkney and Shetland to have their own special situation taken into account," he said after an exchange of correspondence with Prime Minister Harold Wilson in 1975.

"Devolution must not mean more government. Less and better government is what we want. We don't want centralisation in Glasgow or Edinburgh any more than in London. The island authorities must be given greater freedom and discretion. If the UK were to be broken up, as the SNP want, then Orkney and Shetland must reconsider their position," said Mr Grimond.

Vandals halt cinema shows

Kirkwall's Phoenix Cinema would close on October 1, 1975, said director Douglas Shearer, blaming vandals who had slashed 100 seats and damaged toilet facilities.

"If the youngsters had behaved themselves we would have kept the cinema open," said Mr Shearer. "They were like animals. They make a terrible noise during the films and have chased all the others away. It's very disappointing. The youngsters are getting worse all the time. They just do what they like and there is nothing we can do about it."

The cinema, hit by rising costs and dwindling audiences, had been on the market for a year, without attracting an offer.

After a few months, however, Mr Shearer had a change of heart and re-opened the cinema for film shows twice a week. However the cinema was later purchased by the Orkney Islands Council and continued operating until the opening of the new Pickaquoy leisure complex in Kirkwall in 1999.

Orkney's first drugs case

Seven workers, two women and five men from the Scottish mainland, who were employed on the construction site of the Flotta oil terminal, appeared at Kirkwall Sheriff Court accused of cannabis possession after a police raid on the island in April, 1975.

Sheriff Alastair MacDonald said that there had been no instances of any Orcadian or Shetlander appearing in court on drug charges.

"It may be that elsewhere in the country the use of drugs has come to be regarded as just one more disagreeable fact of life. It is not a fact of life here," said the Sheriff. "In Orkney we have no drug problem amongst our young people and I am sure that Orkney parents would want everything possible done to prevent it."

Fines totalling £475 were imposed.

The launch of the inter-island air service by Loganair in 1967 meant that Orkney could claim its own London Airport (situated next to the Bay of London in Eday.) Loganair pilot Captain David Kirkland is pictured (centre) with the airport's ground crew.

(Picture courtesy of Orkney Photographic)

Farewell to our finest artist

Dr Stanley Cursiter, one of the greatest of modern Orcadians and an artist of nationally-acclaimed achievement, died in Stromness, at the age of 88, on April 22, 1976.

He was Keeper of the National Galleries of Scotland from 1930 to 1948, and Painter and Limner to the Queen in Scotland until the time of his death.

He would leave behind him a permanent memorial - not only hundreds of paintings but also his designs which helped create the St Rognvald Chapel in St Magnus Cathedral.

Stanley Cursiter was born at 15 East Road, Kirkwall, on April 29, 1887, (he died a week before his 89th birthday) of a Kirkwall father and a Sanday mother.

He was the youngest of four children and after education at Kirkwall burgh school where he was a contemporary of Orkney writer Edwin Muir for a while, he pursued an interest in architecture and sought to join the drawing office of T.S. Peace, the distinguished Kirkwall architect of the day. However, with encouragement from Mr Peace, he instead joined the Edinburgh firm of McLagan and Cumming on a five year apprenticeship as a designer.

He extended his education by attending evening classes at the Edinburgh School of Art. He came third for the whole country gaining a "Royal Exhibition" which entitled him to proceed to the Royal College of Art in London.

However Cursiter preferred to continue his studies in Edinburgh, where he was elected a member of the Society of Scottish Artists while still at college.

He returned to Orkney most summers and established himself an artist with a series of dramatic land and seascapes.

He married a young Orkney musician Phyllis Hourston from Kirkwall before being dispatched to the front-line on the Somme in World War One with the Scottish Rifles and the 4th Field Survey Battalion. His work helped to revolutionise the preparation of field maps and he was made an OBE and twice mentioned in dispatches.

After World War One, he and his wife settled in Edinburgh where he was elected president of the Society of Scottish Arts, before becoming Keeper of the National Galleries - in charge of the National Portrait Gallery - before succeeding Sir James Caw as director.

At the outbreak of World War Two he had to organise the evacuation of the museum's valuable collections to places of safety. For a time he returned to war work with over 1,000 draughtsmen working at the Ordnance Survey at Southampton, but returned to Scotland to arrange over 80 art exhibitions to brighten the dark days of war.

In 1948, he arranged to return to Orkney in retirement - buying the former Stanger's shipyard at Ness, Stromness, for conversion into a home.

However his skills as a portrait painter still found his work much in demand and he had to maintain a studio in Edinburgh. During 15 years, he painted scores of distinguished people including the Queen Mother.

One of his most important tasks was that of painting a picture of the Queen at St Giles Cathedral shortly after her coronation - a picture that was to hang at Holyrood House.

He was a freeman of Kirkwall and a Deputy Lieutenant of Orkney.

He had more or less given up painting from the age of 75 and he spent his remaining years at another house in Stromness, 75 Victoria Street.

Cursiter was the first secretary of the Royal Fine Arts Commission in Scotland and for some time secretary of the Royal Scottish Academy.

Stanley Cursiter's place as a great Scottish artist was unquestioned. Dr T.J. Honeyman, director of the Glasgow Art Gallery,

Stanley Cursiter - the Orcadian artist who achieved national acclaim. (Picture courtesy of Orkney Library photographic archive)

said: "In his landscapes and seascapes of the Orkney scene, he brings heart, mind and hand to bear on a motif which has become almost exclusive to himself. In the field of contemporary Scottish portraiture he is among the leaders."

A memorial service was held in the St Rognvald Chapel - which he helped design - at St Magnus Cathedral.

Many of his paintings were sought after by private collectors and over the following 25 years, Orkney Islands Council would ensure that several were preserved for the county.

Welcome to Radio Orkney

1976

The biggest step forward in broadcasting that Orkney had enjoyed since the arrival of the television age saw plans announced for the county's own local radio station.

BBC Radio Orkney was to begin broadcasting in 1977, but before that, Orkney teacher Howie Firth - who stood as the SNP candidate in the Orkney and Shetland General Election contest of October, 1974 - was appointed as senior producer and presenter.

By coincidence, Jonathan Wills, the Labour candidate in the same General Election, got the equivalent job for the new BBC Radio Shetland. It meant that both would not be considered as candidates for the following election in 1979.

Assisting Howie Firth at Radio Orkney would be Liz Davies, who had moved to Orkney after presenting her own two hour programme on a commercial station in Sheffield.

The idea of a local radio station - which in the first instance planned only 20 minutes of programmes a day - had been gathering strength for some time and had been enthusiastically encouraged by Jo Grimond MP, and a local advisory committee had been set up under the chairmanship of Eoin Scott, of Redland, Firth, at the start of 1976.

However the man who deserved a major share of the credit, as a real driving force behind bringing the project to reality, was Alastair Hetherington, a former editor of *The Guardian* who had been appointed Controller for BBC Scotland in 1975.

Plane salvaged

A top secret American F14 US Tomcat aircraft was salvaged north of Orkney after the 20 million dollar fighter plane crashed off the aircraft carrier *John F. Kennedy* during an exercise with the NATO fleet in the North Atlantic.

The plane, and her Phoenix missile, had been recovered from nearly 2,000 feet on the seabed by the German salvage ship *Taurus*, and dragged below the surface to Orkney where it was brought to the surface again between Egilsay and Shapinsay.

The missile was recovered 500 yards from the plane, which was taken to the Rosyth Naval dockyard. The salvage cost the US Navy an amazing £1,456,000!

Fish farming trials

Orkney's first fish farming experiments - involving not salmon, which were to become the mainstay of the industry, but turbot - got underway when three tanks of young turbot were delivered to Stronsay where they were to be placed in two floating wire mesh cages.

They would be looked after by Stronsay fisherman John Reid, as part of trials conducted by the White Fish Authority, and financed by the Highlands and Islands Development Board and Orkney Islands Council.

Concorde pioneer

Colonel Malcolm Dennison of Roeberry, South Ronaldsay - then serving in the Sultanate of Muscat and Oman but later to become Lord Lieutenant of Orkney - became the first Orcadian to fly in the supersonic Concorde airliner as he flew from Heathrow to Bahrein.

Howie Firth interviews head postmaster Arthur Reid for Radio Orkney.
(Picture courtesy of Orkney Library photographic archive)

End of the line for Lyness

The last Naval ship to be fuelled at Lyness - the frigate HMS *Penelope* - called on August 13, 1976, as the final link with the Ministry of Defence was broken.

Since the closure of the Lyness Naval base in 1957, the establishment was continued as a Ministry of Defence fuel depot. But now the final axe fell.

It was expected that the five local men - out of a total staff of seven - would be made redundant. It was another blow to the county because the base - with a rateable value of £25,000 - was Orkney's largest ratepayer.

Lucky escape

Seventeen young pupils, aged five to seven, had a miraculous escape as a five ton chimney stack, which was being dismantled, crashed through the roof of their classroom at Stenness School where they were being taught by Mrs Thora Linklater.

No one was hurt but the children were sent home to recover from the shock of the accident which had severely damaged the school roof.

The education authority ordered the immediate closure of the school and lessons were transferred to the adjoining community centre.

Disgrace of 'orgy of drink'

The abuse of alcohol in the county - especially amongst the young - was criticised as "Orkney's Disgrace" in a front page editorial column published by *The Orcadian* of June 3, 1976.

"With every year that goes past comes further evidence of how this canker is undermining the social fabric of Orkney, debasing our lives and corrupting the young," proclaimed the newspaper.

"We cannot claim either that their elders show a good example - one has only to witness the 'debacle' of the last night of any Shopping Week or of a Dounby or County Show day to know this is so.

"There are many aspects of life in these islands that we are proud of and cherish, but this orgy of drinking, especially among the teenagers, is Orkney's Disgrace."

The dawn of the Oil Age

The discovery that was to help change the modern face of Orkney received just three paragraphs in *The Orcadian* of January 25, 1973. A large new oil field had been discovered in the North Sea, 100 miles east of Wick, confirmed Occidental Petroleum. Tests showed a possible output of 250,000 barrels a day. It would be known as the Piper Field.

Orkney's Oil Age had been born - ushering in an era which, although not always ensuring unfettered prosperity, has at least shielded the county from the worst ravages of economic decline suffered by some areas.

It's been a quirk of history that every generation, roughly every 25 years through the 20th century, has produced an economic lifeline for Orkney. Unfortunately, in 1914 and again in 1939, it involved a world war. Thankfully, the discovery of North Sea oil promised Orkney a peacetime bonanza.

The exploration for oil in the North Sea had been going on for five years or more, but it was only at the end of 1971 and start of 1972, as the prospectors moved further north, that Orkney began to be seriously suggested as an oil base. And then the progress of developments was rapid.

It was known that companies had visited Scapa Flow and had looked at the potential of the Naval base at Lyness but the first proposal to be put forward for an oil supply base, in February, 1972, was, in fact, in Kirkwall Bay.

A London oil service company, Hudsons, bought an option to buy the 160 acres of Carness Farm, St Ola, it was reported. A company official, Bryan Nimmo, said: "We are going to build a 1,500 feet pier there. It could take a full range of ships from supply vessels to heavy tankers." The firm hoped to start construction in 1972 and be operating by 1973, employing up to 300 people.

The company's managing director Mr Dave Harrold said the firm had inspected Flotta and Lyness but felt that the area around Kirkwall Bay was ideally suited as a base for serving North Sea oil rigs.

However, it soon transpired that the company had not even sought planning permission.

By March, the focus returned to Scapa Flow as the Ministry of Defence confirmed that it was in talks with a consortium including BP and Shell regarding leasing part of the former Navy base for an oil rig repair yard and a base for oil supply vessels.

That same month, production licences for another 246 blocks of sea round Orkney and Shetland were allocated and, while the major companies of Esso, BP and Shell had the lion's share of the allocation, the successful prospecting firms included Occidental Petroleum (UK) Ltd, which had an area covering six blocks and 316,000 acres of sea.

Perhaps it is the weather to blame, but Orkney has always suffered from the affliction of rumour-tism, and, now, as the county saw an invasion of prospective oil developers, the sight and sound of a trans-Atlantic accent in stetson and cowboy boots was sufficient to start a veritable conveyor belt of rumours around the islands.

Some obviously had some basis in fact. For example, another London-based company Christiani Nielsen put forward a planning application for a construction site and quarry at Houton to construct concrete platforms for use in the North Sea. A public meeting of 200 people at Orphir forcefully dismissed the idea, fearing that as much as 200,000 tons of rock a year would be quarried. The plans were later withdrawn by Christiani Nielsen, citing insufficient water depths in Scapa Flow as the reason.

Another company called Orkney Oil Services Ltd, which had been newly registered in Edinburgh, put in for outline planning permission for the disused Skeabrae airfield. Ministry of Defence officials said they had received "a tentative inquiry" about developing the former World War Two aerodrome for Jumbo jets flying from Texas. The suggestion brought a horrified reaction from members of the National Farmers Union on the West Mainland.

Eventually, in a bid to cut through the burgeoning growth of rumours and oil industry fantasy, Orkney MP Jo Grimond wrote to the Secretary of State for Scotland Gordon Campbell asking the minister to come clean over what was proposed and what was not.

Mr Grimond accepted that, if properly handled, the discovery of oil could bring great benefits and a new variety of employment to the area, but assurances would be needed on environmental and pollution issues, he said.

"Generations to come will not forgive us if we make a mess of our opportunities - least of all if we repeat the mistakes of the 19th century industrial development.

"It is for the people themselves to express a view as to what they want. It is their country. It is the future of their children which is at stake. They want to know what is being considered, even if it is only a possibility."

Everyone seemed to have a view. Even the Church of Scotland weighed in with a report saying: "To sacrifice Scapa Flow for an extremely limited and short term benefit to the community would seem to be absurd."

At the start of 1973, in order to ensure that Orkney had a say over any proposed major oil-related industrial projects, Orkney County Council agreed to seek powers controlling coastal development in certain areas including Lyness, Flotta, Houton, Carness and Hatston. It would also seek council powers of compulsory purchase.

This was slammed by South Ronaldsay councillor Sandy Annal as "blatant dictatorship" and he was the only councillor to vote against the move.

It was eventually decided that to achieve the powers it sought, Orkney County Council would have to put a Private Bill through Parliament. This went before a House of Commons committee, and was eventually approved, in April, 1974. The Bill was essential to protect Orkney's interests, county convener Donald Brown told MPs.

The Bill was opposed by just one objector, Mrs Susan Flint, of Quoyclerks, Orphir, who was the principal teacher of physics at Kirkwall Grammar School and a member of the environmental pressure group Friends of the Earth. She had paid her own expenses to travel to London to voice her concerns. "No case has been made out for the oil developments in Orkney," she said, complaining that the hazards of the industry had been hidden from the public.

To add to the disappointment of her objections being ignored, Mrs Flint travelled home to learn that Orkney Education Committee had ruled that she should not be paid for her leave of absence from school.

By the time Orkney County Council Act became law, the deal had already been done for a major oil terminal on Flotta. (Ironically this sudden elevation to being the home of such a ground-breaking technological development coincided with the news that the island, with a population of 80 was to lose its resident doctor. Islanders threatened to stage a rates strike in protest).

The discovery of the Piper Field by Occidental Petroleum was in January, 1973, and it was four months later that the Occidental - or Oxy as it came to be known - consortium confirmed that a major tanker terminal with oil storage facilities, expected to cost £25 millions, was being planned. The managing director of Occidental in the UK, Mr Robert MacAlister, admitted his company had contacted Orkney County Council about

A Loganair Islander aircraft flies over Flotta as the construction of the oil terminal takes shape.

(Picture courtesy of Orkney Library photographic archive)

establishing such a base, and one of the areas considered was in Scapa Flow. Once established, the base would provide 75 jobs.

By July 26, 1973, the front page headline in *The Orcadian* read: "Oil terminal for Flotta?" A 130 mile pipeline would link the Piper Field to Flotta, with 900 men required for the construction phase, said the newspaper.

The Rev Ewan Traill, councillor for South Walls and Flotta, made a plea that the people of the South Isles should be given a square deal if there was to be such oil development. It could help to arrest depopulation and provide jobs, but he added: "We are no longer willing to be the Cinderella of Orkney, sitting in squalor while the wicked uncles of the Mainland of Kirkwall and Stromness luxuriate in prosperity at our expense. If the council will not help us, we see no reason to be exploited to enrich alien oil companies and uninterested Mainland rate-payers."

In fact the county council granted outline planning permission, subject to Government approval, for the Flotta complex at the start of September, 1973. The terminal would have a capacity for 10 million tons of oil a year.

The county council also approved an application from Shell UK Exploration for a supply base at Lyness to allow drilling to start to the west of Orkney.

Jo Grimond MP said local opinion was "substantially in favour" of the oil project on Flotta but sought assurances that local people would get the jobs, that adequate compensation would be paid for land, with prime agricultural land avoided, that pollution safeguards would be put in place - and that the Oxy consortium would pay a levy on the oil which would be set aside to reinstate the island after the oil installations were no longer needed.

The managing director of Occidental in the UK, Mr Robert MacAlister, confirmed in October, 1973, that negotiations for 250 acres of Flotta, at a reported price of £300,000 were going ahead. (This was at a time when farmland could be bought for around £50 an acre).

Occidental planned five storage tanks - each holding 500,000 barrels of oil - to take the oil from the Piper Field. The pipeline would cost £100 million and the terminal would cost £2 million a year to operate.

"Occidental envisage an operational life of 50 years for the terminal," said *The Orcadian*.

By December, 1973, Oxy officials were in talks with the county council to agree a financial settlement under a so-called "disturbance agreement." This was to be the start of the nest egg which would grow to be worth tens of millions of pounds over the next 25 years.

Under the deal, Orkney would receive a down payment of £500,000 from the oil companies involved in the Flotta terminal.

But in addition, Orkney would receive, at quarterly intervals, a payment of two pence per ton on all crude oil shipped out of the terminal. This figure would be adjusted in accordance with changes in the Retail Price Index, but was guaranteed to be not less than £45,000 a quarter. These quarterly payments could continue until at least 1990 if the Flotta terminal was still in use.

In addition, of course, Orkney would receive money for pilotage, towage and harbour dues from tankers which would use the facilities, which would finance the new Orkney harbours authority, under the directorship of Captain Duncan Robertson.

The council made another £150,000 for allowing a 31,000 ton floating supply base ship - providing pipes for the Brent Field pipeline to Shetland - to be anchored in Kirkwall bay for six months.

After formal clearance from the Government, Orkney County

Council confirmed planning permission for Flotta in January, 1974. Two formal objections were received from the Royal Society for the Protection of Birds and Friends of the Earth, Orkney, but both objections were withdrawn after negotiations with council officials and representatives of Occidental.

Within weeks, work was underway in Flotta - with the expectation that the first oil would be ashore by April, 1975. In fact, it would be December, 1976, before the oil eventually arrived and, by then, the estimated cost of the terminal had increased from the original estimate of £25 millions to something nearer £100 million. In fact, by the end of 1975, the total cost of developing the Piper Field - and the neighbouring Claymore Field discovered in May, 1974 - was estimated at £585 millions.

The influx of Irish construction workers at Flotta saw a twice weekly flight between Kirkwall and Belfast introduced by Loganair, and by the Spring of 1974 the foundations of the new tanks were already laid.

The two main contractors on Flotta were Turriff Taylor Tarmac and Bechtel - while Costain Civil Engineering Ltd was awarded a £5 million contract to build a jetty from the island.

Within weeks, there were rumours sweeping the county that Irish workers were earning £80 to £100 a week while Orkney men were taking home £25 a week, and county convener Donald Brown was forced to deny that the council had made a pact with the Oxy group to regulate the wages paid.

"At present," he said in May, 1974, "There are 17 Orcadians directly employed in connection with the Flotta development but it must be realised that many others are indirectly involved through sub-contractors."

Contractors had given an assurance there would be no differential pay rates for local and incoming labour, he said.

Although this was three years after the advent of decimalisation, Councillor Sandy Annal claimed: "At present, Orkney men are paid 11 shillings per hour while Irish workers can earn double this rate."

Occidental - which had heralded its North Sea find as "the greatest oil discovery of all time" in a promotional film - certainly began to recruit local people to the company's permanent staff. In February, 1975, Mr John Hogg was appointed terminal manager with Captain Arthur MacKay as deputy. Orcadian Captain Max Gunn was appointed marine superintendent while Stromness Primary School headmaster Bill Crichton took up the post of external relations officer for Oxy.

Orkney could now witness at close hand the unique culture of a major industrial construction site. The county had its first drugs case as seven Flotta workers appeared at Kirkwall Sheriff Court accused of cannabis possession after a police raid on the island.

It also saw a series of industrial disputes, which, although not unknown in Orkney, were rare. In February, 1975, several hundred construction workers were laid off - and sent home by air and sea - after the site was closed for a fortnight by a strike of 70 catering staff who complained they worked ten hours a day for 28 days before they got a week off.

A few weeks later, 40 joiners - half of them local - who were earning £2 an hour went on strike seeking £3 an hour. The stoppage lasted a week. There was more industrial strife as 70 electricians and welders were dismissed when they went on strike in support of two colleagues who had been sacked. The men staged a sit-in, but eventually agreed to be flown home on a specially chartered aircraft, only to be later re-instated and brought back to Flotta.

As the biggest oil production platform jacket ever built - weighing 14,500 tons and standing 495 feet high - was towed from the Moray Firth, where it was constructed, to the Piper Field, it was reported that some Orkney fishermen were deserting their industry because it was more profitable to ferry workers to Flotta.

As Oxy agreed to proceed with the development of the Claymore Field, it was estimated that Flotta could provide as much as a quarter of the UK's total oil requirements within three years.

Back in Flotta that brought little cheer to the local population.

In the biggest ever chartered airlift by British Airways in Scotland, 600 men employed on the Flotta terminal construction were flown home for Christmas and New Year. They left behind a "sea of mud."

After reports that mud was a foot deep on the roads, Mrs Laura Grimond said: "Its like the Battle of the Somme and people are furious."

"The islanders have put up with this for two years and they have reached the limit of their tolerance," said Dr Tony Trickett.

To emphasise their dissatisfaction, when Occidental applied to site two more storage tanks on Flotta - each to hold one million barrels of oil - 56 of the 76 electors of Flotta signed a petition objecting to the plan.

Of course, it would be cynical to suggest that had any influence on the decision of Occidental to later present £25,000 towards the cost of a Flotta community centre; a cheque presentation made to 92 year old Tom Rosie, the island's oldest resident, when the terminal was officially opened.

Flotta was also to benefit from the installation of electricity. The Occidental consortium had collaborated with the North of Scotland Hydro Electric Board to construct a power plant using natural gas, which would be provided free of charge, providing the opportunity of electricity for every householder on Flotta as well as being fed into the grid.

The value of this, said Occidental's 78 year old chairman Dr Armand Hammer, was estimated at £500,000 over three years.

"We are very glad to do it, for you have been good neighbours to us and we have every intention of reciprocating and being the very best of neighbours to you," Dr Hammer told the Flotta islanders.

MP Jo Grimond argued that the Scottish Gas Board should have accepted an offer from Oxy to pipe natural gas from Flotta to the Orkney Mainland. The gas could have been used to fuel Kirkwall power station, suggested the MP, who regarded it as an opportunity missed.

And, of course, after the jobs boom came the downside. As completion of phase one of the terminal construction drew nearer in March, 1976, notice was given of more than 700 redundancies among workers employed by the main contractors Turriff Taylor Tarmac and Bateman catering, part of Grandmet. By July, as at least 120 local workers were redundant, an appeal was made to employ as many Orcadians as possible on the second phase. Bill Crichton said Occidental was keen to encourage local labour and 100 of the 160 permanent staff at the terminal would be Orcadians.

The Rev Ewan Traill also proposed that Orkney Islands Council should pay a £10 Christmas bonus to all of Orkney's 2,800 pensioners, out of the oil funds it was beginning to accrue. Councillors agreed to study the proposal and it was later to be adopted - although by the end of the century the value of the bonus had lagged behind inflation.

In November, 1976, just a week before production was due to start, 300 workers at the Piper platform staged a strike. Fortunately it was settled within days and the first commercial oil came from the Piper Field on December 7, 1976 - although it would take 20 days to fill the 130 mile long pipeline to Flotta.

It meant that Piper - the seventh field to come on stream in British waters - had gone from discovery to production in less than four years.

And, what was to become a symbol of Orkney's Oil Age, the Flotta flare, which would burn off excess gas, was lit for the first time at 2am on Tuesday, December 28, 1976. "We're making oil now and it has been a sweet operation," said Captain Arthur MacKay.

The first tanker to take away North Sea oil from Flotta arrived in Scapa Flow on Tuesday, January 4, 1977 - the 800 feet long French vessel *Dolabella* which would load a shipment of 60,000 tons of crude for transport to Shellhaven in the Thames. The five tanks to hold oil from the Piper Field were already half full. By the end of January, 1977, oil was flowing from Piper at a rate of 60,000 barrels a day.

Britain's Energy Minister, Mr Tony Benn, the head of Occidental, Dr Armand Hammer, and piper Mac Robertson enjoy the opening ceremony of the new oil terminal with members of the Flotta community. (Picture courtesy of Orkney Library photographic archive)

The official inauguration of the Flotta terminal took place on Tuesday, January 11, 1977. Oxy chairman Dr Armand Hammer flew to Kirkwall in his executive jet, with his wife, to preside at the ceremony which saw Britain's Energy Secretary Mr Tony Benn pull a lever in the control room to mark the start of oil production.

The oil was appropriately "piped" ashore with a pipe march composed by Mr 'Mac' Robertson, in honour of Dr Hammer and entitled "Flotta Hammer."

Tony Benn said: "This is a great day for all of us - for Oxy and its partners and all those who have worked at Flotta, for Orkney and not least for Britain because it signals another important step towards the goal of security and self sufficiency in energy supplies by 1980.

"Piper is the fourth largest oil field so far discovered round Britain's shores. No field, I believe, has flowed at greater test rates. It is also very high quality crude. We look forward to Claymore oil flowing ashore on Flotta in the Spring.

"Piper and Claymore when in full production will together provide about a fifth - say 20 million tons a year - of United Kingdom's oil requirements. So this makes Flotta a very important oil terminal indeed.

"May I also refer to the speed with which you have brought Piper on stream through Flotta. It has taken less than four years from discovery to production. This is an outstanding achievement in such a hostile Northern environment. I want to say to all concerned companies, contractors, the whole of the work force and Orcadians and Flottarians - how much the Government admires and appreciates this effort.

"I know of the efforts that have been made to protect the environment here in Scapa Flow and to take account of the interests of the people of Flotta who are honoured guests today here in their own island.

"I would also like to extend my congratulations and appreciation to Orkney Islands Council on their good fortune and for the way they have facilitated this important national development." The co-operation between local authority and community and the oil companies had provided a model for the working partnership the Government hoped to achieve, he said.

"The discovery of oil in these northern waters has brought the ships back to Scapa Flow. I should imagine that Orkney has seen nothing like today since the last battle fleet sailed from this fine natural harbour.

"But this time the business is peaceful. And it is bringing Orcadians back to Orkney. It is providing - and will provide - for some decades ahead - new opportunities for the islanders themselves. That is greatly to be welcomed.

"But this and other oil developments around our shores are also breathing new life and hope into our national economy. By 1980 we shall be self-sufficient in oil and energy - security which few, if any, other western industrialised countries will enjoy.

"Altogether we estimate that our oil and gas reserves are worth well over £300 billions. Your ceremony today in Flotta enables me to remind the world of Britain's fundamental strength and potential, endowed, as it is, with resources on this scale. Our job as a nation is how to use these resources to restore our industrial and economic fortunes - not to say pre-eminence.

"And let no one, after this success in bringing a major offshore oil field on stream in less than four years, say it can't be done in Britain. It can and is being done regularly."

"All kinds of records are being broken; frontiers advanced; and human achievements extended in the North sea. Today's is another example of what can be done!"

Armand Hammer said: "My memories and associations with this great county cover many events, but never have I had more feeling of satisfaction and accomplishment than I do at this moment."

Although Occidental held 36.5 per cent of the consortium interest, there were three partners in the project - Getty Oil International with 23.5 per cent, Allied Chemical (GB) Ltd with 20 per cent, and Thomson North Sea Ltd, also with 20 per cent.

Occidental, he said, had been fortunate to find the right partners to help finance the venture in Paul Getty and Roy Thomson.

"I have but one wish and that is that Paul Getty and Roy Thomson might still be here for I know how these two pioneers would have felt to see a dream become reality."

There were some people, he said, who thought the project would bankrupt his company for it was "a pretty daring gamble."

"But great dreams always have their risks and in the world of international oil one must always be willing to face those risks, find the right people to be associated with and get to work."

That was why he had been prepared to "roll the dice for such high stakes."

By 1977, Oxy's investment in the North Sea and Flotta had risen to 1.2 billion dollars, he said. But they had achieved their aims in half the time some people had thought possible.

He paid tribute to the workforce, to the Orcadians who had worked closely with the consortium to establish the development and the islanders of Flotta who had put up with substantial inconvenience.

"The oil that loads today is not just oil from offshore Flotta belonging to a consortium. Rather it is force that will give great new pulse to the lifeblood of the United Kingdom, carrying in its flow a vital assistance at a difficult economic time. I can

The Claymore A platform which would feed its oil to Flotta.
(Picture from the files of *The Orcadian*)

foresee the day - and I hope it will come soon, for I believe it is vital to your national interest - when all the oil produced here will be refined in the United Kingdom, an event of great magnitude, carrying with it enormous additional benefits to all your people."

Occidental had already helped to gift a Steinway concert piano to the Orkney Arts Society, but he now chose the official opening of the Flotta terminal to make the surprise announcement of a £50,000 donation towards the funding of what would become the Pier Arts Centre in Stromness.

Art-lover Margaret Gardiner - a frequent visitor to the islands - had offered her collection of modern and abstract art to the county if suitable premises could be made available to house it.

The collection included sculptures by Barbara Hepworth and paintings by Ben Nicholson and, according to Dr Hammer, who appeared to put a price, if not a value, to everything, was worth more than £225,000.

Dr Hammer said: "These works of art are rare treasures and Margaret Gardiner's gift is a most generous one. Experts in the subject tell me the Hepworths and Nicholsons in this collection are far superior to those owned by the great Tate Gallery in London.

"On behalf of the Armand Hammer Foundation and the Occidental Petroleum Foundation, I herewith donate the necessary £50,000 to make the museum possible. Mrs Gardiner is here with us today and I ask you all to join me in saluting her generosity in donating her excellent collection."

Outside, the real business of the terminal was already proceeding apace. Within eight years, the terminal would handle its first one billion barrels of oil. What the Orkney economy would have been like without the Oil Age is impossible to quantify exactly but there is no doubt that Flotta has made a significant contribution not only to the islands but also the country as the terminal could claim to have handled 15 per cent of Britain's total North Sea oil output.

Occidental would remain the operators of the Flotta terminal until 1991 - a period including the dreadful Piper Alpha disaster of 1988 - when, following the death of Armand Hammer, the American company decided to sell its North Sea interests to the French oil giant Elf which would operate the terminal until the close of the century.

The exultant mood of the early oil bonanza of the 1970s would probably never return, but it was good while it lasted.

Dr Armand Hammer (left) presented a cheque for £25,000 for a new Flotta community centre to 92 year old Tom Rosie, the island's oldest resident when the terminal was opened.
(Picture courtesy of Orkney Library photographic archive)

St Magnus Festival is born

The birth of what was to become one of the most respected and acclaimed events of the musical and artistic calendar in Britain was witnessed in 1977 as the curtain rose on the first St Magnus Festival.

It would continue, and grow, for the remainder of the 20th century - bringing to Orkney some of the world's top names in music and the arts. Over the following 20 or so years, Orcadians would have the opportunity to see and hear the world's top orchestras and soloists - people like Vladimir Ashkenazy, John Williams and Evelyn Glennie - as well as men of letters like Seamus Heaney, who won the 1996 Nobel Prize for literature.

But the name, and work, of one man would be a constant strength behind the festival - Peter Maxwell Davies, the world renowned composer who made his home in Orkney after a fortuitous holiday visit to Hoy in 1970. It was to lead to a meeting with the Orkney writer and poet George Mackay Brown, with whom he was to collaborate in the launch of the first St Magnus Festival.

Peter Maxwell Davies - later to become Sir Peter, but known to most of his friends in Orkney simply as Max - explained that chance encounter: "I was lucky - it was one of those days when all the threads are brought together as if by pre-destination. I went to the island where George Mackay Brown and several other people, who have become very close friends, were staying. We talked for a while and then they insisted that I stay for lunch. I stayed for the day and we became very close friends."

In fact, he was offered a cottage to stay in, and he spent two weeks in Hoy writing the first score to the Ken Russell film *The Devils*.

Inspired by the beauty and solitude, the Lancashire-born composer later renovated an old croft house at Rackwick and, in 1977, he said: "I now have the best working conditions that a composer could possibly wish for.

"I feel very much that it's due to my going to Orkney and having such good neighbours that I have written more music in the last two years than in the whole period before."

The idea of the first St Magnus Festival took shape after he was commissioned by the BBC to compose a work to mark the Queen's Silver Jubilee in 1977. The result was the opera *The Martyrdom of St Magnus* with libretto by George Mackay Brown, based on GMB's novel *Magnus*.

They announced that it would have its world premiere in St Magnus Cathedral in June, 1977, as part of a three day festival during which Peter Maxwell Davies'

Sir Peter Maxwell Davies with young musicians who attended one of his annual summer schools held in Hoy.
(Picture courtesy of Kenny Pirie)

1977

musical ensemble The Fires of London would perform other Orkney-inspired pieces written by the composer.

He said: "I am grateful for the opportunity to show the people of Orkney something of what I've been doing while I'm living and working there - for the opportunity of making contact with a very good audience who will bring excellent common sense. The people of Orkney have been very good neighbours and I wanted to show my appreciation of them and let them have first seeing of the opera."

That year had already seen the premiere of another Maxwell Davies work, *A Mirror of Whitening Light* at the Queen Elizabeth Hall in London which was reported to have received a "rapturous" reception from the audience and critics alike.

The 1977 St Magnus Festival - costing £14,000 to stage - would have a series of concerts and recitals, with the Edinburgh Quartet, Shetland fiddler Arthur Robertson, organists Norman Mitchell and Richard Hughes, the St Magnus Cathedral Singers, Kirkwall Grammar School Choir and Chamber Orchestra and the Orkney Strathspey and Reel Society, as well as an exhibition of paintings by Stanley Cursiter. Orkney Islands Council agreed to underwrite a loss up to £2,000.

Norman Mitchell, the choirmaster and director of music for St Magnus Cathedral, who would be co-director of the first three festivals in 1977-79, said:

"An Orkney audience is very conscious and appreciative of high standards. We look on this as the very first of many festivals and we hope to see Orkney established as a centre for the arts."

Peter Maxwell Davies agreed: "I hope it will be a further stimulus to the artistic life in the islands. I hope too that it will be an annual event." He was already working on an adaption of another George Mackay Brown book *The Two Fiddlers* which would be watched by 1,400 people when staged at the 1978 St Magnus Festival.

Seven performances, in all, were staged in St Magnus Cathedral as part of the first festival. *The Orcadian* wrote: "Its manifest success in transforming the 800 year old Cathedral into a living centre of art - contemporary (and even avant-garde) in manner, but ageless in theme - captured the imagination of all who attended the concerts and recitals this week."

During his years in Hoy (he was to move to Sanday 20 years later) Peter Maxwell Davies was to enjoy worldwide acclaim. He was awarded honorary degrees from the Royal Manchester College of Music, Edinburgh University, Aberdeen University and the Open University. In 1979, he was named as Composer of the Year by the Composers' Guild.

In 1981 he became a CBE and then, six years later, was awarded a knighthood in the New Years honours list. In 1985, he was appointed associate composer and conductor for the Scottish Chamber Orchestra, and, in Orkney, after a decade of sterling service as artistic director, he became honorary president of the St Magnus Festival.

Orkney mourns loss of self-made scholar

Ernest Marwick - who had battled against adversity to become Orkney's most distinquished scholar of the day - died, after a road accident, in July, 1977, at the age of 61.

Born in Evie, the elder son of Mr and Mrs Tom Marwick of Furson, he was self taught after ill health forced an end to his formal education at the age of ten.

Until the age of 26, he worked on the farm, but he battled to overcome his handicaps and, in 1941, a world of literature opened up for him when he moved to Kirkwall where he worked for 12 years in the book and newspaper department of the firm of The Leonards.

His achievements were acknowledged in 1953-54 when he won a place at Newbattle Abbey - where the Orkney writer and poet Edwin Muir was warden - to study history, English language and philosophy. It enabled him to join the staff of the *Orkney Herald* in 1954.

In 1961, he edited the 19th century work *Orkney Folklore and Traditions* by the Orcadian writer Walter Traill Dennison, and he wrote *The Folklore of Orkney and Shetland* published in 1975 - the same year that he shared the honour of being one of the last two men to receive the freedom of the burgh from Kirkwall Town Council before the council was abolished.

He compiled a full length *History of the Orkney People in the Nineteenth Century* published by *The Orcadian*, and made 850 broadcasts for the BBC. And, just a year before his death, the boy who scarcely had a school lesson was awarded an honorary MA degree from Edinburgh University.

The week of Ernest Marwick's death was an especially sad one for Orkney academia as Stromness Academy rector Mr John MacLean also died at the age of 60. He was to be succeeded as rector by Stromness-born Mr Ian MacInnes (55), the depute rector.

Orkney strike stranglehold

Orkney was at the mercy of a series of strikes as the end of the 1970s was marked by industrial strife which left the islands crippled by transport disputes.

In August, 1977, a five day strike by P&O officers, in a pay and productivity dispute, left 300 cars marooned as sailings of the *St Ola* across the Pentland Firth were cancelled. The *St Ola* remained tied up at Scrabster as the strike left holidaymakers stranded without money in Orkney, and disrupted the start of the annual cattle exports.

A week later livestock shipments were delayed again by a two day strike by Aberdeen dockers and, a week after that, a strike by P&O crewmen added to the disruption.

Islanders were also hit by industrial strife within the county in November, 1978, when a two week strike over pay by officers of the Orkney Islands Shipping Company vessels *Orcadia* and *Islander* brought a shipping crisis to the isles with essential supplies of food and fuel running out, and farmers unable to ship livestock.

Ten islands, with a total population of 3,000 were hit as calls were made to the Scottish Secretary Bruce Millan to make emergency transport arrangements before the dispute was settled by arbitration.

The settlement came just in time for a new dispute to surface as the year of 1979 began with a national strike by lorry drivers which saw emergency cargoes having to be shipped to Orkney from Aberdeen to maintain supplies of fuel and animal feedstuffs. A year later, it was a three week strike by Aberdeen dockers which gave Orkney its 1980 dose of transport misery.

The fall of the Labour government in 1979 was attributed largely to the 1978 "winter of discontent." Orkney seemed to have been the victim of a decade of discontent.

Giant cargo ship saved

The 11,000 tonnes American cargo ship *Pioneer Commander*, with a crew of 42 on board, ran aground in thick fog on the Louther Skerry in the Pentland Firth - prompting fears of pollution as her fuel tanks, with 2,000 tons of oil, were ruptured.

The vessel was on passage from West Germany to New York with an 800 tonne cargo of vehicles. The Longhope lifeboat and the Scapa Flow tug *Kessock* stood by, but the crew remained on board, and after a week the ship was refloated by the Dutch tug *Typhoon*.

After temporary repairs at Lyness, the *Pioneer Commander* left for the Tyne to go into dry dock, but her unfortunate visit to local shores was blamed for a number of oiled birds which were washed up. And her master was later fined £1,400 at Kirkwall Sheriff Court for oil pollution.

Orkney's own ship

HMS *Orkney*, a new offshore patrol vessel for the Royal Navy, made her first appearance in her "home" county in April, 1977, when, under the command of Lt Commander Dennis Corless, she visited Stromness where she entertained Orkney's Lord Lieutenant and county convener.

The vessel was virtually the only property of the Royal Navy to be seen in the county by 1977, as Orkney Islands Council concluded negotiations to buy nearly 300 acres of the Naval oil fuel depot at Lyness, from the Ministry of Defence, at a price not exceeding £70,000.

Last Great Auk

A plaque marking the spot where the last Great Auk known to mankind was killed was erected in Papa Westray by Richard Fresson, the son of the aviation pioneer Captain Ted Fresson.

The last Great Auk - a large, flightless bird - was shot on the island in 1813. It was sent by Miss Traill, of Holland House, Papa Westray, to London where the stuffed specimen was preserved in the natural history department of the British Museum.

Football record

Sandwick footballers established a new record when they won Orkney's Parish Cup for the fifth successive season - overtaking Harray's record of four successive victories in 1966-69 - when they beat South Ronaldsay 1-0 in the 1977 final. It was South Ronaldsay's sixth defeat in the final in 22 years. Sandwick made it six Parish Cup victories in a row in 1978.

Bull bonanza

The annual bull show at Kirkwall Auction Mart saw four bulls fetch over 1,000 guineas - the first time that figure had been passed. The top price went to the Aberdeen-Angus champion, the two year old Paragon of Unigarth, bred and shown by D. W. Sinclair, South Unigarth, Sandwick, bought for 1,100 guineas by William Spence, Airy, Stronsay.

Silver jubilee

Princess Alexandra, accompanied by her husband Angus Ogilvy, made a two day visit to Orkney, including a helicopter trip to Westray, as more than 7,000 people turned out at the Bignold Park to see the Princess at a gala organised to celebrate the Queen's Silver Jubilee. Orkney raised £10,317 for the Queen's Silver Jubilee Appeal which was launched by Prince Charles.

Seal wars on Orkney shores

1978

A controversy which had simmered for nearly ten years broke out into open hostility with confrontation threatening on the shores of Orkney as conservationists prepared to form a human chain to save thousands of seals.

Since 1970, a limited cull of grey seals had taken place in local waters each year and around 1,000 pups were killed by local hunters for commercial purposes with the pelts of seal pups fetching up to £12 each.

But in June, 1978, the Scottish Secretary Bruce Millan gave the go-ahead for marksmen to carry out the biggest cull of grey seals yet to be authorised in Orkney, to go ahead in October, 1978.

A Norwegian firm, engaged by the Scottish Office, would kill 4,000 seal pups and 900 breeding females in Orkney and the Western Isles as part of an organised campaign to halve Scotland's Grey Seal population by 1982, in order to protect fisheries interests.

Grey seals were estimated to eat 56,000 tonnes of fish a year.

Much of the opposition to the mass cull was from environmental and wildlife groups in the South, but protests were also heard at the Orkney Countryside Committee where the RSPB officer David Lea said the seals were part of Orkney's wildlife and of international importance, dismissing the cull as "totally unnecessary."

Miss Elaine Bullard, of Orkney Field Club, said she could not see how adult seals could be killed humanely in such large numbers as were being proposed.

Orkney MP Jo Grimond said he had received 118 letters of protest and wrote to the Scottish Secretary: "This proposal to slaughter a great number of pregnant female seals, of a species which throughout the world is rare, has rightly, I think, aroused great indignation.

"If it is necessary to keep down the numbers - though they are animals of singular beauty and of great interest - is it really necessary to have a cull of some 5,000?

"I trust that these shoots will really be supervised. It is one thing to allow local people to shoot some seals, but it is quite another to organise a slaughter on this scale."

A national petition against the cull had raised 28,000 signatures, including 6,500 collected in Orkney, but the Orkney Fishermen's Association came out "reluctantly" in favour of the cull, although questioning the methods of the Department of Agriculture and Fisheries for Scotland.

However, the French film star Brigitte Bardot added her voice to the protests and it seemed that confrontation was unavoidable as the ship *Rainbow Warrior,* oper-ated by the environmental group Greenpeace, arrived in Orkney with a crew of five and 15 volunteers who vowed to disrupt the shoot, a week before the arrival of the Norwegian ship *Kvitingen* with the marksmen who were to carry out the operation.

And as nearly 100 journalists from around the world descended on the islands, the locally-based Loganair pilot, Captain Andy Alsop, a leading opponent of the cull, said: "The cull clearly cannot succeed in the face of so much public opposition."

We will never know what might have happened because at the eleventh hour, Scottish Secretary Bruce Millan called off the mass cull and dispensed with the services of the Norwegians. It was admitted that he had received a total of 2,787 letters from the public - all but seven opposed to the slaughter of seals.

Instead a limited cull of 2,000 pups in Orkney and the Western Isles would go ahead to be carried out by local hunters.

"It is to be hoped that good sense will prevail and that Orcadians will now be allowed to get on with the job, unimpeded," said *The Orcadian.* "We certainly don't need the help of other 'extremists' who now in their turn are threatening to invade us."

And on October 25, 1978, after only 40 hours in Orkney, buffeted constantly by wind and rain, 26 members of the Hunt Saboteurs Association, including a 14 year old girl, left the county after a forlorn attempt at camping at Pickaquoy.

Their spokesman Nigel Crane said: "We are bitterly disappointed. We came here to save the seals and all we got was the cold shoulder. Despite all our good intentions we were treated as outsiders and got no help whatever. It's futile staying here."

By the following year, the seal cull had become the responsibility of the new Conservative Secretary of State for Scotland George Younger. He was immediately lobbied by wildlife groups to scrap the cull for the future.

In October, 1979, he announced that - to allow more consultation with fishery and conservation interests - he would only allow another limited cull of seal pups during the autumn with local marksmen licensed to shoot a maximum of 2,000 in Orkney and the Western Isles.

A mass cull on the scale first proposed by Bruce Millan never did receive the go-ahead, although there would be skirmishes between conservationists and hunters as members of the national Sea Shepherd organisation attempted to sabotage culls by spraying seal pups with red dye to render their pelts commercially valueless. It led, in November, 1981, to 16 protesters, all with addresses outside Orkney, appearing in court at Kirkwall accused of a variety of breach of the peace charges.

Two years later the cull was ended and no government in the remaining years of the century - despite pleas from the fishing industry - ever dared to challenge the weight of public opinion in the South by reintroducing such a proposal.

The old and the new! The St Magnus kirk on Egilsay is the backdrop as a Loganair Islander aircraft flies to the North Isles. (Picture courtesy of Orkney Library photographic archive)

A Royal County Show

It was estimated that two out of every three Orcadians living in the county were in Kirkwall for the day as the 1978 County Show had a record attendance of 10,380 - attracted by the presence of the Queen.

It was the Queen's second visit to Orkney as, accompanied by her youngest son Prince Edward, she visited the 93rd County Show. By coincidence the date was August 12 - the same as her first visit in 1960.

She officially opened the new offices of Orkney Islands Council at the former Kirkwall Grammar School in School Place before, accompanied by Mr Kenneth Eunson, president of the Orkney Agricultural Society, she walked amongst the crowds at the "Royal" show, where the supreme cattle championship went to W. R. Baillie of Biggins, Toab.

In 1979, Prince Charles returned for a six hour visit, after arriving at the controls of a helicopter, during which he toured Robertson's fudge factory in Stromness and the Ortak silvercraft factory in Kirkwall.

And 1980 saw the re-appearance of Orkney's most regular Royal visitor of the century - Queen Elizabeth, the Queen Mother - as, a few days after her 80th birthday, she opened that year's St Magnus Fair.

"As Patron of the Friends of St Magnus, I am especially pleased to learn that thanks to the devoted endeavours of so many loyal supporters, it has been possible to embark on the second phase of the restoration of the Cathedral" she said.

Honour for businessman

Mr John D.M. Robertson (48), of Shorelands, Kirkwall, who, with his uncle Brigadier S.P. Robertson, had built the oil business of S. and J.D. Robertson into one of the biggest private companies in Scotland, was honoured for his record of public service as he was made an OBE in the 1978 New Year honours list.

A former pupil of Kirkwall Grammar School and a graduate of Edinburgh University, where he won a double Blue in athletics, he had worked in the oil industry in London, Aden and South Wales before returning to the Kirkwall-based company which his uncle founded in 1954, and which now served the oil needs of Orkney, Shetland, Caithness and Sutherland. A decade later, the company was to expand its operations as far as the Falkland Islands.

Mr Robertson, who 15 years later was to be also made a CBE, was chairman of the Orkney Savings Committee and a member of the National Savings Committee for Scotland; a member of the Orkney Health Board, of which he would later become chairman; an honorary Sheriff; honorary consul for the Federal Republic of Germany; and Danish vice-consul. He had also been chairman of Orkney Children's Panel, and was past president of the Rotary Club of Kirkwall.

And he was the author of what was

John D.M. Robertson CBE, OBE
(Picture from the files of *The Orcadian*)

regarded as the definitive history of the Kirkwall Ba' game, *Uppies and Doonies*.

Also honoured in the 1978 New Year honours was Shapinsay GP Dr William MacGregor who was made an OBE for his services as Director of Medical Services and Secretary to the Ministry of Health in the Seychelles where he worked for 13 years after previously serving as the doctor on Westray.

Mink farm refused

Plans put forward for a mink farm on Westray by Mr George Drever were blocked by Scottish Secretary Bruce Millan after a public inquiry.

Orkney Islands Council had given permission but there had been protests from conservation and wildlife groups who feared the animals in the fur farming venture could escape.

County convener Edwin Eunson said the Scottish Secretary had surrendered to powerful outside pressure groups. This was just the sort of development that was needed in Orkney, he said.

Hatston ro-ro row

A roll-on, roll-off shipping terminal was proposed for Hatston. It would be built at Crowness and would cost an estimated £2 million, Orkney Islands Council was told in 1978.

It started an acrimonious debate which would continue, on and off, for the next eight years as the scheme was opposed especially by Stromness and West Mainland councillors.

Eventually, after the estimated cost had increased to nearer £6 millions, the whole idea was quashed in the mid 1980s when the Scottish Office refused to support the project. Instead the upgrading of Kirkwall Pier - to what we have in 1999 - would go ahead.

Canadian Indian chief

Senator Joseph Dreaver, for 40 years the Chief of the Mistawasis Cree Indians in Saskatchewan, Canada, died at the age of 86. He was the great grandson of Mr James Drever, who left Westray in 1845, and married the daughter of the Chief of the Mistawasis Indians at that time.

Rugby victory

Orkney Rugby Club returned triumphant after defeating Highland Rugby Club to win the Brin Cup - the only major trophy played for annually between the rugby clubs in the North of Scotland in 1978.

The Hoy menagerie

The new owners of the former Gaskin's grocery shop at North Ness, Lyness, David and Brenda Treasurer, arrived from Faversham, Kent, bringing with them their pets - 34 dogs, 20 cats and a pony - which they had rescued. It cost them £2,500 to carry them in a cattle transporter.

Convener ousted

Councillor George Marwick - the first convener of Orkney Islands Council - was defeated in the Birsay ward at the 1978 local government elections by retired bank manager Jackie Brown. Mr Marwick was succeeded as convener by Councillor Edwin Eunson of Kirkwall.

A real 999 call

Mother-to-be Netta Bain from Sanday became the 999th air ambulance patient to be flown by Loganair since 1967. She was flown by Captain Chris Bartlett en route to the Balfour Hospital where she gave birth to a son. The following day Captain Andy Alsop piloted the 1,000th ambulance flight when he flew a stretcher patient to Aberdeen.

Blizzards black out Orkney homes

Queen Elizabeth, the Queen Mother, visited Kirkwall's St Magnus Cathedral on five occasions after her first visit in 1956, including a visit in 1987 to join the celebrations of the Cathedral's 850th anniversary. She is pictured here being welcomed in Broad Street by the Lord Lieutenant of Orkney, Colonel Robert Macrae, in 1985.

(Picture courtesy of Orkney Library photographic archive)

A marathon three hours 40 minutes of broadcasting by Radio Orkney kept the county updated with emergency messages as the worst weather since the Great Blizzard of 1955 saw the islands hit by three days of snow which left 5,500 homes without electricity or telephones. Helicopters were brought in to help restore power lines. In all, 14 schools were closed in Orkney at the height of the emergency.

Oil gift for hospital

The operator of the Flotta oil terminal, Occidental, announced that the company would finance a £100,000 wing for Kirkwall's Balfour Hospital - to become the Piper Ward - while a covenant from the American company to the St Magnus Cathedral Appeal Fund would be worth an estimated £50,000 over seven years.

Radio protest

As the new BBC Radio Scotland frequency came on the air in 1978, county convener Edwin Eunson complained it was "geared to morons." Orkney Islands Council agreed to register a protest that Orkney could no longer enjoy a clear reception of BBC Radio Four.

Master craftsman dies

An acclaimed Orkney craftsman whose work graced St Magnus Cathedral and the homes of Royalty was tragically lost to the county in 1978.

Kirkwall craftsman Reynold Eunson, whose carvings of Rognvald, his father Kol, and Bishop William adorned the St Rognvald Chapel of the Cathedral, died at the early age of 46.

He had collaborated closely with the Orkney artist Stanley Cursiter on the design of the chapel and was also responsible for the carved communion table and chairs for the Minister and Elders in the Cathedral. He was also a well known maker of the traditional straw-backed Orkney chairs - and his very first chair was presented to the Queen Mother when she visited Orkney in 1956.

Also in 1978, Mr David Horne - who reported football matches and the Ba' game for the *Orkney Herald* under the pen name Cubbie Roo - died in Australia, to where he had emigrated 30 years earlier, at the age of 70.

The year also saw the death at the age of 60 of Mr David Keldie, the first manager of the Kirkwall swimming pool, who, in the previous 30 years, had taught hundreds of young Orcadians to swim.

Fishing plea to oil men

The Flotta oil company Occidental asked all their employees in Orkney to do less fishing in their spare time. The request was in a letter from the company's external relations officer Mr Bill Crichton who said the fishermen who earned their livelihood in local waters were concerned that their income was being affected by part-time fishing by Oxy employees.

He said that it was the company's strong opinion that personnel should be allowed to use their spare time as they wished.

But in deference to the Orkney Fishermen's Association, they would earnestly request that their employers limit their part-time fishing to "sport fishing and a few creels for the pot."

Unknown graves for 27 fishermen

1979

An appalling toll of tragedy saw 27 fishermen perish to unknown graves as, in four separate disasters in as many years, their vessels were lost without trace in the seas of the Northern Isles.

It was a period of unimaginable anguish for the port of Buckie which was home to three of the fishing boats.

The series of inexplicable losses began in March, 1978, when a massive air and sea search, including HMS *Orkney*, was launched to the east of Orkney when the 75 feet Fraserburgh fishing boat *Enterprise* disappeared, without clues, in the North Sea with a crew of eight.

But then 1979 would be forever remembered as a black year of tragedy for Buckie.

In June, 1979, the 58 feet fishing boat *Carinthia*, with six men on board, was lost without trace off Westray. The alarm was raised when a lifebelt was washed ashore in Rousay, and an air and sea search was begun. However the massive search operation had to be abandoned with nothing found.

Just six months later, Buckie was plunged into mourning again as the *Ocean Monarch*, with a crew of seven, was lost off Shetland, after being swamped by heavy seas.

And yet still the grim toll increased when, in March, 1981, the 65 feet Buckie vessel *Celerity*, skippered by Sandy Bruce with a crew of six, was lost in atrocious conditions in the Pentland Firth; the boat again disappearing without trace as an air and sea rescue failed to find any clues.

The loss of life could have been worse but for a major rescue by a Kirkwall skipper in February, 1979. All 11 crewmen of two Grimsby trawlers *Ocean Reward* and *Paul Antony*, which collided and sank while pair-fishing 35 miles off Westray, were rescued by skipper Albert Reid in his trawler *Mount Royal*.

It was a frightening illustration of the risks faced by the fishing fleet in pursuit of a livelihood.

In 1978, Orkney whitefish vessels had landed a total of 30,981 hundredweights - just over 1,500 tons - valued at £578,920.

'Ghost ship' abandoned by crew

The 26 mainly Spanish crew of the Liberian-registered 18,700 ton ore carrier *Vida* abandoned ship in the early hours, leaving their vessel drifting helplessly in thick fog in the sea lanes of the Pentland Firth for three hours.

The vessel was on passage from Canada to Immingham on Humberside with a cargo of iron ore when the master, Captain Jacinto Cuartango, sent out a call for help, two miles off Stroma, after the ship lost power due to a fractured fuel pipe.

Forty minutes later they radioed that they were abandoning ship. The Longhope and Wick lifeboats were launched but the crew were safely picked up from their lifeboat by the tanker *BP Springer* and landed at Scrabster.

Meanwhile the abandoned freighter was drifting in the Pentland Firth. When an Orkney harbours launch managed to put crewman Ken Pirie on board the "ghost ship", he found that the electrical power and radar were still operating, and he was able to assist in the operation as the stricken vessel was taken in tow by the Orkney Towage Company tugs *Kessock*, *Kinloch* and *Keston* which, in a 50 mile rescue, brought the huge vessel to Kirkwall - where the tugmen promptly lodged a salvage claim on their prize ship.

The vessel was owned by the Cement Carriers Corporation of Monrovia, and the owners lodged a bond of £750,000 to allow the ship to leave Orkney. Estimates valued the ship's cargo at £1 million and the total value, with the ship, at £5 millions.

Tug crewmen were obviously expecting a bonanza from the salvage pay-out. Cook Alan Gibson (23) was quoted as saying: "It will be better than working for a living. It will certainly keep us going for a little while."

The 16 tugmen eventually shared £35,890.

Miracle escape in plane crash

All 47 passengers and four crew members of a Viscount aircraft had a "miraculous" escape as it crash landed at Kirkwall Airport at the end of a regular charter shuttle flight from Glasgow for the oil company Occidental.

It brought back painful memories as it was only three months since another oil charter flight had crashed off the runway in Shetland, killing 17.

The incident at Kirkwall Airport on October 25, 1979, saw the plane slither off the main runway and come to rest nose down in the mud, prompting a full emergency alert by fire, police and ambulance services.

The passengers - mainly construction workers and their families - were all able to get out uninjured, some using the emergency exits. They included members of the Tracy Jones Band who were going to Flotta to give a show.

An eye witness said: "I was surprised it wasn't a catastrophe."

The aircraft, in the colours of Guernsey Airways, was operated by Alidair, a charter company based at East Midlands Airport. The plane was a "write off" and was eventually dismantled at Kirkwall.

There had been a previous scare involving a Viscount at Kirkwall Airport in December, 1977, when passengers had to emerge from a British Airways aircraft by the escape chute after the plane slithered off the runway when landing in snowy conditions. The main runway was closed for three days, partially blocked by the Viscount before it could be extricated from the mud where it was bogged down.

And in January, 1980, a BA Viscount, flown by Captain David Lilley, in flight from Shetland to Kirkwall with 24 passengers, was unable to land when the undercarriage jammed. The pilot flew on to Inverness to make an emergency "two point" landing, and everyone again escaped injury.

On a happier note, more than 20 aircraft took part in Orkney's first ever air show on Sunday, August 19, 1979, when a crowd of 4,000 turned out to see a display marking the 25th anniversary of Orkney Flying Club. The weather led to the cancellation of a free-fall parachute display by the Royal Marines but there were flying displays and a RAF Shackleton and a 40 year old De Havilland Rapide on show.

Football cup winners

South Ronaldsay footballers could celebrate winning the Highland Amateur Cup, beating Halkirk 2-1, in the final played before 1,200 spectators at St George's Park, Thurso.

Gas plan rejected

Islanders on Flotta voted overwhelmingly at a public meeting to reject proposals for a £50 million natural gas project which involved grounding two supertankers in Pan Bay to use as a gas processing plant.

The idea had been floated by an Edinburgh-based consortium which included Ben Line Steamers and Liquid Gas Equipment Ltd. However it was condemned by Flotta residents as hazardous to the local population, a pollution risk and of no benefit to the community.

In the event, the application was withdrawn before it could be considered by Orkney Islands Council.

Farmers reel in harvest crisis

Emergency supplies of fodder were shipped to Orkney in a lifeline operation as two successive bad summers caused a crisis for local farmers which was estimated to have cost the county £4 millions.

Scottish Office minister Lord Mansfield flew to Orkney to assess the situation which threatened to leave farmers with insufficient winter feed for thousands of livestock.

Scottish NFU president John Cameron urged Orkney farmers to write to the Prime Minister Margaret Thatcher telling her of their plight. It was an "extremely desperate situation" in which only a fraction of the county's hay and silage crop had been gathered.

The Government eventually announced emergency aid of £500,000 for all the Highlands and Islands, and the European Community said it would match that amount. It would mean grant aid of around £15 per tonne to help Orkney farmers buy in winter feed.

And the year ended on a brighter note as one of the greatest accolades of the farming world came to Orkney.

The supreme champion at the 1979 Smithfield Show in London was a twenty month old cross-bred Charolais/Aberdeen-Angus steer, bred by Mr John Hepburn of Burnside, Tankerness. The steer, which had won prizes at both the East Mainland and County Shows in 1979 was shown by Mr Harry Emslie, of Aberdeenshire, who had purchased the animal from Mr Hepburn on County Show day. It fetched a record price of £8,000 at Smithfield - the equivalent of about £15 per lb of saleable meat.

Boat-building firm folds at Hatston

Thirty nine workers were paid off as the Hatston boat-building firm Orcantic - originally set up as Halmatic (Scotland) Ltd - closed down after producing 84 vessels in eight years. The company, blaming poor trading conditions, went into receivership. No buyer could be found for the firm as a going concern, and the plant and equipment was sold off.

Pier Arts Centre

The Pier Arts Centre at Stromness - home to 67 paintings and sculptures of the Margaret Gardiner collection - was officially opened by Lord Balfour of Burleigh, chairman of the Scottish Arts Council, in July, 1979. Dr Armand Hammer, head of the Occidental oil company, announced that he would also lend 18 paintings from his own art collection.

Golden years

The Orkney-born minister for the parish of Deerness, the Rev Harald Mooney, was given a special presentation by his fellow churchmen, in front of a gathering of nearly 300 well-wishers, as he completed 50 years as minister of the parish, during which time he had completed at least 2,600 sermons.

Orkney sends out home rule blast

Orkney pulled off a constitutional master stroke which rocked the Government - and brought it within the realms of possibility that the islands could claim home rule!

The Labour Government of the day was preparing a Devolution Act to allow a national referendum to decide whether there should be a Scottish Assembly.

However, in January, 1978, Orkney MP Jo Grimond forced through the House of Commons an amendment which would give the people of Orkney and Shetland the opportunity to opt out of the legislation if they voted against the Devolution proposals.

The amendment went through by 204 votes to 118, supported by MPs of all parties, except the members of the Scottish National Party who voted unanimously against. The party which had trumpeted "Scotland's oil" was understandably wary of the implications of it becoming "Orkney and Shetland's oil."

The Grimond amendment called for the setting up of a commission which would consider the future government of Orkney and Shetland and its relationship with a Scottish Assembly.

Jo Grimond's intentions, of course, were not to make a grab for an independent Orkney. He simply wanted to protect Orkney's interests from what, it was feared, would be a Stathclyde-dominated assembly.

The Orkney MP explained: "I remain in favour of devolution but to my mind one of the principal dangers of the current proposals is that there will be a further increase in bureaucracy without enough responsibility being given to Scotland in the running of its own affairs. The Scottish parliament will have no power of tax and it will have very little, if any, power over the economy."

However the implications of the Grimond amendment sent shock waves through the Government. Constitutional experts pointed out that if Orkney and Shetland could opt out of Scottish "nationhood," what was to stop the Isle of Wight, or for that matter Yorkshire, opting out of England.

The Labour Scottish Secretary Bruce Millan needed three meetings with Orkney Islands Council which eventually agreed, by 18 votes to four, not to enforce the Grimond amendment and to accept the Scottish Assembly if the referendum agreed it.

In return, Millan agreed that a commission would be set up to consider the special case of Orkney and Shetland, and he would agree to block any Assembly legislation that was detrimental to Orkney and Shetland.

The referendum was organised for March 1, 1979. Jo Grimond - a supporter of Scottish home rule within the United Kingdom all his life - lambasted the Labour proposal as "a bad Bill" which would lead to conflict between Edinburgh and London. But, he admitted, he would still vote "Yes" for a Scottish Assembly.

"Only if Scotland gets an assembly can we in Orkney and Shetland be sure to get a commission to examine how our affairs should be conducted," he said. "I believe that a Yes vote will at least give us a chance to consider our future and improve the administration as it affects our islands."

As it was, Orcadians rejected their MP's advice. Only 54 per cent of the electorate bothered to turn out and they voted overwhelmingly to reject the Government proposals for a Scottish Assembly. The Orkney result was: Yes 2,104; No 5,439. Nationally, Scotland voted narrowly in favour: Yes 1,230,937; No 1,153,502. But the majority was deemed not sufficient for the Bill to proceed and, with Margaret Thatcher being elected as Prime Minister of a Conservative government a few months later, devolution was ruled out for the next 20 years.

It would be 1999 before a Scots Parliament would become a reality again for the first time in 300 years.

Orkney rages in Uranium battle

One thousand demonstrators took to the streets of Kirkwall to voice their protests as Orkney faced its greatest ever peace-time threat - the prospect of open cast uranium mining cutting an unsightly, and potentially dangerous, gash across the island landscape.

The warning signs had been rumbling for half a dozen years when, in 1979, Orkney was forced to justify to the government why the county wanted to ban any move that could have led to the islands becoming the power house of the nuclear industry.

Orkney's possible use for uranium mining had first been suggested in June, 1973, when, after a five year survey, commissioned by the UK Atomic Energy Authority at a cost of £250,000, 25 geologists, working for the Institute of Geological Sciences, announced they had discovered millions of pounds worth of uranium in Orkney and Caithness.

They stated that thousands of tons of uranium oxide, had been found, down to depths of 1,000 feet in a so-called uranium corridor between Yesnaby and Stromness. It was there in such quantities that mining operations could be started within ten years, they suggested.

Shetland-born Dr Stanley Bowie, assistant director of the Institute of Geological Sciences, said: "The grade of the ore is such that it would be rather more expensive than the uranium which we impart from overseas at present. But I foresee commercial mining in the area within a decade.

"We are going to need all the uranium we can find."

He gave an assurance to Orcadians living there: "The low grade of the ore means there is no danger from radiation."

Eighteen months later, in February, 1976, a team from the South of Scotland Electricity Board came to Orkney to meet 40 land owners and occupiers of land along the uranium corridor.

"We are negotiating with them in order to obtain their consent for trial bores so as to ascertain the quality, quantity and depth of the metal so that we can establish whether it is a viable proposition and in the national interest to extract it," said Mr Alex Cameron, principal assistant secretary to the electricity board.

He had found the people approached to be "most friendly, kind and co-operative," he said.

Obviously not everybody reacted so calmly. Friends of the Earth, Orkney, protested that uranium mining would mean excavation on a massive scale and warned that the pollution and health

County convener Councillor Edwin Eunson helped to lead the opposition to Uranium exploration in Orkney.
(Picture from the files of The Orcadian)

risks were unpredictable and largely uncontrollable. It was claimed that a million tons of rock would be extracted over 25 years, and that uranium miners in the USA had suffered several hundred cases of cancer induced by radioactive dust.

In January, 1977, Orkney Islands Council received an application from the South of Scotland Electricity Board for permission to make 11 exploratory boreholes up to 1,000 feet deep in connection with the possible exploitation of uranium on three different sites along the seven mile corridor between Stromness and Yesnaby. A surge of protests saw the launch of several petitions; the annual meeting of Orkney National Farmers Union voted unanimously against any such proposal; while the Orkney Heritage Society announced it was "totally opposed" to such a scheme.

The Orcadian stated: "It must be made absolutely crystal clear . . . that Orkney wants nothing to do with uranium or the mining of it. If it is under our West Mainland soil, it has been there a long time and should be allowed to stay there."

Nearly 400 people, with placards proclaiming "No uranium poisoners," staged a protest march through Kirkwall to the

council offices (then in Broad Street) where Orkney Islands Council's development and planning committee rejected the planning application. This refusal was confirmed by the full council three weeks later.

The council also agreed that the Orkney Structure Plan should be amended to state that uranium mining was an unacceptable industry in the county. The council decided to promote a Private Bill through Parliament to give the authority greater powers to prevent even exploratory drilling. In the event, this failed to go through after being blocked by the House of Commons Private Bill Committee, some of the members of which were apparently so out of touch they thought Flotta was in Shetland.

The South of Scotland Electricity Board announced it would not appeal against the refusal of planning permission for the uranium test bores, but added: "The board propose to delay, in the meantime, seeking further consents in Orkney, but they reserve the right to make a renewed application at a later date."

This was sufficient threat for Orkney Islands Council to proceed with its amended county structure plan - a move which, in January, 1979, was challenged by the Secretary of State for Scotland Bruce Millan who demanded an explanation why the county should refuse to allow uranium mining. A public examination of the proposed structure plan would be held in Kirkwall, the minister announced.

And now the sparks really began to fly. Ex-provost William Knight of Stromness said he would rather go to jail than see uranium mining come to Orkney. Mrs Marjorie Linklater, chairman of the Orkney Heritage Society, launched a "Declaration of Opposition" in a protest campaign which would culminate in a mass public demonstration on the opening day of the hearing.

Professor Ronald Miller, the Orcadian who had earned a distinguished reputation as professor of geography at Glasgow University and who had been recruited to support the local campaign of opposition, warned that all of Orkney was threatened as the so-called uranium corridor was simply an outcrop of geological conditions that underlay all of the county.

"Uranium never, Orkney forever" proclaimed a big sign which appeared at Stromness as the public examination of the county structure plan began in Kirkwall at the Orkney Islands Council chamber - now in School Place - before

Scottish Office Reporter, Mr W. D. Campbell.

A protest march of 1,000 demonstrators marched in silence to the council offices, on Wednesday, March 21, in a show of united opposition. A white draped coffin was carried to symbolise the death of Orkney in the event of uranium mining being allowed.

Nearly 1,000 Orkney farmers had expressed their opposition to the rape of the countryside, while Orkney Health Board sent a letter to the Government expressing "grave concern" at the possible consequence of uranium mining and the impact of the increase in background radiation. Liberal leader David Steel visited Orkney and pledged full support for Orkney "in protesting at possible wholesale plunder of the landscape."

However, officials of the South of Scotland Electricity Board and the North of Scotland Hydro Electric Board also travelled North to put their case that Orkney's uranium deposits should be investigated as a possible energy source of the future.

To back up the campaign of opposition, a delegation of Orkney Islands Council, Orkney farmers, Stromness Community Council and Orkney Heritage Society later travelled to London to lobby for support at the House of Commons.

County convener Edwin Eunson told the MPs that, at best estimate, the 5,000 tonnes of suitable ore on the islands would only be sufficient to fuel one nuclear power station for ten years - but the mining would be sufficient to destroy the county's main industries of farming, fishing, distilling and tourism.

By this time, there had been a change of government and the decision whether to accept Orkney's amended structure plan fell to the new Conservative Scottish Secretary George Younger.

When he eventually got round to making an announcement in November, 1979, it was fairly apparent that his decision was to sit on the fence. He left it that any planning application for uranium exploration and exploitation in Orkney would be "considered in the light of all evidence available at the time, and the views of the Orkney community."

Pointing out that there was no proposal, presently on the table, to mine uranium in Orkney, the Scottish Secretary recognised "the widely felt concern in Orkney about the effects which uranium mining might have on the environment and the agricultural economy of the islands, and the possible hazards to the health and well-being of its people."

However, he added ominously, there was "a national interest in the exploitation of uranium in the United Kingdom as an indigenous energy source."

Margaret Thatcher - pictured here celebrating the tenth anniversary of Loganair in Orkney in 1977 - became Prime Minister in 1979 and, a year later, told Orkney that the idea of Uranium exploration was "in cold storage."

(Pic: courtesy of Orkney Library photographic archive)

He later tried to reassure Orkney MP Jo Grimond: "I would certainly not wish this stance to be interpreted as a Sword of Damocles hanging over Orkney or as a blight on development." This was backed up a year later by Prime Minister Margaret Thatcher when, on a visit to Orkney, she said: "Uranium is not a live issue. At the moment we have enough to meet our needs. You in Orkney can dispel your fears. The whole thing is in cold storage."

Of course, politicians never say never - and since then there has never been a planning application to put such assurances to the test.

The South of Scotland Electricity Board said, in November, 1979, that it had no immediate plans to proceed with a new planning application to carry out test drilling in Orkney. However, the situation would remain under review and the company could still wish in the future to carry out investigations to establish the extent of uranium deposits in the county.

In the wake of the uranium controversy came the formation of the Orkney Movement with the main aim of securing a measure of autonomy for the islands, similar to that enjoyed by the Faroe islands. Spencer Rosie was appointed chairman of the steering committee which claimed the immediate support of 60 people, including Mrs Marjorie Linklater.

"The first aim is to gain complete control over mineral rights," said secretary Mrs Margaret Flaws.

Tributes for 'adopted' son

Orkney lost a popular member of the community with the death of Tadeusz "Ted" Zawadski of Balfour Castle, a cavalry officer who had escaped from the Nazi invasion of Poland to make his way across Europe, via Dunkirk, to fight with the Free Polish Forces based in Britain.

He had married a Scots wife, Catherine, and the couple had settled in Orkney after the war when he became a leading farmer in the county, as well as county councillor for his adopted home island. He was in the Scotland team which took part in the 1972 International Deep Sea Angling Championships in South Africa.

Back to the future

Orkney's newest primary school - the £330,000 Glaitness school in Kirkwall - was officially opened by county convener Edwin Eunson in 1979 - 77 years after the original Glaitness school was closed. The new school would have a total of 173 pupils.

Just along the road, a new supermarket came to Orkney in November, 1979, as more than 100 shoppers queued for the opening of the Co-operative store at Pickaquoy. The 4,000 square feet shop would employ a staff of 20.

Euro MP elected

The first elections to the European Parliament saw Winnie Ewing (Scottish National Party) elected for the Highlands and Islands constituency which included Orkney. She would remain as Orkney's European MP for the next 20 years.

Helicopter hero wins George Cross

1980

A helicopter pilot was honoured with the George Cross - Britain's highest peacetime award for bravery - after 22 men, women and children were snatched from certain death in raging seas off Orkney's west coast.

The crew, women and children on the 8,700 ton Swedish freighter *Finneagle* had spent three hours huddled on the bridge, amidst 40 feet high waves and a force nine gale before being plucked to safety in one of the most daring and spectacular helicopter rescues seen in British waters.

The one year old ship had been disabled by an explosion and Coastguards described her as a "floating bomb" as fire threatened to ignite her cargo of whisky.

The ship sent out a Mayday message after the drama began on October 1, 1980, and an RAF Sea King helicopter from Lossiemouth - piloted by Flt Lt Mike Lakey - hovered perilously over the stricken vessel as flames shot into the air.

The helicopter lowered a weighted harness to the *Finneagle*, and into this went two of the three women, each clutching a child. At this stage the rescue nearly ended in disaster as the ship rolled badly and disappeared from the pilot's view - but the women and children were even-

tually winched aboard the helicopter.

Within 90 minutes, all 22 survivors were on board the helicopter - now ten people over its normal capacity - with the *Finneagle* master, Captain Bertil Wunnerland, the last to leave after an epic battle to keep his stricken ship into the wind during the rescue operation.

The other four members of the helicopter crew - Flt Lt Dave Simpson, Flt Lt Bill Campbell, winchman Sergeant Rick Bragg and Lossiemouth station medical officer Squadron Leader Hamish Grant - were also to receive gallantry awards for their part in the rescue.

Flt Lt Lakey - he was later named as BBC Radio Scotland's "Scot of the Year"- said: "You can only put your trust in the Almighty and get on with the task you came to do. I still can't believe we got them all off."

Before he set out on the rescue, he had only been back at Lossiemouth for half an hour after returning from London where he received a Queen's

Commendation for an earlier oil rig rescue.

Lossiemouth commanding officer Group Captain Sandy Wilson said: "It is one of the most fantastic rescues I have ever heard of."

The rescue operation was co-ordinated by Kirkwall Coastguards and the 22 survivors - including the second mate Jan-Erik Gustafsson (29) who was on board with his wife Monica (28) and sons Johan (6) and Jonas (3) - were flown to Kirkwall to recover from their ordeal.

Their abandoned, drifting ship was later taken in tow by tugs.

Two months later, four fishermen had a less dramatic but equally fortunate escape from the sea when their Inverness-registered boat *Marandra* grounded in heavy seas on the Kirk Rocks in the Hoy Sound in December, 1980.

They took to their liferaft and were swept ashore in the darkness to escape without a scratch.

The four men - skipper David Bruce, with James Cowie, Kenneth Bruce and Raymond Gardiner - struggled ashore where they had the added good fortune to be given a lift by local veterinary surgeon Albert Spence in his car into Stromness.

A Premier show by Thatcher

Margaret Thatcher became the third Prime Minister in office to visit Orkney in the 20th century - the others were Winston Churchill and Herbert Asquith - when she spent two days in the county, including a five hour tour of the Flotta oil terminal, in September, 1980.

She had made her first visit to Orkney three years earlier as the Conservative Leader of the Opposition when she spent 24 hours in the county, attending a reception by local Conservative supporters, calling at Kirkwall Auction Mart, chatting to dockers at Kirkwall pier and visiting factories in Kirkwall and Stromness.

"The countryside is beautiful and this is a lovely place to live in," she said before flying on to Shetland.

When she returned as Prime Minister in 1980, Orkney's unemployment had just reached a new record level - and would continue to increase to new record levels for the next eight years. Despite the fact that 400 people were employed directly at Flotta and another 200 were in jobs which had developed indirectly from the oil terminal, Orkney's jobless total in the Autumn of 1980 was up to 476 - 327 male and 149 female -

or 7.7 per cent of the insured workforce. Six months later, in March 1981, it had reached 578 - an unemployment rate of 9.4 per cent. This could be compared with September, 1951, when Orkney had just 26 unemployed people on the register. Unemployment had increased more than 20-fold in 30 years.

She was welcomed to Flotta by Dr Armand Hammer, head of the Occidental oil company. It was a meeting of two experts in self-promotion which quickly developed into a scene of mutual congratulation. Dr Hammer would like to nominate Mrs Thatcher as a US presidential candidate "if she was free," while she described him as "a very great man."

On cue, Dr Hammer (82) chose the moment to reveal that Occidental intended to invest a further £620 millions in Britain.

Mrs Thatcher was in fact only the fourth Prime Minister in office to visit Orkney in the previous 100 years. The Liberal Premier William Ewart Gladstone, who visited in the late 19th century, went one better than his successors - he was the only one to be awarded the freedom of the burgh of Kirkwall.

Margaret Thatcher - the second Prime Minister to visit Orkney in peacetime during the 20th century.

(Picture from the files of *The Orcadian*)

The arrival of wind power

What was said to be Britain's first commercial electricity-generating windmill was installed by the North of Scotland Hydro Electric Board at Berriedale Farm, South Ronaldsay, in 1980.

The 40 feet high, 22 kilowatt machine - a quarter of a mile from the home of Mr and Mrs Marcus Wood - was designed to supply enough power for the farm at wind speeds of 12mph upwards.

The £50,000 venture was part of trials being carried out by the Hydro Board.

A few months later it was announced that Britain's first mega-power wind generator would be built on Burgar Hill, Evie, at a cost of £5.6 millions. The largest of the two windmills would be 245 feet high with 196 feet diameter blades which would generate 3 megawatts - enough to supply 1,000 domestic customers.

The year of 1980 also saw Orkney Islands Council open its new £310,000 incinerator at Chinglebraes to burn all the domestic rubbish from the Orkney Mainland and linked South Isles. For years, the Peerie Sea had been used as Kirkwall's rubbish dump - creating an eyesore and a haven for rats - but this had now been given a facelift and created into a recreational amenity as a sailing pond.

Centenarians galore

No fewer than five Orcadian women were aged 100 or more in 1980.

Pride of place went to Miss Jessie Fraser, formerly of Rendall, who in May, 1980, celebrated her 104th birthday in the Balfour Hospital, as Orkney's oldest resident. She died later in the year, six months after her 104th birthday.

Three other centenarians were living in Orkney - Miss Elizabeth Goar (101) at St Peter's House, Stromness; Mrs Jessie Craigie (100), formerly of Cruar, Rousay, who was in the Balfour Hospital; and Mrs Margaret Clouston (100) of Market Green, Dounby.

Another, Miss Mary Burgess, formerly of Garth, South Ronaldsay, celebrated her 101st birthday in Australia.

An illustration of the increased life expectancy over the century is the fact that, in 1900, Britain had 200 centenarians. By 1999, there were 10,000!

Black Building for sale

Kirkwall's "Black Building" - the top secret wartime nerve centre which was commissioned in 1942 to control the aircraft defending the Northern Isles and the Royal Navy Fleet in Scapa Flow - was up for sale, in 1980, at £50,000.

The 17,000 square feet building, which once accommodated working and living quarters for 300 people - had a bomb proof roof and specially steel-reinforced walls. It got its name from the black tar which coated the whole building.

After the war, it had been used by the Post Office as a telephone repeater station.

End of the tangles

The Orkney tangles industry - which had fluctuating fortunes throughout the century but which at one time had been a significant revenue earner for the North Isles as hundreds of tons of seaweed was collected each year for the chemical industry - looked to have met its end.

Alginate Industries Ltd, the company which had bought the tangles for more than 30 years, announced in 1980 that it was ending its operations in Orkney. "We must now face the inescapable fact that Orkney tangle has had its day," said Mr John Sanderson, a director of the firm.

Bakehouse blaze drama

One of Orkney's principal bakehouses, owned by Stromness baker George Argo, was gutted by fire in the early hours, during April, 1980, as flames leapt high in the night sky over the town. Emergency services brought the blaze under control after two hours, after being alerted by neighbour Sydney Omand.

The first Viking arrives

Stromness skipper Angus Sinclair brought his first fishing vessel to be called *Orcades Viking* to the county in 1980 after the vessel had been converted and lengthened to 110 feet at a Norwegian yard. In the following 20 years, he would bring two successor ships - also called *Orcades Viking* - to Stromness, including, ultimately, one of the biggest freezer vessels in the European fleet.

Pilot takes off

After ten years as senior pilot with Loganair, Captain Andy Alsop (39) parted with the company in October, 1980 - after a decade in which he had made 50,000 landings in Orkney and piloted hundreds of ambulance flights.

In March, 1981, a consortium of Orkney businessmen, fronted by Kirkwall accountant Mr Alastair Scholes, launched Air Orkney, with Captain Alsop as company pilot, operating an air taxi service in an Islander aircraft. Unfortunately, it did not prove a lasting commercial success.

Swimming champ

Karen Hourston (14) of Stromness became the first Orcadian to represent Scotland at swimming, in May, 1980, when she competed in an international event in France, at which she won the gold medal. She was the Scottish 100 metres breast-stroke champion in her age group. A year later, another Stromness swimmer, Jimmy Poke became the Scottish Schools butterfly champion.

Folk museum opens

The dream of a generation came to fruition as the official opening of the Corrigal Farm and Rural Life Museum in Harray was carried out by Mr Alexander Fenton, Keeper of the Scottish National Museum of Antiquities in Edinburgh, in 1980.

Former Orkney librarian Evan MacGillivray and the Orcadian writer and historian Ernest Marwick had encouraged the Orkney Education Committee to preserve a traditional Orkney steading as a folk museum 15 years earlier.

Orkney pioneers

Hamish Ross (36), a joiner from Tankerness, was credited with being the first Orkney resident to climb the Old Man of Hoy as he completed the 450 feet climb in 14 hours with Ken Martin, the divisional commander of the Northern Fire Service in Kirkwall, and 29 year old Kirkwall plumber David Moyland.

Richard Jenkins, who later moved back to Orkney to live, had climbed the Old Man in 1976 when serving in the Queen's Own Highlanders.

Sanday shore for an anarchist

The 1970s and 1980s saw the arrival - often temporary - in Orkney of hundreds of people seeking to escape the "rat race" of city life as Orcadians, especially in the isles, sold off unwanted, and usually unmodernised, property that was the legacy of the population drift.

Of all those who settled, however briefly, on Orkney shores, none had a more colourful background than Stuart Christie, a self-confessed anarchist, who set up a printing press at the home he shared with his family at Over-the-Water, Sanday. To be fair, 20 years later, Mr Christie's writings appear no more revolutionary than the Liberal Democrat manifesto.

The son of an Aberdeen trawlerman, Stuart Christie had been sentenced, in 1964, to a 20 year prison term in Spain for alleged terrorist offences. He was freed by General Franco in 1967.

In 1972, he was cleared of conspiracy to cause explosions on behalf of the Angry Brigade after a series of attacks at the homes of prominent public figures.

In 1976, with his wife Brenda, he set up Cienfuegos Press - named after a Cuban revolutionary - and, operating from Sanday, succeeded in raising the blood pressure of Conservative MPs as he published various anarchist pamphlets.

In June, 1980, he published a booklet entitled "Towards a Citizen's Militia" which,

1981

it was reported in *The Orcadian*, gave details on how to make bombs and grenades from household materials.

South Aberdeen Tory MP Iain Sproat protested: "I am deeply concerned at any private individual who, by implication, is encouraging other people to resort to violence." Home Secretary William Whitelaw promised that the police would investigate the alleged "subversive" book.

However, in May, 1981, Stuart Christie became the focus of some sympathy in Orkney as his wife Brenda (30), accompanied by her two year old daughter Branwen, was arrested by German police in Hanover. She was taken into custody as she was about to board a plane to London. The West German authorities said she was being held in connection with a fire bomb explosion at Frankfurt Airport in 1970.

Protests from all over the world poured into the German embassy in London, according to *The Orcadian*, with actresses Vanessa Redgrave, Julie Christie and Frances de la Tour voicing their support for the mother and child.

Stuart Christie said his wife had never

visited Germany before the trip to spend a holiday with his sister, the wife of a British soldier. Christie himself had been banned from entering Germany in 1975, and deported.

Little Branwen was quickly released and flown home, while Brenda Christie was eventually freed after spending seven days in German custody. The Christies moved on from the county a couple of years later.

Population up

The 1981 census gave Orkney's population as 18,425 - an increase of eight per cent, or nearly 1,400 people, over 1971. It was the county's first increase in population to be recorded in the 20th century.

Over 60 per cent of households were owner-occupied while 21.7 per cent were council houses. There were still 680 houses in the county without bathroom facilities, while 30 per cent of households still did not have the use of a car.

Royal wedding gift

Two Orkney chairs - made by Westray Strawback Chairs, run by Mr James Fergus - were presented as wedding presents from the county to Prince Charles and Lady Diana Spencer who married on July 28, 1981.

The Lord Lieutenant, Colonel Robert Macrae, lit a celebration Royal wedding beacon on Wideford Hill - forming a chain of beacons the length of the country. Unfortunately, the Orkney beacon was obscured by heavy mist!

Oh deer, oh dear

Westray man Marcus Hewison brought eight red deer to Orkney to begin an experiment of deer farming on the 400 acre island of North Faray. "I think this is the first time there's been red deer in Orkney," he said.

It did not prove a total success. The deer illustrated their prowess in the water by swimming to Eday!

Power to the isles

The 22 consumers on Egilsay received mains electrical power for the first time in February, 1981, as a submarine cable was laid from Rousay.

In the previous 18 months, mains electricity had been introduced to Westray, Papa Westray and Eday. North Ronaldsay was the last remaining island with a population of any size without mains power. Islanders there had to wait until

November, 1983, for the great switch-on.

Until 1981, Orkney's mains electricity was supplied by the diesel-driven Kirkwall power station and the gas turbine in Flotta. It was now announced, however, that the North of Scotland Hydro Electric Board planned a £8 million, 23 mile long submarine cable across the Pentland Firth, linking Orkney to the National Grid. This was switched on in October, 1982.

Whale of a find

A 45 feet whale which was washed ashore on Papa Westray was identified as a Finn Whale - the first recorded specimen to be seen in the county since 1852. It was towed out to sea to be dumped.

Sunday drinking

Sheriff A.A. MacDonald overturned the decision of Orkney Licensing Board and allowed Kirkwall's Torvhaug Inn - the town's only public house - to open on Sundays for the first time.

Norwegian monarch makes history

King Olav V of Norway created a footnote in local history as the first reigning Norwegian King to visit Kirkwall in seven centuries.

King Olav's informal visit in May, 1981, saw him spend five hours in Kirkwall, during which he attended Sunday morning service at St Magnus Cathedral, met members of the Orkney-Norway Friendship Association, and toured Tankerness House museum before dining with members of Orkney Islands Council.

He was the first Norwegian monarch to arrive in the burgh since Haakon Haakonsson who died in the Bishop's

Palace after the battle of Largs in 1263, at a time when Orkney was still a Norwegian earldom.

(King Olav was not the first Norwegian monarch to enter Orkney waters in the 20th century, however. That distinction fell to King Haakon III who visited Scapa Flow in 1944).

King Olav was to return to Kirkwall six years later when, in what was undoubtedly the most gloriously informal royal visit of the 20th century, he met Queen Elizabeth, the Queen Mother, to mark the 850th anniversary of St Magnus Cathedral.

Falklands War touches Orkney

1982

As the Falklands War exploded in the South Atlantic, an Orcadian became the first captain of the anti-submarine aircraft carrier HMS *Illustrious*. In the following 15 years, he was to rise to the top job in the Royal Navy as Admiral Sir Jock Slater, Chief of Naval Staff and First Sea Lord.

Although he was actually born in Edinburgh, in 1938, his father Dr James K. Slater was an Orcadian and his mother Mrs Billie Slater lived at Stenaday in Finstown for several years. And his Orkney links were further strengthened when he married Ann, daughter of Captain W.P. Scott of Kierfiold House, Sandwick.

His Naval career began when he entered the Royal Naval College, Dartmouth, in 1956. His early service included two years on the Royal Yacht *Britannia*.

He later commanded the minesweeper HMS *Soberton*, a frequent visitor to Orkney waters on fishing protection duties in 1964-65. He became Equerry to the Queen from 1968-70 when he was promoted to commander and took command of HMS *Jupiter* - another visitor to Orkney when the frigate came into Scapa Flow as part of a NATO fleet in 1970.

In 1976, he commanded the guided missile destroyer HMS *Kent*, followed by his appointment as Assistant Director of Naval Warfare, before his appointment to the £250 million HMS *Illustrious* which went to the South Atlantic in August, 1982, to relieve her sister ship HMS *Invincible* at the end of the conflict.

(In 1983, Captain Slater brought *Illustrious*, with 1,000 crew, into Scapa Flow - the fourth ship under his command to come into the Flow in 15 years).

In 1985, as Rear Admiral, he became Assistant Chief of Defence Staff, responsible for policy and nuclear affairs, at the Ministry of Defence in London. In 1987, he became Flag Officer Scotland and Northern Ireland, with the added NATO appointment of Commander Northern Sub Area Eastern Atlantic.

His promotion to Admiral came in 1991 and he became Commander-in-Chief Fleet and the Allied Commander-in-Chief Channel and East Atlantic. He was Knighted to become Sir Jock in 1988. He retired as Chief of Naval Staff and First Sea Lord in 1998.

Heading for the Falklands in April, 1982, was the 16,792 tons Royal Fleet Auxiliary vessel *Stromness* - which had visited Stromness Shopping Week eight years earlier and which took its ship's crest from the motif of the Viking ship on the Stromness burgh coat of arms.

The *Stromness* had been earmarked to be sold before the Falklands conflict broke out, but she now joined the task force sailing to the South Atlantic with a contingent of Royal Marines.

Her commander, Captain Barrie Dickinson, was quoted as saying: "It has lifted moral enormously, and it demonstrates the obvious need for a viable Navy and support vessels."

A year later the *Stromness* was sold to the American Navy!

One of the first shocks of the Falklands War was the loss of HMS *Sheffield* - an occasional visitor to Scapa Flow - which was sunk by the Argentines in the first week of May, 1982.

Among the survivors was a Stromness man, Chief Petty Officer Charles Adamson, whose family lived at Weaverhall, Stromness. A former pupil of Stromness Academy, he had served in the Royal Navy for 24 years.

Tributes after death of Lord Birsay

"There was no better loved man in these islands than Harald Leslie. None of us will ever forget him," said Sheriff A.A. MacDonald in tribute after Lord Birsay died at his home in Edinburgh, aged 77, on November 27, 1982.

Born as Harald Leslie in South Shields, the son of Stromness master mariner Robert Leslie and his wife Margaret Mowat Cochrane, he graduated at Glasgow University before a distinguished record in World War Two in which he was mentioned in dispatches and made an MBE.

After the war, he continued his legal career, becoming a King's Counsel in 1949. He stood as the Labour candidate in the Orkney and Shetland constituency in the 1950 General Election.

He was Sheriff Principal of Orkney from 1961-65 before becoming chairman of the Scottish Land Court, taking the title of Lord Birsay when elevated to the peerage.

He had married Robina "Rena" Marwick, the daughter of Stromness provost James Marwick, in 1945. They were regular visitors to Orkney and their cottage at Queenafiord in Birsay.

Orkney's Sheriff MacDonald paid tribute: "His career is one of great distinction. He held high judicial office. He was Her Majesty's High Commissioner to the General Assembly of the Church of Scotland. He was created a Knight of the Thistle, the highest order of chivalry in Scotland, an honour accorded to very few."

New Isles service

Cornishman Chris Marrow and his wife Rosemary, who had moved to Deerness, set up Wide Firth Ferry Ltd, using the 50 feet mv *Golden Mariana*, a former Flotta work boat, which could carry 65 passengers, which would provide day return trips between Kirkwall and the North Isles.

Three years later, Mr Marrow expanded by setting up Norse Atlantic Ferries to operate a Kirkwall-Shetland service with the *Syllingar*, a vessel which had previously served the Scilly Islands. Unfortunately the venture was not a lasting commercial success - but it was sufficient to push P&O Ferries into re-establishing an Orkney-Shetland service.

End of a lighthouse era

The routine relief of lightkeepers at Suleskerry, Britain's most remote lighthouse, 30 miles west of Orkney, was made for the last time on November 30, 1982, as the lighthouse - built in 1895 - went automatic, leaving the 34 acre island to be inhabited by seabirds and seals.

The last three keepers on duty were David Sutherland, principal keeper for the previous five years, Alistair MacDonald and John Knight.

The programme of automation of the lighthouse service would continue for the next 16 years with North Ronaldsay having the distinction of being the last manned lighthouse in Orkney.

Round-the-world upset

A young Australian couple Ian Johnston (29) and Cathy Hawkins (24), who had invested all their savings to sail round the globe from Tasmania in their 31 feet yacht *Twiggy* to take part in a Round Britain race, were rescued after clinging to the upturned hull of the vessel for 18 hours, 60 miles off Cape Wrath.

The trimaran yacht was later towed into Stromness by Orkney fishermen Alistair Bruce and Alan Jeffries in their boat *Girl May*.

In another rescue in March, 1982, eight fishermen were saved from the Lossiemouth fishing boat *Boy Allan* after she sent out a Mayday call 22 miles east of Copinsay.

A Sea King helicopter from RAF Lossiemouth winched the men to safety from a liferaft as the *Boy Allan* sank.

The same month, the master of a Norwegian-owned cargo vessel, on passage from Denmark to Orkney, died in a North Sea drama as the ship, the *Risnes*, carrying fertiliser for Stromness, sank. The remaining crew of four were rescued and flown to Norway by helicopter.

Final journey for soldier

Nearly 40 years after he died on the shores of Orkney, the body of Italian prisoner of war Giovanni Scarponi was returned to his native country for reburial.

He had died in hospital in Kirkwall in January, 1943, after an accident on the barriers linking the Orkney Mainland to South Ronaldsay. He was buried in St Olaf's cemetery - the only Italian prisoner of war to be interred in Orkney.

However, in 1982, after a request by the man's widow and the Italian Government, the Sheriff gave permission for the body to be exhumed and his remains flown to Viterbo in Italy.

Orkney firm closes

The Orkney firm of Messrs James Flett and Sons of Bridge Street, Kirkwall, was to close after 111 years of trading, it was announced in 1982.

The company, which sold bread, confectionery, groceries and ironmongery, had been founded by James Flett on his return from Canada in 1871

After the closure of the company, much of the building - which was then leased out - was seriously damaged by fire in January, 1985, as firemen fought for six hours into the night to prevent the blaze spreading to neighbouring properties.

Mart trade hits a record

Kirkwall Auction Mart's annual turnover in 1982 reached a new record high of over £9 millions - an increase of £750,000 on what had been a record in 1981. More than 18,000 cattle and 20,000 sheep went through the mart in 12 months.

Also, in February, 1982, a £1 million abattoir opened at Hatston for Orkney Meat Ltd, in which Orkney farmers, represented by Kirkwall and Stromness marts, held a 34 per cent share. The main shareholder was the Fatstock Marketing Corporation, while Orkney Island Council and the Highlands and Islands Development Board also had a stake.

In its first year, it had a turnover of £1 million and a pre-tax profit of £12,538.

It was not at all prosperity, however. In July, 1982, the total of unemployed in Orkney increased to 806 - 553 men and 253 women - or 13.1 per cent of the working population.

And petrol reached £2 a gallon in Kirkwall in December, 1982 - compared with the UK average of £1.73. It would double again in price in the next 15 years.

Mini Mandy

Little Mandy Byers was allowed to return home to Orkney - five months after she was born prematurely at Aberdeen Royal Infirmary - weighing just 1lb 9ounces.

She was born to Mrs June Byers, originally of Eday but living in Kirkwall in 1982, the wife of Garson Byers. They already had two sons, Gary (5) and Trevor (2).

After spending the first few months in the special baby unit at Aberdeen, Mandy - whose weight fell as low as 1lb 4ounces - was eventually allowed home when her weight rose to a heavyweight 8lbs 3ounces.

Blaze brings shipping chaos

Orkney's daily lifeline shipping service across the Pentland Firth was thrown into chaos as the 230 feet P&O ferry *St Ola* was devastated by fire in October, 1982.

She was returning to Orkney following her annual refit when a blaze engulfed her engine room while the ship was off Arran. She was forced to return to the Clyde for vital repairs and would be out of action for two months.

The P&O cargo vessel *St Magnus* was given special dispensation to sail with 50 passengers and the Orkney Islands Shipping Company vessel *Orcadia* made special sailings from Kirkwall to Wick. P&O also chartered the Caledonian MacBrayne vessel *Clansman* as a relief ship.

Sailings of the *St Ola* were again temporarily disrupted at the start of 1984 when the 90 ton vehicle ramp at Stromness collapsed into the sea. Cars had to be loaded by crane until repairs were completed.

Up for the Ba'

When the Doonies won the Christmas Day Men's Ba' of 1982, it was their 12th successive victory. The game lasted seven hours - just failing by minutes to be the longest on record - before the ball entered the Kirkwall basin at 8pm for Sandy Keldie to be acclaimed as winner of the ba'.

The Uppies at last broke the Doonie domination by winning the 1983 New Year Ba', with Jim Cromarty becoming the first Uppie ba' winner since 1976.

Orkney loses a musical great

Ronnie Aim (62), the Holm postmaster who would be best remembered as a musician, composer and a tireless worker for Orkney traditional music as a founder of Orkney Strathspey and Reel Society, died after a motor accident in April, 1982.

He was an acknowledged composer of tunes for the fiddle which included his Silver Jubilee tribute to the Queen, and also his tribute to the crew lost in the 1969 lifeboat disaster, *The Heroes of Longhope*.

He had the honour of playing one of his own compositions for the Queen when she visited Orkney in 1978.

Lifeboat honour

Dr Sydney Peace was awarded the gold badge of the Royal National Lifeboat Institution in recognition of his services, firstly as honorary secretary and medical adviser at Longhope and then as honorary medical adviser to the Kirkwall lifeboat station.

Protests as Old Man of Hoy is sold

Protests greeted the sale of 8,000 acres of Hoy - including the Old Man of Hoy - to the Royal Society for the Protection of Birds; a deal which would go a long way to making the RSPB the biggest single landowner in Orkney.

The decision to sell - for £115,000 - was taken by the trustees of the Hoy Trust in a vote which saw only three of the seven trustees vote in favour of the sale. Two voted against while two abstained.

One of the dissenting trustees Mr Ian MacInnes said: "We will have an enormous sum of money and precious little to do with it."

The term "absentee landlord" had always been particularly emotive in Orkney and Orkney Islands Council voted by 13 votes to five to register their opposition to the sale. Councillor Eoin Scott said: "I feel this is a very serious issue. There has been a total disregard for the wishes of the Orkney people in this matter."

However, the sale was defended by the chairman of the Hoy Trust, Professor Ronald Miller who expressed confidence in the RSPB's ability to fulfil the objects of the trust. He pointed out that local people would retain peat-cutting and grazing rights.

And Hoy councillor Charles Rioch said the decision to sell had not caused a stir on Hoy and he felt the suspicions raised about the RSPB's motives in buying the land were unjustified. The RSPB wanted to buy it to preserve what was one of Great Britain's most important bird sanctuaries, he said.

After two months of controversy and speculation, and threatened legal action to prevent the sale, the transaction was completed in 1983.

The opposition to the deal was symptomatic of a general suspicion, if not outright antagonism, directed at the motives and activities of outside conservation groups in Orkney in the years between 1983-85.

Throughout 1984, what was invariably described as a conservation war waged in the county as a tide of criticism was directed at the way the government-backed Nature Conservancy Council was introducing Sites of Special Scientific Interest throughout Orkney

The designation of such sites often saw restrictions placed on the use of the land - diluting the rights of farmers and landowners stretching back centuries.

It was a public relations disaster on the part of what was seen as an autocratic, authoritarian Nature Conservancy Council. Angry protests saw the effigies of NCC officials hanging from a pole in the West Mainland.

1983

It was claimed that the NCC, with its headquarters 600 miles away in Peterborough, had designated about 15 per cent of Orkney - with areas of Hoy, the West Mainland, Westray and Eday all coming under SSSI controls.

Even the Lord Lieutenant of Orkney, Colonel Robert Macrae, entered the war of words - claiming that the Orkney people were being enslaved by a Nature Conservancy Council which was seemingly "hell bent" on designating as much of Orkney as possible - taking away the rights of Orcadians which stretched back to Viking days.

Colonel Macrae said farmers were particularly concerned about "the infringement of landowners' rights by some bureaucratic authority unconcerned with the economics of Orkney farming."

He added: "Orkney people are genuinely concerned about wildlife conservation and will co-operate but they object to being enslaved."

Councillor Eoin Scott complained that Orkney was in danger of becoming a conservation desert, while Lord Grimond called for a halt and reappraisal of SSSI designations in Orkney and also asked the RSPB to stop acquiring land on the islands meantime. The Wildlife and Countryside Act simply seemed to help wealthy landowners in other parts of the country, he claimed.

Eventually, an uneasy peace did break out in the conservation war as the Nature Conservancy Council improved its beleaguered public image and paved the way for financial settlements with those Orkney farmers who were affected by SSSI designations.

But even the Nature Conservancy Council could not prevent the real power of nature as, in May 1984, the largest and fiercest heath fire ever to burn in Orkney devastated 1,400 acres of moorland in North Hoy as, for 22 hours, huge clouds of smoke could be seen from several miles away.

One thousand acres of the burned out land was within the RSPB's new acquired reserve, and the fire proved fatal for hundreds of birds and Hoy's distinctive mountain hares.

The cause of the fire was blamed on a match discarded by a member of a Stromness Boys' Brigade party cutting peats in the area. Longhope volunteer fire force burnt a fire break round the North Hoy Community Centre and other properties to make them safe.

But about a third of the Forestry Commission plantation at White Glen was burned, and fire fighters saw the ghastly spectacle of mountain hares running from the blaze with their coats on fire.

Call for a tunnel to Orkney

A suggestion that a study be carried out into the feasibility of a tunnel under the Pentland Firth to link Orkney with mainland Britain was made by Stromness councillor Ian Argo.

Commenting that it was only six miles from South Ronaldsay to the Scottish mainland, he said a tunnel could be of benefit to Orkney in the long run.

However Orkney's engineering director Mr Jim McIntosh estimated the cost at around £150 millions, and harbours director Captain Duncan Robertson said it would change the character of Orkney for all time.

Nonetheless, Councillor Alastair Scholes argued: "This could be of major importance. It is not as daft as it would appear at first sight." He claimed that half of the possible cost could be met by European funds, with other money coming from the Scottish Office and Caithness - leaving Orkney to find just £15 millions.

He said the tunnel would "virtually eliminate" P&O Ferries and British Airways and the £3 million annual freight costs that would be saved would finance the interest on a loan.

"Someone leaving this meeting now could be at London airport by breakfast time tomorrow," he told a meeting of Orkney Islands Council in December, 1983.

New era for isles

The first roll-on, roll-off vehicle ferry service within the isles began in April, 1983, when a new ro-ro ship for the South Isles was inaugurated as the *Lyrawa Bay* made her maiden run from Longhope to Houton via Lyness and Flotta. The vessel, skippered by Gordon Watters, had a full complement of passengers and vehicles.

In the first 12 weeks of operation, the boat carried 7,000 passengers - more than double the previous average.

Newspaper stalwarts retire

Two men who, between them, worked for 70 years reporting the news of Orkney, retired within months of each other after distinguished careers on *The Orcadian*.

Chief reporter Bill Hewison retired after 34 years with the newspaper in July, 1982.

Gerry Meyer - or Geremy as he was known to readers - retired in 1983 after 36 years as editor of *The Orcadian*.

He had first arrived in Orkney in World War Two, during which time he edited the forces newspaper, the *Orkney Blast*, for three years, and married his wife Nora from Stromness.

Apart from reporting some of Orkney's most momentous events over four decades along with Bill Hewison, Gerry Meyer could claim to have personally covered every Stromness Shopping Week from 1949-83.

Gerry Meyer was made an MBE in 1984.

He was succeeded as editor of *The Orcadian* by James Miller - a descendant of the newspaper's founding family.

Gerry Meyer MBE
(Picture from the files of *The Orcadian*)

Ditched oil workers saved

Seventeen men on board a British Airways helicopter were rescued as the machine, carrying workers from the Occidental company's Piper Alpha production platform, was forced to ditch in the North Sea.

The helicopter suffered an engine fault en route to Aberdeen with 15 Occidental oil workers and two crew. A distress call was put out and a major rescue operation was started involving a RAF Nimrod and a RAF Sea King helicopter from Lossiemouth.

The oil men were able to remain in the floating helicopter until they were picked up by the Sea King and flown to Aberdeen.

Folk festival takes off

The Orkney Traditional Folk Festival was launched in May, 1983, organised by chairman Johnny Mowat, vice-chairman Len Wilson and Radio Orkney producer Howie Firth, amongst others. Around 2,000 tickets were sold at the 18 events as acts included Shetland musicians Henry Henderson and Bobby Tulloch, concertina player Alastair Anderson from Northumberland, and the Thurso and Dounreay Strathspey and Reel Society.

Warship plundered

The diving support ship *Stena Workhorse*, operating on charter for a film company, working on the wreck of HMS *Hampshire* - lost off Birsay with Lord Kitchener in 1916 - removed the sunken warship's 50 ton propeller and shaft.

The propeller was landed at Peterhead, where it languished for years, but was eventually brought back to Orkney and later became one of the exhibits at the Scapa Flow interpretation centre which was opened at Lyness.

Coastguard nerve centre

Pentland Coastguard's new maritime rescue centre was opened by Chief Coastguard Tim Featherston-Dilke, combining the former Orkney and Wick coastguard operations behind the old headquarters in Cromwell Road, Kirkwall.

The new North of Scotland area was under the supervision of District Controller Tom Coppin and his staff of 15 full-time and 15 auxiliary coastguards.

Whales perish ashore

More than 60 whales perished in two separate stranding incidents on Orkney shores in 1983.

The first, in May, 1983, saw nearly 40 pilot whales - ranging from babies to full grown males of 24 feet or more - beach themselves off the south west coast of Westray.

Some of the females were pregnant, almost ready to give birth, but despite rescue attempts, only six of the whales could be saved and islanders had the grim task of burying the carcases.

Another 28 pilot whales - nine males and 19 females ranging in size from seven feet to 21 feet - stranded on Mill Bay beach in Eday in December, 1983.

Only 13 were still alive when help arrived and these were in such poor shape that the police were requested to shoot them.

Changes in the air

Janet Firminger was the first women to be appointed a Civil Aviation Authority Airport manager when she took over at Kirkwall Airport. She had previously worked at Prestwick, Manchester and Gatwick, where she served for nine years.

Veteran ship is a floating pub

The ship *Earl of Zetland*, which during World War Two ferried 600,000 servicemen across the Pentland Firth between Scrabster and Stromness in the defence of Scapa Flow, began a new career, in March, 1983, as a floating pub in Great Yarmouth, Norfolk, after a £200,000 conversion which saw the ship renamed *Celtic Surveyor*

Kirkwall 'could drown' warning

Twenty eight million gallons of water could descend on Kirkwall from the Wideford Hill reservoir unless £500,000 was spent on shoring up the 70 year old dam which was slowly slipping away, engineering director Jim McIntosh warned Orkney Islands Council in June, 1983. Once the work was done, the reservoir would last another 100 years, he said.

Video chiller

Annie Lennox and Dave Stewart of the chart-topping group Eurythmics braved the weather of December, 1983, to spend four days in Orkney filming a video to accompany their latest musical release.

TV climb conquers Old Man

Millions of television viewers saw 18 year old Zoe Brown reach the top of the Old Man of Hoy as, in a live outside broadcast, she scaled the 450 feet stack.

She was accompanied by her father Joe Brown and his climbing companions Murray Hamilton and Peter Whillance, but it was young Zoe who stole the show - and her cry of "Beam me up, Scottie" when she pulled herself on to the summit was greeted by applause and cheers from the hundreds of spectators on the nearby Hoy clifftops.

Peter Whillance had achieved the climb in just four and a half hours, but there was another spectacular display before the TV broadcast ended.

Hamish MacInnes, the founder of the Glencoe Mountain Rescue team, crossed the 600 feet gap between the Old Man of Hoy and the shore on a single rope in what was known as a Tyrolean Traverse, crossing hand over hand attached by only a metal runner as he dangled 400 feet above the sea.

It was said to be the longest such crossing ever made and took just ten minutes to complete.

Tribute to picture pioneer

The year of 1984 saw the death, at the age of 83, of the well known photographer and pioneer of film shows in Orkney, Mr Jimmy Sinclair.

Born in Sanday, he moved to Kirkwall with his family at the age of three, and, as a young man, became assistant projectionist at the old Electric Theatre, eventually becoming head projectionist.

He then set up a travelling picture show which he took round the Mainland and the Isles. It was the first time that many islanders had seen "movies" and his newsreels included the famous Jack Dempsey - Gene Tunney world heavyweight boxing championship bout.

He later moved into photography business and he was credited with photographing all the winners of Kirkwall's street game, the Ba', from 1923. He also became an entertainments promoter, bringing top musicians like Jimmy Shand to Orkney for several years.

The old Electric Theatre where he began his career had later become Kirkwall's Cosmo ballroom. In 1984, a licence was granted to Robert Swanney to re-open the former ballroom as the Casablanca night club.

A lifetime's labour of love

One of the unsung heroes of safeguarding Orkney heritage during the second half of the 20th century was Norrie Wood, of Graemeshall, Holm, who gathered together one of the most spectacular collections of antiques and memorabilia ever seen in the county.

What began as a boyhood hobby developed into a lifetime labour of love as Mr Wood - who never earned more than £10 a week during his working life - amassed a breathtaking display ranging from china and porcelain, silver and gold ware, jewellery and watches to guns and paintings, furniture and books.

His passion began as a boy of 13 in his native parish of Firth when he persuaded his father to send off for a frog mug he had seen advertised in the *Exchange and Mart* for seven shillings. The items grew until his remarkable collection filled four large rooms of Graemeshall - the house formerly owned by Orkney's Lord Lieutenant Patrick Sutherland Graeme - which the Woods purchased in 1961, specifically to house all the antiques.

Mr Wood never specialised in Orkney items only. In fact, much of his pottery came from Staffordshire, while a Dutch marquetry cabinet, dating from around 1680, was amongst his favourite pieces of furniture.

He also owned the commemorative box which was given to Kirkwall's MP, Sir Arthur Bignold, when he was given the freedom of Kirkwall in the early years of the 20th century. It had never been opened because Mr Wood did not have the key to go with it.

Sadly, at the age of 70, Mr Wood lost his sight, and he was later to move into St Rognvald House in Kirkwall. But he was coaxed into taking part in an edition of the Antiques Roadshow television programme when it visited Stromness in 1991.

The collection, he admitted, was, quite simply, an obsession. "Every penny was spent on what's there," he said.

Acclaim from the Big Yin

Comedian Billy Connolly - a man destined to become an international film star in the following decade - performed at two sell-out concerts in Orkney in November, 1984, giving special credit to a Kirkwall man.

For in the audience was Kirkwall resident George McEwan who wrote the "Welly Boot Song" which the "Big Yin" had more or less adopted as his theme tune.

Mr McEwan, who had moved to Orkney with his Orcadian wife Madeline in 1974, had first met the Glasgow comedian nearly 20 years earlier at an Ayr folk club. He had written the "Welly Boot Song" during his teabreak when he worked at an Ayr brewery, where the women had to wear rubber boots at their work, and Billy Connolly had subsequently recorded the composition.

Lifeboat honours

The coxswain of the Kirkwall lifeboat *Grace Paterson Ritchie*, Captain Billy Sinclair, was awarded the RNLI bronze medal following the rescue of three crewmen and the fishing vessel *Benachie* after she went aground on rocks off Rousay in storm force conditions in January, 1984.

Certificates of commendation were awarded to the rest of the crew: Andrew Grieve, Alex Strutt, Robert Mainland, Robert Hall, Michael Drever, Michael Foulis and Geoff Gardens.

October, 1984, saw the new £370,000 Stromness lifeboat *Joseph Rothwell Sykes and Hilda M* arrive in her home port for the first time to replace the *John Gellatly Hyndman*.

Eight escape plane crash

Eight people walked away unhurt as a Loganair Islander aircraft crash landed in Sanday, hitting a fence in a turnip field, on June 1, 1984. The plane was extensively damaged.

Among those in the plane was Miss Maisie Muir, the travelling cashier for the Royal Bank of Scotland, who was estimated to have made 8,000 flights, carrying out her banking duties in the isles.

New cuisine

Orkney was to have its first Chinese restaurant as the Empire restaurant opened in Junction Road, Kirkwall, in 1984, having been purchased by Mr F. S. Ma who already owned a Chinese restaurant in Shetland.

Council chief

At a salary range of £22,000 - £24,000 a year, Mr Ron Gilbert, Orkney Islands Council's director of finance, was appointed the new chief executive of the council in 1984, to succeed Mr Graeme Lapsley who was retiring.

Football boss

Aberdeen Football Club manager Alex Ferguson - later to become manager of Scotland and then arguably the top football club manager in the world as Sir Alex Ferguson of Manchester United - travelled to Orkney in June, 1984, to open the new Mills Filling Station in Kirkwall.

Pedal power

Two Australians - Kathy McDonald (29) and Paul Marshall (28) - arrived in Orkney after 10,000 gruelling miles as part of a group cycling round the world on a "Bike Ride for Peace."

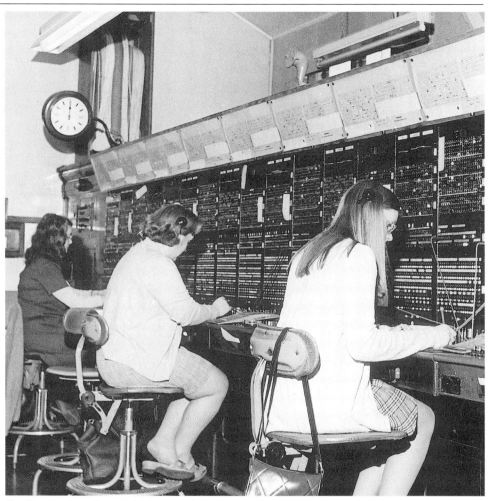

Staff at work at the old Kirkwall telephone exchange.

(Picture courtesy of Orkney Library photographic archive)

Arriving home in style! Brigadier Malcolm Dennison - later to become Lord Lieutenant of Orkney - retired to his home at Roeberry, South Ronaldsay, in 1983 after working in the Sultanate of Oman for twenty years. He is pictured at Kirkwall Airport in front of the huge Hercules transport aircraft of the Omani Air Force which brought all his possessions back to this country.

(Picture courtesy of Orkney Library photographic archive)

1985

The Queen Mother chats to George Eunson, Corse, St Ola, at the 1985 County Show.
(Picture courtesy of Orkney Library photographic archive)

Centenary for County Show

It was a Royal occasion as the 100th Orkney County Show was staged by the Orkney Agricultural Society which received a letter of congratulations from the Queen.

The guest of honour for the 1985 centenary show was Queen Elizabeth, the Queen Mother, making her sixth visit to Orkney. (She had made her fifth visit to the county in August, 1983, when she visited the Pier Arts Centre and attended a dedication service at St Magnus Cathedral for the inauguration of a new lighting system).

The Queen Mother was shown round the Bignold Park by the president of the Orkney Agricultural Society, Mr David Kirkpatrick of Newhall, Stromness, in front of a crowd of 10,300.

The first County Show was held at Sunnybank, St Ola, on August 17, 1875 - but no shows were held for the years of the two world wars.

The supreme cattle champion of the centenary show was an Aberdeen-Angus bull jointly owned by Rognvald Sinclair of Unigarth and Stewart Wood, Garson, Sandwick. A year later, the bull won the supreme Aberdeen-Angus championship at the Royal Show in Stoneleigh, Warwickshire.

Blaze destroys isles mansion house

One of Orkney's most renowned mansion houses was severely damaged as the 19th century Trumland House suffered a fire which destroyed completely the third floor and roof of the building.

The blaze started as work was being carried out to convert the house into a hotel for its owners Thomas Shipstone and his wife Sheila.

The house was built in 1872 to the design of the famous Scots architect David Bryce. Firefighters from Kirkwall and Stromness joined Rousay's volunteer force who worked until the next day, but other floors of the building suffered serious water damage and debris as ceilings collapsed.

Fortunately, most of the library was preserved and the magnificent collection of books which belonged to the original owner, General Sir Frederick William Traill Burroughs were taken out by firemen, along with maps and shooting records of the estate.

Island Games underway

The first Island Games - attracting 766 competitors from 15 island groups around Europe - was held at Douglas, Isle of Man.

Orkney finished in seventh place in the medals table with 15 medals, 14 of which were won in the athletics competitions, comprising three golds, six silver and six bronze.

Top individual performer was Hilary Donaldson (20) who won gold in both the 100 metres and 200 metres. She also won silver medals in the relay and high jump. The other gold medal winner for Orkney was Ian McGruer (19) in the shot put.

Orkney's youngest medal winner was 15 year old Fiona Mackie who got a silver medal in the 3,000 metres.

Pioneer vehicle

The first Sinclair C5 electric car in Orkney was delivered to grandmother Mrs Mina Caithness of Boondatown, Stronsay. The C5 - capable of a range of 20 miles on a fully charged battery - had a top speed of 15mph. Unfortunately, the £399 vehicle did not prove such a success nationally. Only 100 a week were being produced in 1985 instead of an expected 5,000 a month.

Orkney story on film

The film *Down Under*, starring Susannah York and Trevor Howard, told the story of Eliza Fraser who, in 1835, left Stromness to accompany her husband, Captain James Fraser, to Australia.

During the homeward voyage, she was shipwrecked on Eastern Australia, enduring the death of her new born child, the murder of her husband and enslavement by an Aboriginal tribe, before being rescued by a fugitive Irish convict.

Admiral dies

Vice Admiral Friedrich Ruge, who died in Germany on July 4, 1985, was acknowledged to be the last living crew member of the ships of the German fleet interned in Scapa Flow at the end of World War One.

He was a young lieutenant on the German destroyer *B112* and helped to scuttle his ship on June 21, 1919. He again served in the German Navy in World War Two, specialising in minelaying and minesweeping operations.

Shelter blast

There were red faces amongst Army top brass as a 50 year old bathing shelter - which was built by public subscription in Stromness - was blown up by a demolition team of visiting soldiers who mistook it for an unwanted wartime relic.

The team of Royal Engineers from Yorkshire had been in Orkney as part of a clean-up campaign to rid the county of unwanted eyesores. But Councillor Ian Argo said: "This is not an Army structure and I can't understand why it should have been mistaken for a wartime relic."

Fishing giant

Stromness skipper Angus Sinclair and partners, his brother Olly and Joe Nicolson, brought home the £2 million *Orcades Viking II* - the largest purse trawler in the British fleet at 190 feet, and with a capacity for over 1,000 tons of fish.

Island award

Shapinsay was named as the top "Tourism Community of 1985" by the Scottish Tourist Board after the island (population 312) had attracted 6,000 visitors in the year after an effort co-ordinated by the volunteer group Shapinsay Community Enterprises. A year later, the award was won by Shapinsay's neighbouring island of Eday.

Ruby sparkles at the top

Orkney musician and singer Ruby Rendall - known to a generation of children in the county as music teacher Ruby Chalmers - was voted the number one female country artiste in Scotland by the Scottish Country Music Fellowship for three successive years in 1985-87. With her band Cimarron, she had two major British tours during 1985-86, a visit to Germany and an invitation to perform at the Grand Old Oprey in Nashville, USA.

(Picture courtesy of Ruby Rendall)

Duncan Peace at Kirkwall Airport. (Picture courtesy of Orkney Library photographic archive)

Bomb in shipping lane

People in Balfour village, Shapinsay, were asked to temporarily evacuate their homes after a live German World War Two mine was discovered just 200 yards from Balfour Pier in December, 1985.

The discovery was made by Kirkwall diver George Currie who was carrying out a seabed survey.

The mine was right in the middle of the main shipping lane and it was estimated that the island ferries had sailed over the mine about 50,000 times in the previous 40 years.

A Royal Navy bomb disposal team flew to Orkney to detonate the explosive which left "a big hole in the sea bed."

Pilot's career takes off

Kirkwall pilot Duncan Peace became the youngest Loganair captain at the age of 23 in 1986.

He was later to join Air 2000 and then the Virgin Atlantic airline and, in 1999, created a piece of Orkney aviation history as he shared the flight deck with fellow Orcadian pilot Erling Flett on flights from London to Johannesburg and from London to Tokyo.

As one pilot was going up in the world in 1986, another was, unfortunately, heading for a fall.

Orkney's flying farmer Sydney Bichan (68) had a lucky escape after his single seater Jodel aircraft crashed into the sea after taking off from Swanbister, Orphir.

His wife Margaret alerted Police and Coastguards after the crash 400 yard from the shore, and he was pulled from the wreckage by Duncan McNair (22) who rowed to the scene in a dinghy and who managed to get the injured pilot ashore with the help of another neighbour Stephen Groundwater.

Duncan McNair was later honoured by the Royal Humane Society for his bravery while Sydney Bichan recovered to carry on flying.

1986

Royal burgh celebrates

A 500 strong torch-lit procession through the streets of Kirkwall celebrated the 500th anniversary of the granting of a Royal Charter to the burgh by King James III of Scotland on March 31, 1486.

A crowd of 5,000 turned out to watch the proceedings, and 3,000 more spectators gathered in Broad Street, Kirkwall, in August, 1986, as the ancient ceremony of Riding the Marches was revived.

Eighty horse riders, led by Captain Bill Spence, set out on an 18 mile circuit of the burgh boundaries as agreed by King James when granting the Royal Charter.

Isles phone link-up

The smallest digital telephone exchange in Britain was opened by British Telecom, at a cost of £60,000, to link North Ronaldsay to the international telephone network.

Former island GP Dr Sydney Peace made the first phone call to the island's oldest inhabitant Mrs Bella Swanney (100) and then her great granddaughters, eight year old twins Ruth and Gillian Swanney, phoned relatives in Melbourne, Australia.

Tragic sign of the times

In a year of tragedy on Orkney's roads - with six separate fatal accidents - Orkney Islands Council, with the support of the Police, erected signs to enforce the 60mph maximum speed limit at a dozen locations around Orkney. The Scottish Office later ordered the council to take them down.

Marathon effort

The first Hoy Half Marathon, organised by Dr Tony Trickett, was run in 1986 as 40 starters lined up for the 13 mile race which was to become an annual event for the rest of the century.

The first winner in 1 hour 28 minutes was Adrian Askew.

Traffic warden

Kirkwall should have a permanent traffic warden, the Northern Joint Police Committee decided in 1986.

Isles airlift for hedgehogs

An airlift of hedgehogs from North Ronaldsay was begun after complaints that the creatures were eating the eggs of the local bird population.

A survey had shown that the hedgehogs out-numbered North Ronaldsay's human population by ten to one. They had been introduced only in 1970 to help control greenhouse pests but the population explosion began when they escaped. Island GP Kevin Woodbridge said it was better to send them South than cull them. "We have nothing against hedgehogs - they are simply in the wrong place," he said.

Loganair offered to fly the first 42 hedgehogs to the South after the creatures were rounded up by the islanders in a night-time operation. It was hoped that the first 20 would go to the Scottish Centre for Rural Ecology at Penicuik, but Dr Woodbridge added: "There has been no shortage of offers of new homes."

Heritage trail opened

The chairman of the Ancient Monuments Board for Scotland Magnus Magnusson - better known to most people as the presenter of the television quiz programme Mastermind - travelled to Orkney in 1986 to open the Orkney Heritage Walk which included the Vinquoy chambered tomb dating from 2000 BC. (Picture courtesy of Orkney Library photographic archive)

Betting shop a winner

Orkney's first betting shop was given permission on November 26, 1986, as Sheriff A.A. MacDonald reversed the decision of Orkney Licensing Board to refuse a betting office licence for Rails Bookmakers at Junction Road, Kirkwall.

The sheriff said: "It is not apparent to me that there is any feature shared by a Roman Catholic church, a Boy Scout hall, the Phoenix cinema, a footpath to a school, a centre for the handicapped and houses which makes the location of a betting shop in their neighbourhood undesirable."

The betting shop - operated by Lloyd Stockan and Jim Kelly - opened for business at the start of the 1987 flat racing season.

Cathedral yields its secrets

As two reigning monarchs and Queen Elizabeth, the Queen Mother, visited Orkney to mark the 850th anniversary of St Magnus Cathedral, the historic church yielded up a centuries old secret with the discovery of a painted Christ-like face gazing down from the ceiling of the choir nave.

The face was discovered by experts who were in Orkney to examine other paintings which had been detected on the 13th century ceiling at the east end of the Cathedral, near the Rose window.

"It is the first find of this type for a very long time," said Mr Robert Snowden, principal conservator with the Historic Buildings and Monuments department.

The outline of the face appeared - "gazing quite solemnly, surrounded by a halo" - under a coat of lime wash. Painted in a brownish colour, the outline was not complete but was clearly discernible as a face. "I think it could be 13th or 14th century," said Mr Snowden. "However it is very, very difficult to be firm about that because this type of decoration continued to about 1650."

1987

It was thought much of the ceiling painting had been removed in Victorian times. "We are only going to have fragments to conserve," said Mr Snowden.

One of the people able to see the work on the ceiling was the Queen who, in August, 1987, made a flying visit to Orkney to join the celebrations of the Cathedral's 850th anniversary.

(Before her plane touched down, a suspect package found at Kirkwall Airport was detonated in a controlled explosion - it turned out to be entirely innocent).

A crowd of 2,000 waited to greet the Queen in Kirkwall's Broad Street while there were 800 people present in the Cathedral where the centrepiece of the Royal visit was the unveiling of a stained glass window, designed by Scottish artist Crear McCartney, in the west wing of the building.

Outside, the Queen watched as children representing every Orkney primary school presented stones to be used in the building of a new font for the Cathedral.

A week later another Royal occasion marked the Cathedral anniversary as the Queen Mother (87) greeted the 84 year old Norwegian monarch King Olav V as he arrived at Kirkwall pier by Royal barge from the Norwegian Royal Yacht at anchor in the bay.

The Queen Mother, the patron of the Friends of St Magnus, and King Olav both visited the Cathedral before a series of separate events. King Olav paid his respects at the Norwegian war graves at St Olaf's cemetery, and toured Stromness on an informal walkabout, visiting the Pier Arts Centre, while the Queen Mother met Orkney's oldest person - 107 year old Maggie Clouston, a resident at St Rognvald House.

Rousay-born Maggie, who had spent much of her life in Dounby, could claim to be the oldest member of the Scottish National Party!

Woman footballer cries foul

The Orkney football competition for the Parish cup - which dates back to 1929 - made its own piece of sporting history as the captain of the 1987 Rousay team, due to play Sandwick, was sent off before the start of the game - for being a woman!

Mrs Ellen Grieve was told that, under Scottish Football Association rules, she could not play against men in a competitive match. Because of the ban, her Rousay team-mates decided to withdraw

from the competition rather than play without her.

It was the first time in 40 years that Rousay had entered the Parish Cup, and Mrs Grieve said: "The first I knew of it was when the referee came up to me on the field. I was really disappointed. I love playing. I played in the Scottish Ladies League in Motherwell. It's a shame as I started up the Rousay team and got them training."

Rousay team-mate Adrian Davidson said: "It wasn't fair - she's one of the best players on the island, better than 99.9 per cent of the men."

The two teams did go ahead with a friendly match, and Sandwick won 22-1.

The secretary of the Scottish Amateur FA, Mr Ian McTweed, said: "We have to apply the ruling laid down by the Scottish FA that women cannot play in these matches."

New ship for Orkney

Shipping giant P&O marked the 150th anniversary of the company's founding in 1987 with the introduction of a new *St Sunniva* ferry linking Orkney with Shetland and Aberdeen.

The 105 metre ship - formerly a cross-Channel ferry, the *Panther* - had been converted at the Aberdeen yard of Hall Russell and Company. The vessel, with a capacity for 400 passengers, would come under the command of Stromness captain Fred Johnston and Willie Duncan.

Unfortunately, on her maiden voyage as the *St Sunniva*, the ship, while sailing from Aberdeen to Shetland with a party of VIPs on board, was forced to turn back east of Orkney after a giant wave crashed through the bridge, knocking out valu-

able equipment, in estimated 80 feet high seas. The storm ripped off half the ship's new nameplate which had just been fitted.

There had been two previous North ships called the *St Sunniva* - one which ran aground off Shetland and the other lost in World War Two.

The year of 1987 saw another footnote in local maritime history when Barbara Campbell (30) became the first woman deck officer to sail with P&O Ferries as she sailed on the *St Magnus* from Stromness as second mate.

She held a foreign-going master's certificate and was providing two months relief cover on the *St Magnus* – a change from her usual job with P&O Cruises where she sailed to the Caribbean, Mexico and Alaska.

Battle of the Big Tree

Of all the problems in all the world . . . an angry public outburst greeted the pruning of one of Orkney's most famous landmarks, the 200 year old "Big Tree" in Albert Street, Kirkwall.

The tree was cut back - or "pollarded" - to leave not so much a big tree as a big stump. Council workmen had moved in to remove the branches of the Sycamore after it had been feared that the tree would have to be axed completely as unsafe.

The outcry demanded that heads should roll at the council. However, the furore faded as the tree produced new growth which has seen it survive to the end of the century.

Airmen killed in crash horror

The pilot and navigator were lost as an RAF Buccaneer jet plunged into the sea off South Ronaldsay during a simulated attack on Copinsay lighthouse.

A huge explosion was heard through much of Orkney as the plane hit the sea in the crash drama in April, 1987. The jet was based at RAF Lossiemouth where Squadron Leader Norman MacLeod said the danger of night-time low-flying exercises to the Flotta oil terminal was "infinitesimally small."

Orkney was touched by another air tragedy two months later as three men died when a small aircraft which had taken off from Kirkwall Airport hit a mountain on the Faroe islands.

The pilot, Ray Hughes from Leeds, and marine biologists Tim Waters, from Cambridge, and American Fred Fairfield were on their way to make a survey of whales on behalf of the Faroese government when they ran into heavy cloud and fog and hit a mountain on the south west coast of Vagar, and plunged into the sea.

Doomed to global warming?

The first warnings of global warming came at a conference organised by the British Association for the Advancement of Science as Dr William Carter of the University of Ulster warned that sea levels around Orkney and the North of Scotland could rise by between two feet and six feet by the end of the 21st century.

"But," he added, "We have the most severe weather in the North Atlantic so waves may be breaking quite a lot higher than that."

He thought that after the year 2050, planning authorities would have to withhold permission for any building less than 20 feet above sea level.

"The main cause is industrial pollution. We have been burning fossil fuels and that has put a lot more carbon dioxide into the atmosphere.

"It absorbs heat, which warms up the atmosphere and the ocean. The ocean melts the ice caps, and the sea level rises."

Warship joins Orkney rescue

Orkney was at the centre of a major rescue drama as the warship HMS *Ark Royal* helped in an operation which saw 19 people plucked to safety from a sinking trawler off South Ronaldsay.

The rescued - 18 adults and one child - were put aboard the Pentland Firth passenger ferry *Pentland Venture* - which had only begun services the previous month - just minutes before the trawler sank in June, 1987.

The *Ark Royal* had gone to the assis-

tance of the 242 feet long West German factory ship *Hessen* in response to a Mayday message that she was foundering in the Firth after taking water in the engine room.

Two helicopters from the *Ark Royal* took off but they were needed only to winch one man from the water as the Germans transferred to the *Pentland Venture* operated by the ferry firm of Thomas and Bews. The survivors were landed at John o' Groats.

Orkney - a power in the land

Britain's energy minister Mr Cecil Parkinson visited Orkney to formally switch on the world's most powerful wind generator.

Orkney was now "leading the world," said the minister as he inaugurated the £12 million wind turbine at Burgar Hill, Evie, in the autumn of 1987.

As the massive blades of the turbine - standing taller than Nelson's Column in London - began to turn to generate electricity for the National Grid, he congrat-

ulated the 100 engineers involved in the ten year project and said: "This is really a major step forward. I hope from it will come more wind generation capacity in the UK and more exports to different parts of the world."

In 1999, two of the Burgar Hill generators - the 90 feet high 250kw machine and the 150 feet high 200kw machine - were demolished. Scottish Hydro Electric said both turbines had reached the end of their useful life.

Freedom honour for the Grimonds

Lord and Lady Grimond were given the freedom of Orkney in a unique ceremony in April, 1987, on the steps of St Magnus Cathedral. It was the first time that the freedom of Orkney had been conferred -

past ceremonies had simply conferred the freedom of the burgh of Kirkwall.

Lady Grimond said: "This is the greatest honour that has ever been bestowed on me in my life - or is ever likely to be."

On top of the world

Shapinsay soldier Robbie Nelson (19), a sapper in the Royal Engineers, was the youngest member of a 12 man team which headed for a three month expedition to China to challenge the 20,000 feet high Huang Guan, said to be the third highest unclimbed mountain in the world.

The area could be reached by helicopter, so the team had to rely on camels to reach an area which had only been visited by two Western explorers in the previous 100 years - one of whom, Eric Shipton in 1937, reported seeing "gigantic footprints" of the Yeti or Abominable Snowman.

The team had been training on the north face of the Eiger. Team leader Captain Henry Morgan said: "It is, perhaps, truly the last unexplored region on the planet."

Top job for editor

The Orcadian journalist Magnus Linklater - born at Merkister, the eldest son of Orkney writer Eric Linklater - was appointed as the editor of *The Scotsman* newspaper in 1987.

His journalistic career, since leaving Cambridge University in 1965, had seen him work with the *Daily Express*, *Sunday Times* and *The Observer*, as well as writing a book on the Falklands War.

Meanwhile, Mr Robert Cormack, a nephew of Eric Linklater and, in 1987, the British ambassador to Zaire, bought the 18th century Westness House in Rousay. Mr Cormack had previously served in the diplomatic service in Vietnam, India and Sweden.

Top restaurant accolade

Alan and Joyce Craigie of the Creel restaurant in St Margaret's Hope were adjudged the winners of the Taste of Scotland award as the country's top restaurant.

The couple - Alan from Kirkwall and Joyce, whose father was originally from Birsay - had returned to Orkney after working in America where they prepared meals for the British Consul General, meeting celebrities from the film world as well as Royalty and top politicians.

"It was mainly dinner parties and functions for various VIPs, including Prince Andrew - Alan cooked for him and I served him," said Joyce.

Generous Orkney

An astonishing weekend of fund-raising events saw Orkney raise a total of £40,000 for the 1987 BBC Children in Need charity appeal - the equivalent of more than £2 for every man, woman and child in the county. Leading the way was the Ferry Inn at Stromness which raised more than £10,000.

Orkney's nuclear war of words

The threat of the nuclear industry - real or perceived - saw Orkney involved in a war of words throughout the mid 1980s as fears rose that the islands were being targeted as a "soft option" for the location of potentially hazardous developments.

With memories of the controversial uranium mining proposals of 1979-79 still fresh in Orcadian minds, vigorous campaigns were instigated against any suggestion of the county being earmarked for the disposal of radioactive waste, or any expansion of the Dounreay nuclear complex across the Pentland Firth in Caithness.

It culminated in Orkney Islands Council members voting for the county to become a "Nuclear Free Zone" in 1986.

The issue first surfaced in 1984 as a company called ENSEC suggested that North Sea oil technology could be used to store radioactive waste beneath the seabed at Stormy Bank to the west of Orkney.

Opposition campaigners - including Greenpeace - said it would be impossible to monitor the 10,000 feet deep shafts, and argued vocally that such a project would spell disaster for Orkney's fishing industry.

Environment minister William Waldegrave told Orkney MP Mr Jim Wallace that the proposal was "interesting and imaginative" but had only been put forward in the most general terms, and a feasibility study would be needed to assess such a form of disposal.

"Meanwhile," said the minister, "I am not aware of any specific proposal to use any area of the North of Scotland for this purpose, either by ENSEC or by any other organisation."

However, ENSEC director Alex Copson was quoted as saying that his company had already established a relationship of understanding and co-operation with the Nuclear Industry Radioactive Waste Executive, NIREX, and he thought that ENSEC could be in a position to commission the building of a suitable rig within 12 months.

In the event, no rig was ever built - nor, indeed was any specific application ever made to the Government by ENSEC to drill on Stormy Bank, and 15 years later Orcadians can only conjecture how serious or viable the proposal really was.

There was no doubting the reality, however, in the summer of 1985 when plans were announced by the UK Atomic Energy Authority to expand the reprocessing operations of the Dounreay nuclear complex with a proposal to build a £200 million plutonium reprocessing plant on the site. As angry protests were voiced in Orkney, Scottish Secretary George Younger announced there would be a public inquiry into the proposals. "Mr Younger believes the proposed development has implications of greater than regional importance which he would wish to see examined at a public inquiry," said the Scottish Office.

Orkney Islands Council - concerned that any association with the nuclear industry could destroy the islands' reputation for a clean and pure environment for farming, fishing, distilling and tourism - became one of the major objectors to the plans at the ensuing hearings.

The Dounreay public inquiry was based in Thurso, but came to Kirkwall for three days to hear Orkney objections at Kirkwall Town Hall, under the chairmanship of Scottish Office reporter Mr Alexander Bell, in 1986.

The 1986 Chernobyl explosion in the Ukraine had already blighted parts of British agriculture with radioactive fall-out, and scores of personal objectors put forward their concerns that Dounreay's presence just 30 miles from Orkney was a potential blight on the islands.

To coincide with the inquiry hearing in Kirkwall, Orkney protesters launched a "Declaration of Wyre" which challenged the constitutional status of Orkney and Shetland - arguing that the islands could still be part of Scandinavia under the 1667 Peace of Breda, a treaty which gave Denmark the right to redeem Orkney and Shetland.

In that case, argued the Campaign Against Dounreay Expansion, the Pentland Firth was part of international waters and it would be illegal for Britain to dispose of radioactive material.

There was no doubt that Orkney had put its case to the inquiry - but at a cost. There were complaints as the Orkney Islands Council legal bill quickly reached £120,000. After jibes that the issue was becoming a "lawyers' paradise," the council's representative Mr Brian Gill, and his team, offered to continue their work for a reduced fee.

Astonishingly, it was three years after the public inquiry into the Dounreay expansion plans that the then Secretary of State for Scotland Malcom Rifkind announced, in October, 1989, that he would give permission for the £200 million plutonium reprocessing plant. It brought a swift response from Orkney MP Jim Wallace who complained that the minister had ignored the fears of his constituents.

There was also some embarrassment to Orkney's anti-nuclear stance when it was revealed that the Occidental company had been discharging "extremely small" levels of radioactivity from the Flotta oil terminal into the Pentland Firth since 1981.

The Low Specific Activity material - LSA - was the result of naturally occurring radiation in water produced from oil reservoirs under the North Sea.

An Occidental spokesman said: "At no point has the existence of LSA scale either offshore or at Flotta terminal posed any threat or hazard to personnel or the environment. This is due to the extremely low levels present."

A year later, in 1987, Orkney was back on the offensive, however, as a research group at the British Geological Survey identified several Orkney islands as among potentially suitable sites for storing radioactive waste.

A report stated: "More than 100 small islands with areas greater than half a square kilometre have been identified. The majority of the islands lie off the west coast of Scotland, or the Orkneys or Shetlands, although a few are to be found around the coasts of England and Wales."

However, geologist Dr Tim McEwen said: "It is going to take several years to be investigated. I cannot envisage any possible site before the year 2000."

A spokesman for the nuclear industry's radioactive waste organisation NIREX said: "We have simply seen this report from the British Geological Survey team. We have not looked at any islands. We just know that certain islands have good geologies."

County convener Edwin Eunson was in no doubt about the implications, however. "It is another indication that some people seem to regard remote islands as expendable," he said.

In the last decade of the century - with an increasing acceptance that all radioactive waste should be stored on site where it can be monitored - the possibility of island waste repositories, offshore or on land, appears to have receded. Only the future will reveal whether Orkney can forget such concerns completely.

The county has maintained its uneasy relationship with its neighbouring nuclear complex at Dounreay, the reputation of which has been tarnished throughout the 1990s by a series of damning scares over contamination and safety standards which have only served to confirm many of the fears expressed by Orcadians at the 1986 public inquiry.

In fact, in the end, the fast reactor reprocessing plant never went ahead as proposed at Dounreay, as the Government eventually announced that the atomic plant's role would be run down into the 21st century. Orkney, it seemed, was on the way to winning its nuclear war of words.

Epic rescues save crewmen

The 15 crew of the French trawler *St Patrick* abandoned ship off Birsay and took to liferafts after losing the battle to save the vessel which had struck the treacherous North Shoal.

Skipper Claude Raymond told *The Orcadian* that they had been forced to leave the trawler once the water was level with the engines.

Some of the crew were picked up by the Stornoway Coastguard rescue helicopter, and the remainder by another French trawler *Cape St Anne*. Stromness lifeboat attempted to take the stricken *St Patrick* in tow but was forced to release the line as the vessel sank in 60 metres of water.

Three months later, in May, 1988, four shipwrecked crewmen - three of them Norwegian - were plucked to safety by helicopter after the 100 feet converted whaler *Tommeline* went aground on rocks below Noup Head, Westray.

The vessel was on her way from Oban to Shetland with £150,000 worth of salmon smolts. The Shetland Coastguard rescue helicopter landed the rescued men at Kirkwall.

The year saw two new lifeboats arrive in Orkney. In March, 1988, the new £600,000, 47 feet Longhope lifeboat *Lord Saltoun* arrived home, under coxswain Jackie Leslie, to replace the *David and Elizabeth King and EB*. Jackie Leslie retired later that year to be succeeded as coxswain by Billy Budge.

Kirkwall also welcomed a new lifeboat, the *Mickie Salvesen* to replace the *Grace Paterson Ritchie*.

And the *Mickie Salvesen* was soon in action as, in September, 1988, Captain Billy Sinclair, coxswain of the Kirkwall lifeboat, was awarded a bar to his RNLI bronze medal following the rescue of the coaster *BP Mercurious*, with her master and chief engineer, in 20 feet seas and gale force winds.

In the last service before retirement, Captain Sinclair skilfully manoeuvred the lifeboat alongside the *BP Mercurious*, which had lost power off Westray's Noup Head, and secured a line which, despite twice breaking, was eventually sufficient to get the vessel to a safe anchorage.

The rest of the lifeboat crew - Jim Mitchell, Alex Strutt, Robert Mainland, Geoff Gardens, Smith Foubister and Robert Hall - were awarded RNLI certificates for their part in the operation.

Jim Mitchell succeeded Billy Sinclair as coxswain of the *Mickie Salvesen* at the end of 1988, while the former Kirkwall boat *Grace Paterson Ritchie* went on to serve as a lifeboat in Iceland.

Twelve months later, in September, 1989, a dramatic air rescue saw the four man crew of the stricken Kirkwall cargo vessel *Calf Sound* airlifted to safety in treacherous conditions only minutes before the ship turned turtle and sank in 70 metres of water.

An RAF Sea King helicopter from Lossiemouth went to the scene in response to a distress call from the Dennison Shipping Company vessel, carrying a cargo of cement.

The helicopter lifted off crewmen Chris Leitch (23) of Shapinsay and Kenny Fraser (28) of Kirkwall and then the master and mate, Terry Kelly and Brian Woodcock.

Science festival

Orcadian Howie Firth, the founding producer of BBC Radio Orkney, was appointed the director of the first Edinburgh International Festival of Science and Technology in 1988.

He had been succeeded at Radio Orkney by John Fergusson who had moved from Radio Shetland.

In 1991, Howie Firth returned as director of the first ever Orkney Science Festival. The first festival - which was to become an annual event for the rest of the decade - was opened by the well known scientist and television personalty, Professor Heinz Wolff.

The week of exhibitions, outings and lectures would provide a variety of opportunities for Orcadians and visitors alike as the festival "really brought science to life," said Howie Firth. "Orkney has the potential to be in the forefront of science festivals, and we now have a very solid base on which to develop. The extent to which people responded to something new like this was tremendous."

New era for paper

The Orcadian of February 18, 1988, saw the newspaper change from its traditional broadsheet to tabloid style, in response to a poll of readers.

Apart from its earliest issues, and during paper shortages in World War One, *The Orcadian* had been broadsheet for all its existence. The change-over meant the end for the company's Cossar press which had printed the broadsheet paper for the previous 57 years.

The switch to tabloid format saw the circulation of *The Orcadian* reach 10,000 for the first time. And, in 1991, it reached a record 11,000 weekly sales.

Mystery killer destroys seals

Thousands of seals were killed - with hundreds found dead on Orkney shores - as a mystery virus struck in the North Sea.

People in Orkney were warned not to touch seals which appeared ill as the virus - similar to the dog disease of distemper - spread from Scandinavia to Holland and England, and finally to local waters.

In August, 1988, the first three victims of the disease in Orkney were found dead in Scapa Flow, and it was estimated that half of Orkney's common seal population of 10,000 could be at risk.

As the first two weeks of September saw 139 dead seals reported in Orkney, the disease was described as "nature's cull" at a meeting of Orkney Islands Council. Councillor Jim Sinclair said that, around Shapinsay, there had been at least a tenfold increase in seal numbers since 1945.

It was a typically emotive story for the national tabloid press and a Save Our Seals appeal run by the *Daily Mail* raised £300,000 in donations - £20,000 of which was to be given to the work of the Orkney environmental group, the Dunters, it was reported.

Twitchers invade

The island of North Ronaldsay trebled its population - with the arrival of one bird and 250 birdwatchers or twitchers.

The reason was the sighting of a Pallas's Rose Finch - the first time the species had ever been seen in Britain - which was spotted by Dr Kevin Woodbridge at the island bird observatory in June, 1988. The bird would normally be nearer Siberia than the North Isles of Orkney.

The Orkney Islands Shipping company vessel *Orcadia* was chartered twice to go to North Ronaldsay while aircraft and a flotilla of small boats were hired as people arrived in Orkney from all over Britain.

Shopping Week celebration

The 40th annual Shopping Week was marked by a reunion of 27 former Shopping Week queens, who saw the 1988 queen Sandra Ritch crowned by the first ever queen, Ivy Gorn, née Flett, who held the title in 1952.   (Picture courtesy of Alastair Peebles)

Arctic challenge

Kirkwall-born Morag Howell (31), née Nicol, was part of a five strong British team, led by explorer Sir Ranulph Fiennes, which set out to make the first unaided trek to the North Pole.

Morag, who had been educated at Kirkwall Grammar School before moving to Fraserburgh, was communications officer of the team while her husband Laurence was base commander for the expedition.

The team set out, in the first instance, for Canada where the Howells would make base camp at Ward Hunt Island.

Westray stalwart

Norman Cooper retired after teaching in Westray for 38 years, 31 as headmaster. One of his last duties was to welcome the Duchess of Gloucester on a Royal visit to the Pierowall School in July, 1988.

The Duchess also visited Shapinsay, Eday and North Ronaldsay as well as the Orkney Mainland. It was credited as the first ever Royal visit to North Ronaldsay.

Near miss

An investigation was launched in September, 1988, after a Loganair Islander aircraft, flying to Westray with four passengers at 600 feet, reported that two military aircraft had flown underneath the plane, within 200 feet, over Egilsay.

Oldest man

Orkney's oldest man of the day, William Harcus, celebrated his 102nd birthday in the Balfour Hospital in January, 1988.

Born in Faray, Mr Harcus had lived in Eday most of his life before moving to the Orkney Mainland in his retirement.

International footballers

The arrival of David Harvey - pictured above - and his family in Sanday gave the islands an international footballer, albeit retired. In a long and distinguished career, David had played as a goalkeeper for both Leeds United and Scotland. The only Orkney-born footballer to represent Scotland in the 20th century was Andy Wilson, born in Stronsay, who made his name with Middlesbrough and Chelsea in the 1920s.

(Picture courtesy of *The Yorkshire Post*)

Trouble ahead! The Norwegian coaster *Linhav* is pictured after she ran aground, with six men on board, near Roan Head, Flotta, in July, 1979. The vessel was eventually able to refloat herself. (Picture courtesy of Orkney Library photographic archive)

The elected councillors of Orkney Islands Council in 1986. Back row, from the left: Billy Dass, Hugh Halcro Johnston, George Wylie, Alastair Scholes, David Groat, Jack Ridgway, Jack Scott, Allan Taylor, Sydney Peace, Ian MacDonald. Middle row: Spencer Rosie, Jean Crichton, Mairhi Trickett, Phyllida Wright, Brenda Robertson. Front: Jim Sinclair, Eoin Scott, Ian Argo, Edwin Eunson, Jackie Tait, George Stevenson, Jean Marwick and Chris Soames. (Picture courtesy of Orkney Library photographic archive)

Inferno on Piper Alpha -

The world's worst oil disaster brought horror to Orkney as 167 lives perished in a fireball as a series of explosions blasted through the Piper Alpha North Sea oil platform.

For ten years, the platform had fed its oil to Orkney's Flotta terminal, but disaster struck on a summer's night just before 10pm on Wednesday, July 6, 1988, and began the biggest emergency air and sea rescue operation ever witnessed in the North Sea oil industry.

As the magnitude of the human tragedy became apparent, it was revealed that one Orcadian was among the dead, but another was, miraculously, among the 66 survivors of the tragedy.

Mr Alan Miller (31) of Reid Crescent, Kirkwall, an industrial chemist on the platform, was among those who died. He left a wife with three children.

The Orcadian survivor - although badly burned - was 31 year old single men Erlend Grieve, whose home was in Edinburgh but whose mother still lived at Buttquoy Park, Kirkwall.

From a hospital bed at Aberdeen Royal Infirmary - where he was visited by Dr Armand Hammer, the head of the Occidental oil company which operated Piper Alpha and the Flotta terminal - Erlend Grieve gave *The Orcadian* this graphic account of his escape from the doomed platform.

"After the initial explosions on Piper Alpha platform, at around 10pm, I found myself congregated with a small body of men on the north west side of the platform. From time to time some more men appeared until there was a total of about 20. By now smoke was making visibility very poor and it was very plain that no immediate rescue was in sight.

"With no electric power or fire water pumps available to operate the water deluge system, it became impossible to control the fire from the platform.

"It then became necessary to look for a means of escape to a level where we could be picked up. The only apparent means of escape, due to being cut off from the rest of the platform by thick, oily smoke, was to find our way down to sea level. This proved very difficult as visibility was down to zero.

"Finally someone found in a corner, down two flights of stairs, a coiled rope ladder. When this was thrown over the side, the knotted rope was seen to reach the lowest level of the platform.

"No time was wasted in getting the first men over the side and down the ladder. These were mainly the walking wounded who had been injured in the original platform blast. While this was going on, I and others were above on the main deck level, 68 feet above the sea, wearing breathing apparatus because by now the smoke was so thick it was almost impossible to breathe.

"Gathering the remainder of the men, we quickly got them over the side and down the rope ladder to where the inflatable rescue launch of the stand-by vessel was waiting to take them away.

"This left four of us waiting to use the rope ladder. While we were waiting our turn, we unhooked the breathing apparatus and at that moment the fireball hit us.

"Finding myself covered in flames, I tried to cover my face and hands as best I could but getting out of the confined gantry space proved very difficult with three or four of us in the same position.

"As the heat increased, we screamed and pushed our way towards the side. Having learned at our offshore survival training course that any jump over 30 feet was dangerous to the human body, I tried to control my fall so that I would land feet first in the water.

"Within the next second or so I felt a big thump on my back. I thought this was it, I had hit some of the deck support frames before hitting the water . . . but no, it wasn't to be, there was lovely water bubbling all around me and the pain in my face and hands disappeared. As I headed for the surface, I had a dread that the sea would be engulfed in burning crude oil and the heat I felt on reaching the surface certainly made me think so.

"On going under again to avoid the heat I realised I was directly under the platform which was now a complete inferno. So, without a life jacket, I alternated between breathing on the surface and diving and swimming away from the platform to escape from the heat.

"Next, finding myself bogged down by my shredded overalls and boots, I kicked off my boots and tried to discard my ragged flame proof overalls. With this achieved, I found I could make a bit more headway but then a further blast came from behind and I noticed the knot of stand-by and rescue vessels moving away from the blast heat being generated by the platform.

"At this point I thought all my chances were gone with nothing in the near vicinity and no more energy for any further effort. As I pulled my way to the surface for what I thought was my final time, I spotted a piece of expanded polyurethane foam about the size of a rugby ball floating some six feet away. Not believing my luck, I struggled towards it, grabbed it and floated on my back.

"So floating in the sea in this manner I was able to take stock of my situation and looking around I saw 100 yards behind me the devastated Piper Alpha platform; half of the top superstructure completely eaten away and the rest of the platform in flames.

"It was growing darker and visibility was poor but light from the glowing platform lit up the many supply ships and rescue boats in the vicinity. So I kicked out towards the nearest one hoping to encounter other survivors on the way.

"Within a few yards I found a larger piece of foam so I took a hold of this, letting go of the small one.

"Then in the distance, on the crest of a wave, I saw three men perched on a large piece of debris. Kicking out towards them I finally got close enough to pull myself up beside them. Nobody had enough strength to say a word but I could tell by the reaction of two of the men I had worked closely with for the last two or three years that they did not recognise me as I scrambled aboard.

"Within five to ten minutes the Piper Alpha stand-by vessel the *Silver Pit* came alongside but we were so exhausted we were unable to get ourselves on board so we had to wait for the return of her inflatable rescue craft which was still searching for survivors.

"On her arrival we were quickly manhandled on to the launch and transferred on to the *Silver Pit* with the help of other workmates.

"We were wrapped in blankets and taken to the warmest part of the ship. The most seriously injured (including Mr Grieve) were winched up to a Royal Navy helicopter and transferred to the msv *Tharos* which is known to have the best medical supplies outwith a modern hospital. The time was approximately 2300 hours.

"I was given morphine and diet Coke to drink and later put on a saline drip.

"Whilst on board I came across two friendly faces, the first being Garson Miller, a diver medic (an Orcadian living in Dumfriesshire) who had been seconded from one of the nearby drilling rigs and the second was an old school chum who since the beginning of 1988 has been a mate on the *Tharos*, Kenneth Wylie (of Matches Square, Kirkwall). With these two aboard and the treatment given to me by the medics I was at last able to feel I might make it back to the shore.

"The doubt was always there because I could see the skin on my hands had been burnt away and what was underneath was

and a miracle escape

severely swollen. My face felt dreadful and I did not have the courage to look at myself in a mirror but everyone I met assured me that my face would quickly heal as the burns were only superficial.

"At 5 o'clock along with another stretcher case I was loaded aboard a Bristow's helicopter and taken to Aberdeen Royal Infirmary.

"I have since read the list of people lost and it includes many friends. I extend my deepest sympathy to their families and loved ones."

The Lord Lieutenant of Orkney set up a disaster appeal in recognition of Orkney's close ties with the Piper platform. Speaking at the Sunday morning service at St Magnus Cathedral, Colonel Robert Macrae said: "It is all too clear to us now that these oil workers were sitting on a time bomb which the slightest fault could set off - with devastating results."

It was a personal tragedy for Orkney because the men working on the rig had been "working for us and our prosperity." Since oil first started flowing into the Flotta terminal more than ten years previously, the community had perhaps taken for granted the attendant danger of working on an oil platform, he said.

"I think we owe a great debt to the families of the men who lost their lives so horrifically last Wednesday and also to those who will be scarred or incapacitated for life."

Orkney Islands Council pledged to give £20,000 to the disaster appeal. County convener Edwin Eunson said he was writing to Occidental to put on record the council's "admiration" for the company's safe record. The disaster was perhaps the greatest tragedy with which Orkney had been associated since the sinking of the warship *Royal Oak* in 1939, he said.

The Piper Alpha disaster saw the immediate shutdown of operations at the Flotta terminal with the workforce of 390 retained in employment, carrying out maintenance duties, until production could be resumed from Occidental's other fields in the North Sea.

On Tuesday, July 26, 20 days after the disaster, St Magnus Cathedral was full for a memorial service for Alan Miller, who had worked offshore for nine years, two on Piper Alpha.

The congregation heard his sister Alison call on oil companies "to turn the sorrow that they feel now into a real commitment to improve the safety standards on the oil platforms for the remaining 30,000 men still making a living in the North Sea."

She said: "The best memorial Alan could have, the most meaningful and sincerest tribute you can pay to Alan, is to do all in your power to raise the safety conditions in the North Sea to the highest possible standard.

"That is the memorial that Alan and the rest of the men who died on Piper Alpha deserve."

Erlend Grieve was in hospital for six weeks before returning to Orkney to recuperate. Five months later, he was to put the nightmare behind him and return to work offshore.

Occidental announced in August, 1988, that work was to go ahead to bypass the devastated Piper platform so that the flow of oil from the Tartan, Claymore and Scapa fields could resume to the Flotta terminal.

But first Orkney had to witness a grim and tragic operation to recover the bodies that were still in the 1,100 tonne accommodation module of Piper Alpha, laying on the seabed.

The module was lifted on to a barge and brought into the sheltered waters of Scapa Flow to allow a search to be carried out and the bodies to be recovered by Grampian Police and flown to Aberdeen. "Obviously we would like to keep people as far away as possible out of respect for the men and also because it will be a very grim task," said an Occidental spokesman as strict security measures were announced for an air and sea exclusion zone around the salvaged module.

The new Piper Bravo oil platform, with emergency escape craft pictured beneath the helicopter landing pad on the left of the structure, was ready to start feeding oil to the Flotta terminal in 1992. *(Picture courtesy of Elf Exploration UK)*

It was nearly four months before the sad task of retrieving and identifying 74 bodies could be completed, as families of the dead accepted compensation payments averaging £600,000.

Erlend Grieve said: "I was lucky to get off the rig and still more fortunate to have recovered mentally as well as physically. A lot more fortunate than many of my mates."

In December, 1988, he flew back out to the North Sea to take up a job on the Claymore platform. "There will always be bad memories," he said. "But I want to see if I can face working on a rig again."

At the time of the disaster, the Piper field was producing 120,000 barrels a day - contributing to an annual £2 million in oil revenue for Orkney Islands Council. Within six months, plans were on the drawing board for a new Piper Bravo platform while oil supplies to the Flotta terminal were resumed from the Tartan and Claymore fields by early 1989.

At the start of 1992, Erlend Grieve returned to the new Piper B platform to work. He married in May, 1990, and he said his wife Karen accepted and understood his decision. He told *The Orcadian*: "I have got no worries at all about the design of the platform, and its safety standards. It's all been well thought out."

The government gave permission for the tragic Piper Alpha platform to be toppled over on to the seabed and abandoned; a grim underwater legacy of a disaster that had sent shock waves through the oil industry.

Double killer lurked in Orkney

1989

A man who stayed for a week on holiday in Kirkwall was revealed as a double murderer after he hanged himself in a Leeds prison cell because he could not face the guilt of being convicted for his crimes, an inquest heard.

Brian Newcombe (52) had robbed and murdered 88 year old former prize fighter Jack Shuttleworth in Yorkshire in August, 1989, and then went on the run for seven weeks as the glib conman with a criminal record stretching back 30 years travelled throughout Scotland - including Orkney - to elude police.

He met 55 year old Mrs Margaret McOnie - who was to become his second victim - in Inverness and brought her to Orkney on holiday. The inquest was told that Newcombe preyed on lonely middle aged women, offering them the promise of marriage and a life of luxury.

They stayed at a Kirkwall guest house with Newcombe using the name "Dave Kerr" in the week before the 1989 County Show, visiting the Italian chapel where Newcombe was photographed in front of the altar.

A week later, he murdered Mrs McOnie and hid her body in a peat bog in Sutherland. Newcombe later claimed that she had threatened to turn him in to the police for the murder of Jack Shuttleworth.

Newcombe was eventually tracked down by the police to a Nottinghamshire guest house and admitted the two murders to Detective Superintendent Ian Peacock of North Yorkshire Police. However he committed suicide before his case went before the courts.

Detective Superintendent Peacock said: "So far as I am concerned they were both cold blooded killings. He showed no remorse at all during the interviews I had with him about the murders, nothing at all."

Fire hits hotel

One of Orkney's best known hotels, the Standing Stones Hotel at Stenness, was devastated by fire on March 17, 1989.

The blaze was discovered as the owner Mr Bob Ross and his staff were preparing a dinner dance for 100 members of the Strathspey and Reel Society.

The building was evacuated and Mr Ross and his three children got out safely, but Mr Ross then had to pass on the bad news to his wife Linda who was in Shetland for an intercounty netball match.

"It was a very serious fire made worse by the high winds," said Stromness fire brigade officer Paul Hounslow, whose team of firefighters was on duty for nearly 12 hours.

Orkney rescue

The world's worst oil pollution disaster - when the tanker *Exxon Valdez* lost its cargo into the sea after grounding off Alaska in March, 1989 saw five Orkney men recruited to help in the massive clean-up operation.

First to go was Attie Walls of Glaitness Road, Kirkwall, and he was joined by John Thornton of the dive boat *Scapa Courier*, Kirkwall diver John Oxer, Jock Cordock of St Margaret's Hope, and Orphir diver Steve Roberts. They were employed on "skimmer boats" scooping oil from the surface of the water.

Poll Tax battles underway

The Poll Tax - or Community Charge - was imposed on Scotland by the Conservative Government amidst complaints that it would bring hardship and depopulation to Orkney as councillors fixed a rate of £148 - £122 personal community charge and £26 water community charge - for the county.

It would mean big increases, compared with the previous rating system, for the country and island areas which would now be paying exactly the same as Kirkwall, regardless of the fact they enjoyed few of the same services.

County convener Edwin Eunson said Orkney Islands Council would use £1 million from council reserves to hold down the charge to an acceptable level but Shapinsay councillor Jim Sinclair complained: "The whole concept of the Poll Tax is so unfair."

There was certainly a reluctance to pay the charge. In September, 1989, the Orkney Islands Council sent out warning demands to 1,600, out of 15,000 people on the local poll tax register, who had not paid. Ten per cent of the money had not been paid a year later.

In 1993, the Poll Tax was abolished to be replaced by "Son of the Poll Tax" - the Council Tax.

Orkney farm park

Harray farmer Ron Savage set up the Orkney Farm Park, for rare breeds of farm animal, at Harray.

Ten breeds of sheep included the Manx Loghtan, Lewis Blackface and the local North Ronaldsay, while among the five cattle breeds were the Gloucester, a breed thought to date back 13,000 years, short-horned Shetlands and the old British Longhorn.

Unfortunately, the farm park did not prove a long-term commercial success, and closed five years later.

£60,000 shocker for pensioners

Ned Spence (76) and his wife Maisie (72), who had lived in a residential caravan by the Harray loch for the previous 20 years, were told by the North of Scotland Hydro Electric Board that the cost of installing mains electricity would be £60,000!

"I do not know how anyone could reasonably expect an elderly pensioner couple to find £60,000 for vital supplies," Orkney MP Mr Jim Wallace told the House of Commons.

Ned Spence - known to generations of fishermen as a boatman on the Harray Loch - said: "Other people get electricity for next to nothing, and they are asking £60,000 from us. We are severely handicapped during the night, we are here in the dark. We have a generator but we can't run it all night because it is too expensive. The council ought to pay it - we can't. Electricity was taken to Orkney for the people. Why should it penalise them?"

Striking it rich

A coin found in the garden of Harray Stores was identified by a museum expert as being up to 800 years old - and from Ceylon!

The small copper coin was found by Mrs Netta Wylie while digging the vegetable plot at the stores.

The design on the coin closely resembled those issued by Queen Lilavisti who reigned at the end of the 12th century, said Mr Nicholas Holmes of the Royal Museum of Scotland.

A Loganair Islander aircraft flies over Kirkwall Pier as it was until major extension work began at the end of the 1980s.
(Picture courtesy of Orkney Library photographic archive)

Farewell old friend

Mr William Robertson (74) of Myrtle Cottage, Holm, bid a sad farewell to what was believed to be Orkney's oldest goose which died at the grand old age of 43 in February, 1989. He had got the bird from his brother Albert in 1948 when she was already two years old.

Changes at the bar

Mrs Jean Johnston retired as the licensee of the Pomona Inn, Finstown, ending a family link with the premises which stretched back to 1900, as Mr and Mrs David Hutchison became the new owners in 1989.

World champion

Richard Corsie, a 22 year old Edinburgh postman whose grandparents came from Rousay, won the 1989 World Indoor Bowls Championships - and a first prize of £18,000.

Orkney film premiere

The film *Venus Peter*, made entirely on location in Orkney, had its United Kingdom premiere in Kirkwall as part of the 1989 St Magnus Festival.

The film was based on the novel *A Twelve Months And A Day* by Christopher Rush. Produced by Christopher Young and directed by Ian Sellar, the film was set in a small fishing town and revolved around the life of Peter, a young boy played by Stromness schoolboy Gordon Strachan.

Sinead Cusack had the role of his schoolteacher while his grandfather was played by the actor Roy McAnally (63) who tragically died a week before the Kirkwall premiere at his home in Ireland.

Hotel honours for couple

Husband and wife team Henryk and Joyce Zywiecki retired after a total of 82 years service - as head cook and pastry cook - at the Kirkwall Hotel.

Henryk (63) arrived in Orkney with the Polish Army at the end of World War Two. He met Joyce at the old Cosmo ballroom and they married in 1947.

They had prepared meals for two prime ministers, the King of Norway, the Queen and Prince Philip and the Queen Mother.

Call-up for Scotland

Kirkwall athlete Linda Low cut short a visit to the Faroe islands to return home when she was called up to represent Scotland in the javelin in a junior international against Northern Ireland. She still had time, however, to win two gold medals - in the shot and the javelin - for Orkney in the 1989 Island Games.

The man who carried a million

Captain David Pottinger, master of the Pentland Firth ferry *St Ola,* who, it was estimated, carried around one million passengers between Stromness and Scrabster during his career with P&O. A replacement *St Ola* began service on the route in 1993. She was the former Baltic ferry *Eckeroe* and was actually older than her predecessor, which was built in 1973, but she could carry twice as many vehicles.

(Picture courtesy of Orkney Photographic)

Liberal Democrat leader Paddy Ashdown pictured at the controls in the wheelhouse of the ferry *Shapinsay,* with her master Harvey Groat, during a visit to Orkney.

(Picture courtesy of Orkney Photographic)

The year of 1978 and three "men at the top" in Orkney life were, from the left, Mr George Marwick, the first convener of Orkney Islands Council and, twenty years later, to become Lord Lieutenant of Orkney; the Rev Bill Cant, who served as minister of St Magnus Cathedral for more than twenty years after moving to Kirkwall in 1968; and Mr William Thomson, rector of Kirkwall Grammar School, from 1971 to 1991. (Pictures courtesy of Harry Russell, Orkney Photographic and Orkney Library photographic archive, respectively)

Ferry trip to 'financial disaster'

The notion of a "short sea" ferry link between Caithness and South Ronaldsay is an idea which has refused to die for the past 100 years. Its supporters argue that a crossing of just six miles must be preferable to the traditional Orkney route between Stromness and Scrabster which is more than 20 miles longer. And, of course, if it was as simple as that, they would be right.

But in 1989 the whole subject of a short sea ferry exploded into bitter words and recriminations in what was probably to be the most contentious local issue to divide the islands in the 20th century.

Millions of pounds were spent on an ill-fated venture which ended in inglorious failure and even led to a call for Orkney Islands Council to be suspended for "gross mishandling of public money."

The concept of a short sea ferry was not new - it could be traced back to the 19th century - and twice there had been serious discussions about launching such a shipping service in the 20th century.

In May, 1909, Orkney County Council "resolved to do all in its power to further the proposal for the erection of a pier" at Gills Bay as the Caithness terminal for such a link. Two years later, however, the proposed Gills Bay harbour scheme was estimated to cost £140,000 - the equivalent of more than £10 millions at 1999 prices - and support faltered. "Would any sane man dream of such an expenditure for a scheme of this sort?" asked Councillor William MacLennan at a meeting of Orkney Islands Council in May, 1911.

And, by December, 1912, Caithness County Council was complaining that no word had been heard on the Gills Bay scheme from Orkney County Council for "months or years." The idea was dormant for the next half a century.

It revived again in 1968 when the idea was backed by a company called Western Ferries, and a feasibility study was commissioned by the Highlands and Islands Development Board from the firm of consultants, Kinord Associates.

South Ronaldsay councillor Colonel James Goodsir was a keen supporter of the project, and said there was a groundswell of demand for such a service. and, in March, 1969, 400 people packed the Orkney Arts Theatre to hear the case for a short sea shipping link.

However, the consultants' report rejected the idea of a service from John o' Groats to South Ronaldsay as impracticable and too costly, and, in October, 1969, the Highlands and Islands Development Board came down firmly in favour of the Scrabster-Stromness route, operated by a modern roll-on, roll-off vehicle ferry.

And in October, 1970, Orkney Islands Council rejected support of short sea proposals by 17 votes to four.

That might have been the end of it. However, it has to be accepted that Orkney was at the mercy of the monopoly position enjoyed by P&O Ferries at the time. There was a concern that the level of service was too low, while the level of prices was too high.

A summer-only passenger service, between John o' Groats and Burwick in South Ronaldsay, had been successfully established by the Thomas and Bews company, but P&O still dominated the freight market especially.

And, so it was, in the summer of 1985, that Orkney heard of the formation of a new company called Orkney Sealink, backed by Kirkwall and South Ronaldsay businessmen, to operate a year-round short sea crossing between Gills Bay and Burwick. The initial estimates were £1.5 million for a vessel; £600,000 for the terminal at Gills Bay; and £900,000 for Burwick terminal - a total of £3 millions - plus £2 millions for improvements to the South Ronaldsay road.

It was to be the prelude to what one respected councillor was later to describe as "the worst financial disaster our islands have ever experienced."

In January, 1988, Orkney Sealink submitted plans to Orkney Islands Council for a new roll-on, roll-off terminal at Burwick. As outline permission was granted, Councillor Billy Dass said: "I see it as being as important for Orkney as the coming of the oil industry."

The Scottish Office would not fund a study on the potential of the short sea route, saying that it would be better done nearer the time that the P&O ferry *St Ola* was due to be replaced. But by now the band wagon was already rolling.

The name of the company was changed from Orkney Sealink to Orkney Ferries and a 39 page prospectus was launched offering one million £1 shares in the project. In its prospectus, Orkney Ferries said it would approach Orkney Islands Council for a £1 million loan from oil reserve funds, and invite the council to subscribe for £500,000 of shares.

On to the scene as directors of Orkney Ferries came John Rose, a director of the Marine Development company, and Ken Cadenhead, finance director with a ship owning and management company, Harrisons (Clyde).

Already, voices of concern were being raised about the project. "If the council passes this application, it will be a bottomless pit of spending," said Councillor George Wylie. However, opponents of the plan lost by 12 votes to eight in a move to reject any council support, and detailed permission was given for the Burwick terminal while a council working party was set up to negotiate with the company.

In May, 1988, the OIC agreed to take £150,000 worth of shares. The council would grant £2 million to Orkney Ferries to build the terminals at Gills Bay and Burwick, which would then be owned by the council through the auspices of Orkney Islands Shipping Company. The deal between the council and Orkney Ferries was signed in November, 1988, with John Rose and Ken Cadenhead signing for the company and Edwin Eunson and George Stevenson for the OIC.

In the early summer of 1989, the new vessel to operate the service for Orkney Ferries was launched - a £2.5 million, twin-screw ship, the *Varagen*, built at the Selby, Yorkshire, shipyard of Cochranes, and designed to carry up to 170 passengers, four 38 tonne trailer units or 33 cars, at an operational speed of 14 knots

However, by now, the costs of the venture were escalating to worrying proportions. In April, 1989, it was revealed that Orkney Ferries would be taking a £1 million loan, at reduced interest, from the council, and then, in June,1989, that the OIC had doubled its shareholding in the company to maintain a 20 per cent stake.

And a picture of disarray was emerging at the sites of the two terminals. Work had been disrupted by bad weather during the winter, and the terminal construction costs were running ahead of budget. Orkney Ferries said it was to make a new approach to the council for up to £600,000 extra to construct a breakwater at Gills Bay.

It was then that the first real financial bombshell struck home as it was revealed that there had been a total overspend at Gills Bay and Burwick of £3.18 millions above the original estimate of £1.83 millions.

Orkney Islands Council rejected the plea for extra funding and members voted that the council should assume responsibility for the completion of the terminals. More spending would be required as it was revealed that Burwick required further dredging.

And the launch of the new service seemed even more remote when, in July, 1989, the master of the *Varagen*, Gordon Cameron, resigned before a passenger had set foot on board

The *Varagen*, after languishing at Grangemouth for 18 months, was eventually given a role serving the North Isles.
(Picture courtesy of Orkney Photographic)

following a disagreement over whether it was safe to dock at Gills Bay during sea trials.

However, against all the odds, the maiden voyage of the *Varagen* did take place on Tuesday, August 15, 1989, when, without prior warning, the ship sailed, under the command of Captain Chris Irvine, from Gills Bay to Houton in Scapa Flow.

Its only passengers were Tyneside couple Thomas and Mary Marshall and their car. The first vehicle to make the journey in the opposite direction across the Pentland Firth to Gills Bay was owned by Kirkwall motor dealer Edgar Milne.

It was too good to last. Just nine days after the short sea service started, the *Varagen* suffered damage on rocks at Gills Bay and had to sail south for repairs. And worse was to follow. The first gale of the autumn in September, 1989, swept away the vehicle linkspan at Gills Bay, and Orkney Islands Council agreed to suspend all work on the terminals.

The dream had become a nightmare without a single scheduled sailing between Gills Bay and Burwick. "Many people are very angry about the waste of public money and the lack of foresight and specialist knowledge we should have had from the start," said Councillor Brenda Robertson.

There was even a call from Eric Stockton on Sanday to Orkney MP Jim Wallace "to consider possible Parliamentary action to suspend Orkney Islands Council for gross mishandling of public money."

As the short sea crossing became arguably the most contentious issue to ever rock the islands, an opinion poll conducted by *The Orcadian* showed 58 per cent of respondents in favour of the council abandoning the entire project. Instead, at a private meeting, councillors sanctioned £3 million more to complete the terminals. In the meantime, the crewmen of the *Varagen* were laid off. The ship would languish at Grangemouth for the next 18 months.

As a report by consulting engineers Coode Blizard showed that it would cost another £5.9 millions to complete the Burwick

and Gills Bay terminals, on top of the £6.7 millions that had already been spent in total on the short sea project by Orkney Islands Council, Orkney's MP Jim Wallace called for an independent inquiry into the council's handling of the affair - a call backed by the community councils in Kirkwall and Stromness, and a petition signed by 4,500 people.

The OIC agreed to appoint a firm of Edinburgh-based consulting engineers, Posford Duvivier, to carry out an inquiry into the project. The main requirements were to assess the work carried out at the terminals, to decide what was needed to establish a service and to consider the economic viability of such a service. The consultants were also to assess the overall structure of the ferry transport system in Orkney.

In the wake of the short sea episode, six sitting councillors - including four committee chairmen - lost their seats on the OIC in the elections of May, 1990. County convener Edwin Eunson did not seek re-election, and Councillor Jackie Tait was elected the new county convener.

For the only occasion in peacetime, *The Orcadian* published a special edition to report the findings and recommendations of the Posford Duvivier inquiry.

The 350 page document said that a further £5.9 millions would be needed to refloat the Short Sea venture and it would still be "a second best, better than nothing" proposition. The consultants said it would be unreliable as a year-round service and, therefore, they challenged whether it would attract freight.

A bigger ship, probably costing £10 millions, would be required to improve reliability, and, in the meantime, it would be ten years before profits would be achieved.

The report suggested that if the Short Sea service did proceed, the Orkney Islands Shipping Company should not be at the helm. "We do not believe that the company has the commercial, marketing or operating expertise to run a ferry service on a commercial, profit-making basis," said the consultants.

Instead, for the future, the consultants suggested that P&O

Orkney harbours director Captain Bob Sclater suggested that the council could operate its own ship on the Stromness-Scrabster route.
(Picture courtesy of Orkney Photographic)

Scottish Ferries should streamline its operations with two ships operating a Scrabster-Orkney-Shetland service. (This was an option which was immediately and understandably derided in Shetland).

Orkney Ferries had registered a loss of £585,000 in the 1989-90 financial year, company chairman Ken Cadenhead reported, but he said the company would endeavour to find new finance to continue. "It would be a gross injustice to the people of Orkney if the project is not completed," he said.

The option of using the *Varagen* to operate a service between Wick and South Ronaldsay was considered and rejected, but, in the council chamber, opponents failed by 14 votes to ten to effectively quash the OIC's interest in the Short Sea route. Instead, the council would investigate other options, including the suggestion by Orkney harbours director Captain Bob Sclater that the council could build a new £14 millions roll-on, roll-off vessel to operate a rival service to P&O Scottish Ferries on the Stromness-Scrabster route.

Captain Sclater said: "I believe that this would be the best way forward. It would relieve the problems on Orkney Islands Council of building new piers in Caithness. It would be a reliable, economic and safe way of operating a new system, would give competition to P&O, and we would be able to tailor the rates across the Pentland Firth to suit the people in Orkney and also to suit the influxes of tourists which have been envisaged."

On the other hand, the Short Sea crossing would result in a total loss to the council of £20 millions, he said, and there would still be "a grey area" regarding the reliability and feasibility of the project, he said.

The councils first priority, however, was to resolve the future of the *Varagen*. The ship had been built for Orkney Ferries but then sold and leased back from British Linen Leasing to allow Orkney Ferries to clear its overdraft. However, in the leasing contract, there was a £2.8 million penalty clause in the event of the leasing deal being terminated. In the end, Orkney Islands Council made the best of a bad job, and merged the *Varagen* into the North Isles fleet of the Orkney Islands Shipping Company.

Whatever the failings of Orkney Islands Council in its handling of the Short Sea episode, the reasons for OIC support for a rival service to P&O Scottish Ferries were clearly underlined in December, 1990, as P&O announced price rises of up to 23 per cent from the following year.

However, the failings of the Orkney Islands Council had not gone unnoticed. And, at the start of 1992, the watchdog of public spending in Scotland, the Controller of Audit, Mr John Broadfoot, produced a 17 page report listing the council's "deficiencies" in the management of the Short Sea project.

In it, Mr Broadfoot said the council had failed to seek technical advice and viability studies, and had not pressed for independent engineers to look after their interests. These shortcomings had been compounded by the OIC's failure to keep written records or reports.

The initial OIC commitment of £3.15 millions for two completed terminals had increased to potential spending of £17.7 millions, said the report. Councillors in favour of the Short Sea crossing had been so committed to the project that it may have "prejudiced commercial reality."

Four months later, members of the Audit Commission - the official arbiters of local authority spending - travelled to Kirkwall to quiz councillors and officials over the affair, and, in January, 1993, a damning report from the Commission for Local Authority Accounts described the council management of the project as "deficient" and the OIC decision-making process as "inadequate." The report stated:"There is no evidence that there was any monitoring on behalf of the council of the progress of work or expenditure by the council."

Councillor Jim Moar said the report had, for the first time, given the opportunity for the truth to be told, and for the "veil of secrecy" to be lifted. He thought that councillors who had supported the project had been swayed by notions of "romanticism" and added: "It is quite evident that they have followed a false and fanatical philosophy which resulted in the worst financial disaster our islands have ever experienced. Millions of pounds were recklessly and needlessly lost; wisdom and common sense thrown out the window, replaced by extreme ideology and dogma."

Councillors agreed that the dual role of chief executive and finance director Mr Ron Gilbert should be ended with Mr Gilbert continuing as chief excutive and a new finance director, Mr David Robertson, appointed.

Orkney Ferries was struck off the register of Scottish companies on February 5, 1993. The Registrar of Companies for Scotland, Mr James Henderson, said his department had received no accounts from the company since those of March 31, 1990. Three years later, the name "Orkney Ferries" was to resurface, however, as it was adopted as the new name of the Orkney Islands Shipping Company.

And the notion of a regular Short Sea service refuses to die. In 1998, South Ronaldsay businessman Mr Andrew Banks bought a former Caledonian MacBrayne vessel, which he renamed the *Pentalina B*, and set up Pentland Ferries Limited with the intention of operating a Short Sea service between St Margaret's Hope and Gills Bay. Perhaps, at the start of the new century, the dream will finally become true. It seems though that Mr Banks will have to achieve his goal without the financial support of Orkney Islands Council.

Hostage held as 'human shield'

1990

An Orcadian lived through the nightmare of being held hostage as a 'human shield' in an Iraqi munitions factory as the world prepared to face the challenge of Saddam Hussein.

The Middle East had been plunged into turmoil following the Iraqi invasion of Kuwait in August, 1990, and Kenny Linklater (32) formerly of North Tofts, Egilsay, who was working at a Kuwaiti power station when the invasion came, was forced to go into hiding.

He later told *The Orcadian* how the drama began on August 2 as he was woken by the sound of gunfire as Saddam's troops rolled into Kuwait City in the early hours. By 9am, his flat was in the thick of a battle as Iraqi tanks moved down the motorway towards the Kuwait army barracks directly opposite his flat.

Despite the invasion, he and his workmates were able to continue getting to work each day, passing through roadblocks without being stopped. However, on August 20, Iraqi troops started to arrest British nationals.

It was then that Kenny Linklater and his fellow workmates went into hiding in their apartment block, starting a monotonous eight week regime of rationing food as they were holed up listening to the BBC World Service and playing cards.

Mr Linklater, who had worked in Kuwait for nearly two years, managed to smuggle out letters to his parents, Tom (65) and Violet, and sister Marjorie at North Howe, near Peterhead, telling them of his plight.

Living on one meal a day, the men were fast losing weight before they made contact with some New Zealanders who were able to get more food to them.

But on October 18, the soldiers came. "There was a knock on the door and they got us all out of the flat. We were told we were going to Baghdad."

Saddam Hussein had decided to round up the foreigners and transfer them to munitions factories near the Iraqi capital to deter possible attack by the international force building up in the Gulf. (As the tension grew, Orkney's regiment, the Queen's Own Highlanders, was heading to the region to reinforce the "Desert Rats.")

Kenny Linklater and his companions were sent on a ten hour journey across the desert and then, with another 15 men, he was held at a munitions factory where the hostages were forced to endure cramped conditions for six weeks.

However, two weeks before Christmas, 1990, Saddam Hussein dropped his "human shield" tactic and his change of heart saw the hostages released. Without warning, Kenny Linklater was flown home. "When the wheels of the plane lifted off at Baghdad, everybody cheered," he said as he headed home for a family reunion. He planned to take up his old job at the power station in Peterhead.

A few weeks later, however, several Orcadians found themselves caught up in the crisis as the Gulf War exploded, with the Allies moving in to challenge Saddam's forces.

Sanday nurse Angela Seatter (27) was working in a hospital in the Saudi Arabian capital of Riyadh as Iraqi Scud missiles hit the city in early 1991.

By this time, the Queen's Own Highlanders had a contingent of 400 men moving towards the front line and scores of Orkney families were left anxiously waiting for news of their relatives in uniform. Corporal Mike Walker (29) from Kirkwall was there with the Queen's Own Highlanders, along with Army cook Jason Walters, and three Kirkwall privates - Mark Newlands, Cameron Scott and Andy Shearer. Another was Tony Robertson with the Royal Scots, while Private Wayne Gillespie was with the Royal Scots Dragoon Guards.

Lieutenant John Johnston, from Harray, was serving in the Royal Army Medical Corps, while Lance Corporal Robbie Nelson (23) from Shapinsay was there with the Royal Engineers.

Thankfully, they - and all the others with Orkney links - returned home safely after the war.

But it was the last battle that the Queen's Own Highlanders would win in the field. Eight months later it was announced the Queen's Own Highlanders - which incorporated the Seaforth Highlanders, which had traditionally been regarded as Orkney's regiment for the first half of the century - faced the axe under Government defence cuts.

It had been deemed politically correct to allow the regiment to risk lives at war, but politically advantageous to then make some tax cuts.

One of the last duties of the Queen's Own Highlanders before heading for the Gulf War was to travel to Orkney in 1990 to be honoured with the freedom of the county - accepted by Major General J.C.O.R. Hopkinson, Colonel of the Regiment, after a ceremony at St Magnus Cathedral.

Kenny Linklater enjoys a reunion with his mother and father, Violet and Tom Linklater, after his ordeal as a "human shield" hostage of Saddam Hussein in Iraq.

(Picture from the files of The Orcadian)

Farmers suffer the great betrayal

One of the greatest betrayals of Orkney farmers throughout the 20th century was the political prevarication at national level in the wake of what was to become known as the BSE crisis.

It was not a problem of Orkney's making - but Orkney farmers were forced to pay the price.

The disease of Bovine Spongiform Encephalopathy had been identified as far back as 1984 in Kent. But six years of talk, and little action, had seen the national implications of the so-called "Mad Cow Disease" have a shocking knock-on effect in Orkney by 1990.

Orkney had the lowest incidence of BSE in Britain - there had been just six cases (and none of them in beef animals) in the previous four years in the county's total cattle herd of nearly 95,000 animals. The county's BSE rate was 20 times lower than the British average, and all the outbreaks to date could be traced to imported animals.

But Orkney could not avoid the national flak. Cattle prices fell at Kirkwall Mart and the Orkney Meat plant was forced to go on short-time working in May, 1990. Orkney Islands Council was forced to issue a statement saying it would continue to be the policy of the school meals service to offer Orkney beef on its menus.

Orkney National Farmers Union urged its members to adopt a voluntary ban on importing into beef herds all cattle born before July 18, 1988, the date when cattle feed made from animal protein, including sheep, suspected as the source of BSE, was banned.

Cattle prices at Kirkwall Mart in the first July sale of 1990 were lower than the prices farmers had achieved five years earlier. In July, 1989, steers had averaged 136.4p a kilo and heifers 117.4p a kilo. By July, 1990, the respective averages had fallen to 108.7p and 101.7p.

"No industry can operate at those sort of income levels," said Orkney NFU president George Eunson, who warned that approaching £1 million could be wiped off the value of Orkney Cattle by the end of the year.

But still the slide continued. By 1993, a confidential survey, jointly funded by the NFU, Orkney Islands Council and Orkney Enterprise, which analysed the finances of nearly a quarter of Orkney's farms, showed some Orkney farmers were in debt to the tune of up to five times their annual profits - with the worst-hit owing more than £2,000 for every cow they kept.

The results showed that a number of small Orkney farms were making as little as £2,695 a year, but the worst-hit farmers were those with a herd size of 31-40 cattle who, on average, owed £24.959, with an average annual profit of only £4, 877. Some of the bigger farms were paying well over £10,000 a year in bank interest payments alone.

And most Orkney farmers will justifiably claim that things got worse after that!

Then three came along at once

Orkney welcomed three Royal visitors in the course of just two months in 1990.

Princess Anne, the Princess Royal, made her first visit to Orkney since her childhood when she visited Kirkwall - taking the controls of Kirkwall lifeboat - and Stromness in July, 1990.

The Princess visited Scapa Knitwear in Kirkwall, and spoke to young riders at a gymkhana in Stromness, as well as meeting members of the Orkney branch of Riding for the Disabled.

A month later, her brother, Prince Andrew, made a surprise visit when, as a serving officer in the Royal Navy, he airlifted to hospital in Kirkwall a patient from HMS *Campeltown* in Scapa Flow in a Lynx helicopter.

The next day he came ashore and played a round of golf against Orkney Golf Club vice-captain Andy McGinn - to become the first Royal visitor to the club in 101 years.

Prince Michael of Kent made up the Royal treble as he travelled to Orkney to open the extended RNXS headquarters of the Royal Naval Auxiliary Service at Scapa.

There was another Royal appointment for Orkney in 1990 as Orkney Health Board's Stromness-born general manager Dr James Cromarty was appointed Honorary Physician to the Queen for Scotland, an honorary appointment for three years.

In the 1993 New Year's Honours List, Dr Cromarty was also made an OBE.

Shipping revolution for the isles

A new era for the North Isles began with the arrival of two new vessels for the Orkney Islands Shipping Company as part of a massive £23 million programme to introduce roll-on, roll-off vehicle ferries to the isles.

The two new vessels - *Earl Thorfinn* and *Earl Sigurd* - were built at a cost of £5.4 millions to replace the *Orcadia* and the *Islander*.

A new £830,000 ferry *Shapinsay* had begun operating a ro-ro service to her namesake island a few months earlier in 1989.

The new *Earl Thorfinn* and *Earl Sigurd* - which had been given the go-ahead by the Conservative Government just before the 1987 General Election - had to operate as conventional cargo vessels for a time as it was December, 1992, before the new ro-ro terminal at Rapness, Westray, was completed.

The *Orcadia*, which had given 29 years service to the North Isles, made her final run on August 24, 1990, before being sold as a supply boat to a firm with interests in the Caribbean.

It meant that the 20th century would end with North Ronaldsay and Papa Westray as the only two islands with no roll-on, roll-off ferry facilities in Orkney.

Golfing ace

Stromness golfer Dennis Watt (20) scored a hole in one - twice within minutes - at the 186 yard sixth and 105 yard eighth holes of the Stromness course during a medal round in June, 1990. It was a feat that had never been equalled in the 100 years at Stromness Golf Club, which celebrated its centenary in 1990. He eventually completed his round in 67.

New Lord Lieutenant

Brigadier Malcolm Gray Dennison was named, in March, 1990, as Orkney's new Lord Lieutenant to succeed Colonel Sir Robert Macrae who retired.

The son of Captain John Dennison of Shapinsay and Margaret Gray of Roeberry, South Ronaldsay, he was born in what was then Nyasaland in 1924 and returned to Orkney ten years later. He studied at Edinburgh University, before joining the RAF and serving in Bomber Command in World War Two.

After the war, he studied Arabic and, in 1955, he joined the Sultan's Armed Forces in Oman, becoming director of intelligence and then adviser to the Sultan of Oman. He retired in 1983 and returned to the family home at Roeberry to live.

One of his first tasks as the new Lord Lieutenant was to officially open the new St Margaret's Hope school in 1990.

Ashes fall to earth

The Royal Air Force apologised after a special mission to lay a serviceman's ashes in Scapa Flow went wrong. The canister containing the remains was released too soon from a plane and, instead of landing in the sea, came down in a ditch at Tankerness, where it was discovered by local postman Bertie Cromarty.

The canister had been dropped from a Nimrod aircraft at the request of relatives of the deceased. "The crew of the aircraft were horrified at the mistake and it is an unfortunate occurrence they would prefer to forget," said an RAF spokesman.

"Thanks to the vigilance of a member of the public, it was returned to us, and successfully deposited in Scapa Flow."

Mystery drugs haul

A drugs haul seized by police, coastguards and customs officers, prompted a mystery in Orkney in April, 1990, as a consignment of cannabis, weighing 80 kilos and apparently worth £250,000 on the streets, was washed ashore between Stromness and Birsay.

The first discovery was made by a local resident who found a 25 kilo bale of the drug. Glasgow-based customs officer David Bain was quoted by *The Orcadian*: "Clearly drug smugglers have been operating in the area and something has gone far wrong."

Life-saver at 30,000 feet

Jack Sykes (88), known to many Orcadians as the former boss of the Sykes-Robertson electronics company on Sanday, had an amazing escape on a jet airliner at 30,000 feet as his life was saved by a doctor who carried out an emergency operation - with a penknife.

Mr Sykes was on a flight to San Antonia, USA, when he fell unconscious after choking. An anaesthetist with the US Air Force came forward and, using a borrowed penknife, removed the obstruction and got Mr Sykes breathing again.

The jct later made an emergency landing at Memphis to allow Mr Sykes to be taken to hospital.

He had formed the Sanday electronics company in 1967 with Mr George Robertson, although Mr Sykes later moved back to Yorkshire and the company closed down.

Dark horse for Sanday

Seyl the wonder horse was heralded as a potential Derby winner. Instead, he had to settle for winning the horse section of the 1990 Sanday Show.

The thoroughbred stallion - a half brother to the 1989 Derby winner Nashwan - was bred in Kentucky and had been destined for a career as a flat race star when he was purchased as a year-ling for 750,000 dollars by Sheik Mohammed, one of the most powerful figures in world racing, in 1982.

Seyl was entered for 1984 Derby but then a fetlock injury ended his career. He was sold at the 1984 Newmarket autumn sales for just 3,500 guineas, and bought by Marion Gibson who later moved, with the horse, to Sanday from Yorkshire.

Brave new world for plucky Susan

Plucky 14 year old Kirkwall schoolgirl Susan Eccles won the admiration of Orcadians as she was given a heart transplant after an agonising five month wait for a suitable donor for the only operation that could save her life.

The operation was carried out by world famous surgeon Professor Yacoub at the Harefield Hospital in Middlesex in February, 1990. "We never abandoned hope but Suzie was getting worse all the time and we were beginning to despair," her mother, Liz, told *The Orcadian*. "Her survival was being measured in weeks rather than months."

Susan was able to return home in May ready for a new life. "We were confident that Suzie would come through the operation. She is a fighter and we knew she would not give up at that stage," said her mother.

Sadly, in June, 1992, Susan died at the age of 16 after a brief illness. But her short life had proved an inspiration to many others.

Two other Orcadians helped to develop the pioneering heart surgery by receiving transplants in 1990. Stromness fisherman Jim Leslie (44) had a transplant at the Freeman Hospital in Newcastle in May, 1990. Sadly he lost his fight for life three weeks later.

And Mrs Kristine Graham (51) - who lived in Dalcross, near Inverness, but was the daughter of a well-known Kirkwall family - died a few days after a transplant, also at the Freeman Hospital. She was the granddaughter of Mr John Jolly who founded the Kirkwall firm of coal merchants and shipping agents in 1902.

Happy Valley

Orcadian Edwin Harrold - who transformed an area of Orkney pasture into a wooded paradise of trees, shrubs and flowers known as Happy Valley - was given a top national award to commemorate his work.

Shapinsay-born Mr Harrold - he was aged 83 in 1990 - moved to Bankburn, Stenness, in 1948, and immediately began his labour of love to create a landscape unique in the county.

In April, 1990, he was presented with the first David Stephen Award, promoted by *The Scotsman* in memory of naturalist and author David Stephen, a regular contributor to the newspaper.

The presentation was made by Mr Magnus Linklater, the Orcadian editor of *The Scotsman*. "The more we looked at the terms of the award, which is the protection and enhancement of the environment, the more we realised that Edwin Harrold's extraordinary and dedicated contribution had to be the winner," he said.

Freedom

Three prominent figures in Orkney public life were to be made freemen of Orkney in 1990 - county convener Edwin Eunson, who stood down after 40 years in local government; the retiring Lord Lieutenant of the county, Colonel Sir Robert Macrae; and Brigadier S.P. Robertson, the founder of the Kirkwall-based oil company of S. and J.D. Robertson, and Depute Lieutenant of Orkney.

County triumph

The Davidson family of Skaill, Sandwick, won the supreme cattle championship at Orkney's County Show for the third successive year - with a different animal on each occasion.

The 1990 champion, shown by Stewart and Colin Davidson, was a two year old Aberdeen-Angus heifer Nicks Delia, which went on to retain her title at the 1991 County Show.

New rector

Mr Eric Sinclair (42), the son of an Orcadian, was appointed to replace the retiring rector of Kirkwall Grammar School, Mr William Thomson. Mr Sinclair was previously depute rector of the Bridge of Don Academy, Aberdeen. Mr David Sillar became rector of Stromness Academy.

MP dies

Kirkwall Grammar School-educated Mr Norman Buchan, the Labour MP for Paisley South, died in 1990 at the age of 67. His father had worked in Orkney as a civil servant prior to World War Two.

Uproar in the night streets

1991

There was uproar in the night-time streets of Kirkwall as makeshift barricades were thrown up by an "unruly mob" of 300 people who staged a midnight demonstration.

They were protesting over a decision by Orkney Licensing Board to cut back drinking hours, forcing the two major night spots in the town to stop serving drink at midnight. Both Matchmakers and the Casablanca shut their doors for the night, claiming it was no longer financially viable for them to open on Saturday nights.

The crowd which gathered in Kirkwall's Broad Street and then marched to the home of licensing board chairman, Councillor Allan Taylor, was denounced by Orkney's senior police officer, Chief Inspector John Ratter, as an "unruly mob."

However, it was a stark illustration that the low-key (and low-staffed) policing of Orkney - indeed any community - is made possible only with the consensus of the people. Chief Inspector Ratter spelled out the events of the night in a formal statement.

He said: "Just after midnight on Sunday, March 4, 1991, a crowd of approximately 300 mainly young people assembled on Broad Street, Kirkwall, throwing makeshift barricades across the main roads and creating a general disturbance.

"After a time they proceeded en masse through Albert Street, Laing Street, Mill Street and thence to the home of a private individual in a residential area of Kirkwall where a further assembly of somewhat depleted numbers, but still in the region of 100 persons, took place.

"During the course of this incident, a number of windows were broken, taxis damaged, a telephone box vandalised and serious alarm and disturbance caused to residents along the entire route."

He added: "Processions or assemblies of people, as witnessed on Sunday morning, which can best be described as an unruly mob, are unconstitutional and cannot be accepted in any content as a lawful demonstration.

"Parents and young people and all others involved should take stock of the situation now and realise the possible confrontational consequences, resulting from actions which are clearly unlawful and inflammatory, demand appropriate response from the police, and are likely to bring about no good in this community."

The following weekend, a high profile police presence - with extra police and dog teams from the South drafted in - saw no repeat of threatened demonstrations. The drinks curfew was eventually relaxed three months later to allow drinking after midnight on Thursday, Friday and Saturday nights.

Festival rockers entertain the crowds

Orkney's biggest musical event of the 20th century saw 5,000 fans of the Scots rock group Runrig pack Kirkwall's Pickaquoy Park for an open air concert as part of the 1991 St Magnus Festival. The four hour, midsummer event passed without trouble, and Runrig lead singer Donnie Munro said: "It was a real pleasure. Watching that sunset as we performed was something special."

(Picture from the files of *The Orcadian*)

The team from the Rotary Club of Kirkwall which went to Romania. Back row, from left: Bruce Dunnet, Eric Green, Robin Hancock, Bill Groundwater and John Holmes. Front: Alan Peace, Bobby Corsie and Jimmy Croy, and Howard Hazell who accompanied the trip for *The Orcadian*.

(Picture courtesy of Orkney Photographic)

Mercy mission to Romania

With nearly £35,000 in cash - and as much again in gifts of clothes and equipment - raised by generous Orcadians, a team from Kirkwall Rotary Club drove 2,500 miles across Europe, to within ten miles of the Soviet border, to take vital supplies to the orphanages and hospitals of the Romanian city of Iasi.

The mercy mission had been conceived after harrowing pictures reached this country of the desperate plight of thousands of children following the fall of the regime of the Romanian dictator Ceaucescu.

The mission - made possible by the vehicles of Kirkwall businessmen Jimmy Croy and Alan Peace, who both made the trip - was led by Orkney county surgeon

Bill Groundwater, with other Rotary Club members Eric Green, Bobby Corsie, John Holmes, Robin Hancock and Bruce Dunnet, and accompanied by the compiler of this book, representing *The Orcadian.*

The team was given a send-off by county convener Jackie Tait, and a crowd of around 300, from Kirkwall's Broad Street in April, 1991.

The convey arrived at its destination six days later in darkness illuminated only by a thunderstorm at a hospital where the Rotarians unloaded food, clothing, medical supplies and other goods for 50 babies and toddlers who were either HIV positive or suffering full blown AIDS.

Bill Groundwater compared conditions

with those of Victorian Britain a century earlier. The nurses were working for the equivalent of £30 a month. At another hospital, 330 patients of all ages, both sexes and varying conditions, were kept behind barred windows. One 14 year old boy was simply left there by his parents who could not afford to keep him.

"We promised the people of Orkney that every penny that was raised would get to where it was most needed. And that is what we have done. Orkney can be truly proud that its generosity will be helping children who are in real need. We have seen some very grim conditions," said Rotary Club president Bobby Corsie as the team arrived back in Kirkwall to a civic reception.

Bill Groundwater and Bobby Corsie join nurses in a chorus of Auld Lang Syne before the Rotary Club members left one of the hospitals in the Romanian city of Iasi.

(Picture by Howard Hazell)

Airlift from stricken ship

A massive air sea rescue operation was mounted on March 5, 1991, after the P&O cargo ship *St Rognvald* lost power in mountainous seas off Orkney.

The master, Captain Brian Robertson, was injured when heavy seas shattered the bridge windows and cut the ship's power. The vessel, en route from Lerwick to Aberdeen, had been unable to berth at Stromness because of the weather.

Helicopters from RAF Lossiemouth and Sumburgh coastguards joined Wick lifeboat and the Orkney tug *Einar* in the dramatic operation to aid the drifting ship.

Fourteen of the 19 people on board - including the injured captain - were air-lifted off the ship as she struggled through force nine gales.

A replacement master, James Winterburn, was flown out and, with the remaining five crew, battled to steer the *St Rognvald* manually into Sinclair Bay, Caithness, accompanied by the Wick lifeboat and *Einar*.

Angus Sinclair in front of the *Orcades Viking II* which, in 1991, was replaced by the *Orcades Viking III*, a 75 metre freezer trawler. (Picture courtesy of Gunnie Moberg)

Monster in the port

Scotland's biggest fishing vessel, the £9 million *Orcades Viking III* - a 75 metre freezer trawler owned by the fishing partnership of Angus Sinclair and Joe Nicolson, with backing from Orkney Islands Council - arrived in her home port of Stromness for the first time in October, 1991.

The vessel which had been built in Denmark had a catching and freezing capacity of 120 tonnes of fish a day. She would replace the *Orcades Viking II* which the owners had sold to Chile.

By the end of 1994, the total annual catch of Orkney fishing vessels was valued at £15 millions - with the catches of the *Orcades Viking III* alone being worth an estimated £3.8 millions.

An estimated 467 people were employed in Orkney's fishing industry - 364 full-time and 103 part-time - according to Orkney Islands Council statistics in 1995.

Century's drift from the isles

The 1991 census - the last of the century - showed that Orkney's population had increased over the previous ten years, for the second decade in succession.

On the day of the census, the number of people in the county was shown to be 19,450 - the highest figure since the 1951 census, which had been the last to show Orkney's population over 20,000.

The 1991 census results showed that the number of households in the county had increased from 7,894 in 1981 to 8,599 in 1991.

But more than 75 per cent of the population now lived on the Orkney Mainland - a total of 15,128 people. And this increased to over 16,400 if the linked islands of South Ronaldsay and Burray were included.

At the start of the century, the population of Westray alone was over 2,000. But by 1991, the population of all the North Isles - Westray, Papa Westray, North Ronaldsay, Eday, Sanday, Stronsay, Rousay, Egilsay and Wyre, and Shapinsay - was only 2,515, or fewer than ten people for each square kilometre of land.

Billion dollar oil deal

Orkney's 20 year link with the Occidental oil company came to an end as it was announced that the American operator of the Flotta oil terminal had reached a 1.35 billion dollar deal with the French company Elf Aquitaine.

Elf would take over all of Occidental's North Sea interests, and the new operation would be run by Elf Enterprise Caledonia. The French chairman of the new company outlined ambitious targets which, he said, could see the terminal handling one million barrels of oil a day by 2010.

Lifeboat pioneer

Karen Miller (30) of Buttquoy Park, Kirkwall, became Orkney's first woman lifeboat member as she joined the crew of the Kirkwall lifeboat *Mickie Salvesen*. Karen, a clerical officer in the Orkney harbours department, came from a lifeboat family - her father was a member of the former Stronsay lifeboat crew.

President

Mrs Phyllis Harcus, of Messigate, Tankerness, became the first woman to hold the office of president of the Orkney Agricultural Society in its 106 year old history as she took over at the December, 1991, AGM of the society.

Football centenary

A crowd of 1,200 at the Bignold Park saw the Kirkwall football club Thorfinn celebrate the club's centenary with a match against a young Aberdeen side which secured a 1-0 victory. Thorfinn introduced 13 year old goalkeeper Graham Mackay as a late substitute.

Show success

The West Mainland Show at Dounby celebrated 100 years in 1991, as the event had first been held at Dounby Farm in 1891. It was not the 100th show, however. Because of interruptions during wartime, that milestone was not reached until 1998.

A five year saga of sorrow

At dawn on Wednesday, February 27, 1991, social workers and police embarked on a course of action that was to see Orkney's good name smeared around the world. Orcadians would be the innocent victims of a slur for which they had no responsibility and no recourse.

Nine children, from four families, were taken away from their parents and the manse of the local minister was raided. It would become known simply as the South Ronaldsay affair - one of the most controversial chapters in Orkney's modern history, and one for which Orkney Islands Council would stand condemned.

The minister of St Magnus Cathedral, Rev Ron Ferguson, a man of calm and reasoned pronouncements, was later to complain that the allegations in South Ronaldsay had subjected the community to an "outrageous smear" and it was hard to see how there could be reconciliation until the slur was publicly and unequivocally withdrawn.

"The whole case has become a grotesque soap opera in which Orkney's reputation has been dragged through the wringer. The name of Orkney is now linked in the public mind with child abuse and this is grossly unfair," he said in a Sunday sermon. "Anybody with a more than passing acquaintance with Orkney knows that it is a fundamentally decent and caring community, one which cares particularly well for its children and young people."

However, the stigma of a case related to child abuse did not fade easily. It was an episode which was prolonged for five years. And even then the memories would continue.

But to understand the background to the affair it is necessary to go back two years prior to the dawn raids of 1991 to an episode which had no direct link with South Ronaldsay but which illustrates a certain disarray in the Orkney Islands Council social work department in the preceding period.

In 1989, the Reporter to the Orkney Children's Panel, Mrs Katherine Kemp, revealed she was seriously concerned for the children in care at the council's Camoran children's home in Kirkwall, and claimed that the OIC was not meeting its obligations under the Social Work Scotland Act. She said things had become so serious that she had called in the Police, saying: "I regret that I can have no confidence in Orkney Islands Council's social work management."

Council chief executive Mr Ron Gilbert described her allegations as "unfounded and unsubstantiated." Chief Inspector John Ratter said a police inquiry had been instigated but added: "To date, no evidence has come to light which would cause the police to proffer any criminal charges."

However, it was revealed that a government-backed investigation into the operation of the social work department had been carried out, and Mr Philip Cooper, chairman of the Children's Panel, said: "At the moment the home has unqualified, inexperienced staff, no officer in charge and no policy. It makes the whole set-up vulnerable and it is unlikely that the Children's Panel can make use of the home at present."

The previous officer in charge of the home had quit after 74 days in the job, accusing the OIC social work department of a lack of support.

Councillors Spencer Rosie and Ian MacDonald led the criticism of the way the social work department was operating. Mr Rosie said: "I feel ashamed that the Camoran House has not operated properly for a long time." Mr MacDonald accused the OIC of holding secret meetings which he compared to "Kangaroo courts in a banana republic." The two critics were later banned from meetings of the social work committee, accused of leaking confidential documents to *The Orcadian*.

However, in April, 1990, Mrs Kemp was suspended from her job as Reporter to the Children's Panel by Orkney Islands Council. She returned from holiday to find her office in East Road, Kirkwall, locked and a letter, suspending her, from the OIC chief executive. He claimed that she was not carrying out her duties and responsibilities in an acceptable manner, and he said in a council report: "The Reporter is an employee of the council and it is not acceptable for employees to make comments to the press regarding the operational activities of other council departments."

Mrs Kemp described the suspension as "unconstitutional and scandalous."

However, the OIC made a formal request to the Secretary of State for Scotland, Malcolm Rifkind, to be allowed to dismiss her. Mr Rifkind asked for a full report from the OIC and responses from Mrs Kemp to enable him to decide.

Mrs Kemp said that improvements had been made at Camoran House since her complaints, and she now had no reservations about its operation, which now came under the ultimate control of Yorkshireman Mr Paul Lee, previously divisional officer for Grampian Region's Gordon district, who, in March, 1990, became the new OIC social work director, succeeding Mr Hugh MacGillivray who had taken early retirement.

It meant that, at the time of the South Ronaldsay raids, the social work director had been in post for less than a year, and Mrs Kemp, who would have been involved as Reporter to the Children's Panel, was suspended. In her place was an interim Reporter, Mr Gordon Sloan, who had been seconded from Strathclyde.

While she was still in her post, Mrs Kemp's role as Reporter had involved her working with the children of a South Ronaldsay family, whose father was serving a prison sentence for offences of abuse. Following her suspension, three of the children, aged seven, eight and nine, were removed from their mother and taken into care by the OIC social work department. It was the interviewing of these children that was to produce the stories which prompted the dawn raids.

In a two hour operation on Wednesday, February 27,1991, police and social workers removed nine children from four families in South Ronaldsay, and, at the same time, detectives swooped on the manse of the minister, the Rev Morris McKenzie, and his wife Janette.

New Zealand-born Mr McKenzie (64), a former lawyer who came to Scotland to study Divinity in 1974 and moved to South Ronaldsay ten years later, complained to *The Orcadian*: "They were accusing me of lewd and libidinous practices. It's an intrusion into manse life."

It transpired later that the three children in care had told stories of a "hooded master" who hooked children into a quarry to abuse them. Social workers had apparently suspected that Mr McKenzie was the "hooded master."

The police, who had been acting on warrants signed by Sheriff A. A. MacDonald, issued a statement which simply said: "Acting on information received, officers of the Northern Constabulary and staff of Orkney Islands Council social work department are carrying out a joint investigation into alleged offences against children."

Following a series of flawed child abuse investigations in Cleveland and Rochdale in England, alarm bells were already sounding over the way the case was being conducted. The *Daily Record* criticised the dawn raids as an "operation that would have done credit to an SAS raid on Baghdad."

In South Ronaldsay, 300 people packed the Cromarty Hall in St Margaret's Hope to hear the parents tell their story of the raids.

The mother, whose children had been taken into care the previous year, said: "I believe the allegations have come from my children because they have been kept in isolation by the social work department for four months."

Emotions were running high. Former South Ronaldsay councillor Sandy Annal told the meeting: "What is wrong here is the Orkney Islands Council social work department. I will never stop, even if it costs my life, until I have those people removed from office.

"We are in the same situation as the Jews in Nazi Germany - that is the situation in Orkney today - living in fear of the knock at the door. We must prevent this evil, we must stop further action by the social work department - by physical action if need be."

A series of hearings of the Orkney Children's Panel was held to decide that the children would be kept in care until the case could go before a Sheriff Court for proof.

Mr Gordon Sloan, from Strathclyde, who had been acting as Interim Reporter to the Orkney Children's Panel for a year, said: "We have never used the word 'Satanic' or talked about 'Satanism' in connection with this case." However the events were headline news in newspapers, radio and television around the world with lurid headlines like "Devil's Island."

Orkney director of social work Mr Paul Lee backed the dawn raids. "I am satisfied that it was in the best interests of the children. It was done sensitively and sympathetically and, I feel, quite professionally by all concerned."

The Orkney Children's Panel heard from the social work department that the grounds for removing the children included the allegation that in places in South Ronaldsay up until November, 1990, the children were exposed to, as a participant, or an observer, sexual intercourse or simulated sexual intercourse, between adults and children and between adults. These incidents were said to have taken place during the hours of darkness and involved "ritualistic music, dancing and dress."

Kirkwall solicitors John Moir and Alistair Bruce, who were representing the families, published a full page public notice in *The Orcadian* appealing for "any persons who have seen, heard or are aware of any ritualistic music, dancing and dress having taken place."

The solicitors recruited Mr Edward Targowski QC who protested that the children had been taken away from Orkney. He told the Children's Panel: "Unless it can be shown that these children are in danger from the parents, they should be returned. It has never been alleged which parents have taken part in these rather bizarre entertainments. The children have simply been removed, not to other houses within the island but to a totally alien environment.

"If there is the slightest hint of danger to these children, every single person in South Ronaldsay would know about it."

A newly-formed South Ronaldsay Parents Action Committee raised a petition of 2,000 signatures, calling for a judicial review and inquiry, which was presented at 10 Downing Street for the attention of Prime Minister John Major.

There were complaints from members of one family that they had still not been interviewed by police three weeks after their two children were taken by social workers. There were protests from lawyers representing the families at Children's Panel hearings that medical evidence showed that the nine children had not been physically or sexually abused.

The South Ronaldsay affair had been news around the world before, five weeks after the children were taken into care, Sheriff David Kelbie began a hearing to consider the proof of the allegations. Within two days, Sheriff Kelbie had announced that the sooner the children were returned to their parents the better.

Reviewing the history of hearings and interviewing techniques, he said: "I have come to the conclusion that these proceedings are so fatally flawed as to be incompetent."

Interview techniques employed on the nine children - aged between eight and fifteen - could only be described as "cross examination designed to break them down and admit to being abused," said the Sheriff. The statements of the children could not be said to be "spontaneous" but had amounted to "repeated coaching" by their interviewers.

PUBLIC NOTICE

Would any persons who have seen, heard or are aware of any ritualistic music, dancing and dress having taken place at South Ronaldsay, Orkney at any period until November 1990

The Orcadian, Thursday, March 7, 1991

A full page advertisement appeared in *The Orcadian* in March, 1991, after nine children had been taken into care.

The Sheriff said he was unsure what was meant by "ritualistic music." "Depending on which child tells it, it is either Kylie Minogue, Michael Jackson, possibly Andrew Lloyd Webber's *Phantom of the Opera*, the Strip the Willow or the Grand Old Duke of York."

Sheriff Kelbie concluded: "I am in no doubt that the risks to the welfare of these nine children in returning them to their parents are far outweighed by the certain damage being done by their continued detention and the sooner they are returned to their parents the better."

Although Sheriff Kelbie's pronouncements were later rejected as legally flawed by three Appeal Court judges, his dismissal of the case as incompetent was sufficient for the nine children to be flown home in a specially chartered British Airways plane which landed at Kirkwall Airport amid emotional scenes to be greeted by a piper and a crowd of up to 200 family, friends, and media. Calls immediately were reinforced for a judicial inquiry.

No sooner had the children returned home, the astonishing 13 month saga of suspended Reporter Mrs Katherine Kemp took a new turn as the new Scottish Secretary Mr Ian Lang ruled that Orkney Islands Council could not sack her. Mr Lang said that immediate action was required to improve relations between the Reporter and the local authority. A week later, Mrs Kemp was re-instated and returned to work.

However, in August, 1991, there was a bizarre twist in the controversy as a police investigation was mounted after the disappearance, or theft, of hundreds of confidential files from the offices of the Orkney Children's Panel. The files, dating back to the 1970s, apparently vanished while Mrs Kemp was on holiday.

Amidst allegations of conspiracy and cover-up, police established that there were no apparent signs of a break-in. Even Mrs Kemp's husband, Charlie, was drawn into the unhappy situation. He was interviewed and even charged with theft - but the charge was dropped and he was never prosecuted for any offence. Supporters of Mrs Kemp were quick to make allegations of a "bodged frame-up."

In November, 1991, Katherine Kemp gave up the battle and

resigned, saying that she felt she had been harassed and even menaced by the events of the previous months. Some children were "actually being harmed by what is happening in the name of child care in Orkney," she said.

Regarding the disappearance of the files, she said: "The only logic I can make out of it is someone wanted to get at me by making it very difficult for me, by removing the tools I need to work with. Or it was in someone's interest to remove documents or information they thought was there. I can't find any other reasonable explanation for it."

Meanwhile, on May 1, 1991, the Crown Office announced that none of the South Ronaldsay parents - nor the Rev Morris McKenzie - would be charged with any offences. Nor were further inquiries contemplated.

The Secretary of State for Scotland Mr Ian Lang immediately announced there would be a judicial inquiry into the whole South Ronaldsay affair which would be conducted by Lord Clyde. The inquiry got underway at Kirkwall Town Hall in July, 1991.

Even as the Clyde inquiry progressed, however, the curious chain of events in South Ronaldsay continued as police - following a tip-off by officials of the Royal Scottish Society for the Prevention of Cruelty to Children - swooped on a quarry where, apparently, they expected to find a paedophile gang. In the event, no one turned up apart from police and RSSPCC officials.

Councillor Cyril Annal, on whose land the quarry bordered, blasted the police action: "What do they think they were doing? They were having a quarry tour in South Ronaldsay. How bloody stupid can you get?"

The Rev Morris McKenzie - despite the damning blackening of his character - was not permitted to give evidence to the inquiry to stress his innocence. But in an hour long submission, his wife Jan said the OIC social work department had failed to make "reasonably adequate inquiries" into the possible innocent explanations for the allegations made against the four families and other people involved in the South Ronaldsay case.

Evidence at the Clyde inquiry ran for seven months - the second longest running public inquiry in Scottish legal history - running up a legal bill estimated at £6 millions. Suggestions that it was a gravy train for the legal profession led to the inquiry lawyers being dubbed the "Bisto boys" by cynical observers.

In October, 1992, Lord Clyde's 363 page report from the inquiry produced 194 recommendations.

Scottish Secretary Mr Ian Lang told MPs in the House of Commons: "The House should be in no doubt that the report is justifiably critical of the way in which the affair was handled."

He said the report identified "significant failings" on the part of social workers, police and the Royal Scottish Society for the Prevention of Cruelty to Children - "not only in the way in which the decision to remove the children was reached but also how it was implemented and how the interviews were carried out."

The OIC issued a statement a week later which said: "The council unequivocally accept Lord Clyde's view that the parents and children involved, and Mr and Mrs McKenzie, must be accorded the presumption of innocence." However, at that time, there was no word of an apology - either to the parents or the community.

A packed meeting at St Margaret's Hope made calls for the resignation of Councillor Mairhi Trickett, the chairman of the OIC social work committee, and the director of social work Paul Lee. Eighteen individual claims for damages were initiated against the OIC by those caught up in the affair.

Eventually, in May, 1993, social work director Paul Lee was suspended on full pay while disciplinary proceedings were investigated.

Councillor Jim Moar said: "Paul Lee was the leader, he was the captain of the ship. He has to take responsibility if anything happens to it. We feel the buck stops with the director. We based the suspension on 45 recommendations in the Lord Clyde report." Dr Avril Osborne (46), then assistant director of social work for Highland Region, was appointed as the new acting director - later confirmed as a permanent appointment.

A week later, Councillor Mairhi Trickett lost the chairmanship of the Orkney social work committee.

However, the aggrieved South Ronaldsay community was hardly overjoyed in June, 1993, when it was revealed by *The Orcadian* that a "mutually agreed settlement" would see Paul Lee leave his position as Orkney social work director with a £57,000 golden handshake. In August, 1993, he began a new job in Dumfries and Galloway.

Astonishingly, it was March, 1996 - more than five years after the dawn raids - before a line could be drawn under the affair.

It was brought to a close, satisfactory or not, with an out-of-court settlement agreeing compensation averaging around £30,000 for each of the four families - and a "wholehearted apology" from Orkney Islands Council. The OIC would also meet the families' legal expenses, although most of the estimated £250,000 bill would be picked up by Commercial Union, the council's insurers.

A statement issued by the council and families, jointly, said: "Orkney Islands Council regret the long delay but seeks now to compensate the four families for the distress and trauma experienced as a result of the failings in 1991 for which the council are responsible.

"Orkney Islands Council fully accept the criticisms contained in Lord Clyde's report and asks all members of the four families to accept this wholehearted apology. The four families accept Orkney Islands Council's apology.

"Lord Clyde stated in his report that damage was done to the relationship which should exist between the local community and the Orkney social work department. Orkney Islands Council see this statement as a turning point and hope that with this apology a start may now be made to repairing the damage of that relationship."

Still left without any recompense was the much-maligned Rev Morris McKenzie.

The unhappy state of Orkney Islands Council's social work department over ten years was further underlined in 1998 as the county's 51 year old director of social work Dr Avril Osborne agreed an early retirement deal with the council and quit with what was reported to be a golden handshake of £60,000.

Dr Osborne's management style had been called into question on several occasions, and a former council chairman of social work, Councillor Alasdair Thom had called for an official investigation into the running of the department, which had been plagued by problems since the 1980s.

A letter to councillors from chief executive Mr Alistair Buchan said the decision to authorise the deal was based on the grounds of the efficiency of the service.

But Mr Buchan's letter added: "I must emphasise that Dr Osborne has at no time been subject to any disciplinary action, and generally she will leave the council with no stain whatsoever on her professional reputation."

In 1999, the whole affair was thrown into the national spotlight, however, when Dr Osborne sought an interdict at the Court of Session to effectively gag *The Orcadian* and BBC Radio Orkney from revealing details relating to her sexuality, the reasons for her early retirement or OIC policies and practices as her employer.

The petition to the Court of Session said Dr Osborne was "reasonably apprehensive" that material concerning the circumstances and events leading to her retirement had been passed to the press and would be published in contravention of a confidentiality agreement she had made with the council.

However, her motion was rejected by the court after *The Orcadian* and Radio Orkney contested the action.

In a letter to staff, the interim director of community social services, Mr Pat Begley, appealed for a line to be drawn under "the bitterness, division and factions of the past." He wrote: "Unless individuals are willing and able to be tolerant and extend a generosity of spirit to colleagues within this service then the opportunities for healing will be sorely impeded."

Our sportswoman of the century

Four World Championships, one Olympic Games (it could have been two but for injury) and one Commonwealth Games. That was the record of competition achieved by Kareen Marwick, who must surely be acknowledged as Orkney's sportswoman of the 20th century.

Kareen, from Swanney House, Birsay, the daughter of the first convener of Orkney Islands Council, George Marwick, later to become Lord Lieutenant of Orkney, became the second Orcadian of the 20th century to compete at the Olympic Games when she was selected for the Great Britain women's eight rowing crew for the 1992 Olympics in Barcelona.

It meant she had emulated the achievement of Sanday wrestler Tom Ward who had represented Britain at the 1936 Berlin Olympics.

Kareen had started rowing at Cambridge University and won two rowing Blues at university in 1982 and 1983 - success which, in 1984, led her to be selected for the British rowing eights in the World Championships that year. Unfortunately, injury robbed her of a chance of competing in the 1984 Los Angeles Olympics.

However - while studying to be a doctor in London - she returned to the international arena in 1989 when, at the age of 28, she was again selected for the British team in the world championships, this time competing in the quadruple sculls event.

The following year, she was selected for her third world rowing championships - the 1990 event in Tasmania - in which she was rowing in the women's coxless fours. (The British team eventually finished ninth in the consolation final).

Like Tom Ward, who represented Scotland at the 1938 Empire Games in Australia, Kareen also achieved selection for Scotland when in 1994 she took time away from her job as a doctor in Nottingham to compete for the Scottish rowing team in what was now the Commonwealth Games in Canada.

The following year, she was again selected to row for Great Britain in the 1995 world championships in Finland.

There were other sports stars in Orkney in 1992, however, as a host of top names in the rugby world came to Kirkwall to celebrate the 25th anniversary of Orkney Rugby Club, with Orkney meeting an invitation team led by the former captain of Scotland, Finlay Calder. Visiting stars included French ace Pierre Berbizier and Scots internationalists John Beattie, Gary Armstrong and Roy Laidlaw. The All Stars eventually ran out 38-15 winners.

Another rugby player to visit was

1992

Princess Anne's son Peter Phillips who was in the Gordonstown School rugby team which travelled to Orkney in 1992 to comprehensively defeat a combined team from Kirkwall Grammar School and Stromness Academy.

And in a slightly less physical sport, Orkney could claim a new internationalist in 1992 when Mr George Fotheringham, secretary of the Kirkwall Draughts Club, was called up to represent Scotland in an international draughts competition against teams from England, Wales, Northern Ireland, Eire and the Channel Islands.

Orkney could also claim "one of its own" at the highest level of Scottish professional football as, in August, 1992, midfield player Stuart Slater moved from West Ham to Celtic for a fee of £1.5 millions.

His grandmother Mrs Margaret Slater (née Keldie) was born and raised in Thoms Street, Kirkwall. She had moved to England in her early twenties and met and married Albert Slater and settled in Sudbury, Suffolk, where their son Ian - Stuart's father - was born.

Stuart Slater made his senior debut with West Ham in 1987 and played for England at Under 21 and B international level.

He was later to leave Celtic to return to his native Suffolk to play for Ipswich Town, and then moved to Watford, before making a move to Australia.

Two of his grand uncles, Thorfinn Keldie of Stromness, and Dave Keldie from Kirkwall, were both Orkney county players.

The year of 1992 saw the end of a 30 year playing career of one of the stalwarts of Orkney football in the 20th century as Morgan Harcus retired.

He bowed out in winning fashion as Rendall, with Morgan in goal, beat Kirkwall Accies 4-1 in the final of the Oxy Cup.

He played for Orkney in the inter-county against Shetland no less than 18 times, starting in 1964 at the age of 17. He had also been the captain of the Orkney team which won the North Atlantic Cup and, in 30 years, he had never been booked or sent off.

Another Orkney goalkeeper to make headlines in 1992 was Aly Firth (31) of Grainpark, Kirkwall. He played in goal for Orphir against Rendall - unaware that he had broken his neck!

He suffered the injury in a freak acci-

Kareen Marwick who represented Great Britain in the women's rowing events at the 1992 Olympic Games in Barcelona.
(Picture from the files of *The Orcadian*)

dent during the game but did not realise the extent of the damage and it was not until the following day that he visited a doctor who diagnosed the broken neck and sent the goalkeeper to Aberdeen for emergency treatment.

And, on a more leisurely sporting note, Orkney Golf Club's new £200,000 clubhouse was officially opened in September, 1992, by club member Mrs Margaret Mackay who achieved a unique feat with her late husband Jack when they won the men's and ladies club championships in the same year, 1965.

Luckless trans-Atlantic trip

Three Algerian youths stowed away on an oil tanker thinking it was bound for France, and ended up in Orkney - after crossing the Atlantic twice!

They had smuggled themselves aboard the 89,000 tonne Yugoslav-registered *Petar Lekovik* in their native Algeria. But the ship, instead of sailing to France, was bound for New York and then Flotta.

When the vessel arrived in Scapa Flow, the three were put ashore and arrangements made for them to be flown home to Algeria.

Other unexplained arrivals on Orkney shores left the top brass of the Royal Navy with egg on their faces, as well as their caps, in 1992.

The Navy refused to comment on how the log of the class 42 destroyer HMS *Gloucester* came to be washed up on a beach in Sanday - where it was found by former coastguard Geordie Tulloch (62) - while the warship's engineering guide turned up on South Ronaldsay where it was picked up by Mrs Myrtle Thomson.

New ferries for Orkney

The 80 metre, 2,292 tonne vessel *Contender* made her first appearance in Kirkwall, under the command of her master Captain Peter Clarke, to launch a roll-on, roll-off freight service between Orkney and Invergordon, on the Cromarty Firth, for the Orcargo company.

The ship built in France in 1973 had previously operated in the South Atlantic, serving the Falklands. The vehicle deck allowed for 12 articulated trailers while it could carry 500 sheep or 130 cattle.

The new competition brought an immediate response from P&O Scottish Ferries which completed a £9 million deal to buy the former Baltic ferry *Eckeroe* which, after conversion work in Finland, would be introduced on the Pentland Firth service as the new *St Ola*.

The "new" vessel was actually older than her predecessor but she could carry twice as many vehicles.

Triple honour for Papay

When farmer John Rendall (67) received the British Empire Medal in the 1992 New Year honours list, he became the third resident of Papa Westray to receive the BEM in nine years - an impressive achievement for an island with a population of only 80.

Mr Rendall, of Holland, Papa Westray, received the award in recognition of nearly 50 years as custodian of two of the island's ancient monuments, the Knap o' Howar and the Holm of Papa.

He joined neighbours Mr Jim Rendall, the island postman, and former coastguard Willie Groat as holders of the BEM.

Gold theft crooks jailed

Orcadian Detective Sergeant Bill Miller was praised by an Old Bailey judge for his part in bringing to justice some of the villains behind Britain's biggest ever gold robbery.

At the conclusion of a trial which saw three men and a woman jailed for between five and ten years for handling nearly £18 million from the 1983 Brinks Mat gold bullion raid, Judge Henry Pownall commended DS Miller for his work. The investigation had been carried out in the "highest traditions of the force," said the judge.

The following year, Mr Miller retired to his native Stronsay.

Death tragedies

Orkney Islands Council lost two of its senior councillors, within two months, in tragedies overseas.

Councillor Jack Ridgway (57) who originally moved to Orkney as British Airways manager at Kirkwall, died on holiday in Australia in December, 1992. He had set up his travel agency with his son Mark in 1987, the year after being elected to Orkney Islands Council.

Two months later, the council vice-convener Councillor Alastair Scholes died in Lanzarote while attending a conference on OIC business. He had his own Kirkwall accountancy business, and was chairman of Orkney Tourist Board.

Irish premier flies in

By a quirk of fate, the last "international" visit made by the Irish Prime Minister Charles Haughey during his premiership was to Orkney.

He arrived unannounced at Kirkwall Airport in an Irish military aircraft - after deciding to join a training flight of the Irish Air Corps Gulfstream IV - on Saturday, February 8, 1992.

Mr Haughey travelled into Kirkwall to visit St Magnus Cathedral during a short stay in the county.

The following week, dogged by controversy, he was forced to step down as Irish premier.

Generous Orkney raises the roof

The generosity of Orcadians saw an amazing total of £155,000 raised to help bring relief to local cancer sufferers.

The fund-raising campaign was co-ordinated by Kirkwall businessman David Tulloch, and within seven months, the original £60,000 target was reached - and donations continued until the fund closed with £155,000 in the bank.

The Duchess of Roxburghe - the chairman of the Scottish committee of the Cancer Macmillan Fund - flew to Orkney to "turn the first sod" as work began on a new cancer hospice. The hospice - to be known as the Macmillan ward at Eastbank hospital - would consist of three single bed units and a conservatory.

It seems that generosity can be soon forgotten, however. Within three years, Orkney Health Board announced plans for the ward to close and to be switched to the Balfour hospital.

Film debut

After 50 years of appearing in amateur dramatic productions throughout Orkney, retired ship's purser Walter Leask was recruited to make his film debut.

In the feature film *Blue Black Permanent*, set in Orkney and Edinburgh, and made by Orcadian film maker Margaret Tait, Walter - who worked for P&O for 34 years - played the father of the film's central character.

The film, produced by Barbara Grigor, would also feature several other local actors when it had its Orkney premiere at the Phoenix cinema in September, 1992. The professional stars of the film included Gerda Stevenson, Jack Shepherd and Celia Imrie.

The year of 1992 saw the end of another drama enterprise, however, as the curtain fell on the Orkney Youth Theatre when Orkney Islands Council decided not to give £15,000 funding.

In its eight years of existence, over 60 young people had taken part in community plays, pantomimes and school tours, while some of the students had gone on to further their careers at drama colleges in other parts of Britain. The demise of the youth theatre was "a great shame," said the chairman of the board of directors, Mr Chris Matthews.

Royal return

Orkney's most frequent Royal visitor of the 20th century, Queen Elizabeth, the Queen Mother, made her eighth visit to the county - but her first for five years - when she spent 90 minutes in Flotta, a few days after her 92nd birthday in August, 1992. She chatted to locals at Flotta community centre and toured the oil terminal.

Orkney mourns for Lord Jo

1993

Powerful tributes from statesmen in Britain and around the world flowed into Orkney as the county mourned the sudden death of Lord Grimond of Firth, the old-Etonian who represented Orkney and Shetland as MP for 33 years, and graced the international political stage as leader of the British Liberal Party for more than a decade.

Jo Grimond died at the age of 80 in Kirkwall's Balfour hospital on October 24, 1993. His funeral was held at St Magnus Cathedral on October 29, and he was laid to rest in the cemetery in Finstown.

Liberal Democrat leader Mr Paddy Ashdown said: "We have lost a lion of the Liberal cause. Jo Grimond's death will be mourned by millions who shared his beliefs, and by all who value the strength of our democracy and integrity in our politics.

"He brought the Liberal cause back from the verge of extinction, introduced new ideas which have today become commonplace in the agenda of all parties - and inspired a whole new generation of Liberal thinkers and activists."

The former Liberal leader Sir David Steel said: "I do not believe that the Liberal party would have survived at all but for his leadership in the late 1950s when it was down to five MPs. We all owe him an immense debt."

Gerry Meyer, editor of *The Orcadian* during the "Grimond years", said: "Jo Grimond never ceased to illuminate the political arena. As the MP, Liberal leader and elder statesman, he brought distinction to these roles as well as in other spheres of activity, and with it all, never lost the common touch. It was this quality, shared by his wife Laura, that endeared them and won them so many friends in Orkney and Shetland."

Just four months later, Lord Grimond was joined by his wife Laura as, in February, 1994, Lady Grimond died at the age of 75.

Laura Miranda Bonham Carter, the granddaughter of former Prime Minister Lord Asquith, had married Jo Grimond in 1938. She was a founder member of the Orkney Heritage Society, and chaired the Orkney Islands Council social work and housing committee during her time as a councillor, 1974-80. She and her husband had received the freedom of Orkney in 1987.

Her funeral was at St Magnus Cathedral and she was laid to rest at Finstown alongside her husband. "Laura was a remarkable woman who touched the hearts of hundreds of people with whom she came into contact throughout her exceptionally active and energetic life," said the Rev Sandy Horsburgh, who conducted the funeral service.

Jo and Laura Grimond with their youngest son Magnus, pictured at their Finstown home.

(Picture courtesy of Orkney Library photographic archive)

The man who went to the moon

Of all the developments of the 20th century, it is probably the Space Age which sets the benchmark of our progress - the "giant leap for Mankind."

Did the Orcadians of 1900 really believe that, within seven decades, man would walk on the moon? Even the pioneering spirit of Orkney men and women - who had reached new frontiers all around the world throughout the Millennium - could scarcely have considered the final frontier of Space was so attainable.

But, by 1993, the scale of achievement was brought home to Orkney when the county welcomed American astronaut and space shuttle commander John Young - a man who had actually walked on the moon.

A United States Navy officer, Commander Young made his first space flight in 1966 in Gemini 3, and became the first person to fly in Space six times.

It was in 1972 that he explored the surface of the moon with Charlie Duke, travelling further than anyone else.

In 1981 he was the commander of the first space shuttle flight by Columbia, and, in 1993, he was still listed as an active NASA astronaut as special assistant for engineering, operating and safety at the Johnson Space Centre in the USA.

He came to Orkney to pay tribute to another pioneer of flight - Captain Ted Fresson who, 60 years earlier in 1933, had established Orkney's first air services.

"I've been familiar with the exploits of Ted Fresson for a long, long time, so when they invited me to come I was very excited about sharing the celebrations of 60 years of a tremendous feat," he said. "Establishing the first route between Kirkwall and Inverness was really quite an accomplishment in that day and age."

Commander Young presented Orkney with a special montage of space shuttle photographs, including one taken while orbiting over Scotland.

"Even though we've never set foot on Orkney before, we've flown over it," he said.

He made a quick tour of St Magnus Cathedral and expressed his enjoyment of his visit.

"The people have been wonderful, and we have seen a lot of country I've never seen before on the ground."

Not the first man to walk on the moon — but the first man to walk on the moon and Orkney! Commander John Young, pictured here, has visited Orkney twice, in fact. As well as travelling to the county in 1993 to take part in the 60th anniversary celebrations of Captain Ted Fresson's inauguration of Orkney air services, he returned three years later to take part in the Orkney Science Festival. It was in 1972 that Commander Young had landed on and explored the surface of the moon with fellow astronaut Charlie Duke, travelling further than anyone else.

(Picture courtesy of National Aeronautics and Space Administration)

New mart takes shape

It was the end of an era and the start of a new one as the members of Kirkwall Auction Mart and the West Mainland Mart voted to merge into a newly-formed Orkney mart company in 1993.

Sandwick farmer Mr George Wylie was elected the first chairman of the company, the aim of which was to build a new mart worthy of the 21st century.

The contract for the main £2 million phase of the new mart went to Elgin-based Gordon Forbes construction. It was built at Hatston, and allowed the old Stromness-Kirkwall main road to be re-opened to traffic, having been closed by wartime developments in World War Two.

Fishermen protest

Scottish Secretary Mr Ian Lang arrived in Orkney in 1993 - to open the Orkney Opportunities Centre - to be greeted by angry protests from Orkney fishermen.

They feared that Government conservation policies could limit some fishermen to just 80 days a year at sea.

A petition, signed by 300 of the local fishing community, protested at the "immoral imposition of the days-at-sea regime."

They added: "This black Act seriously jeopardises the livelihood of the fishermen and, indeed, the islanders."

Pollution disaster hits home

The New Year dawned with Europe's worst ever maritime pollution disaster, frighteningly close to home, as the tanker *Braer* with 85,000 tonnes of oil went aground on Shetland, bringing devastation to our Northern neighbours.

The year of 1993 began with gales on 21 days of the first 26 days of January with winds recorded up to 107mph in Orkney. About two miles of North Ronaldsay's unique sheep dyke was destroyed or washed away in the storms that claimed the *Braer*. A Royal Navy party from Rosyth arrived to help rebuild the dyke, and Prince Charles made a flying visit to survey the damage. Members of the Prince's Trust later helped on the renovation work.

However it was the devastation at sea which was exercising most minds and the *Braer* disaster immediately prompted calls for a salvage tug to be permanently based in the Northern Isles - a demand that was to be eventually conceded six years later.

Lord Donaldson was appointed to conduct an inquiry into the implications of the *Braer* and shipping safety, and he visited Orkney to hear local concerns.

As if on cue, the dangers in Orkney were swiftly illustrated on February 13, 1993, when the Danish coaster *Bettina Danica* ran aground in the Pentland Firth. The six crew were airlifted to safety by a rescue helicopter from Lossiemouth, but salvage teams had to deal with 30,000 litres of fuel oil on the 70 metre ship which had been on passage from Norway to Greenock.

Lord Donaldson was flown over the Pentland Firth to see the stricken vessel. "With the *Bettina Danica* there, it just highlights a situation where a very sound ship, only two years old, can run aground," said Orkney harbours director Captain Bob Sclater.

If further proof was needed, it came the following year when, in December, 1994, a potentially major oil disaster was averted off the shores of Orkney by a matter of minutes.

The Bahamas-registered tanker *Channel Dragon*, carrying 79,100 tonnes of crude oil, suffered a power failure while less than 800 yards off South Ronaldsay - with one estimate that she was within three minutes of the rocks - after taking on her cargo at Flotta for Wilhelmshaven, Germany.

The power failure was blamed on human error and, fortunately, after a 30 minute alert, power was restored to allow the giant tanker to continue.

Axe falls on Orkney Navy link

Government plans to axe Britain's Royal Naval Auxiliary Service would herald the end of a Navy presence in Orkney for the first time in nearly 100 years.

The decision, announced by Defence Secretary Malcolm Rifkind in June, 1993, would mean the abolition of Orkney's 28 strong volunteer RNXS unit and the redundancy of the full-time RNXS group Naval auxiliary officer for the Northern Isles, Lieutenant Commander Gordon Ivol.

The RNXS unit in Orkney had provided logistical and operational support for Royal Navy exercises in the Northern Isles for a quarter of a century. "Many of the members have given their life to it," said Lt Commander Ivol.

On March 20, 1994, the Northern Isles group of the RNXS disbanded, and the Scapa Port headquarters closed, as Vice-Admiral Chris Morgan, Flag Officer Scotland and Northern Ireland, arrived with HMS *Orkney* for the formal closure ceremonies. A Royal Marines band beat the Retreat, and there was a farewell service at St Magnus Cathedral.

Women welcome

Members of the Orkney Club - an exclusively male institution since its establishment in 1826 as "a society for promoting improvements in husbandry and other branches of industry in the county" - voted at the AGM, by 29-23 votes, to accept membership applications from women.

Women had only been admitted through the doors of the club since the 1970s, and then only as guests of men.

New air tax

Orkney travellers faced a new tax burden as the Government announced the introduction of a controversial Air Passenger Tax - an imposition which would cost Orkney Health Board an estimated £20,000 - £25,000 a year for patients and staff flying to the Scottish mainland. Originally introduced at £5 for domestic flights, it was quickly doubled to £10.

Top university honour

The inauguration of Scotland's newest university created a new chapter in the career of an Orcadian professor in 1993.

Professor William Turmeau - who grew up and was educated in Stromness - became the vice-chancellor and principal of the newly created Napier University in Edinburgh which had grown to an establishment of 9,000 students and 1,200 staff.

After leaving Stromness Academy, William Turmeau had graduated at Edinburgh University with a BSc (Hons) degree in 1952 before going to Canada to work for ten years. His academic career began in 1962 when he became a lecturer at what was then Napier Technical College.

Professor Turmeau, aged 63 in 1993, regularly returned to Orkney with his Orcadian wife Margaret (née Burnett). Three years later, he was chosen to lead the newly formed Scottish Environmental Protection Agency.

Goal crazy

Kirkwall's Thorfinn Football Club went goal crazy in May, 1993. Thorfinn beat Dounby 30-0 in the J. M. Croy Reserve League, while the first team beat Stromness 10-0 in the W. R. Tullock A League.

Drink and drugs shocker

A life-style survey conducted by Orkney Health Board showed that nearly half the senior pupils at Orkney schools admitted they drank to get drunk, some had started smoking as seven year olds, and one in six third to sixth year senior pupils said they had taken drugs or sniffed substances on at least one occasion.

Just two per cent claimed to take cannabis or ecstasy regularly and one per cent said they took amphetamines or LSD often. Twenty two per cent of pupils, aged 11-18, claimed to drink alcohol at least once a week.

Dry distillery

Scapa Distillery - founded in 1885 - would suspend whisky production by the end of 1993, announced a spokesman for the owners, Allied Distillers.

Killer flees murder mystery

1994

The peaceful calm of an Orkney summer's evening was shattered when, in a single act of horror, a man was gunned down in full view of a room full of diners, including families with children, at Kirkwall's Mumutaz Indian restaurant.

Orkney's first murder investigation in a quarter of a century began when restaurant manager Shamsudden Mahmood (26) was shot and fatally wounded by an unknown assailant on the evening of Thursday, June 2, 1994.

Diners watched in horror as the masked and hooded man entered the restaurant in Kirkwall's Bridge Street and shot Mr Mahmood in the face. The killer then made his escape down a nearby lane.

Police mounted a cordon at the airport and ferry terminals with hundreds of people questioned. Armed police were on stand-by if needed, said Orkney's senior police officer Chief Inspector Alistair MacLeod.

"This is an extraordinary and horrific thing to have happened in a community like Orkney," he said. "The local police team was underway in a very, very short time - within minutes. Everything that should be done was done and we reacted as quickly as we possibly could."

As extra police were drafted in from Inverness, Detective Superintendent George Gough, who led the inquiry, said: "There is no obvious motive for the killing." He repeatedly said that he could not rule out the possibility that the killer was still in Orkney. "Indeed," he said, "the inquiry is directed on the possibility that he is, therefore I am concerned that such a person with a firearm remains at large."

Interpol joined the inquiry, with investigations carried out in Bangladesh, the home country of the victim. In its first year, the murder hunt cost £100,000 as 8,000 names went on to the police computer as part of the investigation.

The mystery was no clearer nearly three years later when an Orkney policeman - whose son was named in court as a suspect - was jailed on a charge of concealing evidence in the case. He was freed, after his sentence, still protesting his - and his son's -innocence.

The result was that more than five years after the murder - despite the issuing of a computerised photo-fit picture of a suspect and a national operation that included nationwide television appeals - the killer was still at large.

£15 million oil loan prompts storm

A row exploded after a secret meeting of Orkney Islands Council, convened at one hour's notice, agreed to lend £15 millions to the operators of Orkney's Flotta oil terminal, Elf Enterprise Caledonia.

"This huge amount of money is being lent, without any research, cost analysis or independent reports," complained Councillor Ian MacDonald. "It raises all sorts of questions about why an international company the size of Elf should need to borrow any money from the local council."

The cash - from Orkney's oil reserve funds - was earmarked to help Elf bid for a contract to handle oil from the new Britannia field in the North sea. The loan would be interest free, subject to Elf providing suitable bank guarantees. In the event Elf failed to get the contract, and the loan was never made.

However, a year later, a new era was heralded for Orkney's Oil Age when the future of the Flotta terminal was given a major boost with the announcement that it had captured the contract to land the first oil from the new fields which were to be opened up in the Atlantic to the west of Orkney.

The Elf company secured a five year deal to handle the oil from the new BP Foinaven field. It would help to provide security for the 330 jobs at the terminal, said Elf.

A floating production vessel *Petrojarl 1V* would be used to recover the Foinaven oil which would then be transferred to shuttle tankers for shipment to Scapa Flow.

Viking blood link challenged

A unique study of Orcadian blood groups was begun to help reveal some of the hidden secrets of Orkney's history.

World famous geneticist Sir Walter Bodmer, director general of the Imperial Cancer Research Fund, and his wife Dr Julia Bodmer, asked Orcadians to come forward to give blood samples in the European-funded study to show up the genetic characteristics of indigenous blood groups.

The findings could even show up the influx of Spanish blood into Westray at the time of the Spanish Armada, said Sir Walter. "You can say a lot about where people come from, and the whole idea is to find out about Orkney and how its population derived," he said.

A total of 163 islanders - with Orcadian ancestry back at least as far as all their grandparents - came forward to give blood. However the results rather challenged the accepted view of Orkney's Viking heritage.

"There is no indication that Orcadians are like Scandinavians," said Sir Walter. "It is unlikely they are particularly Viking in origin."

Wild goose chase for Hoy

Grace Robertson, of Glebe Farm, Longhope, created her own niche in history in 1994 - as she was appointed as Scotland's first professional bird scarer.

She was appointed by Scottish Natural Heritage after concerns about the increasing population of barnacle geese causing considerable damage to farm land on the island of Hoy.

After complaints from farmers, Mrs Robertson was given the task of organising her own wild goose chase - marshalling the geese to specially designated refuge areas.

She would work initially for 20 hours a week, said Orkney's Scottish Natural Heritage officer Andy Dorin. "Hopefully, she will be shepherding the geese to where they would go naturally anyway," he said. "The scheme is the first of its type in Scotland - it's both new and innovative."

Tourism chief

Orkney-born Cameron Taylor, who had previously worked at 10 Downing Street during the premiership of Margaret Thatcher, was appointed the new chief executive of Orkney Tourist Board to succeed Josh Gourlay who, after holding the job for 21 years, moved to a new post in the South.

Four years later Mr Taylor moved to a post with the Scottish Tourist Board and was succeeded by Mr Gareth Crichton.

Year of sporting triumph

Orkney sportsmen and women struck gold in 1994 as, in three different sports, the county could claim to have United Kingdom champions.

In addition, one Orkney athlete claimed a Scottish title while four others were selected to represent Scotland in international events. And, for good measure, another Orkney sportswoman achieved success for Australia.

Leading the way in Orkney's year of sporting triumph were eight youngsters who were crowned as the junior champions of the UK in the sport of octopush in July, 1994.

The Orkney Vikings Under 16 team - Finn MacLeod, Andrew Cowan, Matthew Butcher, Bethany Howard, Chris Mainland, Robert Moylan, Dougal Russell and David Sinclair - won the title in the international pool at Crystal Palace in London.

The team members had paid for themselves to have a week's training in the warm waters of the Mediterranean island of Gozo to prepare for the event in which they took part in seven matches in seven hours. The Vikings went on to complete a hat-trick of UK championship victories, also winning in 1995 and 1996.

Their success earned them an invitation to compete as the Scotland team at a tournament in Cape Cod, USA.

Two months later, Orkney was the pride of the British angling world after the county's championship trout fishing team of Sandy McConnachie, Norman Irvine, Ken Kennedy, Stuart Leslie, Sandy Nicolson and Maurice Rendall won the 1994 Benson and Hedges Fly Fishing Championships international final at Rutland Water - repeating the triumph of 1991 when the Orkney team also won the coveted title.

The third British title to come to the islands was claimed by Colin Blake (70) of Seaforth, Burray, who won the veteran's title at the British Short Range Rifle Championships. A shooting enthusiast since 1937 and originally from Hull, he had retired to Orkney and was secretary of the Orkney Shooting Association.

Sanday-based long distance runner William Sichel (40) stormed to a national title as he won the Scottish 100 kilometres championships, beating 40 other runners, and winning in a time of 8 hours 1 minute 10 seconds - 13 minutes ahead of his nearest rival.

It was his first attempt at 100 km after taking up marathon running - but he had previously represented Scotland at table tennis.

It meant that Sanday, a community of just 500 people, could boast two international sporting residents as David Harvey, the former Leeds United and Scotland goalkeeper, moved to the island with his family.

Two Orkney sportswomen represented Scotland in the 1994 Commonwealth Games in Canada. Kareen Marwick - also a competitor at the 1992 Olympic Games - competed in the rowing, while Sarah Burgon (20), who learned to swim in the Stromness pool and whose family still lived in Stromness, was chosen, as the Scottish synchronised swimming champion, to be part of Scotland's swimming squad.

Later in the year, former Kirkwall Grammar School pupil Jamie Crisp (22) was called up for the Scotland trampolining team after taking up the sport just two years earlier, and Kirsty Holden, from Stromness and a founder member of Orkney Fencing Club, was chosen for

the Scotland youth team in a quadrangular fencing international versus England, Wales and Ireland.

And to complete Orkney's sporting success around the world, show-jumper Sharon Ridgway - the daughter of the late Councillor Jack Ridgway, and his wife Janette - landed a success Down Under.

She had moved to live and work in Melbourne, Australia, and, in 1994, she was selected, with her horse Kilkenny Castle, to represent Australia at the prestigious Badminton Horse Trials.

It was an impressive roll of honour. It meant that, in the course of just six months, a total of 21 Orkney sportsmen and women - in nine different sports - could claim to have either won national championships or received international recognition.

Sadly, however, Orkney was to mourn the passing of one of the giants of 20th century British football as Sir Matt Busby died in 1994 at the age of 84. He was remembered by many Orcadians with whom he served in the county during World War Two.

As a player with Manchester City and Liverpool, he had already played in two FA Cup Finals during the 1930s when war broke out and he was posted to Orkney. He was a Sergeant PT Instructor with the 533 Coast Regiment headquarters based at Stangar Head on Flotta.

One of Orkney's finest footballers, Joe Bruce from Shapinsay, an Army comrade of Busby, credited the great man with having the most devastating shooting power he had ever seen.

After the war, Matt Busby had taken the managership at Old Trafford and, surviving the 1958 Munich Air Disaster, built Manchester United into one of the world's most famous football clubs.

The team of Orkney anglers from Orkney Trout Fishing Association who were top of their sport in 1994 after winning the international final of the prestigious Benson and Hedges Fly Fishing Championships. From the left: Norman Irvine, Stuart Leslie, Maurice Rendall, Ken Kennedy, Sandy McConnachie and Sandy Nicolson. (Picture courtesy of Kenny Pirie)

The great North poll

The United Kingdom's most unusual election was witnessed as the great North poll was introduced into Orkney - with as many candidates as there were voters!

In what was the first such scheme in the country, the new style election would decide the membership of the community councils for the islands of North Ronaldsay and Papa Westray.

It meant that the name of every islander was put forward as a candidate, with voting carried out by postal ballot as islanders selected those they wanted to serve. Those with the highest votes were then asked if they were prepared to become community councillors.

Councillor Howie Firth said it would remove the conflicts which arose in small communities where people did not like to be seen to oppose others. "I think it will help democracy and harmony." he said.

Fishermen rescued

Eight fishermen had narrow escapes in two separate incidents within days of each other in February, 1994.

The Buckie-registered *Leandel* sank off Birsay and her four man crew - skipper Jim Thomson, John Orton, Bert Johnston and Raymond Gardiner - were forced to abandon ship and take to the liferaft. They were picked up by the Kirkwall lifeboat after coxswain Jim Mitchell established a satellite fix on the stricken vessel's position from her emergency beacon.

Two days later, the Fraserburgh-registered *Green Castle* ran aground at Rora Head on Hoy's west coast but the vessel, with four crew, was towed off by the tug *Harald* and she was able to make her way to Stromness.

Equally fortunate were the four crew members of the stricken Buckie fishing vessel *Regent Bird* in January, 1995. They were able to clamber overboard and walk to safety after their boat hit rocks at the Bay of Skaill.

Norwegian royal debut

Orkney welcomed King Harald and Queen Sonja of Norway on their first visit to the islands in July, 1994. They toured St Magnus Cathedral and visited Stromness and Stenness before a memorial service at the 19 Norwegian war graves at St Olaf's Cemetery.

(Picture courtesy of Orkney Photographic)

New convener

County convener Jackie Tait lost his council seat for St Andrews and Deerness in the 1994 council elections and was succeeded as OIC convener by Councillor Hugh Halcro Johnston with Councillor Jim Sinclair of Shapinsay becoming vice-convener.

Mass stranding

The island of Sanday witnessed the largest ever stranding of sperm whales in Europe as 11 giant male whales, weighing 40 tonnes each, came ashore at Backaskaill Bay. Measuring up to 50 feet in length, they were towed away to be buried in a mass grave.

Round-the-world trip to trouble

1995

A family who set off from Orkney for a round-the-world trip in a horse drawn caravan found themselves trapped in Mongolia as David Grant (54) was caught up in a bizarre court case, accused of assaulting a man who, he said, tried to steal his horse.

Mr Grant, his wife Kate and children Torcuil, Eilidh and Fionn, formerly of Shortie in Evie, sold their Orkney home to finance their planned travels which began in 1991.

But, in early 1995, Mr Grant was arrested in Ulan Bator. He denied he had assaulted a Mr Bolt, blinding him in one eye with a catapult, but he was given a suspended three year jail sentence, and told he could not leave the country because the aggrieved Mr Bolt was demanding £40,000 compensation.

"There is no way this is straightforward justice," Mr Grant told *The Orcadian*. "I am actually a convicted criminal now. It's just bizarre."

He lodged an appeal against his sentence and eventually an out-of-court settlement of £1,000 for Mr Bolt was agreed to allow the family to leave for China and the last leg of their journey to Canada or USA.

They still faced another headache, however, as they found themselves stranded in Japan as they were ordered out of China. An appeal for funds on Japanese television eventually allowed them to reach America.

The Grants were by no means the first family to embark on a round-the-world trip from Orkney. The Romain family of Robin and Jill, and their seven children, who had lived in Rousay and Papa Stronsay, left Orkney in 1985 to make a similar expedition in a converted bus.

The family narrowly escaped being hit by an exploding missile in Iraq, during the Iraq-Iran war, and managed to travel on to Pakistan and Nepal before, in 1990, reaching New Zealand where they settled.

A more trouble-free global trip in 1995 saw retired Flotta terminal worker Mac Petrie, of Holm, clock up 15,000 miles by cycle - crossing Europe, Asia and the United States.

He set off on May 1, 1995, from Burwick and arrived home on October 21, having lost two and a half stones in weight, cycling up to 135 miles a day, after planning the epic trip for two years. His wife Gill flew out to spend nine days with him in Singapore during a break in the journey.

Unfortunately, on his final leg home, his bike went missing at Birmingham airport!

However, without denigrating the aforementioned achievements, plans were on the drawing board in 1995 for an even more ambitious journey. A venture was launched to prove that an Orkney earl Prince Henry St Clair, sailed from Orkney to arrive in the New World a century before Christopher Columbus.

The organisers said their aim was to demonstrate that Prince Henry had left Orkney in May, 1398, with 12 ships and 600 Scottish and Scandinavian crewmen and Italian navigators, and ventured as far as Nova Scotia and then New England.

The plan, in 1995, was to build a boat to 14th century designs and attempt to re-enact the trans-Atlantic voyage on its supposed 600th anniversary. Fundraising was begun for £250,000 to finance the building of a boat in Stromness. In the end, however, sufficient funds failed to materialise, and the project was dropped.

David and Kate Grant, with their children Eilidh, Torcuil and Fionn, before leaving their Orkney home in Evie to embark on their world trip by horse-drawn caravan. (Picture from the files of *The Orcadian*)

Warship relics return home

Part of Orkney's wartime heritage was returned to the county as the solid brass letters of the name plate of HMS *Royal Oak* - sunk in Scapa Flow with the loss of 833 men in October, 1939 - were formally handed over.

Mysteriously, the name plate letters had been found in Canada after being illegally plundered by divers in the 1960s.

Mounted on mahogany and restored to their original condition, they were presented to Orkney by the Royal Navy at a ceremony in St Magnus Cathedral, where they were handed over by Vice-Admiral Chris Morgan, Flag Officer Scotland, to Rev Sandy Horsburgh, assistant Cathedral minister.

Throne with a view

One of the more unusual property offers of the 20th century saw a unique piece of island history go on the market in 1995 - a communal six seater lavatory in the garden of Tom and Lotty Shearer of Stronsay. The late 19th century building - constructed on the shore for use during the herring boom on the island - was "flushed" twice a day by the rising tide.

Lifeboat veterans

Mr Jackie Groat retired in 1995 as Britain's longest serving lifeboat secretary after 33 years service to the Longhope station.

The UK director for the Royal National Lifeboat Institution, Lt Commander Brian Miles, travelled North for a special presentation Mr Groat shared with former Longhope coxswain Billy Budge and head launcher Anderson Sutherland.

Between them, they had given 100 years service to the lifeboat and the occasion was marked by a letter of thanks and good wishes from the Queen Mother.

Flying Princess

Princess Anne, the Princess Royal, paid a flying visit to Orkney to officially open the Orkney Carers Centre in Bridge Street, Kirkwall. She also toured the Northern Lighthouse Board depot in Stromness before leaving the county by helicopter.

Cathedral pillar

Albert Thomson BEM, curator of St Magnus Cathedral from 1946-78, died in 1995 at the age of 82. His collection of correspondence, cuttings, photographs, scrapbooks, personal notes and other items relating to the Cathedral, was bequeathed as the Albert Thomson Collection to the archives department of Orkney Library.

Ostrich venture

Sanday farmer Ernie Groundwater brought five ostriches to Orkney to begin a new venture for the county - ostrich farming. It was hoped that the birds would make money for their eggs, meat and feathers. (Picture courtesy of Craig Taylor)

Motorcycle aces

The richest sporting prize in Orkney saw £2,000 prize money on offer as top challengers from throughout Britain converged on the county for the annual beach race organised by Orkney Motocross Club, which had grown to become one of the main motorcycle events of the Scottish calendar.

Around 500 spectators saw Barry Gray, a leading Scottish rider, win the 1995 event to compete a hat-trick of victories.

Oops! Ten years early

Enterprising plans by Orkney Trout Fishing Association to celebrate its centenary with a series of commemorative events were called off as it was argued that the celebration was ten years too soon.

It had always been accepted that the association was formed in 1895, but it was now suggested to have begun in 1905.

Survey honour

Former Orkney fishermen's leader David Reid (55), originally from Stronsay, was made an MBE for his services to hydrographic survey. With his survey vessel *Proud Seahorse*, Mr Reid had been engaged in survey work under contract to the Ministry of Defence for the previous ten years - carrying out annual surveys of sand banks around eastern and southern England. His work had resulted in the liner *Queen Elizabeth II* being re-routed into her home port of Southampton.

Show anniversaries

The year of 1995 marked the 150th anniversary of the first St Margaret's Hope Show, believed to be the oldest agricultural show in Orkney. It also marked the 100th anniversary of the Orkney Horticultural and Industrial Association.

Tragic skipper died a hero

Fishing skipper Paul Simpson died a hero as he perished in an inferno as he tried to send a Mayday message to save his crew on their blazing vessel.

Father of two Mr Simpson (46) from the Channel Island of Jersey, was on board his Jersey-registered fishing boat *Inconnu* near the Old Man of Hoy, in January, 1996 when it was devastated by an explosion.

His last act in life was an heroic attempt, undertaken amid thick black

1996

smoke and searing heat, to radio for assistance in the vessel's wheelhouse which was engulfed by flames which reached more than 100 feet into the air.

The rescue operation involved the lifeboats from Stromness, Longhope and

Thurso, an RAF helicopter from Lossiemouth which winched four crew members to safety, and the P&O ferry *St Ola* which rescued the fifth surviving crewman from a liferaft.

The dramatic story involved 32 year old Andrew Watt, of Dunbeath, Caithness, spending a lonely night adrift for seven hours on the raft before being spotted by the *St Ola*, while his four colleagues huddled together on the burnt out shell of the *Inconnu*, waiting for rescue at the foot of 500 feet high cliffs.

The fire was blamed on an explosion in the boat's stove in the galley, and Jersey advocate Mr Frederick Benest told the Fatal Accident inquiry in Kirkwall: "It seems clear that Mr Simpson's last act was a selfless and, indeed, an heroic one as he attempted against all odds to put out a Mayday call."

In his summing up, Sheriff Colin Scott Mackenzie echoed the questions of the surviving crew members as to why at least one ship passed by the disaster scene without going to the assistance of the *Inconnu*.

"It is understandable that the plight of the vessel would not have been seen from that shore on a January night - no one lives there," said the Sheriff. "There was, however, a fishing vessel about four to five miles away which seemingly paid no attention to their obvious distress."

He said this was difficult to explain unless the boat in question had either a very poor, or no lookout. "A deliberate turning away from a fellow vessel in distress is unheard of in the fishing community," said the Sheriff.

There was praise for the RAF helicopter heroes who carried out the perilous rescue operation of the four crewmen from the stricken *Inconnu* - with the rotor blades of the helicopter frighteningly close to the cliffs.

The pilot was an American Lieutenant Bill Oliver, who was on an exchange visit to Lossiemouth from a coastguard station in the USA. He was accompanied by three RAF colleagues, co-pilot Flight Lt Al Dale, winch operator Ted Little and winchman Sergeant Trevor Preece.

An RAF spokesman at Lossiemouth said: "The cliffs of Hoy are fairly daunting and there was the dangerous aspect of sea birds which could have flown into the rotor blades."

The year would bring another tragedy at sea which was to directly touch the people of Hoy.

Despite extensive air, sea and coastline searches, two Longhope fishermen, William Mowat (32) and John Rosie (43) were lost in their 22 feet creel boat *Pentland Spray* in October, 1996.

The stricken *Inconnu* lies trapped on the rocks of Hoy.   (Picture courtesy of Craig Taylor)

Orkney mourns school massacre

The horrific massacre of 16 school-children and their teacher, as a crazed gunman ran amok through the primary school of Dunblane, was mourned in Orkney as the victims included a five year old girl from the county.

Little Victoria Clydesdale had stayed in Deerness with her mother and brothers and sisters until just six months before the appalling day when former scout leader Thomas Hamilton murdered 16 five and six year old children, and their teacher Gwenne Mayer, in a frenzy of bloodshed.

Victoria was fondly remembered at St Andrews primary school where she had been a pupil.

"We still remember her open, trusting and friendly face. She was a delightful little girl," the head teacher at St Andrews school, Ann Gilmour, told *The Orcadian*.

A prayer vigil was held in St Magnus Cathedral as a candle burned slowly throughout the day, symbolising the concern and heartfelt sympathy of Orkney for the people of Dunblane.

Children escape freak waves

Two near tragedies in a week prompted controversy over the safety of the Churchill Barriers as vehicles were swamped by giant waves.

Brian and Marie Corse, and their five children, aged from four months to seven years, from St Ola, escaped unhurt after a freak wave hit their estate car while crossing the barrier between Lamb Holm and Glimps Holm on New Year's Day, 1996.

A few days later, South Ronaldsay taxi operator Alex Rosie, carrying two passengers, was swamped by another huge wave which shattered the windscreen and damaged the roof of his car.

Members of the Barrier Action Group, who were campaigning for improved safety measures on the causeways, claimed that in a period of two and a half hours, more than 20 waves of 40 feet high broke over the wave wall protecting the barrier.

Farewell to Orkney's bard

Writer and poet George Mackay Brown - one of Orkney's most loved sons who, over four decades, secured a place at the very top of the nation's literary tree - was laid to rest, in April, 1996, after a funeral attended by hundreds at St Magnus Cathedral.

The man, who was so often simply known as George or GMB, died at the age of 74 in the Balfour Hospital on April 13, 1996. His funeral was held on April 16, St Magnus Day, which just the week before in his weekly column "Under Brinkie's Brae" in *The Orcadian* he described as "that wonderful day in the Orkney calendar."

Long-term friend and collaborator, Hoy-based composer Sir Peter Maxwell Davies described him as "a staunchly supportive friend, and the most modest and unassuming of men, and an exemplary creator."

"He must be the most positive and benign influence ever on my own efforts at creation," said Sir Peter.

Just a week after the death of George Mackay Brown, Orkney mourned the death of another stalwart of the Orkney world of music and the arts, the director of the St Magnus Festival Chorus, Dick Hughes, aged 55. A Welshman, he took up the post of music teacher of Kirkwall

Grammar school in 1973. He went on to found the Kirkwall Male Voice Choir, serve as musical director and principal of Kirkwall Amateur Operatic Society, and become organist and choirmaster of St Magnus Cathedral.

And, in May, 1996, *The Orcadian* columnist Bessie Grieve, who wrote as Countrywoman for, first the *Orkney Herald* and then *The Orcadian* for nearly 40 years, died at her birthplace, Ostoft in Shapinsay, at the age of 72.

Her published work included *Island Journeys*, *A Countrywoman's Travels*; *A Countrywoman's Calendar*; *Waves and Tangles*; and *A Countrywoman's Diary*.

Round-the-world sailing challenge

Former Orkney policeman Graham Philp embarked as mate on the yacht *Pause to Remember* in the world's toughest sailing challenge as he took part in the BT Global Challenge, a round-the-world race which would see ports of call in South America, New Zealand, Australia, South Africa and the United States.

Graham (41) who had also previously worked at Flotta, set out in the 67 feet yacht on the first leg of the voyage from Gosport on September 29, 1996, and completed the first leg to Rio de Janeiro in 29 days.

The round-the-world yachtsman told *The Orcadian*: "Rio was not a great place. Three of the crew got robbed. The skipper was mugged by a transvestite. A girl had to fend off muggers who were trying to steal her handbag and one of the guys was held up at knifepoint on a bus."

After that experience, the rounding of Cape Horn on the 6,600 mile leg from Rio to New Zealand seemed almost mundane. *Pause to Remember* arrived in Wellington on New Year's Day, 1997, in seventh place, and was up to fifth place when Sydney was reached.

The yacht had to battle against 100 feet waves and high winds in the southern seas - with a crewman rescued after being washed overboard, and having an added problem when the boom broke 3,500 miles from Cape Town. By the time Boston was reached, the yacht was in tenth position in the race.

The crew arrived back in Southampton on Wednesday, July 23, 1997, having completed more than 32,000 miles and spent 175 days at sea. *Pause to Remember* was eventually placed tenth. "I'd do it all over again," Graham Philp told *The Orcadian*.

British Airways quit isles routes

After half a century of serving Orkney, British Airways announced it would no longer operate on the air routes to the county.

Instead, all of the loss-making Highlands and Islands routes would be handed over to British Regional Airlines and Loganair, two independent airlines which would provide the services on a franchise basis for British Airways.

Mr Bob Ayling, chief executive of British Airways, said: "We have been flying on these routes in one form or another for the past 50 years, but, throughout this period, we have never achieved profitability.

"We have looked at a number of ways, and introduced many changes, to try to improve profitability but have reluctantly concluded that we will not be able to do so."

British Airways claimed: "Figures for the last three years of operation have shown a continued decline in the number of passengers carried on these services and increasing losses now amounting to several million pounds a year."

Orkney graduates to a university

One of the most far-reaching developments in the history of Orkney education got the go-ahead in 1996 with a £33 million endorsement of ambitious plans for the county to play its part in a pioneering new university.

It meant that Kirkwall was set to become a university town of the 21st century, after the announcement that the Millennium Commission would provide more than £33 millions towards a University of the Highlands and Islands, a high-tech concept which would see colleges throughout the region linked up by computers to share degree courses.

Work began on a new £5.3 million Orkney College at Weyland, Kirkwall,

which would become part of the new university at the turn of the century. Stromness, which could already claim to be a university town because of its links with departments of Heriot Watt University, would also play its part in the new venture.

It promised a significant boost to the Orkney economy, as Highlands and Islands Enterprise estimated that, across the region, the university would create 800 jobs and generate £70 millions a year for the North economy.

The new Orkney College was designed to accommodate some 300 students, made up of a mixture of local people, who would previously have travelled South, and newcomers to the county.

Lord Lieutenant dies

Representatives of the Royal family joined family, friends and former colleagues who gathered at a memorial service at St Magnus Cathedral to pay their last respects to Orkney's Lord Lieutenant, Brigadier Malcolm Dennison, who died at the age of 72 at his home at Roeberry, South Ronaldsay.

Included in the congregation was the Omani Ambassador to Britain, His Excellency Hussain Ali Abdul Latif, representing the Sultan of Oman.

Brigadier Dennison was succeeded as Orkney's Lord Lieutenant by Mr George Marwick, of Swannay House, Birsay.

Rugby club defeats national ban

Orkney Rugby Club faced its biggest challenge in its 29 year history - as the Scottish Rugby Union banned the club from entering the National League.

Orkney had beaten Ellon 43 - 9 to clinch the 1996 North District League title and qualify for the play-offs for entry into Division Seven of the Tennents National League.

However, the Scottish Rugby Union then announced that Orkney would not be allowed to take part. "The decision follows consultation with other National League clubs, the vast majority of which told the Union that they would find it very difficult to fulfil a fixture in Orkney due to extreme travel difficulties to and from the island, the likely requirement for at least one overnight stay and possibly more depending on the weather, and the consequent unavailability of players, many

of whom could be farmers or shift workers," said the Scottish Rugby Union.

The shock ban produced protests not only in Orkney but also from leading national figures in the game like internationalists John Beattie, Finlay Calder and Sean Lineen. "How pathetic and snivelling of the clubs who have mumped about going there, and how pathetic of the Scottish Rugby Union not to bankroll the cost in the first place," said John Beattie.

The protests eventually forced the Scottish Rugby Union into a U-turn and Orkney won the right to take part in the play-offs. In the event, the national dream was blown away as Orkney lost to Helensburgh in the final play-off match.

However, a year later, the Orkney players did achieve their goal when they retained the North District League championship in 1997 and, this time, found

success in the play-offs - despite having to overcome a new obstacle when the referee failed to arrive for the first play-off fixture.

Fortunately, a stand-in official was found to allow the game to start 40 minutes late, and Orkney went on to beat Strathmore by 20 points to ten. The Orkney team then secured a 24-24 draw with Heriot Watt, and that proved sufficient for the islanders to join the National League Division Seven for the 1997-98 season. (It also meant that the club would have to come to terms with an annual travel bill of around £25,000.)

Orkney's first ever National League game was at home to the Edinburgh side Broughton Former Pupils on Saturday, September 20, 1997. Orkney won 22-9, and went on to finish their first national league season in third place in the division.

Eurovision winner

Orkney musician Aimee Leonard - a former Stromness Academy pupil and Stromness Shopping Week Queen - was the pride of the county as she played her part in the success of the winning entry in the 1996 Eurovision Song Contest in Oslo.

Aimee was part of the backing group to the Irish entry, singer Eimear Quinn, and around 350 million viewers all over the World watched as they scored top marks with their performance of a traditional style Irish folk song, entitled The Voice.

(Picture courtesy of Craig Taylor)

East Kirk anniversary

The 200th anniversary of the congregation which eventually became Kirkwall's East Kirk, was celebrated in June, 1996.

The seccession congregation - which broke away from St Magnus Cathedral -

was formed in 1796 with the Rev William Broadfoot as the first minister. The seccession had grown rapidly to represent a third of the population of Kirkwall and St Ola and the church now known as the East Kirk was built in 1847.

New chapter for newspaper

It was the dawn of a new era for Orkney's newspaper, *The Orcadian*, as the company's new headquarters building at Hatston was officially opened on July 30, 1996, by Lord Younger of Prestwick - a former Scottish Secretary and Secretary of State for Defence.

The ceremony marked the move of the company's printing operations from Victoria Street, Kirkwall, where they had been based for nearly two centuries, and where *The Orcadian* was printed in 1854.

Top teacher

Papa Westray primary school headteacher Christine Hopkins was named as Scottish Teacher of the Year in a competition organised by a satellite television company. She had been nominated by the Papay school board chairman, Mr Ian Cursiter, in recognition of the contribution she had made to the school with only six pupils.

However there was sadness for another small community as Orkney Islands Council decided that Graemsay School - with just one pupil, Kevin Pepper - should be closed.

Top honour

Orcadian Dr Karl Linklater was elected president of the British Veterinary Association for 1996-97.

Dr Linklater, who was born in Stromness in 1939 and was educated in the county, had been director of veterinary services for the Scottish Agricultural College since 1986.

'Catalogue of irregularities'

A "catalogue of irregularities" was admitted by Orkney Islands Council after investigations into the council's former direct services operations.

The council's Direct Services Organisation had lost nearly £300,000 in 1994-95 - leading to the organisation's demise with several job losses and prompting a police investigation.

Councillor Eoin Scott, chairman of the OIC contract services committee, said: "This whole matter was deeply damaging to the council and our relationship with the public. There is no excuse for the disregard of council financial regulations, no matter the circumstances. I am satisfied, however, that a proper and thorough investigation was carried out, and the individuals central to this whole sorry affair dealt with accordingly."

The inquiry had revealed that workers' time sheets had been altered, receipts for the sale of obsolete council vehicles were not properly accounted for, and there had been breaches of financial regulations involving the purchase of materials. "Appropriate disciplinary action" had been taken over the discrepancies, said the council.

Orkney's procurator fiscal, Mr Keith Adam, said: "On the information presently available to me, I am not taking proceedings."

Prince's grief at isles tragedy

Two volunteers of the Prince's Trust - a charity launched by the Prince of Wales - were tragically killed while helping to repair the North Ronaldsay sheep dyke.

The two men - Derek Taylor (20) and Garry Leaburn (25), both from Dundee - were part of a 13-strong team from Tayside continuing the work that the Prince's Trust volunteers had done each year since the sheep dyke was badly damaged by storms in 1993.

Sadly, they were found dead beneath collapsed rubble after a desperate seven hour rescue attempt involving firemen, police, coastguards and islanders.

The Prince's Trust was later fined £10,000 at Kirkwall Sheriff Court, under the Health and Safety at Work Act, for failing to ensure the safety of the two volunteers who died.

Prince Charles - who met the volunteers' families to express his sympathy - had visited Orkney just a few weeks earlier in 1997 when he toured St Magnus Cathedral, the new Orphir community school and twice crossed Scapa Flow - first to Lyness and then to St Margaret's Hope.

Police bravery honours

An Orcadian policeman was commended for his bravery in tackling a murderer armed with two knives.

Sergeant Alastair Bews (48), the son of the late Chief Inspector Samuel Bews of Kirkwall, and a former Kirkwall Grammar School pupil, had completed nearly 30 years service with the Tayside Police when he confronted the killer who was hiding in an attic after murdering his former lover.

Sergeant Bews and a colleague, Constable Michael Whitford, were both awarded the Chief Constable's Commendation for their "courage and professionalism." A 42 year old man was later sentenced to life imprisonment for the murder.

Three Orkney policemen who risked their lives during a dramatic New Year's day rescue of a seaman from the waters of Kirkwall harbour were also honoured.

Constables Derek Fraser (31), John Learmonth (24) and Edward MacKenzie (32) had helped to rescue a Czech crewman who fell 20 feet between his ship and the pier, saving him from almost certain death from drowning or exposure, said a police spokesman as the three heroes received Royal Humane Society testimonials on parchment.

Farewell to Mastermind

A programme which had become part of British television history was screened for the last time as the final episode of the quiz show Mastermind was broadcast from St Magnus Cathedral, Kirkwall.

The show's host for 25 years, Magnus Magnusson, personally chose Orkney as the venue for the very last final. Previous finalists travelled to Orkney for the event and, following the filming, Magnus was presented with the famous black chair in which more than 1,400 contestants had sat.

The last Mastermind winner was Anne Ashurst, a romantic novelist, who answered questions on Barbara Villiers, Duchess of Cleveland.

A 'pillar of Orkney'

Warm tributes were paid following the death, at the age of 88, of Marjorie Linklater, one of Orkney's best known personalities and a woman who became a driving force both in local politics and the arts scene.

She was laid to rest alongside her husband, the Orkney writer Eric Linklater, in the Harray churchyard, overlooking the Harray loch and what became the Merkister Hotel, where they began their married life more than 60 years earlier.

A power behind the Orkney Heritage Society and St Magnus Festival, Marjorie Linklater had been the founder chairman of the Pier Arts Centre in Stromness. She had also been chairman of the Orkney branch of the Scottish National Party.

Dr Winnie Ewing, national president of the SNP, described her as "a pillar in defending Orkney's cultural heritage" and said: "Marjorie Linklater's death has left us all bereft of one of nature's original and beautiful charmers. But her charm hid an iron determination."

Cup winners

Rovers FC became only the third Orkney team to win the Highland Amateur Cup when, in a thrilling extra time battle, the Kirkwall team beat Contin 4 - 2 at Victoria Park in Dingwall. The first ever Orkney winners had been South Ronaldsay, and that feat was later emulated by Thorfinn.

Runner beats cancer to be top of the world

William Sichel in training on Sanday.
(Picture courtesy of Roderick Thorne)

Sanday international runner William Sichel (44) recorded a time of 7 hours 8 minutes 21 seconds in a 100 kilometre time trial - just four weeks after finishing a course of radiotheraphy to beat cancer.

He told *The Orcadian*: "Very shortly after collecting a team bronze medal in Italy at the European 100 km Championships, I was diagnosed as having a testicular tumour. I had immediate surgery and managed to make a rapid return to fitness and was selected to run for Great Britain in the World 100 km Championships in Holland."

There, he was part of the British team which won the silver medal as he finished in a time of 7 hours 27 minutes 56 seconds.

And, after the course of radiotherapy, he knocked nearly 20 minutes off that time in the time trial held at Jarrow in England in November, 1997.

But he was to achieve even greater honours, for, in September, 1998, he could claim to be Orkney's first ever athletics world champion as he returned home in triumph from the Veteran World 100km Road Running Championships in the Netherlands with two gold medals, having completed the course in 7 hours 16 minutes 24 seconds. He finished third overall, but won gold in the over 40 section, and another gold as part of the championship-winning Great Britain team.

William Sichel finished 1998 as the top ranked ultra distance road runner in the United Kingdom and his performance in running 149.31 miles in a 24 hour race in France was good enough to give him a ranking of number twelve in the world.

And in July, 1999, he proved he was the best in Britain as he won the national 100 km road running championships in a time of 7 hours 32 minutes 19 seconds on a gruelling Edinburgh course to become the overall British champion for the first time in his career.

Rugby stars rally for injured Orcadian

Some of the top names in Scottish rugby rallied to help raise thousands of pounds to help a young Orcadian player, Dugald McArthur from Sanday, who had been paralysed.

The tragic injury had been suffered as Dugald was playing in a match in Edinburgh, but several former internationalists - including Iain Paxton, Dougie Wylie, Alan Tomes and Bill Cuthbertson - travelled to Orkney to play against the local club for a Scottish Classics XV.

Dugald, who had been in the spinal injuries unit in Glasgow's Southern General Hospital, flew home to attend a special dinner dance which followed the game, and which raised over £2,500 for the Dugald McArthur Trust.

Theologian, author and devoted follower of Cowdenbeath Football Club, the Rev Ron Ferguson - the minister of St Magnus Cathedral for the last decade of the 20th century. *(Picture courtesy of Craig Taylor)*

Orkney mourns death of a Princess

The tragic death of Diana, Princess of Wales, killed in a car crash in Paris in the early hours of Sunday, August 31, 1997, touched Orkney along with the rest of the world.

A special book of condolences was set up in St Magnus Cathedral to allow people to pay their last respects, and prayers were said in churches across Orkney during Sunday services. Events and sport fixtures were cancelled, and shops closed, as a mark of respect during the Princess's funeral.

Orkney's Lord Lieutenant Mr George Marwick sent a message of sympathy to Buckingham Palace from the people of Orkney expressing the county's "deep sense of shock and devastation."

Farmers' blockade greets minister

The plight of Orkney's farming community was brought home to the public in dramatic style when 500 farmers and their supporters took to the streets of Kirkwall in a mass protest as the Secretary of State for Scotland, Mr Donald Dewar, visited the county.

It was the biggest demonstration by Orkney farmers since an estimated 5,000 people had gathered on Broad Street and the Kirk Green on February 28, 1930, to voice their anger at the agricultural crisis of that era.

Mr Dewar's arrival, on Thursday, December 4, 1997, was greeted by placard-carrying demonstrators and half a dozen tractors, some with trailers or slurry spreaders attached.

The farmers - claiming a total loss of £9 millions to the local economy as prices and subsidies continued to plummet in the crisis in the beef industry - received little reassurance, however.

Mr Dewar said he was aware of figures that showed a considerable deterioration in farm incomes but pointed out there was "no pot of gold" to solve the problem.

That was cold comfort for Orkney's farmers who had endured a decade of doom - a fact starkly illustrated at Orkney Auction Mart in September, 1998, when prime lamb prices were half what they had been in 1988, averaging just 66.5 pence a kilo, compared with an average of nearly 135 pence ten years earlier. Store cattle were averaging 40-50 pence per kilo lower than the previous decade.

Admiral Sir Jock Slater, son of an Orcadian, Dr James Slater, and married to Ann Scott from Kierfiold House, Sandwick, retired as Chief of Naval Staff and First Sea Lord in 1998. (Picture courtesy of the Ministry of Defence)

Record fine for Orkney egg thieves

Two brothers who travelled specially to Orkney to steal rare birds eggs were fined a massive £90,000 each - a record fine for such an offence in Britain - when they appeared at Kirkwall Sheriff Court in 1997.

The brothers, from Portsmouth, had been caught on the West Mainland after taking eggs of such protected species as merlins, hen harriers and red throated divers.

They were warned that they faced up to two years in jail if they did not pay the £90,000 penalties. However, on appeal, the fines were reduced to £6,000 and £4,000 respectively.

Chief executive

Orkney Islands Council chief Mr Ron Gilbert retired after 25 years service to the county as first finance director and, for 12 years, chief executive. He was succeeded as chief executive by Mr Alistair Buchan.

Kicking up a stink

Police gave a "friendly warning" to a 29 year old St Ola man who chose to take direct action to make a protest against Orkney Islands Council.

He walked into the council offices with a bucket full of sewage and slammed it on the desk of the chief environmental services officer.

Mr Peter Laird explained that he made the protest because problems with a septic tank had remained unresolved for nine years.

Lottery jackpot

The dream of millions became reality for members of an Orkney family as they celebrated a near £3 million jackpot win on the National Lottery.

Britain's newest millionaires were Davie and Lana Dunbar, one of the five daughters of former Kirkwall councillor Allan Taylor and his wife Jean. Mr Dunbar, a railway worker of Haster, near Wick, Caithness, said: "I had nothing at 7.50 pm on Saturday except a mortgage, bills and bank loans. Now I've got the biggest smile in Caithness."

Mr Dunbar (43) travelled to Glasgow to collect a cheque for £2,945,989.

Drugs menace

Police appointed a specialist drugs officer for the Orkney area. PC Alec Chisholm would co-ordinate police moves to curb drugs-related offences in the county, in recognition of the increasing incidence of drug abuse throughout the force area, and particularly public concern for the vulnerability of young people exposed to drugs, said a police spokesman.

Model success

Orcadian woman Debbie Flett (23) became a regular face on British television screens as she landed a role as a hostess on the Bruce Forsyth TV show "Play Your Cards Right." Her father Stewart Flett, born in Orkney was a brother of Robert Flett, of the family of agricultural engineers in Orphir, and she was a regular visitor to the county still.

She was also chosen in 1997 to feature as the new "face" of airline tycoon Richard Branson's Virgin empire in a worldwide advertising promotion for Virgin products.

(Picture courtesy of London Weekend Television)

Wallace to a Scots Parliament

Jo Grimond - a winner at ten General Elections - had been MP for Orkney and Shetland for 33 years when he decided to retire from the House of Commons. It would be an awesome task for whoever was selected to take over the mantle.

In the end, the choice was Jim Wallace, who would not only represent the Northern Isles for the remainder of the century but would see Jo Grimond's dream of a Scottish Parliament become reality, and actually take a share in government.

Following Jo Grimond's decision to stand down, the local associations agreed a short list of four contenders to be the Liberal candidate.

They were Shetland businessman Vivien Owers; the Orkney councillor Hugh Halcro Johnston, a 46 year old farmer from Orphir who, a decade later, would become county convener; Richard Jenkins (32) a former Captain in the Queen's Own Highlanders, now farming in Evie; and Jim Wallace, the man who won the nomination on the first count.

Jim Wallace was then a 29 year old Edinburgh-based advocate who had already contested the General Election for the Liberals in his native Dumfriesshire in 1979, the same year that he was called to the bar, having earlier graduated from Edinburgh University and Downing College, Cambridge. He was engaged to Rosie, who would become his wife three weeks after the 1983 General Election.

It had been accepted that Jo Grimond had a huge personal support, but the conjecture now began over whether the voters of Orkney and Shetland had the same allegiance to the Liberal cause. Both the Conservatives and the Scottish Nationalists had hopes that, with the elder statesman gone, they could see off the young pretender.

Winnie Ewing, who was already the MP for the Highland and Islands in the European Parliament, was adopted as the SNP candidate, while David Myles, a farmer in Angus and a former MP for Banff, was adopted by the Tories. Robina Goodlad from Shetland was re-elected as the Labour candidate for her second General Election.

The election was called for June 9, 1983. In fact Jim Wallace was to stand as the Liberal Alliance candidate after a deal agreed nationally with the Social Democratic Party of David Owen, Roy Jenkins, Shirley Williams and Bill Rodgers. Winnie Ewing described herself as the SNP Pro-Islands candidate.

There were many on the eve of the election who believed the result was too close to call. In the event, Jim Wallace romped home comfortably with a majority of 4,150 (a bigger majority than Jo Grimond had managed in either 1950 or 1970).

The result was: Jim Wallace (Liberal Alliance) 9,374; David Myles (Conservative) 5,224; Winnie Ewing (SNP Pro-Islands) 3,147; Robina Goodlad (Labour) 2,665. The turn-out of the electorate was 67.8 per cent.

Laura Grimond, who had campaigned enthusiastically for the young Wallace, told *The Orcadian*: " The result thoroughly bears out what I know to be true about the good sense and good judgement of the people of these islands, and while Jim Wallace is inheriting a great tradition, he has won the spurs through his own efforts. If the Liberal candidate had not been a credible one then he wouldn't have had this tremendous success."

Nationally, Margaret Thatcher's Conservative government was returned for a second term. In his maiden speech in the House of Commons, Jim Wallace paid tribute to his predecessor, Jo Grimond. "He can rightly claim to be described as a statesman and, indeed, an outstanding statesman," he said. He used the speech to make a plea for cheaper petrol in rural areas, as the price in Orkney had now passed £2 a gallon.

Within two years of the 1983 General Election, however, the Orkney political scene was enlivened by a change of party allegiance which was to see Jim Wallace opposed by a man who could have been the Liberal candidate for Orkney and Shetland.

Old Etonian Richard Jenkins, who had been on the short list, along with Jim Wallace, to replace Jo Grimond as Liberal standard bearer, had within months joined the Conservative party and, in May, 1985, he was adopted as the Tory Prospective Parliamentary Candidate for Orkney and Shetland.

Stromness Academy teacher John Aberdein was adopted for Labour and he would contest two General Elections before, as we will see at the end of the century, he too changed his political allegiance.

The Scottish National Party did not contest the 1987 General Election - allowing Shetland Fishermen's leader John Goodlad to stand under the banner of the Orkney and Shetland Movements, seeking greater autonomy for the islands.

It would be the first election in Orkney and Shetland to have five candidates as Grierson Collister, a Manxman living in Orkney, represented the Green Party.

The election was called for June 11, 1987, and the Conservative government did its best to help the party's local prospects by announcing a £10 million scheme to introduce roll-on, roll-off ferries to the North Isles of Orkney.

It was not a sufficient sweetener to sway the result as Jim Wallace was returned with a majority of 3,922 at an election which saw a turn-out of 68.68 per cent. The result was:

Jim Wallace (Liberal Alliance) 8,881; Richard Jenkins (Conservative) 4,959; John Aberdein (Labour) 3,995; John Goodlad (Orkney and Shetland Movements) 3,095; Grierson Collister (Green) 389.

Nationally, Margaret Thatcher again returned to power. A year later, in 1988, the Liberals officially merged with the SDP to become the Liberal Democrats, the banner under which Jim Wallace would stand for the rest of the century.

Kirkwall Grammar School teacher Mrs Frances McKie - already well known in Orkney as a campaigner on green issues and a leader of the opposition to nuclear developments - was adopted as the new prospective candidate for the Scottish National Party, while Hampshire barrister Dr Paul McCormick (40) was adopted for the Tories. He later had to play down the fact that he was a former Labour Party worker.

Margaret Thatcher had been ousted by her own party and so it was John Major, as Prime Minister, who called the General Election of April 9, 1992, which was to see Jim Wallace returned as Orkney and Shetland MP for a third time, and with his best majority to date, 5,033.

The result was: Jim Wallace (Liberal Democrat) 9,575; Paul McCormick (Conservative) 4,542; John Aberdein (Labour) 4,093; Frances McKie (SNP) 2,301; Christian Wharton (Natural Law Party) 115. The turn-out of voters was 65.6 per cent.

The Conservative government of John Major was returned to power, nationally.

Just a month after the 1992 election, Jim Wallace was chosen as the new leader of the Scottish Liberal Democrats - to succeed Malcolm Bruce - leading a team of nine Scottish Liberal Democrat MPs in the House of Commons.

In the run-up to the 1997 General Election, James Paton (35), a former Flotta oil worker and Shetland councillor, who had previously worked for the Labour party in Strasbourg, was adopted as the Labour candidate, while Hope Vere Anderson (38) from Dumfriesshire, would represent the Conservatives. Shetland civil engineer Willie Ross (41), convener of the Shetland branch of the SNP for nine years, was adopted for the Scottish Nationalists.

Christian Wharton would stand for the Natural Law Party, while Arthur Robertson from Stromness stood as an independent, and Francis Adamson represented the Referendum

Orkney and Shetland MP Mr Jim Wallace with his wife Rosie and their young family in 1987. (Picture courtesy of Orkney Photographic)

Party (calling for a referendum on Britain's membership of the European Community) to make it a contest between seven candidates - the most to ever take part in an Orkney and Shetland General Election campaign, and a far cry from the early days of the century when the MP was, on several occasions, returned unopposed.

The result of the General Election on May 1, 1997, saw Jim Wallace's fourth victory and, for the first time, he emulated Jo Grimond's regular achievement of getting more votes than all the other candidates put together. He was returned with a majority of 6,968 from a poll with a 64 per cent turn-out.

For the first time this century, a Labour candidate came second in the Orkney and Shetland constituency, while the Conservatives fell to fourth place with their lowest vote since the introduction of universal suffrage. Jim Wallace could claim 52 per cent of the vote, with the Tories getting just 12.2 per cent.

The result was: Jim Wallace (Liberal Democrats) 10,743; James Paton (Labour) 3,775; Willie Ross (SNP) 2,624; Hope Vere Anderson (Conservative) 2,527; Francis Adamson (Referendum Party) 820; Christian Wharton (Natural Law) 116; Arthur Robertson (Independent) 60.

Nationally, Tony Blair was returned as Prime Minister in a landslide Labour victory. There was not one Conservative MP returned in Scotland, so Jim Wallace could claim to be the leader of the largest opposition party in Scotland.

Labour had campaigned on a manifesto pledge to consult the people on the re-establishment of a Scottish Parliament, and on September 11, 1997, the electorate went back to the polling stations to vote in a referendum on Scotland's greatest constitutional change in nearly 300 years.

Voters were asked, firstly, whether they were for or against a Scottish Parliament and, secondly, whether it should have tax raising powers. Jim Wallace urged a "Yes-Yes" vote to both questions.

Scotland voted overwhelmingly for the reforms. And, in a big turn-about from the 1979 referendum when the islands had rejected the devolution proposals of the time, Orkney also endorsed a new Scottish Parliament with 57.3 per cent in favour (although that was the lowest level of support in the country).

Orkney was one of only two polling areas to register a No vote to tax-varying powers - with 52.6 per cent voting against that proposal.

The referendum result in Orkney (which would be a separate constituency, apart from Shetland, in the new legislature) was: In favour of a Scots Parliament 4,749 (57.3 per cent), Against 3,541 (42.7 per cent). In favour of tax powers 3, 917 (47.4 per cent), Against 4,344 (52.6 per cent). The referendum turn-out in Orkney was just 53.46 per cent.

The massive endorsement nationally saw the Government put in train the arrangements for the legislature. Jim Wallace announced that he would seek to stand as the Orkney Liberal Democrat candidate for the new Parliament - although, for the lifetime of the present Parliament, he would remain as the Westminster MP for Orkney and Shetland.

Christopher Zawadski, of Balfour Castle, Shapinsay, was adopted for the Conservatives, Kirkwall teacher John Mowat for the SNP and Glasgow Labour Party headquarters press officer Angus Macleod was named for Labour.

The election was enlivened a week before the poll when John Aberdein, who had stood for Labour in two General Elections in the Orkney and Shetland constituency, resigned from the Party and announced that he would vote for Jim Wallace.

He was not alone. Two out of every three voters who went to the polls in Orkney voted for Jim Wallace on May 6, 1999, as he became Orkney's first ever member of the Scottish Parliament with 67.4 per cent of the vote, and a majority of 4,619 from a turn-out of 56.95 per cent of the electorate.

The result was: Jim Wallace (Liberal Democrats) 6,010; Christopher Zawadski (Conservative) 1,391; John Mowat (SNP) 917; and Angus Macleod (Labour) 600.

A week after the election, Jim Wallaces, as leader of the Scottish Liberal Democrats, struck a coalition deal with the majority Labour group of Donald Dewar and became Deputy First Minister of Scotland.

It was the first time for 80 years that an Orkney representative had achieved senior ministerial rank; since Robert Munro, the MP for the Northern Burghs (which included Kirkwall) was Secretary of State for Scotland in World War One.

Snow chaos strikes home

1998

All 10,300 houses and businesses in Orkney were left without power as snow storms and gale force winds brought the county to a standstill in January, 1998, in some of the worst weather to hit the islands since 1955.

Motorists were stranded and schools closed as blizzards and drifting snow - up to seven feet deep in places - wreaked havoc across Orkney, and trapped an ambulance, on an emergency call-out, on the Kirkwall-Holm road.

The wind chill factor reduced the temperature to the equivalent of minus 15 degrees centigrade as dairy farmers were forced to pour away thousands of gallons of fresh milk after blocked roads prevented tankers reaching farms.

Ten people had to take refuge for two days at a house in Holm when their cars became stuck - along with a council snow-plough.

A helicopter was brought in to help restore power lines in the county.

However, it would be rain rather than snow that was to have the biggest impact for the next few months as the year of 1998 became the wettest ever on record in Orkney - with more than 330 days when rain fell in the county. The rainfall total for the year at the Kirkwall Airport Met Office was 53 inches, 14 inches more than the annual average over the previous 50 years.

The Rev Marjory MacLean, minister of the Stromness kirk, was the first woman to become moderator of the Orkney Presbytery of the Church of Scotland.
(Picture courtesy of Orkney Photographic)

Max in Antarctica

Orkney-based composer Sir Peter Maxwell Davies spent three weeks in the frozen wastes of Antarctica to help write a new symphony.

Sir Peter embarked on his trip to the British Antarctic Survey Rothera research station to gain inspiration for a sequel to *Sinfonia Antarctica* by Vaughan Williams, after being invited to write the piece by the Philharmonia Orchestra.

He covered thousands of miles during his stay, travelling in a Twin Otter plane, piloted by Andy Alsop from Kirkwall, who was a member of the British Antarctic Survey team. "It was the most dramatic scenery in the world - a once-in-a-lifetime experience." Sir Peter told *The Orcadian*.

The new symphony, also called *Sinfonia Antarctica* will be Sir Peter Maxwell Davies' eighth symphony, and is due to have its world premiere at the Royal Festival Hall in the year 2001.

Death of Lord Orkney

The man who held the title of eighth Earl of Orkney, Cecil O'Bryen Fitzmaurice, died in an English seaside nursing home at the age of 78.

Known as "Ginger" to his friends, Lord Orkney had lived for many years in a modest two bedroomed flat in Ferndown, Dorset. It was believed that he had only visited Orkney on one occasion - and then overcome by nerves, had quickly left without revealing his identity. He also had the titles of Viscount of Kirkwall and Baron of Dechmont.

All three hereditary titles were created in 1696 and had never been held by an Orcadian. Although the eighth earl had made regular trips to the House of Lords, he had only spoken once, on the subject of the armed forces.

On his death, the title passed to a second cousin, a Canadian professor, Oliver Peter St John.

The new Earl, Professor St John (60), from Winnipeg, Manitoba, immediately promised to keep much closer ties with the islands. He, and his wife, the author and historian Barbara Huck, had already visited Orkney in 1990 and arranged to return in 1998. He would be the last Earl of Orkney to succeed to the title before the Labour government of Tony Blair introduced legislation to end the powers of hereditary peers in the House of Lords.

Double celebration

The world's most northerly distillery, Kirkwall's Highland Park, celebrated its 200th anniversary in July, 1998, with a celebration bicentenary dinner for 200 guests.

The same year marked the 200th anniversary of the company which pub-lishes *The Orcadian* (although the newspaper was a mere youngster, having been first printed in 1854).

Stromness Shopping Week celebrated its 50th anniversary with a spectacular display by the Red Arrows aerobatic team.

Double life

The amazing secret double life of a man who moved to Stronsay three years earlier ended in a courtroom in Switzerland as he was sentenced to 16 years in prison.

Described as one of Europe's most notorious gangsters, the 49 year old man - who had been arrested in a police swoop on Stronsay and then extradited to Switzerland - was involved in a kidnap plot to extort a ransom of millions of pounds, the court heard.

Air stalwart

A stalwart of the modern age of Orkney's air service, Mr Bob Tullock, who served as Loganair's station manager at Kirkwall for 26 years, died suddenly at the age of 50 in March, 1998.

Westray-born Mr Tullock - a former member of the RAF - was the man largely credited with the successful operation of Orkney's vital air ambulance service for a quarter of a century.

Epic world flier lands in Orkney

Around-the-world microlight pilot Brian Milton arrived in Orkney on the last leg of an epic flight.

When he touched down at the Lamb Holm airstrip in July, 1998, it was the first time he had stepped on British soil since he set out on his circumnavigation of the world in a tiny microlight aircraft four months earlier,

As well as being the first microlight aircraft to go round the world, it was also the fastest global flight by an open cockpit, single engined aircraft.

His journey of 118 days surpassed the previous record which had been set by two Americans - who had also landed in Orkney - who circumnavigated the globe in 175 days in 1924, a feat recorded in earlier pages of this book.

Brian Milton (55) from Bethnal Green, London, had been inspired to make the trip by the 125th anniversary of Jules Verne's *Around the World in Eighty Days*.

"Eighty days would have been the ideal time," he told *The Orcadian*. "I still do think it is possible for someone to do it in 80 days."

His timetable, he said, had been delayed by problems flying in China, Vietnam and Russia, he said. One of the most frightening experiences was being buzzed by a Syrian Air Force jet and he had been forced to make seven emergency landings in one day as the heat of the Saudi Arabian desert caused the engine to seize. By contrast, he had nearly died when the plane iced up crossing the Bering Sea.

A slightly shorter record was established also in July, 1998, when pilots Robin Clarke, from Inverness, and Syd Utting, from Peterborough, set a new record of touching down on 17 airstrips - seven in Orkney - in one day.

They landed at North Ronaldsay, Sanday, Stronsay, Eday, Papa Westray, Lamb Holm and Kirkwall in their Piper Warrior aircraft as part of a fund-raising effort for the Royal National Lifeboat Institution.

Woman rescued from hotel freezer ordeal

A two and a half hour ordeal in sub-zero temperatures ended in a lucky escape for the owner of the Merkister Hotel after she became trapped in the hotel's freezer.

Mrs Elma MacDonald (59) was inside a walk-in freezer, collecting food, when the door swung shut behind her. She spent the next two and a half hours banging on the freezer door trying to raise help.

It was only then that the delivery man Michael Marwick arrived at the hotel and heard Mrs MacDonald. "It was a very lucky break," she told *The Orcadian*. "If I had been there much longer I definitely would not have survived. Nobody would have been into the deep freeze till the night time when they start the meals."

Westray Valentines celebrate 75 years

Westray husband and wife David (95) and Margaret Burgher (92) celebrated their 75th wedding anniversary as Scotland's longest married couple.

They had lived and worked on the croft at Cubbigoe, Skelwick, since they married the day after Valentine's Day on February 15, 1923.

The couple received a special delivery by Loganair Islander plane in the shape of a telegram from the Queen.

The couple, with two children, two grandchildren and five great grandchildren, said the secret to a long, happy marriage was "to love from the start until the end." David said: "Folk nowadays don't work at their marriages. You have to give and take a little."

(Picture courtesy of Stephen Hagan)

My pen pal - the Empress of Japan

Orkney woman Ross Grant received her first phone call from her life-long pen pal - the Empress of Japan!

Mrs Grant, of Cromwell Road, Kirkwall, first wrote to the Japanese girl who was to become Empress Michiko, wife of the Japanese Emperor Akihito, in the early 1950s when she was a ten year old pupil at a convent school in Edinburgh.

"My teacher at the time asked who would like to have a Japanese pen friend," she explained.

They had lost touch for a while after leaving school but Michiko - who married the emperor in 1959 - re-established contact in 1974, and their correspondence had been resumed.

"I was amazed to hear that she was a crown princess," said Mrs Grant, wife of retired schoolteacher Douglas Grant.

In 1998 the Japanese Royal couple visited Britain and for the first time since they began corresponding, the two pen friends spoke on the telephone.

"We talked about normal things. She is an excellent conversationalist and her English is perfect," said Mrs Grant.

Parish Cup veteran

When Sandwick footballers won the 1998 Parish Cup final, beating Stromness 2-0, it was Sandwick stalwart Calvin Poke's 16th winners medal.

Sadly the year of 1998 saw the death of one of Orkney's footballing greats, Jim "Dook" Donaldson, who had played for Thorfinn from 1946 to 1967. He played in 15 consecutive Orkney - Shetland matches from 1947-61 and gained two further "caps" in 1965-66. His goal tally in these games was 16 goals, while he scored 25 goals in 24 matches against Caithness between 1948-66.

He had once scored a hat-trick for Orkney in a 6-6 draw with the Scottish League side Hamilton Academicals. He was later president of the Orkney Football Association for eight years.

Orkney welcomes QE2 liner

The world's most famous liner dominated the skyline of Kirkwall as the *Queen Elizabeth II* paid her first ever visit to Kirkwall bay on Saturday, August 1, 1998, under the command of her master, Captain Robert Warwick. Over 1,000 passengers were welcomed ashore while thousands of Orcadians took the opportunity to sail round the bay to get a closer look at the 963 feet long vessel of 70,000 tons, the pride of the Cunard fleet since her launch in 1967. The ship created an impressive backdrop for the annual regatta of Orkney Sailing Club.

(Picture courtesy of Craig Taylor)

The £8.25 millions Pickaquoy sports and leisure complex was officially opened by the Princess Royal, Princess Anne, on April 16, 1999.

(Picture courtesy of Craig Taylor)

Floating 'bomb' in sea drama

1999

The impact of the Government's announcement of the imminent shutdown of Orkney's Pentland Coastguard station was brought home as a shipping disaster was narrowly averted in the Pentland Firth after a stricken ship became a floating bomb.

The Cypriot-registered ship *Multitank Ascania*, was carrying a potentially lethal 1,700 tonne cargo of vinyl acetate, when she broke down in gale force conditions in the early hours of March 19, 1999 - prompting an evacuation of homes on the Caithness side of the Firth as a full-scale rescue and salvage operation was launched amidst fears of a potential explosion.

The operation - co-ordinated by Pentland Coastguards - saw the 15 crew airlifted from the vessel, while lifeboats from Longhope, Wick and Thurso, and the Orkney tug *Einar* stood by.

The vessel was eventually towed to the safety of Scapa Flow by the tug *Erlend*.

Deputy Prime Minister John Prescott praised the "magnificent search and rescue co-ordination effort by Pentland Coastguard" but the Government refused to admit that the incident illustrated the recklessness of closing the Kirkwall-based station.

A week later, the first ever ship-to-ship transfer of chemicals in European waters went ahead at Lyness as the cargo from the stricken *Multitank Ascania* was transferred to a sister ship, *Rodenbek*.

Orkney's monument for the Millennium

An £8.25 million sports and leisure complex - the majority of the funding coming from the Millennium Commission and Orkney Islands Council - was officially opened at Pickaquoy by Princess Anne, the Princess Royal, on April 16, 1999.

The main sports hall was designed to double up as a concert hall, capable of seating 1,600, while the complex included a 247-seat cinema, which could also become a lecture theatre, and facilities for printmaking and photography, as well as a health and fitness suite.

Outside, the complex had an all-weather astroturf pitch and 400 metres athletics track. Mr Kieran Henderson was appointed the first manager.

A £2.25 million trust fund was set up to underwrite the expected annual £180,000 a year shortfall in the centre's operation.

Magnus Linklater, chairman of the Scottish Arts Council, which put £650,000 into the new complex, said: "The Pickaquoy Centre is a splendid addition to Orkney's already rich cultural life. It offers Orcadians new opportunities to enjoy performances in the most modern of surroundings with facilities which are second to none in the Highlands and Islands.

Princess Anne said: "This building will be a focal point of these islands, bringing together more people to take part, and I hope this will all contribute to your sporting achievements."

The year also saw the opening of another new sporting facility - a new £470,000 club house for Stromness Golf Club in April, 1999.

Shipping servant

Sydney Scott (84) received a special presentation to mark his retiral after an astonishing 70 years service to shipping in the isles.

Mr Scott, of Antabrek, North Ronaldsay, began working for the old Orkney Steam Navigation Company as a casual docker in 1929, and continued with the company as it evolved into the Orkney Islands Shipping Company and then Orkney Ferries, becoming company agent for North Ronaldsay in the mid 1960s.

He was succeeded as agent in 1999 by his daughter Kathleen. Sadly, Mr Scott died just two months later.

World challenge

Orkney volleyball players Amy Cromarty, from Holm, and Mandy Ross, of Kirkwall, who both took up the sport at Kirkwall Grammar School, were selected for the Scotland Under 19 volleyball squad to compete in the 1999 World Youth Games.

Top Orkney javelin thrower Jeremy Smyth from Kirkwall, who had already represented Scotland at Under17 and Under 20 level, was selected for the Scottish senior athletics squad for the first time to compete at the 1999 Welsh Games.

Lifeboat ceremony

The new Stromness lifeboat *Violet, Dorothy and Kathleen* was officially named by Mrs Margaret Kirkpatrick, widow of the Longhope lifeboat coxswain Dan Kirkpatrick who was lost with his crew in the 1969 Longhope lifeboat disaster. Longhope also welcomed a new lifeboat in 1999 - the *Max Aitken II*, which would be berthed at Longhope pier, ending a 125 year era during which the Longhope lifeboat had been based at Brims.

Trying times

Orkney Rugby Club finished its second National League season in style with a victory of 143-0 over Heriot Watt University.

Final farewell

Orkney's "own" ship, the fishing protection vessel HMS *Orkney*, with 39 officers and crew, made her final visit to the county under the command of Lieutenant Commander Christopher Moore.

The vessel sailed for the last time from Orkney waters, accompanied by local Sea Cadet officer Alex Strutt and four Orkney cadets, to her home base of Portsmouth to be decommissioned and put up for sale or disposal by the Royal Navy.

More for councillors

The concept of full-time, professional councillors moved a step nearer as Orkney Islands Council announced that OIC members would receive increases of up to £5,000 in special responsibility allowances.

On top of councillors' basic annual allowance of £5,400, they would receive an extra £6,348 as committee vice-chairmen and extra £9,529 as committee chairmen.

The total annual allowance of the convener would be £22,857 with the vice-convener receiving £19,683.

"Under the amended scheme the minimum allowance payable to a councillor with a special responsibility allowance will be approximately £11,000 which represents a living wage," said council chief executive Mr Alistair Buchan.

Canadian cousins

Orkney welcomed back her sons and daughters of another age as 170 Canadian visitors - virtually all descendants of Orcadians who had emigrated to the New World - arrived for a five day "Homecoming" visit to the islands.

The occasion was marked by the signing of a treaty of friendship between Orkney and Manitoba.

New Year honour

Orkney jeweller Ola Gorie - whose jewellery business, started in her parents' garden shed after graduating at art school in 1959, had grown to employ 55 people with her designs being exported round the world - became and MBE in the 1999 New Year honours list.

Also made an MBE was 61 year old Angus Hutchison of Stromness, a lighthouse keeper for 36 years, and the last principal keeper at Fair Isle before the automation of the lighthouse there.

(Picture from the files of *The Orcadian*)

Monks return to isle

For the first time since the arrival of the Norsemen, the island of Papa Stronsay was to become the home of an order of monks as an order known as the Transalpine Redemptorists purchased the 250 acre island for its new monastic enclave. Another Orkney island, the 140 acre Linga Holm off Stronsay, was purchased by the Scottish Wildlife Trust as a sanctuary for its colony of grey seals.

Rough waters

Orcargo - the shipping company operating the Kirkwall-Invergordon roll-on, roll-off ferry service - was put into administration, owing £1.7 millions, including £700,000 to the Royal Bank of Scotland and a £200,000 loan to Orkney Islands Council. The administrators announced that the vessel *Contender* would continue sailing and it was hoped to sell the business as a going concern.

Orkney sites achieve world status

Orkney's archaeologically - rich West Mainland, surrounding the Ring of Brodgar, was acclaimed as a World Heritage Site - global recognition that put the area on a par with such monuments as the Pyramids and the Great Wall of China.

The "neolithic heart" of Orkney - including Skara Brae and Maeshowe - was adopted as a site of world importance by UNESCO, the United Nations Educational, Scientific and Cultural Organisation, saying it was an area deserving "protection for the benefit of humanity."

Deal struck over oil cash

Orkney Islands Council agreed a multi million pound deal with Elf, the operator of the Flotta oil terminal which would pave the way for Orkney's Oil Age to continue into the 21st century.

Under the deal, Orkney would waive all oil throughput payments - which had been paid since the terminal began operating and which were worth, by 1999, £16 millions a year - from April, 2000.

In return, Orkney Islands Council would become the sole master of the Harbour Equalisation Fund, an oil reserve fund of £90 millions which had accrued over the years.

The council also agreed that £16.4 millions from the fund would go into an "abandonment fund" to help the terminal operators with decommissioning costs when the terminal eventually closed.

Elf said that the new agreement would ensure the terminal remained a competitive and viable facility for at least another 20 years.

The next generation of Orkney's Oil Age would be under new management, however. Elf announced that it was selling its interests in the Flotta terminal and its associated oil fields and the Canadian company Talisman Energy was in line to take over from the start of the 21st century.

Silver lining

Orkney angler Sandy Nicolson - of King Street, Kirkwall - brought more sporting glory to Orkney as he took part in the 1999 World Fly Fishing Championships in New South Wales, Australia - and finished as the second best in the world and the best in the United Kingdom.

A stalwart of the Orkney Trout Fishing Association, he qualified for the finals after finishing in the top four of 22 Scottish internationalists.

Soldier's farewell

Orkney's Lord Lieutenant for 18 years from 1972-90, Colonel Sir Robert Macrae, of Grindelay House, Orphir, died at the age of 84 in November, 1999.

He had served with the Seaforth Highlanders in France during World War Two before being captured in 1940 and spent five years as a prisoner of war. He later served with the Black Watch in Korea in 1952-53 and in Kenya in 1953-54. He retired from the Army in 1968 and was Knighted in the New Year honours list of 1990.

He had served as a councillor on both Orkney County Council and Orkney Islands Council as well as being a member of Orkney Hospital Board and then Orkney Health Board. He was also an Honorary Sheriff. (Picture from the files of *The Orcadian*)

New rector

Mr Iain Ballantine, the depute rector, became the new rector of Kirkwall Grammar School, succeeding Mr Eric Sinclair who left to take up a new post at Aboyne Academy.

Musical memory

Allie Windwick, the man who composed "Lonely Scapa Flow," one of the best known Orkney songs of the 20th century, died at the age of 85, 34 years after the song was first recorded by Angus Findlater and Allie's nephew Sandy Windwick on the record Owre the Ferry, which featured four of Allie's songs in May, 1965. He had worked in the printing department of *The Orcadian* from 1930-79.

Top potato

Orkney potato grower Claude Peace, Cara, South Ronaldsay, proved he was the best in the land as his selection of prime vegetables helped him to win the Scottish Open Championship for potatoes at the annual competition in Dundee in September, 1999.

Ba' results of the 20th century

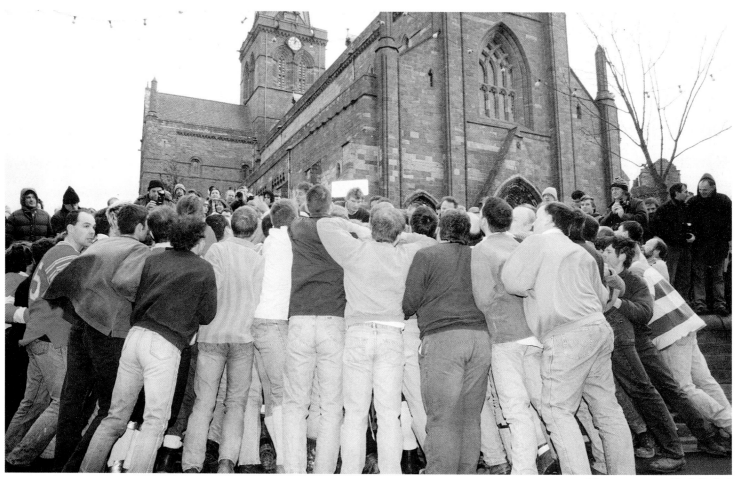

Men's Ba' – (U) Uppies, (D) Doonies

(Picture courtesy of Craig Taylor)

	New Year	Christmas		New Year	Christmas
1901	R. Gunn (U)	Robert Budge (U)	1954	Pat Johnston (D)	Jack Crisp (U)
1902	D.B. Peace (D)	Robert Mowat (U)	1955	John Flett (D)	Tom Shearer (D)
1903	T. Wylie (U)	James Brough (D)	1956	Jock Harcus (U)	Jim Keldie (U)
1904	J. Linklater (U)	John Cromarty (U)	1957	Jim Harrison (U)	Bob Muir (D)
1905	R. Linklater (U)	William Wick (U)	1958	Vincent Linklater (U)	John Sinclair (D)
1906	A. Milne (U)	J. Dennison (D)	1959	Douglas Campbell (U)	Gordon Rorie (U)
1907	William Somerville (U)	William Garrioch (U)	1960	Davie Fox (U)	Bill Stephen (D)
1908	Tom Nicolson (U)	William Costie (U)	1961	Billy Wilson (D)	Bobby Sinclair (D)
1909	William Harrison (U)	W. Park (U)	1962	George Donaldson (D)	Ian Linklater (U)
1910	James Johnston(U)	Alex Voy (U)	1963	Jack Miller (D)	Bill Sim (D)
1911	Jack Scollay (U)	John Mackay (U)	1964	Ronnie Drever (D)	Jack Donaldson (D)
1912	John Mowat (U)	Alex Flett (U)	1965	Jackie Scott (D)	Billy Johnston (D)
1913	Robert Matches (U)	James Kelday (U)	1966	John Robertson (U)	George Craigie (U)
1914	John Herdman (U)	–	1967	Mattie Stephen (D)	Gary Gibson (U)
(World War One)			1968	Bert Grieve (D)	Brian Barnett (U)
1919	–	Peter Hercus (D)	1969	Andy Rendall (D)	Theo Rorie (U)
1920	George Shearer (D)	Alex Walls (D)	1970	Sandy Budge (U)	Jim Dick (U)
1921	Alex Groundwater (U)	Thomas Linklater (U)	1971	Alan Monkman (U)	Ronnie Muir (U)
1922	James Craigie (D)	James T. Herdman (U)	1972	Freddie Rorie (U)	Jim Leonard (U)
1923	Robert Newlands (U)	James Mackay (U)	1973	Brian Smith (D)	Alan Findlay (U)
1924	Andrew Nicolson (U)	J. Harcus (D)	1974	Brian Kemp (U)	Eric Kemp (U)
1925	James Bews (D)	J. Muir (D)	1975	Gordon Rorie (U)	David Sinclair (D)
1926	William Mackinson (U)	William Laird (U)	1976	Calvin Slater (U)	Duncan Currie (U)
1927	Robert S. Robertson (U)	David Fox (U)	1977	Bobby Leslie (D)	Dennis Muir (D)
1928	William Mackinson Jr. (U)	Gillies B. Hercus (U)	1978	Norn Donaldson (D)	Michael Drever (D)
1929	Thomas Sinclair (D)	Robert Gunn (D)	1979	Billy Jolly (D)	David Johnstone (D)
1930	William Bews (D)	James Linklater (U)	1980	Ian Smith (D)	Lyall Flett (D)
1931	D. Johnston (D)	James Linklater (D)	1981	Leslie Tait (D)	Alan Hutchison (D)
1932	William R. Park (U)	James Sinclair (D)	1982	Mike Anderson (D)	Sandy Keldie (D)
1933	Bob Johnstone (D)	John Sinclair (D)	1983	Jim Cromarty (U)	Kenneth Eunson (U)
1934	David Kemp (D)	Andrew Shearer (D)	1984	Fraser Byers (D)	Brian Anderson (D)
1935	David Heddle (D)	David D. Marwick (D)	1985	Davie Johnston (D)	Michael Stevenson (D)
1936	James Thomson (D)	Charles Kelday (D)	1986	Keith Corsie (D)	Erlend Tait (D)
1937	John Miller (D)	Alex G. Webster (D)	1987	Eddie Barnett (D)	Fred Corsie (D)
1938	W.H.B. Sutherland (D)	William Sinclair (U)	1988	John Cromarty (D)	Ian Hutcheon (D)
1939	William Rorie (U)		1989	Sandy McConnachie (D)	John Copland (D)
(World War Two)			1990	Jim Baillie (U)	Evan Monkman (U)
1945	–	Hector Aitken (D)	1991	George Currie (U)	Leslie Manson (U)
1946	John Hourston (U)	Bob Park (U)	1992	Alan Rorie (U)	Alan Craigie (U)
1947	Alie Groundwater (U)	W. Schollay (U)	1993	Jim Linklater (U)	John Stephen (D)
1948	Jim Crisp (U)	Tommy Miller (D)	1994	Benny Thomson (U)	Stuart Leslie (D)
1949	Edgar Gibson (U)	Walter Scott (D)	1995	Barrie Reid (D)	Paul Miller (D)
1950	Tommy Thomson (D)	George Borwick (D)	1996	Jack Leslie (D)	Davie Miller (D)
1951	Johnnie Walls (D)	David Keldie (D)	1997	George Rendall (D)	Stuart Gray (U)
1952	Andrew Thomson (U)	Dan Grieve (D)	1998	Graeme King (D)	Kenny Garriock (U)
1953	George Cook (U)	Tom Sclater (U)	1999	Andy Kemp (U)	Edgar Gibson (U)

Boys Ba' (D - Doonies, U - Uppies)

	New Year	Christmas
1900	George F. Linklater (U)	Tom Shearer (D)
1901	William Rendall (D)	Alexander Smith (D)
1902	David Thomson (D)	James Croy (D)
1903	E. Arthur (D)	John Farquhar (D)
1904	Peter Shearer (D)	Robert Spence (D)
1905	Alex Mitchell (D)	James Findlayson (D)
1906	J. Lennie (D)	John Croy (D)
1907	B. Rendall (D)	John Muir (D)
1908	T. Learmonth (D)	Alexander Morgan (D)
1909	Bob Reid (D)	Herbert Williamson (D)
1910	Johnny Kennedy (D)	Dick Mowat (U)
1911	David Nicolson (D)	Frankie Sinclair (D)
1912	Jackie Nicolson (U)	John Sinclair (D)
1913	William Halcro (U)	James Harvey (D)
1914	Jim Fox (U)	–
(World War One)		
1919	–	James Cooper (D)
1920	Alie Groundwater (U)	Edwin Halcro (U)
1921	David Linklater (U)	Thomas Scott (U)
1922	A. Sinclair (D)	Rognvald Keldie (D)
1923	J. Kemp (U)	M. Thomson (D)
1924	James Mackinson (U)	J. Simpson (U)
1925	Philip Brass (D)	Johnnie Taylor (D)
1926	Archie Findlay (U)	Albert Brough (D)
1927	John Bruce (U)	Albert Thomson (D)
1928	Ronald Muir (D)	Calvin Slater (D)
1929	Bertie Rosie (U)	Tom Cooper (D)
1930	R. Gunn (D)	Charlie Smith (D)
1931	Gordon MacGillivray (D)	John Bews (D)
1932	Johnnie Walls (D)	David Hay (D)
1933	Jim Bews (D)	Jim Norquoy (D)
1934	Jim Duncan (D)	James Thomson (D)
1935	John Sinclair (D)	Herbert Flett (D)
1936	George Craigie (U)	Dan Grieve (D)
1937	James Pottinger (D)	Gordon Linklater (D)
1938	David Flett (U)	Stanley Moar (U)
1939	Norman Cooper (D)	–
(World War Two)		
1945	–	Evan MacGillivray (D)
1946	Jack Donaldson (D)	Ian Argo (D)
1947	Pat Baikie (U)	Cecil Sutherland (U)
1948	Alastair Smith (U)	Gordon & Nelson Rorie (U)
1949	Gary Gibson (U)	Tom Heddle (U)
1950	George Stout (D)	David Campbell (D)
1951	John Mooney (U)	Eddie Craigie (U)
1952	Freddie Rorie (U)	Ronald Muir (U)
1953	Leslie Campbell (U)	Alan Monkman (U)
1954	Jim Leonard (U)	Archie Findlay (U)
1955	Gath Cheyne (U)	Eric Kemp (U)
1956	Alan Findlay (U)	Norman Muir (D)
1957	Brian Barnett (U)	Billy Work (U)
1958	Stewart Urquhart (U)	Chris Norquoy (D)
1959	Douglas Thomson (U)	Tommy Borwick (U)
1960	Dennis Muir (D)	Raymond Borwick (U)

	New Year	Christmas
1961	David Sinclair (D)	Roy Linklater (U)
1962	Attie Leask (U)	Ian Cormack (U)
1963	Tony Monkman (U)	Bobbie Somerville (U)
1964	Archer Kemp (D)	Rognvald Taylor (U)
1965	Raymond Youngson (U)	Leslie Tait (D)
1966	Norman Cooper (D)	Ian Rorie (D)
1967	David Pirie (U)	David Scott (D)
1968	Sandy Keldie (D)	Billy Youngson (U)
1969	Alistair Clunus (U)	George Drever (D)
1970	Stuart Wood (D)	Billy Wylie (D)
1971	Sammy Tulloch (D)	James Donaldson (D)
1972	Maurice Walls (D)	David Miller (D)
1973	George Mowat & Anthony Rees (U)	Kenneth MacConnachie (D)
1974	John Stephen (D)	Brian Hutcheon (D)
1975	Stewart Pottinger (D)	Laurence Leonard (U)
1976	Graeme Smith (U)	Edgar Gibson (U)
1977	Andrew Kemp (U)	Colin Kirkpatrick (D)
1978	Leslie Miller (D)	David Moffat (D)
1979	Neils Newlands (D)	Billy Taylor (D)
1980	Jim Stout (D)	Tam Sinclair (D)
1981	Stewart Ryrie (D)	Alex Findlater (D)
1982	David Flett (U)	Ian Croy (D)
1983	Angus Findlater (D)	Bruce Moar (U)
1984	Gordon Mulraine (D)	Gordon Wilson (U)
1985	Jack Paterson & Rognvald Paterson (U)	Sigurd Gibson (U)
1986	Paul Watson (U)	Ian Gorn (U)
1987	Martin Sutherland (U)	Ian Stout (U)
1988	Derek Sutherland (U)	Greg Rorie (U)
1989	Drew Leslie (D)	Cullen Burns (D)
1990	Alastair Watson (D)	Colin Paterson (D)
1991	Bryan Bain (D)	Christopher Burgess (U)
1992	David Johnstone (D)	Robbie Thomson (U)
1993	Ewan Leonard (D)	Steven Spence (U)
1994	James Baillie (U)	Keith Leonard (U)
1995	Garry Dowell (U)	Roy Keldie (U)
1996	Darren Rendall (U)	Sean Brough (U)
1997	Stephen Kemp (U)	Balfour Baillie (U)
1998	Keith Harcus (U)	Nikki Monkman (U)
1999	Davy Leonard (D)	George Keldie (D)

Youths' Ba' (D - Doonies, U - Uppies)

	New Year	Christmas
1900	No record	James Smith (U)
1901	Jim S. Deerness (D)	Robert Fawns (U)
1902	Robert Sinclair (U)	John R. Miller (D)
1903	J. Spence (D)	George Durno (D)
1904	W. Scott (D)	Robert Harcus (D)
1905	Charlie Russell (D)	William Work (U)
1906	J. Harcus (D)	Stewart Wilson (D)
1907	W.A. Nicolson (U)	Pat Gunn (U)
1908	David Thomson (D)	Jeremiah Wilson (D)
1909	William Groundwater (U)	David Linklater (D)
1910	D. Sinclair (D)	*Youths game abolished*

Intercounty football for the Milne Cup

(The Milne Cup was presented by Mr J. Milne of the North British and Mercantile
Assurance Company of Aberdeen, a man who had once played football
for Woolwich Arsenal - the London club which eventually became Arsenal FC)

1908	Shetland 5	Orkney 1
1909	Orkney 3	Shetland 2
1910	Shetland 2	Orkney 0
1911	Orkney 3	Shetland 2
1912	Shetland 0	Orkney 0 (aet)
1913	Orkney 3	Shetland 2
1914	Shetland 0	Orkney 1
(World War One)		
1919	Orkney 2	Shetland 3
1920	Shetland 3	Orkney 0
1921	Orkney 2	Shetland 1
1922	Shetland 7	Orkney 1
1923	Orkney 1	Shetland 2 (aet)
1924	Shetland 2	Orkney 1
1925	Orkney 2	Shetland 3 (aet)
1926	Shetland 2	Orkney 0
1927	Orkney 5	Shetland 1
1928	Shetland 2	Orkney 3
1929	Orkney 1	Shetland 3
1930	Shetland 1	Orkney 3
1931	Orkney 5	Shetland 2
1932	Shetland 6	Orkney 0
1933	Orkney 1	Shetland 0
1934	Shetland 4	Orkney 0
1935	Orkney 3	Shetland 1
1936	Shetland 0	Orkney 1
1937	Orkney 4	Shetland 1
1938	Shetland 7	Orkney 4
1939	Orkney 2	Shetland 0
(World War Two)		
1946	Shetland 3	Orkney 5
1947	Orkney 2	Shetland 2 (aet)
1948	Shetland 2	Orkney 1 (aet)
1949	Orkney 6	Shetland 1
1950	Shetland 1	Orkney 2
1951	Orkney 4	Shetland 0
1952	Shetland 2	Orkney 5
1953	Orkney 1	Shetland 3
1954	Shetland 3	Orkney 1 (aet)
1955	Orkney 3	Shetland 2
1956	Shetland 1	Orkney 6
1957	Orkney 2	Shetland 4
1958	Shetland 0	Orkney 2

1959	Orkney 4	Shetland 2
1960	Shetland 0	Orkney 2
1961	Orkney 6	Shetland 4
1962	Shetland 4	Orkney 5
1963	Orkney 7	Shetland 9 (aet)
1964	Shetland 3	Orkney 3
1965	Orkney 2	Shetland 1
1966	Shetland 1	Orkney 6
1967	Orkney 1	Shetland 2
1968	Shetland 3	Orkney 2 (aet)
1969	Orkney 0	Shetland 3
1970	Shetland 1	Orkney 1
1971	–	
1972	Orkney 3	Shetland 1
	Shetland 1	Orkney 7
1973	Orkney 3	Shetland 2
1974	Shetland 2	Orkney 1
1975	–	
1976	Orkney 2	Shetland 1
1977	Shetland 1	Orkney 0
1978	Orkney 1	Shetland 2
1979	Shetland 2	Orkney 0 (aet)
1980	Orkney 0	Shetland 1
1981	Shetland 0	Orkney 1
1982	Orkney 0	Shetland 1
1983	Shetland 1	Orkney 0
1984	Orkney 0	Shetland 1
1985	Shetland 6	Orkney 1
1986	Orkney 0	Shetland 1
1987	Shetland 2	Orkney 0
1988	Orkney 1	Shetland 0
1989	Shetland 4	Orkney 1
1990	Orkney 1	Shetland 0
1991	Shetland 4	Orkney 2
1992	Orkney 0	Shetland 2
1993	Shetland 0	Orkney 0
1994	Orkney 0	Shetland 0
1995	Shetland 2	Orkney 0
1996	Orkney 0	Shetland 4
1997	Shetland 5	Orkney 0
1998	Orkney 2	Shetland 3
1999	Shetland 4	Orkney 1

Football Parish Cup Winners

1929	Holm 3	Deerness 2
1930	Deerness 4	Firth 3
1931	Firth 3	Shapinsay 1
1932	Deerness 5	Firth 2
1933	Shapinsay 1	Holm 1
	(Shapinsay won on corners)	
1934	Deerness 6	Sandwick 2
1935	Deerness 3	Shapinsay 0
1936	Stenness 4	Deerness 1
1937	Shapinsay 3	Stenness 2
1938	Shapinsay 4	Deerness 3
1939	Harray 4	Orphir 3
(World War Two)		
1946	Harray 2	Birsay 1
1947	St Ola 6	Harray 3
1948	Shapinsay 4	Harray 1 (after replay)
1949	Holm 2	Harray 0
1950	Holm 3	Harray 1
1951	Harray 3	Holm 2
1952	St Andrews 2	Shapinsay 0
1953	St Ola 4	Harray 2
1954	Shapinsay 3	Harray 2
1955	St Andrews 2	Orphir 0
1956	Harray 3	South Ronaldsay 1
1957	St Andrews 6	Harray 4
1958	Harray 2	South Ronaldsay 1
1959	St Andrews 5	St Ola 1
1960	St Andrews 6	Orphir 0
1961	St Ola 2	South Ronaldsay 0
1962	St Andrews 2	St Ola 0
1963	St Andrews 3	St Ola 2
1964	Harray 6	St Ola 2
1965	St Ola 3	Harray 2 (after replay)
1966	Harray 4	Birsay 0
1967	Harray 2	Sandwick 1
1968	Harray 4	Sandwick 2 (after replay)
1969	Harray 3	Sandwick 1
1970	Birsay 2	St Ola 0
1971	Birsay 4	Sandwick 0
1972	Harray 3	South Ronaldsay 1
1973	Sandwick 1	South Ronaldsay 0
1974	Sandwick 4	Harray 3
1975	Sandwick 1	Birsay 0
1976	Sandwick 3	Harray 1
1977	Sandwick 1	South Ronaldsay 0
1978	Sandwick1	Birsay 0
1979	St Ola 2	Orphir 1
1980	Stromness 1	Birsay 0
1981	Sandwick 1	Birsay 0 (after replay)
1982	Sandwick 1	St Ola 0
1983	Sandwick 3	Orphir 0
1984	Birsay 2	St Ola 0
1985	Sandwick 3	Birsay 1
1986	Stromness 3	St Ola 0 (after replay)
1987	Sandwick 2	Birsay 1
1988	St Ola 3	Sanday 0
1989	Sandwick 5	St Ola 1
1990	St Ola 2	Firth 0
1991	Westray 4	Orphir 0
1992	Firth 2	St Ola 1
1993	Sandwick 3	Westray 1
1994	Westray 2	Stromness 0
1995	St Ola 3	Sandwick 0
1996	Sandwick 3	Firth 1
1997	Sandwick 5	Firth 2
1998	Sandwick 2	Stromness 0
1999	Westray 2	South Ronaldsay 1

Intercounty hockey for the Lady Hamilton Cup

1926	Shetland 3	Orkney 0
1927	Orkney 4	Shetland 1
1928	Shetland 0	Orkney 6
1929	Orkney 8	Shetland 3
1930	Shetland 4	Orkney 6
1931	Orkney 7	Shetland 3
1932	Shetland 3	Orkney 2
1933	Orkney 1	Shetland 2
1934	Shetland 1	Orkney 1 (aet)
1935	Orkney 7	Shetland 1
1936	Shetland 0	Orkney 1
1937	Orkney 3	Shetland 0
1938	Shetland 0	Orkney 1
1939	Orkney 0	Shetland 2
(World War Two)		
1946	Shetland 4	Orkney 0
1947	Orkney 2	Shetland 2 (aet)
1948	Shetland 0	Orkney 1
1949	Orkney 2	Shetland 0
1950	Shetland 2	Orkney 2
1951	Orkney 4	Shetland 0
1952	Shetland 1	Orkney 2
1953	Orkney 6	Shetland 0
1954	Shetland 1	Orkney 2
1955	Orkney 1	Shetland 1
1956	Shetland 1	Orkney 2
1957	Orkney 7	Shetland 3
1958	Shetland 0	Orkney 1
1959	Orkney 2	Shetland 1
1960	Shetland 0	Orkney 0
1961	Orkney 6	Shetland 2
1962	Shetland 3	Orkney 1
1963	Orkney 3	Shetland 1
1964	Shetland 0	Orkney 0
1965	Orkney 3	Shetland 0
1966	Shetland 3	Orkney 3
1967	Orkney 6	Shetland 1
1968	Shetland 3	Orkney 3
1969	Orkney 7	Shetland 1
1970	Shetland 0	Orkney 2
1971	-	
1972	Orkney 3	Shetland 0
	Shetland 1	Orkney 2
1973	Orkney 1	Shetland 1
1974	Shetland 3	Orkney 2
1975	Orkney 1	Shetland 2
1976	Orkney 1	Shetland 1
1977	Shetland 1	Orkney 1
1978	Orkney 3	Shetland 0
1979	Shetland 0	Orkney 1
1980	Orkney 1	Shetland 2
1981	Shetland 2	Orkney 2
	(Orkney won on penalties after extra time)	
1982	Orkney 1	Shetland 2
1983	Shetland 4	Orkney 0
1984	Orkney 2	Shetland 0
1985	Shetland 1	Orkney 2
1986	Orkney 4	Shetland 1
1987	Shetland 1	Orkney 2 (aet)
1988	Orkney 4	Shetland 1
1989	Shetland 1	Orkney 0
1990	Orkney 5	Shetland 1
1991	Shetland 0	Orkney 1
1992	Orkney 2	Shetland 0
1993	Shetland 1	Orkney 0
1994	Orkney 2	Shetland 0
1995	Shetland 0	Orkney 1
1996	Orkney 2	Shetland 1
1997	Shetland 0	Orkney 1
1998	Orkney 3	Shetland 1
1999	Shetland 2	Orkney 2
		(Shetland won on penalties)

Intercounty football for the Archer Shield

1935	Caithness 7	Orkney 0
1936	Orkney 2	Caithness 6 (aet)
1937	Caithness 3	Orkney 6
1938	Orkney 4	Caithness 5 (aet)
(World War Two)		
1947	Caithness 5	Orkney 3 (aet)
1948	Orkney 3	Caithness 4
1949	Caithness 0	Orkney 6
1950	Orkney 3	Caithness 1
1951	Caithness 1	Orkney 2
1952	Orkney 2	Caithness 4
(From 1953-64, the trophy was contested over two games, home and away)		
1953	Caithness 0	Orkney 4
	Orkney 7	Caithness 3
	(Orkney won 11-3 on aggregate)	
1954	Caithness 4	Orkney 2
	Orkney 6	Caithness 5
	(Caithness won 9-8 on aggregate)	
1955	Caithness 2	Orkney 3
	Orkney 2	Caithness 2
	(Orkney won 5-4 on aggregate)	
1956	Caithness 5	Orkney 3
	Orkney 7	Caithness 2
	(Orkney won 10-7 on aggregate)	
1957	Caithness 3	Orkney 1
	Orkney 6	Caithness 1
	(Orkney won 7-4 on aggregate)	
1958	Caithness 1	Orkney 5
	Orkney 1	Caithness 3
	(Orkney won 6-4 on aggregate)	
1959	Caithness 7	Orkney 5
	Orkney 1	Caithness 3
	(Caithness won 10-6 on aggregate)	
1960	Caithness 5	Orkney 4
	Orkney 5	Caithness 3
	(Orkney won 9-8 on aggregate)	
1961	Caithness 4	Orkney 2
	Orkney 4	Caithness 7
	(Caithness won 11-6 on aggregate)	
1962	Caithness 1	Orkney 0
	Orkney 3	Caithness 4
	(Caithness won 5-3 on aggregate)	
1963	Caithness 3	Orkney 2
	Orkney 7	Caithness 5
	(Orkney won 9-8 on aggregate)	
1964	Caithness 3	Orkney 4
	Orkney 3	Caithness 3
	(Orkney won 7-6)	
(In 1965, the competition reverted to one match a year)		
1965	Caithness 9	Orkney 1
1966	Orkney 2	Caithness 1
1967	Caithness 1	Orkney 3
1968	Orkney 4	Caithness 2
1969	Caithness 4	Orkney 2
1970	-	
1971	Orkney 7	Caithness 0
1972	Caithness 0	Orkney 2
1973	Orkney 4	Caithness 0
1974	Caithness 3	Orkney 1
1975	Orkney 0	Caithness 4
1976	Caithness 1	Orkney 0
1977	Orkney 2	Caithness 1
1978	Caithness 1	Orkney 1
1979	Orkney 3	Caithness 1
1980	Caithness 0	Orkney 2
1981	Orkney 2	Caithness 3
1982	Caithness 1	Orkney 0
1983	Orkney 2	Caithness 3
1984	Caithness 2	Orkney 1
1985	Orkney 3	Caithness 2 (aet)
1986	Caithness 3	Orkney 1 (aet)
1987	Orkney 0	Caithness 2
1988	Caithness 0	Orkney 1
1989	Orkney 1	Caithness 0
1990	Caithness 1	Orkney 0
1991	Orkney 0	Caithness 4
1992	Caithness 2	Orkney 1
1993	Orkney 1	Caithness 2
1994	Caithness 4	Orkney 2
1995	Orkney 0	Caithness 2
1996	Caithness 4	Orkney 1
1997	Orkney 3	Caithness 1
1998	Caithness 2	Orkney 1 (aet)
1999	Orkney 4	Caithness 3

North Isles Sports Island Champions 1949-99

1949	Westray
1950	Sanday
1951	Sanday
1952	Westray
1953	Westray
1954	Sanday
1955	Stronsay
1956	Sanday
1957	Sanday
1958	Westray
1959	Stronsay
1960	Sanday
1961	Stronsay
1962	Westray
1963	Sanday
1964	Sanday
1965	Westray
1966	Sanday
1967	Sanday
1968	Sanday
1969	Sanday
1970	Westray
1971	Westray
1972	Sanday
1973	Westray
1974	Eday
1975	Sanday
1976	Sanday
1977	Sanday
1978	Sanday
1979	Sanday
1980	Sanday/Westray
1981	Sanday
1982	Sanday
1983	Sanday
1984	Sanday
1985	Papa Westray
1986	Papa Westray/Sanday
1987	Sanday
1988	Sanday
1989	Westray
1990	Westray
1991	Papa Westray
1992	Westray
1993	Westray
1994	Westray
1995	Eday
1996	Eday/Westray
1997	Westray
1998	Sanday
1999	Sanday

Provosts of Stromness

Andrew Wylie	1900 - 1918
Captain G.G. Baillie	1918 - 1919
Robert W. Clouston	1919 - 1925
James Corrigall	1925 - 1931
James G. Marwick	1931 - 1946
George S. Robertson	1946 - 1953
T.N.F. Hourston	1953 - 1959
Rosetta C.B. Groundwater	1959 - 1965
J.R.T. Robertson	1965 - 1968
William E. Knight	1968 - 1971
J.R.T. Robertson	1971 - 1975

(THE END OF STROMNESS TOWN COUNCIL)

Orkney Agricultural Society Presidents of the century

1889-1907 .Colonel J.W. Balfour of Balfour and Trenabie
1908-18 .....Colonel W.E. Balfour of Balfour and Trenabie
1919 ....R. Scarth, Binscarth, Firth
1920-24 ......J. Johnston, Coubister, Firth
1925 ....T. Clark, Swanbister, Orphir
1926 ....J. Clouston
1927 ..........W.T. Wood, Balfour Mains, Shapinsay
1928 ....G. Learmonth Snr, Pow, Sandwick
1929 ..........J.M.H. Robertson
1930 ....W. Corrigal, Northbigging, Harray
1931 ..........J.R. Hourston, Waterfield, St Ola
1932 ..........J.G.S. Flett, Nistaben, Harray
1833 ....A. Calder, Sebay, Tankerness
1934 ....W. Ritch, Kierfiold, Sandwick
1935 ....T. Clouston, Littlehowes, Holm
1936 ....G. Learmonth Jnr, Pow, Sandwick
1937 ..........A.S. Johnston, Ingashowe, Firth
1838 ..........R.C. Twatt, Upper Scapa, St Ola
1939 ....C. Hourston, Beaquoy, Birsay
(War Years)
1946 ..........G.W.D. Scott, Netherhill, Tankerness
1947 ....W. Corrigal, Northbigging, Harray
1948 ..........W.G. Smith, Hall of Tankerness
1949 ....P. Davidson, Skaill, Sandwick
1950 ..........W.B. Shearer, Sebay, Tankerness
1951 ..........A.C. Rendall, Barnhouse, Stenness
1952 ....J. Tait, Campston, Toab
1953 ..........J.G.S. Flett, Nistaben, Harray
1954 ..........G.W.D. Scott, Netherhill, Tankerness
1955 ....J. Tomison, South Ronaldsay
1956 ....J. Stevenson, Blackha, St Ola
1957 ....W. Wood, Aikerness, Evie
1958 ..........M.W.T. Wood, Berriedale, South Ronaldsay
1959 ..........J.H. Johnston, Gyre, Orphir
1960 ....J. Scott, Caldale, St Ola
1961 ....R. Johnston, Trumland, Rousay
1962 ..........R.G. Bain, Hall of Tankerness
1963 ....K. Flett, Mussaquoy, Orphir
1964 ....B. Bremner, Bendigoe, St Ola
1965 ....E. Heddle, Wester Voy, Sandwick
1966 ..........W.S. Watston, Lynn, St Ola
1967 ....G. Wylie, Swartland, Sandwick
1968 ..........D.G. Spence, Berstane, St Ola
1969 ..........W.D. Kirkpatrick, Newhall, Stromness
1970 ....W. Taylor, Northfield, Burray
1971 ..........J.G. Moar, Bankhead, Sandwick
1972 ..........J.W. Laughton, Easterbister, Holm
1973 ....H. Flett, Boardhouse, Birsay
1974 ..........D.G. Spence, Berstane, St Ola
1975 ....S. Davidson, Skaill, Sandwick
1976 ....J. Tait, Lower Breckquoy, Holm
1977 ..........G.R.T. Scarth, Twatt, Birsay
1978 ....K. Eunson, Keigar, Deerness
1979 ....C. Merriman, Laithe, Sandwick
1980 ..........E.S.H. Harcus, Quanterness, St Ola
1981 ..........J.T.S. Flett, Millhouse, Harray
1982 ..........W.R. Baillie, Biggings, Toab
1983 ..........R.A. Scarth, Twatt, Birsay
1984 ..........J.M. Lennie, Nearhouse, Tankerness
1985 ..........W.D. Kirkpatrick, Newhall, Stromness
1986 ..........J.R. Taylor, St Margaret's Hope, S. Ronaldsay
1987 ....D. Ritch, Brettobreck, Stromness
1988 ....D. Muir, Saverock, St Ola
1989 ..........D.W. Sinclair, Unigarth, Sandwick
1990 ....Jack Cromarty, Roadside, Toab
1991 ....Jim Swannie, Ramsquoy, Stenness
1992 ....Phyllis Harcus, Messigate, Tankerness
1993 ....Arthur Herdman, Linday, Sandwick
1994 ....Scott Harcus, Quanterness, St Ola
1995 ....James Kirkpatrick, Vestrafiold, Sandwick
1996 ....George Eunson, Corse, St Ola
1997 ....Jim Slater, Millquoy, Stenness
1998 ....John Thomson, Muckle Myre, South Ronaldsay
1999 ....Barbara Foulkes, West Nearhouse, Birsay

Provosts of Kirkwall

Nicol Spence ....1892 - 1904
John Sclater ....1904 - 1907
Col James Slater ....1907 - 1913 (the older brother of John M. Slater, who follows)
William S. Baikie ....1913 - 1919
Major John White ....1919 - 1925
John M. Slater ....1925 - 1940
Peter C. Flett ....1940 - 1947
Robert Slater ....1947 - 1954
James Flett...............................1954 - 1957
James Scott ....1957 - 1969
Georgina Leitch ....1969 - 1975
(THE END OF KIRKWALL TOWN COUNCIL)

Challenge Cup Winners SCDA Orkney festivals

1933 ....Dounby (A) SWRI
1934 ....Kirkwall Amateur Dramatic Society (A)
1935 ....Kirkwall Amateur Dramatic Society (C)
1936 ....Kirkwall Amateur Dramatic Society
1937 ....Kirkwall Amateur Dramatic Society
1938 ....Kirkwall Amateur Dramatic Society
1939 ....St Ola SWRI
(World War Two)
1946 ....Kirkwall Arts Club
1947 ....Kirkwall Arts Club
1948 ....Harray Amateur Dramatic Society
1949 ....Kirkwall Townswomen's Guild
1950 ....Stromness Amateur Dramatic Society
1951 ....Phoenix Players
1952 ....Stromness SWRI
1953 ....Stromness Amateur Dramatic Society
1954 ....Kirkwall Arts Club
1955 ....Kirkwall Arts Club
1956 ....Kirkwall Arts Club
1957 ....Kirkwall Arts Club
1958 ....Kirkwall Arts Club
1959 ....Kirkwall Arts Club
1960 ....Harray Players
1961 -
1962 ....Kirkwall Arts Club
1963 ....Kirkwall Arts Club
1964 ....Stromness SWRI
1965 ....Kirkwall Arts Club
1966 ....Kirkwall Arts Club
1967 ....East Mainland Young Farmers Club
1968 ....Stromness Academy
1969 ....Stromness SWRI
1970 ....Stromness SWRI
1971 ....Stromness SWRI
1972 ....Kirkwall Arts Club
1973 ....Harray Players
1974 ....Kirkwall Arts Club
1975 ....Kirkwall Arts Club
1976 ....Harray Players
1977 ....Stromness SWRI
1978 ....Deerness Young Farmers Club
1979 ....Palace Players
1980 ....Kirkwall Arts Club (B)
1981 ....Kirkwall Grammar School
1982 ....Kirkwall Arts Club
1983 ....Kirkwall Arts Club
1984 ....Kirkwall Arts Club
1985 ....Palace Players
1986 ....Kirkwall Arts Club
1987 ....Palace Players
1988 ....Palace Players
1989 ....Kirkwall Arts Club
1990 ....Palace Players
1991 ....Palace Players
1992 ....Palace Players
1993 ....Palace Players
1994 ....Palace Players
1995 ....Palace Players
1996 ....Palace Players
1997 ....Stromness Drama Club
1998 ....Kirkwall Arts Club
1999 ....St Andrews Drama Club

Presidents of the Rotary Club of Kirkwall

1967-68 ....Andrew R. Buchan
1968-69 ....John C. Sclater
1969-70 ....G. Edward Peacock
1970-71 ....John D.M. Robertson
1971-72 ....Alistair Groundwater
..................................William L. Marwick
1972-73 ....Robert T. Tulloch
1973-74 ....James D. Walker
1974-75 ....John H. McDonald
1975-76 ....Alan Bullen
1976-77 ....Marcus W.T. Wood
1977-78 ....W. Michael Edwards
1978-79 ....Hugh Clyde
1979-80 ....John D. Macdonald
1980-81 ....Roy F. Thomson
1981-82 ....James B. Lochhead
1982-83 ....Eoin Leslie
1983-84 ....Ian T.W. Sloan
1984-85 ....Jack Ridgway
1985-86 ....William Groundwater
1986-87 ....Robin Hancock
1987-88 ....Bryan M. Clark
1988-89 ....Eric G.W. Green
1989-90 ....Thomas F. Drever
1990-91 ....Robert W. Corsie
1991-92 ....Bashir I. Hasham
1992-93 ....Peter N. Scott
1993-94 ....Hamish L. Cross
1994-95 ....Philip White
1995-96 ....Bill Cant
1996-97 ....Eric G.W. Green
1997-98 ....John C. Holmes
1998-99 ....Alistair J. Bruce
1999-00 ....Rognvald Johnson

Stromness Shopping Week Queens and Attendants

1952 ....Ivy Flett
..................Elizabeth Robertson, Nancy Linklater
1953 ....Elizabeth Robertson
..................Shirley Seatter, Emily Yorston
1954 ....Elizabeth Guthrie
..................Elizabeth Tait, Violet Cromarty
1955 ....Elizabeth Tait
..................Marjorie Mowat, Elizabeth Groundwater
1956 ....Elizabeth Groundwater
..................Ann Crawford, Marjorie Mowat
1957 ....Ann Crawford
..................Doreen Kirkness, Mary Craigie
1958 ....Constance Groundwater
..................Helen Black, Sheena Barclay
1959 ....Aileen Fiddler
..................Katherine Hill, Kathleen Grieve
1960 ....Grace Stevenson
..................Joan Robertson, Fielda Flett
1961 ....Aileen Harvey
..................Vivienne Fraser, Marion Russell
1962 ....Phyllis Robertson
..................Kathleen Tait, Helen Gibson
1963 ....Grace Rhodes
..................Patricia Meldrum, Kathleen Stockan
1964 ....Ann Brass
..................Helen McLean, Carol Meldrum
1965 ....Carol Meldrum
..................Evelyn Stockan, Moira Sinclair
1966 ....Evelyn Stockan
..................Barbara McIver, Doris Leask
1967 ....Doris Leask
..................Moyra Bain, Eileen Groundwater
1968 ....Moyra Bain
..................Phyllis Flett, Marlene Halcro
1969 ....Helen Moar
..................Arlene Halcro, Irene Mathieson
1970 ....Ida Hourston
..................Alison Bain, Isobel Stove
1971 ....Karen Swanney
..................Ann Marwick, Catrian Sinclair
1972 ....Betty Balfour
..................Audrey Spence, Christina Macdonald
1973 ....Maureen Chapple
..................Eunice Brass, Linda Morris
1974 ....Carol Bertram
..................Ann Ireland, Grace Ritch
1975 ....Ann Ireland
..................Olive Moar, Roma Mowat
1976 ....Jacqueline Cleghorn
..................Ruth Spence, Kristine Moar
1977 ....Eileen Flett
..................Angela Breck, Jean Stevenson
1978 ....Jane McNee
..................Karen Keldie, Carol Flett
1979 ....Belinda Taylor
..................Jacqueline Breck, Lorraine Hutchison
1980 ....Erica Lochrie
..................Maureen Mackay, Margaret Manson
1981 ....Teresa Swanney
..................Melanie Lee, Lorna Isbister
1982 ....Avril Tait
..................Hilary Hay, Kathleen Philips
1983 ....Aimee Leonard
..................Sandra Taylor, Sheena Johnston
1984 ....Sheena Petrie
..................Nicola Brown, Judith Dixon
1985 ....Jacqueline Scott
..................Leona Sinclair, Linda Sabiston
1986 ....Hazel Sinclair
..................Leila Spence, Diane Sinclair
1987 ....Lynn Scott
..................Angela Moar, Paula Spence
1988 ....Sandra Ritch
..................Jenny Moar, Paula Mason
1989 ....Elaine Simpson
..................Genya Harcus, Karen Watson
1990 ....Emma Jane Seator
..................Kirsten Moar, Christine Scott
1991 ....Monica Rendall
..................Vega Rosie, Phillipa Richards
1992 ....Kelly Ireland
..................Claire Beaton, Shelley Richardson
1993 ....Inga Moncrieff
..................Hazel Ritch, Ruth Johnston
1994 ....Inga Moar
..................Sarah Richards, Keri Sinclair
1995 ....Elaine Richardson
..................Kes Eccles, Theresa Omand
1996 ....Jennifer Tait
..................Tory Seyd, Kylie Tullock
1997 ....Sally Kirkland
..................Rachael Scott, Nicola McGowan
1998 ....Christine Sclater
..................Lydia Vincent, Selena Harrison
1999 ....Lorna Flett
..................Alayne Dickey, Carol Rae

Index of Orkney placenames

(Kirkwall, which appears so frequently, is omitted from this index)